MITRES & MISSIONS
IN LANCASHIRE

In Memory of my Mother and Father and my sister Anne

Published by The Bluecoat Press, Liverpool
Book design by MARCH Graphic Design Studio, Liverpool
Printed by Compass Press

ISBN 1 904438 33 4

MITRES & MISSIONS IN LANCASHIRE

The Roman Catholic Diocese of Liverpool 1850-2000

Peter Doyle

The Bluecoat Press

CONTENTS

FOREWORD

In his letter describing this book and asking me to prepare this Foreword, the author Peter Doyle wrote this: 'I will finish with Archbishop Worlock, although I will not be dealing with his years in any great detail since I believe events are too recent for a balanced historical perspective'. When I read that I felt encouraged to offer this Foreword. They reflect that wisdom which knows that history is not about listing facts. It is also about perspective about those events. That same wisdom has suggested to Peter what he calls a thematic treatment, that is, he has chosen facts which, not least from today's perspective, are judged to be profound influences in the past and in the present and therefore have a bearing on our future too. The good thing about this approach is that as we read we may wonder whether we would have chosen the same themes. We will be challenged to enter into a dialogue with what we read. I think it was Archbishop Worlock who alerted some of us to the fact that when he died Pope Paul VI was working on a letter whose title would have been 'Dialogue'. Pope Paul saw this enterprise as essential for coming to secure light and wisdom. A history of this diocese which challenges readers into dialogue must increase wisdom and is always a blessing.

+ Patrick Kelly
Archbishop of Liverpool

November 2003

INTRODUCTION

There is a tendency within institutions to see themselves as more important than they appear to outsiders and to celebrate their jubilees and other landmarks with undue pomp and satisfaction. The Catholic Church in South West Lancashire has travelled a fair distance since it began its journey as the Diocese of Liverpool in 1850. Most outsiders at the time probably regarded it with suspicion, an unwelcome Irish/Romish implant that they hoped would soon wither. Since then it has grown, won recognition and respect and matured as it has moved towards its fourth half-century. There is much to celebrate, but somehow there was a greater air of celebration throughout the diocese in 1950 than was noticeable in 2000, perhaps because Catholics were more aware of underlying problems than their forebears of fifty years before had been, but also because they celebrated the millennium as fully part of English society rather than as a separate group within it. I hope this book celebrates what should be acclaimed, but also gives due consideration to what, with hindsight, might be seen to have been wrong turnings or missed opportunities.

Liverpool has been the most populous English Catholic diocese, served by one of the largest number of priests, churches and schools, since its foundation in 1850 when it stretched from the Mersey to the Lake District and included the Isle of Man. Even when it lost central and northern Lancashire to the new Diocese of Lancaster in 1925, it retained this distinction, although now it was the smallest in mainland area. What happened in the diocese of Liverpool may to some extent be taken as a case study of how the whole English Catholic Church developed between 1850 and 2000, for I would not want to suggest that the issues raised and the problems faced were unique, even though the diocese had its own dynamic as well as its particular complexities.

One of those complexities was the need to fuse into a coherent whole the huge number of the immigrant Irish and to incorporate them into a diocese with its tradition of strong English Catholic recusancy that had developed its own Catholic sub-culture. Part of this task was to provide and encourage a base of regular and commonly shared devotions that would unite English and Irish, well-to-do and poor, and satisfy both the pious and the ordinary practising Catholic. Another was to build a network of parish communities and agencies (secular as well as spiritual) to serve and protect the interests of the people. Chief among these agencies was a Catholic school system; what united Catholics for at least a century was the demand for 'justice' for Catholic schools as the bishops pursued the policy of 'a place for every Catholic child in a Catholic school'. Liverpool was in the van of this provision and sometimes led the struggle at a national level, at a cost that eventually became crippling financially and perhaps distorted pastoral effort in other areas. There was another, and, as it turned out, more difficult, work of integration needed, that of uniting the disparate geographical parts of a diocese that included the different social experiences and dynamics of Liverpool, Preston, Wigan, the rural Fylde and north Lancashire, a unity that was rarely achieved except, perhaps, through the charismatic presence of individual bishops.

After the initial shock and upset of the massive Irish immigration, there were years of slow, grudging social acceptance against a background of bitter Orange and Green rivalry that led too often to street violence and pulpit invective. They were also years that witnessed a remarkable growth in numbers, churches, schools and welfare agencies, and a developing self-confidence and even triumphalism. I have called the contribution of Religious sisters and priests to this provision and growth 'an extra dimension' – an essential and invaluable one. It was a strongly clericalist Church, dominated by priests sure of their approach and secure in their position. Great rallies and demonstrations gave the people some 'voice', but except for the small number who joined Catholic societies or the few who entered local or national politics, they were very much a silent majority, despite some efforts at establishing Catholic Action across the archdiocese. The second World War brought general social upheaval and particular challenges for the Church, but in general terms the 1950s were a time when 'it all seemed to be coming together' for the archdiocese: more diocesan priests and conversions to the Faith than in any other diocese, thriving lay societies, a flourishing seminary and the possibility, at last, of building a cathedral (though not Downey's and Lutyens' ecclesiastical extravaganza).

Then people and priests had to face the same issues that confronted the Church as a whole from the late 1960s: liturgical and other post-Conciliar changes, a steep decline in traditional religious practice, a crisis in the supply and formation of priests, the call for a new approach to authority and the challenges of ecumenism. And all this against a background of rising costs and the burdens left by rapid expansion and heavy debt for the archdiocese and serious economic and social disruption for many of its people. It is too early for a balanced historical assessment of Archbishop Worlock and how successful he was in implementing the decrees and theological insights of the second Vatican Council. How well had 150 years of development prepared clergy and people to meet the uncertainties facing the Church in a post-modern and post-Christian society?

The approach I have adopted in the book is mainly thematic rather than chronological. Like every historian I have been dependent on what records have survived and on what others have written before me. The only previous substantial history was that of Thomas Burke, a successful Connemara-born businessman and local councillor. He called his book simply *Catholic History of Liverpool* and published it in 1910: a great source of information, but written as though anywhere outside Liverpool did not even exist, let alone form part of a single diocese! Since his time and especially in the last thirty years or so, an increasing number of parish histories have been written to mark jubilees and centenaries and, sadly, in some cases the closure of older churches. These have been very useful, as have the annual volumes of the North West Catholic History Society – the result of research into four centuries of Catholic survival and revival in Lancashire and Cheshire. There have also been invaluable studies of the political, economic and social history of the area which have thrown a more secular light (and thus provided a balancing 'second opinion' in some cases) on the development of that part of the English Catholic community that has formed the archdiocese of Liverpool.

~

In researching and writing this history I have incurred many debts of gratitude. I wish to thank Archbishop Kelly for agreeing to write the Foreword. Mgr Provost Peter Cookson, Dean of the Cathedral, encouraged the project from the beginning and provided support and hospitality in Cathedral House. This enabled me to have easy access to the archives where Dr Meg Whittle, the Archdiocesan Archivist, has given unstintingly of her time, patience and expertise. Other archivists who have eased my task have been Sr St Mildred, of the Daughters of Wisdom; Sr Máire Powell, of the Sisters of the Sacred Heart of Mary; Sr Mary Campion, of the Faithful Companions of Jesus; Mr Paul Shaw, of the Generalate Archives of the Poor Servants of the Mother of God; Fr Ian Dickie, archivist of the Archdiocese of Westminster; Fr Thomas Davitt CM for information and a copy of his article on the Vincentians in Liverpool; Dr Kevin Cawley, of the Archives of the

Xaverian Brothers, Notre Dame, USA, for information on St Martin's, Bootle. Sr St Margaret Mary Dudley, of the Sisters of Notre Dame, kindly supplied photographs of St Joseph's Parish, Liverpool.

Others whom I should thank for support and/or practical help include Mr Brian Plumb, whose knowledge of local Catholic history is unrivalled; Mr Tony Hilton, editor for many years of the invaluable *North West Catholic History* and ever-ready to point me in the right direction for information and who supplied me with photographs of Catholic parish life in the 1930s; Mr Terry Duffy, who supported the project from the very beginning and also supplied a detailed account of the development of music at the cathedral and of the Choir School; Dr Susan O'Brien, who generously shared the fruits of her extensive research into the history of Religious Sisters in England; Mr John White, Secretary of the Liverpool Branch of the CEG, and Mr Michael Chitty, formerly of the Merseyside Planning Department; Mr Pat Heery; Mrs N. Neilson; Miss Margaret Peters; Fr Kevin Kelly, Mgr George Mooney, Canon Jimmy Collins, Fr Peter Sibert, Mgr John Butchard and Mgr Austin Hunt. Mr Michael O'Neill has shared his knowledge and enthusiasm for St Anthony's, Scotland Road; Mrs Jo Busby and Mrs W. Byrom provided information on the early history of the Warrington missions and Mr Bernard Waddingham did the same for Preston Catholic College, while Mr Leo Warren provided me with a copy of his history of St Wilfrid's, Preston. Dr Michael Hopkinson kindly supplied the map showing the boundaries of the new diocese. The staff at Ladyewell, Fernyhalgh, also provided me with useful material. Mr Len Hudson, keeper of the marvellous picture archive of Wigan Heritage Services, was very helpful. I am grateful to the Trustees of the Scouloudi Foundation for a grant that helped me to work in the Historical Archive of Propaganda in Rome.

I am grateful to the following for permission to publish photographs and other illustrations: the Sisters of the Sacred Heart of Mary; the Generalate of the Poor Servants of the Mother of God; the Wigan Heritage Services, and Mgr Provost Peter Cookson.

Finally, I wish to thank the following learned societies and their editors for permission to reproduce material that first appeared in their journals or annual publications: the North West Catholic History Society (*North West Catholic History*); the Catholic Record Society (*Recusant History*), and the Ecclesiastical History Society (*Studies in Church History*).

Despite the help and encouragement of all these people (and others whom I may have omitted and to whom I apologise), I would never have finished this book without the continuing support of my son Matthew and the patient and loving care of my wife Barbara – not to mention her reading of it all in draft and her keen advice.

ABBREVIATIONS

AAL	Archives of the Archbishop of Liverpool.*
AAS	*Acta Apostolicae Sedis.*
AAW	Archives of the Archbishop of Westminster.
ABO	Archives of the Birmingham Oratory.
ALP	Archives of the London Province of the Redemptorists.
APF	Archives of the Roman Congregation *De Propaganda Fide; SR Anglia:* letters, reports and papers on English affairs; *Lettere:* letters from Propaganda.
Beck	George Andrew Beck AA (ed.), *The English Catholics 1850 – 1950* (1950).
Burke	Thomas Burke, *Catholic History of Liverpool* (1910).
CR	*The Cathedral Record.*
Cl.R	*The Clergy Review.*
Decreta	*Decreta Quatuor Conciliorum Provincialium Westmonasteriensium 1852 – 1873 (nd).*
Directory	The annual (arch)diocesan directory of parishes, services, clergy, etc., that appeared under various names over the years.
DNB	*The Dictionary of National Biography.*
Flaminian Gate	V.A. McClelland and M. Hodgetts (eds.), *From Without the Flaminian Gate. 150 Years of Roman Catholicism in England and Wales 1850 – 2000* (1999).
JEH	*The Journal of Ecclesiastical History.*
NWCH	*North West Catholic History* (Journal of the North West Catholic History Society).
Plumb, *Arundel*	Brian Plumb, *Arundel to Zabi. A Biographical Dictionary of the Catholic Bishops of England and Wales (Deceased) 1623 – 1987* (1987).
Plumb, *Found Worthy*	Brian Plumb, *Found Worthy. A Biographical Dictionary of the Secular Clergy of the Archdiocese of Liverpool (Deceased) since 1850* (1986).
RCLv	Records of the Archbishop of Liverpool lodged in the Lancashire Record Office (LRO), Preston (mainly pre-1890s).
RH	*Recusant History: A Journal of Research in Reformation and Post-Reformation Catholic History in the British Isles* (Journal of the Catholic Record Society).
SCH	*Studies in Church History* (Annual volumes of the Ecclesiastical History Society).
THSLC	*Transactions of the Historic Society of Lancashire and Cheshire.*

*The extensive archives (currently located in the Cathedral crypt) are principally arranged into a number of Collections (e.g. The Early Bishops; The Downey Collection); each Collection is sub-divided into Series indicated S1, S2, etc. containing papers arranged thematically (e.g. Education); there are further sub-divisions in to Boxes, indicated by Roman numerals, with individual documents listed A/1 etc. See also RCLv above.

Note: Parishes in England and Wales did not become canonically entitled to be called 'Parishes' until 1918 – before that they were 'Missions', with their 'parish priests' either 'priests in charge' or, in some cases, 'missionary rectors'. To avoid confusion I have sometimes used 'parish' of the early years as well.

CHAPTER 1 TRADITION & CHANGE: LANCASHIRE CATHOLICS BEFORE 1850

Lancashire was the gem in the coronet of eighteenth-century English and Welsh Catholicism. Recent critical analysis of the rich heritage that that gem reflected has given it an extra polish and shown that Lancashire Catholicism in the period after 1750 was alive, growing and developing a welcome independence. There were more missions in the county (sixty-nine) than in any other county, amounting to almost half of the 139 in the northern counties; no county outside the north had more than fourteen. This chapter cannot deal in detail with its many facets; it aims instead to pick out some issues and trends that are relevant in the development of the Diocese of Liverpool that was to encompass a very large part of the county.

A FLOURISHING INHERITANCE

Lancashire Catholics from 1750 onwards were not a demoralised or static group, out of touch with the society around them and immune from the social and economic changes affecting the rest of the county. They migrated to the towns when their neighbours migrated to the towns, they changed jobs when they had to or when it seemed in their economic interests to do so. If they had money they tried to make more, if they had large houses and estates they sought to improve them and even pulled down their houses to rebuild on a grander scale as their social friends were doing; some Catholic farmers became gentlemen. As Marie Rowlands has put it:

> there was both tradition and change, prejudice and toleration, separation and integration, danger and security, and individuals managed these contradictions as best they could, responding to changing pressures in different ways from day to day.[1]

What can we say about these missions in detail? The 1767 Returns of Papists made by the Anglican Bishops to the House of Lords are generally reliable and list the known Catholics (men, women and children) in about half of the parishes in the country; it seems likely that the parishes that do not feature were thought by the Anglican incumbent not to contain any Catholics. Overall, Lancashire contained more than two-fifths of all the English Catholics listed in the Returns, and most Lancashire Catholics lived in the western parts of the county. There were, of course, considerable variations:

	Population	Catholics	%
Lancaster	7,000	236	3.4%
Liverpool	34,000	1641	5.0%
Manchester	22,500	287	1.3%
Preston	5,000	1043	20.9%
Wigan	4,500	1194	26.5%
Warrington	2,150	458	21.3%
Chorley	4,000	202	5.5%
Ormskirk	3,000	230	7.6%

These figures illustrate an important point, the transformation of the Lancashire Catholic body from a mainly rural one to an urban one. To take Wigan as one example, half of the Catholic men and women had lived in the town for less than six years; only seven men and fourteen women had lived there for more than twenty years. In nearby Hindley, 75 (69%) of the 108 listed Catholics (about 20% of the total population) were recent immigrants. It is also clear from the returns that in these towns Catholics were numerous enough to form communities and provide at least some group support.[2]

Despite this drift to the towns, 'the heart of Catholic Lancashire's cultural tradition' remained the Fylde, the rural area between Preston and the coast around modern Blackpool. This had more Catholic centres than any other comparably sized area in the country. The major landowners belonged to various branches of the recusant Clifton family, with the senior branch living at Clifton Hall, in Lytham Anglican parish. The neighbouring parish of Kirkham in 1767 contained a remarkably high number of Catholics, 1,275 in total. These were ministered to by Seculars, Jesuits and Franciscans, only two of whom could be described as family chaplains; of the others, five lodged in the houses of yeomen or had their own house with a housekeeper or servant, four lived in Halls but were independent missioners. (The word 'Hall' in this context needs some explanation. Larger, substantial farmhouses were often given this title, which clearly did not in any sense imply the style of gentry living usually associated with a 'Hall'). The few Catholics who lived in the town of Kirkham itself comprised an apothecary, an inn-keeper, a butcher, a malster, a glover, a joiner, a number of servants and some apprentices. In the rural areas there were fifty-four Catholic families of yeoman status, ninety-one classed as husbandmen and sixty-one who were labourers, with a few innkeepers and millers.

The pattern of Catholic existence throughout the Fylde was not uniform. In Poulton le Fylde Anglican parish there was a long tradition of Catholic priests serving a largely pastoral community – as early as 1715 a resident priest had his own house and chapel. Here there seem to have been no Catholic families of yeoman status and Catholics overall formed a smaller proportion of the total population. The small Anglican parish of Lytham, on the other hand, had a total population in 1778 of about 900 people, of whom about 350 were active Catholics. The deciding factor here was the presence of

Wrightington Hall near Standish, the home of the Dicconson family. Rebuilt in classical style in 1748, it had a chapel served by the family chaplain and used for Mass by local Catholics until a parish church was opened in 1894. (Wigan Heritage Services)

the Clifton family. Thomas Clifton had rebuilt his stately hall between 1757 and 1764 and employed forty-seven servants and estate workers (the largest Catholic household detailed in the 1767 Returns). All of these, and their families, seem to have been Catholics. The chapel was in the Hall and this was seigneurial Catholicism of the traditional style, although in the area there were also yeomen farmers, husbandmen and labourers not directly connected with the family.[3]

Robert Banister may be used as an example of one of the independent missioners working in the Fylde in the second half of the eighteenth century, although he was, perhaps, too individualistic to be taken as typical. A native of the parish of Kirkham, he was educated at Dame Alice's school at Fernyhalgh before going to Douai where he was ordained in 1750. He taught philosophy and theology there for about sixteen years and gained a reputation as a good scholar with a very conservative cast of mind – a 'tough, humourless and unimaginative disciplinarian', according to the editor of his voluminous correspondence.[4] He was ready to accuse of mortal sin any young Catholic who courted a Protestant, for example, and there is a mildly Jansenistic air about some of his views. He was also fiercely independent and lamented the almost servile status of his nephew, chaplain to a gentry family in the North East and completely subject to their whims and demands. He was involved in all the Catholic issues of the day, berating the Vicars Apostolic on occasion and a keen champion of the rights of the clergy. He was generally critical of the Catholic gentry (he had spent a year as chaplain to the Dicconsons at Wrightington but left apparently because he objected to the squire's cock-fighting and the local miners' drunkenness).

Eventually Banister became missioner at Mowbreck Hall in the parish of Kirkham, until recently the home of the Westby family. This was a genuine stately mansion, with a private chapel and suite of rooms for a family chaplain, which Banister now occupied as an independent missioner. The mission was endowed with a fund of £1,000, set up specifically to provide an annual salary for a priest by Robert Westby, the last of the family to live at the Hall. So Banister could enjoy the trappings of being chaplain to a wealthy family without any of the normal restrictions of such a post. He opened a Latin preparatory school in the Hall for boys hoping to go abroad to study – it produced fourteen students for the priesthood in twelve years, including both his successors at Mowbreck and George Hilary Brown, the first Bishop of Liverpool. Banister served at Mowbreck for thirty years and became a much respected figure among the northern clergy, many of whom he had taught at Douai. During his time at Mowbreck the number of communicants rose from fewer than 180 to about 270. (The Hall continued as a public chapel until 1809 when a new chapel and priest's house were built nearby at The Willows.) His great-nephew was Alexander Goss, second Bishop of Liverpool; it is not too fanciful to think that he inherited some of Banister's characteristics and outlook.

A feature of Fylde Catholicism that shows in a small way the independence of the people from both gentry and clerical control and their maturity as a community is the Broughton Catholic Charitable Society (Broughton is about four miles from Preston). This was founded in 1787 as a Friendly Society to distribute charity to needy Catholic families. Initially it comprised mainly small farmers and although it had a number of clerical members it was run by laymen and always had a lay president; by 1814 it had 189 members, including some widows, sixteen single women and sixteen priests. Originally it had just £6 to distribute annually but by the 1920s it had given out almost £20,000. It still features in the *Liverpool Archdiocesan Directory* although Broughton is now part of Lancaster Diocese.[5]

Another very strong, though smaller, pocket of traditional Catholicism existed a few miles north of Liverpool and centred around the gentry villages of Ince Blundell, Great Crosby and Little Crosby. Family chaplains based at Ince Blundell Hall and Crosby Hall served the local Catholic communities. (Both Halls were the home of wealthy families named Blundell, though they were only slightly related; that at Ince Blundell after 1837 became known as Weld-Blundell, through inheritance of the estates by the Welds of Lulworth.) The Blundells of Crosby Hall built a separate chapel in 1720, West Lane House (said to be the first public Catholic chapel built since the sixteenth century) and this served the 354 Catholics in Great and Little Crosby until Sts Peter and Paul's, Great Crosby, became a separate mission in 1826 and St Mary's, Little Crosby, was opened in 1847. So strong was the influence of the family that it is claimed that everyone in little Crosby was a Catholic down to the twentieth century. In the case of both families the influence was for the good of Catholicism, through very generous patronage and general non-interference in the work of the missioners.[6]

It is worth looking at what happened at Burscough, near Ormskirk, to see how an independent Catholic mission might develop in the eighteenth century. Initially in the early 1800s a priest, Fr James Gorsuch, lived at

Burscough Hall with his brother, who was the tenant of the Hall. The right of a priest to reside at the Hall and use it for Mass had been established by the Peter Lathom Charity; the priest had his own rooms there (or lived in a nearby cottage belonging to the Hall), with an upstairs chapel open to local Catholics and was supported by the income from the surrounding farmland. So, while Fr Gorsuch lived in a Hall, this was not a case of a gentry family having a chaplain who also looked after the needs of a local community – he was an independent missioner, a 'parish priest' in all but canonical name. The 1767 Returns listed 194 Catholics in Burscough township, with another 250 in the neighbouring Lathom township. In 1784 Bishop Matthew Gibson visited the Hall and confirmed thirty-four people; in the same year there were 190 Easter communicants. A few years later in 1793, his brother, Bishop William Gibson, confirmed forty-eight people there. Here was an active Catholic community made up of husbandmen, farmers, yeoman, a few servants, weavers, blacksmiths and shoemakers.

In 1810 the priest at Burscough Hall was Fr William Coghlan, son of the well-known Catholic printer and publisher, James Coghlan. He decided that the Burscough Catholics needed a proper chapel (the Hall was badly in need of extensive repairs) and so between 1815 and 1819 built the present church and presbytery, dedicated to St John the Evangelist though known for many years afterwards as Burscough Hall Chapel. He had no local patron to call on for funds and in the end subscribed £200 of his own money towards the building costs, and spent a further £300 on fittings, furnishings and laying out the grounds; most of the rest came in small amounts from the parishioners, although the dowager Lady Stanley, an Anglican, did contribute £10. The total costs were almost £1,520 and as late as 1850 there was still an outstanding debt of £800. By the 1820s there were around 620 Catholics in Burscough, making up almost a third of the population of the township.[7]

Catholic provision developed in much the same way in Chorley. Here, between 1755 and 1770 the Catholics were served on a monthly basis by Rev. J. Chadwick who travelled over from Ladyewell (Fernyhalgh) to say Mass at Burgh Hall, his brother's house. He moved permanently to the Hall in 1770 and set about collecting money to build a chapel. The resulting St Gregory's was opened in 1774 at Thurston Hodson's farm, later known as Weld Bank after the Weld family of Lulworth who inherited the estate from Mary Shireburn, wife of the eighth Duke of Norfolk. Chadwick died in 1802 and his successor, Rev. R. Thompson, built the present chapel and later added the schools. St Chad's church, in South Hill, was built in 1791 by Fr George Clarkson. This replaced the old chapel at Slate Delph, on the first floor of an ordinary house and approached by stone steps outside the building so as to be independent of the living quarters of the priest. As the Catholic population had increased this had become too small. According to returns made in 1778, the 202 Catholics of 1767 had already increased to over 400 as the town prospered and its mills provided better opportunities for employment than the surrounding rural areas.[8]

The move from gentry or seigneurial dependence to independent mission could happen in different ways, as the story of the Gillmoss mission shows. The Molyneux family of Croxteth Hall (a few miles north-east of Liverpool) was second only to the Earls of Derby among Lancashire families. They had kept a family chaplain throughout the years of persecution. In 1745 Fr William Molyneux, S.J., became the seventh Viscount Molyneux but continued to live as a missioner at Scholes Hall, near St Helens, another Molyneux residence, where he had founded a mission in the 1730s. (This later moved to Portico in 1790 and became St Nicholas', later Our Lady, Help of Christians). One of his sisters, the Honorable Bridget Molyneux, had founded the first chapel in St Helens, dedicated to St Monica and with a school attached, in 1734 (later replaced by St Mary's, Lowe House, but still standing down to the 1960s). On Fr William's death in 1759 his nephew inherited the title and the estates; as a boy he had been removed from the College at St Omer and brought up a Protestant. He formally and publicly abjured his Catholicism in 1769 and in 1771 became the first Earl of Sefton.

The 1767 Returns showed there were about 750 Catholics in the parish of Sefton which included Netherton, Thornton, Aintree, Litherland, Orrell, Ince Blundell, Ford and both Little and Great Crosby. The Benedictine chaplain at the Hall had ministered to most of these but now had to move out. He settled in Gillmoss, a couple of miles away, and lived in a house attached to a farmhouse. The first Lord Sefton paid for some rooms in the farmhouse to be made into a chapel and continued to pay £40 a year to support the priest and the chapel, as well as making occasional gifts for the same purpose. This support continued down to the 1820s, when the Jesuits (who had taken over the mission in 1773) decided that a new church was required; the then Lord Sefton gave the land for this and provided building materials at a cheap rate. The new chapel of St Swithin was opened in 1824. Of the total cost of over £1,660 only £163 came from the Catholic congregation; the rest came from Jesuit funds and subscriptions. When a new priest's house was needed in the 1830s Lord Sefton again provided the land, as he did also for a school and teacher's house in 1840.[9] Such Protestant loyalty to a family Catholic tradition was rare.

One final example will illustrate the move from dependence on the gentry to independence. In the far north of the county, in the Furness Peninsula, Fr William Strickland, S.J., was appointed to serve the area on his ordination in 1759 and did so as chaplain at the home of his family, Sizergh Castle. He was succeeded by Fr Thomas West, S.J., a respected antiquary and author, who lived at Titeup Hall, near Dalton, owned by a non-Catholic ironmaster named Matson. Clearly West had ceased to be a family chaplain and just lodged in the Hall. He moved again a few years later, this time into the town of Ulverston, where he rented a house where he lived and said Mass for a small congregation made up mainly of workers in the blossoming iron industries. These industries were attracting immigrants from the local rural areas and from Ireland, but while the congregation was growing quite quickly nothing was done to provide them with a proper place for Mass. In the early 1790s we find Dr Rigby, the secular priest in Lancaster, occasionally saying Mass in Ulverston. It was another Secular, Dr Everard, former rector of the Irish College in Bordeaux and later Archbishop of Cashel, who settled in Ulverston in 1794, opened a school for the sons of well-to-do Catholics and built the first permanent chapel in 1806. When he moved on, to become President of Maynooth, care of the mission reverted to the Jesuits.[10] (Barrow, the future centre of Catholicism in the area, was still only a hamlet in the 1820s.)

NEW INFLUENCES AND DIRECTIONS

As the eighteenth century entered its last thirty years or so, the practical tolerance that most Catholics experienced from their Protestant neighbours and local officials was made permanent by Acts of Parliament. The 1778 Relief Act allowed Catholic priests and school teachers to live in the country legally and to exercise their ministries (though it was still illegal to open a Catholic school), although Mass could only be said in private houses with a congregation of no more than five in addition to the members of the household. The 1581 Act which had laid down a penalty of a year's imprisonment for saying or hearing Mass was not repealed. The award of £100 formerly made to informers against priests and teachers was abolished and most of the inheritance laws against Catholics were repealed so that they could inherit or purchase land and property without legal obstruction. As we have seen, in several parts of Lancashire and elsewhere common practice had already gone beyond the strict letter of the law and Mass was said openly in public chapels. While the Act can be seen as the first step towards the acceptance of Catholics as equal citizens, it left a large raft of anti-Catholic legislation on the statute book and did not do away with the anti-Catholic attitudes that were dominant in most sections of English society; the Gordon Riots of 1780 showed how those attitudes could easily turn to destructive violence.

A second Relief Act of 1791 allowed the public celebration of Mass as long as Catholic chapels were registered and the priest took an oath of loyalty – and as long as the chapels did not have a steeple or bell and its doors were not locked during service! Priests were not allowed to wear their religious robes or habits in public apart from saying Mass. It was still forbidden to leave money for 'superstitious purposes' – clearly, this included money for the saying of Masses, but it also covered bequests to most Catholic charities and institutions and could become a legal quagmire. Catholics could now embrace the law as a profession but could not become judges or King's counsel, sit as an MP or even vote in parliamentary elections, hold commissions in the armed forces or hold any office of trust under the Crown; Catholic peers could still not take their seats in the Lords. The position of Catholic schools was unclear, although it was taken that at least the founding of seminaries would be illegal. Catholic marriages still had to be celebrated in an Anglican church (this applied to Protestant Dissenters too).[11]

One factor that increased tolerance towards Catholics was English reaction to the French Revolution and its anti-Christian excesses. An important side-effect was that very large numbers of French exiles, clerical and lay, took refuge in this country. By 1797, about five and a half thousand priests and almost six thousand lay people were here, some of them receiving regular financial help from the Government or from various voluntary bodies that had been set up for the purpose.[12] The irony of French Catholics receiving generous support from the English because they opposed the Revolutionary regime in France, while the same people still looked askance at native English Catholics and refused to give them equal rights under the law, seems not to have been noticed. The exiles opened eight French chapels in London alone and others elsewhere. Most of these soon closed as the exiles returned to France from 1801 onwards, but several hundred priests remained. Many of the English colleges, monasteries and convents abroad were forced to close and about forty of them re-located permanently in this country, despite the 1791 Act that forbade the founding of colleges and monasteries. Of major importance in Lancashire was the founding of the Jesuit college of Stonyhurst, established after the expulsion of the English Jesuit college from Flanders (originally at St Omers) by the French Revolutionary armies in 1794.

Nuns also settled in the county, for the first time for over two centuries. A group of Benedictine nuns from Cambrai resided for a time at Woolton, near Liverpool, where they ran a school until they moved to Stanbrook in 1808. Another house of Benedictine nuns came to England in 1792 and later opened a school at Orrell Mount, near Wigan, which they ran from 1821 until they moved to Rugby in 1835. Benedictines from the English convent in Ghent settled for a time at Fernyhalgh, Wrightington and Little Singleton before finally moving to Winckley Square, Preston, in 1795 where they ran a day and boarding school; the community eventually settled in Staffordshire to lead their contemplative life in greater seclusion than busy Preston allowed.[13]

Unfortunately, none of these communities re-settled permanently in the county. This was rather surprising, given the previous history of the 'Lancashire Ladies', the name given by Dom Odo Blundell to the many daughters of Lancashire families who became nuns abroad. It is a fascinating story in its own right and deserves much more than this brief notice. Blundell identified eighteen convents in France and Flanders (and one in Lisbon) which Lancashire women had joined in the seventeenth and eighteenth centuries. They chose a life of prayer and perpetual exile from their families and, for many, one also of poverty. The most popular convent seems to have been that of the Poor Clares at Gravelines (founded by Mary Ward) where 90 of the 209 English professions came from Lancashire; the names make a roll-call of the noble and gentry families of the county – there were 13 Cliftons, 6 Gerards, 7 Blundells, 3 Molyneux, 3 Andertons and 4 Bradshaghs (and other convents had their Tyldesleys, Westbys, Towneleys, Dicconsons, Haydocks and the rest). By the mid-eighteenth century, recruitment to the English convents abroad was falling off somewhat and a number of them were in financial difficulties. Those in the Austrian Netherlands also suffered from the policies of Joseph II before the final troubles brought on them by the French Revolution. While vocations to the enclosed and contemplative life continued to be a feature of Lancashire Catholicism (and the Ghent community that moved to Staffordshire in 1811 had been replenished by novices and sisters professed in Preston), attention switched increasingly to the active Orders in the nineteenth century.[14]

Nineteen of the exiled clergy spent some time in Lancashire, most of them in Liverpool. A couple of them taught French in the town, one became chaplain to the Ecclestons of Scarisbrick, a few served as missioners and one may have been chaplain to the exiled Benedictine nuns while they were in Woolton; we know very little about most of them while they were here. The majority returned home, but a few spent the rest of their priestly ministry here. One of these was Fr Richebeque (or Le Richebec) who was at Southworth Hall, near Warrington, for several years and ministered to the local Catholics. When the Jesuits built a public chapel nearby at Croft in 1827 it was dedicated to St Louis and put under the care of Fr Richebeque; he served as missioner there until he died in 1845. Another emigré who remained was Jean-Baptiste Gérardot, a Canon Regular of St Augustine. He arrived in Liverpool in 1795, taught in the Catholic Charity School and at Vernon Hall (the predecessor of Ampleforth) until 1803. He had earned enough money to buy a house and piece of land at what was known as Mile End, close by where Scotland Road began. He opened a small chapel for the poor, known as the French Chapel and dedicated to St Anthony of the Desert.

Not used to the quiet approach of traditional Lancashire Catholics to the celebration of Mass, he announced his celebration of mid-night Christmas Mass in 1813 in the local press. For the occasion the front of the small chapel was decorated with candles forming a star and the letters 'J.S.' ('Jesus the Saviour') while the Mass itself included Novello's Adeste Fideles, Handel's Pastoral Symphony from the Messiah, the Te Deum and other classical pieces. Fr Gérardot was in charge of the mission until his death in 1825.[15]

Eventually a Catholic Emancipation Bill became law in 1829 in the face of considerable Protestant opposition. By this date the number of missions in the county had risen to eighty-two (out of a probable total of 383 in the whole of England and Wales). It made little practical difference immediately to the great majority of English Catholics. Indeed, a number of the old penal laws remained on the statute book and the clauses that tried to limit the work of Religious might have meant a step backward from the de facto toleration that had existed from the late eighteenth century. Catholic rites could not be performed publicly, nor could Catholic religious dress be worn in public, while Catholic charities were still regarded as superstitious. What the Act did allow was the election of Catholics to the House of Commons (eight were elected for English constituencies in 1831), and a number of Catholic peers entered the House of Lords.[16]

A closer look at the Catholics listed in 1767 shows that most of them were of humble stock; in the rural areas they worked as husbandmen and small farmers, in the industrialised villages and towns they worked mainly as weavers. It would be a mistake, however, to think of Lancashire Catholics solely in these terms. As Anthony Hilton has pointed out Catholics were also helping to create the new society.[17] John Sadler, a Liverpool printer, invented transfer-printing for pottery and contracted with Josiah Wedgwood to mass-produce the results; Sadler was in partnership with another Liverpool Catholic, Guy Green, and their works was next door to a Catholic brewer's business. Sadler also, interestingly, published both Catholic and Anglican (and one Dissenting) works of devotion, apologetics and sermons and seems to have got on very well with his Protestant neighbours. There were at least two other Catholics among the merchant potters of Liverpool when the industry in the town was at its most successful.

Sir Thomas Gerard of Bryn, later of Garswood, exploited the coal on his extensive estates, transported it to Liverpool by one of the new canals and made a fortune by undercutting the price of coal there. The missions at Bryn and Garswood were served by the family chaplains, at first Jesuits, then Seculars from 1789. It was Fr Thomas Lupton, chaplain from 1819 to 1843, who was the first priest in charge of the new church of St Oswald in Ashton, built in 1822 with Gerard money. The eleventh baronet, Sir William, was responsible for the church of St Mary, Birchley, opened in 1828, which replaced the old chapel in Birchley Hall. Other estate owners, like the Porters of Ackhurst Hall, also set up mining businesses to benefit from the huge increase in the demand for coal and the easy transport provided by the new waterways. James Orrell of Blackbrook, St Helens, was already dealing in coal when he bought the Parr Hall estate in 1781 and developed still further its pits, the main source of coal for Liverpool. Two of his brothers were priests and two of his sons were also ordained. James Orrell also had interests in the glass industry, operating a bottle factory at Thatto Heath. The mission church of St Mary's, Blackbrook, was established in 1845 by Fr James Abraham, with considerable help from the family; he was chaplain at Blackbrook House from 1838 – 1850. When the last of the family died in the 1860s the whole of the estate and the house passed to the diocese.[18]

Further to the east, John Trafford of Trafford and his steward John Brettargh, developed cobalt and other minerals on his estates between Warrington and Manchester, while Robert Gillow, a cabinet maker in Lancaster, opened showrooms in London and was involved in importing timber from the Baltic and the West Indies to feed his successful business. The family moved out of the town to Leighton Hall and after 1830 no longer had any direct interest in the furniture business, although their name continues down to today in Waring and Gillow. They turned instead to producing priests and nuns – at one stage in the nineteenth century nine out of eighteen Gillow first cousins were priests.[19]

The first cotton mill in Blackburn was opened by a Catholic, John Anderton, while it was Thomas Eccleston, with estates in Eccleston and Scarisbrick (and later Wrightington), who was a key figure in the reclamation of Martin Mere to provide more agricultural land to provide food for the growing industrial workers. No wonder Rev. John Barrow, the 'old tar' of

Claughton, stated in 1798 that Catholics would now have to rely on the very pious, rich and charitable families of 'Merchants, Manufacturers, Tradesmen, etc' for funds rather than on the gentry as they might have done up to even five or six years before.[20]

Chapels moved from rooms in private houses and became separate buildings for various reasons, but whatever the reasons, the result was a greater independence for the clergy. The clergy were also trying to break their dependence on the laity in other ways, particularly financially. In 1781 the Lancashire clergy recalled all the monies that had been 'time out of mind lent to farmers, yeomaners, tradesmen, gentlemen, etc.' and often lost or mismanaged, and began to invest the monies themselves. Bishop Gibson declared that he would no longer have lay trustees for church money or property and the clergy gradually took possession of mission funds that had previously been held in gentry trusts. This did not prevent further quarrels, as we shall see, but the overall effect was to increase the independence and self-confidence of the clergy.

Just as with the development of rural missions, no one pattern fitted what was happening in the towns. Additionally, while the clergy were no longer dependent on the gentry, gentry families in several cases were influential and even essential to what happened. In Preston, however, it was a priest who was probably the most influential factor. It would, indeed, be difficult to over-estimate the role of Fr Joseph Dunn ('Daddy' Dunn) in the development of Catholicism in Preston in the fifty years after 1775 (he served there as missioner from 1776 until his death in 1827). He was not slow to acknowledge his own contribution, claiming that Preston was 'the first Catholic mission in England with its chapels, its school, its oratory, its cemetery … its chapel house and school furnished with gas'.[21] His reference to gas is interesting in that he is said to have been one of the first Jesuits in the country 'to face the Industrial Revolution fearlessly'; he helped to found the Preston Gas Light Company in 1815. He opened St Wilfrid's Church in 1793, re-opened a re-furbished St Mary's in 1813, founded a Sunday School in Friargate in 1787 and the Fox Street School in 1814, established a Catholic cemetery, a Catholic Book Society and Library and a Society for the Defence of Catholic Principles. He was widely known and respected in the town, being an original trustee of the Preston Savings Bank and a founder member of the Preston Literary and Philosophical Society.

Meanwhile, the Catholic population of the town rose from about 1100 in the 1770s to 3,500 in 1810 and 5,200 in 1820 – these later totals represented about 21% of the total population. This substantial Catholic body had its lay leaders, men of some wealth who were fully involved in the economic development of the town and its social and cultural enterprises. It was for this body that Fr Dunn produced in 1778 *The Layman's Afternoon Devotion with Litanies and Night Prayers usually said in Catholic Families*, and in 1797 (along with two other priests) *Prayers to be said before and after Mass*, a second edition of which appeared in 1823. There were also a Catholic Choral Society

and a Catholic Band of Music as well as a number of charitable and friendly societies. All in all, as a recent historian has put it, the combination of Dunn's work and personality, together with the presence of large numbers of Catholics of all classes, were the main factors which contributed to the vitality displayed by the Preston Catholic community; it had the confidence to play a full part in the life of the town and the energy and resources to look after its less fortunate members. Not surprisingly, matters did not always run smoothly. Dunn had firm ideas on lay trustees and opposed their having any say in the running of a mission:

> I should be very sorry to meddle with other people's concerns and I should
> not wish for any person to interfere with mine ... I dare affirm without
> fear of being contradicted that when laymen interfere in opposition to the
> Clergy it is seldom to do good.

He fell out with some of the wealthier members of the congregation and feared they would set up a rival chapel. In the end, for the sake of peace, he appointed three lay trustees, but his pioneering spirit did not make him an easy colleague and he quarrelled with his fellow priests, his former Jesuit superiors (he did not rejoin the Order after its re-instatement) and the lay trustees. He wrote to popes, vicars apostolic, Irish and American bishops and the king of Spain – he even got a donation towards the costs of building his school from Sir Robert Peel! He may have been exaggerating somewhat when he claimed to have contributed to making the Preston the leading Catholic mission in England, but not by very much.[22]

Another interesting eighteenth-century town mission was that at Hindley, near Wigan. By the early years of the century there were only about a dozen Catholics in the township served by the Benedictine chaplain to the Langton family of Lowe. Even this arrangement did not last, for the family estate passed to Protestant heirs and the local Catholics had to rely on the Benedictines from Standish and Charnock Richard. The town was growing quickly with the industrial revolution and attracting large numbers of migrants from the surrounding areas. In the 1770s the Trafford family gave their house in Hindley, named Strangeways, to be a residence for the Benedictines and a chapel. The Traffords, along with the Catholic Walmesleys of Ince, were exploiting the coal from their estates in the area, and further employment was provided by factories and mills. The Catholic population had risen to 108 by 1767, most of whom worked in the textile industry (strangely, none of them seemed to have been miners). Only thirteen of them were aged over 50. In 1784 Bishop Gibson confirmed 59 at Strangeways, when there were 259 Easter communicants; by the 1840s the Catholic population had risen to about 1500, 27% of the total population. The congregation got its first proper chapel in 1789 on land given by a local Catholic family named Marsh.[23]

A different situation developed at Fleetwood, a completely new town that grew up around a railway terminus in 1840. It was the entrepreneurial brain-child of Sir Peter Hesketh Fleetwood who saw the profits to be made by developing a port-cum-holiday resort. Within a year it had a population of 2,833, of whom 439 were Catholics. A group of Catholics got together and successfully petitioned Sir Peter for some land and the Vicar Apostolic for a priest. A simple chapel was opened in 1841 and the Rev. Michael Carroll was appointed as its resident priest. He immediately clashed with the laymen who had built the chapel, claiming they had no right to call meetings of the trustees – indeed, he went on, there were no trustees as he alone was in charge of the finances. The trustees had borrowed heavily to build the chapel and wanted an assurance that he would honour their debts by applying the weekly collections to them; they also claimed the right to fix his salary. When it became obvious that Carroll would not agree to any of this, they threatened to sell the chapel and appealed to the local dean. What happened next is not clear, but the lay trustees gave way in 1842; Carroll moved on two years later, and the congregation seems to have accepted the dean's advice that 'peace is valuable and no good can come from extremes'.[24]

It was advice that would have served well elsewhere, especially in the county's largest town, Liverpool. Its population of 34,400 in 1773 increased to 77,650 in 1801 and by 1804 it was the second largest port in the country – the tonnage of shipping using it had increased more than thirty-fold over the eighteenth century and its export of coal alone increased from 14,000 tons in 1752 to 186,000 tons in 1820. Most of the in-migration to the port came from south-west Lancashire and Cheshire. Its mid-eighteenth century Catholic population was the fastest growing in the country. Traditional Catholicism had not been much in evidence in the port, yet by 1767 the number of Catholics there (1,641, or 4.9% of the population) exceeded those in Preston

and Wigan. Of these, 42% were under the age of twenty; of the 899 over that
age, only 78 had been born in the town, while a third of both men and
women had arrived there in the previous five years. Between 1761 and 1770
Catholic baptisms numbered 1,234 and from the 1740s Irish names begin to
occur more frequently in the registers. Catholics lived in both the poor and
better off areas, though they seem to have been under-represented among
the professional classes. There were entrepreneurs among them, too, though
of a different kind: they invested in shipping and took part in the slave trade,
whaling and privateering, as well as the general Irish trade that added so
much to Liverpool's prosperity and made some Liverpool Catholics men of
comfortable means.[25] There was also a small Italian Catholic community, at
least from the 1790s – prominent among them was the Casartelli family,
scientific instrument makers and opticians (and forebears of the future
Bishop of Salford).

A priest had begun to minister to the town's Catholics on a regular basis
as early as 1701. The Jesuits were in charge of the mission and when the
chapel of St Mary's was destroyed in 1746 by an anti-Jacobite mob, they built
another, disguised as a warehouse, in Edmund Street. The priest reported
that it was erected with money 'from friends in other places'. A few years
later, in 1759, this was also destroyed by a mob and was again rebuilt.[26] The
role of the laity in building the chapel led to a major dispute. The members
of the congregation who had paid for the chapel and paid for the services of
the Jesuit missioner, insisted on electing their own trustees and taking charge
of the mission's finances. When the Jesuit superior objected to this practice,

26

the missioner, Joseph Gittins took over the finances, only for a bitter dispute to break out between himself and his assistant, a Spanish priest, Raymond Hormosa, alias Harris, who claimed he was not getting a fair share of the money and who had the support of the lay trustees because he spoke in favour of the slave trade.

In 1779 the congregation voted to go back to the original arrangements for lay control and elected trustees who claimed the right to choose their missioner. Gittins refused to give up the finances and the Vicar Apostolic's arbitrators could not agree on a solution. When the lay trustees tried to take control of the chapel in 1782 there was a riot and the following year the Bishop, in desperation, suspended both Gittins and Harris from working in Liverpool and invited the Benedictines to send a priest to run the chapel – a move apparently supported by most of the ex-Jesuits and a good number of the congregation. Dom Archibald Benet McDonald, OSB, was, however, no more successful as a peace-maker than others had been; after further violence and a civil law-suit (which found in favour of Dom Archibald) two new chapels were built, one named St Peter's, in Seel Street, which the Benedictines ran and the second run by the ex-Jesuits and lay trustees in Sir Thomas Buildings (replacing a former Jesuit chapel in Chorley Street). This second chapel closed in 1813 to allow the building of St Nicholas', Copperas Hill, which opened as a Secular church in 1815.

Of the many claims and counter-claims made during this long-drawn out conflict, two from 1783 give a clear idea of what was at stake. The first came from the lay trustees who argued:

27

no person can serve this congregation as an incumbent without the approbation of the qualified bench-holders ... it is hoped the congregation will never suffer any innovation to take place in a matter of such importance to themselves and posterity as the choice of their own pastors.

The second statement came from the Vicar Apostolic and was addressed to the Catholics of Liverpool: the claims of the lay trustees would:

strike at the very being of ecclesiastical authority and subordination ... an irreligious encroachment upon the rights of the sanctuary, a most preposterous attempt to exalt the sheep above the pastor, to direct your teacher, lead your guide, and overawe your prelate, a sacrilegious effort to disturb the order established by our Blessed Redeemer and disturb the system of Infinite Wisdom.[27]

While the oratorical victory, in this instance, may have lain with the Bishop, were the clergy, free from gentry control in rural Lancashire, about to fall under the spell of a nouveau 'gentry' in the towns, where congregations were stable, relatively well-to-do and contained enough people used to running their own affairs? The Liverpool row was not settled until Bishop Brown, as Vicar Apostolic for a new Lancashire District, abolished the whole system of lay trustees for missions (see below page 32). This bitter confrontation, and later ones between the Secular Clergy and both Jesuits and Benedictines (see pages 145-7) meant that the mission to Catholics in Liverpool went through a difficult and unsettling period, adding additional problems to those accompanying the rapid growth of the town and its Catholic population. Perhaps it also created its own folk-memory, in the minds of bishops and clergy, of the dangers of trusting lay people too much.

One result of Catholic migration to the towns was that some rural missions stagnated or declined. That at Hornby, ten miles to the east of Lancaster, is a good example. From 1811 to 1851 it was in the care of the Rev. John Lingard, the ground-breaking, scholarly historian but better known in ordinary Catholic circles as the author of one of the most popular hymns to Our Lady ever written in English, *Hail, Queen of Heaven*. The mission had already passed from gentry dependence when Lingard became its missioner and its numbers had gradually increased in the last quarter of the eighteenth century, from 183 to 345, with farmers, hatters, weavers and labourers well represented in the congregation. By the 1820s, however, numbers had dropped to 216 and by the 1840s were down to 171. In all, between 1811 and 1850 133 Catholics emigrated and Lingard noted where sixty of them had gone, including forty-two of them to Lancashire towns and six to America. Hornby, however kept going as a mission whereas that in Singleton in the Fylde, established in 1756, eventually closed and the chapel was sold in the 1850s because it had too few parishioners (about forty families) and no endowment to support its priest.[28]

PRIESTS AND PEOPLE

Whoever controlled the finances and appointments to the large number of Lancashire chapels, it was the priest who controlled the services. Here again the pattern of devotional provision was in many cases more varied and richer in the eighteenth century than has sometimes been thought. True, if a congregation was served by a 'riding priest' then they might have Mass only once a month or even less, but in the settled missions that served most of Lancashire's Catholics Mass was at least a weekly event. It might still be referred to as 'Prayers' but that was a hang-over from days of more active persecution. John Gother's missal for the use of the laity was published in 1718 and contained the Latin text and a full English translation, while *The Key of Heaven*, published in Liverpool in 1755, gave prayers for those, like sailors, who could not get to Mass and, interestingly, included prayers for Benediction. Some Mass centres, like Bryn, had all the requisites for the full range of services, including copes, thuribles, incense boats and devotional paintings of the stations of the cross,[29] but that might have been exceptional and due to the local patronage of the Gerards – where Mass was said in temporary accommodation, a room above an inn, perhaps, then presumably liturgical practice would have been cut to the minimum.

Some missioners, especially the Jesuits, encouraged the more devout members of their congregations to join pious societies and confraternities – particularly popular was the Bona Mors society, which involved at least monthly Confession and Holy Communion. For those with more leisure there was the full gamut of Challoner's private devotions – meditation, examination of conscience and lengthy preparation for the reception of the sacraments. Missioners took seriously the duty to instruct their people, as did conscientious patrons – early in the century Nicholas Blundell of Little Crosby felt his chaplain was not doing enough in this regard and asked the Jesuit Superior for a priest who would be 'willing to take pains amongst the poor Catholics, of whom we have a great many'. The new chaplain organised catechism classes after Vespers on Sundays and later put on classes after Benediction for adults to learn more about the Mass and other parts of Christian doctrine. There was a constant demand for catechisms, especially simplified versions for the young and semi-illiterate and while Banister and other conservatives might object to some of them as being over-simplified, they obviously met a need. Indeed, Banister and his nephew often discussed how to instruct young people and ignorant adults. First Communion time was a key period for instruction, according to Banister, and simply teaching the catechism was not enough – it could be learned by heart with little understanding. He himself concentrated on explaining the simplest prayers, the life and miracles of Our Lord and as detailed an exposition of the ten commandments as possible. The lives of the saints were also useful, but

Butler's recently published *Lives* were too remote for most ordinary Catholics, he believed: far more useful as a model would be 'the life of some holy woman, or women, married to an idle husband having 7 or 8 shirtless children, herself too almost naked, neither servant maid to assist her nor anyone to comfort her … or a poor holy man tied to an errant vixen'.[30] He knew the realities of his people's lives.

While these particular forms of religious practice and devotion set the Catholic community apart from its Protestant neighbours, the community in general was increasingly accepted and integrated. Anglican clergymen allowed Catholic priests to use Catholic rites in their graveyards (although sometimes only under cover of dark); Catholic merchants and traders carried on their businesses without hindrance; wealthy Catholics hunted and danced with polite society. How far did they intermarry with their Protestant neighbours, perhaps the truest test of integration and social acceptability? Bossy summarised Catholic attitudes by saying that the clergy opposed mixed marriages, the gentry tended to avoid them, but there seems to have been little prejudice against them in the rest of the community, which is probably true as a general statement. Evidence about the extent of mixed marriages in the eighteenth century is sparse and notoriously difficult to interpret, but some figures are available: at Alston Lane, over a twenty-one year period, 21.5% of Catholic marriages were mixed; at Culcheth, over eight years, 47% were mixed; at Fernyhalgh, over about fifty years, 13% were mixed; at Mowbreck and Kirkham, over twenty-four years when Banister was at Mowbreck, 21.5% were mixed and, finally, at Newhouse, over twenty-five years, 28% were mixed. It should be remembered, of course, that marriages between Catholics and Protestants were as unpopular in certain Protestant circles as in Catholic ones, but these figures show that Catholics in these rural missions were not regarded as social outcasts or even as very peculiar people. Some priests recognised that circumstances played a part and thought it unreasonable to expect all their people to find Catholic partners: they were sometimes scattered and small communities (e.g. Hornby), meeting other Catholics mainly only at Sunday Mass and spending the rest of their time working and socialising with Protestants.[31]

As the eighteenth century passed into the nineteenth, Catholics practised their religion more openly and it began to blossom. By the 1840s the people in parts of the District were experiencing full-blooded revivalist 'missions' given by the Passionists. At Blackbrook, for example, Fr Gaudentius was impressed by the attitude of the country congregation, made up principally of 'coalworking people'. They attended the three daily services when they could and many who had been out of the Church returned to their duties. On the last Sunday there was a general Communion and:

> the three usual nights of Solemn Benediction, when the large new
> beautiful church was filled with people of different congregations and
> denominations, who evinced the greatest satisfaction. Several times
> the church was crowded to excess.

At Billinge, near Wigan, Benediction (with a new, splendid monstrance) was accompanied by processions of children and the Blessed Sacrament was exposed amid 'a blaze of lights on the beautifully decorated high altar'.[32]

THE LANCASHIRE DISTRICT

How was the Church in Lancashire organised? As a missionary country without an established hierarchy of bishops, England and Wales came under the Roman Congregation for the Propagation of the Faith (or Propaganda). In 1688 it had divided England and Wales into four Districts each with a Vicar Apostolic in charge, with the Northern District comprising the whole of England north of the rivers Humber and Dee. It was a very large area, too large for one man to supervise effectively, so that the clergy and the laity had grown used to to a large degree of independence from episcopal control. Increases in the size of the Catholic population during the eighteenth century and the greater legal freedom allowed them argued for a revision of the 1688 arrangements but nothing happened until 1840 when Propaganda decided on eight Districts instead of four, and the former Northern District was divided into the Lancashire District (the counties of Lancashire and Cheshire and the Isle of Man), the Yorkshire District (the county of Yorkshire) and a new Northern District (the counties of Durham, Northumberland, Westmorland and Cumberland). Bishop John Briggs had been Vicar Apostolic of the former Northern District since 1836 and became Vicar Apostolic of the new Yorkshire District. The new Lancashire District passed under the control of Bishop George Brown.

In some ways he must have seemed an ideal candidate for the new post. Born near Lytham in the Fylde in 1786, George Hilary Brown was very much a product of traditional Lancashire Catholicism. After Banister's school at Mowbreck he had gone to Ushaw where he was ordained priest in 1810. He then taught theology at the College, where he was also prefect of studies and vice-rector. In 1819 he was appointed to the mission in Lancaster, where he remained until he became Vicar Apostolic. Most of those who knew him well, however, were surprised at the appointment as he had shown little talent for such a position while in charge at Lancaster. Moreover, he had suffered from frequent bouts of illness and had been often absent in search of the cure that a better climate might bring. John Lingard of Hornby was well-disposed towards Brown (who had been his pupil at Ushaw) but was clearly suspicious of these illnesses for which no one could find a cause: in 1839 he described him as a 'walking shadow' with little hope himself of surviving, unable to say Mass, trembling like a man of ninety 'and all this with a good appetite'.[33]

His appointment as Vicar Apostolic proved to be less than happy. From 1841 onwards Propaganda began to receive complaints about his absence from the District – he was away, for example, from October 1841 to June 1842,

November 1842 to June 1843, and November 1843 to June 1844. When present he caused ill-feeling among his clergy, especially those in the Manchester area: they thought he was a martinet and complained frequently to Rome about his decisions. Part of the trouble here might have been caused by Brown's earlier espousal of causes that he now condemned. In the 1830s he had been one of the leaders among the northern clergy against what some saw as the arbitrary rule of the Vicars Apostolic (nicely described as 'rule by episcopal intuition') and wanted a properly constituted hierarchy. Yet in 1847 a Preston priest wrote of his violence and how 'he pronounced all (as) rebels who petition for what he petitioned for before he was a Bishop!' For his part, Brown seemed to think he was fighting for episcopal rights against a recalcitrant clergy and a threatening laity, and the other bishops should be grateful to him for it.[34]

Yet his period as Vicar Apostolic was not without achievements. In an attempt to regularise finances, in 1844 he had taken the lead among the Vicars Apostolic in abolishing the remaining lay committees that still controlled the finances for church building and the provision of schools in a number of missions. He had put all these finances under the direction of a District Board that contained no lay representatives and insisted that the laity in future could only contribute to collections as individuals. Soon after this he established the Lancashire Mission Fund (it became the Liverpool Diocesan Mission Fund after 1850) to provide money for new building and to help with the maintenance of poorer missions; an annual collection was taken in each mission and an annual report published.[35] He later added similar annual collections for Ecclesiastical Education (the training of the clergy) and the Poor Schools. There were other achievements, too. Between 1841 and 1851 the number of churches in his district went up from 68 to 84, while the number of priests to serve them rose from 87 to 122. New Religious Congregations had been invited to work in the District (the Passionists, the Redemptorists, the Oblates of Mary, the Sisters of Mercy, the Faithful Companions of Jesus) to extend the scope of missionary activity and play a key role in the development of education and works of mercy.[36]

The healthy survival and growth of Catholicism in Lancashire through the seventeenth and eighteenth centuries owed almost everything to the active ministry of the clergy. The Regular clergy made up the majority of the priests in the Northern District (in 1773, only 67 out of 137 priests had been Seculars). By the 1770s, for example, the Jesuits were running fifteen missions in the county. After the suppression of the Society in 1773 they continued to run these as ex-Jesuits but the years of the suppression became increasingly difficult. One important issue concerned the ownership of the Society's funds and property: the Vicars Apostolic believed these should come under their control, to be used as the original donors had wished, while some of the ex-Jesuits believed they should control and benefit from the accumulated funds. In 1790 Propaganda decreed that all the ex-Jesuits must on their deaths leave any property or funds they administered to the

St Mary's Wigan the
Secular church at the
centre of a bitter row.
(Wigan Heritage Services)

relevant Vicar Apostolic. As numbers dwindled the ex-Jesuits gave up some
of their missions, including Liverpool, Little Crosby, Formby and Portico,
but were still able to build St Wilfrid's in Preston, a new church and
presbytery in Leigh and a new church in Gillmoss.

Unfortunately, by the nineteenth century, antagonism between Regulars
and Seculars had become inbred and this general hostility had fed on a
number of bitter local quarrels. Principles as well as emotions had been
involved, and in most cases the laity had taken sides. In 1817, for example, a
public and rather scandalous row had started over the building of two new
churches in Wigan, one by the Jesuits and the other by the Seculars. A public
resolution, signed by about 1,400 people asked for the church of St John to be
rebuilt for Jesuit use and urged the public not to give money for the building
of a Secular church to replace it. The opponents of the resolution opened a

rival subscription list and bought a piece of land for the Secular church. The row escalated when placards appeared on the streets announcing that 'Tates of Wigan (the ex-Jesuit incumbent) is going against the Bishop! Tates gives scandal! Let old Hughes (the Jesuit superior for Lancashire) mind his own flock'. The Rev. Thompson, the Vicar General, met Tate in the street and spent half an hour loudly reviling him and accusing him of lying. His mood was not improved when Charles Walmsley, the leading lay advocate of the Jesuits, wrote him a letter claiming that the Bishop had no right to forbid what the lay congregation wanted. After a 'neck and neck race' to build both chapels, the Jesuit provincial wrote in 1819:

> The Greenough (Secular) chapel is sinking every day: the Secular priest will leave it next month and it is imagined that the chapel will then be closed. Thus ends Bishop Gibson's attempt to invade our property.

The last sentence is particularly instructive in this context. But in the end both chapels were completed and neither collapsed to allow its opponents to claim divine support for their cause. They stood (and still stand) within a hundred yards of each other on the same road. Quarrels continued for many years. No mission boundaries were drawn up for either church and when a second secular mission was opened in 1847 the priest was at a loss to know which were his people: eleven years later they were still debating the issue and in the 1860s the Jesuit provincial was still suggesting that the best way out of the difficulties was for the Seculars to give up all their missions in the town. (St John's became a Secular parish in 1933.)[37]

In 1840 there was another dispute, this time in Liverpool, over the proposed school and church of St Francis Xavier. In both cases the Vicars Apostolic (Bishop Briggs of the old Northern District and then Bishop Brown) had opposed the Jesuit plans, but Propaganda had supported the Jesuits in principle. In the second case the Jesuits seemed to have taken the Bishop's approval for granted and had started to purchase the land before approaching him.[38] This was also the case with the Benedictine mission of St Anne's, Edge Hill, in 1840. Here again Propaganda allowed the building against the wishes of the Secular clergy, imposing a small yearly tax on the mission as a sign that it accepted episcopal authority. There were good arguments on both sides in these cases, and sometimes the Secular opposition appears to have been unreasonable, based perhaps on a determination to make the most of their newly-dominant position.

Clearly, the new diocese of Liverpool would need the combined services of both Regulars and Seculars in increased numbers to serve existing and new congregations of Catholics, and to build successfully on the long tradition of Lancashire Catholicism. In the meantime, Catholic numbers in the county were about to jump to previously unimaginable levels with the massive Irish immigration of the 1840s, bringing in Catholics from an altogether different tradition.

Notes

[1] For eighteenth-century English Catholicism, Marie B. Rowlands (ed.), *Catholics of Parish and Town 1558-1778* (1999); quot. from p.348. See also J.A. Hilton, *Catholic Lancashire* (1994); John Bossy, *The English Catholic Community 1570-1850* (1975). On the old missions and families, Dom F.O. Blundell, OSB, *Old Catholic Lancashire*, 3 vols. (1925-1941).

[2] Rowlands, pp.291, 329.

[3] *Ibid.*, pp.291-6.

[4] Leo Gooch (ed.), *The Revival of English Catholicism: The Banister-Rutter Correspondence 1777-1807* (1995), p.3; F.J. Singleton, *Mowbreck Hall and the Willows* (1983).

[5] Blundell, 1, pp.92-115, and the Society's *Whitsun Newsletter 2003*.

[6] Brian Plumb, *St Mary's, Little Crosby. A History* (1997).

[7] Blundell, 3, pp.125-32; Gillian Goddard, *St John the Evangelist Catholic Church, Burscough, A Celebration of the Tercentenary ... of the Burscough Hall Mission 1700-2000* (2000).

[8] Blundell, 2, pp.91-111; Rowlands, p.353.

[9] J.F. Giblin, 'The Molyneux Family and the Missions at Scholes Hall and Our Lady's Portico', *NWCH*, XXI (1994), pp.1-13; G. Holt, SJ, 'Croxteth-Gillmoss: The Development of a Mission', *NWCH*, XXII (1995), pp.1-8.

[10] Anne C. Parkinson, *A History of Catholicism in the Furness Peninsula, 1127-1997* (1998), pp.39-68.

[11] On the Relief Acts, Bossy, chap.13; Hilton, pp.60-90; B. Ward, *The Dawn of the Catholic Revival in England, 1781-1803*, 3 vols. (1909).

[12] Dominic Aidan Bellenger, *The French Exiled Clergy in the British Isles after 1789* (1986).

[13] M. Panikkar, 'A Catholic Scarlet Pimpernel and the Dames of Ghent: the Benedictine Convent in Preston 1795-1811', *NWCH*, XXIX (2002), pp.50-60.

[14] Blundell, 3, chap.16.

[15] On Gérardot, Burke, p.31; I am very grateful to Mr Michael O'Neill for information on him and St Anthony's. On Richebeque, J. Carus, *History of St Lewis' Church, Croft* (1977); Bellenger, pp.239, 277.

[16] G.I.T. Machin, *The Catholic Question in English Politics,1820-1830* (1964).

[17] Hilton, pp.69-70; L. Hanley, 'John Sadler: An Eighteenth-Century Liverpool Catholic', *NWCH*, VIII (1981), pp.16-24.

[18] J.F. Giblin, 'The Orrell Family and the Mission of St Mary's, Blackbrook, in Parr, St Helens', *NWCH*, VII (1980), pp.6-19; 'The Gerard Family of Bryn and Ince and the Parish of SS Oswald and Edmund', *NWCH*, XVII (1990), pp.1-17.

[19] M. Whitehead, 'The Gillows and their work in Georgian Lancaster', in J.A. Hilton (ed.), *Catholic Englishmen* (1984), pp.21-27.

[20] Hilton, p.70, but see J. Virgoe, 'Thomas Fleetwood and the draining of Martin Mere', *THSLC*, vol. 152 (2004), pp.28-9. On Barrow, D. Milburn, *A History of Ushaw College* (1964), p.68.

[21] T.G. Holt, SJ, 'Joseph Dunn of Preston from his Correspondence', Hilton, *Catholic Englishmen*, pp.29-36; p.29.

[22] Tom Smith, 'Preston Catholics Before Emancipation', *NWCH*, XXVI (1999), pp.33-61; quotation re trustees in Leo Warren, *Through Twenty Preston Guilds* (1993), pp.28-9.

[23] J.A. Hilton, 'A Catholic Congregation in the Age of Revolution: St Benedict's, Hindley', *NWCH*, XVII (1990), pp.20-28.

[24] J.A. Hilton, 'Catholic Congregationalism in Fleetwood, 1841-42', *NWCH*, XXVI (1999), pp.62-9.

[25] Rowlands, p.322; D.J. Pope, 'The Liverpool Catholic and Maritime Business Community', *NWCH*, XXX (2003), pp.28-56.

[26] Rowlands, p.322; Hilton, *Catholic Lancashire*, p.64.

[27] Burke, pp.15-24, includes the Bishop's letter in full; Bossy, pp.341-4.

[28] J.A. Hilton, 'Lingard's Hornby', in *Catholic Englishmen*, pp.37-44; Bossy, pp.374-7.

[29] Rowlands, p.269.

[30] Bossy, p.273; Gooch, *Revival*, passim, and pp.190-1.

[31] Bossy, p.133; M.V. Sweeney, 'Mixed Marriages: Some Statistics of the Eighteenth Century', *Cl.R*, XXIV (Sept. 1944), pp.402-6; for Hornby, RCLv Visitation Return,1865.

[32] Sr Dominic Savio (Hamer), CP, 'Some Passionist Parish Missions in the Victorian North West', *NWCH*, XXII (1995), pp.9-14.

[33] Brian Plumb, *Arundel*; J. Trappes-Lomax, *The Letters of Dr John Lingard to Mrs Thomas Lomax (1835-51)*, Catholic Record Society vol.77 (2000), pp.90,99.

[34] P. Hughes, 'The English Catholics in 1850' in *Beck*, pp.71-2. For Brown's quarrelsome character, Peter Doyle, 'A Tangled Skein of Confusion: The Administration of George Hilary Brown of Liverpool, 1850-56', *RH*, vol. 25 (Oct. 2000), pp.294-303.

[35] Burke, p.79. For the ending of lay control, Bossy, pp.349-54.

[36] Burke, passim; Bossy, pp.349-50.

[37] Francis Edwards, SJ, *The Jesuits in England:From 1580 to the Present Day* (1985), pp.144-72; J.A. Hilton, 'The Case of Wigan: Catholic Congregationalism in the Age of Revolution', *NWCH*, X (1983), pp.1-7.

[38] M. Whitehead, 'The English Jesuits and Episcopal Authority: The Liverpool Test Case, 1840-1843', *RH*, vol.18 (Oct. 1986), pp.197-219.

CHAPTER 2 THE IRISH INVASION

People had sailed from Irish ports to Liverpool for centuries, some to trade and return, some for seasonal employment and some to settle permanently. This migration increased steadily as Liverpool grew in importance as a port and as the new industries of Lancashire and elsewhere drew a growing workforce from rural areas. By 1750 Liverpool ranked second only to London in the importance of its trade with the Americas, including the slave trade. Its trade with Dublin, Drogheda and lesser Irish ports also increased substantially as the century went on and by the nineteenth century it was its control of this Irish Sea trade that provided a secure foundation for its overall prosperity. In the eighteenth century there were Liverpool-based Irish Catholic ship-owners, while other Irish immigrants were to be found in all social levels of the town. By the mid-nineteenth century there were Irish merchant families in the wealthy Abercromby Square area and about 7% of all the merchants, bankers and businessmen in the town were Irish by birth or descent (although not all of them were Catholic, of course). The very important and lucrative Anglo-Irish cattle trade, for example, was dominated by the Liverpool firm of Cullen and Verdon. The two Cullen proprietors were brothers of Cardinal Cullen of Dublin, and were noted for their wealth and charity, setting up temporary hospital facilities for the famine Irish after 1847 on their business premises, and featuring in the top two or three subscribers to Catholic good causes.[1]

IMAGES AND REALITIES

By 1841 there were at least 106,000 Irish-born people living in Lancashire out of a total of 219,000 in the whole of England and Wales. Most of the Lancashire Irish had migrated from Leinster and Ulster. It is important not to think of them all as the poor driven out by famine, hardship and over-population. The ports and provincial towns of Ireland had their own newspapers and these frequently carried adverts for jobs abroad and emigrants' letters, detailing the better life to be found in England. The development of steamships from the 1820s made the journey to England shorter and cheaper and emigration schemes were touted by various agencies; overall, the decision to emigrate was often a positive one, taken by those with initiative. It is interesting in this context that the 1836 Commissioners looking into the condition of the poor in English towns and

St Patrick's Church built for the Irish immigrants in the south end of Liverpool (1821-27).

cities found evidence among the immigrants, including the labouring poor, of a desire to improve their condition. Irish migration to England was part of a chain migration, where the newly arrived could join stable kinship groups that would help them to find work and housing. They would find Irish pubs and Catholic churches that served as social centres and provided formal and informal support groups, thus helping the newly arrived to adapt to what would otherwise have been an alien environment. The massive and unexpected famine migration of 1847 – 1850 upset this pattern and created immediate problems, but it did not destroy it altogether.

Liverpool was used to large numbers of Irish moving through or staying for temporary work before returning to Ireland. Each year saw heavy seasonal migration for harvesting – an estimated 57,000 in 1841 – and for navvying and building work. The census of 1841 gives figures of 49,639 Irish-born people in Liverpool – this equates to over 17% of the town's population (it was very much a 'new' town – only 42% of its inhabitants at that date had been born there). By 1851 the numbers in the county had risen by a massive 81%, to 191,506, and in Liverpool to 86,574 – over 21% of the total. Most of these increases were due to the huge mass of people leaving Ireland because of the potato famine: the numbers are truly staggering – over 280,000 landed in Liverpool in 1846, over 300,000 in 1847, about 200,000 each year in the three years 1848-50, and about 250,000 in 1851. Of course, not all stayed in Liverpool – most moved on to other parts of Britain or re-emigrated to America (130,000 left Liverpool for the United States in 1847 alone).

Strict new poor law regulations meant that several thousand were returned to Ireland, while many died either from the effects of the famine or the awful living conditions in the Liverpool courts and cellars – the registrar general described the town as 'the hospital and cemetery of Ireland'.[2] In 1861 there were 88,732 Irish-born resident in Liverpool and West Derby (a separate Poor Law Union and so counted separately in the census).

1847 was a year of severe economic depression and suffering in England. Even before the famine Irish arrived, living conditions in Liverpool were bad as migrants from rural Lancashire and elsewhere crowded into the booming port. The Town Council started to deal with the problems of over-crowding and disease by having two enlightened Acts of Parliament passed to overcome the worst of these conditions, setting up a statutory Health Committee and taking control of drainage, sewerage, paving, street cleansing and scavenging. The country's first public Medical Officer of Health (Dr William Duncan) was appointed as a result and reported on the living conditions that he found in that year. It was common, he claimed, to find every room in a house occupied by several families, with any sort of privacy impossible:

The father, mother and children of one family sleep together in a corner; the father, mother and children of another family sleep together in another; ditto, ditto, ditto, in a third, etc ... I have latterly seen more cases in which 'litters' are spread upon the floor or pavement, perhaps without any article of furniture in the apartment, or at most a broken chair or two, a log of wood or a stool.[3]

Under Duncan's guidance, and that of a newly appointed Inspector of Nuisances, work began in 1847 on clearing and closing the worst of the cellars. Their efforts were almost immediately overwhelmed as the Irish migrants entered the port in unprecedented numbers and the two severest epidemics ever to hit the town did so in 1847 and 1849. Cellars and other dwellings that had been condemned were re-opened to house the newcomers, over-crowding was inevitable and many of the migrants were already weak and sick from the famine that had driven them out of Ireland. The so-called Irish Famine Fever (in reality, typhus, dysentery and diarrhoea) killed about 7,500 people in 1847 in Liverpool (including ten priests and ten doctors), with another 1,500 succumbing to scarlatina – about 5,500 of whom were Irish. The epidemic of cholera in 1849 killed over 5,200, with another 1,050 dying from diarrhoea.

Apart from those who re-emigrated, many left the port to walk to other parts of England, to find relatives and friends who might provide shelter and find them work. It is not possible to estimate how many died on the way, but we know of enough harrowing examples to show that the roads through Prescot, St Helens, Wigan and Warrington took their toll of the sick and destitute[4]. Moreover, despite its reputation as the 'black spot on the Mersey', Liverpool was not unique in the conditions endured by its poorer inhabitants, whether English or Irish. Preston, for example, suffered from great poverty, with a large number of insanitary cellar dwellings and a terrible cholera outbreak in 1849. As late as the 1880s it had a general death rate higher than Liverpool's, and both its fever death rate and its infant mortality rate were higher than its more notorious neighbour's.[5]

Commentators at the time, and writers since, have tended to concentrate on this part of the truly horrific immigrant experience. While understandable, this has obscured the fact that, once the worst years had passed and the economy picked up, many Irish-born gained jobs that required skill and gave them responsibility, status and some financial reward. These enabled them to move into better housing and to become indistinguishable in many respects from their English neighbours in a similar economic position.[6] A survey of the Lancashire towns in 1872 noted how in St Helens, for example, the newly arrived Irish had started 'in the lowest and most laborious places', but many had already risen to be foremen, some to be managers and even a few to be manufacturers in their own right, while the Liberal newspaper of the town was owned and edited by an Irishman. A similar picture could be seen in Widnes, although there more remained as labourers.[7] The same factors that had enabled their earlier compatriots to rise up the social ladder worked for the newly arrived immigrants as well, though more slowly. The great majority of the new arrivals, however, continued to experience poverty, disease and only low-paid, casual work. A few rose from rags to riches, far more from rags to respectability, but most remained subject to the uncertainties and indignities of the casual labour market.

While Liverpool had by far the largest number of Irish immigrants, by 1851 there was hardly a district in the diocese that did not have its Irish-born inhabitants, as the following table shows:[8]

	Total population	Total Irish-born	Irish-born as % of total population
Prescott	56,074	6,235	11.1
Ormskirk	38,307	1,599	4.2
Wigan	77,539	4,502	5.8
Warrington	36,164	3,629	10.0
Leigh	32,734	812	2.5
Chorley	37,701	944	2.5
Preston	96,545	5,822	6.0
Fylde	22,002	734	3.3
Garstang	12,695	110	0.9
Lancaster	34,660	536	1.5
Ulverston	30,556	374	1.2

Even in Liverpool, the impact of the immigration was not spread evenly. In 1851, Garston had only 3.9% Irish-born inhabitants, Walton 1.4% and Allerton 3.2%, compared with 41.4% in the southern dock area and a massive 59.7% in the northern dock area. As the waves of Irish immigration continued month by month with no sign of the flood ebbing, and as they were blamed for the diseases that wracked the town, English attitudes to them changed and from being rather quaint figures of fun they became an alien menace, somehow spreading moral contagion as well as physical. Even the normally objective Dr Duncan described in emotional language how the newly arrived Irish:

> By their example and intercourse with others are rapidly lowering
> the standard of comfort among their English neighbours, communicating
> their own vicious and apathetic habits, and fast extinguishing all sense of
> moral dignity, independence and self-respect.[9]

Bishop Brown, the Vicar Apostolic for Lancashire, reported to Rome that 'the dreadful plague which the poor Irish have brought into our cities – they are immersed in starvation and squalor – has upset almost everything that relates to religion and the clergy'. They were also vilified as an additional burden on the town's poor law rate, though the evidence does not support the exaggerated press claims of the time, and were thought to work for lower wages, though this should have been some compensation for those paying more in rates; overall, the huge reserve of unemployed labourers was of definite benefit to the port's prosperity.[10] But in these matters perception, not fact, is everything, and adverse ethnic stereotyping lasted well beyond the period of mass migration – it became a staple of certain English attitudes to the Irish and, in too many cases, to Catholics as well.

THE CHALLENGES

About 80% of the new migrants were Catholic, and this posed an immediate challenge to the Lancashire clergy to provide some basic spiritual care for them. There is something heroic in the traditional picture of faithful Irish pastors volunteering to 'go into exile' with their people, working with them in their ghettoes in the industrial slums of England and so helping to strengthen the already strong bonds between priest and people that had been forged in Ireland. We have been told of the priests 'who arrived in scores from Ireland' and who 'brought with them that old tradition of intimate relationship between the Irish priest and his parish'. All this would have been news to the immigrants, for there is no evidence that Irish priests came to England in substantial numbers in the 1840s and 1850s – there were scarcely enough of them to go round in Ireland itself. Some contemporaries believed that the Irish Catholics in England were being seriously neglected. Fr Gentili, a peripatetic Rosminian missioner rather given to exaggeration, reported to Rome that many of the Irish in England were 'abandoned for want of pastors who never put their foot in the areas where they live, and so they miserably perish'. In 1842, 24,000 Irish Catholics in Liverpool signed a petition claiming that very little was being done to help them spiritually and that some English Catholics were even putting obstacles in the way of the few Irish priests who tried to help. The main lack, the petitioners claimed, was of priests who could speak Gaelic, so that large numbers could not go to confession; even the mission of St Patrick's, built specifically for the Irish, had no Irish priest. The petition was got up by an Irish priest, Dr Butler, whose faculties Bishop Brown had refused to renew because of rumours of unsavoury conduct, so it needs careful interpretation. Even so, Butler could hardly have persuaded so many to sign it if they had been happy with the provision being made for them and if there had been other Irish priests available in the town.[11]

Recent research has cast much needed light on how the Irish lived and adapted, or failed to adapt, outside the major centres of immigration such as Liverpool and Manchester. The northern parts of the diocese had its Irish colonies, both Catholic and Protestant, in Barrow-in-Furness and Coniston, where rapid industrialisation from the 1860s onwards attracted large numbers of migrants, especially from Ulster – the towns and villages of Lancashire 'north of the sands' had their street battles as King Billy and the Pope fought for territorial dominance.[12] By 1870, Barrow-in-Furness had around 4,000 Irish Catholics and one writer, with pardonable local pride, has claimed that the town was the epitome of the new Irish-oriented Catholicism that arose in Victorian England.[13] It was also the scene, in 1864, of violent anti-Irish disturbances, caused principally, it seems, by long folk memories of previous conflict between rival navvying gangs and a desire for revenge, as well as perceptions of the Irish as an economic threat. There was further trouble as late as 1903 when a series of lectures and sermons by extreme anti-Catholic preachers in the town (including the notorious Rev. George Wise from Liverpool) aroused latent working-class Protestant and Orange anti-Catholicism and provoked Irish Catholic retaliation.[14]

While we would find it difficult to see the bedraggled immigrants as a threat to England's stability, they were suspect at the time by association with the 1848 revolutionary troubles in Ireland. There were militants among the Liverpool Irish, including some who supported the 'physical force' solution to Ireland's problems, and these had plans to 'rise' in Liverpool once they had news of a successful rebellion in their native land. A new type of Irish secret society, Ribbonism, had grown up – a 'sectarian blend of religion-based nationalism, secrecy and communal solidarity' – and Ribbonmen met frequently in Liverpool Irish pubs, acting as benefit agencies and job centres, while also providing information networks for the more politically committed. In addition, there were the more militant Confederate Clubs (twenty-three have been identified in Liverpool in 1848), each claiming to be able to put 2,000 – 4,000 armed men on the streets at short notice. Informers leaked plans to the authorities; 12,000 special constables were sworn in, army re-inforcements were encamped in Everton and armed marines stood ready on a boat in the Mersey to resist the rebels. Searches by the police uncovered weapons and ammunition. The rising in Ireland collapsed ignominiously and nothing happened in Liverpool.[15] One result of all this was that it sharpened the focus of the image of the Irish as secret plotters and revolutionaries, an alien presence that could not be trusted. This image was further defined by the genuinely dangerous activities of the Fenians revealed in the 1860s. Perhaps it also subconsciously lent support to claims that Catholics could not be loyal English citizens, an age-old shibboleth that was a long time dying. It certainly could make even some English Catholics suspicious of Irish associations and societies, no matter how innocent – Bishop Goss (1856-72) suspected the Catholic Young Men's Society of being a possible republican front (see page 68).

More lasting were worries about the image of the drunken Irish Catholic portrayed too often in the press. The first thing the immigrants saw as they stepped ashore at the Clarence Dock was a statue of St Patrick with a shamrock in his hand. It was not there to offer a spiritual welcome, however, as it adorned the wall of Jack Langan's public house. The owner was a former boxer who died in 1846, leaving a massive £20,000, proof, if any were needed, of his wisdom in placing his pub where it would catch the eye of the immigrant and of the value of the earthly as well as the heavenly patronage of Ireland's favourite saint.[16] In Victorian England the pub played a key role in working-class life, a refuge from terrible living conditions, offering warmth, conviviality and, as we have seen with the Irish Ribbonmen, the support of a range of informal social agencies. It was also the despair of the Victorian social reformer, for whom drunkenness was the major social curse, the wellspring from which flowed most of the real and supposed ills of the lower classes. No matter how kindly one might look on the pub-centred working-class culture of the time and lament that middle-class reformers failed to see its positive values, there is no doubting that excessive drinking was a terrible scourge in Victorian times, and no doubting either that the Irish immigrants made up a considerably higher proportion of those guilty of it than their numbers warranted. Liverpool had the highest number of arrests for drunkenness of any town in the country outside London, with a startling proportion of 1-in-25 of the population arrested for the crime.

As a matter of course, bishops and priests were concerned with the effects of drunkenness on family life, but were as divided as other reformers about whether a teetotal solution was the best way forward – neither Bishop Goss nor his successor Bishop O'Reilly (1873-94) were keen on teetotal initiatives. In general, Catholic leaders were suspicious of the various national abstinence movements because of their strongly Protestant nature; their attitudes began to change slowly after Cardinal Manning's public conversion to the national campaign in 1866, and also because of the apparent failure of piece-meal Catholic efforts. A number of parishes had started their own temperance societies some years before and it was one of these, at St Peter's, Seel Street, that had invited the famous Irish temperance reformer, Fr Mathew, to visit the town in 1843.[17] It is claimed that he persuaded 40,000 Liverpool Catholics to take the total abstinence pledge, and over the next three months about 600,000 throughout the rest of the country – the numbers are impossible to verify, and some people took the pledge each time they attended a meeting during the campaign. Fr Mathew visited the town again in 1849 and 1854, when he was too ill to preach, but little lasting benefit seems to have come from his crusade, perhaps because of a lack of effective follow-up by the clergy. Certainly Fr Mathew and his movement adopted a strongly anti-nationalist stance that made it unpopular with many Irish.

Bishop Goss frequently preached on the topic at visitations, and clearly saw the problem principally in terms of the individual's moral failing; he drew up a list of mortal sins connected with drinking that had to be read out in parishes: going to pubs if excessive drinking usually resulted, enticing others to drink excessively, selling liquor to those likely to get drunk, and so on. Yet by 1860 only two of the Liverpool town churches had specific temperance societies (Holy Cross and Our Lady's, Eldon Street), although it must also have been a constant theme of the many men's societies and guilds up and down the diocese. It was not until 1868 that Goss recommended the setting up of Temperance Confraternities that would provide some mutual help and encouragement to the individual.[18]

The diocesan temperance banner was taken up by Fr (later Mgr) James Nugent, himself the Liverpool-born son of Irish immigrant parents. He was impressed by what he found in the United States and Canada in 1870-71: almost every church had a successful total abstinence society that was also a general benefit society – the 'leaven of each congregation', he called them. With his experience over twenty-two years as a Liverpool prison chaplain, Nugent was in a better position than most to analyse the causes of the high crime rate among the poorer classes, and he had no doubt that the single most important factor was drink – rather like the modern reactions to the problem of drugs, he believed that most thieving and other crime was caused by the need to get money for drink.[19] On occasion he offended his Liverpool compatriots by attacking in public their excessive drinking. He was particularly severe about the effects of drink on women:

> *Drink is making terrible havoc upon the female population of this town;*
> *not only demoralising the young and leading them step by step into crime*
> *and the lowest depths of vice, but destroying the sacred character of*
> *family life and changing wives and mothers into brutal savages.*[20]

He argued that longer and more punitive prison sentences, especially for 'incorrigible women', were one solution to all this. So also, more positively, were education and better after-care of ex-prisoners – in 1865 he established the Reformatory Disposal and Discharged Prisoners' Aid Society. But the only sure way was to stop people drinking excessively in the first place, and so, in 1872, he launched the League of the Cross, a total abstinence association for Catholics. It was to be:

an organisation which takes by the hand the poor drunkard, who was deaf
and dumb, blind and palsied, by drink, and enables him to help himself.
This is its chief work, and it seeks by every means to deliver men from the
curse and slavery of drink, and bring them through the Sacraments to
God Himself.[21]

The League was founded by Cardinal Manning with Nugent's help
(acknowledged by the Cardinal; it is not clear what part each played or who
had the original idea) and was based loosely on the structure of the Salvation
Army in that its members were divided into Officers, Captains and body-
guards who wore a bright red sash at meetings. The first to take the pledge in
Liverpool was John Denvir, the noted Irish nationalist (see page 50) – he tells us
in his autobiography that he had already taken the pledge three times as a boy
during Fr Mathew's campaign. The first League of the Cross hall was built at
the corner of St Anne Street and Rose Place in 1875, and its weekly
'perseverance and re-union' meetings (usually accompanied by a concert) were
well attended. Nugent tried to give the audience the same sort of entertainment
that they would get in a music hall and tried to 'catch the taste of the people,
and to elevate them'. He also gave them cookery lessons himself.[22]

He found it more difficult to persuade the clergy to set up branches in
their parishes and later spoke of the apathy he had encountered. Yet 300 –
400 took the pledge weekly at the meetings, and those who persevered for a
year became League Veterans. Police records show that Irish convictions for
drunkenness dropped considerably after 1871,[23] yet when Bishop O'Reilly
sent in his official report on the diocese to Rome in 1886 he still picked out
drunkenness as the major problem in the diocese and the cause of many
other evils. He went on to say that the same had been true in his report of
five years before and no effective remedy had been found, despite the efforts
of his priests in the towns and country areas through private exhortation,
sermons, sodalities and every other possible means to drive out such a
pernicious evil. It comes as some surprise, then, to see that there were only
ten parishes in 1886 in the whole of the diocese with temperance-linked
sodalities or guilds, including six branches of the League of the Cross. One
place where it seems to have been particularly successful and long-lasting
was Warrington where for fifty years it was the leading Catholic society in
the town. It organised evening classes, picnics, pantomimes, tea parties and
lectures on general religious topics – Cardinal Manning spoke twice there.
The League also had a band that took part in the Walking Day processions
and other events.[24]

The issue of temperance crossed the divide between social and religious
ills. While the Church authorities were concerned about the material
conditions of the newly arrived Catholics, they were naturally far more
worried by their spiritual state. From all sides, apparently, came accounts of
the 'deplorable effects' that the sufferings of the famine had had on the
spiritual condition of the poor Irish: according to the priests and nuns
working among them:

they are not like the same people they were before the famines began …
There are in Liverpool alone a great many thousands who are said to
have abandoned every religious practice with the exception of
abstaining on Fridays.[25]

'Abstaining on Fridays' seems to have become more a folk-custom than a sign of religious observance – and how much meat would these poor people have had anyway? The account raises the important questions of how strongly, and in what ways, Irish pre-famine Catholics had practised their religion. Unlike the Irish Catholicism of the later 19th century, in many parts of rural Ireland, especially in the west and north, the devotion of the people, while strong, had not been particularly 'practising'. Among the reasons put forward for this was a shortage of priests and churches in parts of pre-famine Ireland – the Catholic population of the country had almost trebled in the hundred years before 1841, while the number of priests had risen by less than 50%. The level of 'non-practice' can be exaggerated, and the Irish bishops were addressing its causes actively in the first half of the nineteenth century, with considerable success in the towns and in the east and south of the country. In parts of rural Ireland, however, and especially in the areas where Gaelic was still spoken, there was, perhaps, a level of practice as low as 20 – 40%, with a lack of clear instruction in the Faith and little attention paid to the sacraments other than baptism and extreme unction. So, for example, when the Redemptorists held a mission in Kerry in 1860, 1,000 adults out of about 8,000 received Communion for the first time, while the priest at St Alban's, Warrington, reported in 1865 that many of the immigrant Irish who attended his church irregularly had never been to Communion 'or but once or twice' in their own country, and he feared that half of them were out of the Church altogether. What was strong among the Irish, whatever the level of their formal practice, was respect for the priest and a strong attachment to religion. The priest, indeed, enjoyed cult status among the Irish as the local 'holy man', a 'mine of information and an indefatigable performer of personal services' both spiritual and social – and that whether he himself was English or Irish.[26]

Bishop Goss, responsible for providing priests and churches for the newly arrived Irish, was intensely English – as Cardinal Wiseman reported to Rome, probably with a fair amount of episcopal envy, he was always telling his people, 'I am English, I am a real John Bull, indeed I am a Lancashire man'! Goss gloried in his Englishness and in his loyalty to Queen Victoria and felt his fellow-Catholics should do the same. As he told an audience in Preston:

We have been born on the soil and have all the feelings of Englishmen.
And we are proud of the government under which we now live. We
believe it to be the best, the most perfect government in the world … We
belong to the nation; in heart we are English, in purpose we are loyal.

How did he expect his Irish subjects to respond to this? He was enough of a historian to know that they had little cause to look favourably on English rule, for he had written that after centuries of government of a kind that could hardly be paralleled even in Russia, England had failed to win the affections of the Irish or to reconcile them to her rule. He even wrote that the injustices they had suffered had been so great as to justify rebellion – and that, for the true-blue, reactionary and anti-democratic Tory that he was, was some admission. How, then, did he relate to the Irish in his diocese?

While John Denvir described Goss as 'an Englishman of the best sort', others were critical and believed that he was not interested in Irish affairs. He angered them when he said publicly that the Liverpool Irish stood as much chance of preferment as their English counterparts if only they would abstain from drink and other vices, and on a number of occasions he openly condemned Fenianism and other Irish secret societies. It is clear that he felt that it was only by playing down their nationality that the Irish could be fully accepted in English society and so gain the position that 'their natural ability and the fertility of their mental resources' deserved. On one occasion he went so far as to claim that he had no Irish priests in his diocese, for it was an English diocese ruled by an English Bishop, and the clergy who served it were English, whatever their country of origin.[27]

Goss tried to defend himself against Irish charges of indifference and even hostility by claiming the existence of some ultra-national citizenship in which they all shared. At a St Patrick's night banquet he said that he knew some people said that he was so English and so Lancastrian that he had no sympathy with any problems outside the diocese. He repeated that he was proud to be an English subject, and that he thought this country was one of the greatest in the world. He went on:

> When I say this country I mean England, Ireland and Scotland, because it is perfectly chimerical to attempt to separate them – it is an impossibility. The people are spread and intermixed amongst each other, and there is hardly any work done or great act achieved, which is not equally shared by natives of the three different parts of the country.[28]

However laudable this was as an ideal, it was unlikely to impress those who harboured long-standing feelings of injustice and who felt that they had to fight against prejudice when they tried for jobs or preferment. It is interesting that a later writer of strong Irish sympathies tried to defend Goss's attitude by claiming that the Bishop sincerely believed that everyone had equal opportunities in England (no talk of un-level playing-fields in those self-help days), and that he found it difficult to believe that his own countrymen could be deeply prejudiced against the Irish. It appears that he was prepared to allow a large proportion of his subjects to feel let down by his attitude to them, because to speak otherwise would, for him, have been dishonest and because he felt it was of the greatest importance to convince Protestants that Catholics were fully English and completely loyal.[29] Did he perhaps also hope that his constant repetition of how English he and his fellow Catholics were would somehow effect what it signified?

It is interesting that as late as 1903 Bishop Whiteside (1894-1921) felt he had to move two priests from Barrow, because they had become too involved in Irish politics; one of them, Fr Barry, was also admonished for supposedly anti-English outbursts. Their removal caused a local outcry and an Irish Catholic Association was set up to campaign for their re-instatement; petitions were signed, parents withdrew their children from the Catholic schools in protest and others threatened to withhold financial contributions. Letters to the Bishop spoke of 'another blow aimed at your Irish children', while a letter to all the priests in the diocese argued that Fr Barry had organised his Irish social gatherings and had played the nationalist card to keep young immigrants, mainly from Belfast, in touch with the Church; he had argued, the letter continued, that 'an Irishman who forgets his nationality surely forgets his faith'. It was a minor incident; the people soon accepted the fact that the Bishop was not going to budge and set about organising farewell testimonials for the two priests.[30]

There was further trouble a few years later when the parish priest of St Mary's, Fr John Miller, flew the flag of St George on St George's Day 1908; again there was an Irish boycott of the parish collections and the parish was sharply divided. This time Bishop Whiteside threatened to close the church until peace was restored. Fr Miller left on sick leave the same year and the Bishop replaced him with 'the most English of English priests, Fr Robert Dobson', the future auxiliary Bishop. He succeeded in uniting the parish – perhaps the troubles under Fr Miller had been due to a clash of personality as well as a clash of nationality.[31] Both incidents are indicative of the very careful line to be taken by priests in any community where Faith and Nation were not easily kept apart. It was also a minor indication of the determination of the bishops of Liverpool that their Church should not become an Irish Church, as happened, for example, in parts of the United States and Australia where Irish Catholics had also settled in large numbers. In this context the existence of a strong, well-organised Lancashire Catholic Church into which the Irish gradually integrated themselves was very important; even in places where they came to dominate it numerically, they were not able to create it in their own image. A small indication of this was the very few parishes dedicated to Irish saints throughout the diocese.

MAKING GOOD

It is worth saying something about the Irish who made good – they provided models of integration without any loss of pride in their Irish culture and became champions of Irish and Catholic causes. The most prominent Catholic Irishman in Liverpool for many years was Richard Sheil (1790-1871), a native of Dublin who developed a very successful import and export business, principally with the West Indies. He sat as a Liberal on the reformed town council in the mid-1830s (along with two other Catholics, Henry Sharples, nephew of Bishop Sharples, auxiliary to Bishop Brown, and Robert Roskell, father of the future Bishop of Nottingham) and was the first

Catholic to be elected an alderman in 1836 (Burke suggests he was the first in the country). He was a founder member and first president of the Catholic Club, which was 'to promote unity of purpose, energy in practical charity, and good fellowship in principle'; it also played an important part in local politics, especially in getting Irish voters to register. Sheil remained proud of his 'rich, mellifluous brogue' and of his Irishness: 'He is ever to be found at the head of any movement ... calculated to promote (Ireland's) political or religious welfare, and his enthusiasm on such occasions shows with what heartiness and zeal he espouses the cause of Ireland'. A regular communicant at St Oswald's, Old Swan, he was known for the social events he organised for Catholic charities and could always be relied on to campaign for Catholic causes. Such was his standing in the town that a road and a public park were named after him.[32]

Another successful Irishman who left a quite different mark on the town was Michael J. Whitty, a native of Wexford, who began a career in journalism in London before moving to Liverpool, at the invitation of another Catholic, Robert Rockliff, founder of the well-known printing and publishing firm. There he quickly became a well-known figure, becoming the town's first Chief Constable or Head of the Watch in the 1830s, founding the Fire Brigade as a branch of the police force, and bringing in several useful reforms. At heart always a journalist, he founded the *Liverpool Daily Post* and claimed it was the first penny newspaper in the country. At one time he was sent to Lancaster gaol for defending the freedom of the press to criticise the judiciary. While he remained a Catholic throughout his life and was actively, but very privately, involved in Catholic charitable works, he used his newspaper to attack certain aspects of current Catholicism. In particular he wrote strongly against the way in which support for the temporal power of the papacy had become the latest orthodoxy, and criticised Bishop Goss for attacking the popular press as 'busy purveyors of news, who are paid for gratifying the itching curiosity of busy idlers panting for excitement'. The Bishop had gone on to claim that the penny paper daily laid before its readers 'all that is being done on the great stage of life. Public and private vices alike find room, if they are only thought sufficiently exciting'. Whitty replied caustically that it seemed that the Bishop, 'like used up aristocrats, associates cheapness with nastiness; he is tolerant of papers at threepence, but reprobates papers at one penny'. Whitty also had several run-ins with the *Catholic Northern Press,* normally getting the best of its editor because of his superior skill as a journalist. Many Liverpool Catholics accused him of disloyalty because he was publicly rocking their boat, a vessel that had enough trouble as it was in navigating the shoals of anti-Catholic prejudice, but he generally supported Catholic claims for equal rights and justice in local matters and was generally highly respected in the town. He died in 1873, aged 78.[33]

It was not just self-promotion that moved the successful Irish to leave the wings for a more centre-stage performance. They shared a genuine Irish pride and wanted their Liverpool compatriots to be able to do the same, by enjoying equal rights with the host community and overcoming the ethnic labelling that aimed at keeping them at the bottom of the social ladder. Respectability was a most important civic virtue in Victorian England, and, particularly after the revolutionary debacle of 1848, different groups of Liverpool Irish decided to work to achieve this coveted badge of acceptability. One of the groups was organised by John Denvir (see below); all its members appear to have studied at Nugent's Catholic Institute. Their aim as 'Emerald Minstrels' was to cultivate Irish music and literature, Irish pastimes and customs, and, above all, Irish Nationality. Denvir claimed that they had been successful in improving the tastes of the Liverpool Irish who had for too long, 'through sheer good nature, tolerated an objectionable class of so-called Irish songs, as well as the still more objectionable "stage Irishman"'.[34] John F McArdle, one of the Minstrels, became a well-known local performer, and the group became regular performers at Catholic and Nationalist events in England and Ireland.

In this context, Goss condemned Nugent for encouraging a dangerous sense of nationality by putting on Irish evenings with Irish music and sketches at the Institute. In a mixed community like Liverpool, the Bishop argued, 'we should endeavour to keep down and not keep up a spirit of nationality: we should make men forget that they are Irish or English in the fact that they are Catholic'.[35] This was unfair and misunderstood the situation, since what Nugent was doing was trying to provide a respectable alternative to the pub and to the troublesome street celebrations of the Irish, especially on St Patrick's Day. A sense of pride and self-confidence were important first steps to immigrant rehabilitation.

It was mainly in local politics that the Irish who prospered made public names for themselves and advanced this campaign. Some of the more patrician among them sat as Liberals, but most sat under the general umbrella of Irish Nationalism. Their interests were by no means wholly devoted to single-issue Irish politics, however, and they turned increasingly to the more immediate concerns of their less successful compatriots such as housing, employment and social welfare. A recent writer has identified three distinct groups among them.[36] The first were the professional men, especially the solicitors and doctors – Alexander Bligh, William Madden, George Lynskey, Charles Russell (later Lord Russell of Killowen and Lord Chief Justice), Andrew Commins, are some of the names here. Most of them came from well-to-do Irish families and were educated in Ireland and/or London, moving to Liverpool because of the career openings in that thriving town.

Then there were the successful merchants and businessmen, among them the Harford brothers who had a cloth and woollen business in Richmond Street, and one of whom, Austin, became Liverpool's first Catholic Lord Mayor at the age of eighty in 1943. There was also Lawrence Connolly, son of a County Dublin farmer and Liverpool's first Home Rule councillor; he left £78,000, the result of property development and speculation, particularly in the new resort of New Brighton. Charles Corbally was a nephew and partner

Irish National Foresters
gathered outside Sacred
Heart Church, Hindsford,
c1904 for a walking day.
(Wigan Heritage Services)

of Richard Sheil; he sat on the council for a number of years, was a member of
the Burial Board, treasurer of the Catholic Benevolent Society for thirty years
and a respected J.P. Oliver O'Hara dominated the Anglo-Irish egg trade after
migrating to Liverpool in the 1860s, and later was a Nationalist councillor and
generous party supporter.

The third group consisted of those who started out lower down the social
ladder, as shopkeepers, publicans and other providers of basic services to the
Irish community. John Denvir is difficult to classify. An apprentice joiner, he
set up his own building firm, studied at evening classes at the Catholic
Institute and moved into journalism. Nugent made him manager and editor of
The Catholic Times and he went on to publish a range of Irish Nationalist
publications, including the *Penny Illustrated Library* and the *United Irishmen*,
the short-lived mouthpiece of the Home Rule Confederation, of which he was
a founder and national organiser; he was also a Fenian and some-time gun-
runner. Joseph Clancy began as a hotel 'boots', moved into a successful
tobacconist business and hotel ownership, led the Catholic Representation
Association, served as a councillor and died worth £25,000. More colourful,
but not always taken seriously, was 'Dandy Pat' Byrne, an Irish-born Liverpool
dock labourer who acquired a number of public houses, subscribed generously
to Catholic causes, sat as a Nationalist councillor and died in 1890 leaving a
fortune of about £40,000, some of which went into a legacy to each of his
employees of £5 for every year spent in his service. A public memorial to him
has been restored recently.[37] To show that not all the Irish who prospered
wanted the limelight, we may mention Edward Smith who had arrived in
Liverpool as a penniless migrant from Co. Down, made himself a fortune

through coal mining, lived in merchant-prince style in Abercromby Square and remained a staunch Catholic until his death in 1880; his name does not appear in any charitable, civic or political contexts.

This chapter has not dealt with another sort of Irish immigration, that of Religious Sisters and Brothers, whose multi-faceted contribution to the development of the Church in Lancashire will be covered in a later chapter. There also remains to be covered the legacy of riot and civil disturbance and the pitifully slow acceptance of the Irish Catholics as equal citizens. By way of a conclusion after the first act of the drama, however, it may be said that the massive and in many ways disruptive Irish immigration of the 1840s caused immediate and severe problems for town and Church alike, and Bishop Brown's judgement, already mentioned, that it 'upset almost everything that relates to religion and the clergy' is understandable. But the problems were tackled with considerable energy and success, or faded away of their own accord over time. What was left, in the case of the Church in Lancashire, was a Catholic community that was changed for ever into a community with a rich diversity of traditions and a wealth of ability and commitment to call on in its future development.

Notes

[1] John Belchem, *Merseypride* (2000), p.136. See also his 'Class, Creed and Country: the Irish Middle Class in Victorian Liverpool', in R. Swift and S. Gilley (eds.), *The Irish in Victorian Britain: the Local Dimension* (1999), pp.190-211, and 'Liverpool in 1848: Image, Identity and Issues', *THSLC*, vol.147 (1998), pp.1-26. From the wide range of other works, see especially, W.J. Lowe, *The Irish in Mid-Victorian Lancashire* (1989); R. Swift and S. Gilley (eds.), *The Irish in the Victorian City* (1985), and *The Irish in Britain* (1989); Frank Neal, *Black '47: Britain and the Famine Irish* (1998).

[2] Belchem, *THSLC*, p.10. Neal, *Black '47*, is the best source for statistics about the famine.

[3] Quoted in A. Miller, *Poverty Deserved? Relieving the Poor in Victorian Liverpool* (1988), p.15. On Duncan, G. Kearns, P. Laxton and J. Campbell, 'Duncan and the Cholera Test: public health in nineteenth-century Liverpool', *THSLC*, vol.143 (1994), pp.87-115.

[4] Neal, *Black '47* chap.7.

[5] N. Morgan, *Deadly Dwellings: Housing and Health in a Lancashire Cotton Town: Preston from 1840-1914* (1993).

[6] Colin G. Pooley, 'Segregation or integration? The residential experience of the Irish in mid-Victorian Britain', in Swift and Gilley, *Irish in Britain*, pp.60-83, at pp.70-1.

[7] Alan O'Day (ed.), *A Survey of the Irish in England* (1872, repr. 1990), pp.111-4.

[8] Census, 1851.

[9] Quoted in Belchem, *THSLC*, p.9.

[10] Brown's 'Relatio Status' for 1847 is in RCLv Box 40. Neal, *Black '47*, pp.260, ff, analyses the economic impact.

[11] On Irish priests, see, e.g., D. Gwynn, 'The Irish Immigration', in Beck, pp.265-290; on Gentili, C. Leetham, *Luigi Gentili, a sower for the second spring* (1965), p.293; for Butler, APF, *S.R. Anglia*, vol.10, 225-8.

[12] D.M. MacRaild, *Culture, Conflict and Migration; The Irish in Victorian Cumbria* (1998), p.209.

[13] Parkinson, *Furness Peninsula*, p.60.

[14] MacRaild, pp.175, 192-4.

[15] Belchem, *Merseypride*, chap.3.

[16] Canon Bennett, *Father Nugent of Liverpool* (1949), p.104.

[17] Burke, pp.73-4.

[18] Goss's Visitation Sermons, RCLv 3/B, Visitation Diaries; *Synodi Liverpolitanae I-VIII* (n.d.),

pp.78-9, 82-3; for 1860 churches, *Guide to the Catholic Church Services … for 1861* (1861).

[19] Belchem, *Merseypride*, p.117; John Davies, 'Father James Nugent, Prison Chaplain', *NWCH*, XXII (1995), pp.15-24; Bennett, *Nugent*, chap. 10.

[20] Davies, *NWCH*, XXII, p.20.

[21] Bennett, *Nugent*, p.108.

[22] Canon Bennett, 'Father Nugent', in *Cathedral Record,* May 1948, pp.249-50.

[23] Lowe, pp.

[24] O'Reilly's Report is in APF, *SR Anglia*, vol. 27; for 1886 parish statistics, see *Directory*; on Warrington, Brian Plumb, *Our Glorious Chapter, The Story of St Mary's,* Warrington (1977), p.20.

[25] Belchem, *THSLC*, p.11.

[26] On pre-famine Irish practice, T.G. McGrath, 'The Tridentine Evolution of Modern Irish Catholicism, 1563-1962', *RH*, vol.20, no.4 (Oct.1991) pp.512-23. G. Connolly, 'The Transubstantiation of Myth', *JEH*, vol. 35 (1984). On Redemptorist missions, John Sharp, *Reapers of the Harvest: The Redemptorists in Great Britain and Ireland 1843-98* (1989). On Warrington, RCLv Visitation Returns 1865.

[27] Peter Doyle, 'Bishop Goss of Liverpool (1856-1872) and the Importance of Being English', in S. Mews (ed.), *Religion and National Identity, SCH,* vol.18 (1982), pp.433-447.

[28] *Ibid.*, p.446.

[29] Burke, p.185-6.

[30] MacRaild, pp.125-8.

[31] Parkinson, pp.78-9.

[32] Burke, p.53; Belchem, *Merseypride*, p.138.

[33] Burke, pp.99-100, 158-9.

[34] John Denvir, *The Life Story of an Old Rebel* (1910; re-publ. 1972), pp.118-22.

[35] RCLv Goss's Letterbooks 5/2, Goss to Fr Lans at Bishop Eton, Jan. 1859.

[36] Belchem, *Merseypride*, pp.148-50; also Burke for individuals and political struggles, and see P.J. Waller, *Democracy and Sectarianism: a Political and Social History of Liverpool 1868-1939* (1981) for detailed accounts and analysis.

[37] Sr Margaret Mary, SND, *Treasured Memories of St Joseph's 1845-2001* (2001), pp.12-15.

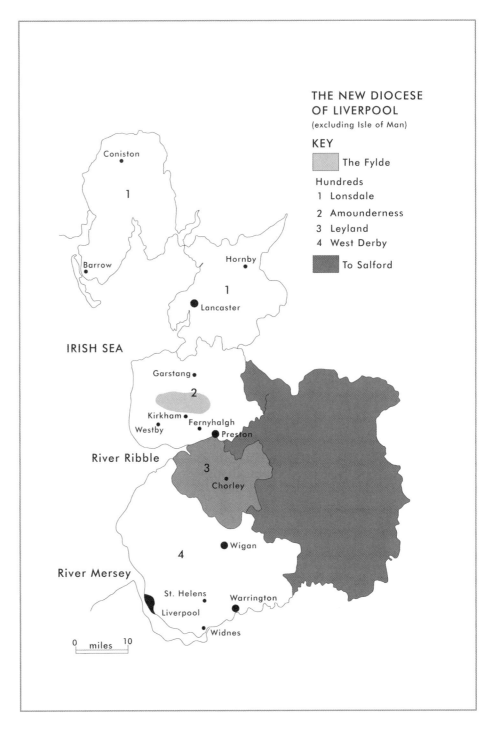

THE NEW DIOCESE
OF LIVERPOOL
(excluding Isle of Man)

KEY

The Fylde

Hundreds
1 Lonsdale
2 Amounderness
3 Leyland
4 West Derby

To Salford

Coniston

1

Barrow

Hornby

1

Lancaster

IRISH SEA

Garstang

2

Kirkham
Fernyhalgh
Westby
Preston

River Ribble

3

Chorley

River Mersey

4

Wigan

St. Helens
Warrington
Liverpool
Widnes

0   miles   10

CHAPTER 3 BISHOPS BROWN AND GOSS: SETTING THE TONE

Some people, including the future Cardinal Newman, argued against the restoration of a hierarchy in England and Wales because it would not be possible to find enough suitable bishops. It was taken for granted that the eight vicars apostolic already in post would become diocesan bishops, whatever their previous record as pastors and administrators, and so George Hilary Brown, Vicar Apostolic of the Lancashire District since 1840, became the first Bishop of the new diocese of Liverpool – despite his quarrelsome character it would have been difficult not to have appointed him. How far was he likely to satisfy the hopes of Cardinal Wiseman, the leader of the new hierarchy, that those appointed would be more than 'soft, good and respectable'?[1]

First, a word about the new diocese and its boundaries. As set up by the papal bull *Universalis Ecclesiae* of 29 September 1850, it consisted of those parts of Lancashire that made up the hundreds of West Derby, Amounderness and Lonsdale, and of the Isle of Man [see map]. The rest of the county (the hundreds of Salford, Blackburn and Leyland) made up the diocese of Salford. Bishop Brown had strongly opposed the splitting of the county between two dioceses (the only example in the thirteen new dioceses where this happened), but the rest of the vicars apostolic (including Bishop Sharples, Brown's coadjutor and vicar for the north) had recommended it to Propaganda on the strength of a petition from the clergy in the north of the county, who no doubt feared that a diocese encompassing the large urban centres of Liverpool and Manchester/Salford would have little room in practice for the needs of the rural north. Brown also objected to having his diocese divided into two sections by the hundred of Leyland – he would have had to travel through another bishop's territory to visit the northern section and he claimed the clergy were confused about which diocese they belonged to. He took advantage of the fact that no bishop was initially appointed to the diocese of Salford – he was to administer it until such an appointment was made – to persuade Propaganda that the offending hundred should be part of the Liverpool diocese and it was transferred in June 1851 (even today some Salford clergy have not forgiven Brown for what they regard as opportunistic skulduggery).[2]

This ensured that the new diocese ran unbroken from the River Mersey to Coniston in the Lake District and comprised large rural areas as well as the important towns of Lancaster, Liverpool, Preston, Warrington and Wigan. It was scarcely a unity, however: the area north of the River Ribble had a character of its own and the vicars apostolic had appointed separate vicars to administer it. As the urban areas of the south increased in size and commercial importance, with all the social problems associated with such expansion in Victorian times, the differences between them and the traditional areas of Catholic strength such as The Fylde only increased. Preston was left somewhat uneasily in the middle; when eventually, in 1924, the diocese was divided, it seemed to many to be ideally placed to become the seat of the new diocese (see chapter 11). The Isle of Man, of course, was an even more distinct area, with its own laws and a history of strong anti-Catholicism – in the 1780s only about thirty Catholics lived there and there was no resident missioner, though priests from Ireland and a French emigré priest lived and worked there on and off, and two Jesuits ministered there for a time in the 1820s. By the 1840s the Catholic population had risen to about 600, but its resident priest, Fr John Gallagher, still reported that nothing grew well there except sectarianism and every barrier was raised against the 'growth of Romanism'.[3] The island had strong trading links with Liverpool and Preston, but little else in common with its mainland neighbour.

Liverpool did not consider itself to be a true Lancastrian town: its status as the country's greatest exporter and its geographical position tended to make it look outwards, and both its merchant aristocracy and its largely unskilled labour force set it apart culturally and socially from other Lancastrian towns, including Manchester. It had more in common with Birkenhead than with Wigan and a sound case could have been argued for seeing the River Mersey as a unifying factor and not a natural frontier (Wiseman argued similarly about the Thames in London). Because the decision was taken in 1850 to use existing county boundaries as far as possible as diocesan boundaries, the opportunity was lost to create a diocese whose people would have shared common geographic and cultural/social characteristics – and the town of Warrington, which spanned the Mersey, was left divided between two dioceses, Liverpool and Shrewsbury.

BISHOP GEORGE HILARY BROWN 1850 – 1856

One of Bishop Brown's first steps was to establish a diocesan Chapter – the first of the restored bishops to do so. His list of provost and ten canons shows that he wanted to make the Chapter reasonably representative, given the size of the new diocese and its very diverse nature – while five of them resided in Liverpool, there were one each from Preston, Claughton, Chorley, Burscough, Lancaster and Old Swan (then a village outside Liverpool). The Bishop, however, soon regretted his haste and only nine months later wrote to Wiseman to say that he wished to drop two canons, one who was useless (it is not clear who this was) and one who was likely to be a trouble-maker – Canon Thomas Newsham of St Anthony's, Liverpool. This could not be done, and later letters claimed that Newsham was openly resisting him and revealing secret Chapter business. Brown wished to suspend the erring

canon and expel him from the Chapter, but Wiseman thought this would be too drastic and would need a formal process of enquiry to prove that Newsham was unfit to exercise diocesan faculties. Brown shied away from such a procedure and one is left wondering at his lack of judgement in choosing Newsham in the first place.[4]

The Bishop's troubled relations with his Chapter were not the result only of the actions of an obvious malcontent like Newsham. By now Brown was increasingly in bad health and also seemed unable to trust anybody fully or to delegate properly; he caused confusion among his advisers by indecision and delay. Having rushed to set up the Chapter, he consulted it formally only once in the first two years of its existence and seemed to have a rooted objection to doing it. The first serious quarrel between them concerned Brown's expenses. He constantly claimed that he did not have enough to live on and suggested to the Chapter that some sort of tax or subsidy should be levied on the diocese to meet his needs. The canons discussed the matter in December 1853 and expressed their opinion very unreservedly. They pointed out that while the Bishop's income was no more than £380 a year, he paid out the large sum of £130 in rent; they did not say so openly, but they clearly believed that Brown could have chosen a less costly lifestyle. In this context it is interesting that Fr Luigi Gentili, the

Rosminian entrusted by Propaganda with the task of reporting on the state of English Catholicism, claimed Brown had a fine country house (Bishop Eton) near Liverpool 'and a carriage, servants male and female'.[5]

The Chapter went on to make a more serious charge against Brown, commenting 'strongly but very respectfully' on the very large amount of charitable trust money that had not been spent upon the objects for which it had been intended, but which had been expended by the Bishop and the late Dr. Sharples.[6] The various trusts and funds, many of them long established, would have been something of a maze for even a careful administrator to negotiate, but such an accusation of financial impropriety could not have been made lightly and reflected Brown's record as an inefficient and careless administrator. Reports for collections did not appear on time and it was very difficult to find out what had happened to the money. In the absence of a regular diocesan structure it was too easy for rumours of misappropriation to be accepted as proven; perhaps it was also too easy for Vicars Apostolic to apply funds to immediate needs, fully intending to settle the accounts properly later. The over-riding concern of any pastorally minded Bishop had to be the provision of enough churches, priests and schools to meet the needs of this rapidly increasing population, and such provision involved finding very large sums of money.

In their discussions on his request for more money for himself the Chapter suggested that he should restrict his expenditure to the *mensa* (maintenance fund) he had at present and that any *caritativum subsidium* (voluntary subsidy) would be inexpedient in the circumstances. At a later meeting, at which he addressed them in person, Brown complained bitterly about their treatment of him: he was, he said, 'left unaided and unassisted'. On this occasion the canons heard him in silence and made no comment; after he had left the room they instructed the secretary of the Chapter to write to say that any positive proposal of the Bishop would receive their best attention.[7]

At the same meeting at which they had first discussed Brown's request for help the Chapter had received a similar request from one of their former members, Alexander Goss, coadjutor to Brown since September 1853. Brown's bitterness may well have been due at least in part to the fact that when Goss had asked for help because no means had been set aside for his maintenance, the canons willingly agreed to provide a suitable income for him from the clergy.[8] The Bishop accused them of acting illegally in helping his coadjutor because they had no right to order any collection to be taken up without his permission. Moreover, he argued, it was his responsibility, not theirs, to provide for his coadjutor. The canons replied that they had not ordered any such collection, but in deference to the Bishop they stopped helping Goss, who, as a result, received nothing from either source for a year. He wrote to Brown in November 1855, setting out his case for some support to cover his expenses. For their part, the Chapter wrote to Propaganda in December 1855 to complain that Brown had done nothing to help Goss: apart from a recent one-off sum of £10 from the Bishop, the coadjutor had received nothing since their own scheme had been stopped. Brown ducked the immediate issue, going over once again the illegality of the Chapter's initial action in Goss's favour. Repeated letters from Goss failed to elicit a clear answer, and he was moved to write:

> Though pained at the contents of your last letter, I cannot but admire the
> ingenious, if not ingenuous, shifts to which your Lordship condescends in
> order to evade giving a direct answer to a plain question, but I assure you
> that I am not to be turned from my purpose either by cunning or sophistry.[9]

It was the only occasion on which Goss dropped his respectful tone, and he apologised in his next letter. But he still threatened to take his case to Rome if Brown refused to help. People said, he claimed, that Brown must have had at least £600 during the year 1855, and yet he had not offered, indeed had declined, to give Goss a penny, recommending him instead to read the life of St Francis de Sales to learn how a Bishop should behave. Propaganda later raised the matter with Wiseman, telling him to see that a fair division of whatever funds were available was to be made between Brown and Goss. Brown's death relieved Wiseman of this embarrassing duty.[10]

In his letter to the Chapter Brown had gone further than just standing on his rights: he had accused the canons of having an 'inordinate attachment' to Goss and advised them to read *The Garden of the Soul* as a remedy![11] He was convinced that Goss had a clique of supporters among the canons and that together they were the cause of all his troubles. He wrote to Propaganda to complain that the Chapter assumed business that rightly belonged to himself; they defended themselves, he argued, *dolis et tergiversationibus* (by fraudulent tricks and delay) 'as the old Appellants did in France', and Goss and a group of them were in conspiracy, tending to 'set up a *Cathedra adversus Cathedram* (a Throne against the Throne) in the diocese'.[12] That Brown was so at odds with his official advisers (all of whom, of course, he had chosen himself) only weakened his authority still further.

The principal cause of contention, however, was Goss's appointment as coadjutor. Brown had not enjoyed the experience of having Bishop Sharples as coadjutor from 1843 to 1850. Sharples was capable and energetic, full of confidence in his own abilities and with a fiery personality that involved him in a number of public controversies – he was more Brown's master than assistant.[13] On the other hand, Sharples' early death in August 1850 (he was only forty-eight) may have made it clear even to Brown that he could not carry on single-handedly, especially as Bishop of the new diocese with all the demands that would make in terms of making episcopal authority a reality. He picked on Canon Cookson, the provost of the new Chapter, as a possible coadjutor and wrote half-heartedly to Propaganda about it. Many of the clergy supported Cookson's appointment, as did the other bishops when they discussed the matter in 1853, but Propaganda appointed Goss in September of that year as Bishop of Gerra and coadjutor with the right of succession – Wiseman had strongly recommended him to Rome while condemning Cookson as 'a real Gallican, an open enemy of Rome'.[14]

Brown reacted to the rejection of his favoured candidate by effectively refusing to recognize Goss's appointment, and so the latter went off to Rome for six months because he had nothing to do. He asked Brown for specific faculties but could get nothing from the Bishop in writing; it seemed to him that Brown was only offering the faculties a vicar general would have. From subsequent correspondence it appears that there was a genuine misunderstanding here: Brown thought he was offering his coadjutor the same faculties (including delegation to carry out the visitation of the diocese) that other coadjutors had been given, and was puzzled by Goss's refusal to accept them, attributing this at first to Goss's *timorata conscientia* (tender conscience). For his part Goss thought Brown was trying to make him into another vicar general to help the ailing Dr Crook and that the Bishop regarded a coadjutor as some sort of private secretary or chaplain, granted for his own personal comfort and not as someone with delegated episcopal powers to help in running the diocese.[15] Presumably the matter could have been cleared up if Brown had been willing to put something in writing; his constant refusal to do so in this and other cases made Goss reluctant to discuss diocesan business with him, as he believed the Bishop frequently changed his mind and mis-represented what had been decided orally.[16]

The trouble came to a head over the issue of the visitation of the diocese. Brown had announced this at the first diocesan synod in December 1853, but had taken no steps to carry it out; he was too ill to do it himself and Goss was obviously the ideal person to do so in his stead. The purpose of the visitation was expressed with simple clarity in the proclamation Goss issued in May 1855: the aim was to enable the Bishop to see:

> *that due and suitable provision is made for the worship of God and the care of souls, that the obligation of Masses are fulfilled, that the instructions of pious benefactors are carried out, and that the temporalities of all Charitable Institutions are beneficially as well as honestly administered.*[17]

The stress on financial regularity is especially interesting in the present context. What Brown objected to most of all was a very detailed questionnaire to be answered by the clergy prior to the visitation, claiming it was too long and asked for needlessly detailed information, including questions about finances. Goss felt that Brown was out to wreck his efforts and that since a coadjutor and his principal should, in Brown's own words, be *quid unum et idem* (one and the same), the Bishop should not lend his name to clerical opposition against the questionnaire. Brown remained opposed and hinted that his coadjutor was not concerned about the happiness of the clergy but was insulting their feelings, and trying 'to ride rough shod over them'; the questions, he claimed, had been hastily put together and rashly published. He had himself read them with 'pain and humiliation', and other northern clergy and the laity 'had sharply twitted the clergy about having to answer them'.[18] Goss claimed that Brown had even sent private letters to some of the clergy, telling them of his disapproval of the questions and forbidding them to answer the question about the number of people married by special licence. Brown had also argued that it was impossible to obtain an accurate status animarum in a town and so Goss was wasting their time in asking them for statistics. Goss agreed that it was difficult to be accurate in many cases, but argued that this was not a reason for not trying – 'hundreds of Catholic children go to no school and thousands of Catholics don't practise; a mass of crime and ignorance has to be dealt with'.[19]

Brown tried to scupper the whole exercise by refusing to give Goss the explicit delegation to carry out the visitation and it needed three very strongly worded letters from Propaganda to force him to do so. The intentions of Propaganda could not have been more clearly expressed than in the first of these letters sent in January 1855:

> the Holy Father ... with the advice of the Congregation (i.e. Propaganda)
> ... has ordered letters to be sent to you so that you may know his mind:
> that the visitation of the Diocese with all the necessary and requisite
> faculties should be committed to Dr Goss ... You will carry out these
> orders with the obedience which you bear towards the Holy See ...

The first part of this letter exhibited a certain exasperation with Brown. The second letter (also of January 1855) was a fuller restatement of the first, since that had crossed with another delaying letter from Brown; the third letter, in March, acknowledged Brown's worries, but repeats, quite curtly, that the visitation should be entrusted to Goss. Propaganda was not satisfied when Brown replied that he would always obey the Holy Father; they wanted an explicit report that the visitation was being carried out by his coadjutor with all the necessary faculties in writing.[20] Goss eventually wrote to Cardinal Fransoni, Prefect of Propaganda, on 26 April 1855 to say that the Bishop had sent him a very kind letter promising, at last, the fullest faculties including those necessary for the visitation.[21]

In an attempt to find out what the clergy did feel about the disputed visitation questionnaire, Goss wrote to the deans asking them to make enquiries at the deanery conferences. Their reply reveals an understanding of the demands of the new situation that had arisen with the changeover to proper diocesan bishops: they believed that the detailed questions would be very beneficial in getting the diocese better organised and would produce spiritual and temporal advantages; moreover:

> the Clergy in general acknowledge that the step taken ... was called for by
> the altered circumstances in which the Hierarchy ... and the Synod of
> Oscott have placed them.

Goss later admitted, however, that the questions had caused a sensation and when he became Bishop he had difficulty in getting all the clergy to complete them.[22]

Goss thought that Brown's opposition to himself arose partly out of jealousy, but he also believed that Brown felt the questions, and, indeed, the whole visitation, would be a criticism of the way he had run the District. He tried to assure the Bishop that every credit would be given to him for all he

The church of St Nicholas, Liverpool, dated from 1815. It served as the pro-cathedral until 1967; demolished 1973.

CATHOLIC CHAPEL, COPPERAS-HILL.

had achieved in very difficult circumstances, but Brown was not won over. In a letter to Wiseman he accused Goss of having deceived the 'Holy Father himself', otherwise Rome would not have supported him in the quarrel.[23] He could not see how a young man, with no experience except eleven years of teaching 'a few boys', should be allowed to:

> set himself above me after my laborious labours for twelve years at Ushaw and twenty years on the mission at Lancaster and fifteen years of being Bishop in the way he has done in violation too of the Canons of the Church. I see much uneasiness looming in the distance.[24]

In the end Brown wrote to Propaganda to ask to have Goss removed, but the move badly misfired: Propaganda replied that not only was Goss to remain as coadjutor but the whole of the administration of the diocese was to be put in his hands.[25] Brown did not tell Goss of this letter but did, for the last month he was alive, treat him somewhat more kindly and gave him the £10 already mentioned towards his expenses.[26]

Meanwhile, Brown had called the first diocesan synod in December 1853, in St Nicholas' church. It was an impressive occasion, full of ceremonial and the first occasion ever on which all the clergy, secular and regular, had been summoned to meet as a body, to receive legislation from their Bishop and to be addressed by him. The solemnity and importance of the occasion were not lost on Brown; in his address to the clergy he spoke of being overwhelmed:

> To find ourselves united with all the Clergy of our Diocese; to stand amongst our fellow-labourers … to behold the alacrity which with all have come to this our first Diocesan Synod … is to us no small consolation amidst the many trials that always await a Bishop.[27]

60

Perhaps one of the trials was the appointment of his coadjutor, Bishop Goss, and another must have been the intransigence of his Chapter, but the euphoria of the occasion discouraged any public recriminations.

Two of the decrees are worthy of some attention. One strictly forbade priests and lay people, even at their own expense, to make significant alterations to churches, schools, presbyteries or any other ecclesiastical property without consulting the Bishop, and this no matter what rights might be theirs in civil law. This strongly worded decree asserted the Bishop's complete control over all church property and goods (the only exception was covered by the words 'without damage to the rights of the Regulars'), and made it clear that lay patrons and priests with private means could no longer act independently, as some had tended to do under the old regime. The other decree concerned priests who held money on behalf of individuals or pious societies: no priest was henceforth to keep more than five pounds for longer than eight days, nor was he to invest any funds in his own name only, without permission from the Bishop or vicar general. In the light of the previous financial scandals in the District the concern is fully understandable.

The secretary also read out the list of synodal and diocesan officials, and a formidable list it must have seemed to clergy used to getting by with a vicar apostolic, a grand vicar or two and perhaps a few deans. Apart from twelve temporary synodal officials, there were the vicar general, the deans, an administrative council for temporalities, three judges for 'complaints and pleas', synodal examiners, a commission of investigation and, finally, the Bishop's archivist. This was not a mere bureaucratic explosion, leaving matters to continue as before once the shot had settled: in addition to the everyday work of the vicar general and the deans, Bishop Goss consulted the council for temporalities regularly and often, and its members examined mission accounts, decided on grants for new missions and schools and, in general, were important instruments in the regularisation of diocesan finances. The synodal examiners were involved in vetting candidates for ordination, in examining newly ordained priests before they were given missionary faculties and in testing the suitability of priests transferring from elsewhere to the diocese. If any of the clergy had believed that the restoration of the hierarchy was merely a palace revolution, they should now have realised that the former days and ways were passing.

After Brown's death Goss felt that some of his letters concerning their quarrels had not been very edifying, and Wiseman, while always taking Goss's side at Propaganda, thought he had sometimes stood too much on principle. Yet Goss's letters to Brown had generally been respectful, and he wrote kindly of him to others, sympathising with his difficulties and excusing his actions as those of a very sick man who was dependent on stimulants.[28]

Despite these difficulties, Bishop Brown's achievements were of lasting value to the young diocese. We have seen in Chapter 1 (p.32) how he helped as Vicar Apostolic to meet the needs of a growing Catholic body, and this work continued when he became Bishop in 1850. He had opened St Edward's

College, a boarding school and the future junior seminary, in 1843, and added the Catholic Institute for the education of the sons of the 'middling classes' in 1853. He had encouraged the establishment of a Blind Asylum (the only one of its kind for Catholic children in the country), an Industrial Lace School, run by Belgian Augustinian nuns, the Birkdale Farm School (a boys' reformatory) and St Elizabeth's Institute for the training of poor girls in domestic service. He may have been a poor administrator but he had not always been an idle one.

His quarrels show a number of interesting features about the years immediately after the Restoration in 1850: the readiness, for example, with which parties to disputes took their cases to Rome, and the equal readiness of Propaganda to be involved in the minutiae of English diocesan administration. What is also clear is the way in which Propaganda referred everything to Wiseman and expected him to be likewise involved, tendencies that were to cause trouble later. More generally, the quarrels illustrate that the Restoration, whatever different groups might have hoped for from it, called for a regularisation of diocesan business and the establishment of proper structures so that episcopal authority would be acceptable to all. The 'tangled skein of confusion' caused by Brown's mismanagement would have to be unravelled if religion were to flourish in the new diocese.[29]

BISHOP ALEXANDER GOSS 1856 – 1872

Bishop Brown died on 25th January, 1856, aged seventy, and was buried in St Oswald's, Old Swan. Goss succeeded him. He had been ordained in 1841 and had served a few months on the mission (perhaps St Wilfrid's, Hulme, Manchester, but more likely at Sts Peter and Paul's, Mawdesley), before becoming vice-president of the newly opened St Edward's College, Everton, where he taught for ten years. As we have seen, Wiseman backed his appointment – Goss had been a student in Rome for a short time during Wiseman's rectorship of the English College, and the future Cardinal seems to have regarded him as a special protegé. Their friendship did not last and the bitterness of their later quarrels may have been due in part to Wiseman feeling that someone who should have been grateful to him had become an open enemy and leader of the opposition. Their relationship cannot have been helped when Goss chose Cookson as his vicar general.

While Goss's outlook and actions as Bishop owed most to his own personality and strict sense of duty, there seems to be little doubt that his insistence on water-tight administration and the most minute attention to detail owed something to his difficult experiences under Brown's chaotic handling of affairs. He had enormous energy and considerable administrative ability and became an outspoken defender of his episcopal rights, and of those of the Catholics of Liverpool, 'strong and resolute almost to vehemence', as Manning put it in his panegyric. He could be a formidable

opponent, with his 'usual rough violence – the crozier, hook and point', as Manning put it on another occasion after experiencing Goss's ire. He was a shy man and perhaps overreacted as shy people often do when they have to speak out. But he bore no grudges and was always open to persuasion, as Manning conceded, 'with a delicacy of the highest kind in balancing justice'. He regarded himself as a 'rough and ready speaker', able to speak his mind to 'plain, homely Lancashire folks' but no more.[30]

The clearest description of him comes from Canon Fisher, President of the college and Goss's last vicar general – they had lived under the same roof for thirty years. Fisher wrote of the Bishop's shyness and retiring character and went on:

> *He lives apart from the world. He has no thought nor care for anything but his Diocese. He busies himself with nothing but his diocese … He may be totally engrossed in affairs, but they are the concerns of his Diocese … He can only think and work for his flock.*[31]

All the evidence points to a life of unceasing work: on visitations he might preach (rarely for less than an hour) three or four times a week, and twice on Sundays, for two months together. He confirmed 69,000 people in 16 years, 11,000 of them in 1871 when he was in poor health. He wrote most of his letters in his own hand as he could not afford a permanent secretary (incidentally, over 4,000 of the letters remain). When not on visitation he said a public Mass and preached at some church every Sunday, often supplying for absent clergy. Fisher said that the Bishop could spend twelve hours a day at his desk on a particular problem and still be up early the next morning to answer a sick call from a priest. All in all, it was the life of an active, missionary Bishop. His way of life was frugal. He had no house of his own and insisted on paying for his keep at St Edward's (he lived in the College Gatehouse) because he was, he said, of no service to it. He could not afford to keep a carriage but travelled to visitation by train and by begging lifts from better-off members of his flock. He gave away to his relations the property he had inherited, supported a former servant of his parents with a weekly allowance and sent money when he could to poor relations. He would not, however, use his position to help a nephew or anyone else find employment lest he compromise his independence.[32]

Finally, lest he seem a man dulled by devotion to duty, he had scholarly interests that he tried to keep alive and to encourage in others. In 1856 he published a scriptural work that he had translated from French; in 1864 he edited two works of recusant history for the Chetham Society, and the Manx Society published his translation of the *Chronicles of Man*. He corresponded with the British Museum and a number of learned Catholic historians and wrote manuscript histories of the Kirkham Mission in the Fylde and the Harkirk Cemetery at Crosby. He collected a large number of transcripts of records from the British Museum, the Public Record Office and the Duchy of Lancaster for a projected history of Lancashire Catholicism. He was keenly interested in natural science and built up a fine collection of birds' eggs, shells and fossils. He was invited to join the committee of the Liverpool branch of the National Association for the Promotion of Social Science. He urged his clergy to develop like interests and wanted them to 'stand at the head of education' in secular as well as theological subjects.[33]

As an outspoken defender of his rights as Bishop he fought off interference of any kind, whether it came from inside or outside his diocese. This determination to be allowed to exercise unquestioned authority came from his belief that a diocesan Bishop was answerable, under God, only to the pope – and, as we will see in a later chapter, there were limits to what even a pope could order him to do. His authority as diocesan Bishop did not come from the pope but from God and belonged to him by divine right. Hence his opposition to any moves towards centralisation, whether among the English bishops or in Rome. He claimed that he was in the best position to know what was needed in his diocese to advance religion: he visited it conscientiously and relied on his trusted deans, 'the men on the spot' as he referred to them, to see to day-to-day administration and keep him in touch. His searching eye covered every aspect of diocesan life and it all came under his control. He put his case clearly when writing to the Jesuits at St Wilfrid's, Preston, in 1864: 'I care not who is Bishop, but there can and must be only one, and as I am in possession, it is my duty to maintain my position'.[34] No doubt his determination to be a decisive helmsman had been strengthened by his experience of Bishop Brown's wayward hand on the tiller, but it also suited his anti-democratic temperament: just as those who were best suited to do so by birth or wealth should steer the ship of state, so the barque of Peter in Lancashire should be guided by the one with both the divine right to do so and the surest knowledge of the currents and crosswinds that might endanger it.

Some of the northern clergy had hoped that the Restoration of the Hierarchy would regularise their position and free them from what they saw as the arbitrary rule of the vicars apostolic. Some had even hoped that they would be allowed a say in the appointment of their bishops. How widespread these radical ideas were is impossible to say, but Goss was aware of them. What happened at the third diocesan synod in November 1857 seemed to be proof that the ideas were strong enough to call for decisive action to convince his clergy that he would tolerate nothing that seemed to allow his subjects to question his authority. The cause of the initial quarrel was relatively minor (how much should the clergy pay as the cathedraticum tax to the Bishop and who should fix it?), but it led to an appeal to Rome by some of his clergy and a counter-appeal by the Bishop and a key statement of the principles involved.[35]

Behind the quarrel lay a claim by the clergy to have the right to discuss matters of concern to them at their Conferences, and to have a spokesman at synods to put their case against what was being proposed as legislation – or were they there just to hear the Bishop legislate? The self-appointed leader of the clergy was Fr (later Canon) John Worthy, a native of Nova Scotia and cousin of the future Bishop, Bernard O'Reilly; he was missionary rector of St Mary's, Euxton, from 1851 to 1893. After failing to persuade the deans to have the question of the tax discussed at their conferences, he drew up a petition to the Bishop. About a third of the clergy from all parts of the diocese signed it, including Seculars and Regulars (although none of the Jesuits). When the synod opened in November 1857 Worthy put himself forward as a spokesman of the clergy, but Goss refused to allow this and used every canonical technicality to support his case. Worthy and his close supporters (one of whom was Bernard O'Reilly), were as respectful as possible and withdrew their petitions once they saw how determined Goss was. The Bishop was quite clear on the role of a synod, it was:

> an assembly of clergy called together to receive from the Bishop, modestly and reverently, words of reproof or encouragement, according as he is satisfied or not with their discharge of the duties he has entrusted to them during the last year.[36]

Part of Worthy's error was that he thought the clergy at synod had a right to argue, but in Goss's eyes the right to petition did not include a right to question the legality of the Bishop's acts. Goss could always exaggerate to make his point and in letters written to the chief petitioners after the synod he spoke of having been baited by the Secular clergy for the amusement of the Regulars. He described how there had been complete silence at the synod as the Regulars 'leaned forward with ill-concealed glee to watch the gladiatorial show' and spoke of the petition as a 'bill of indictment' – even in political matters, he went on, there was nothing to parallel the scene except when Charles I had been arraigned in Whitehall to be tried by his own subjects! If the clergy objected to his actions they could appeal to Rome, but they had no right to expect the Bishop to defend his decisions and still less any right to question those decisions in public. 'Not even in England', wrote Goss, 'where liberty verges on licentiousness', could it be tolerated that a judge's acts be questioned in open court. Worthy's actions might be based on principles, but for Goss these principles were 'the very essence of ecclesiastical radicalism' and could 'arouse feelings that will not be allayed for years'. Whatever the failings of the clergy, Goss had at least hoped that they were free from the taint of radicalism in their ideas about Church government, but now he wondered whether he had been mistaken.[37]

Worthy did not give up. He printed and circulated to the clergy a paper justifying his case, in which he reminded his readers that if the clergy thought an error had been committed by their superiors they had a duty to get the error corrected; if this were taken as 'factious opposition' then they might as well believe that every Bishop was inspired in word and action and infallible.

Secondly, Worthy dealt with the loyalist objection which said, 'Oh, the Bishop knows better than we do. I do not understand the question. But I like to stick to the Bishop'. He said this was a dangerous argument and if it had been encouraged in the past one would not have heard of Rome's having to correct the bishops, as 'they might have done as they pleased for ever'. Finally, Worthy answered those of his opponents who said that the Bishop's reactions were understandable as the whole matter had seemed to be 'only the uneasy crotchets of a few of the clergy'. He argued that the conscientious belief that something was wrong, even if held only by a few, called for an answer. To treat people indignantly because they were few in number was, he went on, to put a premium on agitation so that the few could become many.[38] Worthy's tone throughout was reasonable and Goss himself admitted that he was 'civil', and praised the 'spirit of peace' breathed by his letters but the principle of the independence of episcopal rights was at stake, and no matter how reasonable Worthy might sound, and no matter how 'calmly and respectfully' he might put his honest doubts, what he was doing was 'mischievous' and 'dangerous' because it would undermine episcopal authority by setting up the clergy as judges of the legality of the Bishop's decisions.[39]

Worthy finally appealed to Propaganda and the Bishop sent in a counter-petition. Propaganda considered the case thoroughly and found against Worthy on every point except the amount of the tax, but even here it stated that any decision on the matter by a Provincial Synod would not be retrospective; in the meantime the clergy had to obey the Bishop's decree. Even after Worthy had lost so comprehensively, however, the Bishop was a little wary. He would not be surprised, he wrote, if the opponents of the tax were to form 'a permanent radical clique in consequence of their defeat'.[40] Worthy was not a radical (and, anyway, soon lost support when he was seen to be 'against the Bishop'), nor was there any danger in his proposals. In the rapidly changing situation of the Church in Liverpool it surely would have been useful for the clergy to have been able to discuss matters of concern and for the synod to have been more than an occasion for rubber-stamping the Bishop's decrees.

BISHOP AND LAITY

And what about the laity? For the great majority of Catholics these arguments about rights and authority were of no interest. They would see the Bishop perhaps every three or four years when he came on visitation. When that Bishop was Goss these must have been impressive occasions as he paraded in full episcopal dress, standing about six feet three inches tall without his mitre and preaching powerfully for at least an hour – most of the people would not have seen or heard anything like it before. He used these occasions to explain to his people that one of the necessary results of 'the reconnecting of the chain of episcopacy was the reducing of all things to order in harmony with the laws of the Church', and he was fond of explaining the ceremonial used on visitation as a 'token of the Bishop's supreme jurisdiction over the churches in his diocese'.[41] To the historically minded it was, perhaps, reminiscent of a medieval monarch on royal progress, providing a sense of unity and exuding an aura of unquestioned authority, convincing them to be proud that they were part of something larger and grander than their local community. A few, however, of the wealthy and influential Catholics in the diocese were more personally affected by the changes that 1850 brought and called from Goss another explicit defence of his episcopal authority.

The issue here was the existence of private chapels or domestic oratories throughout the diocese. There were a surprising number of these – Goss reckoned there were at least thirty. As we have seen in Chapter 1, a number of them had developed into mission churches serving a locality, but others were of different origin and the cause of greater concern. These seem to have been private or domestic oratories in the strict sense: a room in a house set aside for worship, for use by the members of the family or an individual. Some of these were in the houses of the gentry, for example at Garswood, near Ashton-in-Makerfield, the home of the Gerards; some were in farmhouses (or 'halls'), while that of Mr Bushell, at Myerscough near Garstang, was in a cottage. Some of these may have originally been of the chaplaincy-cum-mission type, but the dual function had ceased when a proper chapel for public use had been built – e.g. at Thurnham, south of Lancaster, where the Daltons retained a private oratory. Some were quite recent: those belonging to the Orrells at Blackbrook, St Helens, the Gillows at Leighton Hall, near Lancaster, and the Andertons at Heighton Hall, near Preston. Preston, indeed, and its surrounding area had the lion's share of these: a Mr Gillow had a chapel in Frenchwood Street, Councillor Segar in Fishergate, Mr Pyke, a corn merchant, in Winckley Square, while Mr Sidgreaves had one near Alston Lane Chapel, as did Mr Chadwick; Mr Roskell, a banker, had one at West Cliff. Finally, a Mr Edwards had one near Old Swan, outside Liverpool.[42]

The privilege of having a private chapel had in some cases been granted for the sake of a sick member of a family and had continued in use afterwards. Some of the grants seemed to have no written approval – perhaps another sign of Bishop Brown's carelessness, although in general he, too, had been worried about the possible abuses that might arise from multiplying private chapels and especially if the owner claimed the right to reserve the Blessed Sacrament; probably a number of the chapels went back before his time, anyway. Goss was also worried on this score and felt that it would be better for the ordinary laypeople to see their social betters receiving Communion publicly. Moreover, of course, too frequent use of private chapels meant that their owners and families missed sermons, pastoral letters and collections. He also believed that some of the chapels served only as status symbols and tied up the services of priests unnecessarily.

In addition to his own feelings on the matter, it seems that Propaganda was much less willing to give the new bishops the same faculties in this regard that it had given the vicars apostolic. Goss claimed that he could not even allow Mass to be said in private chapels unless the owners had written permission from the pope himself, let alone give permission for the reservation of the Blessed Sacrament. When the chaplain of Sir Robert Gerard asked the Bishop for permission to reserve the Blessed Sacrament in the family's private chapel, Goss had to refuse. He was immediately accused of 'sacrificing the liberties of the English Church to Italian notions acquired by a Roman education' and had to explain that he no longer enjoyed the extensive authority of his predecessors. In the times of persecution, he went on, the laws of the Church were in abeyance in England and 'hence many things were allowed which are now prohibited'. Not all the chapel owners were convinced and he met with open hostility when he insisted on officially visiting the chapels and checking the owners' right to them – at Haighton Hall his reception was 'cold and distant', while at the Chadwick chapel it was 'scarcely civil' and he felt he was being treated as an intruder.[43]

Only two owners, in the event, could produce papal indults, the Orrells and the Gillows. He did not take the drastic step of closing all the other chapels but he made it clear that any previous grant only applied to an individual and not to a family or house; once that individual died, the chapel would have to close. Only the genuinely sick could receive Holy Communion in them; he sometimes asked for a medical certificate, though he was generous in allowing it if he felt the people concerned had 'earned it' by being generous benefactors and patrons. He also insisted on having a veto on the appointment of chaplains to the bigger houses and exercised it firmly, particularly if the patron wished to appoint a member of a Religious Order, even if his refusal might offend a powerful and generous patron such as Major Blundell of Crosby Hall, Little Crosby, who wished to appoint a Capuchin or a Vincentian in 1860.[44] Whatever privileges and precedents the laity might appeal to in these matters, Goss was determined that they could only be exercised in accordance with the laws of the Church and his own overall control. He saw the parochial missions of the diocese as a spiritual grid, providing the laity with all the sacramental aid they needed and linking everyone to the source of spiritual jurisdiction, the Bishop. He believed private chapels constituted a tradition that remained when its usefulness had passed.

Perhaps, in a few lay minds, their chapels were also reminders of days when there had been greater lay independence from, and even control over, the clergy. Here Goss was of the same mind as his predecessor, intent on keeping any element of control away from the laity. He advised a priest who was about to build a school to consult the 'respectables' in his congregation, but to do so informally and without constituting them a committee or putting anything to the vote – in that way, after the school was built the group would 'die a natural death'. He was against having lay trustees for land or funds used for school or church building, but as the government insisted on them for schools, he was in the habit of appointing the diocesan representative on the Poor Schools Committee to avoid having local people who might think that their trusteeship gave them some say or authority.[45]

A small number of people could become members of the lay committees that helped to run diocesan institutions such as the reformatories, the blind asylum, the Industrial Schools and the Catholic Benevolent Society. Most of these organisations had clerical chairmen or chaplains, and Bishop Goss insisted that in the case of confraternities all decisions had to be taken by the chaplain and his power must be 'absolute'. Given this degree of clerical control it is welcome to find the Bishop telling the poor Irish colony in Coniston who were without a resident priest that they should gather on Sundays in one of the cottages to say the Rosary and other prayers and to listen to some pious reading; a weekly collection was to be taken and the Bishop appointed six people to be responsible for taking the money to the bank.[46]

There was, finally, the Catholic Young Men's Society (CYMS). This was a very popular parish organisation – in 1905, for example, there were forty-eight branches up and down the diocese, in both rural and urban areas. The Society saw itself mainly in spiritual terms; by its presence in each parish:

> *a social and intellectual side could be developed inside each separate society, suited to the rank and characters of its members, which served as an antidote to outside temptations, and carried on under the banner of the Church, minimised the possibility of any weakening of their faith.*

Members were encouraged to take part in retreats and could gain plenary indulgences twice a year – as long as their branch had been properly erected by the local Bishop, who also appointed their chaplain and decided on their patron saint. Although he had some fears that a few of the Liverpool branches might be covers for illegal Irish activities (the Society had been founded in Ireland by a strongly nationalist priest, Fr O'Brien), Bishop Goss approved of the Society and Liverpool became the home of its governing body. While it was a lay society, the Bishop insisted on firm clerical control: once again he stressed that the chaplain was to be in charge and it is interesting that of the thirty-five branches listing their treasurer in 1905, over half of them (nineteen) had the chaplain or another priest in the parish holding that office.

CYMS activities extended well beyond the narrowly spiritual and various branches between them ran reading rooms, lending libraries, public lectures and a few evening classes in the three Rs. All had burial funds and some had sick funds, while one (run by Mgr Nugent) had its own building society. The Society had its magazine, *The Catholic Circle*, and was well-organised, with a national structure and diocesan central councils. When its National President, Lord Edward Howard, however, suggested that the Society might help to relieve the clergy of some of their heavy parochial work, Goss replied that it would not work in Liverpool where often an entire congregation consisted of the 'poorest and most depraved', unable to provide members for societies such as the SVP (the St Vincent de Paul Society, see Chapter 9) – though he did allow that the members might help with listing house numbers for the clergy.[47] It was an excuse rather than a reasoned answer: he feared giving lay people any authority in church-related matters and the formation of spiritual élites did not imply for him any corresponding active function in the Church.

One area in which the early bishops gave their lay people full support and encouragement was that of local politics. It was essential to have Catholics on town councils, School Boards and the Board of Poor Law Guardians (known in Liverpool as the Select Vestry), especially in Liverpool where there was a strong and effective anti-Catholicism. The Bishop was the protector of his people – from the evils of current society, and also from the prejudice and discrimination they faced in a largely anti-Catholic society. Schools, of course, became the major issue where Catholic rights were concerned, but that struggle lay in the future. Bishop Brown and Bishop Goss were more concerned with getting equal treatment for Catholic inmates in prisons and the workhouse, in the form of Catholic chaplains and the right to attend Mass. Even when government legislation allowed for these, the authorities in Liverpool, dominated by Protestant and Orange interests, refused to allow them. There was a constant battle, sometimes carried on by Goss himself in the press and in sermons, but more usually by Catholic councillors on his behalf. In 1856 he publicly attacked the Select Vestry for their refusal to allow Catholic children in the workhouse the services of a Catholic chaplain: they had, he claimed, taken to religious persecution 'in a small way'. They were 'strong and valorous and fiery with religious zeal' against poor children, but cowardly when they come face to face with men. If there was to be war, he continued, it should be in the open.[48]

In the circumstances it was difficult to reduce the tension between Catholics and Protestants in the city, but Goss did what he could to prevent that tension leading to public demonstrations and violence. He was well aware that some Catholics were willing to try to combat anti-Catholicism with a show of force and, if possible, get their retaliation in first. It was always easier to get Protestant and Catholic working men onto the streets to defend their rights than to get them to attend church or chapel. The presence of anti-Catholic speakers was likely to cause Catholic reaction and Goss warned his people in 1867 to keep away from any building where such speakers were due to appear and not to gather in nearby streets; they were not to organise counter-lectures or to answer 'in the public prints or by placards the calumnies and slanders they may utter'. The Irish Catholics in Liverpool did not like it when he forbade processions and demonstrations in the same year in honour of the Fenians executed in Manchester – it took two appeals on his part to have any effect.[49]

Generally the Bishop was more concerned with local than with national elections, but in 1859 he tried to influence the way Catholics of the diocese should vote in the coming parliamentary elections. His interference caused a public row. His secretary, Canon John Walker, wrote to all the clergy in Lancashire to say that Lord Derby, the Tory Prime Minister, had promised to make concessions to the Catholics over prison and workhouse chaplains if he should remain in office. This was clearly a bribe to try to wean Catholics from their traditional allegiance to the Liberals. Not surprisingly, Walker's confidential letter was leaked and the Liberal Press, led by the *Liverpool Daily Post* under its Catholic editor, Michael Whitty, attacked the Bishop for undue interference. It printed Walker's letter, but got it slightly wrong, and this allowed Walker to claim, rather dishonestly, that he had not written it and that it was a forgery. Goss later claimed that he would have done the same if the promise of concessions had been made by the Liberals, but he was being disingenuous – he strongly supported the Tories and regarded Catholics as their natural allies. In a letter to the Tory agent he wrote that he would try to get the co-operation of his clergy, and if he could do anything to persuade the people he would, but neither he nor his priests interfered in politics![50]

In 1872 he did issue a notice to be read in all churches telling people whom they should support in the forthcoming School Board elections – he would not, he wrote, have said anything if it had been a Parliamentary or a Town Council election, but since it concerned the education of the poor he told his priests to instruct their people to vote for religious education in the person of the Anglican/Tory candidate, Mr Bailey, standing against the Liberal, Mr White. This advice reflected the disillusion of Catholics generally with the Liberals' support for the 1870 Education Act, with its establishment of non-denominational schools. Many Catholics did support Bailey, but White won. By this time the alliance between Catholics and Liberals was weakening, at least in Liverpool: the Irish were turning more towards Irish Nationalist candidates and in the 1876 municipal elections Home Rule candidates defeated the two Liberals put up by the Catholic Club. The Catholic/Liberal alliance in Liverpool had always been somewhat artificial: the Liberal élite was just that – its leaders never had, or wanted, the common touch. They supported Catholic rights out of an intellectual conviction about civil rights in general and not out of sympathy with the mass of poor Irish Catholics: it was unthinkable for most of them to support radical working-men against Tory gentlemen.[51]

Perhaps Goss was not too wide of the mark in claiming that Lancashire Catholics were natural Tories – if only the party in Liverpool had not so openly played the Orange Protestant card; in Warrington and Wigan (which both had large Catholic minorities) the Tory candidates could attract strong Catholic support. As later chapters will show, the inability to control how their people voted did not prevent future bishops on several occasions from trying to do so, by issuing clear instructions on how Catholics should vote to support their religious interests locally and nationally.

~

Fr John Worthy had been out of step when he had tried to introduce a small element of clerical democracy into the running of the diocese. At the start of the dispute with Bishop Goss, Dean Greenhalgh of Chorley had tried to console Worthy by saying that, although the clergy had been used to discussing all sorts of matters at their Conferences:

> now that Conference is constituted under the regular laws of the Church,
> it is beyond its province, as Conference, to discuss questions of this kind.
> (This would be) obnoxious at first sight to our former notions and the like
> of which must often meet us whilst we are in a state of transition to
> regular discipline.[52]

Goss was determined that that transition should occur as quickly as possible and be accepted without question. While a few liberals might continue to lament 'episcopal coups' and talk of the 'triumph of arbitrary rule', it was undoubtedly the day of the Bishop. The confusions of Bishop Brown's years were over and the scene was set for further expansion under firm episcopal direction, with both priests and people in their proper, subordinate, roles.

Notes

1 J. Derek Holmes, *More Roman than Rome* (1978), p.84. English text in Beck, pp.107-115.

2 B. Ward, *The Sequel to Catholic Emancipation 1830-1850*, 2 vols. (1915), pp.205-22. *Decreta*, pp.123-4; *Synodi Liverpolitanae I-VIII* (n.d.), pp.15-16.

3 AAL Chancellor, Parish Boxes, Fr Gallagher to Bp Brown, 15.1.1841.

4 Doyle, 'Tangled Skein'.

5 R. Schiefen, *Nicholas Wiseman and the Transformation of English Catholicism* (1984), p.149.

6 AAL Chancellor, Chapter Minutes, 1.12.1853.

7 *Ibid.*, 31.9.1854.

8 *Ibid.*, 1.12.1853.

9 AAL Early Bishops, Additional Letters (Goss), p.36, Goss to Brown 23.11.1855.

10 AAW, 140/1, n.1, 9 Jan 1856; AAL, Additional Letters (Goss), p.41, Goss to Brown 5.1.1856.

11 AAL Chancellor, Chapter Minutes 25.10.1854; Early Bishops, Additional Letters (Goss), p.32, Goss to Brown 9.11.1855.

12 APF, *S.R. Anglia*, vol.13, nn. 1111-13, 31.12.1854.

13 Milburn, *Ushaw*, p.210.

14 AAW, R79/6, Wiseman to Brown 16.02.1853.

15 APF, *S.R. Anglia*, vol.14, nn. 207-8, for Brown's account; for Goss's letters to Propaganda, RCLv 5/1 (at end); also pp.28-31, Goss to hierarchy's Roman agent, 10.11.1855.

16 AAL Early Bishops, Additional Letters (Goss), various.

17 AAL Early Bishops, S1 II, B: Pastoral Letters of Bishop Goss, 18.5.1855.

18 AAL *Questions Addressed to the Clergy … at the Visitation of 1855*, (Liverpool 1855); Early Bishops, Additional Letters (Goss), p.24, Goss to Brown 11.9.1855; AAW, R79/6, Brown to Wiseman 28/30.11.1855.

19 RCLv, 5/1/26, Goss to Bishop Clifford 8.11.1855.

20 APF, *Lettere*, vol. 346 (1855), nn. 49b,50; 84; 213b; 310; 321; 359.

21 RCLv, 5/1, Goss to Fransoni, 26.4.1855.

22 RCLv 5/1/26, Goss to Cornthwaite, 10.11.1855, and 5/3/26, Goss to Bp of Shrewsbury, 14.3.1859.

23 AAW, R79/6, Brown to Wiseman, 28.11.1855.

24 Milburn, *Ushaw*, pp.213-4.

25 APF, *S.R. Anglia*, vol.14, Fransoni to Wiseman 7.12.1855.

26 RCLv 5/1/53-4, Goss to Cornthwaite 15.1.1856.

27 *Synodi Liverpolitanae I-VIII*, pp.12, ff, for the address and decrees.

28 RCLv 5/1/112-3, Goss to Bp Turner 1.3.1856; 59-60, Goss to Cornthwaite 25.1.1856.

29 *Ibid.*, Goss to Gibson 20.3.1856.

30 H.E. Manning, *The Good Soldier's Death* (1872), pp.9-10; Beck, p.196; RCLv 5/2/348, Goss to Bamber, 9.10.1858.

31 English College Archive, Rome, TAL.313, Fisher to Talbot, 15.6.1868.

32 RCLv Goss's Letterbooks, letters to various priests 1856-64.

33 *A Sacred History, comprising the leading facts of the Old and New Testament …* (1856); *Abbott's Journal 1689-91*, and *The Trials at Manchester 1694*, (1864); *Chronica Regum Manniae et Insularum …* (1874). His transcripts and MSS histories are in the diocesan archives. RCLv 5/1/440,446, to Turpin and Corless, 7/9 March, 1857.

34 RCLv 5/4/619, Goss to Cobb SJ, 24.12.1864.

35 Peter Doyle, 'Episcopal Authority and Clerical Democracy: Diocesan Synods in Liverpool in the 1850s', *RH*, vol. 23 (May 1997), pp.418-33, gives a full account. Unless otherwise noted, references are to AAL St Joseph's Seminary Collection, Cathedraticum Folder, sections I-X, given as Cath. with section no. The petition is in Cath. I.

36 RCLv 5/2/106, Goss to O'Reilly 21.11.1857

37 RCLv 5/2/94, Goss to Taylor; 99, to Brown; 149-54, to Abp. Errington, Nov. 1857-Jan.1858.

38 Cath. V, pp.23-4.

39 Goss to Errington – see note 37.

40 RCLv 5/3/26, Goss to Bp of Shrewsbury, 14.3.1860. For Propaganda's replies, Cath. VII.

41 RCLv Visitation Diaries 3/B, 1856, sermons at Lancaster and Preston.

42 Peter Doyle, 'Bishop Goss and the Gentry: the Control of Private Chapels', *NWCH*, vol. XII (1985), pp.6-13.

43 *Ibid.*, pp.7-10.

44 *Ibid.*, p.12.

45 RCLv 5/1/137, Goss to McCormick, 11.4.56; 399, to Hickey, 21.1.1857.

46 RCLv 5/6/2/62, Bp's secretary to Donnelly, 4.1.1865; AAL Early Bishops, Mss Pastorals for Special Occasions, 'To the Irish at Coniston', 30.8.1855.

47 Ryan Dye, 'The Irish Flood: Famine, Philanthropy, and the Emergence of Duelling Catholic Identities, 1845-1865', *THSLC*, vol. 150 (2001), pp.97-120; 'Report of Second General Conference, Liverpool 1861'; *Directory*, 1906; RCLv 5/6/2/62, Goss to Lord Edward Howard 4.1.1865.

48 Burke covers all the battles; see p.130. See also Waller, *Democracy and Sectarianism*.

49 Burke, pp.179-80.

50 *Liverpool Daily Post*, 7 May 1859; RCLv 5/3/58-9, Goss to Lord Campbell, 12.4.1859; 5/6/1/326-38, Walker to *Daily Post* and others.

51 Burke, p.200; Waller, *Democracy and Sectarianism*, p.13.

52 Cath. I.

CHAPTER 4 THE CHALLENGES OF EXPANSION

In 1847 disaster had struck the Catholic clergy in Liverpool when ten of the twenty-four priests had died in a few months from fever caught while attending the sick and dying during a typhoid and dysentery epidemic. The ten became known as Liverpool's 'Martyr Priests'; a memorial was erected in their honour in St Patrick's graveyard, and a silhouette of them became a best seller, helping to keep alive the ideal of Liverpool priests dying in the course of duty, 'true champions of the Cross and valiant heroes of Christianity' as another memorial put it (in St Anthony's). Eight other priests caught the fever but eventually recovered, including Fr Bernard O'Reilly, the future Bishop of Liverpool, whose ordination at Ushaw was brought forward without notice (he was just twenty-three) so that he could be posted to St Patrick's to fill the gap left by the death of the first of the three priests to die there.

Two priests had also died of fever in Wigan in 1848; three Christian Brothers who were teaching in the poorest Liverpool schools also died, as did ten medical practitioners. The conditions in the courts and cellars where the priests ministered were truly horrific and in the most vulnerable streets up to a third of the inhabitants died – Fr Nugent, at St Nicholas', Liverpool, noted forty-three sick calls in one day.[1] The loss of priests came just as the Church in Lancashire needed to provide extra priests and build new churches to cope with a huge increase in its numbers.

PROVIDING PRIESTS

No wonder Bishop Goss, soon after becoming Bishop in 1856, was 'well nigh in despair' at the impossibility of meeting the demand for priests, especially that created by the convents, workhouses, gaols and industrial schools. Just to take the example of convents: in 1855 there had been four convents in the diocese and one Religious house for men (apart, that is, from the houses for Religious priests); by 1865 this had increased to twenty-five convents and two houses for men, and by 1872 to twenty-nine convents and three houses for men. While the great majority of these establishments did not need a full-time chaplain, they did need Mass to be said daily if possible, confessions to be heard and other services to be performed. Moreover, the number of schools run by Religious had increased from thirty-three in 1860 to eighty-one in 1872, and Goss was

insistent that priests should visit the schools within their missions regularly: he suggested that where there was more than one priest in a mission one of them should be in the school every morning.

Liverpool's 'Martyr Priests' of 1847.

The following table of ordinations and deaths perhaps gives a realistic picture of the situation during his years as Bishop:

	Ordinations	Irish included in total	Secular deaths
1856-60	5	0	9
1861-65	32	12	14
1866-70	40	4	13
1871-72	13	1	4
TOTALS	90	17	40

So, in the first five years of his episcopate, Goss lost nine priests through death and gained only five through ordination. This left a back-log of vacancies and of expansion not undertaken, so that even the big increase in the next five years to thirty-two ordinations was already partly spoken for, and was, in any case, matched by a rise in the number of Secular deaths to fourteen. The outstanding year was 1869, when all eighteen ordinations were from the English colleges, but there had been none the year before and there was to be only one the following year. There is no way of telling with any accuracy how many priests over these years retired through illness, but in 1864, in addition to the six deaths, four priests were too ill to work and another two had left the diocese to join Religious Orders.[2]

Clearly, the main reasons for the need for more clergy were the increase in the Catholic population and the migration of Catholics to find employment. The following table shows the increase in the Catholic population, churches and chapels and the increase in priests (Secular and Regular). It has to be said that the numbers given for the overall Catholic population of the diocese, while not completely accurate, are generally reliable; they are taken from Bishop O'Reilly's very comprehensive returns to Propaganda in 1887 covering the previous thirty years, which were based on the baptismal records of each mission; the total for 1851 is the most open to question.[3]

	Est. Catholic Population	% increase	Churches / Public Chapels	% increase	Total Clergy	% increase
1851	197,500		84		122	
1861	236,912	20%	110	17.0%	202	65.6%
1871	286,312	21%	120	10.0%	215	6.0%
1881	316,210	10%	140	17.0%	286	33.0%
1887	322,622	2%	152	8.6%	372	30.0%

At first sight these figures show a satisfactory situation, with the increase in the clergy outstripping the increase in churches and chapels they were to serve. Of the 215 clergy in 1871, however, eighty-eight were Regulars. While the increase in their numbers was welcome, it did not help the Bishop to staff new missions. There was only one new Regular mission opened in these years, that of Holy Cross, St Helens (run by the Jesuits, who also ran the new mission at Tyldesley for a short time); indeed, during these years the Regulars gave up six missions and the Bishop had to find Seculars to take their place. Most of the increase in the numbers of the Regulars was among the Jesuits (twenty-four in 1856, thirty-six in 1872), who followed a policy of leaving one-man missions and making their remaining houses into proper community houses, and the Redemptorists (from five to eleven), who did not run any missions at this period. The missionary expansion of these years was staffed by the Secular clergy.

There were a number of sources a Bishop might look to to increase the number of his priests. First of all, there was Ireland. Some Irish-born priests were working in the diocese in the 1850s – we know that in 1855, twenty-three, or 17.7%, of the total of 130 priests were of Irish birth – four of them Regulars and nineteen Seculars. By 1865, this number had risen to forty, nine of them Regulars and thirty-one Seculars – the Irish-born now made up 22.8% of the total. So there had been an increase over the ten years, but at no time did the Irish-born amount to a quarter of the priests in the diocese or a third of the

Secular clergy. (In this context it is interesting that over a much longer period, from 1850 to 1986, the proportion hardly changed: Irish-born priests made up 29% of the Secular clergy working in the diocese.) The percentage of the Irish-born priests trained in Irish colleges was also increasing (from 47% to 67%); the Irish element among the clergy was rising by the recruitment of priests straight from college who had no pastoral experience in Ireland.[4]

It is interesting to look briefly at the deployment of Irish priests in the early years. St Patrick's, Liverpool, with a large congregation of nearly 13,000, almost all of whom were Irish, was served in 1865 by three English and one Belgian priest. At the same time, St Oswald's, Old Swan (then just outside Liverpool) had three Irish-born priests for a congregation of 3,000, few of whom were recent Irish immigrants. There were also cases of individual Irish priests serving small missions where the number of Irish Catholics was tiny – Little Crosby had a young thirty-three year old to look after its 67 families, and Blackbrook, near St Helens, had a forty-three year old to look after 120 families.[5] What is clear from all the evidence available to us is that there were no significant differences in religious practice and general spiritual health between the two groups of Catholics. One can only conclude that the presence or absence of Irish priests made no essential difference to the Irish Catholics in the diocese: if any special bond existed between the Irish immigrants and their priests, it existed because of the priests' office and not because of their nationality. It is also clear that English priests were as willing as any others to care for the spiritual needs of the immigrants and were just as effective in doing so.

With this evidence before him, perhaps Bishop Goss saw no reason to worry about where to appoint Irish priests. He was aware of the language problems that could arise, especially in the early years of the immigration – in 1856 he moved Fr Gerald O'Reilly (brother of the later Bishop) from the Isle of Man to Our Lady's, Eldon Street, Liverpool, where his knowledge of Gaelic would be invaluable. He refused, however, to allow the priest in charge of St Anthony's, Scotland Road, to recruit an Irish-speaking priest directly from Ireland, offering him instead the services of Fr Van Hee, a highly recommended Belgian priest! He added that the Irish were not the only group with special needs, and he had recently sent two of his students to train in Germany so that the spiritual needs of 'the many German immigrants' could be met.[6] It should perhaps be added here that the language problems of the Irish have probably been exaggerated: Gaelic had been dying out for some years in Ireland, and the majority of the immigrants, especially those from the east and north of the country, would by now have been English speakers.

The early bishops of Liverpool were more reluctant than some other bishops to rely on Irish priests. In 1841, Bishop Brown had written that he was in great straits to find enough priests yet did not think it prudent to 'place more Irish priests among the people' – he confided this to Bishop Briggs, since he knew the country 'would be in a blaze' if his sentiments were widely known.[7] By the 1850s, however, he was writing to All Hallows College in Dublin begging for some Irish priests, though with little success – Australia and America were competing for them, and there were fewer of them available anyway. For Bishop Goss it is clear that the main reason against employing more Irish priests was that he wanted to build up a native English clergy; as he wrote in 1857:

> Now if we are to preserve the vantage ground gained by those who have preceded us … it can only be by having a regular supply of native clergy, educated from the people amongst whom they have to labour.

He felt that this was particularly necessary in rural areas where the need was for men who would be acquainted with the 'feelings and habits of the people and have their welfare at heart'. If 'altogether English' priests were not available, then at least they should be 'bred up in England and formed in (English) habits'. In 1856 he wrote to Dean Greenhalgh of Chorley that he was finding it difficult to find another priest to send there: there was one available, but he was Irish, and he did not want to appoint another Irishman to the town. Later on he lamented that there were very few English subjects suited to the priesthood and when Herbert Vaughan (later Cardinal) asked him for priests to help set up the Mill Hill Missionaries, the Bishop replied that he felt he must hang on to the few English candidates he had – even in his 'most Catholic' diocese many of the boys being educated for the priesthood were of Irish parentage.[8] He should, perhaps, have been consoled that those of Irish parentage would at least be 'acquainted with the feelings and habits', and concerned for the welfare, of many Catholics in different parts of the diocese.

In this respect, it is interesting to see how Bishop O'Reilly, himself born in Ireland and educated there before going to Ushaw, regarded the Irish clergy in the diocese. In his report to Propaganda in December 1887 he noted that there were 235 Secular priests working in the diocese; of these, 93 were 'foreign' or 'non-native', composed mainly of 81 Irish priests (there were also ten Belgians and one German permanently attached to the diocese and one 'exiled' German). Many of the Irish, the Bishop continued, had lived in the diocese from childhood or had at least been educated in English colleges and this was particularly true of the 55 Irish priests permanently attached to the diocese. The other 26 were on temporary loan for set periods and would eventually be returning to their Irish dioceses. While the Bishop was more willing to use Irish priests than his predecessor had been, his Report gives a definite impression that he was at pains to show how 'English' most of these Irish priests really were! Perhaps he had accepted Goss's ideas on the necessity of building up a native English clergy. Certainly he hoped that having a Liverpool seminary would persuade his people to give more money for the training of priests and encourage more local vocations and so he devoted much of his energy and resources to building one at Upholland. In that way, he wrote to Propaganda, he would not have to rely on borrowing priests from elsewhere and could look forward to a steady twelve or so ordinations a year just from his own seminary.[9]

Why did the bishops not turn to other religious Orders and Congregations for assistance? When the diocese had been set up in 1850 five such bodies were already working there: the Jesuits and the Benedictines (both of very long standing), and the Oblates of Mary Immaculate and the Passionists (both introduced by Bishop Brown) – all four ran missions. The fifth body was the Redemptorists, also introduced under Brown; their house at Bishop Eton, Liverpool, was not a mission although it was open to the public for Mass and confession. Others could have been invited, for example the Rosminians, the Vincentians and the various branches of the Franciscans – and certainly the last were very eager to be allowed to open houses in the diocese. Neither Goss nor his successor, Bishop O'Reilly, adopted this apparently easy way out of some of the manpower problems they experienced.

Goss admired both the vocation of the Regulars and the work they were doing in the diocese, but believed that their presence there as missioners raised serious issues. He was convinced that there was a fundamental conflict between the pursuit of the Religious ideal and the life of a missioner. Above all, he was strongly opposed to Religious living in one-man missions, a practice that existed throughout the diocese for historical reasons, but, as he wrote to Major Blundell of Crosby Hall who was keen to appoint a Capuchin or Vincentian to the chaplaincy-cum-mission of Little Crosby, it was an anomaly that the Regulars themselves were keen to get rid of. Furthermore, he could not deploy Religious to meet fresh needs or at times of crisis. There was always the danger that they would withdraw at short notice, leaving him to find replacements, and at times they seemed unwilling to take on duties that he felt were part of missionary life but which they claimed were inconsistent with their vocation as Religious (see Chapter 7). Finally, the Bishop believed that he was being deprived of the services of a number of elderly or sick clergy who could not cope with a busy mission but would have been happy running a small country mission if so many of these had not been in the hands of the Regulars.[10]

Another source of priests were those who wanted to transfer to Liverpool from other dioceses or religious orders. Obvious caution was needed here and Goss seems to have turned down about thirty applications in the sixteen years he was Bishop. It was difficult to be sure of the good standing of the priests concerned and some who were accepted left almost as quickly as they had come. Goss was necessarily concerned about the reputation of his clergy and wrote:

> In a town like Liverpool with a hostile press we require to be prudent, and
> (there are) sufficient reasons for caution with regard to strange priests.
> The people cannot decide nicely, and if they see a Priest at the altar they
> will treat him with unbounded confidence.

His cautious, long-term policy of slowly building up his clergy with his own candidates as far as possible, prevented the diocese from becoming the kind of *refugium peccatorum* (refuge of sinners) that Nottingham was said to be under Bishop Bagshawe later in the century.[11]

We have seen that Bishop Goss refused to send any of his priests to help the new missionary venture at Mill Hill. In general he had no sympathy with priests who asked to leave the diocese to work on the foreign missions. He argued that there was more than enough work to be done in Liverpool and other Lancashire towns; he wrote to a Fr. Bridges in 1858 that he was sure he could achieve greater good and save more souls in Blackstock Street than in India. As far as he was concerned, the priest's work was the same everywhere and it was a matter 'not worth the enquiry' whether it was in one place or another; he thought that one of the worst signs of the times was the 'daintiness of the clergy' about where they were asked to work.[12]

During these years the diocese was not short of clerical students. In 1859 it had a total of seventy-eight while by 1887 this had risen to 151 – probably about half of the latter were junior students.[13] Their training, of course, cost money. When he had been Vicar Apostolic Bishop Brown had attempted to regularise the provision of finance for clerical training by initiating an annual collection in all missions. This had become the diocesan Ecclesiastical Education Fund, with the annual collection every Lent, the occasion for a pastoral letter on the subject and a detailed list of private donations and church collections. The annual accounts show a rise in the amounts spent on training, but there was no similar rise in donations and collections in the early years:

	subscriptions	collections	training costs
1850	£286	£467	£132
1860	£183	£364	£510
1870	£163	£386	£535

Given the overall rise in the Catholic population over the same period, these figures can only have been depressing.[14]

About £120 a year was needed to keep a priest once he was ordained – 'the wages of a common book-keeper in an ordinary establishment', according to Goss – and at times he had to turn down good priests applying from elsewhere because there was no mission that could afford to support them. In 1859 he wanted to place a priest of good repute in St Vincent's, Liverpool, where he estimated there was enough work for four priests, but the mission could support only three. In the same year, the rector of the Isle of Man asked the Bishop either to remove one of his curates or to send extra money for his support. Finally, in 1867, the Bishop took the extraordinary step of post-poning the ordination of two students because there were no places available that were suitable for newly ordained priests and that could also afford to keep them.[15]

Canon Bernard O'Reilly became third Bishop of Liverpool in 1873. While taking Bishop Goss as his model in many things he was more approachable than his predecessor and more likely to be accepted by the Irish sections of his people – he had been born and educated in Ireland and had spent all his priestly ministry among the poorest of Liverpool Catholics;

'this gave a stamp to his ministry and a bent to his episcopal action' as a *Daily Post* leader put it when he died. He seems to have been the first to have experienced that peculiarly Liverpool phenomenon, the 'Lime Street Accolade', designed to show Catholic loyalty and even devotion to their leaders. It happened in 1883 when he returned to Liverpool after six months' absence due to illness. He was met at the station by a 'huge and enthusiastic assemblage of his devoted people'. The streets in the Catholic areas of the city were decorated with banners and triumphal arches and the Pro-Cathedral was crowded to overflowing when the Chapter received him back; the Te Deum was sung in thanksgiving for his return.[16]

Like his predecessor he did not have enough priests to meet the insistent demands of an expanding and changing community. In his 1874 report on the Ecclesiastical Education Fund he told the faithful that it was much more difficult to find priests than to build and maintain churches: he had needed 24 extra priests over the previous year to staff new parishes and provide additional support in expanding areas and, of course, to replace those who had died or had become too ill to continue working. The following year he could report a large increase in the parish collections and individual subscriptions, though he also pointed out parishes where he felt the collections were too small. There was a big rise in the collections in his early years – the total in the 1873 Report was £643, in 1877 it was £1,194. The total then stayed about this level or slightly higher throughout the 1880s. Each year there were more individual subscribers listed in each parish and considerably more from the clergy. The huge demands on people's pockets and purses for the new seminary (opened in 1883) perhaps explains why the collections for the Ecclesiastical Education Fund did not continue to rise at any substantial rate.[17]

BUILDING CHURCHES

Most missions began in poverty – the traditional picture is of the missioner faced by a field and with little more than a spade to turn the first sod – and almost any building could serve as the first place in which to say Mass: the disused office of a glass factory in Newton-le-Willows, an old warehouse in Tyldesley, a room over a shop in Barrow, or even a large room over a cow-shed for Holy Cross mission in Liverpool. Some people argued that there was no need for expensive buildings when it became time to replace these temporary arrangements, but Bishop Goss said he saw no reason why God should be expected to live 'in a hovel' while men lived in palaces, and he believed that the poor expected to worship in good churches as a compensation for the awful conditions in which they lived. He wrote to one priest:

Your people are zealous, though not rich; and they are mostly composed of those faithful Irish who, banished from their own country by poverty and persecution, can hardly find a home except in the temple of God, and who, therefore, take a pride in providing for God and themselves a suitable dwelling place on earth.[18]

Well-built and 'respectable' churches improved the social reputation of Catholics, and may possibly have improved attendance. They also gave members of a congregation a greater sense of belonging and enabled them to talk feelingly of 'our church' as something to be proud of.

Much has been made of the willingness of the poor to contribute to building churches and of the 'pennies of the poor' being the mainstay of this activity. Yet in the mission to which the above quotation refers the plans had to be considerably modified because money was not forthcoming. The Bishop also had a long correspondence with the architect, E.W. Pugin, in which he referred to the 'fickleness of the people' and the despair of the missioner.[19] What seems to have happened in a number of cases is that the people initially showed great enthusiasm for a building project and collected enough money for the down payment on a piece of land or the laying of a foundation stone. After that it became difficult to raise the steady sums required to pay off the remainder of the debt. So at St Joseph's, Liverpool, which had been opened in 1845, nothing had been paid off the debt for years,

The fine interior of St Anthony's, Scotland Road, Liverpool, opened in 1833.

The 'temporary' church of Our Lady of the Rosary, Plank Lane, Leigh, opened in 1879; it was still in use in the 1930s. (Wigan Heritage Services)

according to a report in 1863. At the famous laying of the foundation stone of St Vincent's, Liverpool, in 1856, where £6,500 had been collected to pay for the site, the day was marked by Irish ship carpenters passing in single file, each laying on the stone a day's wages, followed by the dock labourers with their offerings, the total amounting to £101. 9s. Yet fifteen months later the Bishop was appalled at the size of the debt: income barely covered running costs. In some cases the Bishop felt that the priests had not pushed their appeals for money hard enough, but one good reason for not doing so may well have been their knowledge of the poverty of their people and perhaps the latter's opposition.

The value of the contributions of a small number of wealthy Catholics in founding missions and building churches was all the greater in such circumstances. In Chapter 1 something was said about these generous benefactors in the eighteenth century and the tradition continued. In 1877, for example, the Bishop reported that the 'generosity of the proprietor' had provided a magnificent site for a church at Blundellsands, while the quaintly named 'lord of the soil' had given suitable plots of land in Birkdale and Preston for the same purpose. The church of The English Martyrs in Preston is another excellent example. The money raised between 1865 and its opening in 1867 came to £2,000, of which Joseph Gillow gave £1,000. Over the years the parish priest gave a further £1,000, but the main credit for keeping the mission solvent goes to the local Pyke family of successful corn millers. They built the presbytery, paid for additions to the church and school, and by 1902 had contributed over £7,200 to the total expenditure since the opening.[20]

Another feature of fund-raising was the bazaar, usually organised for a specific project and usually held over a few days in a prominent public venue – no petty jumble sales or car boot sales these! An individual parish or charity might hold one only every ten years or so, but in a town like Preston the public (Protestant as well as Catholic) would be expected to support them much more often. In 1894 the English Martyrs' bazaar raised £2,400; in 1896 St Walburge's, £4,000; also in 1896, St Ignatius', £2,600; in 1898, St Augustine's, £4,000. The bazaars also attracted good coverage in the local press.[21]

While he wanted churches to be as beautiful as possible, Bishop Goss drew the line at certain plans and developments. He claimed that the people objected to elaborate Gothic designs, partly because of the expense and partly because they could not see as well in them as in the older churches. The main objection, he claimed, was to pillars: commenting on the plans for a new church at Westby he said that the country people would 'consider it heaven after the pillars of the Willows'. He admitted that if he had to build the chapel at St Edward's (part of Pugin's Gothic design for a cathedral and the parish church of Our Lady) he would not have a pillar in it, and that, he added, was a great deal for a 'Goth' like himself to admit. On another occasion he wrote to the architect:

Words cannot convey to you the aversion of the people to whatever prevents them seeing. The Clergy too are of the same mind, and a reaction in favour of the old barn style is inevitable, unless we strive to make Gothic more suited to our wants. We must cease to be antiquarians ... [22]

I have not been able to find Pugin's reply.

Some of the new churches were of a different order altogether. At St Charles, Aigburth, the first church erected in 1892 was an 'iron church', one of those mass-produced in the Midlands and assembled in a very short time on site. The outer walls were painted (usually green or ochre) and the windows bore some resemblance to a Gothic design, while inside an arch separated the chancel from the rest of the space. Such constructions were meant to be temporary and St Charles' lasted only six years before being dismantled and re-assembled at Platt Bridge, near Wigan, as the church of the Holy Family; this, surprisingly, was in use until 1956. [23]

Whether the building was simple or grand, it was up to the priest to make it as attractive as possible so that people would want to use it. We know from visitation reports that on the whole the churches were well kept and in good order. What could go wrong can be illustrated by two examples. At Hindley, the incumbent was 'quite inadequate'. The altar linen was in a bad state, an old vestment was discovered at the back of a drawer which the priest had not seen before (he had been incumbent there for four years), and the Holy Oil stocks were in 'a most disgraceful state of dirt', not having been cleaned for very many years, despite a decree to do so at the previous visitation. The buildings were in a ruinous state, the roof timbers were rotten and the walls saturated with rain: 'the whole, inside and out, are (*sic*) damp, dirty, desolate, and in disorder; nothing is well kept. The Incumbent seems to have no idea of cleanliness or order' – in his defence it was stated he had been a professor of theology for twelve years. The only way forward was for the priest to be moved and a new church built.

At South Hill, Chorley, the parochial books were all defective; vestments condemned at the previous visitation were still there, though new ones had been bought; there was ample altar linen, but all of it had a dingy look and the sacred vessels were seldom cleaned. The roof was dilapidated and the sanctuary needed repairs to make it fit for Mass. There was more to this case than just neglect by a careless or elderly missioner. When the Dean suggested to the people that they should give money for the repairs, more serious trouble came to light: they had quarrelled with the priest 'on several points' and refused to contribute – they claimed he had already built schools he could not pay for and pulled down parts of the church on the pretext of repairing it, adding to the costs. Finally, they added, his language in the pulpit had been intemperate and he had angered the congregation more than once. The priest was moved shortly afterwards. [24]

It was unrealistic to expect poor or small congregations to be able to pay for a new church without outside help. If that did not come from wealthy individuals it had to come from the Diocesan Mission Fund, originally set up by Bishop Brown when he was Vicar Apostolic of the Lancashire District. Bishop O'Reilly used his annual reports on the Fund to get support across the diocese for new and struggling missions, outlining in considerable detail the needs of new congregations and explaining the difficult choices that faced him in deciding which should get help. The money contributed 'was but as the five barley loaves and the two fishes' when he had to provide for so many Catholics. Some missions had missed out on funding that year because there seemed little prospect that a start could be made on building in the immediate future, while some were passed over because 'others were deemed more helpless'. So, St Joseph's, Preston, was not helped because St Joseph's, Wigan, was in greater need and Rainford, Walton, Ashton, Catforth and Dalton were 'more destitute'. Pilling was a mission that had to be helped because its people were far removed from church and school and there was a danger that 'the Faith become extinguished' – a later letter referred to it as 'a wild district' that could not be left to become wilder still because there was no one to tend it.

His letters are full of graphic detail. To provide more accommodation for the 'teeming population' of the north end of Liverpool a wooden shed had been set up, with an altar and seats for five hundred worshippers and about eighteen hundred people heard Mass each Sunday in this new mission of St Sylvester's. The Bishop hoped to replace the shed with a 'commodious church, roomy in its proportions and plain in its details'. The same letter spoke of the 'spiritual destitution of one quarter of Chorley' that had been partially solved by building a school, part of which doubled as a church. Nor was it just expanding working-class congregations that had to be catered for: St Marie's, Southport, had been greatly enlarged to cope with the heavy influx of visitors that thronged to the growing town during the summer. Yet the workers, especially those who were migrating to fill new industries or following the movements of old ones, were the Bishop's chief concern. At Barrow-in-Furness, for example, the prospect was, according to the Bishop 'most sad'. Large numbers of Catholic labourers worked in the various industries in the district and soon grew negligent in the practice of their religion, and weak in their faith without a priest to help them – the embryonic mission received a larger grant than usual in the hope that something could be started in the coming year.[25]

Reading the letters one can almost see Bishop O'Reilly sitting at his desk and moving little piles of money across a map of the diocese, inviting the people to share his hopes and problems as he did so. It was a successful approach and the amounts contributed went up from year to year, though never by enough to enable him to allocate a pile to each new mission. From a total of £640 at the start of his episcopate the amount at his disposal went up to £1,200 in a few years, with the list of those subscribing £5 or more individually going up by 50% (Mr Weld-Blundell of Ince Blundell regularly headed these names with £50 or £60). Perhaps listeners to these annual letters developed a feeling of belonging to something larger than their own mission or town and for a brief moment at least were united around their bishop as a diocese ought to be.

There is an interesting passage in the Bishop's report to Propaganda in 1887, justifying his approach to providing new missions with Mass centres. Over the previous five years in particular, he argued, he had addressed the need for more churches and schools, 'to be centres from which the light of faith would shine out to surrounding areas'. Some of the new missions had started in very humble ways while others had started in dual-use buildings such as schools. Gradually the first type of accommodation had been replaced by proper dual-use buildings and the latter replaced by fine churches, all to the greater benefit of the faithful. It was much better, the Bishop was certain, to proceed in this way from very small, humble beginnings and at little cost, but to the benefit of large numbers of the faithful, than to build a few grand churches at great cost that would benefit only a few.

It was not just the thriving industrial and commercial centres that demanded extra resources. Southport may be taken as a good example of a new town that developed gradually over the nineteenth century. Deliberately founded in 1792 as a commercial venture to take advantage of the new interest in the seaside and sea-bathing, over the century its total population rose from 2,500 to over 60,000, with Catholics increasing from single figures to 8,000 in 1900, served by five churches. The town also provides a good example of the continuing role played by the gentry in the development of Catholicism. A Fr Pope, OSB, had said Mass regularly in a cottage from about 1830. St Marie's church was opened in 1841, with a capacity of 203; it was enlarged in 1852 and rebuilt in 1875, with a capacity of 700. The national Religious Census of 1851 reported that 320 people attended morning Mass and 208 the afternoon service. The town had its 'Little Ireland' area, with sub-standard, shanty-town accommodation, but half its inhabitants were English. No Irish-born are listed in the census for 1841 or 1851, but ten years later 13 are listed (including the Anglican curate), and in 1871 fifty Irish families are listed. Between 1868 and 1877, Anglican services were held every Sunday in St Patrick's Catholic school in 'Little Ireland'. There was some local anti-Catholic (or anti-Irish) feeling when the diocesan authorities tried to buy land for a Catholic church there in the early 1890s, but the whole area was demolished soon afterwards.

The growth of the Catholic body in the town is most easily seen from this table:

	Catholic Baptisms	Catholic Marriages
1830s	33	
1840s	99	
1850s	286	34
1860s	555	108
1870s	921	193
1880s	1,346	213
1890s	1,807	269

After St Marie's, the next church to be built was St Joseph's, in Birkdale, a well-to-do suburb of Southport. It was opened in 1867 on land given by Mr Thomas Weld-Blundell who also gave £1,000 towards the estimated building costs of £3,000. (He had previously given a plot of land for an Anglican church.) He also gave land for a school, built conveniently near the Notre Dame convent that had opened in Weld Road in 1868 (the Sisters taught in the school), and for Birkdale Farm School, opened in 1872. When another church, Sacred Heart, was planned for Ainsdale in 1878, he gave the land and £625 towards the building costs. Finally, in 1887-88 the family gave £3,200 to build the shell of St Teresa's church, while the congregation raised over £1,900 to fit it out and furnish it. [26]

~

New missions, additional priests, substantial churches: can we estimate what the overall effects were? Bishop O'Reilly's 1887 Report to Propaganda gives an overview of the state of religion across the diocese and of what had been achieved since 1850. He believed that over the previous twenty years the faith of the people had gradually increased and that levels of practice had improved. Obviously it is very difficult to assess this accurately, though the increase in the number of priests, churches, pious societies, and more than the minimum in the way of devotions, are some sort of measure to support the impressions of a very experienced pastoral Bishop. The returns help to underline the very diverse nature of the diocese and the widely varying levels of practice to be found within it. The smallest mission, at Hornby, had a Catholic population of only 50, with a regular Mass attendance of 22 or 44%, while St Francis Xavier's, Liverpool had a Catholic population of 9,720 and a regular Mass attendance of 5,794 or 59.6%. Other missions, selected at random from around the diocese, were:

	Catholic population	reg. attendance	%
Coniston	99	47	47.5%
Clifton Hill	57	46	80.7%
Rixton	90	27	30.0%
Lt Crosby	528	435	82.4%
St Patrick's, Wigan	5,615	2,302	41.05%
St Alexander's, Bootle	9,247	3,254	35.2%
St Patrick's, Liverpool	9,022	4,475	49.6%
St Joseph's, Liverpool	14,130	3,293	23.35%
St Anthony's, Liverpool	10,845	3,095	28.5%

The returns included the following table:

Town / Area	No. of Missions	Catholic Population	Regular Mass Attendance	Level of Practice
Liverpool*	37	177,893	68,449	38.5%
St Helens	3	16,086	5,670	35.2%
Warrington	2	7,604	2,731	35.9%
Wigan	4	14,885	6,705	45.0%
Widnes	2	6,772	2,962	43.7%
Chorley	2	4,317	2,548	59.0%
Preston	6	30,350	17,361	57.2%
Lancaster	1	2,700	1,118	41.4%
Rural Amounderness	18	7,068	4,714	66.7%
Southport/B'dale	3	2,857	1,660	58.1%
Blackpool	2	1,575	718	45.6%
Isle of Man	4	1,914	926	48.4%
Rural Lonsdale	7	1,801	737	40.9%

* I have included the figures for Bootle, Walton, West Derby, Old Swan, Ford, Garston, Waterloo, Wavertree, Woolton, Seaforth and Great Crosby here although they are entered separately in the returns as not being at that time within the city boundaries.

Overall, Bishop O'Reilly opened 42 new missions during his twenty-one years in charge of the Diocese and the number of priests increased from 221 in 1873 (of whom 135 were Seculars), to 383 in 1894 (of whom 247 were Seculars) – an increase in the number of Seculars of 83%.[27] He also opened a diocesan seminary at Upholland and launched a system of Poor Law Schools. The *Daily Post* commented that the Bishop was 'consistently and persistently occupied with his own business … and was far more successful than appeared from any display that attracted the attention of the general community'.[28] His achievements as a devoted and energetic pastor completed the laying of the foundations begun by his predecessors and enabled the diocese to enter the twentieth century not as a struggling newly born but rather as a sturdy, well-nourished young adult.

BUILDING COMMUNITIES

By the 1890s the vast majority of Catholics in the diocese had access to the sacraments regularly and could send their children to a Catholic school. Moreover, missions were settling down and expanding from being Mass-centres to becoming communities, visited regularly by their priests who were increasingly providing a range of non-spiritual activities for their people. There were boys' clubs, plays and concerts, tea-parties, outings, debating societies, tennis and other sporting clubs, whist drives, and smoking concerts. Some of these were for fund-raising, some were a reward for parish workers – some just a natural development of having parish communities. They were also, in the mind of the clergy, a means to stop the 'leakage', especially among the young – to make the Church more attractive to those who would not attend for purely religious reasons. This extension of the role of the clergyman was not restricted to Catholic churches but was a feature of the age in all the major Christian denominations, all of whom by the last quarter of the century had passed the period of substantial growth and were increasingly worried about the failure to hold on to their younger members. In the early years of the diocese, there is some evidence that an additional aim was to provide an alternative to the Irish pub, where Ribbonism was both a political and a social movement and provided a focus for immigrant nostalgia and desire to mix with their own. There was also a temperance side to some of these activities. It is interesting here that the Chapter in 1899 asked Archbishop Whiteside formally to consider whether he would allow further facilities for evening 'Social Gatherings' amongst Catholics; it is not clear what they had in mind, perhaps the use of school premises for dancing, prohibited by his two predecessors. The laconic secretary of the Chapter recorded his reply as 'he had encouraged and still wished to encourage Social Gatherings'.[29]

A few examples may help here. Burscough was a small agricultural town of about 5,000 people, a thousand of whom were Catholics. It was by no means a model parish, with low attendances (about 25%) at Mass and a high number of mixed marriages taking place outside the church. A 'tea party' held on New Year's Eve, 1888, became rowdy after 10.30pm when the local pubs closed and 'doubtless many got into the room not paying'. Fr Eager decided that he should pay for the services of a constable the following year and that was, he reported, 'of advantage'. But in 1891 the party was again rowdy and disreputable, this time till about 2.30am; the fault was 'laid on people smuggling in spirits'. Owing to a misunderstanding, 'the police were merely onlookers'; what was needed was to have someone in charge of the room to 'direct the police whom to eject, etc'! This seemed to work. When Fr Eager put on a dinner for parish helpers it was far from teetotal, with beer, sherry, port and whisky available.[30]

Things could go wrong in other ways and priests could be disappointed at the response. Fr Burge of St Austin's, Grassendale, tried to set up a debating society in the parish in 1907; a few parishioners tried to make a go of it but 'the men of the Congregation would not attend, and it fell through like the other attempts to provide an Association of the Parish'. Much the same happened when he tried to set up a sewing circle – attendances started off well but fairly quickly fell away and when the La Sagesse nuns began evening classes in French and sewing 'only four could be induced to attend'. If this has a modern ring about it so has another entry in Fr Burge's log: the church collection boxes were 'again rifled'; when a parishioner supplied steel replacements, 'attempts were made with whalebone and birdlime to draw out the coins', but the would-be thieves were thwarted by a 'little arrangement' inside each box.[31]

In clerical eyes, clubs and societies might also have the added advantage of providing more possibilities for young Catholics to meet other Catholics and so help to prevent the spread of mixed marriages. Generally, however, they attracted the already committed; it was difficult to work-in any religious message, without immediately spoiling the atmosphere and causing an exodus. But they were a useful addition for those who were committed. They provided respectable entertainment when respectability was not just the preserve of the better-off middle-classes but was also desired by many skilled manual workers, clerks, shopworkers and others who strove to keep themselves and their families a rung or two above the bottom of the social ladder.

One example may be taken here to illustrate both the success and the failure of the attempts to attract boys and young men. In 1865 the Jesuits of St Francis Xavier's, Liverpool, set up a Boys' Guild (also known as the Guild of St Stanislaus) for boys aged between ten and twenty. From the beginning it had a choir that sang at the Sunday evening services and a brass band. It was well organised and enjoyed the dedication of a number of priest-directors who were assisted by elected wardens (older boys). These had the added responsibility of visiting defaulters in their homes, helping boys in trouble and visiting the sick and dying. The purely recreational side of things was slower to develop, but by the end of the century there was a football team, outings, an annual picnic and regular winter concerts. A report in 1914, however, pointed to an underlying problem when it ended with the words, 'Unless the boys themselves are keen on the Guild, and unless their parents see to it that they attend, no amount of visiting or looking up will secure their attendance'. Another report commented that it was very difficult to keep older boys in the Guild: 'As soon as they have been emancipated from … elementary education, and have begun to wear trousers' they cease to be members and give up the practice of 'all good customs' learned in the Guild. Blame for this falling away was put on the parents: the Guild was dying because 'the appreciation of things spiritual had lost its sensitiveness in the home'. No matter how much it provided by way of football teams, boxing, swimming and music, the Guild had failed to give most of the boys a deep enough appreciation of the Faith to enable them to cope with their entry to the adult world of work. The Guild struggled on until finally buried in the blitz.[32]

While these activities provided opportunities for encouraging Catholic solidarity, they were essentially within the 'family' of the parish. As the century progressed, Catholics also took to more public demonstrations of their presence in local society. The Guilds of St Wilfrid's, Preston, took part in the Preston Guild Week of 1842, walking second in the procession of Friendly Societies. By the next Guild, in 1862, the Catholic walkers numbered over 4,500. Cardinal Manning and other bishops attended that of 1882. These were essentially civic occasions and it would have been odd if the Catholics of the town had not taken their proper part in them. The Guilds also took part in the Whit Walks as early as the 1840s, and by the end of the century the Guilds walked in the parish processions that marked important feastdays each year, although by far the most important of these remained the Whitsuntide Procession, when they were led by the clergy of the town and important laymen. Each Guild wore its regalia and carried banners; occasionally in the late 1860s there were clashes between the Catholic and Orange Whit Walks.[33]

Elsewhere walks and processions seem to have been one-off affairs. In Burscough, for example, the parish priest organised a Gala Day procession for the benefit of the school children.[34] The procession took place through the town, accompanied by the Skelmersdale Old Brass Band and carrying banners. It was similar to the local Anglican and Methodist processions usually held annually and did not have any obviously aggressive element, unlike the public processions and marches organised in, say, Liverpool, where they formed part of the bitter Orange and Green confrontations. They were also different from the mass 'demonstrations' organised to protest over particular issues, such as denominational schools, which will be dealt with later.

Were Catholics consciously asserting their equality with other religious groups when they marched or 'walked'? Or were they just following the tradition of Lancashire industrial towns, where Whit Walks were an important element of popular culture, and doing what came naturally to them while providing some fun and a feeling of religious well-being in the process? Where Anglican processions were made up mainly of children, the Catholic ones were more representative of the average congregation; parish priests might lament the low number of marching men, but onlookers were often surprised that so many took part.[35] Where the religious and the secular fused it is not easy to separate the mixed motives – celebratory, doctrinal, demanding, or just 'one in the eye for the Protestants'. Certainly there was an increasing note of confidence and even triumphalism, a feeling of strength and pride, an unconscious demand to be granted equality of respect with their non-Catholic neighbours. It was the coming-of-age of the new Catholic body, fused from Lancashire tradition and Irish immigration.

Notes

1 Bennett, *Nugent*, pp.15-19; Burke, pp.86-7.

2 *Directory* for relevant years; RCLv 5/1/193, Goss to James Whiteside Esq, 17.4.1856; 5/2/99, Goss to Dean Brown, 20.11.1857.

3 APF *S.R. Anglia*, vol. 27, nn.483-529, Dec. 1887.

4 RCLv Visitation Returns, 1855, 1865; Plumb, *Found Worthy*, pp.i-ii for later figures.

5 RCLv Visitation Returns 1865.

6 RCLv 5/4/285, Goss to Power,13.3.1862.

7 Dye, *THSLC*, p.103.

8 RCLv 5/1/440, Goss to Turpin, 7.3.1857; 444, Goss to Crowe, 9.3.1857; 452, Goss to Penswick, 13.3.1857; 5/2/303, Goss to Greenhalgh, 3.9.1856; 5/6/1/399, Goss's secretary to Herbert Vaughan, 14.9.1863.

9 See note 3.

10 RCLv 5/3/328,347,399 and 5/4/34, Goss to Blundell, July 1860-March 1861. 5/2/418, Goss to Greenhalgh, 30.12.1858.

11 RCLv 5/3/219, Goss to Vandepitte, 20.10.1859. Holmes, *More Roman*, pp.174-5.

12 RCLv 5/2/405, Goss to Bridges, 18.12.1858; 5/2/440, Goss to Maguire, 15.1.1859.

13 APF *S.R. Anglia*, vol. 15, nn. 1250ff, May 1860.

14 *AAL Liverpolitana*, Annual Reports on Ecclesiastical Ed. Fund.

15 AAL Early Bishops, S1 II, B: Pastorals of Bp Goss, Lent 1861; RCLv5/6/2/171, Goss to Berry, 26.5.1867.

16 Burke, pp.249-50; AAL Chancellor, Chapter Minutes, 13.6.1883.

17 AAL *Liverpolitana*, Annual Reports on Ecclesiastical Ed. Fund.

18 RCLv 5/1/228, Goss to Vandepitte, 10.5.1856.

19 RCLv 5/2 and 5/3 contain several letters to Pugin from 1858-59; quotation from 5/2/360. For St Joseph's, 5/6/1/410-11, Goss to Duggan, 14.11.1863; for St Vincent's, 5/1/476 to Holmes, 8.5.1857, and Burke, p.127.

20 AAL *Liverpolitana*, Annual Diocesan Mission Fund Reports. Tom Smith, 'Turning the Century: Catholics Decadent and Prestonian', in J.A. Hilton (ed.), *Turning the Last Century: Essays on English Catholicism c1900* (2003), pp.10-26.

21 Smith, 'Turning the Century', p.18.

22 RCLv 5/2/374, 378, Goss to Pugin, 27 and 30 Oct. 1858.

23 Margaret Peters, Brian Plumb, et al., *St Charles Borromeo Parish Centenary 1892-1992* (1992), p.8.

24 RCLv 3/B, Visitation Diaries, 4/117 and 3/202-6.

25 AAL *Liverpolitana 1873-78*, Diocesan Mission Fund Annual Reports.

26 P.F. Lynch, 'Southport and the Catholic Church in the Nineteenth Century', unpublished M.A. thesis, Liverpool Hope University College (2002). See also Harry Foster, *New Birkdale: The Growth of a Lancashire Seaside Suburb* (1995).

27 *Directory* for relevant years.

28 Burke, pp.249-50.

29 AAL Chancellor, 52 Chapter Minutes.

30 Gillian Goddard, *St John the Evangelist Catholic Church, Burscough* (2000), pp.35-7.

31 John Davies (ed.), *Thomas Anselm Burge: St Austin's Log 1899-1929* (1999).

32 N. Ryan, SJ, *St Francis Xavier's Church Centenary, 1848-1948* (1948), pp.102-7.

33 Smith, 'Turning the Century', pp.21-2.

34 Gillian Goddard, 'St John's, Lathom: The Sociology of a Parish as Viewed Through Fr Eager's Log Book 1880-1918', *NWCH*, XXIX (2002), pp.90-1.

35 S. Fielding, *Class and Ethnicity: Irish Catholics in England, 1880-1939* (1993), pp.72-8.

CHAPTER 5 DIOCESAN INDEPENDENCE: LIVERPOOL, ROME AND WESTMINSTER, 1850-1950

A fter 1850 England was once again a fully-fledged member of the world-wide Catholic family. That certainly gave cause for celebration, but the bishops knew that the devil was, as usual, in the small print: this made it clear that the commitment of the Roman authorities to a fully-independent set of English bishops was far from wholehearted. The Church in England was to remain under Propaganda, whose normal brief was to look after missionary territories considered not stable or mature enough to rule themselves. Why did the Roman authorities think that such continued surveillance of the new bishops was necessary? They feared that English Catholics, and especially the priests and former vicars apostolic, had been cut off from Rome for so long that they had become too English in outlook and had developed an unhealthy spirit of independence from Rome.[1]

RELATIONS WITH ROME

Under a different pope this surveillance, and the interference it led to, might not have been very important, but at a time when there was a positive drive towards centralisation in Rome it could be dangerous. Blessed Pius IX's pontificate witnessed a tendency to interfere directly in diocesan affairs and to impose an all-embracing uniformity. Many Catholic bishops did not object to these developments and accepted in practice a diminution of their own authority and a corresponding increase in that of the Roman Curia. The Roman Congregations' consulatative role gradually changed to an authoritative one. Moreover, the Pope deliberately used his charm and personal popularity to win over wavering bishops, calling them to Rome either as individuals or for great emotional gatherings, as in 1862 and 1867. He revived the practice whereby bishops paid regular *ad limina* visits to report on the state of their dioceses, and regarded both the visits and reports as very important. In various letters he wrote on this topic there is a presumption that it was his duty to look after every diocese and to provide the means for the local bishops to do their work, as well as a strong suggestion that all problems should be taken to Rome for solution.

Bishop Ullathorne of Birmingham, another of the new bishops, was clear about what was happening and complained to Manning in 1862 that Rome was always trying to limit the rights of the bishops while they wished to be as limited as possible. Manning called this remark 'the pure fruit of Gallicanism' and stated that the bishops owed any privileges they had to delegation from the Holy See and not to any divine institution.[2] For his part, Bishop Goss complained about the 'backstairs influence' of English clerics living in Rome and had a low opinion of Propaganda's ability and its reliance on Wiseman and Manning for information about England. He added:

> *Rome is only Manning in Italian. It learns all from him and acts by his suggestion … Rome lives in an ideal world, in a cloud of incense offered by the nauseous Tablet, Universe (sic), Civiltà and Osservatore. Who is Herbert Vaughan or Veuillot to dictate a Catholic policy to the world?*[3]

Goss, however, in opposing what was happening at Rome, was concerned about something much deeper than the attention paid to Talbot and Manning. The first important occasion on which he voiced his opposition was in connection with the condemnation of the liberal Catholic review, *The Rambler*. Cardinal Barnabò, secretary of Propaganda in Rome, wrote to the English bishops ordering them to issue pastoral letters against the review. Goss was indignant and wrote to Bishop Brown of Shrewsbury; his reactions were based on a mixture of expediency and principle:

> *What next? I suppose you have received Cardinal Barnabò's instructions about pastoralising the Rambler, a sure plan to rekindle the gallican spirit among Catholics, to alienate the Converts and to bring down the whole Protestant press upon us.*

He then asked why the periodical, if it was so bad, had not been forbidden by Cardinal Wiseman, as it had been published in his diocese. This led him on to his main complaint:

> *If Rome has thought it necessary to censure it, why has it not done so in its own name? Why throw the odium and the responsibility upon us? Is it not unusual to prescribe to bishops to issue pastorals on particular subjects? Does it act so with France or Germany? If not, why are we treated so exceptionally?*[4]

Goss was now in full flow and brought up something that had been rankling for some time. Propaganda had refused to ratify the decree of the Third Provincial Synod on the constitution of the English seminaries, even though it had been carefully drafted and agreed to by nearly all the bishops; instead, each Bishop had been ordered to send his ideas in separately to Barnabò. Goss commented to Bishop Brown:

> *Provincial Synods are never set aside unless they contain enactments contrary to faith or morals … like a set of schoolboys we have been ordered to send up our themes to Propaganda: and now we are ordered to write pastorals on a given theme within a given time! Verily, anything better than VGs? Does Talbot or Manning or Cardinal Barnabo govern our dioceses? We certainly do not.*

Goss did not write a pastoral letter on *The Rambler*, the only English Bishop not to do so.

What Goss wanted was to be left alone to get on with his main task, the advancement of religion in his diocese. Undue interference by others meant an unnecessary increase in business, long delays and decisions which did not take into account all the local circumstances. In some cases it could also lead to injustice, as he claimed had happened over the disputes about how to divide the old Vicariate funds between the new dioceses.[5] In 1863 he wrote to Bishop Grant of Southwark to complain of 'the child's play' going on over the funds: the bishops were being bandied about from Propaganda to York Place (Wiseman's residence) and had to waste time arguing and defending 'the petty details' of their administration over and over again. Goss, who could always exaggerate to make his point, said they were being treated like:

> Our Lord … sent from Pilate to Herod, a way of proceeding which made
> … Saint Thomas of Canterbury declare that it was as hard for a Bishop
> to obtain justice in the court of Rome, as for Our Lord to meet with it in
> the courts of Pilate and Herod.[6]

In part, Goss's attitude stemmed from his low estimate of the ability of the Roman curial officials. He spoke of them as 'little men' who had hardly enough ability to run an English mission, and who covered up the weakness of their reasoning by constantly using the Pope's name and appealing for loyalty: if there was a danger of Gallicanism in England, said Goss, then such cavalier action was a sure way of arousing it. Moreover, Rome was full of what he called 'frightening gossip', and a Bishop's good name was readily blackened if he did not say just what those 'fussy busy bodies chose to dictate'. Goss was always outspoken and honest, and he hated the intrigue of the curia; he wrote later to Cardinal Newman that nothing ever wounded the simplicity of his faith so much as the trickery with which he became acquainted on his official intercourse with the Curia.[7]

To Goss, Newman was a great champion, too humble and retiring to defend himself; efforts to assail a name that was 'without stain' were 'lamentable'. In 1867, in a reference to Propaganda's prohibition of Newman's plan to work in Oxford, Goss wrote that it was 'infamous'; what had Newman done to be 'cast aside in so contemptuous a manner'? At the same time Goss commented on Propaganda's decision that the bishops should issue pastoral letters against Catholics attending the English universities. He was not in favour of Catholics going to the universities, but Propaganda had no right to order the English bishops to prohibit something under pain of mortal sin. He wrote:

> … we should sustain our position by presenting a firm remonstrance,
> couched not in the flattering mode of the day, but in the more English
> style of Saint Thomas … if we publish (the Roman brief) we should do so
> simply, leaving to Rome the responsibility of its own act. If Germans and
> Americans are allowed to attend mixed universities, how can we condemn
> of (sic) mortal sin those who do (so) in this country?

Goss also complained about the last sentence in the Roman brief, which had said that the Archbishop of Westminster was to see that the pastorals issued by the bishops should be uniform in content and style.[8] Goss's belief was that each Bishop should be left to interpret Roman rulings (and decisions taken in common by the English bishops, for that matter) as he thought best.

On this occasion he did write a pastoral. In it he quoted the two most important paragraphs of Propaganda's letter and added a little about the dangers faced by Catholics at the universities; he also referred to the general teaching of the Church about avoiding occasions of sin. Most of the pastoral, however, was about the dangers that faced Catholic children who attended Protestant schools, a far more pressing problem in Liverpool.[9] The whole pastoral is a good example of how a Bishop could interpret a general ruling to suit the circumstances of his people.

It is not surprising that Goss was in the lists again in 1870 during the First Vatican Council. He did not attend the Council because of bad health (he got as far as Cannes); had he done so he would have been another voice arguing against any definition of papal infallibility. In the course of a letter to Newman about the Council he explained what he thought the role of a bishop was in defining doctrinal matters. A bishop should not judge according to his own theological opinions, but should be a witness of the tradition and teaching of his Church. Goss implied that the general view in England was against a definition of infallibility. Unfortunately, he went on, anyone who spoke against it was being branded a heretic by 'an aggressive and insolent faction' – Manning, *The Dublin Review* and *The Tablet*. What was being done by Manning's faction in Rome smacked of the intrigue that Goss hated, and he complained:

> *Truth, simple English truth, seems to have departed from the whole faction.*
>
> *I generally believe any assertion which they are unanimous in contradicting.*

He also feared that the Council would result in a lessening of the bishops' rights, because they would be subordinated even more to Rome, and the 'patriarchal sceptre' would be changed into 'the dictator's truncheon'. The bishops who had gone to the Council to confer with the Pope would, he felt, return to find waiting for their obedience the very decrees that they had refused to sanction in Council.

Part of the trouble, Goss thought, was the Pope's judgement had been spoilt by flattery and the excesses of the pro-papalist party; for years no one had dared to contradict him, and his amiability had won a 'sort of hysterical affection from ladies and young priests', so much so that he felt that the bishops would succumb to the same fascination. Moreover:

> *the Pope has been so much flattered by four great assemblages of the Bishops … that he has been led to think that he can rule them as a pedagogue rules his pupils. The dealings of Rome, at any time, with the Bishops have been of the ferula and bonbons type: they are not treated as grown-up men but as difficult children.*[10]

Goss tried to keep clear of the papal charm. He did not attend the great gathering in Rome in 1862 to celebrate the canonisation of the Japanese Martyrs. As he wrote to Bishop Errington, he had a good excuse because his health would not stand a Roman summer, but there was another reason for not going as well. He did not want to sign an address to the Pope which he did not agree with and in Rome he could hardly refuse to do so. The address would not contain what the bishops 'really thought best', but would be drawn up by 'the officious few' who hoped to gain increased influence as a reward. This letter is additionally interesting in that it makes clear that pressure was put on the bishops to attend. Cardinal Rinaldini had written to Bishop Grant of Southwark to say that 'offence would be given in high quarters' if he and Goss did not go to Rome. Goss's letter of excuse was accepted by Barnabò, who wrote to say that the Pope had been pleased by the Bishop's expressions of love and veneration; clearly, Goss did not push his independence too far.[11]

Propaganda questioned his loyalty again in 1870 when he refused to allow his clergy and people to have anything to do with an address and petition in favour of the Pope which was circulated throughout England He was afraid that accompanying demonstrations or public meetings might cause an outbreak of anti-Catholicism in a town marked by bitter sectarianism. As local ordinary Goss believed he was in the best position to judge the seriousness of such dangers, and he told Propaganda so.[12] There was, however, a more serious reason why he had objected to the petition and here we touch on something fundamental in Goss's thinking and in his approach to the question of episcopal independence. He had been intensely annoyed to find that the petition had argued that all Catholics, whatever their nationality, were 'citizens of Rome', an idea put forward by some extreme papalists. For his part, the Bishop was always concerned to stress that English Catholics were citizens only of England, and that in no sense could the Pope claim even the smallest degree of that obedience and respect that a civil ruler could demand from his subjects. Extreme pro-papal arguments would not only resurrect old accusations of divided loyalty against Catholics but would strengthen in English people's minds the prejudice that Catholicism was something foreign and un-English.

The Bishop frequently touched on these matters in his sermons, especially when there were Protestants present. More than once he said of himself and his fellow Catholics, 'we are not Italians, but Englishmen'; Catholic ceremonies were not, he insisted, 'foreign superstition'. On one occasion he wrote:

> To the Sovereign of these realms we own allegiance, and we give it … It would be as great a sin to give to the Pope what belongs to the Crown as to give to the Crown what belongs to the Pope.[13]

Both Wiseman and Manning thought that Goss was among those who were too English ever to be truly Roman. Those who supported Newman, Manning believed, held 'low views' about the Holy See, were 'cold and silent', to say no more, about the temporal power, and were 'national' and 'English'.[14] Such a statement only underlines the lack of subtlety in their judgements of people and ideas, for Goss, despite all that has been said, was not anti-papal.

He believed that the Pope held the primacy over the whole Church, that his person was 'august and sacred' and that the Catholics of Liverpool, as his devoted children, owed him 'profound respect, veneration and dutiful obedience', and shared in his sufferings; the Pope was the supreme visible head of the Church in matters of faith and morals. In 1859 when the Pope needed special help and support Goss arranged for a diocesan collection to be taken and for an address to be circulated for signatures, as proof of 'the deep interest which we feel' in the Pope's welfare. The address was signed by over 53,000 people and the collection raised a staggering sum in excess of £7,000. The Bishop presented the address and the money in person in Rome and on his return wrote to the people to pass on the Holy Father's gratitude and blessing. Privately, however, he had been very disappointed with the papal response and wrote that he had hardly been thanked at all and had taken nothing back to his diocese but his independence. Yet four years later he gave full support to the launch of a papal loan and said that the contributions from the diocese showed that clergy and laity were unequalled in 'their attachment to the person and office of the Holy Father'.[15]

In 1867 he issued a very strongly worded pastoral on the Temporal Power of the papacy, incorporating a papal encyclical on the subject. Goss's views were very straightforward, even simplistic: Garibaldi, the great Italian anti-papal hero who had been feted when he had visited England, was a pest to society, and governments that had failed to stop him were unfaithful and untruthful. It was, he went on, simply puerile to say that the Pope would have more respect without his territories and hypocritical of Englishmen to claim that spiritual and temporal power were incompatible in one ruler or that Rome most obviously belonged to Italy; what about Queen Victoria and what about Gibraltar? He authorised a triduum of prayers and another collection; the latter raised almost £2,000.[16]

Goss fully accepted the papal primacy, but the expansion of curial business and of Roman interference could so extend that primacy as to undermine the position of diocesan bishops, who were, in his eyes, 'princes of the household' to be consulted and conferred with, not given orders.[17] Moreover, the contemporary heavy stress on papal infallibility meant that there was an added danger of its being so extended as to claim some sort of administrative inerrancy for the Pope and the Roman Congregations. Goss feared that, as a result, the Church in England would be dominated by curial thinking, that Italian solutions would be found for English problems and that, in the process, the Church would lose its Englishness and its ability to appeal to English people.

Goss's successor, Bishop O'Reilly (1873-1894), had a happier relationship with Propaganda, although at times he, too, felt he was unfairly treated and his views misrepresented (for example, over the case of the Franciscan Tertiaries – see page 123). When Propaganda wrote to complain about his actions towards some of the Regulars, the Bishop replied rather plaintively that it gave him great sorrow that the Secretary of Propaganda seemed to look with little favour on his undertakings. Indeed, he went on, he would say that he seemed to be altogether without the Secretary's protection when every complaint and statement from whatever quarter was immediately accepted as true. In a plaintive plea for understanding he stated that he was almost overcome by grief and oppressed by labours beyond his strength; to whom could he speak heart to heart if not to His Eminence and whose help and protection could he claim for himself and his diocese if not his? One cannot imagine Goss uttering such a cry for understanding and sympathy. When the Prefect of Propaganda sent him some kind and re-assuring words, O'Reilly was duly grateful: they dispelled his worries and brought him great solace, he replied.[18]

Archbishop Whiteside (1894-1921) followed the line of interpreting Roman decrees and documents as he believed best suited the needs of his people. When Pope Leo XIII issued an Apostolic Constitution on The Prohibition and Censorship of Books in 1897, the Archbishop wrote to his clergy to say that its use should be restricted mainly to the confessional and even then should be interpreted according to the guidelines laid down by approved authors. Priests should, of course, warn their people from the pulpit of the dangers of contemporary 'pernicious literature', but to talk about the ecclesiastical laws on the subject 'before a mixed congregation might be fraught with danger'. He took a similar line in 1907, when Pope St Pius X issued his extremely important condemnation of Modernism in the encyclical *Pascendi*, and the Holy See published a decree on Mass stipends. The decree pointed out some abuses that had grown up in connection with stipends, particularly to do with sending surplus stipends to unknown priests and letting large numbers of stipends accumulate. Whiteside told his clergy that he did not think it advisable that any of these documents should be read to the people, presumably because he felt that neither issue was a problem in the diocese and that raising them would only encourage his people to find out more and cause scandal. In the case of Mass stipends there was the added danger that Protestants would use the admission that there were abuses in the system as an additional shot in their anti-Catholic armoury, already well stocked with accusations that priests extorted money for their services and the sacraments.[19]

RELATIONS WITH WESTMINSTER

The English and Welsh bishops ceased to be responsible to Propaganda in 1908 and became as other independent national hierarchies were, responsible to the Consistorial Congregation. But there could still be trouble and complaints that their views were not taken into account and that Roman decisions were influenced by behind-the-scenes string-pullers. In general, bishops considered the archbishops of Westminster to be the principal string-pullers throughout, suspicions that went back to the 1850s. As well as learning how to live with Propaganda, the new bishops had had to learn how to live with each other and, in particular, how to live with the archbishop of Westminster, their Metropolitan. Canonically, the archbishop was little more than the president of a body of bishops over whom he had no direct

Nicholas, Cardinal Wiseman, first Archbishop of Westminster, 1850-65.

authority; in practice, everything depended on the character and diplomatic skill of the individual archbishop.

The first archbishop was Cardinal Wiseman, an outstanding man in many ways but a hopeless administrator and a poor judge of people. He put off difficult decisions as long as possible and delayed dealing with routine business to an embarrassing extent. Gradually Bishop Goss had lost patience with him and their former friendly relationship disintegrated into bitterness as the Bishop felt Wiseman's lack of action was causing him more and more troubles. At one stage Goss was threatened with legal action by some of his laypeople who wanted to know what had happened to certain charitable funds that should have gone to training apprentices – they were, in fact, tied up in a dispute that Wiseman had been empowered to settle years before but about which he had ceased even to answer letters after a time. As with the major dispute over the Ushaw Funds, which again involved Wiseman, and in which many thousands of pounds were at stake, all the financial cases were eventually settled in Goss's favour.[20]

There was, in addition, Wiseman's autocratic manner, which led Bishop Goss to claim that the Cardinal could only be propitiated 'by having the hierarchy prostrate before him'. His basic fear was the same as with Propaganda: episcopal authority would be diminished and undue outside interference would cause damage. When the Cardinal refused to allow the bishops to meet without him to discuss the choice of a new Bishop for Beverley, Goss expressed his views in his usual forthright way:

We stand before the world as a body of incapables, who cannot or dare not move hand or foot unless His Eminence is there with his wand to direct our movements.

Some of the issues at stake were of little lasting importance, but underneath them was a key principle that was to cause trouble between Westminster and the other dioceses for many years: did the bishops have a decisive voice or only a consultative one in matters of policy that were of common concern to them? When Wiseman asked Propaganda to quash the decrees of the Third Provincial Synod (1859), because he felt the bishops did not have the right to legislate about the English seminaries, Goss led the opposition. He went to Rome in 1860 to plead their case and in 1862 organised them in a final attempt to convince Propaganda to find in their favour, even writing draft letters for his episcopal colleagues to send to Rome. In the meanwhile he decided that it would be dishonourable to attend Low Week meetings of the hierarchy and so organised a partial boycott of them in 1862 and 1863.[21]

Propaganda must bear some of the blame. It had enough information to make sound judgements in all the disputes, but indulged in turns and twists of policy that bewildered everyone. There was simply no excuse for the seven-year delay in settling the college question (it also took seven years to settle a funds dispute between Bishop Grant of Southwark and the Cardinal), nor for quashing the bishops' decrees in 1860 and then re-instating them in 1863. Propaganda misread both the situation in England and Wales and the minds of the bishops; it thought there was danger of schism and that Gallican beliefs were strong among the bishops – even when the Prefect of Propaganda thought the bishops were in the right, he felt it necessary to uphold Wiseman's authority against them. Goss, however, probably over-estimated Wiseman's influence in Rome – as Wiseman himself did.

Unfortunately, these attitudes and Wiseman's failures coloured Goss's attitude to Manning when he succeeded Wiseman as archbishop in 1865. Manning had been Wiseman's agent in Rome during the colleges dispute and seemed to have undue influence there – to Goss he seemed like an 'arch-intriguer'. While he was an incomparably better administrator than his predecessor, and a much more sensitive diplomat, he had a tendency to want and expect united action from the other bishops, even when there seemed to be room for different approaches and policies to suit local conditions. In general, Goss's relationship with Manning may be summed up as one of unenthusiastic co-operation: he might complain about the Archbishop's way of doing things but he rarely refused to do what had been suggested. An example of what he saw as Manning's deviousness occurred over the appointment of an English theologian to help with preparing the schemata for the 1870 Vatican Council. Goss, along with the majority of the other bishops, suggested Newman, only to be told by Manning that they could only recommend Secular priests with pastoral experience in their own dioceses. Goss could find no justification for these restrictions, which certainly had not come from Rome, and smelt a rat, adding that 'missionary experience and great theological knowledge seldom go together'. Manning, however, got his way and had one of his own supporters, Dr Weathers of St Edmund's, Ware, appointed instead of Newman.[22] As it happened, Newman had already turned down an invitation from the Pope to attend the Council and so could hardly have gone at the request of the bishops.

Goss saw himself as an independent member of a body of bishops, retaining his freedom to join in common action or to take unilateral measures, and no one else must presume to act for him unless expressly delegated to do so. He objected to Manning's habit of lobbying bishops individually to get common action – it smacked to him of an unhealthy 'divide and rule' approach. At times, with both Wiseman and Manning, Goss could be petty and exasperating, but he felt that some of his fellow bishops seemed too willing to let the archbishops have their way and to do little except murmur about injustices afterwards. He knew his diocese as well as any Bishop could; outsiders and their suggestions were more likely to be hindrances than helps. He was not the last of the Liverpool bishops to think so. There is something attractive in the image of the diocesan Bishop as a rugged individual fending off with his crozier outsiders who wanted to interfere, but with it went the dangers that the diocese would become too inward-looking and that English Catholicism would fail to develop a positive corporate role in national society.

THE TWENTIETH CENTURY

The failure of Cardinal Bourne (Archbishop of Westminster 1903 – 1935, Cardinal from 1911) to consult his fellow-bishops and his tendency to take advice from a very small group of intimates were likely to cause hostilities between himself and the hierarchy. He has been described as a 'moderator, lonely, intensely cold in disposition' and, ironically, suspicious of what was going on in Rome behind his back.[23] The position vis-à-vis the other bishops changed somewhat after 1911 when Westminster ceased to be the Metropolitan See for the whole of England and Wales. The Diocese of Liverpool became an Archdiocese, with metropolitan jurisdiction over the northern dioceses of Salford, Hexham and Newcastle, Leeds and Middlesbrough, and Birmingham also became an Archdiocese, with jurisdiction over Clifton, Plymouth, Shrewsbury, Newport and Menevia. In Rome, however, despite these changes, the Cardinal-Archbishop of Westminster was still treated as the sole leader of the hierarchy and some of the other bishops resented his influence there.

The main quarrels arose over Bourne's desire to increase the number of dioceses in the country, something he worked on for several years. Bishop Keating of Northampton (later Archbishop of Liverpool) declared in 1912 that Westminster had always been autocratic and seemed to forget that the Cardinal was only the spokesman of the bishops, with no authority over them. In 1917 he complained that whenever Bourne spent a prolonged period in Rome there was likely to be trouble: some project 'disturbing our peace' would be the result, sprung on the other bishops as a fait accompli. In a letter to Bishop Amigo of Southwark he described Bourne as 'an autocrat of the most Prussian type, who consults no one but himself and wishes to stifle all opinion opposed to his own'. Amigo agreed, saying that whenever Bourne wanted something he discovered it was the will of God![24] Archbishop Whiteside wrote to Bishop Casartelli of Salford:

I have felt for some time that the Bishops' meetings have not been for a frank discussion and settlement of things by ourselves, but meetings merely to confirm the Cardinal's decisions. I have told the Cardinal privately he is getting out of touch with the Bishops. For that reason I have advocated regular Executive meetings. But His Eminence won't see it.[25]

It was Archbishop Keating, Whiteside's successor, who had to deal with these issues as they affected Liverpool when the question of dividing the archdiocese arose in 1921 (see Chapter 11). After it was all over, Keating continued to blame Cardinal Bourne for the way the division had been made 'without one word' to himself. It was, he believed, only the latest instance of a continuing problem: 'H.E. simply cannot keep his fingers out of other people's business and his interference is seldom to the good'. He ended this letter, to the rector of the English College in Lisbon, with a warning: 'Don't let him get a hold on the government of Lisbon'.[26]

During Cardinal Bourne's declining years the leading Bishop in the country was Archbishop Downey of Liverpool. Many Catholics and much of the press regarded him as the only possible domestic candidate to replace Cardinal Bourne, who died in January 1935 (see Chapter 13). That honour went instead to an outsider, Bishop Arthur Hinsley, who had no recent first-hand knowledge of English ecclesiastical politics and, in his seventieth year, might have thought he would end his days quietly in Rome. Instead, he immediately ran into a north-westerly squall when Downey took him to task over matters of protocol. It was a silly matter, involving the new Archbishop's grant of an indulgence of 100 days to all English and Welsh Catholics and the question whether he had precedence over the other three archbishops. Downey was in the wrong and the squall blew itself out as quickly as it had arisen, but it was a sign that there were still unresolved problems connected with the relationship between Westminster and the rest of the hierarchy.

Cardinal Hinsley tried to open windows to allow light and fresh air into English Catholicism, especially in its relations with other Christians, but he lacked both personal and canonical authority to carry the rest of the bishops with him. One of Hinsley's biographers speaks of his being 'hemmed in' by the three archbishops, Godfrey (the Apostolic Delegate), Amigo (of Southwark) and Downey.[27] Archbishop Downey is usually said to have taken the lead in wrecking Cardinal Hinsley's 'Sword of the Spirit' movement, at least in the north of England, but what he (and the other bishops) objected to was its ecumenical aspects, where Hinsley was moving too far ahead of his episcopal colleagues without consulting them (see Appendix to this chapter).

As Cardinal Hinsley's health deteriorated in the early years of the war (he died in March 1943) he asked Downey to deputise for him, and Downey came to the fore again as de facto leader when he took over the chairmanship of the bishops' negotiating committee for education – always the most important issue in Catholic circles. R.A. Butler, in charge of drawing up the new Education Bill, and sincerely hoping to be fair to the Catholic case, found it impossible to deal with a committee that changed its membership too often and seemed to have no central planning or authority behind it. The whole episode revealed not only a lack of leadership and planning from a dying Cardinal, but tensions between the other bishops as well – if they could not get along co-operatively with Westminster, neither could they get along very purposefully among themselves. They seemed able to act together defensively when they thought their rights were under threat from Westminster or the secular state, but unable to act positively and coherently when a united voice was needed.

We come back to the authorities in Rome. In the early years of the new hierarchy they mis-read the signs coming from England and Wales and relied over-much on reports from foreigners and English ex-pats in Rome. By the 1930s and 1940s, given the right leadership, the Catholic Church in England and Wales should have been ready for more than its customary bit-part on the national stage. Cardinal Hinsley had the imagination to see the possibilities and was free of the traditional fortress outlook of so many English and Welsh Catholics. But he was too old when he was appointed and out of touch with his fellow bishops. To succeed him, Rome chose Arthur Griffin (1943-56), rather cruelly but not altogether unfairly described as 'a nice, hard-working nonentity'.[28] He was unlikely either to impress the nation or persuade his epsicopal colleagues to move outward from their diocesan city-states. On one occasion Archbishop Downey told him, 'Don't forget, Your Eminence, that I rule the North'. Perhaps he did; he certainly ruled the archdiocese of Liverpool and was as jealous of his episcopal rights there as ever Bishop Goss had been.

APPENDIX

ARCHBISHOP DOWNEY AND THE 'SWORD OF THE SPIRIT' MOVEMENT

Archbishop Downey's initial doubts about Cardinal Hinsley's movement arose partly from the belief that it would not last, a belief that Bishop David Mathew, Hinsley's auxiliary, strengthened in two letters of September 1940. Mathew is normally portrayed as a keen supporter of the scheme but in a letter to Downey he said he steered clear of it because it was not his 'line of country' and he was not sure if it would last at all. He was at pains to stress that it was purely personal to the Cardinal and existed only to promote knowledge of the Cardinal's standpoint as revealed in all his public statements; rather disparagingly, he said that it had started with 'some CSG women plus the Plater Dining Club women plus Fr O'Hea' – the Jesuit head of Plater College in Oxford. Finally in this particular letter he said that he quite appreciated Downey's attitude and that of the northern bishops. In a second letter of the same date to an unknown northern Bishop (copied to Downey), Mathew promised to raise with the Cardinal the bishops' worries about possible repercussions on already established Catholic Action movements. Again he stressed that he had no direct connection with the movement and repeated his idea about how it had started, adding this time that the head of the Religious Section of the Ministry of Information had also played a part – the Ministry had already distributed copies of the Cardinal's original speech and would pay for further leaflets to keep it going and increase awareness of the Cardinal's views – which was what the movement was all about. Both letters clearly played down the importance of the movement as something that Catholics nationally should support with any enthusiasm or energy.[29]

Downey also felt that the movement seemed to be aiming at something very similar to Catholic Action, and indeed could be seen as just another form of it. Along with some of the other bishops he feared that the introduction of another movement would disrupt what had been achieved in establishing Catholic Action and divide Catholic effort to impact on society. This was a point made by Mr P. Taggart, a leading and well-respected member of the Liverpool Catholic Action Board, but he added that the circumstances of the war might make it more attractive to people than organised Catholic Action. It would also have the benefit of having clergy and laity working together – Catholic Action had as yet not sorted out the different roles to be undertaken by each. It might also, he continued, help the development of Catholic Action in that the new movement would be focused on immediate ends while Catholic Action was more interested in general principles and 'ultimate ends'. On the whole, Taggart thought the 'Sword' could be encouraged in the Archdiocese, as long as it worked under the general aegis of the Catholic Action Board. It was presumably because of this memo that Downey saw Taggart as a suitable person to represent the northern bishops on the national Executive Committee of the 'Sword' and persuaded the bishops to accept him.[30]

The Archbishop was not opposed to Hinsley's initial aims (what he could understand of them – the Cardinal admitted that the 'Sword' had got off the ground too hastily and its own Committee was divided on its aims[31]). But the movement very quickly attracted the interest and enthusiasm of other Christians, specially the Anglicans, and this raised two key issues: could non-Catholics become full members of a Catholic organisation and, more crucially, could the combined members say prayers in common? The founders had not had an ecumenical movement of this kind in mind, but some people seized on it as an opportunity to develop closer links between the main English Christian denominations; even the Cardinal initiated the recitation of the 'Our Father' at a joint meeting (for which he was strongly taken to task by his fellow bishops).[32] Nobody should have been surprised when Downey and the other bishops objected to these developments and made it clear that they would withdraw their support completely if the 'Sword' became a 'mixed' movement and/or there was any suggestion of prayers being said in common. Even so, it was not a knee-jerk reaction – Downey initiated some proper consultation with theologians in his diocese, and their report was very similar to that received by the Cardinal when he consulted Canon George Smith and Canon E.J. Mahoney, probably the two best known Catholic theologians in the country: there was total and unanimous opposition to anything that might even remotely link the Cardinal with 'heretical religious worship'.

Taggart also developed doubts about the movement, but for different reasons. He felt there was a danger that the 'Sword's' (and Catholic Action's) general principles on which society should be built would, because of the war, become infected with a spirit of nationalism, so that what was considered good for England in its present dangers would become elevated into a general good. He resigned his position and Downey replaced him with Charles Doyle, the builder of the cathedral and acting-president of the Catholic Action Board. Interestingly, Fr (later Canon) Joseph Cartmell, a highly respected theologian in the archdiocese and former lecturer at Upholland, changed his mind in the opposite direction: he felt they had, perhaps, been too dismissive of the 'Sword', which could well attract a good many people and, more importantly, highlight things more important than the social question that had, he felt, become the concern of Catholic Action. That question had been the nineteenth-century question; now the issue in the twentieth century was internationalism – on what principles should states relate to each other and how should states treat their own citizens and respect their individual rights – what universal Christian principles should apply? He continued with an interesting observation: 'The problems of the day are a guide to the line which Catholic theology must particularly concern itself with at any given time; and Catholic theology must get right into the problems, and try to take the lead in solving them'.[33]

Despite his initial hesitations, in February 1941 the Archbishop allowed the Catholic Society of the University of Liverpool to interest itself in the movement, which he praised as aiming at the restoration in Europe of a Christian basis for public and private life, 'by a return to the principles of international order and Christian freedom'. He did not want the 'Sword' to become a large new movement and so laid down that the Catholic Society should act in this matter under the general supervision of the Catholic Action Board.[34] Shortly after this he wrote to deny a report in the *News Review* paper that claimed he was totally opposed to the new movement, pointing to his permission to the Catholic Society and to his appointment of Doyle to replace Taggart. Later, in 1942, the Catholic Action Board tried to enlist the co-operation of the 'Sword' in a campaign against the sale of contraceptives, but not even Hinsley was clear whether that was the proper work of the 'Sword' or not. By September 1943 the Liverpool Catholic Action Board reported that it had distributed 130,000 copies of the Cardinal's original letter about the 'Sword'.[35]

The 'Sword' was still being discussed favourably by the Catholic Action Board in 1947, when Doyle reported that some measure of success had been achieved in putting the 'Sword' on a sound financial footing nationally. There was a move to hold a joint conference of the 'Sword' and the Catholic Action groups in Liverpool and Middlesbrough. Doyle spoke of the splendid work of the 'Sword' and of the support that it was receiving in various parts of the country, but he felt it had drifted away from its initial aims. The Board decided that there was more than enough to do to put Liverpool's own Catholic Action house in order before meeting with other bodies – the conference idea was postponed, indefinitely as it turned out.[36]

Hastings is quite mistaken in his judgement that Downey scuppered the 'Sword' movement because it was lay, ecumenical, intellectually progressive, decidedly English and fairly upper class.[37] Downey's opposition was based solely on the Cardinal's ecumenical elements and not on its original aims, which he shared.

Notes

[1] Doyle, 'The Importance of Being English'.

[2] C. Butler, *The Life and Times of Bishop Ullathorne*, 2 vols. (1926), 1, p.237.

[3] Archives of the English Benedictine Congr., Ampleforth, Misc. box: Goss to Bishop Brown of Newport, 19.12.1870. Vaughan was editor of *The Tablet*; Veuillot was editor of the *L'Univers*; the *Civiltà Cattolica* and *L'Osservatore Romano* were pro-papal Roman publications.

[4] RCLv 5/4/246, Goss to Bp of Shrewsbury, 14.1.1862. J.L. Altholz, *The Liberal Catholic Movement in England* (1962), for *The Rambler*.

[5] Milburn, *Ushaw*, for the disputes. Goss's letterbooks, 1859-61, contain numerous letters on the subject.

[6] Archives of the Archbishop of Southwark, B.13, 1.6.1863.

[7] RCLv 5/5/147, Goss to Canon Oakley, 24.4.1867; Archives of the Birmingham Oratory (ABO) Goss to Newman, 28.3.1870.

[8] ABO Goss to Ullathorne, 10.9.1867.

[9] AAL Early Bishops, S1 II, B: Bishop Goss's Pastorals, Advent 1867.

[10] F.J. Cwiekowski, *The English Bishops and the First Vatican Council* (1971), pp.169-72, 293, 322-4.

[11] RCLv 5/4/340, Goss to Abp Errington, 1.7.1862; APF *S.R. Anglia*, vol.16, n.580, Goss to Barnabò, 4.6.1862; APF *Lettere* 1862, 24.7.1862, Barnabò's reply.

[12] AAL Early Bishops, S1 III, C: Ad clerum 31.10.1870; ABO Goss to Newman, 24.1.1871.

[13] Sermon in *The Preston Chronicle*, 3.9.1864; see also the pastoral letter of 14.2.1871.

[14] Butler, *Ullathorne*, 1, pp.358-9.

[15] AAL The Early Bishops, S1 III, A Roman Documents, Address to the Holy Father 1860 (1860); pastoral letter 14.2.1871; Ad clerums 3, 25.12.1859 and 13.3.1860; RCLv 5/4/311, Goss to Grant, 16.4.1862.

[16] AAL Early Bishops, S1 II, B: Pastoral 11.12.1867.

[17] Cwiekowski, *English Bishops*, pp.169-72.

[18] APF *S.R. Anglia*, vol.24, nn.485, 574, O'Reilly to Propaganda 25.3.1882 and 29.7.1882.

[19] AAL *Liverpolitana I*, 1897; Early Bishops, S1 VII, C: Whiteside ad clerum November 1907.

[20] Milburn, *Ushaw*; Schiefen, *Wiseman*.

[21] RCLv 5/4/25, Goss to Bp of Shrewsbury 28.2.1861. Schiefen, *Nicholas Wiseman*, pp.296-8, 313-7.

[22] RCLv 5/5/204, Goss to Ullathorne, 29.9.1868; ABO Goss to Newman, 12.5.1869.

[23] Adrian Hastings, *A History of English Christianity 1920-1985* (1986), p.145.

[24] Kester Aspden, *Fortress Church: The English Roman Catholic Bishops and Politics 1903-63* (2002), pp.113-4.

[25] Casartelli to Cardinal Gasquet in Rome, 10.11.1917, Gasquet Archive, Downside Abbey.

[26] AAL Keating Collection, S4 I, A: Letterbooks, 25.1.1925, Keating to Dr Cullen.

[27] Thomas Moloney, *Westminster, Whitehall and the Vatican: The Role of Cardinal Hinsley 1935-43* (1985), pp.31, 203.

[28] Hastings, *English Christianity*, p.478.

[29] Moloney, *Westminster*, chap.10,

for the movement; Michael J. Walsh, 'Ecumenism in War-time Britain', *Heythrop Journal* XXII, no. 3 & 4 (July & Oct. 1982). Mathew's letters in AAL Downey Collection, S1 II, A/8, 30.9.1940.

[30] AAL Downey, S1 II, Other Bishops A/1.

[31] *Ibid.*, S2 II A/12, Hinsley to the bishops, 25.3.1941.

[32] Hastings, *English Christianity*, p.395.

[33] AAL Downey, S1 VI Diocesan Social History, C/16, Taggart to Mgr Adamson, 20.6.1941; S2 II A/10, Cartmell to Mgr Adamson, 21.11.1940.

[34] AAL Downey, S1 III, B Letters to Clergy: Feb. 1941.

[35] AAL Downey, S1 VII Diocesan Social Action, A/1: C.A. Board Minutes 1943-47, various dates.

[36] AAL Downey, S1 VII A/1, July 1947.

[37] Hastings, *English Christianity*, pp.393-4.

CHAPTER 6 THE DEVOTIONS AND DUTIES OF THE PEOPLE

What did it mean to be a committed Catholic in Lancashire in the second half of the nineteenth century and beyond? Just to ask the question is to raise so many issues that it is immediately obvious that no single set of answers is possible. For some, the most important practical effect of being a Catholic was probably determined by how they related to their Orange neighbours and how much prejudice they faced in seeking a job. For others, it may have been how often they could get to church and develop their piety through taking on devotional extras, such as attending Benediction and joining a confraternity or guild. Still others, probably the majority, satisfied their religious needs by attending weekly Mass and receiving the sacraments reasonably regularly. If Catholics listened to pastoral letters and sermons they would also know that they should be helping the expansion of their religion by contributing to diocesan collections. They should, as well, be giving to the poor, providing for abandoned and delinquent children and ensuring that their own children had as much chance of remaining within the Church as possible by sending them to Catholic schools. In this chapter an attempt will be made to examine the religious ideals put before the laity by bishops and priests, to see how the people responded to the helps provided and what made them 'tick' as Catholics.

Opposite: Devotion to the Blessed Sacrament: the altar of St Patrick's, Wigan, during Quarant'Ore. (Wigan Heritage Services)

A SACRAMENTAL CATHOLICISM

Bishops and priests in the mid-nineteenth century wanted 'practising Catholics' and practising meant regular attendance at church on Sundays and regular reception of the sacraments, along with the performance of practical works of mercy – although this last was never regarded as an essential part of the definition. In many ways that seems to state the obvious, but it may not have been so obvious to many Catholics in England and Wales at the time. A key factor here were the immigrant Irish – as we have seen earlier (Chapter 2) the devotion of pre-famine Irish Catholics to the Church had not been particularly sacramental. This may have been true of certain English Catholics too. A Redemptorist missioner in Formby in 1850 reported that 'an infinite number of sinners were converted to God … (including) young men and women from twenty to forty years of age who had never received Holy Communion before' – whether they were Irish or English is not stated, but Formby was not a particularly Irish town. So for these people, Irish immigrants and English Catholics, developing a rich sacramental life and warm devotions was an important step in providing a Church they wanted to attend regularly: it was a new situation for the English Church, dealing for the first time with a large urban population which if it did not go to church to pray was unlikely to do so at all.

The Lancashire clergy were keen to encourage strong eucharistic devotions among their people. In the Clergy Conferences held in the mid-1860s, for example, there was general encouragement to frequent Communion, with no hint of the rigorist or Jansenist approach that English Secular clergy had rather tended to in the 18th century. Attitudes were not uniform – the priests in one deanery were unanimous in recommending confessors to tend towards frequency in their advice to penitents, while in another deanery only four priests out of eleven were of this opinion; almost all were against admitting serious sinners to Holy Communion every week once they had been absolved, though the members of one deanery thought the practice was acceptable. But every deanery declared itself in favour of frequent Communion (without defining 'frequent'). Several of the answers included references to St Francis de Sales' saying that two types of people should communicate frequently, the perfect 'that they may continue so', and the imperfect 'that they may become perfect'. Even careless Catholics, some argued, should be allowed to receive once or twice a week. One deanery quoted the Council of Trent on the duty of parish priests to exhort their people 'to frequent and even daily communion'. There was, of course, a stress on people being in a state of grace and having the necessary dispositions before receiving, but the tone throughout was very positive and encouraging, perhaps to a surprising degree.[1]

From several points of view Bishop Goss was a rigorist and in the matter of devotions he lamented that the old tried and tested ways of *The Garden of the Soul* were giving way to what he called a 'multiplicity of prayer books' and that this had led to a lessening of the habit of prayer 'as a multiplicity of dainties destroys healthy appetite'; elsewhere he referred to 'the more flippant style of modern devotions'. But he had no doubts at all about the value of devotions to the Blessed Sacrament and frequent Communion. When, for example, a priest could not get help for a second Mass on Sundays, the Bishop advised him to hear confessions after his own nine o'clock Mass and to give out Communion 'until twelve, as they do in Italy'.[2]

Some of his warmest approval went to the practice of the Quarant'Ore or Forty Hours Exposition of the Blessed Sacrament: he urged this as most beneficial and laid down careful rules for its proper celebration. The Liverpool churches celebrated it during Lent: so, in 1861, for example, the Bishop himself officiated at the solemn opening of the Exposition, in the church of the Immaculate Conception on 17 February, and at the ending at the pro-cathedral on 27 March; between these dates the other 17 churches in and around Liverpool ensured that there was a continuous daytime rota, with the dates and times published in a special pamphlet. In this context the Bishop spoke of the sacramental presence of Christ as 'the dearest token of God's love', and continued:

> we exhort you to come and fall down before the Lamb that was slain and has redeemed us in his blood … Do not limit your devotion to the Exposition in the church of your own district, but follow Jesus, if you wish to be healed, to every church in which his presence is manifest.

He recommended a Preston priest to advertise the times of the Quarant'Ore in the local newspaper so that as many people as possible would be able to visit the church. Sanctuaries were highly decorated with flowers and candles for the Exposition which became one of the great annual occasions in parish life, often with a grand closing procession.[3]

Benediction was another non-liturgical devotion that Bishop Goss urged as much as possible; he willingly gave permission to have it every week, and even twice a week on special occasions, for it was 'an attractive service' to the people and would bear fruit in 'an increased frequentation of the sacraments'. On another occasion he said that there was no other service that 'so effectively warms the devotion of the people'. It was a very English devotion, given prominence in *The Garden of the Soul* for a century or so before 1850, and was sometimes held every night during parish missions and during May Devotions. It proved to be extremely popular with all sections of the English Catholic body, undoubtedly the most popular form of 'optional extra' – it was colourful, concise, convenient, theatrical, and mysterious all at once. It was a very powerful affirmation of the Real Presence and a sure witness to the people's devotion to the Blessed Sacrament. A note of caution is, perhaps, called for here. There is no doubt that for more than a hundred years Benediction was the most popular extra-liturgical service, but it was never more than a minority interest if the numbers attending it are compared with those attending Mass. At St Austin's, Grassendale, for example, those attending Benediction on a Sunday evening amounted on average to a third of the morning Mass attendances in the early 1920s; by 1929 the percentage was below 25%. Moreover, these figures related to attendances on the Sundays in Lent, when some would have made a special effort to attend the evening service as well as Mass.[4]

Processions of the Blessed Sacrament were also popular, although Goss wrote that it was one of the abominations imported from France to have women or girls occupying a prominent position in these processions: they must only join in with the body of the congregation. Nor did he approve of boys and girls dressing up specially to receive their First Communion: shirt sleeves were preferable to 'gewgaws and finery' obtained by pawning everyday apparel (so it must have been happening even then – 1855).[5]

There are signs in all this of what might be called a Sacramental Fundamentalism that gave a feeling of security and certainty to Catholics – and of satisfaction to the priests. It also differentiated Catholics from any other religious group at the time: daily services and frequent Communion were very distinctive features of Catholic churches – unknown in the Church of England and among Non-conformists. Especially distinctive were very early daily Mass times, and devotion to the Real Presence leading to private visits to the Blessed Sacrament and the raising of one's hat or crossing oneself when passing a Catholic church. Protestant churches were often described by Catholics as 'empty', 'lifeless' – and locked. Lancashire Catholics did not live in geographical or social ghettos, but their spiritual outlook and practice did create their own mental ghetto.

One result of this sacramentalism was a tremendous attention to rubrical correctness on the part of the clergy, a stress on what was necessary for the validity of a sacrament. It also lessened the importance of preaching and may have led to Catholics being over-sacramentalised and under-evangelised. Goss himself warned against seeing the Sacraments as ends in themselves: 'Many mistake the means for the end, and suppose that frequent communion is the very essence of virtue, whereas it is but a means of obtaining graces that so we may practise virtue'.[6]

Despite all this stress on the importance of receiving Holy Communion and on devotion to the Blessed Sacrament, the Sacrament of Penance loomed so large in the preaching and practice of the day that one could be forgiven for believing that it, and not Holy Communion, dominated clerical thinking. If one looks at the hours that priests were expected to spend in their confessionals it is easy to understand why the preparation of expert confessors played such a key role in the training of the clergy. A few examples will suffice. At Barrow-in-Furness confessions were heard every morning on which Mass was said, from 6.30am to 8.00am; on the eve of holy days and feasts of devotion from 5pm to 10pm; every Friday and Saturday from 5pm to 10pm, and in Lent every evening. At Leigh the confessional was manned every morning, every Friday evening, the whole of Saturday and on Sunday before the two Masses (there were two priests in residence). At Great Crosby confessions were heard every Saturday from 3.30pm to 10pm, every Sunday and weekday before Mass if people presented themselves, and on alternate Fridays from 2.30pm to 6.00pm for children; before special feastdays and for the whole of Lent they were heard from 2.30pm to 10.00pm on two weekdays and on Saturdays. A final instance of the important role given to confession was a circular to schools in 1864: very child over the age of seven had to answer five questions on a Monday morning, and the replies were to be summarised for the Bishop (unfortunately the returns have not survived). There were three questions about attending Mass, and two about confession; none mentioned Holy Communion.[7]

Many Catholics developed a devotion to the Sacrament of Penance; they went weekly to confession even when they had no need to do so. Confession and Holy Communion were the surest physical experiences they could have that they were receiving God's grace.[8] It is not surprising that fifty years later Archbishop Whiteside, in his campaign to increase frequent reception of Holy Communion, had to urge his priests to try to rid people's minds of the idea that they always had to go to confession before they could receive Holy Communion.

While such an approach to confession could easily have led to rigorism, the over-riding attitude of the clergy seems to have been one of a positive, pastoral concern. This can be seen, for example, in the discussions on hearing children's confessions, when it was stressed that the confessor needed special qualities to carry out this task successfully; among those mentioned were 'great sweetness', mildness, prudence, patience and charity. Penances should be short, light and suited to the capacity of children, and an important aim should be to convince them of the value of the sacrament so that a habit of receiving it could be developed.[9]

When a priest asked Goss to make it compulsory for people to attend their proper parish church rather than a neighbouring one, he refused, saying that it was up to the priest to make his church attractive enough for the people to want to attend it. For, in the end, people voted with their feet, and 'no power or authority in the Church' could make them attend where they felt uncomfortable or where they felt the priest was negligent or slovenly. This included seeing that it was clean and well-kept, the services properly carried out with dignity, and the priest being punctual on both Sundays and weekdays; in the pulpit the priest should not scold, and should 'preach and not talk' – then the priest would find that his church would be full. The Bishop ended, 'Ordinarily, it is through the Confessional that the Church is filled' – an instructive remark in the circumstances.[10]

From time to time lay Catholics would have experienced retreats or missions in their churches – this work was usually undertaken by newly introduced Congregations such as the Redemptorists and the Passionists, who had been active in the diocese since the 1840s. Goss highlighted their importance by trying to open the missions himself with a special sermon, and even to attend some of the spiritual exercises alongside the people. He did this on a few occasions as coadjutor, but it soon became impossible and so he tried to ensure that his vicar general, or some other representative of standing, did it in his stead. At the same time no one expected a mission to work wonders, especially where a congregation had been neglected for some years. The Bishop was also cautious about the more extreme methods used by some retreat-givers: over-enthusiastic preachers tended to ignore ordinary restraints and to override or ignore the local clergy, yet if the missions were to do any lasting good it could only be through the co-operation and painstaking follow-up work of the latter.[11]

The stress was on getting people to the sacraments, and in this the mission-givers were successful. At Old Swan so many flocked to confession that the Redemptorist preachers had to send for reinforcements, and even then could scarcely cope. At Wigan it was reported, 'many came to confess their sins', while at Woolton the mission was 'very successful', with 687 communicants (ninety-five of them first-timers) and thirteen converts. The number of penitents at St Anthony's, Scotland Road, was again so large as to require extra priests, even though seven Redemptorists were in action. Finally, a special children's mission (these were not uncommon) resulted in 600 communions, 400 confirmations and twenty baptisms, while the subsequent mission for adults resulted in 4,000 communions and twelve converts.[28] A Redemptorist mission in St Anthony's in 1875 resulted in 10,000 communions and 2,500 confirmations; on St Patrick's Day, 4,000 people crowded into the church, while 2,000 were turned away and the doors locked to stop gate-crashers! There could be other striking effects: at St Vincent's, Liverpool, the average Sunday Mass attendance during a Lenten mission was 4,352, compared with a normal average of 2,837 (a 53.4% increase). At Lytham, in 1865, the parish priest reported that there had been a mission recently in the parish and that as a result 'nearly all are in the Church'; he thought that not more than 'ten or twelve of the regular Catholics' were missing.[12]

His reference to 'regular' Catholics is interesting: were missions becoming more useful in keeping already practising Catholics up to the mark than in winning back the lapsed? Later in the century some of the Redemptorists voiced their own doubts about the effectiveness of missions as a means of reaching the uncommitted. Missioners reported on indifference and materialism among nominal Catholics and a greater integration into the wider society in which they lived; some of them felt helpless in the face of these features. In St Helens in 1879 only 3,000 Catholics out of 17,000 in the town made their confession and received communion during the general mission and the missioners picked out indifference and drunkenness as causes of an 'almost total neglect of Mass and of parental duties'. A mission in St Mary's, Wigan, in 1894 seemed to leave the parish in exactly the same state as it had been beforehand; the missioners found 'very little faith' among the people and what faith there was 'was worse than no faith at all' – and all this in a parish which had experienced a mission about every four years over the previous twenty. A similar picture was given of St Vincent's, Liverpool: while missions in the 1850s had done much to build local Irish Catholics into a community, the good effects on their morals and religious practice did not last and later missioners found it impossible to rouse the majority from torpor and their 'supreme indifference' to religion: only a quarter of the parishioners were making their Easter duties by the late 1880s and only the 'best people' attended the missions, despite conscientious home visiting by the parish clergy. Things were much better outside the big towns, and missions at Scarisbrick in 1882 and Burscough in 1893 were very successful, although there was a high level of practice already in these places; rather worryingly to the modern ear, perhaps, the reports of the missioners spoke of the docility and pliability of these people compared with their townie counterparts.[13]

It was not only during missions that preachers dwelt on 'the guilt and enormity of sin'. People were frequently reminded that they were living in an age which was 'reeking of iniquity'; towns were especially bad, and Liverpool was 'this great Gomorrah of the plain'. The whole age was marked by Godlessness. As Goss put it in usual forceful style:

*They are corrupt and are become abominable in their ways; there is none that
doth good, no, not one. Their throat is an open sepulchre; with their tongues
they act deceitfully; the poison of asps is under their lips. Their mouth is full
of cursing and bitterness … there is no fear of God before their eyes.*

The sacraments were proof of God's love and of his desire to save mankind,
but life remained a battle and salvation was difficult to achieve: people
would often have the worse of it in their spiritual conflict against the world,
the flesh and the devil. Moreover, death was inevitable and often sudden; all
were 'children of rottenness, the brothers and sisters of worms', and it was
terrible 'to fall into the hands of the living God, merciful though he be'.[14]
Bishop O'Reilly devoted a whole pastoral to death and its terrors, asking his
hearers how many of those who had died over the previous twelve months
had thought as little that that year would be the last for them 'as many of us
now think that this will be the last for us'. He ended with a quotation from
Proverbs, addressed to the unrepentant sinner: 'You have despised my
counsel and my warnings, I also will laugh at your destruction and will
mock when that shall come upon thee which you feared'.[15] Death-bed
conversions, so common in popular Protestant literature of the period,
played no part in either Goss's or O'Reilly's account of the divine plan.

The only belief that could give the sinners hope and support was that they
had been redeemed by the blood of Christ and made members 'of his body, of
his flesh and of his bones' – Christ had made himself their brother and had
incorporated all believers in himself. Because all believers were branches of the
same vine, they shared in the merit of all the good works performed in the
Church. God, of course, was standing by, ready with all the graces necessary,
but, as Goss put it very plainly, 'He helps us, but only in proportion as we help
ourselves'. Baptism was no guarantee of salvation: 'if we want it, we must live
so as to deserve it'.[16] Basically, the embattled Christian was on his or her own
and the struggle was an individual one, a truly Victorian sentiment.

GOOD WORKS AND LEVELS OF PRACTICE

Among the best ways to 'deserve it' were personal mortification and good
works. Bishop Goss was no advocate for the rigorous fasts of former times,
and admitted that there were many extenuating circumstances, including,

*the excitement and restless activity of commerce and manufactures, the
increased comfort of domestic life and the capriciousness of climate.*

At the same time, he thought that 'constitutional debility' was a suspicious
excuse, too easily admitted by an 'obsequious family doctor', and that many
of the better-off owed their ailments to a luxurious diet, late suppers and all-
night dancing, rather than the effects of fasting. His letters were full of
scriptural arguments in favour of fasting, but he also justified it as being
good for the body as well as for the soul.[17] In all this there was a certain
accommodation to the world and a realisation that, while Catholics were in

a sense a people set apart, they were also living in a secular world and could not adopt a way of life wholly at odds with it. The majority of Catholics, engaged as they were in heavy manual labour, could not be expected to fast very much – and, anyway, for many their normal daily consumption would hardly have exceeded what was allowed.

Chief among the good works expected of Catholics was alms-giving, to support the expansion of the Church in the diocese and to help the poor and suffering. There were three annual diocesan collections: the Diocesan Mission Fund, the Ecclesiastical Education Fund and the Poor Schools Fund. When the Bishop spoke to the people about these he was often scathing and sarcastic, trying to shame them into giving more by contrasting their small contributions with their obvious comfort or by contrasting their fine chapel and plentiful supply of priests with the spiritual destitution of those parts of the diocese where there were neither priest nor chapel. For example, at St John's, Wigan, he urged the congregation which was 'so able ... to judge from the costliness of its apparel', to look compassionately on places like Barrow, Coniston, Skelmersdale, Tyldesley which were 'completely destitute'. It is rare to have any audience feed-back to the Bishop's sermons, but at The Willows it was noted that after he had spoken for some time 'in a low and impressive tone' and had appealed 'in a most earnest and burning language' to their feelings, one parishioner was moved to comment, 'Didn't his Lordship come out on the penny a head? My word, he did give it us'.[18]

He could be just as outspoken with regard to alms-giving. To leave money in one's will was not enough, he claimed, for 'it is no great act of charity to give to God what you cannot carry away'. Too many Catholics, he argued, excused themselves from helping the poor on the grounds of not being able to afford it, yet:

> do not people dress, dine, entertain and furnish their houses in a style far beyond their present or probable means? Are there not hundreds of middle-class families who have learned to sneer with vulgar contempt at the simplicity which becomes a modest fortune?[19]

Thriving, mercantile Liverpool in the mid-nineteenth century was a socially upward society and those Catholics who could do so no doubt hankered after the same status symbols as their neighbours.

Another reason why Catholics did not give enough money to the poor was, according to Goss, the tendency to glorify the unknown: too many closed their eyes and hearts to:

> the Irish or the Highlander, driven from their wrecked cabins to seek a home in a foreign land ... Tears are shed over the exiles of Siberia and the Wanderings of Evangeline, whilst men behold with dry eyes thousands of exiles ... yearly leaving ... for America or Australia ... Men would sooner scratch their names on the great pyramids of Egypt than engrave them in the hearts of the suffering poor.[20]

The full range of Catholic charitable institutions gave more than enough scope for traditional alms-giving throughout the diocese (see Chapter 9).

Missions raised the levels of practice, but the effects were generally short-lived. Can anything be said about normal levels of practice in the nineteenth century? Certainly, support for 'good works', official and unofficial, continued and increased over the years. With regard to weekly Mass attendance, it is impossible to be accurate, partly because generally we do not know how many Catholics there were within parish boundaries, how many of them could or should have been at Sunday Mass and how many did attend. Busy priests filled out returns conscientiously enough but with what degree of accuracy we do not know. Estimates for overall Sunday attendance in 1871 vary between 37% and 43%; do these averages mean very much when dealing with such different parishes across the diocese – from small rural parishes with only a few hundred Catholics to 'inner-city' ones with many thousands? The following table gives what priests at the time might have thought was a more accurate impression of religious practice in the mid-1860s. The parishes have been chosen at random, but with the proviso that care seemed to have been taken in making the returns.

Parish	Catholic Population	Average Sunday Mass attendance	Numbers regularly neglecting to attend
Euxton	520	220 (42.3%)	50
Fernyhalgh	388	230 (59.3%)	4
Fleetwood	–	440	290
Golborne	506	241 (47.6%)	105
Liverpool: St Anne	–	1,742	1,420
St Peter	7,537	2,017 (26.8%)	2,500
Preston: St Joseph	1,480	600 (40.5%)	435
Thurnham	405	200-225	25-30
Westby	492	250 (50.8%)	115
Woolton	1,496	680 (45.5%)	140

The conscientious parish priest in St Patrick's slum parish in Liverpool reported in 1865, 'Half of the Catholics who should attend Mass, do so'; it was a satisfyingly high level of practice.[21]

A STRICT MORAL CODE

What moral code were these Catholics expected to follow? Catholic reformers, clerical and lay, were influenced by the ethos of the society in which they lived and shared the general concerns of Victorian reformers; one of the keenest felt of those concerns was about the family. In the minds of Victorian social and religious commentators, working-class family life was far from being satisfactory, and promiscuity and sexual immorality were common. They blamed a great deal on the terrible living conditions in courts and cellars: privacy was impossible because of multi-family occupation of inadequate living space. Bishop Goss spoke openly about these evils in his pastoral letters and sermons, constantly stressing the need for improvement among the poor. He saw the connection between bad living conditions and grinding poverty on the one hand and immorality and crime on the other: he spoke of the temptations that faced those who had 'to fight in the battle of life for a crust to eat and a rag to cover them', and from which the better-off were exempt through no efforts of their own. On a number of occasions he attacked the existence of a double-standard approach to morality, most strongly in the matter of prostitution and of the fashionable wrong-doer who was acceptable in society because he was cleverer than the uneducated at concealing his crimes. He excused in public the large number of Catholics in prison in Preston on the grounds of the poverty in which they were forced to live and wrote with understanding and some sympathy of the economic pressure that drove women and young girls to prostitution.[22] But sin was still sin and God did not tempt people beyond their power to resist.

His most frequent attack, however, was on the general neglect by parents of their duties toward their children, and here he believed that both rich and poor were at fault, although his most vivid picture can have applied only to the poor:

> Whoever passes through the streets of our large towns cannot but feel how wretchedly parents discharge (their) duties ... Their children are wandering through the streets badly clothed and worse fed; they are not sent to school; they are allowed to mix with companions as bad or worse than themselves; they learn to curse and swear and blaspheme, to lie and to steal, to use bad words and do worse things ... It is much to be feared that children have been schooled in vice at home before they are turned adrift ...[23]

We do not know what went through the minds of parents who sat and listened to his pastoral letters and visitation sermons. They heard condemnations of abortion, concealment of births and even infanticide, and, of course, of parents who encouraged their children to turn to prostitution to support themselves and the rest of the family. The Bishop's strongest words, however, were directed against the practice of parents and children sleeping together. He apologised for raising such 'revolting' matters in public, but duty compelled him to do so, as the results of the practice were so terrible. The practice went on, the Bishop claimed, in rural areas as well as in towns, but was worse in the latter because lodgers were often allowed to share the children's bed; was it any wonder, he asked, that prostitution was not unknown in children not yet in their teens?

In this grim catalogue of parental sins and crimes, company-keeping by their children before marriage must have seemed a relatively minor offence, but it, too, aroused the Bishop's suspicions because it led to mixed marriages and illegitimate births – every baptism register in the diocese, he claimed, showed its evil results. Parents had even to be careful about Sunday evening services, for these were often just an excuse for children to meet friends, and their minds were far from prayer. On the other hand, when young people reached marriageable age it was up to their parents to provide opportunities for them to find suitable partners. Parents did great harm by wanting to keep children at home as extra earners, something which, he stated, happened all too often in manufacturing districts.[24] Such outspoken pastoral letters, including one on the issue of prostitution, support Cardinal Manning's tribute to Goss as a Bishop who, in an age of refinement, 'spoke out like a man where he saw vice to denounce or follies to extinguish'. John Denvir wrote that 'the Bishop had a blunt, hitting out from the shoulder style of speaking that compelled attention. But you could hardly call them sermons at all: they were rather, powerful discourses upon social topics …'[25] In all this, how far was Goss accepting uncritically, and re-inforcing, middle-class myths about the wickedness of the lower classes? We can only assume that he spoke about what he learned from listening to his clergy, who certainly knew the realities of their people's lives.

He may have been more outspoken than most, but the sexual code he laid on Catholics was not unusual at the time. Moreover, he believed that a number of external constraints would help them to live up to it. Among these was separation of the sexes in 'free' parts of churches (i.e. those parts for the use of the poor); especially on occasions of 'great pressure' in smaller churches, priests were to take care that the stairs and aisles were not occupied by 'a miscellaneous crowd': the sexes must be separated. Indeed, this kind of precaution was to operate as early as possible in Catholics' lives: priests had also to take care to keep school girls and boys apart; communicating doors between the different playgrounds were to be kept locked, and the priest was to hold the only key. Finally, priests were to take care that they did nothing to encourage 'promiscuous dancing' and did not allow it in Catholic school rooms – Goss claimed that too many mothers mourned for their daughters' virtue after Catholic dances.[26] Neither he nor Bishop O'Reilly would lift this ban even when some clergy argued that dances made good fund-raising events.

CONFRATERNITIES AND PIOUS SOCIETIES

External aids and constraints of a much more positive kind were also available. There were always Catholics who wanted more by way of commitment and spirituality than they could find in the normal parish, something more regular than the boosts provided by missions every few years. After all, nineteenth-century Catholics were Victorians too and could be affected by the same seriousness and desire for personal religion as other Christians. Group support and communal aids to devotion abounded for the committed, for, despite all the stress on Victorian individualism and the need to work out one's own salvation, it was also the age of the confraternity and pious society for English Catholics. To take St Wilfrid's, Preston, as an

The Children of Mary,
Sacred Heart Church,
Hindsford, c.1890. (Wigan
Heritage Services)

example, there was the 'Holy Guild of the Blessed Virgin Mary, St Aloysius and St Agnes' for school children who had made their First Communion. Its stress was on frequent reception of the sacraments and careful counts were taken each Sunday, but the Guild had social and moral concerns as well. There were Sick Relief, Medical Attendance and Funeral Funds; if a Sister were unfortunate enough to be in the workhouse, she was absolved from paying Guild fees but could receive no Guild benefits. When she left the workhouse she was to be in the same position with regard to the Guild as if she had never entered it, 'the time passed there being considered as not having happened'. Rules of conduct were extremely strict and enforced the same sexual code outlined above: frequent attendance at common dancing rooms could 'easily' be a matter for expulsion; the chaplain complained in 1863 that some of the smaller girls had been frequently seen playing with boys and that 'sometimes in the dusk of the evening', while the full rigour of the Guild fell on one member for 'long public misbehaviour ... for frequenting Friargate in a disorderly manner late at night, she having no ostensible employment whereby to gain her living'. Her solemn expulsion took place in the presence of the Guild's Council wearing their regalia, 'with bell, book and candle, the Chaplain wearing his surplice and purple stole and erasing her name from the lists, the Warden tearing her collar in the presence of the Guild'.[27]

It is worth staying at St Wilfrid's to see something of the range of guilds and sodalities that could exist in an active parish. It is also interesting in revealing the class-based membership of some of these groups. Some Catholics did not want to be connected with pious sodalities that were also benefit societies and so a Gentlemen's Sodality was formed, consisting of 'the more respectable young men of the town'. The Children of Mary likewise was 'composed of Ladies of the better classes'; the ninety or so members met in the Sodality Chapel (a feature of Jesuit churches) at 3pm on the first Wednesday of the month, thus ensuring that no working women or millgirls could attend.

Like many parishes, St Wilfrid's also had an Altar Society, with its members contributing 1d a week to supply and clean altar linen, pay for wine and hosts for Mass and part of the sacristan's salary and vestments. The Purgatorial Society's members contributed the relatively large sum of 1/- a week, met in the sacristy after evening service on the first Sunday of the month and prayed for the Holy Souls, arranging Masses for them as well. At that same evening service the members of the Bona Mors (Good Death) Confraternity made their special devotions. Another confraternity was that of the Immaculate Heart of Mary, dating from 1842 and so one of the earliest in the parish. Finally there was the Confraternity of Christian Doctrine, with the twin aims of instructing children (and occasionally adults) in the Faith and of keeping them practising after they left school. The active members of the confraternity were expected to run special Sunday classes, morning and afternoon, in the nearby schools; the children were then taken to Mass or Benediction and absentees were 'sought out and visited'. A series of Christian Doctrine prizes were awarded annually to the children who attended most regularly and knew their catechism.[28]

Some lay people trusted in membership of the Third Order of St Francis to satisfy their spiritual needs, with its call to a more intense prayer-life and more regular mortification. The Franciscan Order, however, had no presence in the diocese and this made things difficult for the would-be Tertiaries. Bishop O'Reilly, who was firmly opposed to the friars being allowed into the diocese, shared the general suspicion of the older Religious Orders that was common among many of the secular clergy, and sincerely feared that new foundations would lead to a loss of money and clerical manpower. There had also been earlier cases of friars begging in Liverpool and perhaps some scandal – the details are not clear and, anyway, they related to something that may have happened many years before. The Bishop encouraged the people to join confraternities and sodalities and held the newer Congregations, such as the Redemptorists and the Passionists, in high regard. But for whatever reason, he held out against the Franciscans and told Propaganda so in forceful language. One of his complaints concerned the Tertiaries' visits to Pantasaph monastery in North Wales to gain the Portiuncula Indulgence each August. Both sexes left Birkenhead together by boat at night, he claimed, and returned also at night, with no care being taken to keep the sexes apart; the people then had to make their way home in the dark through a dangerous city.[29]

The next shots were fired by some Liverpool Tertiaries themselves. No doubt prompted by their spiritual directors to make the right noises, they described themselves as belonging for the most part to the artisan and working classes residing in Liverpool; they then reminded the Bishop that the Third Order was directly opposed to 'Materialism, Rationalism, and Nationalism, and all condemned propositions', and so was hated by those opposed to the Holy Father. For them to be faithful followers of their Rule they required an oratory where they could go to confession and receive instruction from a Capuchin priest who could give them the numerous general absolutions and papal benedictions that Tertiaries were entitled to. They hoped for a favourable response since their request concerned 'the morality, the good behaviour and improvement of a class of people whose vices and whose neglect of their religious duties we mean to correct by means of our holy Order'.

In the end, Propaganda's decision went against the Bishop and an oratory in St Francis Xavier's church was the result. By 1882 there were several groups of Tertiaries in the city, of which that attached to the Jesuit church was particularly healthy. Its director was a Capuchin who came across from Chester on Sunday afternoons; it numbered about eighty brothers and met every Sunday afternoon and Wednesday evening. A special Mass was offered for them on the first Sunday of each month in the church, and this was thought to be responsible in part for the increase in numbers. Female members became a separate Congregation in 1881.

The Third Order slowly became established throughout the diocese. By 1899 the Franciscan superior could write amicably to Bishop Whiteside announcing his intention, with the Bishop's 'kind approbation', to write to all the parishes where the Third Order was established to arrange for the annual visitation to be made more regularly. For their part, the Tertiaries believed that they were doing great work in the city of Liverpool by offering another form of spirituality, half way in its religious intensity between that of the full Franciscan way of life and that of the ordinary Catholic lay person. In no sense did they regard themselves as opting out of normal parish life and its duties; rather, they saw themselves as an asset to the diocese by offering their services to the clergy in their individual parishes, and the bishops after O'Reilly accepted this. By 1940 the Third Order had branches in twenty-two parishes, sixteen of them in Liverpool, three in Wigan and one each in Warrington, St Helens and Chorley.

By 1886 there were a total of forty-three different sodalities, confraternities or guilds throughout the Diocese. The most popular by far was the Living Rosary Society (with 71 branches), followed by the Children of Mary (47), Altar Societies (24) and the Sacred Heart Confraternities (21), although if one were to count the variously named men's and young men's groups they would take second place with about 50 branches. It is not surprising that the Living Rosary Society should be so popular since the saying of the rosary became the major non-eucharistic devotion for the next hundred years for Catholics – often recited during Benediction and making up a key element in that most popular of Sunday services outside Mass itself – Rosary, Sermon and Benediction. It had long been a feature of English devotions, featuring as it did in those classics of traditional piety, *The Garden of the Soul* and the *Penny Catechism*.[30]

Confraternities could wax and wane in popularity. In 1894 Mgr Canon Joseph Clarkson, parish priest of St Alban's, Liverpool, (better known to generations of Upholland students as the person responsible for buying many of the pictures that adorned its walls) reported to Bishop Whiteside that the Pious Association of the Holy Family was flourishing: it existed in twenty-six parishes and had enrolled over 1,500 families. He had sent the returns to Rome. Only the following year, however, he was reporting a big decline – membership was down to 620 families and several branches had closed, despite his reminding every parish about it. He asked the Bishop to give it a special push, perhaps in the Advent pastoral. The Association's main advantage, according to Clarkson, was that it brought the family together for night prayers. About the same time a new confraternity was established, that of Our Lady of Compassion, connected with the Guild of Ransom and the conversion of England. The Bishop received about a dozen letters asking for permission to erect it canonically, and for it to be affiliated to the archconfraternity in Paris. The parish priest at Wrightington reported that he had already enrolled 143 names.[31] In this, as in so many things, everything depended on the support of the parish priest.

SPECIAL DEVOTIONS

Bishop Brown had dedicated the new diocese to Our Lady Immaculate and had urged his clergy to celebrate the feastday in a fitting way, referring to Mary as 'the Throne of Mercy' and 'the destroyer of all heresies' – he had written to Propaganda to support the definition of the Immaculate Conception in 1854. The Redemptorists played an important part in increasing devotion to Our Lady. They preached about it regularly and introduced the practice of 'May Devotions' at Bishop Eton, with a sermon every evening during the month and a stress on saying the rosary. This was important, for not all the older clergy were particularly in favour of it (including Bishop Goss). When some Redemptorists were giving a mission in Mawdesley in 1858 they found that the parish priest was of 'the old school' and opposed to what he called 'new fangled devotions'; in particular, he refused to erect a special altar on which a statue of Our Lady could be exhibited for veneration – they built one anyway with books from the library and decorated it with flowers and candles for the ceremony of consecration to Our Lady. From the late 1860s the main form of devotion preached by the Redemptorists was to Our Lady of Perpetual Succour and copies of the supposedly-miraculous icon in their church in Rome became common. Huge crowds attended the public inauguration of a shrine in her honour in Bishop Eton in 1869; special indulgences were attached to visiting it and members of the confraternity wore the medal of Our Lady of Perpetual Succour and had a copy of the picture in their homes. A choir of sixty students from Mount Pleasant Training College sang at the event, starting the tradition of an annual pilgrimage of the Notre Dame students, some of whom at least must have spread the devotion to their pupils.[32] By 1870 a quarter of the new churches opened in the diocese had been dedicated to Our Lady under one title or another and by 1875 Bishop O'Reilly could write of the 'tender devotion of all the Clergy to our Holy and Immaculate Mother'. It was a year of Jubilee and May Devotions could be used to gain the Jubilee Indulgence; he recommended that devotions be held three times a week during May, with Benediction.[33]

Another devotion that grew rapidly in these years was devotion to the Sacred Heart of Jesus. The Apostleship of Prayer was especially favoured by the Jesuits in this regard. Founded in France in 1844 and first established in England in St Helens that same year, it existed to 'promote the glory of God and the salvation of souls through a programme of constant prayer, particularly to the Sacred Heart'.[34] It was responsible for the very popular *The Messenger of the Sacred Heart* (the English edition was founded in 1868), which listed the intentions that members were to pray for, including the pope's intention for that month. By 1886 there were six branches of the Apostleship throughout the diocese. Devotion to the Sacred Heart became one of the defining devotions of English Catholics. In 1875 (the year in which Blessed Pope Pius IX exhorted all Catholics to consecrate themselves to the Sacred Heart to celebrate the bi-centenary of the original revelations) when the Confraternity of the Sacred Heart was established in the parish of Lytham, over 350 Catholics joined straight away.[35] The practice of consecrating the first Friday of each month to the Sacred Heart and of receiving Holy Communion as an act of reparation went back beyond the nineteenth century. It was only after 1870 that special significance was attached to doing this nine times in an uninterrupted row, according to the 'Great Promise' revealed to St Margaret Mary Alocoque. This offered a tangible target for the devout to aim at and the re-assurance that those who reached it would have the grace of final repentance and would not die in sin or without the last sacraments. The fact that people went on making 'the nine' repeatedly shows that the assurance of the promise was not taken too literally – it became just another form of devotion. The evening before the

First Friday became a time of extra confessions (a practice that lasted down to the 1970s) and in some places very early Masses were celebrated on the First Friday for those going to work. A number of new churches were dedicated to the Sacred Heart, fifteen of them between 1854 and 1904.

Those hostile to Catholicism at the time claimed that there were strong elements of superstition in Catholic devotions – the repetitive, automatic saying of the rosary, the Nine First Fridays, prayers to St Anthony and St Jude for special favours, the veneration of relics and an over-readiness to believe in miracles. Irish Catholic immigrants in particular were assumed to be strongly attached to some undefined folk religion that was also superstitious to a large extent, although it is worth noting that that bastion of English piety, *The Garden of the Soul*, was very popular in Ireland, too. Evidence in these matters is difficult to find and very difficult to assess – to what extent do what have become cultural practices impinge on a person's basic beliefs; how far, for example, do Catholics who 'touch wood' or 'cross their fingers' genuinely believe it will safeguard them from trouble? Certainly, in the years under discussion here some preachers could go over the top when attempting to rouse their congregations to piety. Fr Bernard, a Passionist from Sutton, near St Helens, preached at a Confirmation ceremony in the town in 1859. His main message was the importance of Catholics wearing the scapular of Our Lady. A person doing so would find it almost impossible to commit sin – 'If a person, for instance, wanted to fight, he would feel he could not do so until he had taken it off'. He followed this rather ambiguous statement by relating how when fire struck a particular town the houses of those wearing the scapular were not burned down.

Even more startling was his tale of a French girl named Lucy. While she was saying her rosary before a statue of Our Lady and the infant Jesus, the baby came down into her arms, no longer a stone image but alive. Lucy took the divine baby home for three days and nights. While she was asleep he returned to Our Lady's arms 'and submitted to petrification'. What the congregation made of all this is not recorded, but the preacher clearly did not expect them to reject it out of hand. When the local newspaper printed the sermon it provoked outraged condemnation by a correspondent who wrote that it might have passed without comment in Italy or Spain, or even in this country in times past 'when darkness covered the people'; now it smacked of the worst excesses of Mariolatry.[36]

In 1866, Bishop Goss reacted somewhat similarly in a letter to a nun in which he condemned 'superstitious practices' – they might, he said, have been suitable for 'simple people' in an age of faith, but were not suitable for the present day. What was he objecting to? Firstly, 'superstitious prayers'. The only time in all his voluminous correspondence (over 4,000 surviving letters) that he mentioned the penalty of excommunication was in a letter to a printer, Mr Cullen, in connection with the printing of superstitious prayers or pictures. Presumably these were similar to the 'chain-letters' that can still be found, offering special graces and rewards to those who said the particular prayers, and, perhaps more importantly, sometimes threatening with temporal and even eternal penalties those who refused to do so and failed to pass on the letters. The content of the letters was often linked to the revelations of a holy person or saint – St Bridget of Sweden was a favourite in this regard in the nineteenth and early twentieth century in England.[37] Secondly, in his letter to Sister Lucy he had condemned the use of a live baby in a Christmas crib – it was, he claimed, an impiety made all the worse by the use of incense. Nor should living people ever be used to represent Our Lord or the saints. It seems that the crib in question had been in the convent chapel, which in the eyes of the people must have lent it an air of official approval. Finally, he wrote in very strong language to some nuns to forbid the practice of giving old altar linens, including purificators, to miners to bind their injured hands with. As the priest at nearby Standish also did this the nuns probably felt they were in good company in doing so. It is not altogether clear, but it seems the linens were regarded as having some special healing power attributed to them because of their previous use. In Preston, likewise, Sister Lucy was in the habit of giving away old altar linen to be used as baby linen; the Bishop strictly prohibited this as well.[38] It could be, of course, that the Bishop was seeing superstition where the Sisters saw only a work of mercy in providing clean bandages to people who could not afford them.

PRAYERS, HYMNS AND PILGRIMS

If it is true that 'to be religious is to pray', we should make some attempt to find out about Catholic prayers. Something has already been said about the popularity of Benediction. Another popular devotion was the Way of the Cross or the Stations. By 1861 ten of the Liverpool town churches listed it as one of their devotions, sometimes held every Friday, sometimes only during Lent and Advent. It is not clear what form the public devotion took at this time, but it is likely to have been based on St Alphonsus Liguori's short meditations and prayers that were later incorporated into the official *Manual of Prayers* and into later editions of *The Garden of the Soul*. It was also a devotion that could be practised privately, again especially during Lent, and was heavily indulgenced – it carried all the indulgences that pilgrims to Jerusalem had previously enjoyed.[39] Gradually sets of the Stations became a feature of every parish church; some consisted of simple crosses, some were carved in stone or moulded in plaster, and some were works of art such as those erected in Our Lady of Mount Carmel, Liverpool (by local artist May Greville Cooksey, at a cost of £30 each in 1928).

We have already seen that the rosary was the most popular non-eucharistic prayer for a very wide range of Catholics. Other popular prayers were the Act of Contrition, the 'Out of the Depths', the *Memorare*, the 'Hail, Holy Queen', the Angelus and the Apostles' Creed. Far and away the most popular prayerbook was *The Garden of the Soul*, which went through many editions and gathered new prayers as it went, especially prayers for the conversion of England, prayers to St Joseph, devotions to the Sacred Heart and prayers for the Forty Hours. *The Catholic's Manual of Instructions and Devotions* was published in Liverpool in 1867. In 1886 the bishops published the first official *Manual of Prayers for Congregational Use*, heavily dependent on *The Garden of the Soul*. Also popular were *The Key of Heaven* and *The Treasury of the Sacred Heart*. How many people in a typical parish congregation would have their own copy of these prayerbooks and follow the prayers they contained during Mass? There seems to be no way of knowing, but cost may not have been the barrier one might expect: by 1904 Catholic publishers like Burns Oates and Eason's of Dublin were trying to cater for every pocket, with editions of *The Garden of the Soul* running from 6d to 17/6 and of *The Key of Heaven* from 6d to 5/-. *The Child's Key of Heaven* was advertised as 'the cheapest prayer book in the world' at one penny for its 94 pages. The rosary was often said privately during Mass; some might have used *A Simple Prayer Book*, first published in 1886 and costing very little. By the 1890s English missals were becoming more available – *The Roman Missal Adapted to the Use of the Laity* appeared in 1887, with *A Popular Missal for the Use of the Laity* in 1893 and *The Missal for the Use of the Laity*, arranged by Provost Husenbeth in 1897.[40] In the absence of evidence, one may assume that their use was limited less by cost than by levels of liturgical literacy.

Some of these prayerbooks contained special devotions known as novenas, the saying of a prayer or set of prayers on nine successive days in order to obtain some special favour. While the commonest novenas were to the Sacred Heart and Our Lady, any prayer or devotion could be used in this way. Some became more formalised, and *The Treasury of the Sacred Heart* gave special prayers for novenas to St Joseph, St Patrick, St Dominic, and one's Guardian Angel. Increasingly as the nineteenth century went on indulgences were attached to particular novenas – over thirty in all. The number and type of indulgences attached to individual prayers and special devotions was truly staggering and created a whole sub-culture that was uniquely Catholic. As has been said, the saying of the Stations of the Cross could obtain for the participant with the right dispositions all the indulgences ever granted by the popes to those who went on pilgrimage to the Holy Land. Some indulgences were plenary, some for a number of days or years or 'quarantines' (forty-day remissions); some could only be gained once a day, some as often as a particular devotion was repeated over a period; some required a visit to a particular church. Some could be applied to the souls in Purgatory, some could not. There was a Roman publication, the *Raccolta*, that listed them all (an English translation first appeared in 1856)[41] but to become an expert on indulgences and the Canon Law controlling them would have been even more perplexing than becoming an expert on recognising nuns' habits; most Catholics, it seems, just accepted them as a welcome bonus that would help someone somewhere.

Medals were another feature of popular Catholic devotion, especially the extremely popular Miraculous Medal. Its design had been revealed to St Catherine Labouré in 1830: it contained the prayer, 'O Mary, conceived without sin, pray for us who have recourse to thee'. Its popularity was helped by its becoming the official medal of the Children of Mary who wore it on a blue ribbon.[42] The Guild of the Blessed Sacrament also had a distinctive medal that could be worn as a lapel badge. Many pious Catholics wore collections of medals attached to their underwear or on a simple string around the neck but under their clothing – medals of the Sacred Heart, Our Lady, St Francis, St Joseph, St Anthony of Padua, St Patrick, St Christopher, and so on almost without end. Special medals could be obtained at places of pilgrimage and taken home as presents for friends. The wearing of some medals carried with it an indulgence, especially when they had been blessed. It was not always easy to distinguish between the wearing of a medal as an act of devotion and carrying it as a protective, and even lucky, charm.

Scapulars, or two small pieces of coloured cloth joined by ribbon and carrying a picture and prayer, were also worn around the neck. The most popular was the 'Brown Scapular' of the Confraternity of Our Lady of Mount Carmel, but there were also a number of white scapulars, including that of the Immaculate Heart of Mary and one of the Sacred Hearts of Jesus and Mary. Along with having at home holy water, blessed candles and pieces of blessed palm, sometimes thought to have special protective powers because they had been blessed, these devotional objects added a certain physicality to one's faith and could be useful reminders of a commitment to follow a particular way of life.

Vernacular hymns played an important role in public services. *The Crown of Jesus Music* appeared in 1864, with the aim of providing hymns that would be 'simple, plain and quite untrammelled with musical technicalities, so as to come within reach of all, even the unskilled'.[43] Among its 174 vernacular hymns it included some that were to become long-term favourites, such as 'Daily, daily, sing to Mary', 'O Mother, I', 'Full in the panting heart of Rome', 'I'll sing a hymn to Mary', 'Sweet Sacrament Divine', 'Hail, glorious St Patrick' and 'O come and mourn with me awhile', as well as such awful offerings as:

O happy flowers, O happy flowers,
How quietly for hours and hours,
In dead of night, in cheerful day,
Close to our own dear Lord you stay,
Until you gently fade away.
O happy flowers what would I give,
In your sweet place all day to live,
And then to die, my service o'er,
Softly as you do, at His door.

Unfortunately, it is not possible to say how many churches in the diocese used this hymnal – there were other smaller collections available – and the English bishops appear not to have imposed a particular one on their flocks (at their synods in 1852 and 1873 they contented themselves with trying to encourage the use of plainchant as the main form of congregational singing). The Notre Dame Sisters edited a collection of forty-five hymns in 1891 (published by Rockliff Brothers, Liverpool), including 'Bring flowers of the rarest' and 'Ave Maria, O Maiden, O Mother'. Since the Sisters taught in a number of schools and trained hundreds of teachers, their collection became very widely used. Another collection, *The Parochial Hymn Book*, was published by Watsons of Preston about 1898; its contents were similar to those in the *Crown*, but with a greater stress on hymns for children about to make their First Communion, including:

> *O Mary dearest Mother,*
> *Of heaven's immortal bowers,*
> *Will you gather for a little child*
> *A bouquet of sweet flowers.*
> *I wish my little heart to be*
> *A cradle fair and gay,*
> *Where my blessed Jesus may repose*
> *On my First Communion Day.*

Finally in 1912 there appeared *The Westminster Hymnal*, the official collection issued by the English and Welsh bishops and edited by Sir Richard Terry, Master of Music at Westminster Cathedral. In his preface Terry made it clear what he thought of some of the hymns and tunes that he had included:

> *Some of these tunes are good, some are indifferent, and some bad. But it has been felt that since those of the latter named class have been ... bound up with many pious associations of so many holy lives, this is hardly the occasion for their suppression, but this retention cannot be justified on musical or other artistic grounds!*

We may mention to end with another form of devotion that had not died out altogether during penal times and which enjoyed a revival in the second half of the nineteenth century – going on pilgrimage. The first English pilgrimage to Lourdes took place in 1883, but it was to be another forty years before the Diocese organised one (see page 265 below). Lancashire, however, had its own Marian shrine, at Ladyewell, Fernyhalgh (near Preston), a very ancient place of pilgrimage with a holy spring and a fourteenth-century chapel. The well was said to have miraculous properties and had continued to be a place of pilgrimage after the Reformation. The chapel was re-built at different times and 'quite large' pilgrimages took place in the second half of the century, although the well seems to have fallen into disrepair; the Holy Child Sisters took over the shrine in 1905 and restored it.[44]

St Winefride's shrine at Holywell in North Wales also had a continuing popularity with people from the North West. In 1895 alone pilgrims lit thirty thousand votive candles there and the local railway company collected 96,000 tickets in three years (1894-6).[45] Bishop O'Reilly led a number of pilgrimages there, sometimes accompanied by the band from St Vincent's parish, Liverpool, in what must have had something of the air of a gala procession. Numerous cures were claimed, including some from Preston, Liverpool and Lancaster. These were well-publicised in the Catholic press and, surprisingly, in the national press as well – the great London journalist, W. Stead, compared Holywell with Lourdes, which was, he claimed, 'but of yesterday' in comparison. Those who were thought to have been cured became the focus of great local interest and were sometimes besieged at home by pious or just curious visitors. Claims that the cures were miraculous were played down with due caution, but they were seen to be at least a providential answer to prayer. A more regular feature of the pilgrimages to Holywell were the very large numbers of confessions heard by the priests who looked after the shrine: it would seem that going on pilgrimage had something of the nature of a mission about it, with most coming away with renewed faith and a fresh purpose to amend their way of life.[46] It seems to have fallen off in popularity in the 1930s but revived again in the 1960s, with about 25,000 pilgrims a year visiting it.

Little changed in the self-contained world of Catholic devotion down to the 1950s. It remained strongly eucharistic, a trend re-inforced and developed by Archbishop Whiteside, but with a continuing stress on sin and the confessional. Many of those who practised their religion regularly joined confraternities and sodalities, all of them said the rosary and contributed to parish and diocesan collections and did what they could to ensure that their children followed in their footsteps. A passive role, perhaps, but one that provided its own satisfactions and seems to have been rarely questioned.

Notes

1 RCLv Conference Reports, 1863-4 and 1864-5. See Peter Doyle, 'Missed Opportunities: Clerical Conferences in the Nineteenth Century', *Downside Review* Oct. 1982, pp.263-73.

2 RCLv 5/1/140, Goss to Dawber, 18.3.1856. AAL Early Bishops, Pastoral Letters, Lent 1864,1868,1872.

3 *Guide to the Catholic Church Services and Quarant'Ore in Liverpool for 1861* (1861). AAL Pastoral Letters, Lent 1857; RCLv 5/1/461, Goss to Gillow 1.4.1857.

4 J. Davies, *St Austin's Log*, pp.34, 43. Mary Heimann, *Catholic Devotion in Victorian England* (1995), esp. Chapter 2.

5 RCLv 5/1/471, Goss to Callaghan, 17.4.1857; 5/1/1, Goss to Carr, 15.6.1855.

6 AAL Early Bishops, S1 II, B: Pastoral Letters, Sexagesima Sunday 1863. Doyle, 'Clerical Conferences', pp.268-9.

7 RCLv Visitation Returns; *Directory* for various years.

8 Heimann, p.150.

9 RCLv Conference Reports 1864-5, pp.63, 99, 207, 243, 315, 351.

10 Heimann, p.170.

11 Of many letters on these topics, see RCLv, 5/1/267, Goss to Vincent, 14.6.1856; 5/1/361, Goss to Dowding, 24.10.1856.

12 ALP Chronicles II, pp.88, 131-2, 158; Sharp, p.186; RCLv, Visitation Returns, St Vincent's Lent 1869; Heimann, p.147.

13 Sharp, pp.227-34.

14 AAL Early Bishops, S1 II, B: Pastoral Letters, 25 Feb. 1857, Feb. 1869, Feb. 1864.

15 AAL *Liverpolitana 1873-78*, Pastoral Letter, Lent 1878.

16 Pastoral Letters; see note 14.

17 Pastoral Letters, Feb. 1872.

18 RCLv Visitation Diaries, 3/B, St John's, Wigan, Nov. 1864; The Willows, Sept. 1864.

19 Pastoral Letters, 14 Feb.1857, quoting an anonymous moralist.

20 *Ibid.*, Nov. 1857.

21 Figures from RCLv Visitation Returns 1865.

22 Pastoral Letters, June 1856; Feb. 1868. *Preston Chronicle and Lancashire Advertiser*, 2.7.1864.

23 Pastoral Letters, Feb. 1866, Feb. 1869, Feb. 1870. RCLv Visitation Diaries, 3/B, have 22 sermons on the topic between Oct. 1860 and Sept. 1861.

24 RCLv Visitation Diaries, 3/B, Sept. 1862-Aug. 1865, pp.29-32,41-4. AAL Pastoral Letters, Sexagesima Sunday 1863.

25 Pastoral Letters, Feb. 1866; Manning, *Good Soldier*, p.12; Denvir in Burke, p.130.

26 AAL *Synodi Liverpolitanae*, p.24; RCLv 5/1/162, Circular to all clergy, 18.3.1856; 5/4/154, Goss to Hines, 18.12.1857.

27 Leo Warren, *Through Twenty Preston Guilds. The Catholic Congregation of St Wilfrid's*, Preston (1993), pp.63-5.

28 *Ibid.*, pp.63, 66-7.

29 Peter Doyle, 'Bishop O'Reilly and the Franciscans', *NWCH* XXVII (2000), pp.45-54.

30 Heimann, p.63.

31 AAL Early Bishops S1 VII A/12, Establishment of Confraternities, 1894-99.

32 Sharp, p.94-6; F. Goodall, CSSR, 'Celebrating the Redemptorists at Bishop Eton 1851-2001', typescript of sermon of 11.6.2001, pp.5-6 (kindly supplied by Bishop Eton).

33 AAL *Liverpolitana 1873-78*, ad clerum 26.4.1875. *Directory* for dedications of churches.

34 Michael Walsh, *A Dictionary of Devotions* (1993), p.28.

35 Heimann, pp.151-3.

36 John Bridge, *The Lowe House Story 1743-1993* (1993), pp.81-3.

37 RCLv 5/6/2/163, secretary to Mr Cullen 30.7.1866; Heimann, pp.64-6.

38 RCLv 5/5/64, Goss to Sr Lucy 26.1.1866; Visitation Diaries 3/B, St Wilfrid's, Preston, and Standish.

39 Walsh, pp.250-2.

40 Heimann, pp.71-5. I am grateful to Brian Plumb for information on this topic.

41 Walsh, p.213.

42 *Ibid.*, pp.176-7.

43 I am indebted to Brian Plumb for allowing me to quote from his comprehensive article, 'Hymnbooks Revisited', *NWCH* XXVII (2000), pp.68-91.

44 *Ladyewell, Past and Present* (nd, but c.2000).

45 Judith Champ, 'Bishop Milner, Holywell, and the Cure Tradition', *SCH*, vol. 19, pp.153-164, at p.162; H.Thurston, SJ, 'Holywell in Recent Years', *The Month*, vol. 128 (1916), pp.38-51; Janet Toole, *The Parish is a Beehive* (2002), p.21; Anon., *St Vincent De Paul's, Liverpool* (1952), p.27.

46 M. Maher, 'Holywell in 1894', *The Month* (1895), p.154.

CHAPTER 7 RELIGIOUS SISTERS AND REGULAR CLERGY – AN EXTRA DIMENSION

Astory is told of how in 1794 Squire Dicconson of Wrightington (an improving landowner), in his efforts to help the displaced Benedictine nuns of Ghent, sent his coachman to Wigan to collect them. When the coachman asked a fellow-servant, 'What are nuns?' he received the answer, 'I dunno – some sort of new potato perhaps'![1] Even fifty years later there were only four convents in the area that was to become the diocese of Liverpool, despite its being the most Catholic part of the country. There was nothing new, of course, in the presence of Regular clergy in the diocese. The survival of Catholicism in Lancashire in the seventeenth and eighteenth centuries had owed a great deal to the active and often heroic ministry of Jesuits and Benedictines. Both had long-established missions and chaplaincies and by the 1850s the Jesuits still ran twelve missions and the Bendictines twenty-one, and altogether the Regulars accounted for 48% (66 out of 137) of all missionary priests in 1856. This chapter examines the work of some of the Sisters and Regular clergy in the diocese.

RELIGIOUS SISTERS

A rare sight before 1840, the Sisters soon became ever-present figures in the Catholic landscape, especially the urban one. If the buildings silhouetted on the skyline were predominantly schools, that reflected the dominant part that education played in Catholic thinking. In reality there was a rich variety of enterprises and the Sisters proved to be extremely adaptable when facing the changing needs of the English Catholic Church: some ran schools, hospitals, nursing homes, orphanages and reformatories and looked after those with physical and mental disabilities while also nursing the poor in their own homes. Others undertook parish visiting, instructed children for their First Holy Communions and prepared adults for reception into the Church, while still others cared for the domestic needs of seminarians, priests and bishops. Between 1850 and 1870 the number of convents in England and Wales increased fourfold, with thirty Congregations making their first English foundations, and by 1905 twenty-three female Congregations in sixty-two houses served in various parts of the diocese:[2]

Congregation	Convents
Adoration Réparatrice	Liverpool
Augustinian Sisters	Waterloo
Bon Secours (of Troyes)	Liverpool
Carmelites	Orrell
Daughters of Wisdom (La Sagesse)	Liverpool, Preston
Faithful Companions of Jesus	Liverpool (x2), Preston
Good Shepherd	Liverpool (x2)
Holy Child Jesus	Blackpool, Preston
Little Sisters of the Poor	Liverpool (x2), Preston
Sisters of Mercy	Liverpool (x4), Blackbrook, Douglas (IoM), Lancaster
Most Holy Cross and Passion	Lytham, Sutton, Warrington
Notre Dame	Liverpool (x3), St Helens, Wigan, Birkdale
Poor Servants of the Mother of God	Liverpool (x2), St Helens
Poor Clares	Liverpool
Poor Sisters of Nazareth	Gt Crosby, Ditton, Lancaster
Sacred Heart of Mary	Barrow, Blackbrook, Liverpool
St Joseph's Missionary Sisters	Freshfield
Sisters of Charity	Liverpool (x5), Little Crosby, Freshfield, Preston
Sisters of Charity of Our Lady of Mercy	Preston, Birchley
Sisters of Charity of St Paul	Garstang, Gt Crosby, Rainhill, Southport
Sisters of St Catherine	Liverpool, Lancaster, Preston
Sisters of the Sacred Hearts of Jesus and Mary	Liverpool
Ursulines	Blackpool

Numbers continued to grow steadily:

1925	64 convents (75 in 1924 before the division of the archdiocese)
1930	65 convents
1935	71 convents
1940	82 convents
1950	84 convents
1955	85 convents
1965	92 convents
1980	108 convents

The number of Congregations also increased, though slowly, from the twenty-three of 1905 to twenty-five in the mid-1930s and twenty-seven in 1950. The following years saw a large increase so that by 1965 thirty-eight different Congregations were working in the diocese, and by 1980, forty-three. At the time of writing (2003) there are thirty-nine, with eighty-one convents. This chapter can only look at a few examples in any detail to try to illustrate the general contribution that these Congregations and Orders made to the life of the diocese in its first fifty years or so.

What these Congregations offered spiritually to women who joined them can only be written by those on the inside. Some went out of their way to recruit working-class and lower middle-class women, providing a spiritual home for many otherwise excluded. Each Congregation followed the spiritual inspiration of its foundress and between them they offered a variety of devotional approaches sufficient to satisfy every applicant. Moreover, they offered opportunities not otherwise available to women in the nineteenth century – something Florence Nightingale commented on favourably: 'their training, their discipline, their hopes, their home ... There is nothing like the training which the Sacred Heart or the Order of St Vincent gives to women'.[3] Although self-effacing in their dedication, they were a public witness, a distinctive presence that evoked respect from all but the most bigoted after initial suspicion and opposition.

How did they come to the diocese? By invitation to take on particular work (see later chapters on Social Agencies and Education) or they asked to be allowed to enter – Catholic Lancashire was an obvious field for their apostolates. Initiatives sometimes came from individual priests – Mgr Nugent was most influential here, but there were other priests as well, like Fr Parker of St Patrick's, Liverpool, who wrote to the Mother General of the Faithful Companions of Jesus (FCJs) almost demanding that she send some Sisters to work in Liverpool. When they did arrive in 1844 he wrote to her again, 'In our many heavy parish duties it is a relief for us to be able to hand over these poor women to your sisters and to feel that we can rely on their ready and willing co-operation'. There is evidence that some of the English Clergy were more willing to call on the services of French and Belgian Congregations than on the new English or Irish ones.[4]

By 1887, thirty-two of the sixty-two Congregations working in England had come from France, with another five from Belgium.[5] Interestingly, between 1840 and 1900 a total of sixteen Congregations were founded in England. In the 1890s and early 1900s there was a large increase in the number of applications from Religious to open houses in the diocese. It was probably not a coincidence that they began as soon as Bishop Whiteside became Bishop, since Bishop O'Reilly had not looked too favourably on such an expansion, although he did introduce the Little Sisters of Poor in 1874 – Goss had refused them a place. All the applications were discussed by the Chapter, a way of ensuring that no Congregation was allowed into the diocese without the approval of the senior clergy. Some common features are evident in how the Chapter was likely to respond: they did not like mendicant Religious (those that relied on begging for their upkeep), they preferred applications from Congregations that proposed to take on a specific work of mercy, and they wanted the Bishop to have the final say in where the new house was located (this was particularly so in the case of male Religious). At the same time, they welcomed applications from contemplative female Orders. While Whiteside was in charge (1894-1921), about twenty-five applications were discussed by the Chapter; some of these were from female Congregations suffering under the anti-religious laws in France.[6]

In 1896 German nuns of the Order of St Catherine were unanimously accepted into the diocese to teach the Polish community in Liverpool (it was claimed that 700 of them lived around Eldon Street alone) and to work among the German immigrants; their application stressed that they were not a mendicant Order.[7] The nuns later took on the running of a Children's Home (Knolle Park, Woolton) but had to leave because of anti-German feeling during the First World War (see Chapter 9 below). Also in 1896, Mgr Nugent asked for the Servants of the Sacred Heart to be admitted: they would visit and nurse the sick poor and look after pregnant girls. He hoped their convent would provide both a Foundling Hospital and a Maternity Home. The Chapter approved his request, and also a slightly later one that the Sisters of the Good Shepherd (in the diocese since 1858) should open a convent and asylum for fallen women near Preston, especially since the local clergy had apparently long felt the need of such a foundation.[8] An interesting case arose over the Daughters of the Heart of Mary, a Congregation bound by religious vows but not wearing a distinctive habit; they wanted to take up the work previously done by the Catholic Girls Aid Society in Preston. They were approved by the Holy See and strongly recommended by Cardinal Vaughan, but some of the Chapter were unsure about their not wearing a habit and so not being recognisable as nuns. The matter was adjourned for fuller discussion and then approved a few months later.[9]

About 1905 two Sisters from the Daughters of Wisdom Congregation (also known as the 'La Sagesse' nuns – Les Filles de la Sagesse, founded by St Louis Marie de Montfort in France in 1703) opened a small convent in Preston. They worked initially in St Wilfrid's parish at the invitation of the parish priest, looking after the sick poor in their own homes and supplementing the work of the SVP. The Congregation had come to the diocese in 1904 with an apostolate to care for the poor in any capacity and taught in a number of parish schools in Liverpool, later opening a secondary school for girls in Grassendale, Liverpool (this lasted until 1985-86).[10]

An altogether different apostolate was that of the Sisters of Our Lady of the Cenacle who were allowed into the diocese in 1906 when they opened a convent in Lance Lane, Wavertree. They ran a Retreat Centre for girls and women that provided preached retreats for women, girls and children of all classes, the whole year round. There were also specialised retreats for teachers, private retreats by arrangement and days of recollection for married women each month and for the Children of Mary, also monthly; the nuns also offered facilities for a small number of lady-boarders. It is an apostolate that has lasted down to the present day.[11] The Franciscan Sisters of Calais, who described their apostolate as 'works of mercy and the foreign missions', were admitted in 1911 to work among the poor, on the understanding that they would be self-supporting and would work in Leigh – which they did until 1917 or 1918.[12]

A minor disagreement occurred between Archbishop Whiteside and the Chapter when they discovered that he had given permission to some Benedictine nuns to open a convent at Morton Grange, Aughton, without

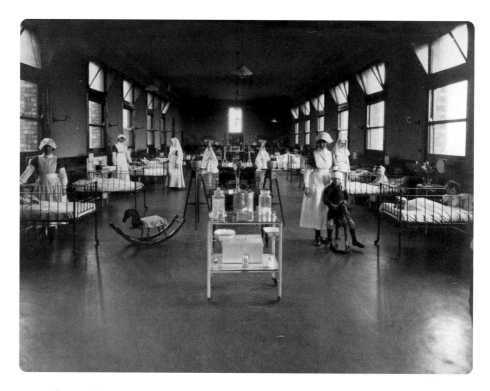

Providence Hospital, St Helens: a children's ward, and opposite, fund-raising in the town.

consulting them. The nuns, who took simple vows and were aggregated to the Olivetan Benedictine Congregation, came under the Archbishop's jurisdiction. What particularly annoyed the Chapter was a circular from the nuns appealing for £5,000 as a 'Foundation and Sustenation Fund', accompanied by a letter from the Archbishop wishing them well. As well as objecting to the appeal for money the Chapter pointed out that none of the nuns was qualified to teach. The school (variously known as Morton Grange Priory and St Ann's Benedictine High School) went ahead and flourished – it was bringing in about £1,000 a year by 1923 and the nuns, who were also receiving about £500 in alms, had been able to pay for a new chapel the previous year. Despite this early success the school closed and the nuns left Ormskirk in 1928 or 1929.[13]

One of the newly founded English Congregations was the Institute of the Poor Servants of the Mother of God (SMGs), founded in London in 1869 by Mother Magdalen Taylor – as Fanny Taylor she had worked in the Crimea with Florence Nightingale and become a Catholic, inspired by the example of the nuns she was working with.[14] She wanted a Congregation that would accept as postulants women from poor backgrounds who had no dowries to offer. Their convents had to make money to support themselves, largely through running laundries as commercial enterprises. They had no specific apostolic work but responded to the needs of the day – catering for the sick poor, children, the destitute, prostitutes and ex-prisoners. At the request of the Jesuits they opened a house in St Helens in 1882 and nursed the sick in their homes. The following year they started the Providence Free Hospital, which became a major medical facility for the whole town and lasted until

138

1982. Attached to it the Sisters opened a free Night School for miners, many of whom were illiterate not only in the ordinary sense but also in their knowledge of the Faith they professed.

The Sisters moved into Liverpool in 1891 at Mgr Nugent's request to run a refuge for women (see Chapter 9) – the buildings became the Lourdes Hospital in 1929, which is still providing acute health care (in Greenbank Road). They opened another refuge, Rosemont, in the city in 1900; then, at Archbishop Whiteside's request they took over a nursing home for deprived and sick children (mainly TB sufferers) in Freshfield in 1915 and in the same year Knolle Park Children's Home from the German Sisters. Again at the Archbishop's request, they ran St Lucy's Eye Hospital for Catholic Children, Fairfield, in 1918 (this closed in 1925), and, finally, Nugent House refuge for girls in 1923 and in 1924 St Saviour's, Mossley Hill, as a refuge and later as a home for those with learning disabilities. Throughout these years and later the Sisters were also running a home for discharged prisoners and young offenders and working as district nurses. In later years a small number of the Sisters taught in parochial schools.

Another English Order, the Sisters of the Most Holy Cross and Passion, settled in Sutton, near St Helens, in 1855 and later taught in elementary schools in Lytham, St Anne's-on-Sea, Sutton and Warrington. Founded in Manchester by Elizabeth Prout in 1851-2 and initially known as the Institute of the Holy Family, their first aim was to care for poor factory girls by providing hostels for them, but they soon moved into teaching. Like the SMGs, they provided an entry into the Religious Life for daughters of lower middle-class and poor Catholic families – they had no dowries and no wealthy members to support them and so the members of the Institute continued to work to support themselves, a few in the Manchester cotton mills but most of them by needlework and teaching; their apostolate was 'to be both Martha and Mary'. By 1912 they were asking for either a dowry or a teaching qualification.[15]

Part of their teaching work lay in running Sunday Schools – a general feature of teaching congregations such as the Notre Dame Sisters and the Christian Brothers at the time. It is worth remembering that a Sunday School in mid-Victorian times meant something quite different from its later forms. The following description comes from a Christian Brother of the time:

> On Sundays, after ... breakfast ... immediately off to school to lead the boys to Mass. After Mass, Sunday School in which reading, writing, arithmetic and religious instruction continue until 12.30. Then dinner, after which school again at 2 until 4.30. Then tea, and back to school to lead the boys to church at 6.30 for evening prayers.

The Sunday Schools were generally well-attended by girls as well as boys. They did not interfere with the children's working week and charged no fees; they met both an educational and a religious need. A number of Congregations were involved in this particular apostolate – the only way, they believed, that they could get across to working girls and have any hope of influencing them.[16]

Several successful bids to move into the diocese were made by contemplative Orders – the Poor Clares Colletine in 1902, a French Order of Carmelites nuns in the same year, and the 'English Carmelites' from Kensington, London, in 1904. French Carmelites from Carcassonne were driven out by French anti-Catholic laws and about 1906 settled in Orrell Mount, Orrell, which for a time (1821-35) had housed a community of French Benedictine nuns who had been exiled under a previous anti-Catholic regime. The Carmelites stayed in Orrell until 1917, when they moved into the purpose-built Carmel in Upholland, opposite the grounds of Upholland seminary – their apostolate included prayers for priests. Later a second Carmelite community opened a convent in Honeygreen Lane, West Derby and another in Eccleston, St Helens (all three Carmelite monasteries are still there at the time of writing). The Poor Clares (Colettines) settled in Green Lane, Liverpool. There were also the Sisters of the Adoration Réparatrice Congregation, who opened their convent in Edge Lane, Liverpool. Their apostolate was essentially one of perpetual (night and day) adoration of the Blessed Sacrament. They supported themselves by making altar breads, vestments and altar linen, and ran days of recollection for women, especially their 'Association of Lay Adorers'.[17]

Most of the new Congregations were independent of direct episcopal control, though they all needed the Bishop's permission to open a house in his diocese and were subject to visitation. This relative freedom allowed them to be more flexible in their responses to missionary needs. Moreover, a considerable percentage of the new founders were converts (60%) or Irish and so not shackled by either recusant traditions or undue regard for traditional convent practices and customs. A number of them were run at various times by wealthy, upper-class ladies, able to use their influence and position to further the development of their apostolic work: they proved to be formidable foundresses and superiors, and quarrels between them and bishops and clergy were not unusual. Goss and the Good Shepherd Sisters fell out over property rights. When they were about to move into their new Magdalen Asylum in Ford, their Provincial, whom Goss referred to as Madame Weld, argued that they could not do so unless ownership of the house was made over to them. Goss exploded: the house had cost £12,000 and the money for it had been raised on his authority and belonged to the diocese – he would sooner make the Mayor and Corporation of Liverpool trustees of the property than allow 'her to get the property into her hands'! If she insisted and threatened to withdraw, he would call her bluff and use the building as a reformatory without their involvement. In this instance, Madame Weld gave way and the Sisters moved into the new house as tenants.[18]

We have seen that the ability to support itself without begging for alms was an important criterion when the Chapter and Bishop were deciding whether to allow a Congregation into the diocese. Opposition from the bishops to Religious begging had always been strong, even though on occasion they might allow it in special circumstances. Some Orders and Congregations could claim a canonical right to beg (sometimes done openly house to house or by visiting friendly shop-keepers, sometimes by sending out written appeals and advertising), but the English bishops felt this was a practice more suited to Catholic countries than to England. The issue was complicated by the continuing problem of impostors begging under the guise of Religious – the diocese, Goss believed, had been overrun by 'vagabonds', who, under the guise of religion, 'filch from the poor their hard earned wages, in order to spend the money in dissipation and debauchery'.[19] In 1888 O'Reilly warned the clergy against two women pretending to be Sisters of Mercy who were begging in the Liverpool neighbourhood without any authority. He even opposed the SMGs and their hospital in St Helens because he was sure they were begging for alms – he turned down their request to open a similar institution in Liverpool. Mother Taylor explained that they had sent out no appeals to Catholics but only around the town in general, and that most of the money they received came from Protestants (though, she noted, they faced some Protestant bitterness as well) – in the end, but reluctantly, the Bishop accepted that this was not begging, at least in the ordinary sense.[20]

Begging was not, of course, restricted to the female Orders. When the Capuchins asked Bishop O'Reilly for a licence to beg he refused them, referring to some trouble and possibly scandal connected with friars begging in Liverpool a long time before. Interestingly, he also quoted the fact that the Passionists had been granted such a licence, as they were very poor and needed all the money they could get – it would be unfair to allow the Capuchins to encroach on what was Passionist territory. Despite his refusal, some friars appeared in the diocese on begging missions, causing, he claimed, scandal to Catholics and non-Catholics. He quoted the example of a begging letter sent by a friar: it asked for money to help one of them go to Italy to visit his sick mother and promised to bring back articles blessed by the pope – 5/- would obtain a crucifix, 2/6 a rosary and 1/- a medal; the writer of the letter hoped that its recipient would 'get him a good collection among her dear friends in Southport'.[21] The Bishop's opposition to begging seems to have become an obsession, but he was an experienced pastor and knew the impact that the practice had on the people, especially the poor – they had to be protected from their own generosity.

Orders and Congregations that worked in the diocese hoped that it would provide a harvest of vocations as well as providing outlets for their apostolic work. It is not possible to be sure how far those hopes were fulfilled but there is some evidence that their expectations had been over-optimistic. We know that by 1900 almost all the 500 postulants who had sought entrance to the Poor Servants of the Mother of God, a very English Congregation, had come from poor families in rural Ireland. The Sisters of the Sacred Heart of Mary (SHMs), with a large girls' grammar school in Seaforth, Liverpool, (opened 1884; the Sisters had been working in the Bootle area since 1872) recruited only thirty-two postulants from Lancashire between 1880 and 1949, compared with a staggering 620 from Ireland. The Sisters of Charity of St Paul the Apostle (the Selly Park Sisters) worked in several parts of the diocese; between 1847 and 1947, 440 of their professed Sisters were from England or Wales, 783 from Ireland. Recruitment patterns differed from Congregation to Congregation – the Cross and Passion Sisters were rapidly 'Hibernicised', the Sisters of the Holy Child Jesus were not and drew strongly from Lancashire. Overall, it seems that the proportion of Irish-born in many Congregations working in England was very high.[22]

In this context, it is interesting that, much later, Archbishop Heenan asked why so few girls and women from Lancashire were taking up a vocation to the Religious life. In a startling pastoral letter of Feb 1962, while pre-Vatican II Catholicism was still riding high in the religious charts, he gave some statistics: he had recently visited a large convent that had 33 Sisters, of whom 32 had been born in Ireland; another large one, where young sisters were being trained for teaching and nursing, had 28 sisters, 21 from Ireland, 5 from Malta, one from Wales and one from Liverpool. He spoke of girls who complained to him that their parents would not allow them to enter a convent – even practising Catholics, he said, sometimes spoke as if a religious vocation for their daughters were a disgrace rather than a blessing. They would rather see their daughter marry an unbeliever than become a spouse of Christ. 'Why', he asked, 'are Lancashire boys ready to offer themselves to God's service while the girls are so reluctant'?[23] It was a telling question. Whatever the answer, there was here a second, very different, 'Irish invasion' that had its own distinctive impact on the Church in Lancashire.

THE REGULAR CLERGY

A number of Orders and Congregations of men also applied to work in the diocese. In 1894 the Dominicans were given leave to open a house as long as they accepted the locality appointed them by the Bishop, but they did not follow it through. The Brothers of Charity wanted to open a house near Preston and run a home for epileptics and a hostel for working boys. The home for epileptics was approved without question but the Chapter was doubtful about the hostel because the SVP was already running one in the town. The Chapter decided to consult the local parish priests who approved of both the home and the hostel, and so permission was granted. In 1908 a request from the Carmelite Friars was unanimously turned down by the Chapter, but no reasons for the decision were noted – was it possibly because they were a mendicant order?[24] In other cases far more detailed conditions were required of the applicant, especially in the case of Orders whose members were priests. Two of these cases occurred in 1907.

The first concerned the Friars Minor who were allowed into Liverpool to open and run a mission (St Mary of the Angels, Fox Street). As we have seen, Bishop O'Reilly had been implacably opposed to any of the Franciscans having a house in the diocese and the conditions now imposed on them are interesting. First of all, they were to relinquish formally their canonical right to beg and, secondly, the congregation of the new mission were not to be asked to support more Friars than were necessary for the efficient running of that mission. Finally, if the Friars left the mission it should revert to the Bishop with no financial burdens. The Friars accepted the conditions and St Mary's was opened in 1909, soon developing into one of the major inner-city parishes. Presumably they helped to get rid of any remaining anti-Franciscan feeling, for in 1925 another branch of the Order, the Friars Minor Conventuals, was given leave to launch a new mission at Mossley Hill, Liverpool, dedicated to St Anthony of Padua, which opened in 1926.[25]

The second case concerned the Congregation of the Fathers of the Holy Ghost. They wanted permission to open a novitiate somewhere in the diocese and this was granted, on condition that they did not beg, educated only their own students and undertook no missionary work except at the Bishop's request. A few years later they wanted to open a mission in or near Liverpool, or at least to have a house there, presumably to recruit more candidates for the novitiate (at Grange-over-Sands), but this was refused. A few months later they were offered and accepted the mission at Peasley Cross, St Helens. Three years later they returned to their request for a foundation in Liverpool; this time the Chapter strongly opposed the idea of their having another foundation in the city or anywhere else in the Archdiocese.[26] Strict control was the norm for the Chapter, and especially so, it seems, where cases of admitting Regular priests into the diocese were concerned.

The Benedictine Church of St Mary, Highfield Street, Liverpool. The original A.W. Pugin building (1845) was destroyed in the 1940s Blitz; this new church, by Weightman & Bullen, was opened in 1953. It closed in 2000.

The older Orders of Jesuits and Benedictines both had distinguished long-service records in Lancashire and from the start of the diocese had provided a source of essential clerical man-power, particularly important in the major centres of population: the main Jesuit missions were in Preston (3 missions), Liverpool, St Helens and Wigan, while the Benedictines had four missions in Liverpool and one in Warrington. More importantly, they added an invaluable and different dimension to the spirituality 'on offer' to the people and the Jesuits were at the leading edge of secondary school development in Preston and Liverpool. When Bishop O'Reilly reported to Propaganda on the state of the Diocese in 1887, he picked out the missions run by Regulars for special note:

Missions run by Regulars: (the figure in brackets is for the number of priests):

	Missions	Catholics	Regular attendance	%
Benedictines	18 (34)	33,840	15,810	46.7%
Jesuits	13 (41)	43,106	24,698	57.3%
Passionists	2 (8)	1,917	931	48.6%
Oblates	1 (4)	6,705	2,907	43.4%

Attendances in Jesuit missions were consistently higher than in similar missions run by other clergy, for reasons that are not altogether clear; the 'pulling power' of the special devotions they put on must have played a part.

Unfortunately, there was also a long history of feuds between the Seculars and Regulars. Perhaps the Regulars remained wedded to their recusant traditions, and their former privileges and independence, for too long and so indulged in constant sniping at episcopal authority when it was imposed after the Restoration of the Hierarchy – there was among some of them a paranoid reaction to every scratching of an episcopal pen! As an extreme example, a petition of 1839 had reminded Propaganda that in pre-Reformation England the Benedictines had held at least a third of all parochial churches in England and in some dioceses had had the right to elect bishops – their former position and privileges should be restored along with any restoration of a hierarchy.[27] Even to have penned such a petition was indicative of a refusal to accept that a different situation was developing.

The Secular clergy for their part had long feared the influence of the Regulars, and these traditional fears had been increased by two Roman decrees of 1838. One of these had allowed the Regulars to attach special indulgences to certain devotions and to set up lay confraternities in their missions. The second decree had seemed more ominous: it allowed the Regulars to build public churches and to retain them as their own property, without any reference to the local Bishop. The vicars apostolic objected most strongly: the decree on indulgences was, they claimed, unnecessary, unsuited to English conditions and would only be a source of discord. The decree on the building of churches was, they argued, 'subversive of episcopal jurisdiction' and would cause 'dissensions and scandals'. Animosity towards the Regulars was strongest in the north of England and a number of resolutions about the two decrees were presented by the Secular clergy in Lancashire, Yorkshire, Northumberland and Durham. These abounded in such phrases as 'altar being raised against altar', 'open war' between the two sets of clergy, the 'annihilation of subordination to episcopal authority', 'storms of strife, anarchy and confusion'; finally, the Seculars argued, the decrees would be a gift to the enemies of the Church and would increase Protestant prejudice.[28]

Unfortunately, the delicate relationship between the two sets of clergy was not improved when the famous Fr William Faber preached at Goss's consecration in 1853. The Secular clergy, he claimed, were the life of the Church, while the Regulars were only its ornament: the Church could exist without the latter but not without the Seculars whom Christ himself had founded: throughout the ages they had done the work of the Church and had suffered persecution and martyrdom.[29] The sermon was, at least, a tactless gaffe and caused ill-feeling among even the newer Congregations who generally kept themselves free of the bickerings and controversies.

The main issues at stake were not particular to the Liverpool Diocese, but were more important there because of the large numbers of Regular priests and missions. Among those issues were the visitation of Regular missions and property; the division of Regular missions; the attendance of Regular clergy at clerical conferences; the right of Religious superiors to

move their subjects at will; the attitude of some of the Regular clergy to synodal regulations, especially those concerning the celebration of marriages, and the holding of collections for diocesan causes. There was, too, the fundamental issue of whether Regular clergy should be running one-man parishes at all. A number of disputes led to appeals to Rome by both sides and the issues were not finally settled until the papal Bull *Romanos Pontifices* of 1881 found almost entirely in favour of the bishops.

The Regulars' stance on some of the issues in contention shows their basic attitude to episcopal authority: they accepted it in principle but went in for a continual questioning of its practical implications, as though trying to assert their former independence. One relatively minor but indicative issue was that of diocesan collections. In 1864 a Jesuit at St Wilfrid's, Preston, advised the congregation not to give more than a penny a head to the Diocesan Mission Fund and expressed his joy that the total was down on the previous year's, 'for it was quite enough for the Bishop'. In the same year the Benedictines of St Augustine's, Liverpool, refused to hold a collection for the support of the Public Institutions, and the senior priest, Fr Bulbeck, claimed it was 'a piece of impertinence' for the vicar general or anyone else to tell him to hand over money for a particular purpose. When Goss threatened to withdraw his faculties, Bulbeck apologised and excused his letter on the grounds of the hardship and ill-health that the priests in that part of Liverpool faced. Goss agreed that priests working in the slums needed a comfortable home and sympathised with their situation, but still insisted on the collection.[30]

At other times it seemed that the Jesuits were on the one hand claiming that their churches should be regarded as full missions while on the other refusing to carry out ordinary missionary duties. In 1869 Fr Porter of St Francis Xavier's, Liverpool, complained that one of his curates had been asked to become confessor to the nuns at the Blind Asylum. As exempt Religious, argued Porter, they were not required to undertake any duties 'beyond the strictly quasi-parochial duties of their own church' and he had been advised by his Provincial to refuse the appointment. The tone of the letter is strange: Porter wrote as though the Society were doing the Bishop a favour in taking on any missionary duties at all and implied that the appointment had been an attack on their rights. Goss simply replied that duty required the Fathers to obey their Rule and he would find another confessor for the nuns. He had not, however, suddenly become meek, and shortly afterwards he removed the care of the military barracks from the Jesuits in Preston and gave it to the Seculars. When the local Jesuits objected, he replied that as Bishop he must never ask Religious to act against their Rule. Perhaps he had a quiet laugh about it all: the work at the barracks carried a government-paid salary, that at the Blind Asylum no stipend at all.[31]

Much more serious was a disregard of, or cavalier attitude to, the diocesan regulations concerning the celebration of marriages. It is interesting that all the cases where these regulations were ignored or flouted involved members of the Regular clergy and all took place in Liverpool town missions where there were particular problems in making sure that Catholics married according to the laws of the Church. Cases of flouting the law continued under Bishop O'Reilly, who complained that people were beginning to think that he and the Seculars were rigorists because the Jesuits were acting so leniently in such important matters.[32]

One of the means at a Bishop's disposal to ensure uniformity of practice was the holding of clerical conferences in each deanery. These took place annually and consisted of six or eight sessions when all the clergy met to discuss set questions laid down by the Bishop; if clergy were absent for any reason they were expected to submit written answers to the questions. There was a heavy stress on practical pastoral issues such as taking Holy Communion to the sick, hearing confessions, how to interpret the regulations on marriage, and so on. There was also a social dimension to the meetings in that they enabled the clergy to get to know each other; sometimes the sessions ended with a communal meal. In the circumstances it was a pity that the Jesuits asserted their independence by refusing to attend the conferences – in 1855 they boycotted the Preston conferences altogether and in 1856 did almost the same in Liverpool.[33] In the end the Jesuits accepted the demands of the new situation and the Bishop won his case that all those exercising missionary faculties under his jurisdiction should take the normal means of ensuring that they exercised them properly.

THE NEWER CONGREGATIONS OF MEN

By 1905 there were eight Orders or Congregations of men serving in the diocese:

Benedictines:	Liverpool; Brindle; Clayton Green; Goosnargh; Grassendale; Hindley;Leyland; Netherton; Ormskirk; Parbold; Scarisbrick; Warrington; Woolton.
Jesuits:	Liverpool; Blackpool; Leigh; Portico; Prescott; Preston; St Helens; Wigan.
Oblates of Mary Immaculate:	Liverpool.
Passionist Fathers:	Sutton.
Redemptorist Fathers:	Liverpool.
Society of St Joseph for Foreign Missions:	Freshfield.
Brothers of Charity:	Preston; Liverpool.
Irish Christian Brothers:	Liverpool.

Among the newer Congregations, mention may be made first of all of the Redemptorists. In 1844 Bishop Brown and his co-adjutor, Bishop Sharples, had moved into Eton House, an eighteenth-century mansion on the road from Liverpool to the village of Woolton. The house became known as Bishop Eton and in 1851 the Redemptorists took it over as their principal missionary house (Bishop Brown moved to Catharine Street in Liverpool). It had been Bishop Brown, apparently at the prompting of Mgr Nugent, who had invited them to settle in the diocese, although individual priests had used them to give parochial missions before that. One of the missioners described how they took to the streets to reach the people. Preceded by sodality members in uniform and carrying a banner, he soon had an audience:

> to whom I preached … we had no altar, no Mass, no tall black mission cross with its nine yards of drapery drawn over the arms; an empty egg-box served for a pulpit. My audience was all that could be wished in numbers and respectful attitude, not only looking up to me, but down at me from tiers of windows on every side.[34]

Bishop Eton became the Congregation's English novitiate in 1860. The Congregation was relatively small throughout the nineteenth century, its numbers in England and Ireland never rising much above sixty, but its influence was great through its dedication to the giving of parish missions and retreats. Cardinal Manning thought them the 'most evangelical men he knew', while Bishop Goss also thought very highly of them: 'the only truly religious community of men under his jurisdiction, all the other religious orders being more secular priests than religious'. He also believed that they were the best givers of clergy retreats and that any priest who made a sincere retreat with them would come to no spiritual harm. Bishop O'Reilly, himself a Redemptorist Oblate, described their work in the diocese as bearing 'truly the greatest fruit for religion and piety'.[35] Their chapel, dedicated to Our Lady of the Annunciation, did not become a parish church until 1962, but many Catholics used it for Sunday and weekday Mass and devotions, especially to Our Lady of Perpetual Succour.

Altogether, between about 1860 and 1900, over 920 missions were given by priests from Bishop Eton, with some remarkable effects: in 1862 at St Patrick's, Liverpool, the Redemptorists rejoiced because in that 'wilderness of sin and impiety and irreligion' the heart of the exiles were roused 'to the warmth of the Faith' and religious practice. Nine years later in the same parish the missioners reported that innumerable 'exiles from the Sacraments', some of whom had been away for anything from 10 to 60 years, and some of whom had never been to confession, flocked back to the church.[36] But, as we have seen, these 'glory years' did not last and new methods were needed to meet changing audiences.

Another Congregation that came to the area just before the diocese was established were the Passionists. Founded by St Paul of the Cross (1694-1775), they had a special zeal for the conversion of England and by 1849 had opened houses in London, Aston Hall (Staffs) and Woodchester (Gloucs). Blessed Dominic Barberi had already given missions in Liverpool, Preston and Blackbrook and Bishop Brown wanted to give the Congregation a permanent house in the area. At the same time, Mr John Smith, a self-made wealthy businessman and philanthropist, wanted to build a church at Sutton, near St Helens, for the small community of Catholics living there. After meeting Fr Ignatius Spencer, a leading Passionist and convert English aristocrat, Smith offered to build a small monastery, with twelve acres of land, for the Passionists as well as the church. The new church of St Anne was opened in 1851. It was a parish church from the start, although the work of giving missions and retreats was the Passionists' priority.[37]

In 1850 Fr Ignatius was twice attacked by crowds in Liverpool because he was wearing the distinctive Passionist habit. Bishop Brown reported the matter to Propaganda and blamed Spencer for going against his advice, banning him from the diocese until he ceased wearing it – it was technically illegal under the 1829 Catholic Emancipation Act to wear religious habits in public. Propaganda told the Passionist Superior General to order him not to wear it in public. Later, Fr Ignatius sided with those Regulars who objected to attempts by the bishops to curtail the Regulars' privilege of exemption from episcopal control: he believed that the Holy See's policy in allowing exemption was to 'prevent the Bishops from becoming so many Popes'![38] The work of the Congregation prospered, and Sutton became a successful retreat centre and the base for an extensive mission-giving apostolate throughout the diocese and across northern England. Its early rectors were Italians: Fr Honorius Mazzini, 1851-52; Fr Bernadine Carosi, 1852-63 and 1864-66 (after Fr Ignatius Spencer, appointed in 1863, had died in 1864), and finally

Fr Salvian Nardocci, 1866-69. It was Fr Bernardine who invited the Sisters of the Cross and Passion to open a house in Sutton in 1855, the year that the incorrupt body of Bd. Dominic Barberi (who had died in 1849) was moved to St Anne's church from Aston Hall. At some stage Bishop Goss received a report from a local parish priest that made him think that an unlawful devotion was developing around the body of the holy Passionist. He ordered it to be buried in a vault in the crypt that was not to be opened without the Bishop's permission.[39]

By 1860 the number of Catholics in the Sutton area had grown to about 2,000 from the 30 or 40 for whom John Smith had built the first church. Fr Bernardine established a second school at nearby Peasley Cross (the Sisters of the Cross and Passion taught there as well as in St Anne's) and in 1862 added a large lecture hall that was used for Sunday Mass – St Joseph's, Peasley Cross became a separate parish in 1878. He also enlarged the monastery at Sutton in 1860 to take in students for the priesthood and by 1879 there was a community of nine priests, four clerical brothers and eight lay brothers. The parish had the usual complement of the Catholic Young Men's Society, the Children of Mary, a Women's Guild, a men's club and, later, a branch of the Total Abstinence League of the Cross; there were annual Corpus Christi processions and 'Catholic Demonstrations' – a form of Catholic witness meant to parallel the Protestant Sunday School Whit Walks. It remained the only Passionist foundation in the diocese until 1933, when they opened St Gabriel's Retreat, Blythe Hall, near Ormskirk – a centre for training their postulants and for clergy and lay retreats. A Mass-centre and school was opened in Burtonwood in 1886, dedicated to St Paul of the Cross; this was staffed from St Anne's until it became a Secular parish in its own right, with a new church, in 1898. In the following year a special shrine for the conversion of England was built in St Anne's, dedicated to St Paul of the Cross. In 1921 Archbishop Keating spoke there of Fr Dominic Barberi and Fr Ignatius Spencer as:

> *two men who sounded the trumpet which announced the birth of a new and better day for Catholics; who were the apostles and the first labourers in the glorious work of the reconversion of England to the Catholic Faith … Many here present may live to see the name of Father Dominic and I hope also the name of Father Ignatius upon the roll of the Church's saints.*

It was the start of regular pilgrimages to the tombs – on 'Dominic's Day' in 1925 about 2,500 people took part and by 1939 this had risen to 10,000. Fr Dominic was beatified in 1962 – the original church is now dedicated to St Anne and Bl. Dominc – and the causes of Fr Ignatius and Elizabeth Prout (foundress of the Cross and Passion Sisters) were formally introduced in 1992 and 1994 respectively.[40]

The third of the original 'new' Congregations to work in the diocese were the Oblates of Mary Immaculate, a French Congregation, approved in 1826 and dedicated to evangelisation of the poor, through the giving of missions and running parishes. Bishop Brown invited them to work in Liverpool in 1850 and they took over the mission of Holy Cross, founded the previous year in one of the most crowded and poorest parts of Liverpool. They said Mass first of all in the space over a cow-shed and their work was successful so quickly that within a year they were reputed to have totally reformed some of the worst streets in the area from being notorious dens of vice and infamy, largely through intensive house-visiting and the building of schools in Fontenoy Street – lay teachers ran the boys' day school and night school; the girls' day school was under the Sisters of Mercy. The foundation stone of a large Gothic church was laid in 1859 and the church opened in 1860. Unfortunately it was destroyed by enemy action in 1941; it was rebuilt in 1954 but population movement brought about the closure of the parish in 2001. In 1928 the Oblates had taken charge of a new parish, dedicated to St Teresa of the Child Jesus, in Norris Green, one of the new post-war suburbs.[41]

So much dedicated work has not been dealt with in this chapter and so many devoted Religious orders and Congregations have received little more than a mention. The following chapters on education and the Catholic social agencies will redress the balance to some degree. What this account has shown is the strength and value of the Religious presence, female and male, throughout the diocese. They were much more than the 'voluntary sector' of the day: without their input the whole Catholic evangelistic enterprise would have been that much poorer and certainly less entrepreneurial; their rich spiritual and practical inputs to the development of the diocese were outstanding.

Notes

[1] Hilton, *Catholic Lancashire*, p.83. There is a technical difference between 'nuns' and 'sisters' but for ease of treatment I have used 'sisters' throughout this chapter.

[2] The titles given here are those used in the 1906 *Catholic Directory*. Other figures are from later *Directories*.

[3] Susan O'Brien, 'Religious Life for Women', in *Flaminian Gate*, p.115.

[4] Susan O'Brien, 'French Nuns in Nineteenth Century England', *Past and Present*, 154 (Feb. 1997), pp.142-64, at pp.149-50.

[5] O'Brien, 'Religious Life for Women', p.114.

[6] AAL Chancellor, *Acta Capituli Liverpolitani III*; Early Bishops, S2 V C/42 (1903) for French exiles.

[7] AAL Cancellor, *Acta Capituli*, 24.2.1896.

[8] *Ibid.*, 15.12.96; 26.1.1897.

[9] *Ibid.*, 1.3. and 6.6.1899.

[10] Information on the La Sagesse Sisters in Liverpool from their Provincial Archives.

[11] AAL Cancellor, *Acta Capituli*, 6.11.1906; subsequent *Directories*.

[12] *Ibid.*, 2.5.1911 and 12.6.1911; *Directory*, 1918.

[13] March 1916; subsequent *Directories*.

[14] Information from the Generalate Archives of the Poor Servants of the Mother of God.

[15] Edna Hamer, *Elizabeth Prout 1820-1864. A Religious Life for Industrial England* (1994), p.205; O'Brien, 'Religious Life', p.117.

[16] Hamer, p.108.

[17] AAL Cancellor, *Acta Capituli*, 30.1.1902; 5.11.1902; 7.11.1904; 3.11.1915, and subsequent *Directories*.

[18] Archives of the Archbishop of Southwark, B.13, Goss to Grant, 18.11.1867.

[19] AAL Early Bishops, S1 III, C: ad clerum 22.9.1865.

[20] SMG Archives, Mother Magdalen Taylor to Bishop O'Reilly, Aug. 1884 – May 1888.

[21] APF *S.R. Anglia*, vol. 20, nn.992,ff.

[22] O'Brien, 'Religious Life', p.117 (SMGs); SHM statistics from their archives, kindly supplied by Sr Máire O'Donnell; J.J. Scarisbrick, *Selly Park and Beyond* (1997), p.87. I am grateful to Dr O'Brien for her help on this question.

[23] AAL Heenan, S1, II Documents A/19.

[24] AAL Cancellor, *Acta Capituli*, 6.11.1894 (OPs); 26.1.1897 (Brothers); 5.11.1908 (Friars).

[25] *Ibid.*, 4.6.1907 and pp.138-41; for later foundation, 3.2.1925.

[26] *Ibid.*, 8.11.1907; 21.1.1908; 7.11.1911; 13.3.1912; 15.3.1915.

[27] Ward, *Sequel* 1, pp.254-7; the petition may not have been presented.

[28] AAL Early Bishops, Misc. vol. VI, Letters etc. of Bishop Briggs, pp.25-58.

[29] *The Tablet*, 1.10.1853.

[30] Peter Doyle, 'Lancashire Benedictines: The Restoration of the Hierarchy', *EBC History Symposium 1983*, pp.4-21, at pp.14-15; also, 'Jesuit Reactions to the Restoration of the Hierarchy: the Diocese of Liverpool,1850-1880', *RH* vol. 26, 1 (May 2002), pp.210-28, at p.219.

[31] Doyle, 'Jesuit Reactions', pp.219-20.

[32] *Ibid.*, p.221.

[33] *Ibid.*, pp.222-3.

[34] Sharp, p.19.

[35] *Ibid.*, pp.33, 63, 98.

[36] *Ibid.*, pp.146-8, 193, 271.

[37] Sr Dominic Savio (Hamer), CP, *St Anne's, Sutton, 1850-2000* (2000).

[38] Burke, p.97; Doyle, 'Lancashire Benedictines', p.11.

[39] RCLv 5/2/367,371, Goss to Fisher, 23 and 25.10.1858.

[40] Sr Dominic, *St Anne's; Directories*.

[41] Burke, pp.94, 107-8; *The Lamp, A Magazine of Instruction and Amusement*, VII, no.6 (Feb. 1860), pp.81-2; *Directories*.

CHAPTER 8 EDUCATION AND SCHOOLS: THE FIRST HUNDRED YEARS

On the success of this our common effort in behalf of the children of the Poor, not only our religious progress and prosperity, but also the eternal salvation of thousands, does depend.

So proclaimed the Vicars Apostolic when they set up the Catholic Poor School Committee in 1847 to help provide schools in their Districts. They were followed by the new Bishops in 1852 who urged their clergy to put the building of schools before the building of churches in new missions,

for the building raised of living and chosen stones, the spiritual sanctuary of the Church, is of far greater importance than the temple made with hands. And it is the good school that secures the virtuous and edifying congregation.[1]

No other concern so united the Catholic body as 'the schools question', or kept its leaders, clerical and lay, so regularly in the public eye and at odds with successive governments. As far as one can see, there were no dissenting Catholic voices to question this new test of orthodoxy, and the purses of the rich were as open in its support as the pockets of the poor. The century after 1850 was punctuated by great national educational debates and key Acts of Parliament in 1870, 1902 and 1944, and the history of the Catholic community could be written with these dates as the milestones in its development. Parochial schools became a central feature of parish life for nearly all Catholics across the diocese, and those in Liverpool who entered public life almost always cut their political teeth on educational matters, whether on the Select Vestry, the School Boards or the City Council.[2]

The financial burdens involved in implementing the 1852 ideal were heavy and bishops understandably spoke of the injustices of the system and of the crises facing their dioceses whenever new legislation meant increased expenditure. It was a considerable achievement that Archbishop Downey could boast in 1943 that while the Church of England had had to give up 2,700 elementary schools between 1902 and 1942, the Catholic Church had not surrendered a single one to local authority control and had, indeed, opened new schools in every year of that period except during the war years.[3] This may have been something of a pyrrhic victory, however, since governments never believed that Catholics would not go on meeting the costs of their schools. At the same time it must be pointed out that the various Acts brought benefits that the Catholic body was very reluctant to acknowledge – more Catholic schools for children to attend, an improvement in academic and material standards in elementary schools and a wider provision of secondary and grammar schools, with a consequent increase in the numbers going on to higher education.[4]

With the diocese of Liverpool having the largest Catholic population in England and Wales and the largest number of parishes, it is not surprising that its bishops were fully involved in the struggle to provide schools and often led the Catholic forces into action. On the whole, the need for the schools was taken as proven; where theory was invoked to justify them, it was usually in terms of parental rights and the need for religious teaching if the 'whole child' were to be educated. In the early days, Catholics shared some of the pragmatism of others who pushed for a national system of schooling: the need to keep the children off the streets and so out of the magistrates' courts, and to give them enough education to help them become a more effective workforce and have a better chance of finding a job.

In a Pastoral of November 1885 on Education, Bishop O'Reilly argued that if the Secularists had their way then the rising generation in England would be one of atheists, and the country, which had been 'robbed three hundred years ago of her Catholicity', would within the present generation be robbed of her Christianity'. The Church, and the Church alone, had the right to 'the exclusive teaching of her children'; she would never delegate this to others, and the Bishop grew unusually oratorical in his description of the Church's Divine commission to teach the truth – she could never give up absolute control of the religious teaching in her schools.[5] It is interesting that in all this he made no appeal to the parents' right to have their children educated in the type of school they wanted.

If most Victorians came to support the provision of schools in which the children of the lower classes should be taught the 'three Rs', there can be no doubt that for the clergy the chief R had to be Religion. Some, indeed, were dubious about the other supposed benefits of education and there is in some of Bishop Goss's writings what can only be called praise of 'Holy Ignorance' – he wrote, for example, that ignorance was a 'great preservative of innocence' and 'the safeguard of virtue'. Education in itself did not make people better: it might just make them cleverer villains, and sin was not the result of ignorance but of a lack of moral restraint, found as often in the educated as in the uneducated. Moreover, the inventions and discoveries of the age, whether it was travelling by steam or conversing by electricity, did not improve a man's moral sense nor 'throw light and peace into the dark and troubled conscience'. The ability to read brought with it a craving for news; the press and books served only to introduce the young to fashionable vice, and he was sure it would be better to remain ignorant than to expose one's virtue to shipwreck. The 'quiet old times' had gone, however, when Catholics had been content because they had been forced to be so; he believed that the effect of education on the children of the poor was not always beneficial and it often seemed to make them 'both saucy and indifferent'.[6]

In this depressing context it is interesting to read some of the replies to the questions sent out by the 1886 Royal Commission on the Education Acts. Bishop O'Reilly wanted uniformity in the answers from clerical managers of the Catholic schools so that nothing would be 'given away' when they were compared with the

Board Schools; the principles behind the model answers were overwhelmingly approved by the clergy. When the Commission asked about the value of what it called the higher educational requirements, the suggested answer was that these were wasted on the majority of the children in Catholic schools and made them unfit for manual employment; by giving the children tastes that could not be gratified it made them discontented with 'what must be their natural position in later life'. With regard to the teaching of particular subjects, the model answers suggested that the standard of arithmetic should be lowered, especially for girls and 'half-timers' (those aged eight to thirteen who worked half-time in the mills and factories), while if the equivalent of domestic science were introduced (which was considered quite undesirable), then the instruction given should be no more than would fit them to cook for the working-man's family. Overall, in a statement that has a modern ring to it, 'constant changes' were said to be injurious to education.[7]

1870 – EDUCATION FOR ALL

Despite these official doubts about some of the supposed value of education for the lower classes, pre-1870 Catholics had done great work in building schools and there were places available in Liverpool for about 14,000 of the estimated 20,000 children between five and twelve years of age, although only an average of 6,200 actually attended. In Preston, too, the problem was non-attendance, with the mills proving to be a more attractive option to poorer families. The Elementary Education Act of 1870, the first step towards a national system of elementary education for all, showed what Catholics would have to do if they were to compete and prevent their children from being drawn into a largely secular system. A detailed return to the Government in November 1870 gives some interesting data for Liverpool and its immediate neighbourhood:[8]

(the table shows the entries for a selection of parishes; the percentages in the final column are for the average daily attendance as a percentage of the number on roll)

Mission	Children between 5 & 12	Children on Roll	Existing places	Places needed	Average daily att.
St Michael's	461	nil	nil	461	nil
Mount Carmel	600	338	300	300	231 (68%)
St Joseph's	2,480	1,091	945	1,535	626 (57%)
St Anthony's	3,161	1,473	1,028	2,133	1,176 (80%)
St Augustine's	1,200	1,208	1,500	—	748 (62%)
Eldon Street	1,599	1,216	991	608	763 (63%)
Old Swan	542	415	605	—	260 (63%)
Formby	233	90	170	53	60 (66%)
Aigburth	170	97	219	—	69 (71%)
Gillmoss	70	72	200	—	60 (83%)

To plan for the required extra funding, Bishop Goss called a meeting in the Theatre Royal, Liverpool. It was an outstanding occasion, attended by Archbishop Errington and Archbishop Kenrick of Baltimore, the Duke of Norfolk, the Marquis of Bute, Lord Howard of Glossop, Baron Vasconcellas, Sir Piers Mostyn and representatives of most of the Lancashire gentry families. The meeting decided to set up a National Fund, to which the Duke of Norfolk and the Marquis of Bute each pledged £10,000 and Lord Howard £5,000, with seven other pledges of £1,000 each. At the same time, a Liverpool Crisis Fund was set up to meet the local demands.[9]

By 1877 additional accommodation for more than 10,000 children had been provided in the inner-city areas and in Bootle, Huyton and Waterloo; accommodation for a further 10,000 or so children had been provided in other parts of the diocese. The total cost had been a staggering £109,560, met by £5,400 from the Liverpool Crisis Fund, £12,100 from the London (or central) Crisis Fund, and the Committee of Council grants of approximately £10,000 (government grants were given on a per capita basis to schools that had been approved by HMI; no public money was available for building, repairs or maintenance, or teachers' salaries). The balance of about £82,000 had come from, or been promised by, 'private benevolence, the charity of the Faithful which never fails, (and) the labours of God's Priests that are never wearied'. The Report continued that visitors to the schools would see children whom they had previously seen 'loitering in the gutter' now gathered in a 'happy home under affectionate care and (especially) under the guardianship of Religion'; those who were ragged and shoeless were beginning to gain self-respect and were thinking it was 'high time to abandon a life of idleness and wandering', and benefactors would be consoled to know that the children whom God loved were being shielded from danger and that some of them might eventually take 'high place and position' in society.[10] Leaving the emotional rhetoric aside, the provision of so many additional places in so short a time was the result of tremendous effort by the Catholic community, an effort it was pledged to continue with the consequent heavy burdens of debt. It should be mentioned here that despite all the extra provision, Bishop O'Reilly had to report to Rome in 1887 that a major problem for the diocese was the large number of Catholic children attending the Board Schools.

Among the schools helped by the Liverpool Crisis Fund were the two Bishop Goss Memorial Schools. Bishop O'Reilly's choice of schools as a memorial to his predecessor was apt, if a little ironic given some of Goss's views on education. They were attached to the parish of St Joseph in Liverpool. The land cost £4,000 and the buildings £6,000. The subscription list was headed by Lady Stapleton Bretherton with £500, and there were six other subscribers of £100 each. The schools were opened in April 1877, with the boys under the care of the De La Salle Brothers (also known as the Brothers of the Christian Schools) and the girls under the Sisters of Notre Dame. Both schools

One of the Bishop Goss
Memorial Schools opened
in 1877 and still
flourishing in the 1950s.

prospered; by 1883 they had 1026 on their combined rolls, although the average attendance over twelve months was only 756 (or 74%).[11]

Some Protestant bodies made strong protests after 1870 against Catholic schools receiving any public money by way of government grants. As part of its campaign, the extremist Protestant Alliance demanded close monitoring of Catholic Schools to ensure that religious teaching was kept quite separate from secular teaching; they argued that only if religious teaching and any related rites or prayers took place at pre-agreed times of the school day (the beginning and/or the end) could parents know when it was happening and so be able to withdraw their children, as the 1870 Act allowed. This ran counter to the Catholic ideal that religion was not just to be taught like another subject but should permeate the whole school and become part of its atmosphere. The Alliance also raised the issue of statues, religious pictures and even altars in classrooms and elsewhere in the schools – according to a strict interpretation of the Act these should not be in evidence during 'secular' periods. To try to find out what did go on in Catholic schools, and how they compared with other schools in similar social areas, the Education Department commissioned special reports from HMI (including Matthew Arnold).[12]

Among other things, they reported that Preston had probably the best Catholic schools of anywhere in the country, while in Liverpool the boys' schools seemed below the average for the area, although no worse than those run by other denominations dealing with the same class of pupil. Discipline was acceptable in these schools but 'order and organisation' less so, and the pupil-teachers were not satisfactory. In general, boys' schools were less good than the corresponding girls' schools. Nuns got mixed reports as teachers: some were too gentle, some not quite up to standard in teaching secular subjects, although the Notre Dame nuns and the teachers they trained were generally praised. The inspectors found that the managers and the teachers in Catholic schools in Preston and Liverpool were keen to improve and to make the post-1870 system work. With regard to the 'religious atmosphere' in Catholic schools, one of the inspectors made the interesting point that only those fired by religious zeal would take on the very difficult task of educating the type of child ('chiefly noisy, unwashed, young Hibernians') to be found in Catholic schools in the large manufacturing towns, and since almost all of them had Catholic parents, there was not likely to be any objections to the Catholic influence in the schools.

THE ROLE OF THE RELIGIOUS ORDERS

Members of Religious Orders, male and female, made a vital contribution to the development of the Catholic school system. They tended to work more in the larger towns, where a single Community could serve a number of different schools. They ran parochial schools and fee-paying secondary schools and some of the Congregations were in the van of developing teaching methods and educational theory – the *Book of Studies* (1863) used by the Sisters of the Holy Child Jesus (the SHCJ) was the work of their foundress, Cornelia Connelly, who approached education with a 'mind fresh and unfettered by the bonds of established attitudes and customs'. The Sisters of Notre Dame of Namur (the SNDs) were also pioneers: in 1856 they opened Mount Pleasant Training College for girls in Liverpool, under the gifted Sister Mary of St Philip Lescher. It was the only training college for Catholic girls in the country until 1874 and grew rapidly in size and reputation. By the 1890s the convent in Mount Pleasant had over sixty Sisters, 110 student teachers, sixty resident pupil teachers, nearly 200 day pupils and 300 pupils in the 'demonstration' school, and was having a decided impact on Catholic teaching throughout the country and in Scotland. Both sets of Sisters were especially important in developing the education of girls at a time when most still regarded it as something not to be encouraged.[13]

One of the first Congregations to pioneer the education of the Catholic poor had been the Irish Christian Brothers, who had opened their first school in England in Preston in 1825 and in 1837 took over St Patrick's school in Liverpool. In 1843 Fr Parker of St Vincent's, Liverpool, rented a Penny Theatre in Blundell Street and the Brothers used it as a school during the week while Fr Parker used it as a Mass centre on Sundays. They opened three more schools in 1844 and another in 1845, by which time they estimated they had nearly 1700 boys attending their schools in the town. It is interesting that they also opened Night Schools for adults from 1842 onwards in an attempt to prevent adults from giving up their Faith.[14]

It is worth looking at their organisation in Preston between about 1850 and 1875. They ran the school attached to St Augustine's – in fact, it was three separate schools, because it consisted of a poor school for full-time pupils, a 'lower school' for the 'half-timers' and a more 'select' school for full-time pupils who paid 6d a week.[15] There was a Christian Brother in charge of each of these schools or departments and the teaching depended on the use of a monitorial system, a system that had generally been discarded in other schools as inefficient because it relied on untrained pupils to pass on to their fellows what they had learned from the master.

The Brothers refused to accept any government inspection or grants, lest they lose full control over their schools. These principles brought them into conflict with school managers who looked to the grants system (with its attendant inspections) to help with the heavy cost of providing the schools – this was the main reason why the Brothers were asked to give up St Peter's schools in Liverpool in 1864. It should be said that the Brothers inspected their own schools very thoroughly, but gradually lost touch with what was happening elsewhere. A government inspector of 1870, after seeing St Nicholas' and St Patrick's, Liverpool, described their monitorial system as 'very bad', 'obviously unsatisfactory' and 'defective', with too many inherent defects to be acceptable. By 1870, only six schools run by the Brothers remained in England; they left Preston in 1875 and relations between the Brothers and the local clergy became so unpleasant that Bishop O'Reilly in the end asked the Brothers to leave Liverpool altogether in 1878.[16] They had done a marvellous job in providing an elementary education for the poorest Catholics, and their dedication and hard work still won praise, but Catholic schools needed government inspection and grants if they were to compete with the new Board Schools and, furthermore, there was now a steady supply of Catholic lay teachers. The Brothers returned to Liverpool in the early 1900s, but to do an altogether different job (see below, page 165).

By the mid-1850s Liverpool had three communities of Sisters working in elementary schools. The first of these, the Faithful Companions of Jesus (FCJs), had started a small boarding school for girls in Great George Square in 1844 and also ran the girls' section of St Patrick's parish school; by 1857 they had 600 in the day school, sixty in the evening classes for women and 700 in the Sunday schools. The second Congregation, the Sisters of Mercy, had set up a convent in Mount Vernon in 1842 and taught in the schools attached to St Joseph's, St Oswald's, St Francis Xavier's and Holy Cross. Thirdly, the SNDs had arrived in 1851 at the invitation of Mgr Nugent and opened a convent in Islington Flags, from where they taught in the schools attached to St Nicholas's, St Peter's, St Anne's, St Mary's and St Anthony's. Their next foundation in the diocese was in Wigan, in 1854, where the Jesuits of St John's and 'an enthusiastic crowd' welcomed them; they worked in the poor schools attached to the parish. Four years later they opened a house in St Helens, again at the request of the Jesuits. Other SND foundations in the diocese were at Birkdale (1868) and Everton Valley, Liverpool (1869).[17]

Another Congregation prominent in running schools were the Religious of the Sacred Heart of Mary (RSHM). A French Congregation, they opened their first house in Marsh Lane, Bootle in 1872, at the request of the local dean, Fr Thomas Kelly. Eventually they were to work in nine parochial schools, run evening classes for adults and an industrial school. In 1884 they took over Seafield House, a huge hydro hotel on the river front at Seaforth, where they had a secondary day and boarding school for girls and a training centre for pupil teachers. The Mersey Docks and Harbour Board bought Seafield for dock expansion and the Sisters moved their convent and grammar school to Crosby, keeping the name 'Seafield' – a highly successful grammar school that had over 250 pupils by 1911.[18]

An early report from an HMI highlighted what was special about these schools run by Religious:

> the intellectual work they accomplish, however valuable and effective, is
> uniformly accompanied by a more precious moral and religious triumph
> of which they alone seem to possess the secret.[19]

By 1905 Religious Congregations ran 64 elementary schools across the Diocese, from Liverpool to Barrow-in-Furness.

This left the majority of parish schools in lay hands – and, of course, there were lay assistants in the Sisters' schools as well. The thirty or forty years after the 1870 Act witnessed a massive increase in the demand for trained teachers and provided for thousands of Catholic young men and women a satisfying, if extremely demanding, career – Mount Pleasant alone had trained over 1300 by 1897. Intending teachers were told that they would stand between the priest and the parents and, like them, would derive their authority from God.[20] Their dedication, sense of vocation and willingness to work for poor salaries in often over-crowded conditions were key elements in building up the Catholic school system just as much as the work of the Religious Congregations. In many ways they became part of the parish, teaching for years in the one school (it is not difficult to find service records of anything from thirty-five to forty-five years), getting to know the great majority of children in the parish, well known to parents and even grandparents whom they had taught, and accompanying children to church on Sundays for the children's Mass in the morning and Sunday school in the afternoon. They earned less than their counterparts in the Board Schools and often less than skilled manual workers – in Bootle in the 1890s, bricklayers could earn £100 a year while experienced assistant teachers were fortunate to earn £50 – £70.[21]

We can see something of what post-1870 schooling was like from snippets in the school log-books and diaries. The schools had an important social role – indeed, to judge from some reports, this was as important as their educational work. In Mount Carmel school in 1881 poor children

*The Religious of the Sacred
Heart of Mary opened their
first school in England in
1872, at Marsh Lane, Bootle.
This very early photo shows
pupils and teachers there.
(RSHM Archive)*

received soup and bread every day and the clergy contributed money to buy clothes and clogs for the poorest. In St Alexander's, Bootle, where over 80% of Catholic parents were labouring poor or casual workers, the children regularly received second-hand clothing and clogs, and free-dinners were available in the severest winters.[22] The new school of St Charles's, Aigburth, under the FCJs, opened in 1896 with accommodation for 150 pupils in just two rooms, one for the infants, the other for all the children aged 7 to 11 – sick children sat near the fire, the only heating available. St John's School, Burscough, was extended in the 1880s to three rooms, with 100 pupils in one, 21 in another and 44 in the infants' room; there was a Headmistress (on £60 a year) and one assistant teacher (on £30). At St Joseph's, Wrightington, one teacher looked after 88 pupils, though her task was made easier by a good deal of absenteeism as many girls were part-timers and worked in the local basket industry. At St Lewis's, Croft, where most of the Catholics worked as silk-weavers, farm workers and labourers, absenteeism was also common, along with ill-discipline: a mistress complained in 1884 of great irregularity in keeping school hours, 'most imperfect discipline' and three or four boys who were noisy, disobedient and the cause of a great deal of trouble to the teachers. Lack of discipline was also a problem at St Austin's, Grassendale, where Fr Burge rejoiced when the Headmistress resigned – she could, apparently, handle HMIs very well but not young boys![23]

These problems were not in the least confined to Catholic schools at the time and it is a wonder that teachers did as well as they did with large classes of mixed ages. Absenteeism may have kept the over-crowding down but it brought its own problems. In both rural areas and towns it needed several years before many parents were convinced of the value of regular attendance by their children. It is not clear whether higher rates of attendance when they came towards the end of the century were the result of a change of heart or better policing by School Attendance Officers. The average attendance in Bootle in 1881 was only 65%, with St Alexander's at about 67% and St James' about 60% – interestingly, it was St Alexander's that served a somewhat less deprived area of the borough. Both schools had average rates of about 82% by the end of the century.[24]

EDUCATION AND POLITICS

The elected School Boards that resulted from the 1870 Act created a new arena for political activity and participation, of more meaning for many people than parliamentary elections, and helped to bring about a change in Liverpool's old alliances. Traditionally, Catholics in Liverpool had supported Liberals because they would not support Tory/Orange interests; the other strong supporters of the Liberals were the Non-conformists. As the latter were supporters of non-denominational schools after 1870 and supporters of the non-denominational religion taught in the new Board Schools, their alliance with the Catholics weakened, and there seemed to be more political sense in Catholics allying with Anglicans, who supported denominational schools. But how could Liverpool Catholics support Anglicans who were so strongly linked to anti-Catholicism, and who opposed any moves towards Home Rule for Ireland? The arrival of the Irish Nationalist Party eventually provided a way out of this dilemma, but in the immediate aftermath of the Act two issues proved particularly contentious and problematic for those trying to read the political runes.

The first concerned the version of the Bible to be used in the new Board Schools: the Liverpool Board laid down that it should be the King James Authorised version, but Catholics asked that their children who were attending the Board Schools should be issued with the Douai version. Secondly, the Act allowed local Boards to pay the fees of poor children attending denominational schools out of public funds. Both issues were red rags to Liverpool's Orange bulls. In 1871, J.J. Stitt, a Liberal Non-conformist who opposed both the payment of fees to Catholic children and the provision of Douai bibles, was defeated in Exchange ward after appealing to the Catholics of Holy Cross parish for their traditional support – they elected a Tory instead. In the next School Board election, Bishop Goss urged Catholics to vote for the Anglican Tory candidate against a Liberal Non-conformist (Irish Presbyterian); the latter was successful overall, but the Tory polled well in strongly Catholic wards – the traditional loyalties could no longer be trusted.[25]

A battle slogan to be heard incessantly down the years whenever new legislation or a change in educational policy was mooted by a government, was that Catholics faced an imminent crisis. While the initial demands of 1870 were met, it was clear that the financial drain would be a continuing and increasing burden. For this reason, Bishop O'Reilly urged Catholic voters (increased in numbers since the electoral reforms of 1884) to get a clear commitment from all parliamentary candidates that they would support putting denominational schools on the same footing as the Board Schools and would vote for a Royal Commission to enquire into the working of the 1870 Education Act. Catholics, he argued, should vote for those candidates who gave clear assurances on these issues, even if it meant voting against the party they had traditionally supported – an open plea that Catholics should give up their traditional support for the Liberals if necessary to save the schools, since the Tories were more in favour of denominational schools; his 'conscience above party' became another useful slogan. One Catholic Councillor in Liverpool referred rather confusedly to the Liberal minister, Joseph Chamberlain, as 'that socialist, confiscator, leveller and Oliver Cromwell of the present day'.[26]

It was just as important to organise the Catholic vote for local School Board elections and the Bishop wrote to the clergy in 1885 to ensure that Catholics divided their votes evenly to get all their favoured candidates elected – in the previous elections all had been returned at the head of the poll by large majorities. The only enemy, according to the Bishop, was apathy – 'all must work, each one must do his duty by recording his vote' (sic); at least 12,000 Catholic voters would be required. The clergy should tell their people who the Catholic candidates were.[27] In the event all six candidates were returned, though on a reduced Catholic turn-out.

In the 1890s it became clear that some central diocesan organisation was necessary to represent Catholic schools and their needs at a local and a national level. A Liverpool Conference of Catholic School Managers was set up in 1895, followed by Catholic School Managers' Associations in Liverpool, Preston, Wigan, St Helens and other autonomous boroughs in 1904, and a County Association to cover the remaining areas the following year. The value of these Associations lay in their success in interpreting national legislation to suit local Catholic needs – the Liverpool Association could claim in 1905 that they had succeeded in getting the city's Education Committee to recognise holydays of obligation and that the Committee had no right to vet the training in Catholic training colleges. They had also fixed set times for religious instruction in their schools – from 9 to 9.45 in the morning and from 1.30 to 2 o'clock in the afternoon and had decided that they could take children to church during those times as appropriate, until the Committee could prove such action illegal. Finally they had federated with Catholic Associations in other dioceses to strengthen their position nationally and learn from 'best practice' elsewhere.

None of this was particularly striking, but the Associations provided a new opportunity for clergy and laymen to work together and gained recognition as legitimate negotiating bodies both locally and nationally. These had hardly been established when the hierarchy decided that a single national body was required – The Catholic Education Council (1905 – 1991)

– with each diocese having a single Diocesan Education Committee. These diocesan committees probably carried more clout when dealing with secular authorities, but their creation involved a certain loss of local involvement in areas outside Liverpool.[28]

The 1902 Education Act allowed Catholic schools to receive aid from Local Education Authorities – the subsequent 'Rome on the Rates' controversy ignited sectarian fires even in areas where relations between Catholics and Protestants had been relatively peaceful. In Wigan, for example, Non-conformists became very agitated about an application to build a new school in the rapidly developing St Andrew ward. This had seen a rapid expansion in its population so that by 1901 it had a population of over 9,000 but still only one school, that belonging to St Andrew's Church of England parish. Local Non-conformists lodged an appeal against the application as part of their campaign against the provisions of the 1902 Act – their agitation had already led to about fifty summonses against local Non-conformists for conscientious non-payment of the education rates. The Local Education Committee, however, decided that a new Catholic school with 450 places was justified and appealed to the national Board of Education. The Board replied that in the light of the opposition, it might be preferable to build a Catholic school for 200 younger children only, while the older children could attend one of the five existing Catholic schools in the town. In the end, the school was to be limited to 200, but children of any age might attend. The school opened in 1906 and soon had 173 pupils on its roll. The Non-conformist opposition had failed to stop the building of an all-age school but had succeeded in reducing its future usefulness to the Catholic community. Twenty years later an extension for an additional 160 children had to be built, this time without any local opposition.[29]

SECONDARY EDUCATION

The 1902 Act also gave a boost to secondary education in that it obliged the Local Education Authorities to give tuition grants to approved secondary schools and colleges (although in the case of denominational or 'non-provided' schools, there was still nothing available for building or alterations or maintenance). After 1907 a scholarship scheme obliged all grant-aided secondary schools to take in 'free-place scholars' who passed a qualifying examination and who had spent two years or more at a public elementary school; each secondary school had to reserve at least 25% of its places for such pupils. The result was a large increase in the number of elementary children going on to secondary schools and staying on until they were sixteen or, more rarely, eighteen, and an overall increase in the provision of secondary or grammar schools. The diocese already had a number of such schools – seven for girls and five for boys (although the Jesuit college in Leigh was to close two years later). All of these schools were run by members of Religious Orders and were the property of the Orders, not of the diocese. It is worth looking at a few of these schools in greater detail.

In Preston, there was Winckley Square convent school for girls. As long ago as 1853 Fr Henry Walmsley, SJ, had negotiated with Mother Cornelia Connelly to have the Sisters of the Holy Child Jesus (SHCJ) teach in the town's schools. They opened convents in St Wilfrid's, St Ignatius' and St Walburge's parishes, ran the parish schools and took over the Select School for Girls, also in St Wilfrid's. By 1876 there were 26 SHCJ Sisters in the town, with an amalgamated convent in Winckley Square, where the Select School had also relocated. This school had a Pupil Teacher Centre attached to it and by the early years of the twentieth century had 105 girls on its roll and 66 pupil teachers. By 1909 it was recognised officially as a Secondary School and its numbers and reputation grew rapidly after that. Elsewhere in the town, in 1860 a lay committee had bought Lark Hill mansion and given it to St Augustine's parish to use for its schools. The FCJ Sisters ran these and a small fee-paying boarding and day school for girls – when proposing to open the latter the Sisters said it would offer 'no accomplishments, but such knowledge as would make farmers' and tradesmen's daughters useful in their people and place' and lead some to become pupil teachers. The first few years were very difficult because of the effects of the 'cotton famine' in Lancashire – the Sisters could collect no fees and worked as much as social workers as teachers, but eventually Lark Hill became a successful grammar school.[30]

For their part, the Jesuits founded a Catholic Grammar School or College for boys in Winckley Square in 1865. The initial aim was to counteract the effects of the successful Protestant Grammar School that was attracting the sons of Catholic parents. Whatever the value of the education they received there, it was claimed, 'the poison of heresy' was being instilled and they had to listen to the 'calumny and ridicule' heaped on the Church by their teachers. Various attempts had already been made in the town to set up a school for the sons of better-off Catholic parents, though many even of these had difficulties in paying the fees. The Xaverian Brothers had opened a Higher Grade Boys' School (in reality, a higher grade elementary school) in St Ignatius' parish in 1861, offering a sound commercial education and charging only low fees. The new College found it difficult to compete: numbers rose for a time but then fell back to a mere twenty-four in the early 1880s as Preston parents seemed to prefer the practical education offered by the Brothers. Only when the Jesuits engineered the take-over of the Higher Grade School in 1899 did the College begin to prosper.[31]

In Liverpool, St Francis Xavier's College for boys, owned and staffed by Jesuits, opened in October 1842. It was England's first Catholic Day Secondary School, described in the language of the time as a Preparatory, Classical and Commercial school, situated in Soho Street. The advertisement in *The Liverpool Mercury* announced that the first care of the staff would be the religious and moral instruction of the pupils, who would also be taught the range of subjects normally taught in such schools, and, when parents desired it, French, Latin and Greek at no extra charge (*sic*). It opened with only two pupils and two months later still had only three; when it moved to Salisbury Street (its home for the next 135 years) in 1846 it had twenty-four on its roll. Also in 1842, Bishop Brown decided to establish a boarding school for boys – St Edward's opened in January 1843 with just one pupil! (see pages 230-3). In 1853 Fr Nugent and Fr Worthy founded the third Liverpool secondary school, the Catholic Institute in Hope Street, to be run by the Secular clergy – a more direct rival to St Francis Xavier's as it also had preparatory, classical and commercial sections.[32]

What do these foundations tell us of the Catholic body and its attitudes to secondary education? To judge from the numbers on roll in the schools (see the figures below), there was no great demand for secondary education in the early years; what interested lower middle-class parents wanted was a good enough commercial education to fit their boys for a white-collar job. Boys often only spent two or three years in the schools and could then get employment; why pay for more years? Why, indeed, go to a secondary school at all, when 'higher grade' elementary schools were offering commercial training at a lower cost? From the clerical authorities' point of view, of course, the provision of Catholic secondary schools would keep boys out of the parallel Protestant schools, and they also hoped that there would be a steady flow of vocations – certainly a motive behind the Religious Orders who set up such schools. When Mgr Nugent set up the Catholic Institute he had a grand and inspiring vision of the school becoming a centre for Catholic culture, but most Catholics were not yet ready for such forward-looking ideas and ideals. To judge from the serious lack of support on the part of bishops and priests for the Institute, neither were most of the clergy.[33]

At Bishop Whiteside's invitation the Irish Christian Brothers returned to Liverpool and took over the pupil-teacher training centre in Great Mersey Street in 1900. The Brothers then decided that the training would be more efficiently carried out if the Centre could be attached to a small secondary school, as the Notre Dame Sisters were doing already in Mount Pleasant and Everton Valley. The Bishop suggested that the Brothers might like to take over the ailing Catholic Institute and so the pupil teachers moved to Hope Street in April 1902 and the Catholic Institute opened under its new management on 1st September 1902, now with a mere 27 boys.

Whereas the 1890s had been a bad time for Liverpool secondary schools, with both Catholic and Protestant schools losing substantial numbers, the 1902 Education Act was a sign that the atmosphere was changing. The Brothers were determined to make the most of the new climate and by early 1904 numbers at the Institute had risen to 113 and the buildings had been improved and extended. After the first major government inspection of the school in 1905 it was recognised as a 'Class A' school by the Board of Education; shortly afterwards the title of this type of school was changed to Recognised Secondary School.[34]

These early Inspectors' Reports on secondary schools are interesting because they give us some idea of the social background of the boys' fathers and other details and therefore some idea of the make-up of the Catholic body that felt a need for this sort of education. There are difficulties in comparing the lists because of differences in how occupations were named, but they give a reliable impression.

The Catholic Institute: 1905, 201 on roll:

Occupations of fathers

professional and Independent	16
merchants, bankers, etc	24
retail traders	35
farmers	1
clerks, etc.	75
elementary teachers	2
artisans	25
not stated	23

residence:	Liverpool	150
	Rest of Lancs	35
	Cheshire	16

St Francis Xavier's: 1904, 311 on roll:

Occupations of fathers:

professional & independent:	49
merchants, manufacturers, etc.	36
retail traders	97
farmers	4
commercial managers etc.	94
elementary teachers	1
artisans and labourers	30

residence:	Liverpool	244
	Rest of Lancs	45
	Cheshire	22

Preston Catholic College: 1904, 126 on roll:

Occupations of fathers:

retail traders	41
commercial managers, etc	23
merchants & manufacturers	18
professional & independent	11
artisans and labourers	15

residence:	Preston	109
	Rest of Lancs	17

Age-range in each school:

	under-10	10	11	12	13	14	15	16	17	18
SFX	22	18	35	52	54	62	46	14	7	1
CI	18	24	26	36	32	44	18	3	0	0
Preston	8	13	16	29	36	13	8	3	0	0

The two Liverpool schools flourished after 1902; indeed the increase in numbers was striking: by 1910-11 the Catholic Institute had 390 boys on roll, St Francis Xavier's 380. Preston Catholic College had about 130, but suffered from the large number of boys who left early – 40% of the boys at the college were under 12 and only ten boys were over 16. All three schools received good reports from the Inspectors and from local observers – one example of this came in 1907 when the Catholic Institute could report what the local *Daily Post* headlined as 'A Chapter of Success'. Not only was the school now recognized by the Board of Education, all the local councils recognized it as a school where their scholarships could be held. Moreover, the success of the pupils in gaining scholarships to Liverpool University was, according to the paper, 'most remarkable'.[35]

The later development of secondary education for boys down to 1944 may be summarised here. Fr Martin, SJ, spent the last years of his life in Leigh, where he founded a Jesuit secondary school about 1900. It soon had 100 boys on its roll but unfortunately this success did not last and it closed in 1907. The Irish Christian Brothers opened St Mary's, Crosby, in 1919. St

The Catholic Institute in Hope Street, Liverpool. The original building was the two-storey block with the arched doorway; the third storey was added in 1902 to house the Christian Brothers; the wings were later additions.

Martin's, Bootle, run by the Xaverian Brothers, opened in 1932 (it had been a central School run by the Irish Christian Brothers) but closed in 1947 (it may have stopped taking in pupils by 1942). The Vincentians opened a small secondary school in the south end of the city in Belvidere Road in 1932, in what had been Archbishop's House. The school took in boys between eight and fourteen years of age and had about forty on roll. The priests, however, lived out in Gateacre Grange, the Order's house of studies for their own senior students, and to avoid the travelling in and out to the school they moved the boys out to Gateacre as well. Although numbers rose to about seventy and the school became more popular with 'the better class Catholics of Liverpool', it could not compete with St Francis Xavier's or St Edward's and closed in 1939. The Vincentians withdrew altogether from the archdiocese, selling the Grange to the Sisters of Charity. By 1940 there was a Catholic Grammar School for boys at West Park, St Helens, run by the De La Salle Brothers, with about 300 pupils, but nothing between that and the Catholic College in Preston or Thornleigh Salesian College in Bolton (both outside the archdiocese) for boys to attend.[36]

Girls fared better, though some of the schools were surprisingly small:

		pupils
Liverpool	Bellerive (FCJ)	200
	Broughton Hall (Sisters of Mercy)	320
	Everton Valley (SND)	445
	La Sagesse High School (D of Wisdom)	156
	Mount Pleasant (SND)	443
	St Anthony's High School (Sisters of Mercy)	45
	St Vincent's Convent School (Sisters of Mercy)	40
Blundellsands	Overdale House (Ursulines)	65
Crosby	Seafield (Sisters of the Sacred Heart of Mary)	380
Penketh	St Joseph's High School (Sisters of Charity of St Paul)	40
Rainhill	St Mary's High School (Sisters of Charity of St Paul)	33
St Helens	Notre Dame High School (SND)	278
Southport	Notre Dame High School (SND)	129
Wigan	High School (SND)	304
Douglas, IOM	Convent School (Sisters of Mercy)	36

Two other convent schools, one at Layton Hill, Blackpool (SHCJ), and one at Lark Hill, Preston (FCJ), had been in the archdiocese when founded.[37]

MORE POLITICS: 1906 – 1944

Archbishop Whiteside coped with the continued expansion and its costs. By 1905 the Diocesan Education Committee had responsibility for:

177 Elementary Schools

7 Pupil Teachers' Centres (in Liverpool, Preston, St Helens and Wigan)

5 Boys' Secondary Schools or Colleges (in Liverpool, Preston, Leigh and St Helens)

7 Girls' Secondary Schools or Colleges (in Liverpool, St Helens, Preston and Wigan)

The Liberal landslide victory in 1906 brought a serious threat to this carefully constructed system. The Non-conformists (returned to Parliament in large numbers) saw an opportunity to overturn the 1902 Act. The Education Bill of 1906 would have meant the end of the Catholic elementary provision that had been so painfully built up since 1870.[38] Catholic agitation against the bill started in Liverpool, with Whiteside giving the lead. He addressed a mass meeting in St George's Hall in March – a meeting, according to contemporaries, such as had never been seen in Liverpool before: up to 60,000 people were said to have failed to get into the hall and to have been addressed by other speakers while the Archbishop spoke to those inside. He prophesied that if non-denominational schools became the norm:

> *it will mean for Christian England the handwriting on the wall ... one Church will be left to bear witness to Christ's revelation ... the undying Catholic Church, and with her will remain her Catholic schools, Catholic in name, Catholic in reality.*[39]

Catholic reaction to the threat led to a number of mammoth rallies and demonstrations throughout Lancashire. To take just one example: in Preston over 10,000 attended a demonstration in the Public Hall, with a large overflow outside. A Parental League was set up and another demonstration organised for a Sunday afternoon in May. The clergy led their parish groups, complete with banners, to the market where platforms had been erected for each group. Hymns were sung and the national anthem; as someone who had been there later put it, 'It proved that Catholic Spirit had been stirred to its very depths and that full account must be taken of it'.[40] Whether Catholics had as much political clout as they imagined is open to some considerable doubt, but at least they left candidates and MPs no room to question their commitment to the cause, and Whiteside was seen nationally as the foremost opponent of the Liberal government on educational questions. Birrell called him 'the mildest man who ever slit a throat', though he was probably unmoved by the Bishop's threat to lead a new Pilgrimage of Grace made up of northern Catholics.[41] In the end the government withdrew the Bill because the Lords had altered it so much. When, in 1936,

Archbishop Downey took a less bullish approach over the education bill of that year and urged 'restraint in agitation', Bishop Amigo of Southwark lamented, 'I wish we had a Whiteside in Liverpool' – though Downey was later to prove as stout a defender of the cause as anyone.[42]

We can get an insight into Archbishop Downey's (1928-53) ideas on education from a speech he made in 1932. The occasion was the opening of St Martin's College, Bootle, run by the Xaverian Brothers. It is an interesting speech in that it was not devoted to particularly Catholic issues. He first of all attacked the amount of money being spent not on education itself but on the 'appurtenances of education' – palatial council schools with a million surplus places – and for what? Despite general education since 1870, there had been a clear decline in popular culture – he spoke of the 'vulgarians of the sea-side', street hooligans, roadhogs, and those who exhibited rude and boorish behaviour in public places and on trams, buses and trains. These people might have plenty of specific information, he admitted, but they had no culture.[43]

The main cause of the problem, he continued, lay in leaving no scope for developing individualism. Secondary schools, he argued, should offer different pupils different courses of study: there was too much stress on order and uniformity, not enough on freedom and initiative. Turning to elementary education (i.e. the education that most children would receive at that period), he believed that it should be 'really elementary' – just the three Rs and English grammar; the last, unfortunately, was being excluded on the grounds that children imbibed it with their mother's milk. Elementary education, he continued, had to blend in with the ideals of the children's parents: thus the farmer would second the teacher's efforts to teach his child the principles of irrigation, but would be unlikely to bother about 'clay-modelling and drawing'. The modern reader might welcome the stress on 'freedom and initiative' in secondary schools, but wonder how far these attributes were fostered in Catholic schools, or parishes, for that matter, of the period. What strikes a discordant note is the divide between this sort of educational ideal and the deadening functionalism advocated for the majority of children – but was this, perhaps, what most parents wanted? There is substantial evidence that at least skilled working-class parents, and their lower middle-class counterparts, regarded education instrumentally, as the way to improve the chances of their children becoming white-collar workers – the lure of the office stool was strong.[44]

A Social Survey of Merseyside (undertaken by the University of Liverpool in 1934) noted the success of the Catholic efforts to provide schools in Liverpool. It referred to this provision as the 'most conspicuous characteristic of juvenile education in Liverpool and the other Merseyside boroughs'. Throughout England and Wales, the Survey reported, two-thirds of children in elementary and central schools were in local authority schools, while the figure for Liverpool was only a little over a half; again, throughout England and Wales, a quarter of children attended Church of

England schools, while only 17% did so in Liverpool; the corresponding national figure for Catholic schools was only 7%, compared with 30% in Liverpool.[45] No wonder Downey and other Catholic leaders claimed that Catholics were saving local authorities substantial sums of money.

The number of places may have been impressive but the standard of some of the schools, at least those in inner-Liverpool, was far from satisfactory. The Board of Education felt obliged to write to the Archbishop in 1933 to point this out – the main complaint was substantial overcrowding, which was so serious that the Board would have to ask the managers either to exclude children or provide extra places, despite the difficulty of finding suitable sites in congested areas; it hoped slum clearance would deal with the worst of the black-listed schools.[46] Perhaps part of the reason for Downey's complaints about 'palatial Council Schools' lay in the fact that they high-lighted the poor condition of a number of Catholic schools and made it even more difficult for them to compete (although in 1935 thirty-four Liverpool Council schools had been black-listed). It is of some interest that thirty years on Archbishop Heenan was urging Catholic managers to spend money on improving some of the most basic facilities in their schools because the lack of decent lavatories brought real suffering to sensitive children.[47]

The 1936 Education Act empowered local authorities to pay denominational schools between 50% and 75% of the costs involved in upgrading schools and raising the school-leaving age to 15. When Liverpool Catholics asked for the higher figure, the Tory/Protestant controlled Council offered them nothing (the only authority in the country to do so), making the interesting position that the Tories opposed denominational schooling while the Labour group on the Council supported it, despite the latter's traditional support of secular education – Liverpool's politics never fitted easily into the national mould! In the end it took threats from the Board of Education and a special Liverpool Act of Parliament to resolve the issue, by which time the war was too close to do anything about it.[48]

It was not only physical standards that might be lower in some Catholic schools. Downey complained in 1941 that the Catholic elementary schools were failing to get enough children into secondary schools: in the previous year they had received only an 8% success rate in the Scholarship Exams compared with the 13% achieved by non-Catholic schools. Indeed, he continued, some Catholic schools entered no children at all for the scholarship, even though there were plenty of places in Catholic secondary schools. Furthermore, the places available at St Elizabeth's Central School (for those who passed the Scholarship Examination but not well enough to go on to Grammar School) were not being taken up. Clergy should inform parents that maintenance grants and free transport were available for poorer families sending their children to secondary schools.[49]

But Downey's main call to arms and his fiercest campaigning came with the issue of the wartime government's plans for education, leading eventually to the momentous Butler Education Act of 1944. For a short period the Archbishop led the negotiations on behalf of the hierarchy, but his influence was not beneficial. In the end Butler felt he could not altogether trust him as he seemed to say one thing in private and another in public – witness the public campaign of outrage against the government's proposals orchestrated by Downey in Liverpool that same year – and he seemed unwilling to use his authority to keep more militant Catholics in check. Lord FitzAlan Howard, a leading representative of the old English establishment Catholics, told Butler that he also greatly mistrusted the Archbishop.[50] The Act envisaged a national system of primary, secondary modern and secondary grammar and technical schools and the government offered grants to denominational schools that opted for 'aided' rather than 'controlled' status. As a result, Catholics would be able to transfer to the LEA the cost of teachers' salaries, and school maintenance and upkeep costs; in addition, they were eligible for 50% grants towards the repair and reconstruction of schools, and 75% towards the costs of modernisation that fell within the 1936 Act's scheme; Catholic managers would control the appointment of teachers. No grants would be available for new schools, unless these were needed as replacements for existing schools because of population movements brought about by official policies, and then only for the exact number of places in the old school and only at 50% of the building costs. The bishops pushed for 100% grants (completely unrealistically) and for the proposed grants to be extended to new schools.

In 1943, as part of his campaign against the proposed Act, Downey gathered statistics on the financial outlay on education since 1918 by Catholics across the archdiocese. On elementary schools the amount spent had been £490,000, on secondary schools, £200,000, and on Mount Pleasant Training College, £10,000. In addition to this £700,000, the archdiocese had proposed to provide an extra 28,480 places to raise the school-leaving age to 15 in accordance with the 1936 Act – this would have involved spending an additional sum in the region of £350,000. Downey took up the fight for 'justice for our schools' with his usual gusto when it came to public campaigning; a fighting speech of his at a rally in the Liverpool Boxing Stadium in October 1943 got national coverage and was later used as a joint pastoral on the subject by the Hierarchy.[51] Butler, for the government, thought the bishops, and Downey in particular, were not doing enough to moderate the more extreme Catholic campaigners who risked arousing anti-Catholic and anti-voluntary schools feelings, thus jeopardising even the 50% offer. He also believed that the Catholic campaigners were not giving a true picture of what the government was offering and were exaggerating the costs that Catholics would have to meet. The Act passed into law and began a new era in the provision of Catholic schooling.

After the war, when it came to implementing the Act, Downey still spoke in the militant terms of former campaigns. Before the 1950 (February) election he arranged for a day of 'prayer and protest', when a special service of Benediction in all churches and chapels across the archdiocese would be followed in Liverpool by an evening 'monster demonstration', with similar meetings in Chorley, Leigh, St Helens, Southport, Warrington and Wigan. About 25,000 people attended the Liverpool demonstration on a large blitzed site in the city centre, when Downey's main theme was that Catholics were not asking for privileges but only to be treated as other citizens who paid rates and taxes. Again, his speech received national press coverage. The meeting passed a resolution asking the government to pass an amending Bill to allow Catholics to educate their children without penalty.[52]

In October 1951, in order to emphasise Catholic determination 'to fight for justice and to enlighten public opinion', he organised another 'monster' outdoor rally followed by a meeting in the Liverpool Stadium; evening services were to be adjusted to allow people to attend. Estimates of the size of the crowd that gathered outside St George's Hall varied wildly, from 10,000 to nearly 50,000, with over 6,000 attending the Stadium meeting. Catholics from Shrewsbury took part, and the meeting was addressed by the Archbishop, Bishop Murphy of Shrewsbury and Bishop Beck of Salford, who was rapidly becoming the Hierarchy's expert on educational questions. In a typical tongue-in-cheek fashion Downey suggested that politicians should be encouraged to come up with an agreed syllabus in politics to match that in religious teaching – it would eliminate all the differences between the parties and do away with the need for elections, thus saving the country a lot of money. There were parallel meetings and demonstrations in Southport, Warrington, Chorley, Leigh and St Helens.[53] Clearly, education was still the single issue most likely to unite Catholics and keep alive the feeling that they were being treated as second-class citizens.

In February 1952 the Archbishop claimed that in the battle for our schools 'we are as near to open and flagrant persecution as we have ever been', and in that battle it was 'the precious Faith of our children' that was at stake.[54] Such exaggerated language can only have puzzled those in charge of making educational policy and reminded Butler of the negotiations over the 1944 Act. Without doubt, the Archbishop enjoyed the element of showmanship in these demonstrations and the national coverage they attracted; he also believed sincerely in the cause.

The full development of the Catholic School system across the archdiocese after a century of endeavour is evident from some mid-twentieth-century statistics. In 1955 there were:

166 Primary and All-Age Schools in the Archdiocese
 16 Secondary Modern Schools
  6 Secondary Grammar and 8 Direct Grant Grammar Schools
  1 Secondary Technical School
 15 Special Schools
  8 Independent Schools

The Primary and All-Age schools catered for 75,000 pupils, and the various voluntary aided Secondary schools for 9,250; the Direct Grant Grammar Schools had 4,740 on roll and the Independent Schools 1,334; the Special Schools, 1,929. There were still 5,675 Catholic children attending non-Catholic schools, but no analysis is available of the ages of the children or type of non-Catholic school they were attending.[55] Catholic parents who sent their children to non-Catholic schools faced excommunication if they did not have permission from the Bishop to do so. 'A Catholic place for every Catholic child' had finally, to all intents and purposes, been achieved.

With hindsight it may seem that the stress on the provision of places for Catholic children was at the expense of Catholic adult formation – when a pupil left a Catholic school at fourteen or sixteen he or she was expected to have a sound enough foundation in the Faith to last throughout adult life, and only a few bothered or had any opportunity to build on that foundation. Moreover, all the clergy knew that large numbers of Catholic children either had already ceased to practise their Faith in any meaningful way before they left school or did so immediately afterwards. This was not a modern development or the result of the break-up of well-established Catholic communities – neither the schools nor the clergy had ever found it possible to counter the influence of family and social peers in this matter. In some cases, of course, it might have been that very influence that had kept them going to church when there was little or no personal commitment; probably most of those who stopped practising continued to regard themselves as Catholics. Certainly it is difficult to envisage any other system that would have given 'better results' over the century after 1850 than the elaborate one of the Catholic Schools.

Notes

1. Maurice Whitehead, 'A View from the Bridge: The Catholic School', in *Flaminian Gate*, pp.217-44, at pp.218,219.

2. A.C.F. Beales, 'The Struggle for the Schools', in Beck pp.365-409.

3. Whitehead, 'A View', p.220.

4. Hastings, *English Christianity*, pp.421-2.

5. AAL *Liverpolitana 1885-90*, Nov. 1885.

6. AAL Early Bishops, S1 II, B: Pastoral Letters, June 1856, Nov. 1857, Feb. 1865, Sept. 1870; *The Weekly Register*, 5.11.1857.

7. AAL *Liverpolitana 1885-90*, ad clerums 27.9 and 30.10.1886.

8. AAL Early Bishops, S3 I, B/1.

9. Burke, p.191.

10. AAL Early Bishops, S3 I, B/2, 'Crisis Fund Report', Nov. 1877.

11. Burke, pp.219-20; the 1997 *Directory* gives 79 on the roll of the Bishop Goss JMI school.

12. Maurice Whitehead, 'Briefly and in Confidence: Private Views of HMI on English Catholic Elementary Schools, 1875', *RH* vol. 20, no. 4 (Oct. 1991), pp.554-62.

13. W.J. Battersby, 'Educational Work of the Religious Orders of Women: 1850-1950', in Beck, pp.337-64, at p.342; Sr Jennifer Worrall, SND, *Jubilee: Sisters of N.D. de Namur celebrate 150 years in Britain* (1995), pp.34-7.

14. Burke, p.70.

15. W. Gillespie, CFC, *The Christian Brothers in England 1825-1880* (1975), p.188.

16. *Ibid.*, Chapter 8.

17. Burke, pp.72, 76, 104-5; Worrall, *Jubilee*, pp.79-80.

18. SHM Archives, Anglo-Irish Province: *Prospectus* of 1894 and 'RHSM Foundations in Liverpool', with copies of original correspondence, kindly supplied by Sr Máire O'Donnell.

19. Burke, p.105; original italics.

20. B. Aspinwall, 'Catholic Teachers for Scotland: the Liverpool Connection', *The Innes Review* XLV no.1 (Spring 1994), pp.47-70, at p.49.

21. W.E. Marsden, 'Social environment, school attendance and achievement in a Merseyside town 1870-1900', in P. McCann (ed.), *Popular education and socialization in the 19th century* (1977), pp.194-230, at p.197.

22. M.J. Hewlett, *Our Lady of Mount Carmel, Centenary of the Opening* (1978), p.5; for St Alexander's, Marsden, 'Social environment', p.203.

23. M.D. Peters, 'St Charles' Schools', in *St Charles Borromeo*, pp.41-4; Goddard, *St John the Evangelist, Burscough*, pp.47-9; Carus, *St Lewis*, p.10; *St Austin's Log*, p.15.

24. Marsden, p.212.

25. Waller, pp.28-9; Burke, 199-200, 217.

26. AAL *Liverpolitana 1885-90*, Pastoral Letter, Nov. 1885; Waller, p.55.

27. AAL *Liverpolitana 1885-90*, ad clerum 7.11.1885.

28. AAL Early Bishops, S3 I B/6, 9.

29. D. Mallin, 'Rome on the Rates in Wigan: the Founding of the Sacred Heart School,1904-6' *NWCH* V (1978), pp.34-41; *Catholic Times*, 27.1.1927.

30. Warren, p.55; Margaret Burscough, *The History of Lark Hill, Preston, 1797-1989* (1989), pp.37-45.

31. Alban Hindle, *A Centenary History of the Catholic College, Preston* (1971), chs. 1-3.

32. Pat Heery, *The History of St Francis Xavier's College, Liverpool, 1842-2001* (2002); Peter Doyle & Leslie McLoughlin, *The Edwardian Story* (2003).

33. Hindle, p.12; Warren, p.107-9; Doyle & McLoughlin, pp.28-31.

34. Doyle & McLoughlin, pp.35-6.

35. Data from Hindle, Heery, Doyle & McLoughlin, as above. For *Daily Post*, Doyle & McLoughlin, p.38.

36. *Directories*; Doyle & McLoughlin, p.41; Thomas Davitt CM, 'St Vincent's, Gateacre, Liverpool', in '*Colloque', Journal of the Irish Province of the Congregation of the Mission*, no.22, (Autumn 1990), pp.273-95.

37. *Directories*.

38. Beales, 'Struggle', p.386.

39. E.K. Bennett, *Archbishop Whiteside* (CTS 1926), pp.22-4.

40. Smith, 'Turning the Century', pp.24-5; M. Savage, *The Dynamics of Working-Class Politics. The Labour Movement in Preston 1880-1940* (1987), pp.159-60.

41. Plumb, *Arundel to Zabi* (1987); Waller, p.234.

42. Moloney, p.158.

43. *The Tablet*, 10.9.1932.

44. Marsden, p.225; John Davies, 'Rome on the Rates: Archbishop Richard Downey and the Catholic Schools Question, 1929-39', *NWCH*, XVIII (1991), pp.16-32.

45. *The Tablet*, 28.4.1934.

46. AAL Downey, S4 II B/23, 30.6.1933.

47. AAL Heenan, S1 III, Documents, A:Miscellany: ad clerum 1962.

48. Waller, p.340-4.

49. AAL Downey, S1 III, A/3 ad clerums 1940-53: 1.2.1941.

50. John Davies, 'Palliative and Expedients: The 1944 Education Act: Archbishop Downey and the Catholic Response', *NWCH*, XX (1993), pp.47-70.

51. AAL Downey, S1 III, A/3 ad clerums 1940-53: no. VI, 1943; pastoral letter, Lent 1943.

52. *Ibid.*, ad clerum 26.1.1950.

53. Reports in *The Times, The News Chronicle, The Irish Press,* etc., 22.10.1951. AAL Downey S1 III, A/3 ad clerums, Oct. 1951.

54. AAL *Liverpolitana*, Lent pastoral 1952.

55. *Directory*, 1956; AAL Downey Collection, S1 IV A/89.

CHAPTER 9 THE POOR, THE DESTITUTE AND THE DELINQUENT

There was plenty of organised charitable effort among Lancashire Catholics before 1850. A committee of Liverpool lay people had set up a Girls Orphanage in 1816 and launched an annual Charity Ball in 1824 to help support it – a highlight of the town's social scene. The Catholic Benevolent Society had started its unsung operations to counter the worst effects of poverty in 1810 by providing 'active practical benevolence, guided and administered by the Clergy'. Almost a hundred years older was Preston's Catholic Brethren, or First Catholic Charitable Society, founded in 1731 and whose forty members pledged themselves to work 'for the benefit of the poor and to the increase of Christian Morality'. From 1753 the clergy of Lancaster were arranging apprenticeships for Catholic boys, while the Broughton Catholic Charitable Society, formed by a group of small farmers in 1787, assisted widows and orphans. In 1841 a ground-breaking Blind Asylum had been established in Liverpool. In St Helens, the Lowe House Men's Guild of 1847 aimed to increase the holiness of its members and 'to provide assistance during times of sickness and distress'.[1] This chapter will outline how by the end of the century Catholics had moved from this ad hoc provision and created for themselves an astonishing cradle-to-grave welfare system, remarkable in its completeness and for the amount of charitable giving that it involved. But if better-off Catholics (and Protestants) were to support these ventures, then they wanted them run properly, with representation on boards of management, annual reports and full accountability. If this meant the end of spontaneous alms-giving to help one's neighbour in need, so be it – one of the Victorian gods, after all, was efficiency.

At parish level the lead was given by the clergy. In this context, a special report of 1883, commissioned by the City Council and entitled 'Squalid Liverpool', commented that the Catholic priest was 'the parson, the policeman, the doctor, the nurse, the relieving officer, the nuisance inspector, and the school board inspector all in one', the only influence for good reaching the 'depths of squalid poverty' in the town.[2] It is worth noting here that the Catholic Benevolent Society in 1893 was giving 100 priests 10/- a month each to give to the poor in their slum parishes.[3] But the body that the clergy relied on most of all to organise relief at parish level was the St Vincent de Paul Society (the SVP).

NIGHT SHELTER.

THE ST VINCENT DE PAUL SOCIETY

Founded in France in the 1830s by two laymen, Bd Frederick Ozanam and Emanuel Bailly, the Society was ideally structured to 'search out hidden sufferers, heal sorrows that do not cry out, visit the attic where the sick man suffers in silence, penetrate the prisons'.[4] Each parish group was known as a Conference and consisted entirely of lay workers under a clerical chaplain. They were men of their generation; they had no political aim to change the socio-economic status of society and tried to distinguish between the deserving and non-deserving poor in true Victorian fashion. Some examples of their work may be mentioned here. Two Conferences were set up in Preston in 1859. In its first 18 months, that at St Wilfrid's recorded the names of 14 Brothers, who had between them relieved 87 poor people and had made over 1300 visits. They had paid for 80 poor children to attend school, distributed 1645 ounces of tea, 2968 loaves, 66 pairs of clogs and 59 other items of clothing. The members, or Brothers as they called themselves, met weekly, heard reports on the previous week's visits and decided on visits and other duties for the coming week; a secretary kept minutes. For funds they depended entirely on donations, occasional church collections and weekly donations from the Brothers themselves. It was all admirably simple and effective – and long-lasting: by 1936 St Wilfrid's Conference was holding its 3,000th meeting.[5]

The SVP Brothers knew the struggles of those in work and earning as much as 30/- a week who suddenly got sick or injured; they were too respectable to ask for outdoor relief, but their condition was helpless and they formed part of the 'silent, invisible poor', impossible to quantify.[6] There was always a shortage of funds for these voluntary agencies to work with; they had to make decisions between one case and another – for example, the Liverpool Central Council decided it was better to help men with large families earning less than 30/- a week, even though this meant other deserving cases being passed over. The Conference attached to St Mary's, Highfield Street, served some of the most deprived parts of the town and its minute books show the difficult decisions facing the Brothers every week about who should and who should not be helped, and, inevitably, there were those who tried to work the system. Help might be given indirectly, as happened when the parish school teacher, Mr Kelly, asked for help for twelve poor children attending his school; the Brothers granted him six tickets (exchangeable at local stores for food) to use as relief. St Francis Xavier's Conference tended to give immediate help to almost all cases and then to investigate and decide whether the relief should be continued; later it decided to reject long-term cases, no matter how deserving, because the short-term demands were so pressing.[7] While there was much talk about 'deserving' and 'undeserving' cases, in practice the Brothers faced an impossible task and had to take on the spot practical decisions. When Bishop Whiteside urged them in 1902 to be prudent in selecting the cases they helped it was not an ideological stance but a practical one forced by shortage of funds; he went on to say that it was better to relieve a few impostors than to reject a genuine case through over-zealous scrutiny.

While individual Brothers became immersed in the needs of their own parishes, the Liverpool Central Council had an opportunity to deal with wider needs. In 1861 it established a Home for Destitute Boys in Everton Crescent, offering accommodation, clothing and instruction to seventy boys who earned some sort of living by street trading. It is not clear how long this Home remained in operation. The Council had another attempt at opening and running a home in 1891 – St Vincent's Working Boys Home and Night Shelter. This was the idea of Mr P.E.J. Hemelryk, a leading cotton broker, JP and President of Central Council. His aim was to provide an alternative to the common lodging houses that working boys (some as young as twelve or thirteen years of age) had to use. More will be said about this venture later.

The active members of the SVP saw themselves essentially as providers of material assistance. No doubt they shared the general Catholic desire to keep their poor away from the dangers of Protestant charity, contaminated, it was always alleged, by actively anti-Catholic proselytising. The majority of the Catholic poor, when desperate, did not enquire into the religious persuasion of any gift-horses that came their way, and were probably immune to Protestant proselytising anyway. Catholic-administered relief could reach only a minority of those in need and most of the rest were as subject to the pawnbroker, the money-lender and the Poor Law Guardians as their Protestant neighbours.[8]

There is no direct evidence that the SVP tried to influence those they visited to attend church, though some Conferences asked applicants to get a note of good standing from the local priest and this probably involved attendance at church on a regular basis. Some of the leaders of the Society seemed to have become increasingly conscious of the need to put across a spiritual message. It would help their public image (and so get them more financial support) if they were seen to be helping in Christianising the poor and helping to stop lapsing – the St Francis Xavier Conference opened a Boys' Club in 1899 for these purposes, and the motive behind St Vincent's Working Boys' Home seems to have been largely spiritual. When a Catholic Dispensary was opened in St Francis Xavier parish in the 1890s it provided consultants, medicines and some domestic visiting; its organisers could claim later that it led to a few conversions from Protestantism and to a large number of Catholics returning to their religious duties, but such benefits were secondary to its main work of helping the poor cope with their suffering.[9]

An important, if little noticed, side effect of the SVP was to provide for a small number of men in each parish an opportunity for active involvement and a level of responsibility beyond what most of them would have experienced otherwise. Although they worked under a clerical chaplain, in practice they were, more often than not, independent of clerical control.

FR JAMES NUGENT

The worst effects of poverty and the street crime that so often accompanied it could not be dealt with by small groups of SVP Brothers working in segregated parish units. Here we come to the work of one of Catholic Liverpool's great heroes, Fr (Mgr from 1892) James Nugent, the only Catholic priest to have a public statue erected in his memory in Liverpool city centre. Born in Liverpool of Irish parents in 1822, he had studied at Ushaw and at the English College, Rome, before being ordained in 1846. He was in Liverpool during the terrible epidemics of 1847 that killed ten of his fellow-clergy. Inscribed on the plinth of the statue is his famous slogan, 'Save the Boy!' and his fame rested principally upon his work for destitute and delinquent children, though his achievements in setting up the Catholic Institute secondary school and his twenty-two years as the first Catholic chaplain to Walton Gaol were also remarkable and ground-breaking. The inscription on the plinth also extols him as the:

> *Apostle of Temperance, Protector of the Orphan Child, Consoler of the*
> *Prisoner, Reformer of the Criminal, Saviour of Fallen Womanhood,*
> *Friend of All in Poverty and Affliction, an Eye to the Blind, a Foot to the*
> *Lame, the Father of the Poor.*

Fr James Nugent, 1822-1905.

In 1889 he topped a local newspaper poll as the 'most popular man in town'.[10] Not everyone was so full of praise. The local newspaper, the *Liverpool Daily Post*, edited by a Catholic, Michael Whitty, described him as 'a divine of exuberant benevolence … an excellent theatrical manager. No one knows better than he does the value of a sensation and no one knows better how to tickle the public into liberality'! It was meant as a back-handed compliment, but they were useful qualities as Catholics strove for recognition. Much more importantly, Bishop Goss also had his doubts. In a letter to Nugent, he said that he found an 'incomprehensible vagueness' in some of his suggestions (in this case to do with extending the Catholic Institute school into an ambitious centre for Catholic culture in Liverpool). Again, a couple of years later, he claimed, 'There is however more of restlessness than of useful activity about him: he seems ever straining at new things, instead of consolidating the old ones, and thus keeps up an unhealthy excitement'. The Bishop clearly found it difficult to pin the good Father down and to say what his views were: they seemed to change so often that he concluded he must be 'inconstant and changeable'.[11] One gets the impression that Goss preferred a steady P.C. Plod to a mercurial Hercule Poirot!

Another of Nugent's contemporaries, himself a City Councillor for one of Liverpool's poorest wards, saw him differently and felt that Nugent's greatest achievement lay in breaking down the barriers between Catholics and Protestants: 'to enlist the aid of enlightened Protestantism in Liverpool for the salvation of the child was Father Nugent's greatest service to the Church in Liverpool, if not the whole of England'. The writer referred to public meetings called by Nugent in the 1860s and attended by the Stipendiary Magistrate, the Mayor and nearly every member of the Town Council, and the Protestant chaplain to Walton Gaol; the aim of the meetings was to gain support for his rescue work in Soho Street. The reference to 'enlightened Protestantism' is important: Nugent and those who worked with him in setting up relief agencies continued to face strong Orange opposition. When the Town Council gave Nugent £1,500 towards the Clarence Reformatory Ship it was objected that the boys would be taught Roman Catholicism, whose doctrines were contrary to the spirit of the Constitution 'as established at the Reformation (and) which has made this country the most wealthy, happy and free of all the nations in Europe'.[12]

The wealthiest and happiest country, of course, had its darker side. Nugent's description of those he came to call 'Nobody's Children' makes a suitable introduction to his work:

> They roam unheeded about those crowded thoroughfares ... desolate and
> homeless wanderers, without a heart to love them or a hand to guide them
> ... these poor little ones huddle together under railway arches, in empty
> boxes, over baker's ovens, in fact anywhere to get a little heat and
> protection ... The streets are the schools of crime, where the girl scarce in
> her teens is degraded into a fallen outcast, the boy into a rowdy, duffer,
> thief and convict.

On another occasion he lamented the loss of ability, invention and energy to the city and the country, claiming that he could find among 'the newsboys, shoeblacks, fuzee-sellers and ballad singers' a match in physical and moral qualities for the 'young aristocrats or nobs of Eton, Harrow and Rugby'.[13]

Nugent first came across the problem of these children when he was appointed as curate to St Nicholas', Copperas Hill, in 1847. Two years later he opened a Ragged School, to keep some of them off the streets during the day and to give them a rudimentary education – throughout his life Nugent believed that education, while not a panacea by itself, provided one of the best ways to avoid a life of crime and destitution. He was not alone in his concern, of course, and others opened similar schools. The Jesuits' Ragged School, run for them by the Sisters of Charity, was at least as important for the meals (at times quite openly a reward for going to Mass) and the clothing it dispensed as for its education; it lasted until 1874 and the tradition of giving free dinners to the children continued in the ordinary parish schools long afterwards.[14]

At the time there were two types of school for those who had been in trouble with the law. A Reformatory School took in those children who had been in prison, while an Industrial School took in those who had appeared before the magistrates for some offence but had been deemed not to deserve a full prison sentence (after 1933 both types of institution became known as Approved Schools). There were neither children's courts nor young offenders' prisons in those days – it was not until 1908 that the Children's Act set up Juvenile Courts – but many magistrates were enlightened enough to want to keep young offenders out of the gaols. Sometimes there was overlap in the non-prison provision – a Refuge or an Orphanage could apply for an Industrial School certificate and so take in both young offenders and those who had not broken the law at all, the advantage being that children in

Industrial Schools attracted public funding and so helped to keep the institution financially stable.

In 1854 Nugent became secretary of the newly formed Catholic Reformatory Association, to provide an alternative to prison for boys and girls brought before the magistrates for often petty offences. At first the association was content to use reformatories elsewhere, principally Mount St Bernard's Reformatory in Leicestershire, run by the Cistercians, who agreed to take 200 Liverpool boys in return for the Association investing £2,000 in the project. When the Fathers of Charity (the Rosminians) took over from the Cistercians, however, they refused to honour the arrangement, the Liverpool boys left the Reformatory and the diocese spent several years trying to get some of its money back – in the end it recovered £500.

It was clear that a local reformatory was needed – apart from issues of control, Liverpool townies had not taken kindly to the supposed virtues of life in the country. Nugent, now president of the Association, turned to the idea of using a ship berthed in the Mersey as more suitable for training local delinquents. This was not a new idea – when Cardinal Wiseman had visited the town to give a lecture in 1858 he had visited the Corporation reformatory ship Akbar accompanied by a number of clergy, including Nugent. Eventually the Association secured from the Admiralty a former man-of-war, HMS Clarence. The costs of this enterprise were, and remained, high and were met by the grant of £1,500 from the Town Council and collections among Catholics in Liverpool, Preston, Wigan and St Helens.[15]

The ship, which despite its retirement from active service had certainly not seen the end of violence and insurrection (after a number of mini-riots she was eventually destroyed in 1884 when some of the boys set her alight), was quite successful as a training ground and many of her inmates saw later service in the Merchant Navy. In 1885 she was replaced by another former man-of-war, HMS Royal William, renamed the Clarence. More riots and some years later the ship went the way of her predecessor and was deliberately burned and sunk in a very serious disturbance led by a group of the boys (while the Bishop of Shrewsbury was on board to confirm them). Instead of finding another ship the Association opened St Aidan's, in Farnworth, near Widnes, as a reformatory school specialising in naval training. Already, in 1872, it had opened a farm school in Ainsdale, near Southport, on land given by Thomas Weld-Blundell; apart from the difficulties already encountered at Mount St Bernard's in trying to train the boys for farming, there was the additional problem that the land around the school was too sandy for successful agriculture. Despite these difficulties, the school enjoyed a golden age that lasted thirty years under the guidance of its second governor, Mr Daniel Henry Shee.

The Reformatory Association was also committed to establishing a reformatory for girls. Eventually the Sisters of Charity opened a school for sixty girls in Old Swan in 1876. Relations between the Sisters and the Association's committee were always strained, and the Sisters withdrew three years later. The first lay superintendent resigned after a period of rioting by the girls, during which considerable damage was done to the buildings and a number of girls absconded. A Miss Donovan restored order and reigned successfully and more or less peacefully until 1900; on her retirement the Sisters of Charity returned.

In 1864 Nugent turned his attention to the non-delinquent but destitute boys among Liverpool's 'Nobody's Children'. He opened a Night Shelter and Refuge in Soho Street, and two years later could report that it was serving over 48,000 suppers a year and providing nearly 3,000 nights' accommodation. He decided, however, that the boys who used it needed something more long-term and in 1869 changed it into the Boys Refuge and Night Asylum, offering residential accommodation and aiming 'to save Boys from Pauperism, Ignorance and Crime'. The first superintendent was John Denvir, better known as a journalist and Irish Nationalist; it then passed under the care of the Brothers of the Christian Schools, who ran it for some years. The Refuge later gained an Industrial School certificate and claimed that it was one of the first Industrial Schools in the country to give its boys practical training in a trade – it ran a printing works, joinery, bakery, paper-bag manufactory and wire-mattress works. A number of its boys were among those who were later helped to emigrate to Canada.[16]

While Nugent's own schemes were aimed at helping boys and young men, he also took some interest in what could be done for girls and young women, especially after his experiences as prison chaplain showed him the extent of female destitution, crime and prostitution in the city. He was particularly impressed by the work of the Good Shepherd nuns who had opened a Home, or Asylum as it was known at the time, for Penitents – women who had been in prison for prostitution. They had to enter voluntarily and be over sixteen years of age. The nuns began in Netherfield Road, to the disgust of the surrounding population – Victorian 'nimby-ism' was one of the factors behind the physical attacks on the house in its early days, though Orange opposition to convents in that strongly Protestant neighbourhood seems to have played a larger part. The nuns moved to Mason Street in Edge Hill, where they had accommodation for fifty-six 'penitents', and eventually to a new site in Ford, helped considerably by the fund-raising efforts of Nugent (he helped to raise nearly £3,000 for them) and the generosity of Miss Rosson, a member of a prominent Catholic family that had been active in Catholic causes, political and social, for many years.[17]

It would have been remarkable if all these enterprises had been immediately successful. There was no special training for those who staffed them and in most cases no models for them to follow. Religious dedication could supply for some deficiencies but at times failed to cope with the practicalities, which seemed on occasion to take second place to making sure the children kept up the practice of their religion. One case involved St George's Industrial School, opened originally by Belgian Augustinian nuns to protect and instruct poor and destitute girls. Initially successful, they began to take in boys as well but very soon major problems became evident – the boys were said to be 'in a wretched condition, miserable looking, with a spirit of discontent pervading the whole of them'. It was a complex case, with more than local interest in that it brought out the government inspector's general opposition to Reformatory and Industrial Schools being run by Religious, apparently because of their vows. Nugent and Archbishop (later Cardinal) Manning met the inspector, who at first insisted that no institution managed by Religious would in future be certified and funded unless there was a separate committee of management; the only nuns he considered qualified for such work were the Sisters of Charity. It would be far better, the inspector argued, for schools like St George's to be run by a husband and wife team. Certainly, he continued, male Religious should not be in sole charge of such institutions – there should always be some female staff to ensure cleanliness and household order in the kitchen, infirmary, and dormitories, 'and that personal kindliness of discipline which keep a school in a permanently satisfactory condition'.[18]

When it was decided to separate the boys' and girls' sections completely, the Brothers of the Christian Schools were invited to take charge of the boys, with a lay manager and an agreement with the Sisters of Bon Secours (whose mission was to nurse the sick of all ages at home, an invaluable service at the time) to cover any necessary nursing. The system did not work, the Brothers withdrew and the School passed under the control of a lay superintendent – and flourished. Meanwhile the girls formed the new St Anne's Industrial School, under the Sisters of Charity, at first in Mason Street, Edge Hill and then in Freshfield. It closed in 1922 and the premises became the final home of the St George's Industrial School for boys, who moved there from their West Derby premises. No matter how successful this and other institutions were, however, reformers worried about what the boys and girls would find when they left. What 'after-care' could be provided – or would it be better to move them away altogether from the society that had failed them in the first place?

EMIGRATION SCHEMES

Enlightened social reformers of the day encouraged emigration schemes for the young and Trade Unions encouraged them for the unemployed. It seemed a sensible policy for both the 'empty' countries looking for more people and the emigrant who was being given a new start. Talk of such schemes was in the air as early as the 1850s, and a small number of the Liverpool children who had been sent to Mount St Bernard's Reformatory had emigrated of their own accord to the USA and Canada on being discharged. 1870 was the year of the first organised scheme for the emigration of children, but it is not altogether clear whether Nugent was the very first to go with a group or whether it was another Liverpool philanthropist, Miss Annie MacPherson of Mrs Birt's Homes in Myrtle Street (strongly criticised by Catholics for their supposed proselytising approach). Whatever the inspiration, he decided to take a group of children (twelve boys and twelve girls in the first instance) to the United States in 1870 as the start of an organised scheme. After finding places for the children (he claimed all the girls had been placed within two days of arriving in Montreal) he spent nine months touring around the USA and Canada, selling the idea of organised emigration as good for both the destitute children and the receiving country. He stressed that the children had been well instructed in their religion and had had some education and basic training; nine of the boys already had a trade. He wanted to set up a small committee in each locality to look after the project, to be responsible for the welfare of the children and report to him from time to time on their progress, but the scheme did not get off the ground and would have been far too loose a system – Nugent accepted too readily the initial enthusiasm of others.[19]

In the end Bishop O'Reilly set up the Liverpool Catholic Children's Protection Society in 1881, to take charge of destitute or abandoned children, give them some training and send them to Catholic families in Canada, 'to preserve them in their religion' and help them find a respectable place in society. It was an emigration agency, with a Home for training children in Liverpool (at 99 Shaw Street) – this gave it an edge over other societies, some of whom were criticised for their failure to prepare the children for emigration. The Society organised its first sailings in 1881; the ages of the children taken ranged from two or three years to fourteen (for boys) or sixteen (for girls). Those who supported the scheme argued that emigration was much preferable to the Poor Law Guardians' practice of sending children and adults away from Liverpool to work in the mining and manufacturing districts of Lancashire and Yorkshire where there might be no Catholic provision for them, little supervision of the children and quite unhealthy working conditions.

The first superintendent of the Home was a Mrs Lacy. As well as taking two or three parties of children to Canada each year she was expected to visit as many as possible of those already placed there. In 1885, for example, she reported on 140 children of the 650 in Canada, having visited them personally. She felt that 120 were satisfactory, the rest being lazy, deceitful or, in one case, accused of theft. These attempts to check on the condition of the children once they were in Canada, and to find new places for them if necessary, contrasted with some of the emigration agencies who seemed to think their job was done once the children were placed. Mrs Lacy was succeeded by Miss Yates, the daughter of John Yates (see below) in 1894, by which time the Society had been responsible for moving 1,500 children and had a proper system in place, with a home in Montreal run by a superintendent who did the work of finding new places and reporting back on the children. Just over a third of the children had been helped to emigrate by the Select Vestry who paid £10 per child. By 1900, however, the number of children sent out had dwindled and the Society's funds had diminished; three years later the Home was handed over to Father Berry's Homes (see below) and the Society used what money it had to pay other agencies to undertake the movement of children. It struggled on in this way for some years, finally joining the general amalgamation of children's societies in 1924.

Arthur Chilton Thomas, manager of Father Berry's Homes, suggested that it would be sensible if the various diocesan emigration schemes amalgamated, and went to Canada on a fact-finding mission to see what could be done. He and Fr Bans of Westminster interviewed over 300 former emigrants. As a result, in 1905 the Catholic Emigration Association was formed, and the Canadian scheme became the joint responsibility of the dioceses of Westminster, Southwark, Birmingham and Liverpool. Father Berry's Homes looked after any Liverpool children who were to emigrate. Altogether, Nugent made over a dozen visits to Canada and the United States, establishing himself as a popular speaker and expert on emigration schemes for the young. Not all the children took to farming and some of them were badly placed and mis-treated, specially those who went into service, while others found they could get back to England as stowaways or by working their passage – Mgr Pinnington later claimed that he had helped a number of boys emigrate from Liverpool to Bootle by way of Canada! It would be quite wrong to judge that the organisers of these schemes were unaware of the these issues or indifferent to what happened to those they helped to emigrate. Whatever the problems and the individual cases of failure, most people at the time agreed with the findings of the 1902 report that 'the farms and corn-fields of Canada offer advantages, both material and moral, which could never be guaranteed at home'.[20]

POOR LAW SCHOOLS

By the second half of the nineteenth century official and voluntary bodies were looking for ways to remove children from the oppressive atmosphere of the workhouses and to provide them with some suitable care and training. Poor Law Guardians in Liverpool housed children in the Kirkdale Industrial Schools and Catholics had set up a Workhouse Children's Fund about 1860, with the aim of providing for Catholic children after they left the schools. Its President was Canon Walmsley but most of its Committee members were laymen; the Sixth Annual Report claimed that 795 Catholic children were receiving education and training in the schools. The chaplain to the schools, Fr Henry Gibson, had been responsible for getting the Guardians to take a more co-operative attitude and to provide a list of the Catholic children leaving the schools so that he could place as many of them as possible with Catholic families and employers. Every effort was made to find Catholic places for the girls when they entered service; it was more difficult to do this for the boys who got jobs in offices or in various trades, and Fr Gibson had resorted to providing accommodation in his own house for fifteen of them, in effect setting up the first Catholic 'Home for Boys', as he called it.

Fr Gibson was in some respects a 'mini-Nugent' – he had taught under him at the Catholic Institute and been its vice-principal. He was deeply concerned about the fate of Catholic children, and worked for some years as chaplain to Kirkdale gaol. At times, perhaps, his enthusiasm overcame his prudence, but his contribution to child care in Liverpool was important; indeed, it was claimed that he was half a century ahead of all social reformers in starting the system of working-boys' homes to help the young wage earner. In his work to get a better deal for Catholic workhouse children he had the assistance of Mr James Whitty, one of the two Catholic representatives on the Select Vestry from 1853 – 1865, who had an intimate knowledge of the workhouse system. Whitty served the Catholic body well as a Town Councillor and later as a member of the School Board; on his monument in Ford cemetery, erected by public subscription, he was described as a 'man of rare talent, persuasive eloquence, and untiring zeal; these qualities he devoted to the service of the poor of Liverpool, irrespective of creed or country'.[21]

Given the range of agencies, official and unofficial, that existed in the Diocese to help children, it is strange that it was one of the last in the country to set up Poor Law Schools. These had come into existence through Acts of Parliament in the 1860s that enabled Poor Law Guardians to allow children in their care to attend residential schools outside the workhouse; the schools were, in effect, orphanages. The Guardians were to pay the fees of the children and were to see that Catholic children should attend Catholic Poor Law Schools – if such existed and were properly certified. When Poor Law Schools became increasingly popular, most Catholic dioceses established at least one of them as soon as possible. For whatever reason this did not happen in Liverpool – while Westminster had thirteen Poor Law Schools by 1887, Liverpool had none, though its needs were almost as great as London's. It has to be stressed here that the Guardians of the three Liverpool Unions had become much more tolerant towards Catholic claims than the bitter sectarian battles of the mid-century might lead one to believe. The Toxteth Park Union had boarded out a number of Catholic girls at St Clare's Convent, Pantasaph, North Wales, while the other two Unions allowed a Catholic chaplain and a number of Catholic staff in the Kirkdale Poor Law Schools to cater for the special needs of Catholic children. But the numbers involved were small and the great majority of the Catholic children were not provided for.

Finally, in 1888, Bishop O'Reilly issued two pastoral letters on the subject, pointing out that there were over 1,200 Catholic children in the sixteen workhouses throughout the diocese who needed accommodation.[22] He had made a start by purchasing Leyfield (a mansion with twenty-five acres of land in West Derby) to be a Poor Law School for girls – the total costs would be nearly £6,000 and he had only £1,700 in hand. A second possibility, the Bishop went on, was the establishment of a Poor Law school for boys in Preston – the Poor Law Guardians in the town had ignored the legislation regarding

Catholic children and there was an immediate need to provide for them – and so in 1889 a committee organised a public meeting there to promote the foundation of a local Catholic Poor Law School. Difficulties arose at once because, people claimed, there was confusion about the relationship of Preston to the diocese. Would the diocesan authorities be contributing to the cost of the proposed school? If they did, would they have the right to place children in it, or would the school serve only children from the town?[23]

Bishop O'Reilly was known to be keen on a scheme that would establish a system of schools open to children from anywhere in the diocese. When he heard of the Preston plan he made it clear that he doubted the value of local initiatives, and argued, without any evidence, that there were not enough children in Preston alone to justify a local school, and if such a school were established then there could be no diocesan financial help for it. If, however, the Preston Protection Society committee agreed to join in a diocesan scheme, he would see to it that they would receive as much support as he could afford. The Society went ahead and bought land for a school at Fulwood at a cost of £4,500. Local priests were soon reporting to the organizing committee that they were finding it difficult to raise money from their congregations because places in the proposed school would not be reserved for Preston children; the least people wanted was for children from the town to be given priority. Matters reached a stalemate and in 1890 a deputation waited on the Bishop in an attempt to clear up the differences. They put their case for the transfer to their Protection Society of the land that had been purchased and for all monies collected north of the Ribble, including church collections, to be under their control, and for them to control admissions. All that O'Reilly would agree to was that any money collected in the north would go to them; he resolutely refused to give them control of the land or buildings or admissions. When the school opened it was soon clear that the Bishop had total control over all aspects of it and it was even designated as one of the Bishop O'Reilly's Poor Law Schools. It seemed to locals that he had hi-jacked the whole enterprise and this was proved by the fact that from its opening in May 1897 until mid-December 1899, not a single boy from Preston Union Workhouse was admitted to the school; all 133 of those admitted in that period were from Liverpool Union Workhouses. By December 1899 over 200 boys in Preston had been identified as in need of places in the Poor Law School and ten were finally admitted that month.

It may be added here that this was not the first time that people in the town had opposed what they saw as interference by the diocesan authorities. In 1872 Maria Holland, a wealthy Catholic, had funded a Catholic orphanage for girls in Preston. In 1877 she followed this with the foundation of St Joseph's Institution for the Sick Poor, and drew up a joint scheme for the administration of both establishments. She was determined not to allow the Bishop of Liverpool to have any say in the control, management and admissions of the two places and made arrangements for the Jesuits in Preston to have the principal say in these matters; if the Jesuits failed for any reason, then the Benedictines were to act in their place; if they failed, then lay trustees were to take over – whatever happened, the Bishop of Liverpool was to be excluded altogether.[24] The people's lack of trust in the Bishop is noteworthy, as is his lack of sensitivity about their legitimate point of view. They did not see themselves sharing in a united diocesan enterprise; was this a result of geography or of the long stand-off between the dominant Jesuits in the town and the bishops?

Meanwhile, 1889 saw the start of a diocese-wide campaign by the Bishop to raise awareness of the need for Poor Law Schools. He addressed meetings in Liverpool, Wigan, Warrington, Chorley, St Helens, Leigh, Barrow-in-Furness and Kirkham. The campaign worked in that large sums of money were collected for the two schools, Leyfield and Fulwood, with all the money collected north of the Ribble going specifically to the Preston establishment. In the end Leyfield opened first, in December 1894, while Fulwood did not open until May 1897, mainly because the Local Government Board inspectors believed the plans were for too large a single building where the children would be all housed together – they preferred the Cottage Home or 'Pavilion' approach that would allow for smaller and therefore more homely units – a sign in itself how far social thinking had moved away from the old workhouse system.[25]

Bishop O'Reilly died in April 1894 and so did not see the completion of any of his plans for Poor Law Schools. By 1910, there were seven certified Poor Law Schools in the diocese:

St Edward's Orphanage, Broadgreen, Liverpool:
    300 boys: Brothers of Charity
St Vincent's Home, Fulwood, Preston:
    300 boys: Sisters of Charity of S.V. de Paul
Leyfield School, West Derby, Liverpool:
    350 boys & girls under 8: Sisters of Charity of S.V. de Paul
Greenfield House, Billinge, near Wigan:
    113 girls and boys under 8: S. of Charity of Our Lady of Mercy;
    later, Sisters of Charity of St Paul of Chartres
Knolle Park, Woolton, Liverpool:
    120 girls and young boys: Sisters of St Catherine; after 1915, Poor
    Servants of the Mother of God
Moorfield Orphanage, Ribbleton Avenue, Preston:
    60 girls: Daughters of Wisdom (La Sagesse)
Pontville, Aughton, Ormskirk:
    15 ESN girls: Sisters of the Sacred Hearts of Jesus and Mary

All these schools received glowing reports from the inspectors, but they continued to be a heavy financial burden for the diocese. Perhaps there was some over-kill in provision – not all the places were taken up (average attendance at Moorfield, for example, was only 31 and at St Edward's around 270), and the schools took in children from outside the diocese (though this might have been on a reciprocal basis).[26]

OTHER NEEDS, OTHER INITIATIVES

Reformatory and Industrial Schools and now the Poor Law Schools – the delinquent and the officially destitute were being cared for, but how much had been done to help 'ordinary' orphans, the long-term sick or incapacitated, and the elderly? Even a summary account of Catholic provision shows the needs that existed in Victorian society and which were met only by voluntary bodies. It had long been recognised that orphans were one of the more deserving groups and a Catholic orphanage for girls had been established by a lay committee as early as 1816 to cater for those orphaned as a result of the Napoleonic Wars. (A similar institution for boys for some reason did not survive.) In 1843 the Sisters of Mercy took charge when it moved to Falkner Street; from 1851 it was under the care of the Sisters of Notre Dame who later moved it to Druids Cross, where it remained until the 1960s.[27]

Dr Youens, in charge of St Nicholas', Copperas Hill, had brought the Sisters of Mercy to Liverpool in 1842, to teach and evangelise the poor through home visiting and nursing. They soon developed another apostolate that throws some light on the needs and difficulties of poorer working girls at that time. The aim of this 'School for Girls and Infants' was:

1. To train up respectable young females for domestic service, by constant inculcation of habits of order, industry, and obedience;
2. To afford a refuge for such as for the time being are out of a situation from accidental circumstances and so prevent them spending their small earnings on lodging houses, or what is still worse, parting with their wearing apparel, which raises a special obstacle against securing a future situation;
3. To instruct them in their religion and their moral duties.

The girls worked in a large laundry attached to the school to make the institution partly self-supporting. After their period of training they were helped to find suitable employment. Another Convent of Mercy, in Hardy Street, provided a Night School for 'a class of women' (unspecified).[28]

Outstanding among the many charitable institutions in the diocese was the Catholic Blind Asylum. Founded in 1841 by Dr Youens and Mr John Rosson, brother of the Miss Rosson already mentioned, the asylum was the only Catholic institution of its kind in the British Isles for poor boys and girls. Its aim was to give the children an elementary education and training in some trade or occupation – and, of course, a thorough grounding in their religion. It had its premises at first in St Anne Street, then in Islington and eventually in Brunswick Road. A mixed clerical and lay committee of management with a lay matron was responsible for its day-to-day running before it passed under the care of the Sisters (now the Daughters) of Charity of St Vincent de Paul, who are still responsible for its present day successor. For many years as far as one can see it received no public funding and was frequently in debt, mainly because of building and extension costs.[29]

Destitute children were not always orphans. When a Miss Gordon opened St Elizabeth's Institute in Soho Street in 1854 it was to provide a home for destitute girls under the age of twelve (later changed to eleven to sixteen years of age), who were either orphans or whose parents 'were so demoralised as to make their condition still more wretched'. The girls were given a simple education and training for domestic service under the guidance at first of a group of Catholic laywomen of means and then, from 1871 until its closure in 1920, under the Sisters of Mercy. The problems did not necessarily cease when girls found employment, for their wages could be so small that finding a respectable place to live was difficult. It was to meet this need that the Sisters of Charity opened two institutions in Everton Crescent – St Joseph's Home for Female Servants and St Mary's Hostel for Working Girls. The latter soon began to take in girls of school age who had nowhere to live; this part of the work became a separate Voluntary Home, housing sixty girls, and lasted until 1924.[30]

There was no organised provision for orphaned boys until 1859 when a 'Refuge for Destitute Boys' opened under lay management, again in Everton Crescent. After a move to Beacon Lane the committee of management handed it over 'in a deplorable state' to the care of the Sisters of Charity of St Vincent de Paul in 1863, who renamed it St Vincent's. The boys had to be at least four years old to be admitted, 'born in holy wedlock and duly baptized'. The orphanage obtained an Industrial Schools certificate five years later, but continued to be heavily in debt for some years – it is said that the boys had to go Sunday Mass in relays as there were not enough good clothes for all of them to go together![31]

FATHER BERRY'S HOMES

Another social need was to provide for boys and young men just above the poverty line – in work but, like the girls, still at risk because of a lack of suitable accommodation at affordable prices. This work was undertaken by Fr John Berry, who had taken over St Philip Neri's parish in 1887, becoming in the process Principal of the Catholic Institute. In some ways he was a second Nugent, establishing a series of homes for boys that became known as Father Berry's Homes. He also succeeded Nugent as owner of the *Catholic Times*. In the end the Homes proved too large an undertaking for him: he retired from their management in 1897 and from St Philip's two years later, a sick man, disillusioned and heavily in debt because of the monies he had spent and borrowed to keep the Homes going – in five years he had collected over £10,000, but it had not been enough.[32]

The scale of his ambitions is obvious from a list of his foundations. In December 1892 he opened St Philip's House for street-trading boys, off Williamson Sq; in November 1894 this moved to 31 Everton Crescent, but closed in May 1897. In 1893 the Bishop asked him to take over St Vincent's Home from the SVP because it was nearly bankrupt and in danger of closing; Fr Berry found that its debts were even heavier than the Bishop had thought. In October 1894 he opened St James' Night Shelter; this also closed in May 1897. A year later, in October 1895, he started St Bernard's Training Home, Bute Street, which closed in October 1897. Not surprisingly, perhaps, that same month Fr Berry and his committee resigned.

A new committee of four priests and eight laymen took over St Vincent's Home, under J.P. Reynolds and J.J. Shute (both became MPs later). Fortunately, Mr Chilton Thomas agreed to stay on as honorary manager – a remarkable person who had given up his work as a QC to devote his life to the cause of destitute children. At one stage he wanted to found a Religious Order of Brothers to help in the work; he was only forty-three when he died in 1906. St Vincent's was a success story, remaining open until 1945. In 1898 St Bernard's Home re-opened; it moved in 1903 to 119 Shaw Street. The following year St Philip's House in Everton Crescent re-opened for street traders, but for some reason was never used. This conglomeration of homes and hostels was at first named 'Homes for Catholic Friendless Youth (late Father Berry's Homes)'; then in 1901 they became 'Late Father Berry's Homes (Homes for Catholic Friendless Youth)', and in 1903 'Father Berry's Homes', the name they kept until 1924 and by which they were commonly known.

In 1900 Chilton Thomas opened Newman House at 99 Shaw Street – a hostel for working boys who were independent but preferred a Catholic atmosphere and the club facilities attached to the hostel. A different project was launched in 1903 when the Hon. Mrs Molyneux opened Our Lady's Home for Homeless Babies in 93 Shaw Street; it became part of Father Berry's Homes in June 1906. They now owned 95, 97, 99, 105, 119 Shaw Street and rented 93! In 1905 Chilton Thomas organized a six-day Great Bazaar in St George's Hall: it raised £4,305 net to meet the capital debts of £4,500 on all the Homes. Fr Berry kept up his connections with the homes for some years, even though he had retired from active work in the diocese, regarding himself as a failure. It was not that his vision of what was needed was too great, but that he was too keen to do things quickly and would not wait for a proper financial base on which to build.

His failure helped to persuade Bishop Whiteside that the time for some degree of centralisation had come. In 1899 he set up the Catholic Children's Aid Committee, with offices at 1a Trueman Street, Liverpool (part of the estate of James O'Byrne, architect and patron of Upholland), in an attempt to bring together the multifarious charitable activities under Fr (later Mgr) William Pinnington – his experience as a Poor Law Guardian made him the obvious choice as secretary of the new committee (it was taken for granted it would be a priest). Some may have lamented the loss of spontaneity and the bravura approach of a Nugent or a Berry, but their piecemeal approach had achieved as much as it could, and the endless closures and movings and changes of regime can have done little to create the stability that many of the children needed.

The Aid Committee functioned for 25 years. Again, Preston felt it needed separate provision and set up its own Committee, no doubt fearing that the diocesan one would be too occupied with the many problems of Liverpool. By 1909 over 3,600 children were being catered for in the various homes and institutions of the diocese. In 1924 Father Berry's Homes and the Catholic Children's Aid Committee dropped their names and amalgamated with the Liverpool Catholic Children's Protection Committee, with Mgr Pinnington as Administrator and Fr John Bennett as Secretary. Fr Bennett (later Canon and Nugent's biographer) became Administrator in 1930, a post he held until his death in 1965, at the age of seventy-four. His long experience made him a national expert, consulted by the Home Office and other dioceses and agencies dealing with children's care and welfare; he was a member of a Papal Commission on Emigration.[33]

ARCHBISHOP WHITESIDE

While Bishop Whiteside had a great belief in providence and was rarely dissuaded from starting a project by want of money, he also knew that the multiplication of institutions put considerable strains on the funds available from occasional donations and ad hoc legacies. This was the thinking behind the launch of his Good Shepherd Appeal for Waifs and Strays: this became an annual appeal, made directly to the children of the diocese each Lent to collect money for less well-off children and those in Catholic Poor Law Schools. His message was simple, even simplistic, and sentimental: poverty was the will of God and so the poor were especially dear to Him – poor children were like Jesus himself who was 'poor, hungry and homeless' as a child. They should take Jesus as their model:

> Would you not have loved to play with Mary's Son in the pleasant fields
> of Nazareth? How gladly you would have shared with Him all you
> possessed – your toys, your sweets, your little pocket money? ... this
> privilege can still be yours – Jesus lives in His poor.[34]

It is interesting that Fr Berry rejected this view of the poor quite explicitly, and it sits uneasily with Whiteside's own statements when he was dealing with social evils (see pages 206 below).

The appeals were increasingly successful. In 1909 the collection amounted to just over £800; by the last year of the united diocese (1924) it reached almost £3,000. In his pastoral letter of Lent 1910 Whiteside reported that during the previous year over 200 poor children were provided for, 'more than 100 of whom were in danger of being robbed of their faith and

being lost to the Church'.[35] His use of the word 'robbed' is telling – it was a constant theme of Catholic appeals for schools and other social agencies that children who were not looked after in Catholic institutions would be the victims of active Protestant proselytising. Many of the Catholic statements on this topic make it clear that it was considered more important to save the child from loss of the Faith than it was to rescue it from the suffering and degradation caused by poverty. But Whiteside was not content just to appeal for money; he launched into widening the provision for children and adults, in so comprehensive a manner that he deserves to stand alongside Nugent as the founder of Catholic social service provision in the diocese.

If the Catholic body wanted to build a comprehensive system of care some groups were still not catered for adequately. Bishop O'Reilly had invited the Little Sisters of the Poor into Liverpool in 1874 to care for the elderly poor who otherwise had only the workhouse to look forward to. The Sisters opened their first home, for sixty elderly people, in Hope Street; five years later they moved to larger premises in Belmont Road, which remained open until the 1980s. A recent writer has described them as perhaps the 'most saintly and street-wise' in managing their various operations through carefully organised begging; they very quickly won widespread respect for their selfless dedication.[36] They opened a second home in St Charles' parish later – again still in operation in the 1980s.

Bishop Whiteside was also concerned about the lack of provision for the long-term incapacitated and the elderly and so in 1897 he invited the Poor Sisters of Nazareth to open a house in the diocese – on the day he decided to ask them, he received a letter from them asking for his leave to work in the diocese, and he regarded this happy co-incidence as the answer to prayer. The first Nazareth House opened in 1897 in Crosby, for 'girls, cripples and the elderly'. Mgr Nugent, despite being retired and seventy-five years old, took a strong interest in the work and was involved in supervising the building alterations. Two years later the Sisters opened another home for girls and the elderly in Lancaster (at first in Dalton Square, then, from 1902, in Ashton Road). Their next foundation, in 1903, was a boys' orphanage in Ditton, near Widnes, where the Sisters took over the house that had been given in 1872 by Lady Stapleton-Bretherton to the exiled German Jesuits who had founded the parish of St Michael's, Ditton.[37]

Another important area of social work for the charitable in Victorian society was the reclamation of 'fallen women' or 'penitents'. There was a Liverpool Female Penitentiary open to all, but it allowed only Anglican services on Sundays. By 1890 the Good Shepherd Home in Ford had accommodation for over 200 women, but then in 1891 the Liverpool police launched a campaign to close as many brothels in the city as possible and prosecuted over 800 brothel-keepers in one year. This resulted in a very large number of prostitutes being made destitute and homeless; since many of them were at least nominal Catholics, Bishop Whiteside decided that further provision was required. Nugent approached the Poor Servants of the Mother of God (SMGs) and in 1891 the nuns opened a temporary refuge in Limekiln Lane and the following year moved into a large building in Bevington Bush that had been bought for them through Nugent's fund-raising efforts; this became St Saviour's Refuge, while the original house became a Night Shelter – by 1905 more than 19,000 women had used it. The Good Shepherd Sisters opened another home, at Eton Lodge, Wavertree, in 1903, while the Sisters of Our Lady of Charity opened one at Redcliffe, Aughton Park, Ormskirk, in 1914.[38]

Catholic provision seemed to accept no bounds to its expansion and one of Nugent's last initiatives was in the area of infant mortality. For much of the nineteenth century Liverpool had the highest rate of infant mortality in England and Wales – more than that twice that in what were considered 'naturally healthy' areas, and almost four times as high for infants. Reformers at the time considered that the infants most at risk were illegitimate babies, either from natural causes, desertion by the mother or deliberate infanticide. Infanticide, indeed, was not restricted to such cases and many of the infants who died as a result of being overlain by their (often drunken) parents were thought to have been deliberately killed. How far these accusations were true is impossible to quantify, though there is enough evidence to show that they were not just a middle-class horror story about the terrible habits of the lower classes. In all the reforming effort to improve the general health of the population very little thought went into providing specific medical care and provision for mothers and their babies, and it was not until 1918 that a Maternity and Child Welfare Act allowed local authorities to spend money on them.

Nugent was convinced that unmarried mothers and their babies needed special protection and should be kept together for at least a year. He looked to the Sisters of the Sacred Hearts of Jesus and Mary to help him in this work

St SAVIOUR'S REFUGE & NIGHT SHELTER.

and they opened the first House of Providence in the Dingle in 1897 – helped by a donation of £1,300 that he gave them from the money he had been given for his golden jubilee. It was a rule of the house that the mothers had to remain there for twelve months and that only first cases should be admitted; moreover, every effort was made to get the fathers to contribute to the costs. Thirty-three mothers were in residence at the end of the first year, doing laundry work to help support the venture. Nugent resurrected his old Association of Providence to help and then toured some of the south Lancashire towns to raise funds; at a meeting in Southport the Mayoress stressed that the fathers of the children should do more: 'the partners in their sin ought to be partners in their sorrows'.

A well-publicised trial in December 1898 involved a case of abortion and Nugent took the opportunity to write to the local press about the need for a Maternity Home to care for unmarried mothers before they had their babies. He described the plight of the young pregnant girl: 'Deceived, ruined, deserted, possibly almost penniless, in her critical condition, what was to become of her?' He offered all his help to raise the necessary funds but no one came forward. Eventually in 1903 he used the occasion of the Annual Conference of the Catholic Truth Society to show the delegates round the House of Providence and got some support. He opened a Maternity Home nearby in 1904, with a qualified lay staff, but when he died the following year no one was willing to carry on the necessary work of fund-raising (the Home had proved to be even more expensive than expected) and it closed.[39] The House of Providence eventually moved to Kelton, in Woodlands Road, Aigburth, where it remained for many years.

Finally, mention should be made of a prisoners' aid society in the shape of the Liverpool and County Police Courts Catholic Aid Society, formed in 1904. Its members interviewed men and women in the courts and in prison or on release, gave them aid, food and clothing and found them work to try to prevent re-offending; some were discharged from the magistrates' courts on condition the Society took care of them. By 1910 it had dealt with an amazing thirteen thousand individuals.[40]

It is amazing that Mgr Nugent had the energy and commitment to be actively involved in rescue work in his eighties. When he died:

> *flags at the Town Hall, municipal Buildings, the White Star (Shipping) Offices, and the various clubs … were lowered half-mast. Tributes were made … in the City Council, the Chamber of Commerce, the law courts and by official bodies. The local newspapers contained many columns … detailing his life-work for the most neglected and abject classes …*[41]

In many ways he was a man of his times, with what today would be considered reactionary views, especially on drunkenness and women prisoners; at the time he annoyed some of his Liverpool compatriots by unflattering remarks about their thriftlessness and addiction to alcohol. In no sense a social revolutionary, he was certainly a revolutionary Christian – or was he all that revolutionary, except in his drive and energy? He would have achieved little without the commitment of hundreds of lay men and women, Religious Orders and Congregations, priests and bishops – the many who sat on humdrum committees, raised thousands of pounds each year and did the day-to-day thankless work of running the institutions. It was a gigantic effort on the part of a fledgling Catholic community (with some help from its Protestant friends) that was also busy providing new churches and schools for its needs.

There is some evidence that a few Catholics believed the Church was providing not only a comprehensive system of care but also a model for others to follow.[42] But there was little theorizing: those involved were practical people, hoping to safeguard the Faith and relieve the suffering of those they helped. I have come across no references to Leo XIII's great social encyclical, *Rerum Novarum* (1891), or to any of the more advanced socio-economic ideas of some Catholic writers. Sectarianism, Irish nationalism and the Victorian virtues of individualism and voluntaryism determined the shape of Catholic social endeavour.

LATER YEARS

By the time Archbishop Whiteside died in 1921 the archdiocese had a more or less complete system of social care agencies in place, along with an acceptance on the part of Catholics that the system was worth paying for. More institutions were to be added in the inter-war years, especially in the area of hospitals for the poor and residential care for the elderly, but the system itself was adequate and well-founded. At the same time, the need for such a comprehensive system was diminishing as attitudes in the wider society changed and both central and local authorities extended their remit to take care of their citizens. Old age pensions (no matter how meagre) from 1909, National Insurance against unemployment and sickness from 1911, a centralised Ministry of Health from 1919 – these were major indicators of a slow change in philosophical outlook. The Liverpool workhouse on Brownlow Hill, one of the largest in the country, closed in 1928 and the Poor Law Guardians, for so long the arbiters of dignity and despair, lost their powers to Local Authorities. The last of the Poor Law went effectively in 1935, when the Public Assistance Authorities could give relief to people in their own homes. Security with dignity was the aim of the post-1945 changes.

The elderly poor and sick were not, of course, immediately freed from the fear that had been for so long a blight on British society and many of them were still grateful for the care they could receive at home from the Little Sisters of the Poor and the Little Sisters of the Assumption, or the residential care proffered by the Sisters of Nazareth. Educational changes and compulsory schooling cleared the streets for the most part of Nugent's 'street arabs'. Yet the welfare state and universal schooling did not do away with the need for Approved Schools, Orphanages, Homes for Unmarried Mothers and their Babies, Hostels and Homes for young men and women, or facilities for those with Special Needs, and Catholic Social Services developed and adapted in the new atmosphere while continuing to be motivated by the desire to care for the material and spiritual needs of the vulnerable.

There were organisational changes. As a result of the findings of the Curtis Committee and the 1944 Education Act, the English and Welsh bishops decided in 1947 that one authority was needed in each diocese to look after all children's institutions. By this date the archdiocese had nearly 2,400 children in four types of Institution: Voluntary Homes, Residential Schools for the Handicapped, Approved Schools, and Certified Schools for Poor Law Children. These had come under the aegis of six different Government departments, but now they passed under the Children's Branch of the Home Office. Archbishop Downey decided that the responsible body in Liverpool should be the Rescue Society, better known as the Liverpool Catholic Children's Protection Society. It later dropped the word 'Protection' from its title.

Other changes reflected what was happening in social work throughout the country. By the 1970s, under the umbrella of Liverpool Catholic Social Services, the Catholic Children's Society (with Mgr J. Dunne as Administrator) as well as running ten residential homes/schools for boys and girls of all ages and two homes for unmarried mothers, provided a number of 'services': a Family Advice Service, Social Work Services to the Magistrates Courts, A Child Guidance Centre, a Family Casework Service providing long-term intensive support to individual families with difficulties, an Adoption Service and an Advisory Service for people with severe learning difficulties. Religious Orders continued to run their own residential homes for children and provided a wide range of other institutions and services, catering for the deaf, dying, physically and mentally handicapped, the elderly, unmarried mothers, training homes for women and girls and general residential accommodation for men and women. They also ran five hospitals and provided home visiting and nursing. Some societies and institutions changed in rather subtle ways – the Catholic Needlework Guild had been set up to supply clothing and house linen to the poor; by 1977 it had renamed itself Ancilla with the aim of providing 'new clothing and house linen to those in need'.[43]

Despite all the changes, there is a sense of continuity. The Liverpool Benevolent Society (founded 1810) still featured in the *Directory* for 1972, with the aim of assisting 'the sick poor through the clergy', and the even older Broughton Catholic Charitable Society (1787) is still there in 2004, helping 'needy persons, families and charitable organisations on petitions from its members' and offering all its members, clerical and lay a 'share in Masses both during life and after death'.[44] In 1997 the SVP celebrated 150 years of work in Liverpool and had two Central Councils (South West Lancashire and Liverpool) and a presence in most parishes. The Catholic Blind Institute has become Christopher Grange, but its new buildings are in the aptly named Youens Way. Finally, it makes a fitting end to this chapter to note that the Archdiocesan Catholic Social Services are now the Nugent Care Society.

Notes

[1] Warren, pp.19-20; Rowlands, p.125; Bridge, p.71.

[2] Belchem, *Merseypride*, p.121.

[3] L. Feehan, 'Charitable Effort, Statutory Authorities and the Poor in Liverpool, c.1850-1914', unpubl. PhD thesis, University of Liverpool (1987), p.55.

[4] Ozanam, quoted in Warren, p.63.

[5] Warren, pp.61-3.

[6] Feehan, p.30.

[7] John Davies, 'Parish Charity: The Work of the SVP, St Mary's, Highfield St, Liverpool, 1867-8', *NWCH*, XVII (1990), pp.37-46; Feehan, p.49.

[8] Belchem, *Merseypride*, p.126.

[9] Feehan, p.215.

[10] Canon Bennett, *Father Nugent of Liverpool* (1949), is full but uncritical; Burke; Belchem, *Merseypride*, p.119.

[11] Burke, p.183; RCLv 5/2/83, Goss to Nugent 14.10.1857; 5/3/64. Goss to Lans 15.1.1859.

[12] Burke, p.174.

[13] Bennett, pp.30-1.

[14] Ryan, p.47.

[15] Bennett, chaps 5 and 6.

[16] Burke, p.166.

[17] *Ibid.*, p.152.

[18] Bennett, pp.84-92.

[19] *Ibid.*, chap. 9; also, Canon Bennett, 'The Catholic Emigration Association', in *CR*, vol. XX (1950), pp.208-11.

[20] V.A. McClelland, 'The making of Young Imperialists; Rev. Thomas Seddon, Lord Archibald Douglas and the Resettling of British Catholic Orphans in Canada', *RH* 19, no.4 (Oct.1989), pp.509-29, at p.522.

[21] Burke, pp.165, 216.

[22] AAL *Liverpolitana 1885-90*, pastoral letters, Lent 1887 and July 1888.

[23] The best coverage of the case is in M. Whittle, 'Philanthropy in Preston: The Changing Face of Charity in a Nineteenth Century Provincial Town', unpubl. PhD thesis, University of Lancaster (1990), pp.314,ff. I am grateful to Dr Whittle for allowing me to use her thesis.

[24] Whittle, pp.130-8.

[25] Series of articles on the Poor Law Schools by Canon Bennett, CR, XX (1950), p.377.

[26] AAL Early Bishops S1 VII, *Annual Report of the Catholic Certified Poor Law Schools* for 1910.

[27] Burke, p.105; *Directories*.

[28] *Guide to the Catholic Church Services ... for 1861* (1861), p.34.

[29] *Ibid.*, p.37; Burke, p.65; AAL *Annual Reports*.

[30] *Guide to the Catholic Church Services ... for 1861*, pp.37-8; Bennett, *CR*, XX (1950), p.408.

[31] Bennett, *Nugent*, p.93.

[32] The best source is Canon Bennett's six articles, 'The Story of Father Berry's Homes', *CR*, XXI (1951).

[33] Plumb, *Found Worthy*, p.9.

[34] AAL *Liverpolitana*, pastoral letter, 14.2.1912

[35] *Ibid.*, 1.2.1910.

[36] Belchem, *Merseypride*, p.117; Burke, p.223.

[37] Bennett, 'Fr Berry's Homes', pp.408-9.

[38] Bennett, *Nugent*, pp.114-6; Belchem, *Merseypride*, 113-5.

[39] Bennett, *Nugent*, pp.117-26.

[40] June Rockett, *Held in Trust: Catholic Parishes in England and Wales 1900-1950* (2001), p.26.

[41] Bennett, *Nugent*, p.142.

[42] Belchem, *Merseypride*, p.115.

[43] *Directories* 1984, 1997, 2003.

[44] *Ibid.*, 2004, p.199.

CHAPTER 10 CONFRONTATION & CONSOLIDATION: c.1890-1930

By 1900 a network of parishes and a system of social care and education showed how far the diocese had consolidated its position since 1850. General acceptance of Catholics as equal citizens varied, however, no matter how much individual Catholics might be highly regarded by their non-Catholic neighbours. Mgr Nugent's death in 1905 was marked by the erection of a statue by public subscription in his honour in a prominent position in the centre of sectarian-riven Liverpool. Wigan had a Catholic mayor, Thomas Fyans, in 1900, but Liverpool had to wait another forty years for one (the octogenarian Austin Harford, 1943-4) At a more humble level, Fr Thomas Keeley was parish priest at Euxton, near Chorley, from 1898 to 1939 and served as chairman of the parish council for thirty years.[1]

Yet that most English-Catholic of towns, Preston, had only seven councillors out of forty-eight in 1905, and when Catholics pushed for a Catholic mayor in 1909, the Conservatives turned against them and decided that the office should remain an Anglican monopoly. The Catholic move provoked a strong Protestant backlash, with the Rev. Urquhart stating that he hoped the day would never come 'when the regalia of the municipality' would be carried into a Roman Catholic chapel. (It was 1937 before the town had a Catholic mayor and 1951 before it had a Catholic MP).[2] Bigotry was still evident, especially when it came to accepting such essentially Catholic institutions as convents. When the Sisters of the Sacred Heart of Mary opened a house in Ulverston in 1913, the local Anglican rector warned his fellow citizens that he regarded the convent with great unease despite 'the outward charm, culture, quietness and gentleness of these devout ladies' – it sounds like a knee-jerk psychological reaction from the past.[3]

The conflict in Liverpool could on occasion be much more serious. It was not fundamentally anti-Irish so much as intra-Irish and anti-Catholic – there is no doubt that the Orange cause won considerable support from English Protestant workers and hangers-on. Nor is there any doubt that a section of the Tory interest in Liverpool saw it as an advantage that they could rely on this almost inbred anti-Catholicism. Sorting out who was directly responsible for particular outbreaks of street violence is not always straightforward. One such occasion, which may be taken as an example, was the 'Home Rule' election of July 1886. After polling had ended, an Orange band marched from Toxteth to Lime Street, accompanied by a large crowd; the police turned it back but failed to stop the marchers attacking St Patrick's church and breaking its windows. Catholics retaliated by doing the same to Toxteth Protestant churches. Street battles followed over the next few days, leading to eighty casualties who needed hospital treatment; roofing slates were the preferred weapon. Elsewhere, in the North End, Protestants attacked four Catholic houses, ransacking them and beating up the wife of a Catholic whom they wanted but could not find (he was hiding in the cellar). In Toxteth an old Catholic woman led a mob of about 150 men and boys from Norfolk Street to stone the Anglican school in St James Place, while three men broke into the premises of an Orange cobbler and stabbed him. On 12 July Catholics burned effigies of William and Mary and there were more street clashes. As usual, the police were blamed for losing control of the events, but the Chief Constable replied that he would need another 200 men to keep the peace; Orangemen threatened to set up their own vigilante groups. Neal claims that 'hot summer days, boredom and drink' all played a part in these disturbances. While the damage done was relatively minor and casualties few, to the people facing the anger of either a Catholic or an Orange mob the danger was real and there was the constant threat that some similarly minor incident would start the round of violence once more.[4]

It was altogether different when the violence, or at least the threat of it, was deliberately manipulated and in 1909 parts of inner-Liverpool experienced several weeks of religion-inspired communal violence and disorder: 'Religious pageantry touched off murderous assaults' as mounted police charged rioters, women and children brawled outside schools, and men were attacked on their way home from work (one died). 'The authority of the city's police hung by a thread'.[5] Again, basic issues were complex, tied in with Catholic political and social advancement, Orange fears, and generations of street disorder, but the violence was not random or set off by the annual marches on St Patrick's Day or the Twelfth of July – though 'where you could walk' was always a key factor.

The immediate cause of the trouble was not Liverpool-based but was the international Eucharistic Congress in London in 1908 and its planned Blessed Sacrament procession through the streets. A large Protestant rally in Liverpool, led by the fire-brand Pastor George Wise (who had already been in prison for his anti-Catholic abuse and incitement), called for the procession to be banned – it was technically illegal, since the 1829 Emancipation Act had outlawed the public parading of Catholic symbols, though this had never been enforced. An additional red rag were sermons and messages that called for Catholics to pray for the conversion of England – 'to bring back Protestant England to the worship of the Eucharist' was how the *Catholic Herald* put it.[6] In the end the government said that the Blessed Sacrament should not be carried and the procession went ahead without it.

Despite this, in 1909 there were public Blessed Sacrament processions in Manchester, Reading and London, in open defiance of the law, while Catholics were also trying to get Parliament to change the royal Accession Declaration that contained a denunciation of the doctrine of

Transubstantiation. It seemed to many Protestants that English Catholicism was on the march, trying to subvert the laws that protected England's Protestantism. In retaliation, the *Liverpool Protestant Standard* proclaimed 'War Against the Church of Rome'. The first occasion for hostilities came with a huge jubilee procession to mark the sixtieth anniversary of Holy Cross church: streets were decorated, temporary altars set up along the route, banners and statues carried by about 4,500 marchers, and Bishop Whiteside took part in an open carriage. There were, in the end, only a few minor scuffles as mounted police kept the two sides apart. The Protestants claimed that the police were favouring the Catholics, since they had allowed the procession and the altars, but the Chief Constable argued that any breaches of the law had been minor and purely technical.

A few weeks later, another large Catholic procession, this time organised by St Joseph's parish, caused more trouble. Some of the violence was led by Protestants against Catholic houses, but the fiercest of the fighting was against the police, again accused of favouring the Catholics. Over the following months, Pastor Wise preached regularly at the 'St Domingo Pit', the main place for Protestant outdoor meetings, and his hearers took part in sporadic violence against Catholic homes and shops, Everton Valley convent, St Edward's College, the Bishop's house (in the College grounds) and St Alphonsus's church. In the end Wise was imprisoned for refusing to be bound over to keep the peace; this caused more outbursts of violence and things settled down only after his release and a parliament-backed enquiry was set up. Bishop Whiteside forbade any Catholic processions for a year, and promised that in future they would try not to antagonise Protestants; at the same time he called for curbs on Wise's anti-Catholic insults. He was himself stoned in June 1910 as minor clashes continued to break out. Even in the great transport strike of 1911, when Catholic and Protestant workers joined hands in common action, there was bitter fighting between the two sides that was stopped only by armed troops. The fear of general disorder at last persuaded the City authorities to pass bye-laws (enabled by a Liverpool Corporation Act of Parliament of 1912) giving them control over processions, demonstrations, public meetings and the use of religious emblems and music, while it also taught all but the more extreme politicians the danger of fomenting discord by overtly or covertly relying on sectarian voting power. Catholics and Protestants in the sectarian parts of the city retired into what have been called their 'sectarian cocoons', still suspicious of each other but limiting their violence to occasional outbreaks and brawls.[7]

Most Catholics had not been involved in the troubles or even directly affected by them – and this was true also, of course, of the great majority of their non-Catholic neighbours. And there was co-operation as well as conflict, with joint philanthropic enterprises and common subscription lists to charities, including even the building of Catholic orphanages and schools. Less eye-catching than the conflict and less colourful than the sectarian rhetoric, this co-operation was nonetheless part of the relations between the two communities.

The majority of Catholics, however, took it for granted that attending their own schools was an essential part of being 'a good Catholic'. They were proud of their schools, just as they were proud of their parish and its church, even though past pupils often remembered poverty and overcrowding as the key features of those schools – and in 1930 St Malachy's, Liverpool, cancelled its outdoor procession because of 'excessive poverty'.[8] And the clergy were fully aware that the success of the schools, which cost so much, was limited. In 1907 Fr John Wright, SJ, of St Wilfrid's, Preston, noted that a very considerable number of boys who left the parish school never entered a church or received the sacraments again. A few years later he asked what the point was of all the sacrifices made for the schools if each year 'ten thousand drift away from the faith' as soon as their school days were over. He called for a national scheme of Care Societies to keep registers of each year's leavers and try to keep in touch with them – he had started them in St Wilfrid's.[9] Along similar lines, both Mount Carmel and St Patrick's, Liverpool, had what were called 'After Care Committees' (formed in 1917) attached to the Guild of St Agnes (the guild was for young girls up to 16 years of age). Committee members visited the girls who had left school and who were thought to be in danger of falling away, to encourage them to frequent the sacraments and attend the school on one evening a week, for dancing, games, dressmaking, and reading.[10] It seems that none of these initiatives lasted very long.

In some of the larger parishes non-liturgical societies and events flourished with a life of their own and helped to provide a Catholic alternative to secular leisure activities, without however removing Catholics from the latter. How these activities were to flower is evident from a report in the *Parishioner* for February 1922. This carried a section headed 'Carmel News', detailing some of the events at Our Lady of Mount Carmel, Liverpool.[11] A 'gigantic concert' before Christmas had raised money to provide poor children with toys to 'save them from disappointment owing to the hard times'; the Mount Carmel Orchestra had played and accompanied a large number of solo performers. Also before Christmas a 'delightful entertainment' had been presented in Carmel Hall, given by a group known as 'The Carmels' (Pierrot Entertainers), who had also given charity concerts over the previous eighteen months. Whist Drives were held in the boys' club every Tuesday and Irish Dancing taught every Wednesday, while 'The Popular Players' had recently presented their first play in Carmel Hall.

The parish also had its boys' club, called rather grandly the 'Mount Carmel Papal Cadets'. Its founder was Fr John Hayes, an Irish priest who served in the parish from 1915 to 1924 and who was remembered for many years for his work with the Cadets and men's Confraternity – said to be the largest any parish had ever seen. When he left the Home Office wrote to thank him for his work on behalf of the youth of Liverpool.[12]

Parish loyalties united and kept even some nominal Catholics together in some sort of bond. The parochialism they engendered, however, had weaknesses as well as strengths and it was much more difficult to create a sense of belonging to a wider Catholic community. Back in the mid-nineteenth century Mgr Nugent had felt that a Catholic newspaper would help and had launched the *Northern Press and Catholic Times* (in 1872 it became the *Catholic Times* and four years later the *Catholic Times and Catholic Opinion*). He also founded the *Catholic Fireside* and the *Catholic Family Almanac*, forerunner of the diocesan directory. Almanacs were a very popular type of Victorian publication, full of facts, statistics, biographical sketches and, in this case, some quite open Catholic propaganda. Only the *Almanac* was truly diocesan in its news and coverage, but it was published only annually and did not fill the need for a regular Catholic popular journal for the archdiocese, especially when it became the *Diocesan Directory*. This led to the launch of *The Parishioner*, a monthly magazine published in Liverpool between 1917 and 1934.[13]

It was never an official publication but a private commercial venture, although Archbishop Keating gave it some official backing for a few years. It claimed to be a parochial magazine and a means of communication and link between priest and people, giving times of services, accounts of special events, interesting snippets of news and short articles. Archbishop Keating also used it to give a monthly message to its readers and explain new projects and other developments. By the end of its first year it was appearing in different sections for Seaforth and Formby, Bootle and Walton, and North Liverpool. There does not seem to have ever been an 'outside Liverpool' section, although in later years it covered news from Wigan, Leigh and Newton-le-Willows – the presence of the *Wigan Catholic Herald* and the

Preston Catholic News probably goes some way to explain this. It was well-produced and readable and clearly met a need, though it would be interesting to know what the clergy, who boasted of how well they knew their people and how close the bonds with them were, thought of the need for a newspaper to keep them in touch. It gave way in 1934 to Downey's official *Cathedral Record* – this had first appeared in 1931, when Downey had commented favourably on the *Parishioner's* aim to link up the various parts of the archdiocese 'into social and spiritual unity', something he hoped the new monthly would continue to do.

Meanwhile, Bishop Whiteside faced the question of whether to allow his priests to attend St Edmund's House, Cambridge, and study for university degrees, as part of a closer integration of the Catholic body into English society. At first he was strongly opposed, as were the other northern bishops except Wilkinson of Hexham and Newcastle, the only one of them who had graduated from an English university (Durham), and Casartelli of Salford. Whiteside wrote to the Master of St Edmund's in 1897 to say that the hierarchy had declined to approve any general scheme. While they agreed with the aim – the raising of the intellectual standard of the clergy – they feared the risks involved. But about 1905 he had a change of heart and began to send some of his priests to Cambridge – a practice that continued for many years. One of them, Fr Cuthbert Waring, left St Edmund's in 1914 but returned to be Master from 1929 – 34, though not very successfully, it turned out; the historian of St Edmund's claimed that he was far more suited to the 'ecclesiastical Shangri-la of Birchley', where he was parish priest from 1935 to his death in 1961, than the to the 'rough and tumble of Cambridge'.[14]

POLITICS

No one could be Bishop of Liverpool and not be involved in local politics, but both Whiteside and Keating were also called on to state their positions on a number of national issues as well. Perhaps surprisingly, given his general caution in political matters, Whiteside took a somewhat pro-Boer stance in the Boer War, as did many of his flock who were Irish or favoured home rule for Ireland and could not see why the Boers should not have it too. There were strong denunciations nationally of supposed 'Catholic disloyalty', and a local newspaper called the pro-Boers, 'a heterogeneous collection of Anarchists, Socialists, Revolutionists, Screeching Sisters, and cranks of every description', but Whiteside publicly added his name to those who called for a Day of National Humiliation and Prayer to atone for the injustices done to the Boers.[15] At the same time, in January 1900, 200 volunteers from the Liverpool Irish regiment went to Mass at St Patrick's and heard their long-serving chaplain, Mgr Nugent, preach; they then received a great send-off as they departed for South Africa.[16]

Archbishop Keating, second Archbishop of Liverpool, 1921-1928.

On the broader political front, both Archbishop Whiteside and Archbishop Keating had to deal with the growth of Socialism and the rise of the Labour Party as a competitor for the votes of Catholics. For his part, Whiteside believed that a new English Socialism was evolving, which English Catholics could 'clasp hands with' and be friends with – he had even given qualified praise to Snowden's book, *Socialism and Syndicalism*. When the Labour Party adopted nationalisation in 1918 (the famous 'Clause 4'), some Catholic commentators argued that it had become fully Socialist and so should be condemned. Whiteside dealt with the issue sensibly in his Lenten Pastoral of 1919: Catholics were free to join the Labour Party because it had not been explicitly condemned by Rome. There was no reason, he argued, why Catholics should not co-operate with non-Catholics to promote the 'social and even the moral regeneration' of their society, as long as principles were not compromised. He listed some of the areas where such co-operation could be fruitful: housing, temperance, sweated labour, divorce and secular education. When Cardinal Gasparri consulted him and some of the other English bishops in 1919 about the Labour Party he replied that it was more important for Catholics to judge the individual measures that the Party might try to introduce rather than engage in arguments about its theories.[17]

Most of Archbishop Keating's statements on the topic dated from his time as Bishop of Northampton (1908-21). He took part in Catholic Social Guild and Catholic Women's League meetings – he was the CSG's first president – and showed a willingness to engage with social issues and debates that marked him off from almost all of the other bishops. He favoured state intervention on issues such as pensions and national insurance, though he could also criticise it for trying to 'make men moral by legislation'. He believed that modern poverty was so bad it needed special treatment that went beyond traditional approaches: it was 'hopeless, without expectation of the life that is now or of that which is to come'; later he claimed that 'the degradation of the slums' was not only an injustice that the Church was bound to voice but also a barrier that checked all her efforts to do good. He wanted to mend the industrial system rather than change it radically, and he still feared Socialism because it was so materialist in its philosophy. But he welcomed the fact that there were representatives in Parliament of 'such a large class and such a suffering class' as the workers. On the issue of membership of the Labour Party he argued that it was the duty of Catholics to stay in the party to fight the extremists; the Party, he felt, was not against all forms of private property, and nationalisation was not necessarily evil in all circumstances. Any condemnation of the Labour Party would give workers the message that the Church was siding with the rich against the poor and that would make even docile Catholics 'grow cold in their loyalty'.[18]

In 1926 he made it quite clear where he stood on the issues of the General Strike: he wrote to his clergy:

> *Our clear duty is to stand by lawfully constituted authority … Obeying implicitly and refraining from all violence and provocation we must make our conduct square with our religious profession, not rendering evil for evil …*

This was not, however, a statement in favour of the mine-owners, for he made it equally clear that he believed nationalization of the mines might be the only viable Christian solution to the ongoing problems in the industry; no 'decent country', he was sure, should tolerate the wholesale devastation of the mining areas and the breaking up of mining communities. When a layman had written to him about Cardinal Bourne's open condemnation of the Strike, Keating had replied that the statement had been purely Bourne's own view and was only a theological opinion: Catholics should treat it with respect but were not committed to agreeing with it. He personally agreed with those TUC leaders who had repudiated the General Strike as an unlawful weapon, and he urged Catholic trade unionists (his correspondent was presumably one) to fight hard keep the trade unions away from 'extremist politicians'.[19]

The issue of 'the priest in politics' was a delicate one: Catholics could easily be offended and Protestants have a field day if they scented priestly interference – they already regarded Catholics as 'priest-ridden' and the more extreme of them believed that Catholics received their orders in the confessional if not more openly. For this reason Whiteside had taken a very strict line on priests taking sides in public. The vocation of the priest, he had argued, was to serve and save everybody, and so he must stand aloof from political differences among his people and give no weight to political meetings by his presence or allow parish buildings to be used for political meetings. At the same time the priest should encourage any of his flock who were so inclined to devote themselves 'heart and soul' to political movements. Here Whiteside was following the line laid down by his predecessor, for Bishop O'Reilly had insisted on political neutrality because in England every congregation would contain members of every political party; the Church, he had argued, was 'the impartial mother of all, embracing all, rejecting none, as long as they are guided by her counsels'.[20]

This did not mean, at least for Whiteside, that the clergy should not be politically aware and even at times extremely active. In June 1900, for example, he had called together the parish priests of the Liverpool missions and re-activated the Catholic Registration Association that he had set up in 1897 to ensure that those Catholics entitled to vote in local elections would be properly registered. The Bishop was president of the Association and he wanted parish committees to be set up to encourage Catholics to register and to help them take disputed cases through the Revision Courts.[21] Just before the School Board Elections in November he stressed to the clergy that the elections were 'purely a Catholic question' and ordered them to remind their people to call at the Catholic Committee Room in their parish and collect a voting card, on which would be printed the name of the candidate he or she was to vote for. In 1906 he went further and obliged Catholics under conscience not to vote Liberal in the elections because he was so opposed to the Liberal Government's plans for education. Neutrality clearly had its limits.

By the mid-twenties Archbishop Keating had become more interested in local issues. The political situation in Liverpool was complex. After the establishment of the independent Irish state, Irish Nationalism lost its power as a rallying force and the Irish National Party rapidly declined into insignificance, despite the fact that it had espoused general issues such as housing and had become popular as a working-class movement apart from its Irish policies. Some of its former members tried to keep it going as the Irish Democratic Party but with no success, and the way was open for the Labour Party to win over its former supporters.

Some Catholic commentators were concerned that the Catholics in Liverpool would lose whatever cohesion they had had and cease to be the force their numbers warranted in local elections. As early as April 1922 the *Parishioner* was commenting on the apathy of many Catholics in the recent elections of Poor Law Guardians: in some districts more than half had not voted. Archbishop Keating shared these concerns, claiming that the solid block of Catholics on various municipal bodies had been the result of the work of the Irish Nationalists, and with their demise Catholics had it in their own hands to 'cherish or to squander' that heritage. In late 1923 he hoped that the Catholic vote in the November (local) elections would be cast for Catholic candidates because he believed that no political party could be trusted to safeguard Catholic interests as loyally as Catholics could do themselves.[22]

The Archbishop was moving towards some way of ensuring the return of candidates who would put religion above party when Catholic interests were at stake: he could not rely on the Liverpool Conservatives because they had too close a link with the Orange Order and extreme Protestantism, and he feared the socialism to be found in some sections of the Labour Party and its avowed opposition to denominational schools. He announced that priests and people had set up a new Catholic Representation Association (the CRA) in the six wards of the Scotland Road district. He went out of his way to stress that this was not to be thought of as a Catholic political party, and he rebutted charges in the local press that the action was 'provocative', 'aggressive' and 'sectarian', although, surely, in the Liverpool context it was the last of these, intentionally or not. It re-awakened Protestant militancy and complaints about 'the priest in politics'; almost inevitably it became known as the Catholic Party – even some Catholic councillors referred to it as such.[23]

Keating regarded it rather as a defensive move, to protect Catholic interests in the various municipal bodies by returning 'our own' candidates. So it was more than a matter of just ensuring that Catholics would be fully registered to vote: the Association would choose its list of candidates, 'who might belong to any political party or to none', as Keating put it, and Catholics in the six wards that made up the Scotland Road area (where they constituted a majority of the population) would be expected to vote for those candidates and so return a 'Catholic contingent'. Catholics, he argued, would gain nothing by apathy or disunion but contempt, and would put the Catholic vote 'in the pocket of political wire-pullers who will use it for their own ends'.[24]

While officially neutral between all parties, Keating was taking action in reality against the Labour Party that was beginning to capture the Catholic vote. What he was objecting to, apparently, was that the Labour Party insisted on its representatives voting according to the party line, so that Catholic representatives would not be free to support Catholic interests if these were not in agreement with party policy. He spoke of Labour in terms of open warfare but blamed Labour for this and for wanting 'to carry on the feud'; when he wrote to Mgr George, parish priest of St Joseph's and a CRA candidate, his language was extreme:

> *you have no choice but to teach them the stern lesson they are asking for. You can give no quarter ... We have no use for political dictators. The Catholic voter must be master in his own house – especially when he lives in Scotland Road!*[25]

But, of course, he wanted all the elected CRA representatives to vote as a block, and encouraged the clergy to get Catholics to the elections where they would vote for the names on the card they had been given.

The Constitution of the CRA (not formally agreed until September 1927) set up ward and parish committees, the latter consisting of clergy and representatives of adult parochial societies, with an overall Central Council that would select candidates. It was a strange document. On the one hand it quoted papal statements on the need for Christian Democracy to stay clear of politics and ensure it did not serve political parties and political ends, and, of course, to be totally subservient to the local bishop – it is interesting that in an earlier speech Keating had described party politics as a menace. At the same time, it pledged itself to work for the social betterment of the working classes on such issues as a living wage and better working conditions 'so that work proportionate to their strength, age and sex be given them'. The CRA was also to push local authorities to provide decent sanitary, and sufficiently large, houses. Finally, the CRA pledged itself to uphold the principle that employers could expect their workers to do their work 'fully and honestly' in accordance with a 'free and equitable agreement'. How the CRA could achieve these aims without getting involved in politics was, to say the least, unclear. The constitution ended with a pledge to be signed by every CRA candidate that he would 'sit, act and vote' with other CRA members on all Catholic matters.[26]

While Liverpool Protestants objected vociferously to this Catholic action, Keating faced the strongest opposition from those Catholics who had espoused the Labour cause and hoped to benefit from the end of the Irish National party. Six leading Catholics of the Scotland Divisional Labour Party wrote to the Archbishop in 1925 to voice their concerns about the reported launch of a 'Catholic Party'. There was even stronger opposition when the CRA put up Catholic candidates to oppose Catholic Labour candidates, especially when these were men of proven loyalty to the Church – in October 1927 Keating apologised to James Sexton (see page 212), saying that it was deplorable that the CRA should be putting up a candidate against him after Sexton's many years of faithful service to the Church – 'Catholic fighting Catholic is a sorry spectacle and ought to cease'; but what did Keating expect? Sexton was standing for Labour and Keating seemed to blame the Labour Party for putting up Catholic candidates against the CRA – 'If your party persists in trying to oust our 'sitting members', the CRA cannot be blamed for retaliation'. He would see if he could get the CRA to drop its opposition in this particular case, but expected Sexton to use his influence on the Labour Party to come to a friendly understanding and not stand against sitting CRA members.[27] But there was no likelihood that this would happen – the Labour Party was determined to try to replace the defunct Irish National Party as the first and obvious choice for the city's working-class Catholic voters.

The CRA was successful in four of the five wards in which it opposed Labour in November 1925 and managed to get its candidate, P.J. Kelly, elected as an alderman against the Labour candidate W.A. Robinson (a convert and later a faithful Catholic MP), but it would be a mistake to think that it had the support of all the Catholics in the areas concerned – there was no single Catholic response in these matters, nor would they necessarily follow the lead given by the clergy.[28] Robinson had condemned the formation of a Catholic Party as he would, he claimed, condemn any other party based on religious adherence, for such moves only served to divide and weaken the working-class. The case of P.J. Kelly is instructive: formerly an active member of the Irish National Party and a strong trade union champion, he had supported the Irish Democratic Party (an attempt to keep the Nationalist Party going under a different title) in 1924 but had lost his seat on the City Council; he resigned the leadership of the IDP and joined the CRA. This supported the impression that many people had that the CRA was just a vehicle manufactured to keep former Nationalist politicians in power.

The *Parishioner* gave a brief biography of Mgr Thomas George, parish priest of St Joseph's, Liverpool, 'whose triumphant return to the City Council was the outstanding feature of the Liverpool Municipal Elections' – he beat the ex-Nationalist-turned-Labour candidate by 3,400 votes to 617. Another priest, Fr T Rigby, parish priest of St Sylvester's, Liverpool, was also elected, but in the same ward (North Scotland) the Labour Party won back the seat the following year with Robinson as its candidate, and overall CRA representation on the Council diminished. It was successful again in 1927 in the Poor Law elections, getting six candidates in the Exchange Ward elected – including two priests, Frs O'Ryan, OMI, and Fr O'Shea – a victory hailed by the *Catholic Times* with the comment that the attempt by the Labour Party to 'capture' the Catholic seats had 'failed miserably'.[29]

A key meeting of inner-city clergy in January 1928 discussed the future of the CRA. Some argued powerfully against its continuance in any form – it had caused bitter divisions among their people, some of whom had stopped attending church and the sacraments as a result, and its anti-Labour line and obvious clerical interference were destroying the traditional respect for the clergy. Other priests argued just as strongly for its necessity – only lax or already lapsed Catholics were criticising it, and the Labour Clubs throughout the area were doing great damage to people's loyalty; one priest spoke of the need to 'smash socialism just as Central Liverpool had smashed Birrell'. In the end a small majority voted to continue the CRA, but only on condition that it was extended to all the parishes in Liverpool and changed its character (19 voted for, 13 against and 15 abstained).[30] Keating died unexpectedly on 7 February 1928 and the advent of Archbishop Downey put an end to the CRA altogether.

Keating had been naive if he had believed that Catholics would automatically vote as the clergy told them to, especially if people thought their social and economic betterment were at stake, and they were far being a united or consistent body. Just what the experienced and fairly worldly-wise Keating had in mind is not clear – he certainly did not see the CRA operating outside a very small part of Liverpool and that only in local elections. Despite what his opponents (and some historians) claimed, he had not set out to found a Catholic Party, but he had failed to understand that local politics, and Catholic voters, were far more complex than he had thought – or been led to believe. It may be that he had been taken in by

Nationalist politicians anxious to keep their careers going by organising the Catholic vote in their favour and promising the continuation of the useful Catholic influence on boards of Poor Law Guardians and the City Council.

Returning to the national scene, a small number of Catholic Members of Parliament held seats in the archdiocese. The first Irish member of parliament winning an English seat was T.P. ('Tay Pay') O'Connor who had won the Scotland Division in Liverpool in 1885. He was adopted by the Liverpool Irish as one of their own although he had no earlier links with the city (he had first been elected for Galway in 1880). He held the seat until his death in 1929 and became a highly respected member of the Commons (he became president of the national board of film censors in 1916) – such was his popularity that he was given walk-overs from 1918 onwards. He had founded the Irish National League in 1882 and his abiding interest was in the politics of Home Rule, in which he followed a strictly constitutional, anti-violence line. Despite his great popularity in Liverpool he seems to have been hardly interested in local or specifically Catholic issues; in the 1920s he spoke in the Commons in favour of Catholic schools on a number of occasions, but saw education more as an urgent need for his poor constituents than as a strictly Catholic issue – and the Commons politely ignored him, anyway. It is said that the first World War, when he shared a recruitment platform with Churchill and urged the Liverpool Irish to fight for 'Our free Empire', made him a Liverpool rather than an Irish MP.[31]

Another Catholic who gained something of a national reputation as an MP was James Sexton, the 'Dockers MP', who represented St Helens for Labour from 1918 to 1931. A rather old-fashioned Christian Socialist in many of his views, he was a keen trade unionist and a fervent patriot, being awarded a CBE in 1917 for his support of Lord Derby's 'Liverpool Dock Battalions' which put the dockers under military discipline (and gave them uniforms and extra pay) to help the war effort. His parliamentary career was devoted in large measure to Labour and Trade Union interests, but he spoke in support of Catholic schools and opposed his party's proposals for secular education. He was knighted in 1931.[32]

Francis Nicholas Blundell of Little Crosby represented Ormskirk as a Conservative from 1922 to 1929 and was the main mover in getting the Roman Catholic Relief Act passed in 1926 – it removed almost all the remaining legal disabilities from Catholics. Also in the Conservative camp was Sir James Philip Reynolds who represented the Exchange Division of Liverpool from 1929 to 1932 and was High Sheriff of Lancashire from 1927 to 1928. A recent historian has argued that Catholics in England were prone to exaggerate their electoral clout; the small number of Catholic MPs representing the most Catholic part of the country would seem to support this view.[33] It had not always been clear to the electorate at large how far Catholics, if elected to either Parliament or local Councils, would represent a wider community and not just their own sectional interests; O'Connor and Sexton at least showed that this could happen.

MIXED MARRIAGES

One issue that was a lasting source of confrontation between Catholics and their neighbours was that of mixed marriages – indeed it could be argued that no other single issue aroused so much bitterness. It was also an issue that divided Catholics, despite the official tirades of the Church against them. Where Catholics were a small minority there were bound to be problems in finding suitable Catholic partners, and even where they were living in predominantly Catholic areas, as in parts of the larger towns and cities, it was impossible to think of confining their social contacts entirely to their co-religionists. For the clergy, too, there were conflicts between a desire to see Catholics more integrated into society and the obvious dangers of a resulting increase in mixed marriages. Nor were the clergy united in condemning mixed marriages out of hand: some saw them as opportunities for a fruitful apostolate and a few even saw them as a useful or even necessary tool in the conversion of England.

Under Bishops Goss and O'Reilly Catholics found it relatively easy in practice to obtain a dispensation for a mixed marriage, no matter how fiercely they might be condemned from the altar. The Rev. James Swarbrick of Preston had summed up the traditional arguments in a sermon in 1858 (later published as a pamphlet at the request of his fellow clergy): two things, he was sure, were pre-eminently destructive of children's welfare, heresy and adultery, and the Church abhorred both. A wide difference of opinion on the 'very first duty of man' created a broad chasm between the partners, and could neither strengthen their union nor generate love. Moreover, he went on, they 'could have no sure hope of meeting each other in the next life'. They could not strengthen each other in faith, no matter how naturally virtuous the Protestant might be, and the children could hardly ever acquire thorough religious principles: he concluded, 'alas! alas! many are the instances where children sprung from such marriages end their days expressing no belief ...'[34]

The whole issue of marriages caused severe pastoral problems. Priests found it very difficult to keep track of Catholics in the large town missions with their crowded courts and cellars and the custom of easy flitting from residence to residence. There was also the ease of access for any Irish people who wanted to take advantage of a less strict attitude to mixed marriages and who could easily pass themselves off as recent immigrants with an address of convenience. Alternatively, they might want to avail themselves of the legal anomaly resulting from the fact that Tridentine legislation had not been promulgated in England, and so marriages that would have been invalid in Ireland were valid if contracted in this country. There was, in addition, the normal difficulty of Liverpool being a major port, with sailors and others passing through or staying for only short periods.

Mixed marriages were only to be expected in a predominantly Protestant country such as England, even in towns like Liverpool, Preston and Wigan, where Catholics were at least likely to have plenty of social contacts with other Catholics. Outside the towns they were even more likely to occur, as the priest reported from Hornby: his people were too poor and scattered to have a Catholic school and hardly ever met other Catholics except at Mass on Sundays.[35] It was a point that all the bishops felt strongly about and said so to Rome when asked for their views in 1867: to prohibit mixed marriages would only result in more serious evils and drive more Catholics into marrying outside the Church altogether. It was not a point, however, that Propaganda accepted: the English bishops received a severe rebuke for not having taken more notice of an earlier Roman condemnation of mixed marriages and were told that the granting of mixed marriage dispensations should be a burden on episcopal consciences; they were to be allowed only for the gravest of reasons.[36]

Despite this, pastoral practice continued much as before in the diocese and Bishop Goss refused to make it more difficult to gain a dispensation. He had consulted his clergy and their general view was that to tighten the regulations would only cause trouble. A number of priests, indeed, believed the Church gained rather than lost from mixed marriages, and gave statistics to prove it. In fifty-eight missions, for example, there had been 2,716 mixed marriages, and in 859 of these the Protestant partner had become a Catholic and only 395 Catholic partners were neglecting their duties; in 1,727 cases all the children were being brought up in the Church, and in seventy-nine others at least some of the children were.[37] What is striking is the widely differing effect of mixed marriages in different missions. At Huyton there had been twelve mixed marriages and in every case the Catholic partner was neglecting his or her duties and there had been no converts. At Newton-le-Willows thirty-one mixed marriages had produced one convert, and twenty-eight of the Catholics involved had become negligent or had left the Church. On the other hand, at Great Crosby, ninety-four mixed marriages had produced forty-five converts, one apostate and none who were negligent, while the inner-city mission of St Mary's, Liverpool, had seen 155 mixed marriages, one convert, and 152 faithful Catholic partners.

Mixed marriages, clearly, could have provided a fruitful apostolate, but, equally clearly, that apostolate was being neglected in many cases. This is not surprising, for the strongly-worded condemnations of mixed marriages were self-fulfilling prophecies and led many to believe they were doomed to failure from the outset and not worth the investment of any pastoral energy. The Bishop felt unable to give positive guidance, leaving his priests trying to impose a law that ran counter to the social demands of the situation in which most of their people lived. An intriguing comment was added by the Bishop's secretary to the account of a sermon on the evils of mixed marriages given by Goss at Southport: 'The Bishop (was) himself the son of a mixed marriage, therefore he did not speak from feeling but from duty'.[38]

214

This relatively tolerant approach continued under Bishop O'Reilly. In his reports to Rome he lamented the number of mixed marriages, of course, putting the main blame for them on those Catholics who attended the Board Schools, where education was free, or the workhouses, where Catholic provision was lacking. There was also the difficulty of priests keeping track of young Catholics who moved around on a regular basis to wherever work could be found. Moreover, he believed, one mixed marriage started a line of subsequent mixed marriages as children followed their parents' bad example. For most of the 1880s mixed marriage dispensations ran at an average of 110 a year; for the last seven years of O'Reilly's episcopate the average rose to 195 a year, with a thirty year high of 227 in 1894. So, despite his 'very frequent and most vehement' denunciations of the practice and his urging his priests to do everything to prevent it, and despite opening a school for the workhouse children in Liverpool, the number of Catholics contracting mixed marriages was increasing. Indeed, reading the Bishop's reports to Rome one gets the impression that the strong language and almost strident denunciation of mixed marriages may have been intended mainly to deflect likely Roman criticism of the growing numbers of dispensations, and that neither Bishop nor priests really felt there was much that could be done to prevent them, especially as Catholics were gradually becoming more integrated into the wider society around them.[39]

His successor, Archbishop Whiteside, firmly opposed any hint of pragmatism in this matter and insisted on adopting a strictly orthodox line. His ideal would have been a diocese in which no dispensations for mixed marriages were either asked for or granted: as he put it in a letter to the clergy, 'A favourable or lenient attitude (to them) is irreconcilable with the teaching and the laws of the Church.' He went on to warn his priests, 'If such an attitude is taken by a pastor of souls, let him beware!'[40] His stricter policy was successful in that he reduced the number of dispensations quite markedly: the annual average fell to 57 between 1896 and 1907, with an all-time low of 29 in 1904.[41] Whether he had reduced the number of mixed marriages is, of course, a different question.

He opened his public attack in 1900 with twenty-page Instruction to be read at all Masses: after the traditional arguments against mixed marriages he pleaded with the people never to forget their inheritance: they were the descendants of those 'who in bitter times have suffered hardships untold, rather than tarnish in the least the faith they prized so much'. They should follow the example of their noble ancestors, and, whatever the cost, see that they handed on to their children and their children's children their faith vigorous and unimpaired.[42] At the Diocesan Synod in 1905 he imposed the normal law of the Church for the 'few mixed marriages' in the diocese. They had to take place in the sacristy, without any religious rite at all – without cotta and stole and omitting all the blessings and prayers, including blessing the ring and even the words 'ego vos conjungo' (I join you together). There was, however, a let out: if in a particular case the head priest judged that in the circumstances grave evils would result from following these strict regulations, then he was at liberty to use the form of ceremony previously in use – i.e., the ceremony could take place in the church, with the priest wearing a stole, but not at the high altar and without any sign of outward celebration.[43]

It is not clear how many priests made use of this escape clause, but there is some later evidence of how they regarded the stricter approach. In 1913 Whiteside had to collect statistics on the prevalence of mixed marriages across the northern province to compile a return requested by Rome. The returns for the archdiocese contain comments from the clergy: ninety-nine parish priests declared themselves in favour of the stricter approach, with comments such as, 'it has improved the tone of the parish' and has had 'good effects'. The twenty-five that declared against the regulations commented, 'nothing gained'; 'does not prevent the marriage'; 'harmful' and 'impaired the religious life' of the parish. One argued that mixed marriages were necessary 'for the Conversion of England' and that the regulations 'improved the good people, but injured the bad – extreme strictness harmful', causing great loss to the faith.[44]

Whiteside returned to the issue in 1920 with another lengthy letter (20 pages) to the clergy, again urging a very strict line and ordering his priests to 'stop them at all cost' – it reads as though his previous instructions on the matter had not stopped enough of the clergy from asking for dispensations. The spiritual future of any diocese, he wrote, depended in very large part upon the spirit of faith 'animating the upgrowing generation'. To keep this spirit alive, children must live in 'a Catholic atmosphere, both in school and in their own homes'. The generosity of the people had ensured that about 97% of the children in the diocese experienced 'the invigorating atmosphere' of a Catholic school. Yet only if both parents were Catholics could the same atmosphere exist at home; otherwise the religious atmosphere there 'is never bracing, is generally enervating, and is sometimes noxious'. He claimed that 80% of the Catholic homes in the archdiocese were 'truly Catholic', but attacked those priests who, either through a misguided leniency, or, worse still:

> *a cowardly fear of offending certain members of his flock, or, again, through a misplaced sympathy for the worldly prospects of an individual, ranges himself against the Church and her laws, and instead of defending her against her rebellious children, takes their part against her.*[45]

The strict line prevailed down to the 1950s. Whiteside's successor, Archbishop Keating set up a special commission to examine 'thoroughly and conscientiously' the results of his predecessor's policy. The members of the commission reported that they themselves, and an overwhelming majority of the rest of the clergy, were convinced that the policy had had beneficial results and they would 'deprecate any serious relaxation in our practice'.[46] They may have been satisfied with policy and practice, but both were soon to cause a public row between Catholics and Protestants under Archbishop Downey (see pages 252- 5 below) .

PASTORAL PROVISION AND GROWTH

A rigorist in many ways, the positive side of Archbishop Whiteside's pastoral concern for his people is best seen in the matter of Holy Communion, where he was perfectly in tune with the thinking of the Pope, St Pius X. The Pope's two decrees on the subject (in 1905 and 1910) were considered truly revolutionary in their positive encouragement of frequent Communion and on the matter of children's First Holy Communion. In 1907 and 1908 Whiteside reported that frequent Communion had taken on well in the diocese, but he thought more should be done to encourage the people – for example, a triduum of prayers and devotions during the octave of Corpus Christi. He had already taken the initiative, before the papal decrees, with a pastoral letter of 1901: this dealt with the question of why more Catholics did not receive Communion frequently. He reported that to mark the start of the new century there had been special midnight services in churches throughout the diocese and these had been remarkably successful, with reports from all sides of:

> churches unable to contain the crowds which flocked to them, of devout adorers of the Blessed Sacrament, and of unprecedented numbers that approached Holy Communion … (focusing) on Jesus Christ the Redeemer; not as he is to so many around us, the merely historical personage … but Jesus Christ, true God and true Man, as really present and living on our altars, as He was with His Apostles.

If only those numbers would receive regularly, he went on, what a change in their lives and the lives of those around them. Yet so many only received a few times each year when they could easily do so more frequently. Holy fear might be an obstacle for some, but they should remember that no matter how gravely or frequently a person had sinned, if he or she received absolution in confession then monthly Communion was not only lawful but advisable, and everyone should be encouraged to reach at least this standard of frequent Communion.[47] Towards the end of his life published annual statistics to show both the overall diocesan total of Communions received and the figures for each parish; he claimed that whereas the total diocesan figure in 1910 had been just in excess of 2.7 million, by 1919 the number had risen to 5.7 million. Figures from individual parishes were striking: whereas 125 girls made their First Communions in 1910 in Mount Carmel parish, over 700 did so the following year, while at the Peace Festivities in 1919 over 800 children received Communion at the 9 o'clock Mass.[48]

A feature of parish life in these years was the holding of General Missions. In 1910 Whiteside announced one that was to last for three weeks in some 47 churches, with about 120 missioners brought in 'to preach the truths of salvation' – a massive logistical exercise in itself, including moving curates out of presbyteries to accommodate the visitors. The Bishop arranged to administer confirmation on eleven occasions during the second two weeks, temporary confessionals were put up to cope with the large numbers of penitents expected and curates were asked to do confessional duty in other churches where demand was the greatest. The second Sunday of the Mission was to be kept as a day of Reparation for the insults offered to the Blessed Sacrament: each church should hold a General Communion of Reparation and Exposition of the Blessed Sacrament.[49] Acts of Reparation to the Blessed Sacrament were a common feature of Redemptorist missions: a modern Redemptorist historian has written that they had an element of quite deliberate theatre, in that they included a dramatic form of preaching about the horror of sacrilegious communions, with a clear suggestion that all present were guilty of them; the act of reparation was itself a catharsis, allowing the pent-up emotions to be released and expressed as 'penitential distress'.[50] By the 1920s the city deaneries had to be divided into three groups, each having its general mission at a different time to ease the burden on the mission-givers and make the logistics more manageable.

Despite the interruptions caused by the war of 1914 – 1918, Whiteside's years saw a considerable growth in the provision of churches and priests throughout the archdiocese. In 1895 there had been 383 priests (247 Secular, 136 Religious) serving the diocese, with 162 churches and public chapels, and 37 convent and other private chapels; in 1921, the number of priests had increased to 504 (322 Secular, 182 Religious), with 204 churches and public chapels, and no fewer than 69 convent and other private chapels.[51]

~

Archbishop Whiteside died unexpectedly as the result of stroke on 28 January 1921. His funeral was marked by a great demonstration of grief at the passing of a pastor who had never hesitated to defend Catholic rights: the streets from the pro-cathedral were lined by school-children and teachers for a distance of five or six miles towards Ford Cemetery, and a large crowd of men and women followed the cortège on foot.[52] Nothing on such a scale had been seen in the city before and it was another example of the peculiarly strong feeling that Liverpool Catholics developed for their bishops. His successor, Bishop Keating of Northampton, was to claim that English Catholics respected rather than loved their bishops; they might value them as spokesmen and official standard bearers and pray for them when they were sick or dying, but otherwise they tended to be forgotten and even unknown.[53] Keating himself had made something of a name on the national Catholic stage and had probably been the most energetic of the bishops on the social and political front;[54] at Liverpool, however, he was to be totally taken up with local issues and internal affairs, the first of which was the division of the archdiocese, the subject of the next chapter.

Notes

1 Plumb, *Found Worthy*, p.78.

2 Savage, pp.159-60; Smith, 'Turning the Century', p.24.

3 Rockett, pp.93-4.

4 Frank Neal, *Sectarian Violence. The Liverpool Experience 1819-1914* (1988), pp.186-7; John Bohstedt, 'More than One Working Class: Protestant-Catholic Riots in Edwardian Liverpool', in John Belchem (ed.), *Popular Politics, Riot and Labour. Essays in Liverpool History 1790-1940* (1992), pp.173-216 – my account is based on this article.

5 Bohstedt, p.173.

6 *Ibid.*, p.178.

7 *Ibid.*, p.209.

8 Mary Campion McCarren FCJ, Frances Trotman & Marion Piggin, *With Devotedness and Love – 150 Years of service to Catholic Education* (1994), p.43.

9 Warren, pp.71-2.

10 McCarren FCJ, p.37.

11 *The Catholic Parishioner*, Feb. 1922, p.20. (see note 14).

12 Hewlett, *Mount Carmel*, p.14.

13 Peter Doyle, 'A Link Between Priests and People: The Parishioner Magazine', *NWCH*, XXIX (2002), pp.101-8. It was called *The Liverpool Catholic Parishioner* for a time.

14 Garrett Sweeney, *St Edmund's House, Cambridge, the First Eighty Years* (1980), pp.8, 36, 170.

15 Waller, p.182.

16 M. Snape, 'British Catholicism and the British Army in the First World War' *RH*, vol.26, no.2 (Oct. 2002), p.321; John Davies, 'British Catholics and the South African War. 1899-1900', Hilton (ed.), *Turning the Last Century*, pp.47-65.

17 G.P. McEntee, *The Social Catholic Movement in Great Britain* (1927), pp.99, 133; Aspden, *Fortress Church*, pp.131-7.

18 Aspden, pp.55-8.

19 AAL Keating, S2 I C:, ad clerum 6.6.1926; S4 I, A, Letter Books1921-8, Keating to Robert Georgeson, 13.5.1926; *Parishioner*, June 1926; Aspden, pp.170-2.

20 AAL Early Bishops, S1 VII, ad clerum 25.2.1903; S1 V A: O'Reilly to Walmsley, 22.10.1882.

21 *Catholic Times*, 1.6.1900, p.4; AAL Keating Collection S5 Social Issues, II, B/3, 'Instructions for Canvassers etc.'

22 *The Parishioner*, April 1922 and Nov. 1923; Sam Davies, 'A Stormy Political Career: P.J. Kelly and Irish Nationalist and Labour Politics in Liverpool, 1891-1936', *THSLC*, 148 (1999), pp.147-89.

23 *The Parishioner*, Nov. 1925, p.1; AAL Keating Collection, S5 II B/4, CRA 1925-28: Councillor Luke Hogan to Keating, 12.10.1925.

24 *The Parishioner*, as n.23.

25 AAL Keating Collection, S4 I, Letter Books, p.514, Keating to VG, 26.2.1926; pp.541-3, Keating to George, 18.3.1926.

26 AAL Keating Collection, S5 II B/4, 'Constitution of the Catholic Representation Association', 22.9.1927. Aspden, p.132.

27 AAL Keating Collection, S5 II B/4, letter of 6.10.1925 to Keating; S4 I, Letter Books, Keating to Sexton, 5.10.1927.

28 S. Davies, 'P.J. Kelly', p.187.

29 *Parishioner*, Sept. 1925, p.3; Waller, p.299; Apden, p.159; *Catholic Times*, 8.4.1927.

30 AAL Keating Collection, S5 II B/3, 24.1.1928.

31 L.W. Brady, *T.P. O'Connor and the Liverpool Irish* (1983).

32 John Davies, 'Catholic Representatives in Parliament: the North West of England 1918-1945', *RH* vol. 26, no.2 (Oct. 2002), pp.359-83

33 Dermot Quinn, *Patronage and Piety. The Politics of Roman Catholicism, 1850-1900* (1993), pp.86, 153.

34 *Marriage, A Sermon Preached at St Augustine's by the Rev. James Swarbrick … 1858* (1858), published by clerical request.

35 RCLv Visitation Returns, 1865, Hornby.

36 *Decreta*, pp.315-7.

37 RCLv Conference Reports 1863-4; Visitation Returns, 1865.

38 RCLv Visitation Diaries, 3/B Oct. 1864.

39 APF *S.R. Anglia*, vol. 25, pp.16-64, report of Jan. 1883; vol. 25, p.482-529, Dec. 1887.

40 AAL *Liverpolitana*, ad clerum ?Feb. 1896.

41 AAL Early Bishops S1 VII A/14, *Responsa ad Quaesita de Matrimoniis Mixtis*, 13 Sept. 1914; the returns are extremely detailed.

42 AAL Early Bishops S1 VII, C/6.

43 *Ibid.*, C/3, Synod 1905.

44 See note 42.

45 AAL Early Bishops S1 VII, ad clerums 1907-1921, Jan 1920.

46 E.K. Bennett, *Whiteside*, p.26.

47 AAL Early Bishops, S1 VII, C, ad clerums, 28.5.1907, 12.6.1908, 3.9.1908; *Liverpolitana*, pastoral, 21.2.1901.

48 E.K. Bennett, *Whiteside*, p.27; M.C. McCarren FCJ, *With Devotedness*, pp.36-7.

49 As note 48, also, AAL S1 VII C: ad clerums Oct. 1910 and Oct. 1915.

50 Sharp, *Reapers*, p.167.

51 E.K. Bennett, *Whiteside*, p.19.

52 *Ibid.*, pp.31-2.

53 Quoted in Aspden, p.1.

54 *Ibid.*, pp.117-8.

CHAPTER 11 DIVIDING THE ARCHDIOCESE

I t is not clear when talk of dividing the Archdiocese of Liverpool began in any serious way. It was in the air as early as 1911 when the diocese became an archdiocese – Cardinal Lépicier of the Consistorial Congregation spoke to Archbishop Whiteside and asked him to supply statistics and a map for a new diocese based on Preston, although the Cardinal thought nothing would happen 'for the present'.[1] When Whiteside died unexpectedly in January 1921 the Congregation in Rome took the opportunity to discuss the possibility of a division, so that any decision would be a fait accompli for his successor. The basic argument in favour of dividing the archdiocese was its size and the number of parishes it contained: to visit these properly was very demanding and even the ultra-conscientious and energetic Whiteside could only complete a full visitation in five or six years. Cardinal Bourne believed that smaller dioceses would lead to better evangelisation, which he thought was dormant in most parts of the country.[2] There was, additionally, the different nature of the archdiocese in its northern and central parts, where there was little geographical or social affinity with Liverpool and its immediate hinterland. One has to be careful here: these separatist feelings may have been strong in the mid-nineteenth century when the diocese had originally been set up, and the actions of O'Reilly on occasion had not helped to cement the different parts, but by the 1920s Archbishop Keating could claim that there was no desire among the northern clergy for separation – though this, of course, might have been special pleading on his part. This time, unlike what had happened over the setting up of the diocese Brentwood in 1917, Rome insisted on wide consultation and refused to accept Bourne's proposals without question – perhaps the strong protests from the bishops after 1917 were bearing fruit.

Bourne, of course, was among those whose views were sought. He argued for a scheme similar to what he had wanted for Brentwood: the designation of the area of a new diocese and the appointment of an Apostolic Administrator who would choose the best place for the seat of the diocese and begin to gather funds – a new diocese should expect no financial help from its parent. There was also the question whether a new diocese in the north should include parts of the diocese of Hexham and Newcastle in addition to the northern part of Liverpool. Bourne consulted Archbishop Mostyn of Cardiff, perhaps on the grounds that Mostyn had worked in Birkenhead and knew something of 'the north', but the Archbishop was not sure that any but the bishops immediately concerned should be consulted. Personally, he did believe that a new diocese was urgently needed and was sure that if it were based on Preston it would receive ample support. Bourne commented that he himself was against wide consultation: if it had taken place in 1917 the vote, he was sure, would have been against the setting up of Brentwood.[3]

Bishop Casartelli of Salford was also consulted. He believed England and Wales had too many dioceses already for the resources available, not too few, and he provided some comparative statistics to prove his point. In general he thought that all the bishops should be consulted on such matters and not just a hand-picked few. For himself, he admitted to knowing nothing about the finances of Liverpool and so was altogether incapable of answering the questions asked by the Consistorial Congregation. It is interesting that Bourne wrote to Cardinal De Lai asking for specific instructions so that he could avoid having the matter discussed by the bishops at their Low Week meeting.

When in April 1921 the Consistorial Congregation took the decision in principle to divide the archdiocese, it asked for more information on two questions: was the division wise, and where should any new bishop be based? They asked for answers to these questions from the three priests whose names had made up the Chapter's 'terna' for the Liverpool appointment: Dr Joseph Dean (later rector of Upholland), Fr Robert Dobson (soon to become auxiliary Bishop), and Canon Pinnington, the Vicar Capitular. Dean replied that a new diocese was necessary, but it should include the hundred of Leyland as well, with the Bishop's seat being at Preston; this interesting suggestion would have given the new diocese an area south of the Ribble including the towns of Chorley and Leyland. Pinnington also believed that a new diocese was necessary, both for the progress of religion and the health of the new archbishop. He was sure that Preston was the right place and claimed that 'all but three priests' agreed with him about this; he added that the Catholic families that had given Lancaster its former importance were becoming 'fewer and fewer'. For his part, Dobson opted for either a Coadjutor Bishop in the north or a new diocese, but thought Lancaster would be the best seat. The Congregation was still not satisfied and so discussed these replies with Mgr Hinsley, rector of the English College in Rome; he thought a new diocese was desirable and on the whole favoured Lancaster as its seat.

Archbishop Keating wrote at length to the Congregation in Rome.[4] He was not new to the issues involved because while he had been Bishop of Northampton in 1917 he had received notice that his diocese was under threat if Bourne's ideas went ahead. This time he thanked Cardinal De Lai for allowing him to see all the relevant documentation and expressed himself basically in favour of a division. On the question of how much should be included in a new diocese, he felt there was no argument in favour of including the hundred of Leyland but believed that sooner or later the two northernmost counties would have to be included, with the River Ribble forming the southern boundary. He felt that the claims of Preston, as the most Catholic town in England, were so strong that only the most invincible reasons could justify not choosing it. Answering an argument of the pro-Lancaster party, he believed that the Jesuit influence in Preston should not be exaggerated as the Seculars had large parishes in the town as well, and the presence of a Bishop would be likely to unify the two sets of clergy; the final decision, however, should be left to the new Bishop.

He favoured Cardinal Bourne's plan of appointing an Apostolic Administrator in the first place, as this would allow time for him and Keating together to explore the possibilities of both dioceses and to draw up a joint agreement about resources and obligations. With regard to the division of funds, Keating did not know enough about the position in Liverpool to say whether this would be possible or not; he knew that he would have the additional expense of the new archbishop's house that Archbishop Whiteside had purchased in Belvidere Road, but he needed time to sort these and other matters out. And so he asked for a delay in the appointment of even an Apostolic Administrator until he could prepare a full report on the health of the archdiocese.

So far Keating's letter read as an understandably cautious approach by a newly appointed Bishop in a difficult situation, but in the final two pages he launched into a strong attack on Cardinal Bourne and his interfering ways. He defended the bishops' request to be allowed to consult among themselves on the question of the division of their dioceses, and asked why the Cardinal was so much afraid of his fellow-members of the Hierarchy; he also asked why the Congregation had agreed with him that the bishops should not express their joint opinion. The reason could only be, Keating concluded, that Bourne despaired of winning the bishops' assent to his plans and was determined to ensure success for his own views by systematically stifling theirs.

Despite the Archbishop's pleading, the Congregation decided to go ahead with the division straightaway and asked him to choose an Apostolic Administrator from Dean, Dobson or Pinnington.[5] Keating's next step was to write a very long report on the state of the archdiocese. Not surprisingly, this gave a very favourable summary, claiming that the archdiocese was the best equipped of all the English dioceses, that no Catholic family was prevented from hearing Mass because there was no nearby church, and that almost all 100,000 Catholic children attended Catholic schools. He gave full praise to the administration of his predecessor, which had been more thorough than anywhere else in the country, with the result that everything was in perfect order. Any suggestion, he went on, that the northern parts had been neglected was 'a rash and baseless falsehood'. The reason behind all this euphoria was that the Archbishop had decided to fight the Congregation's decision: he did not see any reason for dividing such an admirably run archdiocese – above all, no valid reason could be put forward for doing so at that particular moment. Moreover, he claimed that the clergy in the northern parts thought the same: they had spontaneously asked not to be separated from the archdiocese, which they would not have done if matters had been neglected.[6]

Returning to his predecessor, Keating claimed that the only flaw in his administration had been his total refusal to delegate; despite the existence of very able and experienced priests who could have assisted him, he had preferred to keep everything in his own hands, including even the investigation of matrimonial cases and routine correspondence. Keating made out that he was not going to fall into that particular trap: he had already devolved the supervision of Religious houses to Ecclesiastical Superiors and was contemplating similar devolution to his Deans. By doing this he hoped to carry on the highly efficient administration of Whiteside, without the strain that had shortened his career. What he needed was not an Apostolic Administrator in Preston or Lancaster, with all the worries of setting up a new diocese, but an auxiliary Bishop residing in one of the Liverpool parishes and so able at an hour's notice to take over some routine engagement – after all, Cardinal Bourne had two such auxiliaries and at one time had had three of them! He recommended the appointment of Fr Robert Dobson to the post.

Keating was obviously determined to put forward as many arguments as possible to delay the division. In his letter he explained that there were, indeed, two gaps in the otherwise excellent provision in the archdiocese, both of which all agreed it was urgently necessary to make good: the re-constitution of the seminary, and the building of a metropolitan cathedral. Both of these projects had been launched, with the full support of the people, the clergy and his Chapter. Funds were being collected and, in the case of the seminary, plans were well advanced to deal with a matter that was of the utmost urgency to the well-being of the archdiocese. In connection with the proposed cathedral, the Archbishop claimed that both clergy and laity had long felt ashamed of this 'glaring deficiency, so much out of keeping with the efficiency of the archdiocese in all other respects'. Both projects were matters of vital interest to the spiritual progress of the whole archdiocese and could not be delayed 'without disaster' (true, one might think, of the seminary, but somewhat doubtful in the case of a cathedral). The Archbishop went on to argue that both also required the united effort of an undivided people – an actual division or even the shadow of a coming one would blight both projects. The 'northerners', he argued, were foremost in wanting the cathedral as a memorial to Archbishop Whiteside who had been one of their own, but they were hardly likely to contribute if they knew their connection with Liverpool would be severed 'before the walls of the cathedral could appear above ground'. Similarly with the seminary at Upholland: talk of division would, at the least, cause interminable delays, while there would be no problem in allowing a new diocese sometime in the future full use of the new seminary, with its Bishop sharing in its government and administration. Finally, the Archbishop made the point that whenever the time came for the creation of a new diocese, there would be no difficulties in providing for it financially: it would receive its share pro rata of all general funds, as well as whatever funds were ear-marked for its special benefit – whatever Cardinal Bourne had said to the contrary. Keating followed up this letter by talking to the Pope personally while in Rome to receive the pallium. When he reported to the Chapter on his return, he claimed that the Pope had listened carefully to details of the two projects and was sympathetic to the idea of deferment. The Congregation then granted Keating's main requests without hesitation: the division of the archdiocese was put off, apparently *sine die*, and Robert Dobson was appointed as Auxiliary Bishop, a post he held until his death in 1942.[7]

After all this, one can easily understand Keating's astonishment when he suddenly received two brief letters from Cardinal De Lai, dated 3rd and 6th December 1924, announcing that, since the agreed period of postponement had now passed, a new diocese was to be established without delay and that the new Bishop was to be a Benedictine, Thomas Wulfstan Pearson. In his New Year message in the semi-official magazine, *The Parishioner*, Keating referred to the news as a 'surprise packet' from the Holy See, adding that it was his plain duty to make the decision 'yield all the spiritual fruit anticipated', and to put up with any temporary inconveniences it might cause.[8] The letters also settled that the seat of the new Bishop should be Lancaster – there was no mention of the discussions about the suitability of Preston; had the choice of a Benedictine as Bishop excluded 'the most Catholic town in the country' from consideration because the Jesuits were in such a strong position there? Perhaps the reason for the choice of the more northerly town lay simply in the decision to include Westmorland and Cumberland in the new diocese: Lancaster was geographically central whereas Preston was on the southern border.

The formal decree setting up the diocese, *Universalis Ecclesiae sollicitudo*, was dated 22 November 1924: it stated that the counties of Westmorland and Cumberland were to be included in it, that the Ribble should be its southern boundary, and that St Peter's Church, Lancaster, was raised to the status of cathedral. The new Bishop would be a suffragan of Liverpool and the clergy currently serving in the new area would automatically become subjects of the new Bishop. These arrangements were, the decree claimed, being made 'for an increase in religion and the greater good of souls'.[9] Keating immediately issued a Pastoral announcing the fact of the division. In this he made clear that the division had come as a shock to everyone and outlined how he had been promised that nothing would be done until the cathedral project had been completed. He called the decision an unexpected set-back to his carefully constructed plans to collect funds for the cathedral, a set-back that was bound to cause discouragement and delay. However, it had been done and now they had to accept it in faith. He promised ungrudging support to the new Bishop and his diocese which he was sure would flourish: its people had the blood of the Lancashire martyrs in their veins and would surely 'yield a still richer and more abundant harvest when their chief Pastor is resident in their midst' – a half-admission at least that pastoral needs had made the change desirable.[10]

The Bishop-elect, Dom Wulfstan Pearson, was a native of Preston. Educated at Douai, he had joined the Downside community in 1887 where he served on the school staff until 1912. He was then appointed as curate to St Mary's, Highfield Street, Liverpool, where he stayed for four years until he was made Prior of St Benedict's, Ealing, London. His years at St Mary's were, he claimed, the happiest of his priestly life: he was deeply interested in pastoral work and was very unhappy when he was appointed to Ealing; while there he constantly asked to be allowed to undertake pastoral work.[11] He was to rule the new diocese until his death in 1938.

The new diocese took from Liverpool 46 parishes, containing 67,647 Catholics and served by 91 priests (60 Seculars, 25 Jesuits, 1 Benedictine and 5 Holy Ghost Fathers), and from Hexham and Newcastle a further 18 parishes in the counties of Westmorland and Cumberland, with 21,098 Catholics and 32 priests (16 Seculars and 16 Benedictines). Keating estimated that these combined figures made the new diocese eighth in size out of the eighteen English and Welsh dioceses. In a letter to Cardinal De Lai he explained how as Apostolic Delegate he had established a Lancaster Chapter and seen to the new Bishop's formal installation. He had also arranged a suitable *mensa* (maintenance) for him and put in train an equitable division of the temporalities and the ecclesiastical students who had formerly all belonged to Liverpool.[12] Keating's generosity in these arrangements was in clear contrast with Cardinal Bourne's insistence that the new diocese of Brentwood, established from Westminster in 1917, had to rely on its own resources and could expect no help from him.

While Keating carried out his duties as Apostolic Delegate to the letter and as quickly as he could, and in his correspondence with Bishop Pearson showed a welcoming spirit of warm friendliness that went far beyond mere courtesy, he was very angry with the way in which the Consistorial Congregation had acted. He made these feelings abundantly clear in his letter to Cardinal De Lai. He had, he wrote, been genuinely taken by surprise by the Congregation's letters of December 1924 announcing the setting up of the new diocese, since his last dealings with them had indicated that they accepted his arguments for a delay in doing so. Neither he nor his agent in Rome, Mgr Redmond of the Venerabile, had picked up any intimation that a decision was imminent, although in the summer of 1924 Keating had commented on 'gossip' caused by the delay in appointing a Bishop to Hexham and Newcastle – he asked Redmond to rub it in that any revival of the division idea would drive him mad as he was 'in the thick of my two great undertakings'. Keating felt justified, therefore, in uttering a strong protest against 'the undeserved humiliations inflicted on myself and my office as Metropolitan of this Province'.

He continued by asking De Lai whether, given the earlier assurances, it was considerate or just for the Congregation to yield so suddenly to outside influences, and to sacrifice his interests and those of the diocese simply to free the Consistorial Congregation 'from the constant importunities of people who would be much better occupied with their own business'. He felt justified, he went on, in complaining of broken faith: De Lai had chosen to leave him deliberately in the dark both in regard to the division of the archdiocese and the appointment of a Benedictine as the new Bishop. Surely, he argued, both as

Metropolitan and as Archbishop of the diocese most affected, he had a more valid claim to information than any other bishop in the country, and his fellow bishops found it difficult to believe that he had not been consulted. These were, indeed, strong words.

The depth of his feelings was also revealed in a second letter written a few days later, this time to the Pope himself. He asked for 'sympathy and redress' in the hardships and humiliations inflicted on himself and the archdiocese, and re-iterated the point that as Metropolitan he was surely more entitled to the confidence of the Congregation than 'irresponsible parties who have only their own private ends to serve'. The main interest of the letter, however, is that Keating used it as an opportunity to complain about the attempts that had been made since 1911 to dismember the English dioceses against the wishes of the bishops concerned. Again he attacked Cardinal Bourne, the prime mover in these 'objectionable practices', whose aims throughout had been to break up Southwark in order to incorporate the whole of London in a the single archdiocese of Westminster and to increase the number of dioceses through divisions. Many of the bishops, Keating claimed, had objected to what they believed was a mistaken policy and, still more, to the secrecy with which Bourne pursued his ends – 'he refuses us his own confidence, and robs us of the confidence of the … Congregation'. Finally, he claimed that things had been better under the authority of Propaganda prior to 1908: then any decisions about the creation of new dioceses had only been taken at the suggestion of the whole hierarchy; now, not only were they not consulted as a body, but when they had tried in 1917 to get a hearing and correct Bourne's misleading statements, they had been told by Rome not even to discuss such matters at their Low Week meetings.[13] Keating had obviously been very hurt by the plans to divide Northampton, even though nothing had come of them in the end.

He was clear in his own mind that the 'outsiders' who had interfered in the case of Lancaster had been the Benedictines, and this view was supported by De Lai in his reply when he said that one of the reasons why the Congregation had acted as it had was the need to keep the promises made to the English Benedictine Congregation in the 1920 Bull, *Praeclara gesta*.[14] This had promised the English Benedictine Congregation that, in the light of their distinguished contribution to the Catholic Church in England, and also because they had given up the 'cathedral' status that had been granted to Belmont in 1911, as far as was humanly possible there would always be a Benedictine among the English bishops. Keating and Redmond thought the Benedictines in Rome had been pushing for such an appointment (apparently they were spreading rumours there that Keating had said it would take fifty years to complete the cathedral), and the division of Liverpool was the easy way out, especially as the new Bishop was a native of Preston and had had pastoral experience in Liverpool and so would be acceptable to the Lancashire clergy – though how acceptable he was is open to some question. Shortly after his appointment he planned an early unofficial visit to his new diocese 'to break the ice', as he put it, adding 'and there's a lot of ice about!'[15]

For the rest, De Lai dismissed Keating's complaints more or less out of hand: he had not been consulted again because his views were already known and he had agreed in principle to the division; two years was a long enough delay and other provision could be made for the seminary and the cathedral. Moreover, it was urgent that episcopal rule be put on a sounder footing in the north of England.[16] It is not clear what the Cardinal was referring to here; Bishop Collins of Hexham and Newcastle (1909-1924) had been in ill-health for some time and it could be that De Lai had this in mind rather than any criticism of how Liverpool had dealt with its northern areas. After Bishop Collins died in February 1924 it was appropriate to settle the future of the counties of Westmorland and Cumberland before his successor was chosen. Anyway, De Lai denied that the English bishops had ever been forbidden to make their views known on such subjects and claimed that both the Congregation and the Holy See had the fullest confidence in them – and in the case of both Brentwood and Lancaster had listened to their views. Keating may have exaggerated his belief that a key decision had been taken entirely behind his back (and may not have paid enough attention to Redmond's hints in the summer of 1924), but the apparently sudden decision late in 1924 does contrast rather oddly with the careful consultations of 1921 and 1922, the willingness of the Consistorial Congregation at that stage to let Keating see all the documentation that it had collected, and the obvious desire not to do anything to upset either Liverpool or Hexham and Newcastle. It must have seemed to Keating and others at that time that at last the English and Welsh bishops' insistence on being fully consulted had been taken seriously in Rome; now all that had, it seemed, counted for nothing.

While Keating continued to feel badly done by, the tone of his letters to the new Bishop continued to be friendly, and agreement on the division of funds was soon reached between Canon Dennet, for the archdiocese, and Canon Vaughan of St John's, Poulton-le-Fylde, for Lancaster.[17] The same was true about the allocation of seminarians – Pearson kept all those with a domicile in the new diocese. With regard to the clergy, those actually in post in the new district at the time of the establishment belonged automatically, and without the right to object, to Lancaster – though Keating allowed that there might be a possibility in future of parish priests exchanging parishes on either side of the boundary. In a later letter, Keating explained that Liverpool was the loser by this arrangement, because Pearson had all his parishes bar one staffed by secular clergy and no 'spares', whereas Keating had the sick, the sinners and the misfits, including 'some that are a very heavy charge to us'. This letter shows a slight change of tone and even a note of exasperation – Keating could not get Pearson to meet him to talk about all the matters that needed sorting out. There was also a hint in the letter that Pearson did not realise his good fortune either over the allocation of the clergy or over the funds for his upkeep – according to Keating, the new diocese would be better off than most in the country, with a healthy *mensa* for its bishop and a sound basis for an administration fund, a sixth of the archdiocese's General Funds and a sixth of the funds set aside for educating students at Ushaw. Loans that had been made by the archdiocese to parishes and other institutions that were now in the new diocese would continue to be at a preferential rate of interest.[18]

How the news of the setting up of the new diocese was received north of the Ribble is difficult to assess. If the *Preston Catholic News* is anything to go by there was no particular rejoicing over the event, and certainly no feeling that at last the area had received its due recognition. Perhaps Keating had been correct in claiming that the clergy had not wanted the division, but it is still strange to note that in the issue of the newspaper after the announcement more space is devoted to the life of the Venerable Beatrice of Silva than to the establishment of the new diocese! Keating's statement that the whole issue was 'a serious matter' for the archdiocese was quoted from *The Parishioner;* a week later he was quoted again, this time saying 'We have no misgiving' and the division was 'inevitable', and he hoped for renewed effort for the cathedral despite the reverse (these were statements taken from his New Year pastoral). More attention was paid by the paper to the new Bishop of Hexham and Newcastle than to Bishop-elect Pearson, though there were pictures of him and quotations from *Praeclara gesta* of 1920 on the contribution of the Benedictines to Lancashire Catholicism. Later there was full coverage of the ceremony of consecration.[19]

As the new diocese settled down relations between it and the archdiocese seem to have been amicable. There appears to have been no serious trouble over either the division of diocesan funds or the seminary at Upholland, which always had a large number of Lancaster students, though very few members of staff were appointed from the new diocese and this rather upset Bishop Pearson and some of his clergy. When the question of a successor to Canon Walmsley as rector came up in 1926 Keating insisted on appointing Dr Dean, whereas Pearson wanted Bishop Dobson. But in October of that year it was Bishop Pearson who officiated at the laying of the foundation stone of the new (professors') wing even though Keating was present at the ceremony. There were later disagreements over some of the policies of the new Rector; in particular, Pearson was not happy with his very strict disciplinary line and thought that erring students should be regarded more leniently and given a second chance, while Keating believed that it was better to support the college authorities in such cases.[20] But these were minor differences, unlikely to cause very much trouble between the two dioceses.

Keating had suggested that Upholland should become a joint seminary for Liverpool and Lancaster, since it had been planned to serve the whole of the county except for the parts in Salford diocese. He claimed that Cardinal De Lai favoured the idea, which would make the Bishop of Lancaster jointly responsible for the management of the seminary. For his part the Bishop of Lancaster would have to agree to tie up a substantial part of its priest-training funds in Upholland. This would put the Lancaster students on the same footing as the Liverpool ones; they would, for example, benefit from the higher education funds available for post-ordination study at the universities and then could be appointed to the seminary staff as required.[21]

Bishop Pearson asked for time to consider this idea but nothing came of it; perhaps he feared that his diocese would also become responsible for the massive expansion then taking place at Upholland and that the whole enterprise was something of a financial gamble.

The new diocese flourished and Bishop Pearson opened twelve new parishes and established twenty-one new Mass centres. Its growth can be seen from the following statistics:[22]

	Secular priests	Catholic population
1926	80	88,536
1936	124	98,212
1946	163	101,835

After seventy-five years, then, the archdiocese lost the Catholic heartlands north of the Ribble, including Preston. In return it gained a greater cohesiveness and unity, and still had enough traditional parishes to ensure that Lancashire Catholicism remained a key element in its composition. On the wider front, Cardinal Bourne and the bishops seemed to have reached some agreement in 1925 on the principles that should govern the future division of dioceses, but the official acta of the meeting do not give any details. They did not prevent Bourne from making another attempt the following year to divide Northampton against its Bishop's will, but he dropped the idea in the face of opposition from the other bishops. Keating was too ill to attend the meeting and the Cardinal refused to allow Bishop Dobson to attend in his place.[23] In the end, no other new dioceses were set up by division until after the second World War.

Notes

1 AAL Early Bishops, S1 VII A/7, Lépicier to Whiteside 8.9.1911, with some added statistics.

2 Aspden, pp.111-6.

3 AAL Keating, S2 I A/1, headed *Consistorial* 14 April 1921, is a full summary of the correspondence and consultation, written by Keating in Rome.

4 *Ibid.*, 21 June 1921, from the English College.

5 AAL Keating, S2 I A/3, Consistorial Congregation to Keating, 21.2.1922.

6 *Ibid.*, 'Report on the condition and requirements of the Archdiocese. May, 1922'

7 AAL Chancellor, Chapter Minutes, 21.6.1922; letter from the Consistorial Congregation, 24.6.1922.

8 AAL Keating, S2 I A, letters from the Consistorial Congregation, 3 & 6 Dec. 1924; *The Parishioner*, Jan. 1925.

9 *Acta Apostolicae Sedis* (AAS), vol. 17 (1925), pp.129-31.

10 AAL *Liverpolitana*, pastoral letter 6.1.1925.

11 R. Kollar OSB, 'The Reluctant Prior: Bishop Wulfstan Pearson of Lancaster', *RH*, vol. 20, no.3 (1991), pp.403-13; Plumb, *Arundel to Zabi.*

12 AAL Keating S2 I A: Pastoral, 6.1.1925 (note 10 above); Keating to De Lai, 2.4.1925.

13 AAL Keating, S2 I A: Keating to the Pope, 5.4.1925.

14 *AAS*, vol.XII (1920), pp.265-7.

15 Kollar, p.413.

16 AAL Keating, S2 I A, De Lai to Keating, 1.5.1925.

17 AAL Keating, S3 I A/2, Finance and Administration.

18 AAL Keating, S4 I A: Letterbooks, Keating to Pearson 4 & 8 Feb., 18 Mar., 2 June 1925; to Fr Delaney, 24.1.1925 re changing dioceses.

19 *Preston Catholic News*, 10 & 17 Jan. 1925; 31 Jan. (Hexham and Newcastle); 21 & 28 Feb. (Consecration).

20 AAL Keating, S4 I A: Letterbooks, Keating to Pearson, 7.8.1926.

21 *Ibid.*, Keating to Pearson, 2.6.1925.

22 Brian Plumb, 'The Founding Fathers of Lancaster Diocese' in Hilton (ed.), *Catholic Englishmen*, pp.53-8, at p.56.

23 AAW Acta of the Bishops' Meetings, April 1925, item XXIII; AAL Keating, S6 II B/2: Bp of Northampton to Keating, 19.4.1926.

CHAPTER 12 TOWARDS A DIOCESAN SEMINARY

ST EDWARD'S COLLEGE

St Edward's College in Everton opened in January 1843 as a 'classical and commercial school' for boarders under the care of the secular clergy. It was in a fine situation outside the town on the 'verdant slopes' of Everton and housed in St Domingo House, acknowledged to be the grandest mansion in the area. From all accounts it developed into a small, successful school under the presidency of Dr John Henry Fisher, assisted by Dr Alexander Goss. The College was planned to take fifty boys but recruitment was slow. There were 13 in residence in its first year (having opened in January 1843 with no students – the first arrived from Newcastle-on-Tyne the next day) and an average of 32 during the first ten years; the highest total in these years was forty-five. The intake was strongly international in the early years, witnessing to the importance of Liverpool's international trading links and evidence that the school was better known outside Liverpool than it was in the town itself. In 1846, for example, there were two Irish students, ten from Central and South America, four from the West Indies and only one from Liverpool among the 37 in residence.[1]

One of those to arrive in 1843, at the age of eight, was a boy named Alfred Austin, destined to succeed Tennyson as Poet Laureate. In his Autobiography he had high praise for St Edward's:

We were most comfortably housed and fed, Dr Fisher personally superintending our needs, and amply providing for them. I could not praise too warmly the thoroughness, as far as it went, of the education I received …

He tells us that he was well-grounded in Latin and French, though less so in Greek – even here, however, he had read before the age of fourteen some Xenophon, St Luke's Gospel, Plato's *Symposium*, and the *Antigone* of Sophocles; under the personal supervision of Dr Goss he had coped with the Odes of Anacreon. The teaching of English was, he claims, still more thorough (unfortunately, this excellent grounding did not prevent him from writing some terrible poetry later in life).[2] Austin also praised the general high level of culture at St Edward's, Fisher's opposition to rough games and the stimulating international atmosphere of the school, as well as the freedom from excessive supervision. He went from there to the Jesuit school at Stonyhurst, which, he thought, compared poorly with St Edward's on those grounds.

It is not clear whether Bishop Brown had in mind all along that St Edward's would become a junior seminary. In this context it is interesting that the establishment of the college had been strongly opposed by the

The first advert for St Edward's College, opened in Everton in 1843. It later became the Junior Seminary and then a grammar school run by Irish Christian Brothers.

president of Ushaw College who saw in it the first move towards the setting up of a separate seminary for the Lancashire District, with a subsequent withdrawal of funds and students from Ushaw. In May 1850 Brown chaired a meeting of his senior clergy that resolved that the lay college of St Edward's should become a diocesan seminary 'to prepare students for the higher branches of Humanities, as well as Philosophy and Theology, to be read elsewhere'.[3]

A committee was set up to carry out this resolution and came up with suggestions for how it should be funded: each priest should contribute £1 per annum; the faithful should contribute by way of an annual collection, to be preceded by a pastoral letter, and each church should have a box for occasional offerings for the 'Ecclesiastical Education Fund'. Brown promised to choose two senior priests as 'consultors' in matters concerning the administration of the seminary, and to set up a board to supervise the funds and property of the new institution – interestingly, no doubt because of previous criticisms of Brown's handling of funds, the clergy were to have the right at their general meeting to appoint two of the five members of the board.

St Edward's College,
Everton, opened in 1843.
The new wings added in the
1870s are visible to the rear
of the original mansion.

This time opposition came not just from Ushaw but from many of the clergy of the Northern District. They said that the new plan was derogatory to Ushaw, which could take more than all the students Lancashire was likely to supply and which was well-established with a true ecclesiastical spirit, whereas a new college was untried and would cost extra to establish. Moreover, St Edward's could never be a proper Tridentine seminary, because the ideal was to have all the training of students, from boyhood to priesthood, in one establishment. Some of the Lancashire clergy were among opponents of the scheme and one of them, the future Bishop Turner of Salford, thought it was the 'height of folly' given the other problems facing the District. There was a marked difference between the support Brown received from the priests working in the city of Liverpool, who presumably thought of St Edward's as 'their college', and the, at best, ambivalent attitudes of those from other parts of the District. Those in Manchester were non-committal on the whole, but doubted the suitability of St Edward's for the training of priests; the priests who met in Preston to discuss the matter suggested an appeal to Rome for arbitration, a sign that there were serious differences of opinion on the subject among the clergy.[4]

Brown was unmoved and went ahead with his plan, announcing that he intended to turn the highly respected College of St Edward's into an Ecclesiastical Seminary, devoted exclusively to the education of young men for the priesthood. As justification, he quoted an increase of baptisms in the district of 37% since 1801 and of Easter Communions of 38% over the same period; he referred to the loss of priests in the terrible epidemic of 1847 and to the thousands of destitute Catholics who needed assistance. His aim, he said, was to 'train up pastors chosen as youths from among the people they will later serve'. To raise funds Brown altered slightly the methods suggested by his committee: he himself promised £5 annually and asked that every

family above the class of labourers should contribute 1d per week, with labouring families contributing 1d per month. Probably the clergy felt it would be impossible to collect these contributions, for Brown shortly afterwards altered them again: now bench-holders were to pay 1/- quarterly when they paid their bench rents and the 1d per month from labourers was to be collected by lay collectors. He concluded by saying that there were bound to be difficulties and opposition, as there were in all initiatives, but 'why should we be terrified?' he asked; 'we will hope in God and persevere. The work is His, not ours'. Large posters were put up in each church, with details of the funding arrangements.[5]

Brown was nothing but enthusiastic about his new scheme, but it seems to have met with less than full support from his clergy. Only 29 priests subscribed the £1 to the first annual collection and this dropped to 24 in 1853. Perhaps the clergy were wary of trusting the Bishop with more funds when his handling of other funds had been criticised severely by the Chapter. A far bigger blow to the Bishop's hopes was the fact that St Edward's remained a mixed college; by 1859 it had only six ecclesiastical students there, and it was not until the early 1900s that it became exclusively a junior seminary. Clearly, in the early years, there were not enough boys wanting to be priests to take up the places there and at Ushaw. Did the clergy, most of whom had been educated at Ushaw themselves, prefer to send likely lads to their old college? There was no attempt to withdraw Lancashire boys from the northern seminary to make up the numbers.

While the main disputes over the English seminaries had to do with episcopal control and the division of funds, there was also a growing concern with the fact that they continued to educate lay students alongside the church students. Some of the bishops felt that this necessarily created a more worldly spirit in the seminaries than was desirable – Newman, the product of an altogether different tradition, had called for something 'more strict, more monastic' in the way of training; Oscott, he wrote, was 'a place of dissipation (with) tribes of women and hosts of visitors. The want of rule is felt'.[6] Others believed it meant a dissipation of funds when every penny should be spent on the training of priests to meet the needs of expanding Catholic populations. Some argued that it was time to provide proper diocesan seminaries, dedicated exclusively to educating and training clergy. At the third Provincial Synod in 1859 the bishops passed a resolution that each of them should apply himself 'carefully and earnestly at once to the task of founding a seminary in his diocese the best way he can'. At the fourth Synod, in 1873, the resolution was repeated: each Bishop should do everything possible to set up a diocesan seminary, in which 'the Church students may be taught their philosophy and theology apart from any intercourse with laics'.[7] Few admitted how unrealistic such a resolution was, given the lack of suitable manpower and the unnecessary overlap in provision that would result.

When Canon Bernard O'Reilly became Bishop of Liverpool in 1873 he adopted the idea of establishing a diocesan seminary as his main objective – 'the cherished child of the Bishop's heart, even to his last breath' was how Mgr Nugent described it.[8] He convinced his Chapter in 1875 that steps should be taken without delay in that direction, so that, as he argued, he could provide adequately for the increasing needs of religion across the diocese. Possible sites were suggested for purchase, but the majority of the Chapter favoured turning St Edward's into a major seminary and setting up a new junior house some miles outside the city. As a first step, in 1875 St Edward's was enlarged to accommodate double the existing number of students, at a cost of almost £20,000. This resulted in the addition of new wings to the original house, designed by the architect James O'Byrne. Born in Waterford, Ireland, in 1835, he had served his apprenticeship in Pugin's workshop in Bristol before becoming official architect to the Cheshire Lines Railway. His main interest, however, was in church architecture. At the same time the classical and humanities side of the curriculum was extended and a sixth form (in the shape of Poetry and Rhetoric) added, so that students no longer had to transfer elsewhere if they wished to study beyond the age of sixteen. Two years later a priest was appointed to teach philosophy, in order to prepare students for the theology courses they would undertake at Ushaw or in the new senior seminary in Leeds, opened in 1878.[9] St Edward's was gradually becoming more geared to providing the courses suitable to a junior seminary, but it continued to take lay boys for several years – the last (rather lonely) lay student left in 1910, when there were a total of 97 students in attendance.

A SEMINARY AT UPHOLLAND

Meanwhile the Bishop and his Chapter looked at various buildings that came on the market as possible places to re-locate the junior seminary. Amongst these were Woolton Hall (turned down after an unfavourable survey), Burscough Hall and its estate (there were problems with the water supply) and other properties at Blundellsands and Lydiate. It is not clear from the records when the decision was taken to change the original plan and to look for a new site for the major seminary instead of having it at St Edward's. In March 1877, O'Reilly began to consult his clergy formally about the feasibility of establishing a full diocesan seminary, without giving any details of where it might be or what might happen to St Edward's. He announced the results of these consultations the same month:

> The clergy of the diocese have emphatically declared their conviction that the establishment of a Diocesan Seminary is an immediate necessity. Wherever I have met them and have had the opportunity of speaking to them upon the subject (and this I have done in Liverpool, Preston, Lancaster, Chorley and Kirkham), they were unanimous in expressing their opinion that this great work should be at once undertaken.[10]

This clerical support was not a figment of the Bishop's imagination, for he was able to add a list of subscriptions promised by the clergy which amounted to £5,615. No wonder he concluded, 'In the name of God, and trusting to the prayers of our Mother, Mary, and our Protector, St Joseph, we will begin'.

A few weeks later he issued a pastoral letter in which he asked for support for the new seminary. As with the clergy, the response was overwhelmingly positive and subscriptions of over £34,717 were pledged. A possible site had been found, a property known as Rough Park (also referred to sometimes as Walthew Park, a name that survived) just outside the village of Upholland, about four miles from Wigan. Purchase of this was completed in December 1877 and a neighbouring piece of land was added to it early in the following year, the whole totalling about 150 acres. There was no building available with the property and so the Bishop had the opportunity of starting completely from scratch in the design of his seminary. The Chapter advised him to plan for an eventual intake of 200 students, with initial space for 120 if contributions would allow. Canon John Worthy (the Bishop's cousin) was appointed site manager and spent the next six years preparing it; he was able to purchase for £20 the rights to quarry stone nearby and this provided stone for the main building, a lodge and two cottages.[11]

Mr James O'Byrne was again the chosen architect. His plans for the new seminary were approved by the Chapter in March 1879 and the foundation stone was laid in 1880 on 19th March, the feast of St Joseph to whom the college was to be dedicated. The initial plan was to provide accommodation for forty or fifty students; some urged the Bishop to build for larger numbers, but he felt constrained not to build beyond the resources available. Then a large legacy from Mr Gilbert Heyes enabled the Bishop to add a whole north wing to the original plans and so accommodation for seventy students was provided; a large marble plaque outside the dining room was erected to commemorate the generosity of the donor. The builders were a Liverpool firm, Robert and Robinson, and most of the workmen came out from the city, staying in lodgings and going home at weekends.[12] The new college was in a commanding position, with wide views across the Douglas Valley to the Lancashire fells. The building itself was serviceable and built to last rather than to strike the on-looker with external beauty or decoration; the local grey stone was hard-wearing but unfortunately darkened with the years and gave the building a rather forbidding exterior. Inside was spacious and remarkably light for a Victorian institutional building. The new college received its first students on 22 September 1883; of the thirty-one who entered on that day, twenty-nine went on to ordination – a remarkable record.

By then, £58,006-3s-1d had been spent in all. This was more than had been anticipated, largely because of the cost of ensuring an adequate water supply: the College needed its own reservoirs and filter bed which cost over £3,870. Towards these costs, £27,700 had come from church collections and clerical and lay donations; a legacy of £2,000 had been received from a Mrs Santamaria, and the £17,000 from Mr Heyes There had been other donations and gifts of books, furniture and pictures which helped to reduce the costs. Outstanding among these early donors was the architect. In his will he left an extraordinarily rich collection of china, coins and medals (said at one time to be the finest private collection in the country), pictures and other works of art. The residue of his estate realised £130,000 in 1923, making the extensions of the buildings in the 1920s a possibility: a plaque inside the new entrance carries a fine relief bust of the donor and a record of his generosity. The Bishop, in a pastoral letter of 1885, also paid special tribute to 'the late Mrs Mary Agnes O'Byrne, a most generous benefactress'.[13]

Two years after the opening the Bishop had to appeal for more money to help clear the remaining debt. His pastoral letter of April 1885 dealt with

a subject than which nothing is dearer to our heart, nothing dearer to you, nothing so important for the salvation of souls in this Diocese, nothing that can so promote the honour of God in this portion of his vineyard … our New Diocesan College.

After a detailed account of the purchase of the site and the building works, he moved on to financial matters. He was very disappointed that of the initial £34,600 promised, only £27,700 had materialised. The small number of students (by now twenty-five divines and eleven philosophers) would produce only a very small income, with nothing to spare to pay off debts, hence this appeal for £6,000.[14] He made a special appeal to the younger priests of the diocese who had not been among the initial subscribers in 1878.

One suggestion was to sell St Edward's and move the junior seminary to Upholland as well, or to find another site for it while realising the value of the city site. An opportunity to consider this occurred in 1885, when the Liverpool Corporation was looking for a site for an isolation hospital and asked if St Edward's were available. The Bishop had the site and buildings valued at £56,000 and was recommended to ask a market price of £75,000. The Chapter agreed to the sale but it turned out that the Corporation had no use for the whole site and wanted to buy only three acres or so; the Bishop refused to consider a partial sale and the deal fell through.[15] It is interesting that ten years later a suggestion was made by Canon Taylor that St Edward's should be sold and amalgamated with St Joseph's; this time, however, the reason was not financial but to give the new college, which was experiencing some problems, 'a tradition and history' which it all too clearly lacked.[16] In the end, St Edward's remained the junior seminary until 1919 when it was sold to the Irish Christian Brothers for use as a secondary school.

One change that was made in 1885 was a decision to extend the school by taking in day boys: this 'high select school' as it was called lasted for ten years. It is not clear who decided to close it, as this was done in the interregnum between Bishop O'Reilly and Bishop Whiteside, and the Chapter were annoyed that they had not been consulted.[17] Presumably the decision was taken by the President, the autocratic Canon Evan Banks, who ruled St Edward's from 1894 to 1919. Described as 'a *Garden of the Soul* Catholic touched by Jansenism',[18] Banks was the sternest of disciplinarians and, under his nickname 'Bunker Banks' (given to him because of the speed and readiness with which he expelled or 'bunked' students), became a bogey figure to generations of future students. It was under him that St Edward's became exclusively a junior seminary that had to follow the Tridentine ideal of being a *hortus conclusus* (an enclosed garden), cut off from the society it lived in and which its future priests were to serve; the boys even dressed differently and in the words of Canon Tom Turner who had been one of them,'must have looked freaks', in their short pants, stiff Eton collars and a heavy 'blocker' or bowler-type hat. At times there was a touch of arrogance in this desire to be different: when the government ordered two minutes' silence to be observed on 11 November 1919, Banks refused to have anything to do with it and ordered the boys to continue with their football. Unfortunately, three trams stopped in St Domingo Road outside the college wall; as Canon Turner noted, 'Passengers must have had their own thoughts about us'.[19] Whatever the state of the boys, when the college was handed over to the Christian Brothers the surveyor noted that he had never seen the fabric of a building in better condition.

The Bishop had some trouble in finding a suitable rector for the new college in 1883 and enough priests to staff it. This difficulty had always been put forward by those who doubted the wisdom of each diocese having its own seminary, and if a diocese the size of Liverpool could hardly provide enough priests, suitably qualified, to teach philosophy and theology, the doubters had a point. In the end the Bishop chose Canon Charles Teebay as rector and Fr John Bilsborrow as vice-rector and professor of moral theology.

Canon Charles Teebay (1824-1892), controversial first rector of Upholland College.

Fr Bilsborrow had been on the staff at Ushaw prior to this appointment, and also from Ushaw came the new procurator, Daniel O'Hare – in himself a proof of the Bishop's difficulties in finding staff for St Joseph's as he was still only a deacon. The other two members of the teaching staff were both Germans. Dr Ernst Commer was to develop a European reputation as a scholar; ordained in 1872, he had left Germany because of the Kulturkampf. He had started to lecture in philosophy (in Latin) at St Edward's; when asked by the Bishop to move to Upholland he persuaded a friend, Dr Steffens, to join him there. Dr Commer went to Rome in 1879 for three years to take his doctorate. He spent only one year at St Joseph's, teaching philosophy, before leaving to take up a professorship at the university of Münster, where he led the neo-scholastic revival and was active in the anti-modernist campaign; he died in 1928. Dr Franz Steffens had been born in 1853 and had studied theology in Rome before his ordination in 1878. He then spent four years as chaplain to the Notre Dame nuns in Birkdale, before teaching dogmatic theology at Ushaw for a year. After a year at Upholland he left because of ill health, moved to Fribourg in Switzerland and stayed there for the next forty-six years until his death in 1930.[20]

There was, of course, more for the Bishop to be concerned with than the buildings and the finances. In 1882 he agreed with the Chapter's suggestion that a board should be set up to draft a constitution for the new college. The members of this board were Canons Walker and Teebay, Mgr Gradwell and Fr James Swarbrick.[21] The last-named produced his proposals in July 1883. They might have formed something of a 'minority report' as we do not have any indication whether the other members agreed with him or not, but in the light of later troubles it is worth examining his ideas, especially on general discipline. His guiding principle was that advanced students should have as few rules as possible, consistent with good order and regularity. In correcting students superiors should try very carefully to bring out what was good in the individual and avoid suspicion, mistrust and harshness. The writings of St Francis de Sales should be the 'classics of St Joseph's, supplemented by the practical spirit of St Vincent de Paul'. It was a surprisingly enlightened approach that he applied also to academic matters: lectures should be limited to an hour, 'to prevent tedium in listeners and diffusiveness in speakers'. In philosophy and theology lecturers should follow approved authors and 'lean always to the side favoured at Rome'. He clearly believed that students had to be mentally stretched and not just given a practical training: lecturers should ensure that students' minds be not 'cramped by confinement to the practical only; some speculation is needed to develop the mind'. Finally, he recommended that some branch of science should be studied alongside moral philosophy, not only because of the increased attention that was being given to scientific studies in general, but 'mainly to foster precision in thought and expression – a requisite most important in Philosophy and Theology alike', and not always present even when students knew their subject reasonably well.[22]

How far these ideas were accepted is not clear, but they were probably too liberal for most of the clergy. They had something in common with the principles of Canon Charles Teebay, the college's first rector, and it was clear within a few years that some of the clergy had little confidence either in him or the institution. The number of students fell, so that in 1892 there were only seven studying philosophy and the same number studying theology. Part of the solution, suggested in a report to the Bishop, was to increase the number of junior students at St Edward's, which was still being praised for its excellence, but this did not deal with the basic issues – the loss of confidence in Teebay and stories of ill-disciplined and worldly students. The attack was led by Canon Carr, the president of St Edward's, who visited Upholland and was so horrified by what he saw that he threatened to resign if matters did not improve: what was the point, he asked the Bishop, of providing a good education in an ecclesiastical atmosphere at his college if his students were then to lose everything when they entered St Joseph's?[23] To help to get a sense of proportion about his complaints it should be added that one of his severest criticisms related to seeing the students playing football in coloured gear, including white trousers and what he called 'variegated jackets', a sign, he was sure, of the completely worldly spirit that the rector was allowing to develop! When the Bishop raised this last point with the rector, Canon Teebay replied that he thought it might help to preserve their clothes.[24]

It was not just Carr, however. A member of staff at Upholland, Fr J. O'Reilly, added other details: Teebay was inadequate as rector; there was poor discipline, the students were allowed to read newspapers including 'the most revolutionary and anti-religious of dailies', the *Pall Mall Gazette*. There were charges of favouritism and too much communication with the servants. The whole place compared badly, in Fr O'Reilly's view, with both Ushaw and Lisbon. As part of his argument, he reported the views of an American student who had studied at Ushaw before going to Upholland. He compared the new college favourably with the older institution, arguing that it had no hard and fast rules because Canon Teebay did not want them. Instead, he felt, the system was 'beautifully broad, general and liberal, so different from Ushaw where the students were mere machines'. At Upholland everything depended on the rector, whose slightest nod was law and who was never severe, trying instead to follow the example of St Francis de Sales. Ushaw, he went on, had been an unpleasant shock after the freedom of American life, but at St Joseph's he noticed hardly any change at all. Also, there was more intellectual activity among the students than at Ushaw, and he felt the new seminary would turn out priests of liberal views, priests who would be 'immensely popular', and who would make themselves 'all to all'. The student also implied that there were major differences between Teebay and the rest of his staff over discipline with perhaps only Dr Commer adopting the same liberal stance.[25] What was praiseworthy in the student's eyes was enough to condemn Teebay in those of many of the clergy.

More worrying for the Bishop than Fr O'Reilly's complaints was a list he drew up himself of the complaints he had received from various quarters: students claimed they could go where they liked and, when staff were out of the way, could do as they liked; they were frequently seen in Wigan calling at private houses and shops, sometimes late at night and on their own, while others were known to visit their parents. They had also been seen singly or in twos and threes on the railway at a considerable distance from the college, while during the vacations some were known to read 'objectionable Novels' and when reproved said there was no supervision over them at college. One priest reported that other members of the clergy said they regretted having subscribed to the college building fund, when they saw its fruit as judged by the 'tone of conversation of students during the vacations which showed a want of Priestly discipline and Priestly spirit'. Another priest feared the Bishop was 'rearing a crop that would give endless trouble when ordained', while another reported a complaint shared in his district of the independent tone of the students who showed by their conversation and conduct that they had no respect for authority. The Bishop was annoyed that those who made these reports would suggest no remedy for the ills and for this reason he refused to meet those who composed a Memorial to him on the subject. It is of some interest that one of the things the Memorialists wanted was to test clerical opinion on the relative advantages of a college in the country compared with one in the town; the Bishop refused to allow them to circulate this and other questions.[26] Perhaps any suggestion that he might have been mistaken in siting his major seminary at Upholland instead of developing St Edward's would have been too painful for him to deal with. There is also an air of anonymous 'Have you heard the latest about Upholland?' rumours in some of the reports.

Differences about the proper approach to seminary discipline and the most fruitful way of training priests for their future ministry seem to have been ended with the resignation of Canon Teebay, and the stance adopted by future rectors and bishops was both strict and marked by a strong fear of the world and the temptations it held. The English bishops as a whole had supported this position when they had met for the fourth Provincial Synod in 1873. They had condemned the *pestifer spiritus* (destructive spirit) of private judgement which was propagated everywhere by books, pamphlets and newspapers. They had also laid down that only those books approved by the bishops themselves should be read in seminaries, and students studying philosophy and theology must be separated from lay students; moreover, boys from the age of eleven, who hoped to be priests, should be educated apart from other children.[27] Although a few writers feared that such an approach did nothing to equip the clergy to deal with increasingly educated lay Catholics or answer the arguments of increasingly secular opponents, the majority view prevailed.

Whiteside, for example, inveighed against seminary students reading secular newspapers. He wanted to prevent students from picking up unorthodox ideas and diluting the solid doctrine they should receive from reading the authors approved by the Bishop of the diocese. Moreover, he continued, the reading of secular newspapers only distracted the students from their studies, encouraged a less than healthy interest in political questions with the added danger of causing dissension among them, and caused too great an interest in sport, so that priests would want to attend public sporting events – he had been on the staff at Upholland under Canon Teebay and so perhaps was speaking from experience. He did not think a total ban could be imposed in England, however, where education was based on a spirit of free enquiry (!), but it should be left to the Bishop to decide what the students might read, with the same rules applying to secular newspapers as applied to books on the Index.[28] In practice, down to the 1950s students at Upholland were not allowed to read secular newspapers. On a different tack, Mgr Dean insisted on keeping the junior students (aged eleven or twelve to eighteen) at the college and so 'away from the world' over the whole Christmas break (see below).

Meanwhile, the rows had been too much for Canon Teebay, a gentle man who was more liberal in his views than most of the clergy. He also had to deal with troublesome quarrels with the local people: a miller complained he was being deprived of his water supply; there were disagreements over rights of way, and a long-running row over the amount of rates the college should pay. Two brothers named Brindle left the Church because of a quarrel over a supposed right to quarry stone in Jolly Wood. Teebay's health had not been sound for some years and in 1886 he resigned as rector, to be replaced by Canon Bilsborrow who remained in post until 1892 when he became Bishop of Salford. Canon Teebay continued to live at St Joseph's until his death in the same year.

A period of stable rule would have helped the new seminary to settle down, but the third rector, Dr Whiteside, was in post for only two years when he was appointed Bishop of Liverpool in succession to Bishop O'Reilly who died in 1894. Provost William Walmsley became the fourth rector to be appointed in eleven years; he was to provide the desired stability, remaining in post until 1926. He became something of an institution in his own right, a 'shrewd, gruff, kindly-hearted man', known as 'Old Bill'; one of many stories of his no-nonsense approach concerned a student who was rather tearful and sorry for himself after a painful operation: 'You'd have made a right fool of yourself at Tyburn!' was the rector's comment.[29] In 1906 he was asked to become patron of the Upholland and District 'Annual Horse, Dog, Poultry and Pigeon Show' – was the college at last being accepted as part of the local scene?

The stability promised under Provost Walmesley was interrupted by the war and by 1918 there were only ten students left in the college; four of them were ordained in July, and the rest transferred to Ushaw. The buildings became a temporary home for seventy orphans from Liverpool under the Sisters of Mercy, who were joined later by some Sisters of Charity with more children from St Helens. When the college re-opened as a seminary in 1920 it was completely changed in character for it now housed the junior seminarians from St Edward's, the first stage in Archbishop's Whiteside's plan to have one all-embracing diocesan seminary. On 29 December 1919 the 'great trek' started: the 'Pioneers' (fifteen senior boys), led by the Prefect, Fr Tom Turner, walked from St Edward's to Upholland. They arrived late, hungry and very tired, but rather proud of their achievement, only to be told off by Provost Walmsley, who called them 'silly fools', rebuked them for their late arrival and told them they had missed dinner; he later relented and let them eat. The remainder of the older boys (the 'Diehards') and the younger ones travelled more conventionally a few weeks later. The total number of students starting a new life at Upholland was eighty-eight, with seven priests and five 'minor professors' on the staff.[30]

So ended the old St Edward's. It had educated a total of 1,365 students between 1843 and 1919, among whom had been seven future bishops: Archbishop Whiteside of Liverpool (St Edward's 1868-73); Bishop Dobson, auxiliary Bishop of Liverpool (1879-86); Archbishop Downey of Liverpool (1894-1901); Bishop Barrett of Plymouth (1890-1900); Bishop Flynn of Lancaster (1893-1902); Bishop James Bilsborrow, OSB, Bishop of Port Louis, Mauritius, and Archbishop of Cardiff (1881-2). Many others had gone on to become priests, of course, at least 250 of them for the diocese of Liverpool, while lay boys had played their part in building up the English Catholic

body throughout the country.[31] The buildings continued in use as a secondary school under the auspices of the Irish Christian Brothers, who at Whiteside's suggestion bought the site and transferred the Catholic Institute from its old premises in Hope Street to St Domingo House. One of the conditions imposed by the Archbishop, at the request of the clergy, was that the Brothers should adopt the name of St Edward's for their school, and so started the successful new St Edward's, still flourishing although not on the old site in Everton – that was sold in the 1930s for Corporation housing.[32]

A NEW START

Archbishop Whiteside died in 1921 and it was his successor, Archbishop Keating, who undertook the massive building program that was required if St Joseph's were to become large enough to house both junior and senior seminarians. The architect chosen was Mr Pugin Powell, a grandson of Augustus Welby Pugin, the great Victorian enthusiast for everything Gothic. Powell planned a large quadrangle to go in front of O'Byrne's original wing and a new chapel, all in a Gothic style and built of attractive red sandstone. The foundation stone of the first of the new wings was laid in October 1923 (to house the 'Higher Line' or older boys of the junior seminary); by 1927 this and a new east wing had been completed, so there was now room for the philosophy and theology students, who in the meantime had been studying mainly at Oscott. A new south wing, to complete the quadrangle, was started in 1926 and, when completed with its three large towers, formed an impressive new entrance facing the college lakes; it housed teaching staff and the Gradwell Library. The foundation stone of the new chapel was laid in 1927, and the completed building was consecrated by Cardinal Bourne in 1930. One historian of this great expansion has said that it was the greatest accomplishment in building by English Catholics between the wars, and it would be difficult to disagree.[33] The diocese at last had its Tridentine seminary, as grand as any of the older colleges – in a typical flight of oratory Archbishop Downey claimed it was 'the pride of the North, the envy of the South, the admiration of the East and the West'.

Archbishop Keating was justifiably proud of what he had started and should be regarded as Upholland's co-founder. As well as being responsible for the massive building project, he had had to decide on the staffing of the new seminary. In 1926 he appointed Mgr Joseph Dean as Rector, a scripture scholar of ultra-conservative views and a severe disciplinarian well in tune with the *hortus conclusus* (enclosed garden) ideal of seminary training. On the academic side he was determined to appoint well-qualified staff – mainly priests who had studied in Rome for doctorates, a few of whom also had external degrees from London University. Two of them already had something of a wider reputation. One of these was Dr Thomas Flynn (later second Bishop of Lancaster), who had studied at Upholland and Fribourg, and then, after ordination, had read natural science at St Edmund's, Cambridge. He taught science at St Edmund's, Ware, and became something of an expert on medical ethics; he later became joint editor of the *Clergy Review* when it was launched in 1931. He was on the staff of Upholland from 1924 – 1932, and was vice-rector for the last four years.[34]

Fr Richard Downey was another obvious choice. He had studied philosophy and theology in Rome after ordination at Upholland, gaining both a PhD and a DD. He returned to England in 1911 and worked for 15 years as a member of the Catholic Missionary Society (CMS), preaching and giving missions all over the country and developing a reputation as an effective and often witty preacher and public speaker. He founded the CMS's *Catholic Gazette*, wrote articles for a number of journals and in 1921 published his first book, *Some Errors of H.G. Wells. A Catholic's Criticism of the 'Outline of History'* (a new edition in 1933 included some correspondence between the two). He became a member of the British Aristotelian and Psychological Societies and an Honorary Fellow of the Philosophical Society of England.[35] Downey's preference would have been to teach philosophy, but the Archbishop wanted him to teach Dogmatic Theology: 'I want a man who can work-in the positive and the apologetic theology (*sic*) with the speculative and your long experience on Missions to non-Catholics makes you peculiarly suited to the work'.[36] He became vice-rector of Upholland shortly after joining the staff in 1926, and there is one amusing, and perhaps revealing, story told of him while he was there: he and Dr Flynn tried to have the address of the seminary changed so as to omit the name of nearby Wigan, on the grounds that it would not be good for the reputation of the place to be connected with a town that was the butt of music hall jokes![37]

The Archbishop also laid down an ideal, or 'mission statement', for the seminary and its staff, whom he addressed formally at the beginning of the new academic year in 1926. Not surprisingly, he began by stressing that he had great expectations of the recently expanded institution: it was to be a centre of sacred learning, an exemplar of religious observance, a treasure-house of ecclesiastical culture. To realise these ideals the staff would have to be of the highest quality, with a faith unsullied by liberalism and adorned by 'deep and accurate learning, defended ... by patient study' – the phrase 'unsullied by liberalism' is a telling one in the post-Modernist period of the 1920s, as is the complete obedience to the Holy See and the hierarchy that Keating went on to advocate They should, he stressed, always *sentire cum ecclesia* (be of one mind with the Church) and accept the authority of the Holy See and the hierarchy. In academic matters they must continue what was an excellent tradition in 'lower studies', and he congratulated them on the achievements to date in the University Joint Examinations; they should also, however, take special care of the backward students. In 'Higher Studies' (i.e. philosophy and theology), for the present 'they would have to create their own' (his meaning not clear here); they should leave no room for slacking, and while lectures would be in English he would welcome the introduction of the Syllogistic Disputatio (*sic*) in Latin. At all times members of the staff should be careful to preserve 'professorial dignity' by wearing academic dress, and insisting on proper forms of address and observance of the rules. At the same time, he would welcome the development of a respectful familiarity with the students through informal contacts with them and taking an interest in student associations.[38]

Most of the rest of the Archbishop's talk was taken up with the internal organization of the seminary: the rector was the Archbishop's representative and in overall charge in all matters of discipline; the prefects of studies were responsible for drawing up syllabuses and timetabling which had to be approved by the archbishop and then adhered to strictly at all times; all staff should normally return to the college before 10pm, and should not normally take on regular supply work in parishes. Finally, the Archbishop wished to see the development of an 'esprit de corps': this should not result in the narrowness of mind that refused to see good in other institutions, but should encourage a strong sense of loyalty and devotion to their Alma Mater. He ended:

> *Believe in yourselves – in your ideal – in your power to attain it. Hence do not belittle the work nor the workers – be generous in your esteem of each other – a mutual admiration society (is) better than a mutual contempt society. Guard yourselves in conversation about the affairs and personnel of the house – it is the criticism that is repeated.*

He was here showing an awareness of the difficulties of establishing a new institution that could not rely on an inherited tradition stretching back centuries, as was the case with the older English seminaries. This was both a challenge and an opportunity, to develop a justifiable pride in its achievements and to seize the opportunity to develop something new that would not be hidebound by tradition or complacent because of past glories; the outlook of archbishops and rectors would be all important.

Archbishop Keating died in February 1928 and so did not see the completion of his great work. He was buried, fittingly, in the private cemetery at Upholland. Mgr Dean remained Rector until 1942. He welcomed the Beda students who arrived as refugees from Rome under Mgr Duchemin and stayed for the duration of the war, occupying the Gradwell Library and the Philosophers' corridor, and no doubt comparing their new home unfavourably with what they had left behind.[39] Mgr Dean's concerns were two-fold, to ensure the strictest orthodoxy in what was taught to the theological students, especially in the area of Scripture, and to enforce the strictest discipline on the students' way of life. He gave in reluctantly to the Archbishop's demand that the senior students should be allowed to smoke, but resigned in 1942 after a decision on whether the junior students should be allowed home for a break at Christmas went against him. All the staff and the special commission set up by Archbishop Downey were in favour of this relaxation, and the commission also 'encouraged' the rector to consult his Council more often and trust them more fully.[40] In his retirement he was chaplain to the Sisters of Our Lady of Charity in Ormskirk. During the Liverpool blitz he took over as temporary priest-in-charge of St Anthony's, Scotland Road, where the two curates had been killed and the parish priest seriously injured. He died in Ormskirk in October 1960, aged 85. Those who visited him in his latter years, and had known him as students or members of staff, still found it difficult to relax in his company, such had been the aura of unbending discipline that had surrounded him as rector.[41]

Presumably Mgr Dean was working out the wishes of Archbishop Downey, who laid out his ideals for the seminary in a Lenten Pastoral (1934): the candidate for the priesthood was not encouraged to be clever or smart, 'to uphold strange and original views, to be abreast of the fleeting novelties of the day, to break away from the abiding, age-long traditions of the Church'. Hence, according to the Archbishop, at an early age the candidate was withdrawn from the world and its dangers to within 'the sheltering walls' of the seminary, and the intensive culture of charity, chastity, humility and obedience began by means of the constant round of prayers, daily Mass and Communion, frequent confession 'that the soul lose not its lustre' and constant encouragement, exhortation, admonition and correction.[42] Here was the 'enclosed garden' of the seminary, junior and senior, in its all its glory – and all its limitations.

What contribution did the new seminary make to the supply of priests for the archdiocese? The number of priests ordained for Liverpool in the early years was not high and even by 1937 only amounted to a third of the total ordained for the archdiocese. During these years the Archbishop was recruiting regularly from the Irish seminaries and there was a steady number of ordinations from the English colleges abroad, especially Rome.

Upholland Ordinations

	Liverpool	Lancs	Salford	Total ordained for Liverpool	Upholland ords. as % of total
1934	4	2	0	22	18%
1935	3	1	1	12	25%
1936	7	3	5	21	33%
1937	5	0	6	14	36%
1938	10	1	6	14	71%
1939	6	4	2	7	86%

The total number of clergy in the archdiocese in 1939 was 616, of whom 450 were Seculars (including twenty-six sick or retired and thirty-six on temporary duty elsewhere). Altogether this represented the largest number of clergy in any of the English dioceses – grounds for some justifiable pride in what had been achieved so far in providing sufficient priests, and confidence that future pastoral developments would not be held up because of any shortage.

Notes

[1] J.F. Turner, 'St Edward's' in *Upholland Magazine* (1943), pp.71-86; also, A Diehard, 'The End of an Epoch', pp.87-97. *The Upholland College Magazine* Dec. 1923 and July 1924 has an article by Canon Cosgrave, written in 1880, 'The History of St Edward's College'. Statistics in P. Phillips, 'St Joseph's College, Upholland. A Brief History', *Ushaw Magazine* (1983), pp.3-17.

[2] Alfred Austin, *The Autobiography of Alfred Austin Poet Laureate, 1835-1910* (1911), pp.25-34.

[3] Milburn, *Ushaw*, pp.198-200.

[4] *Ibid*, pp.200-1.

[5] AAL St Joseph's Collection, S3 III G: Pastorals of Brown, June and Sept. 1850.

[6] Peter Doyle, 'The Education and Training of Roman Catholic Priests in Nineteenth-Century England', *JEH*, vol. 35, no. 2 (April 1984), pp.208-19, at p.209.

[7] *Decreta*, pp.154-72; 214-24.

[8] Burke, p.236.

[9] Turner, pp.78-81; J. Garvin, 'James O'Byrne', *Upholland Magazine* (Jan. 1934), pp.3-5.

[10] AAL St Joseph's, S3 III G/14, typescript, 'St Joseph's Diocesan College, Walthew Park', pp.1-2.

[11] *Ibid.*, 'The Diocesan Seminary': typescript account of Chapter involvement, 1868-1920, pp.4-5.

[12] Phillips, p.7.

[13] AAL *Liverpolitana*, pastoral letter April 1885, with accounts sheet attached.

[14] *Ibid.*

[15] AAL St Joseph's Collection, S3 III G/20.

[16] *Ibid.*, S3 III F/6, Taylor to Whiteside.

[17] Turner, p.83.

[18] Plumb, *Found Worthy*; 'The End of an Epoch', pp.94-5 (see note 1).

[19] Canon Tom Turner, Prefect of Discipline at the time, gives excellent detail; AAL St Joseph's, S3 III G/19.

[20] List of original staff, AAL St Joseph's, S3 III G/20; for Commer, obit. in *Upholland Magazine*, Spring 1928, pp.76-7 (also mentions Steffens).

[21] AAL Chancellors' Collection *Acta Capituli Liverpolitani* II, 14.11.1882.

[22] AAL St Joseph's, S3 III G/20, 'Proposals from James Swarbrick 14 July 1883'.

[23] *Ibid.*, S3 III F/4, 21.9.1885, Carr to O'Reilly.

[24] *Ibid.*, Teebay to O'Reilly, n.d.

[25] *Ibid.*, J. O'Reilly to Bishop, 3.3.1885.

[26] *Ibid.*, list of complaints in O'Reilly's hand.

[27] *Decreta*, pp.216,.219.

[28] AAL Early Bishops, S1 VII A/5, Consistorial Congregation to Whiteside about a ban, 11.1.1911; the copy of Whiteside's reply is undated.

[29] Phillips, p.10; Plumb, *Found Worthy*, p.154.

[30] Turner, p.85.

[31] *Ibid.*, p.86; Plumb, *Found Worthy*.

[32] Peter Doyle & Leslie McLoughlin, *The Edwardian Story. The remarkable history of St Edward's College, Liverpool* (2003).

[33] AAL St Joseph's, S6 XII, *The Upholland Magazine*, 1924-30, covers all the new building; F. Callon, 'A History of the College Grounds, Pt. I', *Upholland Magazine* (New series), vol.II, no.2 (1965), pp.11-15.

[34] Plumb, *Arundel*.

[35] *Ibid*; *DNB* 1951-60, pp.309-11; *The Times*, 17.6.1953; *Upholland Magazine*, vol. XVII (1953), pp.11-4.

[36] AAL S4 I A: Keating Letterbooks, Keating to Downey 14.2.1925.

[37] AAL St Joseph's, S3 III, G/19: Canon Turner's Diary, under 1926.

[38] AAL Keating, S7 IV A/107, Keating's Address, 18.9.1926.

[39] 'The Beda', in *Upholland Magazine*, 1947, pp.53-4.

[40] AAL St Joseph's, S3 III G: petitions started about 1933; the final one from the staff to Downey is dated December 1941; private memo by J.F. Turner, also Dec. 1941; the Commission reported to Downey in March 1942.

[41] Plumb, *Found Worthy*, p.34; personal reminiscences of Upholland staff.

[42] Quoted in Plumb, *Found Worthy*, p.vi.

CHAPTER 13 ARCHBISHOP RICHARD DOWNEY – 'THE RULER OF THE NORTH', 1928-1953

THE NEW ARCHBISHOP

In August 1928 Fr Richard Downey succeeded Keating as Archbishop of Liverpool. It was an unusual appointment in that he was only forty-seven years of age and the youngest archbishop in the Catholic world. In addition, he had been appointed without any previous experience as a Bishop or a parish priest, although his years with the Catholic Missionary Society had given him some pastoral experience. He was consecrated Bishop in the pro-cathedral in September 1928 by Cardinal Bourne. Over the years, he became a freeman of a number of towns and cities in Ireland, an honorary Doctor of Laws of Liverpool University and an honorary Doctor of Divinity of the University of Toronto. He undertook a number of lecture tours – in Canada, the USA and Australia (mainly to raise money for his dream-child, the cathedral), and was always received rapturously, especially by journalists, with whom he got on well and was at ease.

He was one of the very first of the English bishops to take to the new medium of broadcasting and could use it very effectively. In 1931 he was invited to give a radio talk, one of a series entitled 'What I would do if I were Dictator of the World!' His talk covered a wide range of issues, including how to deal with the current moral decadence. First of all, he claimed, he would restore the 'simplicity of family life' by a gradual process based on Christian education. Part of this would involve banning divorce from all Christian countries, if only because of the 'moral canker' that a light view of marriage spread through society. In addition, he would 'cheerfully provide millstones' for the necks of those who scandalised little ones by plays, films or books, and he would discourage 'the peculiar genius … which can express itself only in obscenity'. He went on to state his objection to sterilisation of the unfit, euthanasia and birth-control and all the other proposals of the eugenicists of the day – eugenics, indeed, in the hands of cranks and fanatics could easily become a deadly anti-social weapon: those who wanted to give the world 'a muscular Keats' could just as likely end up giving it 'an intellectual Bill Sykes'. Turning to the question of inequality in society, the Archbishop claimed that he would tax out of existence the 'absolutely leisured class' and insist on everyone doing some work for the good of society – it was no good preaching the dignity of labour, he went on, if the pleasures of idleness were flaunted in public. Finally, he would find some way of bringing about a juster distribution of wealth in each country, although he was opposed to interference in ordinary business affairs by the state.[1]

The talk illustrates Downey's light, witty touch that endeared him to audiences even when he was dealing with serious issues. This was, no doubt, a legacy of his days spent travelling up and down the country for the Catholic Missionary Society and talking to largely uncommitted groups of people whose attention he had to capture and hold. Once, while visiting the HMV studios in London, he was invited to make a record and without any preparation he spoke about the new cathedral he was planning for Liverpool. When he finished he was applauded by everyone in the studio for the quality of his impromptu talk – the recording was good enough to be sold to raise funds for the building.[2] His 1932 Christmas message on 'The Prince of Peace' was broadcast to the nation. As his 'novelty value' wore off the invitations to appear or speak in public declined, but his ability to attract wide press coverage remained to the end.

He had a reputation as a scholar, a reputation, it must be said, that he helped to foster. He shared the high esteem for the academic standard of Roman institutions, especially the Gregorian University, that was common among many who studied there. Its system was as remote as could be from that of intellectual life and expectations in an English university and some who experienced both systems lowered their estimation of the Roman one considerably. His first book, a critique of H.G. Wells' *The Outline of History,* shows how well read Downey was in subjects such as evolution and the anthropology of religion, though there is evidence, too, of a tendency to sarcasm and point-scoring that marked many of his writings and speeches – he was ever the controversialist. It is also somewhat strange to find the Archbishop describing himself in print as a 'professional psychologist' and as one who had studied zoology 'seriously'.[3] His published works were mainly collections of his talks and broadcasts, some rather ephemeral in nature, others apologetic in Catholic Missionary Society style, such as *Critical and Constructive Essays* (1934) and *Pulpit and Platform Addresses* (1933). He wrote forewords to a small number of books and edited a volume of essays to raise money for the cathedral called, *Rebuilding the Church in England; The Liverpool Cathedral Book* (1933), to which he contributed a chapter justifying the building against the timid and the doubters. Two of his longer pamphlets in the *Treasury of the Faith* series, one on Divine Providence and the other on The Blessed Trinity, were reprinted as chapters in the definitive *The Teaching of the Catholic Church.*[4] The chapter on the Trinity (originally written in 1930) is a straightforward scholastic treatment in line with the textbook dogmatic theology of the day. It is as clearly written as an account dealing with divine processions, essences, divine spiration, appropriations and visible and invisible missions could be.

The chapter on Divine Providence (dating originally from 1928) was more open to a modern treatment that would deal with such issues as blind evolutionary chance, free will, the purpose of prayer and, of course, the problem of evil. Despite passing references to the laws of thermodynamics and to writers such as Hume, Huxley and Nietzsche, he made no attempt to deal with objections to the traditional Christian stance to be found in contemporary writers or arising from the first World War. Man, according to Downey, was still largely the architect of his own misfortunes, and his conclusion, that every 'healthy-minded man and woman' was forced to see that the universe simply teemed with the evidences of the infinitely good God who had called it into being, 'not for our satisfaction, but for his own greater honour and glory', begged more questions than it answered.

By the mid-1930s Downey's leading position among the English and Welsh bishops was the result of a number of factors. There was his undoubted ability and willingness to speak out and engage with the media. There was also Cardinal Bourne's illness and decline before his death in 1935, when people looked to Liverpool rather than Westminster for leadership and comment. What some have called his 'Liverpool power-base' was built on sound statistical foundations: by the outbreak of war in 1939 the industrial North-West contained about 820,000 Catholics, twice as many as the industrial North-East and eight times as many as the industrial Midlands. Not all of this area came directly under Downey's control, of course, but he was secure in thinking that he was the major player in the Catholic heartland of England and Wales. It was not a security based mainly on numbers, however, but a deeply psychological one as well, supported by the absolute certainty of his beliefs and his unbending conviction that Catholicism provided the only reliable champion of Christian orthodoxy in the country. The Catholic Church in England and Wales had only to hold fast to its doctrines and traditions for the fruit of the return of the country to the faith of its fathers to drop into its lap, and he was proud to be its principal spokesman and defender.

When Cardinal Bourne died in January 1935 Archbishop Downey was in Australia – he had stayed on after the Eucharistic Congress of 1934, mainly to raise funds for his new cathedral. He had given a highly successful series of lectures and proved extremely popular with the Australian press who loved his quick-wittedness (when asked whether he approved of trial marriages, for example, he replied that he did not, but was all in favour of test matches) and his high praise for their country, which he saw as fresh and invigorating and a sign of hope for the future. When news of Bourne's death became known he was immediately picked out as his successor, and cut short his engagements to 'hurry back' to London (the phrase was *The Universe's*). There, incredibly, he stayed in Archbishop's House and even had a photograph taken of himself obviously at ease there; it was published in the *Daily Sketch* and the *Universe*. Most of the English secular press made him the hot favourite in what they thought was a three-horse race: himself, Bishop Myers, Auxiliary to Cardinal Bourne, and Bishop McNulty of Nottingham. The *Evening Standard* quoted in Downey's support the words of the Pope on the occasion of the Archbishop's silver jubilee of ordination: his services to the Christian world were 'conspicuous' and he was a 'pattern of virtue to his flock'. The value of this press support was somewhat reduced when the *Daily Express* announced that 'well-informed Vatican circles' had named Bishop Amigo of Southwark as Bourne's likely successor![5]

Downey was certainly the outstanding internal candidate: as Moloney says 'his personal magnetism matched his brilliance as a scholar and speaker'.[6] But Rome surprised everyone by choosing instead an outsider, Bishop Arthur Hinsley, former rector of the English College, Rome, and Apostolic Visitor to the Missions and later Apostolic Delegate in Africa. In his seventieth year he was clearly a stop gap appointment and no one was more surprised than himself. Immediately on the day his appointment was announced in Rome he wrote to Downey to say that he had only accepted the post under strict obedience and totally against his own will – it was as though he felt he owed the favourite candidate an explanation.[7] We do not know why Downey was passed over, or even whether he was ever a likely

candidate in Rome's eyes. His lavish praise of Archbishop Mannix of
Melbourne, a fiercely Irish maverick and a bête noir of the British
government for his anti-British sentiments (he had the distinction of being
the only Catholic archbishop in modern times to be intercepted on the high
seas by the British navy to stop him speaking in Ireland in 1920), cannot have
done his cause any good, and the English Catholic establishment never took
him to its narrow nationalistic bosom, either.

Meanwhile the Archbishop was back in Liverpool, where he had been
welcomed by crowds variously estimated at between 20,000 and 30,000
strong. He was also given a civic reception by the Lord Mayor. He spoke
about the wonders of Australia, about the strength of Catholicism there and
how much people had been interested in the building of the new cathedral.
While he had been away special collections had been taken up and he was
given a home-coming present of about £4,000 for the building fund.[8]

PUBLIC CONTROVERSY

While undoubtedly a fighter and public controversialist, he started in
Liverpool by trying to reduce the heat of sectarianism in local politics. He was
also determined to end the trouble that Keating's CRA had caused both with
local Protestants and local Labour politicians. Downey was very keen that
Catholics should take part in civic life and be active in politics, but he regarded
an exclusively Catholic party as an obstacle rather than a help in achieving
this. He met Labour leaders in October 1928 and afterwards declared that no
priest should stand as a candidate in any election or take an active part in any
election; nor should any priest allow parish buildings to be used for political

purposes. Furthermore, he promised that sitting Catholic members would not be opposed in local elections that year by other Catholic candidates. Finally, he stated that he would not recognise the right of any political party to use the word 'Catholic' in its title or official publications.[9] This effectively killed off the CRA, though a few of its members continued to be active, changing its title to the 'Centre R.A.' Downey, however, developed his own brand of combative Catholicism and certainly did not act as though he believed that the meek would inherit the earth.

Sectarian civil war smouldered on, and could easily be fanned into flame. The dispute over the purchase of the workhouse site for the cathedral roused bitter opposition (see pages 293-5), and at the beginning of December 1930 there were outbreaks of street violence. A demonstration by about 200 Protestants prevented the Archbishop from attending the prize-giving at the Notre Dame school in Everton Valley. Bricks were thrown at the convent windows which were broken despite their protective wire shields. A little later on the same evening a large crowd attacked a van that was trying to deliver furniture to the new presbytery belonging to Our Lady Immaculate church in St Domingo Road, Everton. In the end the van had to drive away, while bricks and railings from the site were torn up and missiles thrown at Fr Denis O'Shea, the parish priest – the presbytery door was damaged and he lost his hat but was otherwise uninjured. These events received national coverage.[10]

At the same time, the Archbishop was involved in a long-running and very bitter public quarrel with the Anglican Bishop of Liverpool, Dr Albert David, on other issues. One of these was the street preaching of the Catholic Evidence Guild (the CEG): the Bishop claimed that its speakers poured scorn on the Anglican Church and its ministers, inciting their Catholic hearers to insults and, indirectly, to violence. Archbishop Downey seems to have taken this seriously and ordered the CEG to ensure that its speakers did not attack other denominations but just put its own Catholic message across positively, though in some of his later statements he was less willing to accept that the charges had been substantiated.

The principal issue between the two leaders, on which Downey would not yield at all, was that of mixed marriages contracted outside the Catholic Church. The Bishop publicly accused Catholic priests of 'terrorising' the non-Catholic wives (the Bishop frequently stressed this element and how it had led to nervous breakdowns), using foul language to tell them that their marriages were invalid and their children illegitimate; in one case a priest was said to have told a Catholic husband that he was quite free to leave his wife because they were not validly married. Moreover, the Bishop claimed that the priests reserved this treatment for the poorest and least educated of the people and dealt with their middle-class parishioners quite differently.

Downey demanded details of individual cases, with the names of the priests concerned, and when the Bishop gave details of six cases the Archbishop poured scorn on the lack of genuine evidence that would ever stand up in a court of law – in some cases no priest of the name given existed, or the case was thirteen years old and based on hearsay, or the witnesses were known to be trouble-makers and unreliable (including one case of a Protestant woman claiming to have 'laid the priest low with a poker' when he questioned the legitimacy of her children!). He claimed that the one genuine case was eleven years old and had concerned the marriage of two Catholics, not a mixed marriage. Overall, Downey claimed that the allegations were incapable of proof, while the one about particularly bad treatment of the poor and unlearned was 'beneath contempt'. He also accused the Bishop of inconsistency in that he complained of terrorism by Catholic priests but did not condemn his own spiritual allies who repeatedly tried to wreck a Catholic presbytery and threw stones at defenceless nuns and the children in their charge.

The quarrel lasted about two months, with claims and counter-claims. What is amazing is the way it was taken up by the press across the country from Penrith to Penzance. All the national papers covered it and many local ones as well, giving details of the Catholic laws about mixed marriages and, in particular, the changes brought about with the implementation of the *Ne Temere* decree in 1908. This made the marriages of Catholics (mixed or not) invalid if not performed in a Catholic church before a priest and two witnesses, whereas previously they had been unlawful but valid. In his final statement Bishop David claimed that since the decree the Catholic Church had greatly intensified 'its aggressive propaganda', paying no heed to Christian charity or the laws of the land – this was, he stated, a matter of common knowledge in Liverpool and he was prepared to publish in full any future cases of harassment brought to his notice. Perhaps, he continued, Roman priests 'and other agents' would learn from the publicity of the controversy to be more careful and would be deterred from their previous excesses. In his final statement to the press Downey said he had no objection to the publication of details, especially if they were as amusing as those of the 'unknown female warrior with the poker'. He believed that the controversy would not have been in vain if it made the Bishop 'and his abettors' more careful and a little less hasty 'in bearing witness against their neighbours'.[11] No doubt some priests had been over-zealous in their efforts to 'put right' mixed marriages that were invalid according to Church law, without making due reference to the laws of the country. In the 1930s there were about 500 of these a year that were subsequently validated by dispensation; Downey continued the strict line of his immediate predecessors on the granting of dispensations before marriage, but there were still about 200 of these a year.[12]

In 1932 Downey told a *Times* correspondent that he had tried for four years to keep his people quiet but it was proving very difficult when they faced 'wanton provocation'; it was sad to reflect, he continued, that the 'gospel of religious hate was preached with impunity' in the city.[13] He referred to an 'unoffending priest' being dragged off his bicycle and forced to spend the night away from the presbytery, but the immediate occasion was an attack by twenty youths on St Bernard's presbytery and church in Kingsley Road (the bicycle incident might have been part of this). This was followed, probably as retaliation by Catholic youths, by an attack on the windows of the Lady Chapel of the new Anglican cathedral and a nearby council school. Downey deplored these attacks and hoped Catholics had not been involved, while Bishop David professed himself at a loss to understand them since Liverpool Anglicans had given no grounds for offence. In the light of these differences it is interesting that Bishop David was one of the guests of honour and spoke 'delightfully' at the banquet given by the Archbishop for Cardinal MacCrory and other Catholic bishops on the occasion of the laying of the cathedral foundation stone in 1933.[14]

ECUMENICAL RELATIONS

While outbreaks of street violence became less frequent as the decade wore on, relations between Catholics and Protestants remained edgy. A special cause of ill-feeling was the refusal of Catholics to take part in joint civic services, whether it was Armistice Day services at a town's war memorial or a civic service to mark the installation of a mayor. A particular case of the former had occurred in Southport in 1926 when the Catholic clergy were attacked in the local press for refusing to join the town's Anglicans, Non-conformists and Jews. Local resentment was all the higher because it seemed that the Catholics were being inconsistent – they had attended the inaugural service at the war memorial three years before. Canon John Turner, parish priest of St Marie's, explained that the non-attendance was not a discourtesy to the town council but a decision based solely on religious grounds. It was true a Catholic priest had attended previously, but only for the civic part of the ceremony – he had left 'unobtrusively' before any prayers or hymns. Their non-attendance might appear narrow and bigoted, Turner added, but was 'the logical outcome of principles which we believe have God as their author'.[15]

With regard to common civic services, one of Downey's main arguments was always that attendance by Catholic VIPs at such services would only confuse the people, but there were some very sensitive occasions when the Catholic attitude appeared to many people to be unjustified. When, for example, the Liverpool Cenotaph had been unveiled in front of St George's Hall on Armistice Day, 1930, no Catholic representative was present and Downey later snubbed the Anglican Bishop of Liverpool when he invited Downey to an ecumenical service: 'an Archbishop of the Catholic Church', Downey was reported to have said in reply, 'can hardly be expected to accept the spiritual leadership of an Anglican Bishop'. One result of this snub was that Downey was 'buffeted' or stoned – something that happened to him again in the September when he was walking in procession to lay the foundation stone of a new school in Edge Hill; he was not hurt, but a Catholic girl guide lining the route was – and a Protestant gang attacked a Catholic presbytery.[16]

Downey was involved in another spat in December 1940. The occasion this time was an extremely sensitive one – the mass burial in Anfield cemetery of the victims of enemy air-raids. Downey was present, but refused to give a blessing, which led to what the Anglican Bishop said was 'a painful scene at the graveside'. He regarded Downey as lacking in courtesy in not letting him and the Lord Mayor know of his attitude beforehand. There seems to have been a genuine confusion over what had been agreed in the initial phone calls between Downey and the Bishop, and Downey apologised if he had misunderstood what the Bishop had asked him to do – he did not like answering the phone because of his 'catarrhal deafness'.[17]

Occasionally there was an element of the bizarre in these matters. A National Day of Prayer was held in September, 1942, and the Ordnance Factory in Kirkby wanted to broadcast a fifteen-minute service to all its workers. When the Factory manager approached Downey to see if this would be acceptable, the Archbishop said 'no' – the Catholic workers would have their own prayers and services that day. But he would agree if part of the fifteen minutes could be devoted to a purely Catholic service; the manager agreed and allowed a local priest to use the official factory microphone for the purpose.[18]

The Armistice Day services after the war raised the same sensitivities. In 1946, when the Lord Mayor was a Catholic, the arrangement was for him to attend the wreath-laying part of the service but then to retire to the Pro-Cathedral for a Catholic service. Interestingly enough, Downey sent an official representative to the services in 1946 and 1947 and had a wreath laid at the memorial, but subsequently told the Town Clerk that it would be better for Catholics to concentrate on the Mass at the Pro-Cathedral and so he would not be sending a representative in future. Again, in 1951, when there was a dedication service for the memorial placed over the communal grave of 559 blitz victims, Downey insisted on having a separate Catholic service on the following day, claiming that he could not possibly join in 'a common dedicatory service'.[19]

POLITICS

When it came to defending Catholic principles on the national stage, Downey could usually rely on a small number of local Catholic MPs (usually three or four at any one time) to put the Catholic point of view in Parliament and in some cases to subordinate their party loyalties to their religious interests. The legendary T.P. O'Connor, was succeeded by David Gilbert Logan (1871-1964), who held the Liverpool Scotland seat from 1929 to 1964 for Labour – a Liverpool-born Catholic of Irish-Scots parentage and a pawnbroker by profession. He was outspoken in Parliament on Catholic issues, declaring in his maiden speech, 'To me God means everything and all things … in this House it is essential that we should understand what true religion means'. He voted against his party in 1931 on its Education Bill because it would lay extra burdens on Catholic schools. In 1932 he opposed any moves to make divorce easier even in cases where one partner had been insane for more than five years, and in 1935 and 1936 he opposed any government grants to clinics that gave information about birth-control – 'scurrilous literature only fit for the gutter … (not) decent homes'. He was also, however, very active in constituency matters, especially housing and unemployment benefit.[20]

Among other Catholic MPs during Downey's years was W.A. Robinson, a convert, who represented St Helens as a National Labour MP from 1935 – 1945. Colonel Sir John Shute succeeded Sir James Philip Reynolds in the Exchange Division of Liverpool in 1933. He was an indifferent speaker but a successful businessman, and had been chosen by the local, strongly Protestant, Conservative party machine precisely because he was a Catholic – the Exchange Division included the business heart of Liverpool but also wards with the highest Catholic population; he was supported quite openly in the parishes by the clergy and described his Labour opponent as one of a 'poisonous Socialist cum Communist crew'.[21]

Finally, there was J.T. (Joe) Tinker, Labour member for Leigh from 1929 to 1945, 'a blunt, unsophisticated British working man' who played a significant part in the parliamentary stages of the 1944 Education Bill, although Downey had earlier excluded him from the official Catholic delegation.[22]

By Downey's time it had become established practice to try to obtain pledges from non-Catholic candidates before an election or to get them to answer a series of questions on Catholic issues – the schools question above all, of course. As we have seen, these attempts were usually highly organised, with parish priests sifting the answers from local candidates and announcing the results to their people – in practice advising them how they should vote. Archbishop Downey followed the practice of his predecessors, sending a questionnaire to fifty-nine parliamentary candidates in and around Liverpool. The practice, however, caused sectarian bitterness and, in any case, seemed to make little difference to how Catholics actually voted – priests might on occasion be able to influence how some of their people voted, but on the whole could only lead them in the direction they wanted to go.[23] Moreover, pledges that were easily given were just as easily forgotten. In the late 1930s Downey seemed to move towards allowing Catholics to make up their own minds on the basis of the candidates' manifestos. Even when a number of candidates tried to win his support by promising to vote for a 75% grant for Catholic schools, he refused to back them; as he wrote to the Conservative election agent, he had no intention of trying to appraise the pledges and promises made by candidates. All he would say was that he believed that Catholics should make a stand against anyone who opposed all grants to Catholic schools.[24] But after the war he followed the other bishops in organising calls on local candidates to ensure that they understood the Catholic case and to find out how they would vote on any measures designed to bring relief. He asked for the results of the interviews to be sent to him, but appears not to have taken any subsequent action.[25]

The general election in October 1951 resulted in a Conservative majority of seventeen, overturning a Labour majority of five won in February 1950. These narrow margins led the Archbishop to make an ill-considered political claim in November 1951. He hoped that the almost-stalemate situation between the two main parties would continue, because that would give Catholics the opportunity to hold the balance of power and obtain concessions from whatever party was in government. The press immediately portrayed the statement as an attempt to organise Catholics into some sort of political party or, at least, as a 'separate influence' that would mean that Catholics would go to the polls seeking to sway the result of elections for Catholic purposes. This, *The Tribune* argued, would be a 'development of deadly seriousness' that would result in a threat to the principles of religious toleration. Voters had to take into account a whole range of national and international issue when they were deciding how to vote and not vote simply as members of particular denominations. The paper ended by asking other Catholic leaders to repudiate Downey's statement. *The Church of England Newspaper* thought that the Archbishop 'must be going crazy' – nothing was more likely to inflame Protestant passions and to support the idea that for all its talk the Roman Church was more interested in political power than in the Kingdom of God; somebody 'should take Dr Downey in hand …'[26] The press reactions were unnecessarily hysterical, but the Archbishop should have known that any suggestion from him that Catholics might be able to dictate the shape of politics would arouse ancient fears and traditional bogeys. He was naive if he believed that he or the other bishops could persuade Catholics in post-war England and Wales to drop traditional party allegiances and vote together on a single sectarian issue.

The education issue was principally a national one. Locally, Catholic councillors had to deal with another 'hot' topic, the funding of birth-control clinics. In 1935 Luke Hogan, the Catholic leader of the Liverpool Labour Party and a future Lord Mayor (1945-6), criticised the City Council for its decision to award a grant to a birth-control clinic. When the grant came up for renewal the following year, Hogan stated that he acknowledged the difficulties that women faced in childbirth and paid tribute 'to the clean-minded women who endured them', but birth-control was not the right approach and was 'the negation of socialism'. His main opponent was the formidable Bessie Braddock who argued that the only safeguard against often fatal abortions was 'clean, scientific advice' on birth-control. She was supported by the leader of the Protestant Party, the Reverend Longbottom. The motion to renew the grant was easily carried, though 34 Labour Councillors (about 27 of whom were Catholics) voted against it (nationally the Labour Party was split on the issue in the 1930s).[27] In 1936 Downey instructed the forty Catholic voluntary workers of the Personal Service Society to resign because the Service decided to provide birth-control information to non-Catholics.[28] It is not clear how many followed his advice.

SOCIAL ISSUES AND RECONSTRUCTION

Downey's early years as Archbishop had co-incided with the worst years of the 1930s depression. In 1931-32 there were 110,000 insured unemployed on Merseyside, plus another 30,000 uninsured and 90,000 under-employed; the overall unemployment average was 28%. As a port Liverpool suffered from the world-wide depression in trade more than some other parts of the country and since the first World War had been losing traffic to other British ports. Moreover, Liverpool's small manufacturing base and large, unskilled workforce meant that it could not attract the new industries that were doing much elsewhere in the country to soften the effects of the depression and even to raise living standards. In 1936 50% of those who volunteered for the army from Liverpool were medically unfit and the following year 30% of all those who volunteered for the three armed services were also rejected on medical grounds. An economic study in 1932 concluded that there was no hope of getting rid of heavy unemployment in the city within ten years; there were still 80,000 insured unemployed in 1939, despite increased opportunities in the armed services and much civil defence construction work.[29]

Other parts of the archdiocese suffered, too: the mining and textile industries, already with unemployment averages considerably above the national average in the 1920s, had levels over 41% (coal) and over 31% (cotton) in 1932. There was some improvement as the decade wore on, but in 1938 the unemployment rate in the cotton industry was still over 27%. Pit villages around Wigan were particularly depressed, and the heavy chemicals industry around Widnes and St Helens stagnated or declined, although the glass industry in the latter fared better. In several places the standard of living of the poor dropped to pre-1914 levels, and with long-term unemployment went a long-term decline in nutrition and health and other social ills as people coped with chronic poverty and its consequent insecurity.[30] In these circumstances the Archbishop's fervent adoption of the Land Association scheme has to be seen as a desperation tactic (see Chapter 14). His decision to build the largest cathedral in the world at such a time of economic crisis for the majority of his people was, to say the least, unreal.

At the same time, the decades after the First World War saw a continuation and quickening of slum clearance in Liverpool and other towns. About 140,000 people (15% of the Liverpool population) were re-housed and the process of breaking up some of the old inner-city and slum communities was under way by 1939. This played its part in diminishing outbreaks of sectarianism as people moved out to new estates in Fazakerley, Norris Green, Croxteth, Speke and Huyton – 30,000 were re-housed in the last-named alone. The poor, however, did not benefit to the extent they might have done because of their need to stay close to traditional sources of casual labour and their inability to pay higher rents.[31] These changes also called for a new building campaign to provide churches and schools for the displaced Catholics: this was part of a significant expansion across the archdiocese as a whole that saw forty new missions established in the twenty-three years from 1919 to 1941, twenty-four of them between 1930 and 1941 – a remarkable allocation of resources in a difficult economic period.[32] The old problems of the inner-city and slum areas were alleviated but not conquered, and priests on new estates, usually built with no community or social facilities and very poor transport links, found themselves dealing with the 'modern' problems of alienation, loneliness and the loss of informal support groups.

Downey was well aware of the social ills that affected the majority of his people and was interested in steps to alleviate them, but his political leanings and involvement were determined more by the two issues of Catholic schools and anti-Communism (on the latter, see the chapter on Catholic Action). Like his predecessor, the Archbishop did not want former Irish Nationalist voters to turn automatically to Labour, because he disagreed with the party's general support for secular education and was frightened of its socialist wing. He supported many of the social reforms that Labour promised, however, and, in 1943, welcomed the Beveridge proposals for a national health service: he was strongly in favour, he said, of a health service that would provide full preventive and curative treatment of every kind 'to every citizen without exception, without remuneration limit and without an economic barrier at any point to delay recourse to it'.[33] At the same time he wanted the voluntary Catholic hospitals to continue and had some fears that the Beveridge system would do away with 'the painful necessity of thinking' on the part of its citizens. Writing at a time when he and others were condemning the all-powerful state in fascist countries, it is hardly surprising that he was on the lookout for any signs of undue state influence at home – the sovereign will of the people must not, he stated, be overridden by bureaucracy. Some have seen in this an ultra-conservative and negative approach to the welfare state, out of touch with the general attitudes of English society; perhaps the voluntary principle and the sacredness of the patriarchal family had ruled English Catholic thinking for too long.[34] Others might have wondered what the 'sovereign will of the people' meant when faced by ecclesiastical bureaucracy.

Downey was one of the first English Catholic leaders to inveigh against the evils of fascism, at least in its German form. In his foreword to a book by Graf von Galen, Bishop of Münster, he made a straightforward attack on Hitler and Nazism as anti-religious, totalitarian and evil. He praised von Galen's great courage in standing up to the Nazis in the pulpit and in print. Hitler, Downey claimed, could not win – Christ cast out paganism, and even though the demon had returned with seven more evil than itself, 'Christ's promise guarantees the final collapse and destruction of that which is false and evil'.[35] On this occasion the Archbishop made no direct reference to the persecution of the Jews, though he referred to the 'sadistic and perverted cruelties of the Gestapo', but the following year he shared the platform at a meeting in the Liverpool Town Hall to protest at the treatment of the Jews by the Nazis. It was, he declared, at once a crime against humanity and a menace to civilisation. The Jews, he went on, were human beings with the God-given rights of human beings; the extent and the enormity of the atrocities inflicted on them had to be condemned.[36] He claimed to have been the first English Bishop to denounce the persecution of the Jews and had appeared on platforms in that connection as early as 1933 – in that year he had addressed Liverpool University's Jewish Society and attacked the 'exaggerated and pseudo-nationalism' being fostered in Germany, and shortly afterwards he joined other Church leaders in Liverpool to declare that 'on broad religious principles which transcend all differences' they must protest against the persecution of the Jews.[37] It is interesting in this context to read of the Chief Rabbi's reaction on hearing of Downey's death: he sent a telegram to Westminster expressing his deep regret on the death of a distinguished 'cleric, humanitarian and friend', and added that the Jewish community would always remember 'his active championship of the victims of Nazi persecution'.[38]

In 1942 and 1943 there was a strong feeling in many quarters, religious and secular, that the issue of the reconstruction of British society after the war needed serious and early attention. In the political arena this led, among other things, to the Beveridge Report and its plans to eliminate the causes of poverty and ill-health, and the Education Act of 1944 and its plans to provide more equal and improved educational opportunities. In religious circles, attention turned to Christian renewal: what could be done to ensure that post-war society would be influenced by Christian principles? That could only come about if more people were committed privately and publicly to Gospel values and to achieve this many religious leaders felt that they could take advantage of the heightened religious awareness evident in the darkest days of the war. A letter to *The Times* in April 1943 called for a return to 'God the Father of all' as the only remedy to the rivalries and strife that do so much to 'ruin life and culminate in the insensate horror of war'; these sprang from sources in human nature too deep to be controlled by human planning. The need in society, according to the letter's signatories, was for everyone to lay aside self-seeking as individuals, as families, as classes in society, as nations or as races and to return to God by submitting to his law and accepting his love.[39] Downey signed the letter as the chief representative of the Catholic Church in the country, alongside the Archbishop of Canterbury, the leaders of the free Churches and a surprisingly wide range of leaders or representatives of foreign Churches, as well as the French Secretary of the Interior and the French National Commissioner. The question, of course, was what to do to bring these changes about.

In 1943 the Anglican Church on Merseyside launched a mini-revivalist campaign to begin the re-Christianisation of local society, under the general heading, 'Religion and Life'. Downey, of course, refused to join in any common Christian endeavour of this kind, but did promote his own Catholic version of the campaign called 'Christ in Society'. In May he announced that the parish missions then in progress, which the people were responding to enthusiastically, would be followed by a great public meeting in the Philharmonic Hall on Whit Sunday. Downey had invited Cardinal Hinsley to be the main speaker and he had accepted, but his death in March had meant that the Archbishop of Edinburgh would speak instead; other speakers would be Vice-Admiral Sir Robert Hornell and the National President of the Catholic Women's League. This meeting was to be followed on Whit Monday by a 'Catholic Youth Demonstration of Loyalty to Christ the King', to be held in Liverpool's Boxing Stadium.[40]

To keep up the momentum, he planned a series of public lectures to show how religion and religious principles could be brought into every aspect of life. The titles of the lectures – 'Christ in the Home', 'Christ in Education', ' Christ in Business and Professional Life', 'Christ in the State' and 'Christ in the World' – give a fair indication of the flavour of the project. Different diocesan organisations were to be responsible for different lectures and non-Catholics would be welcome to attend. The Archbishop concluded by asking Catholics on Merseyside to make a special effort to follow the annual novena to the Holy Ghost for the success of the whole venture, because its success would, he believed, confer a lasting benefit on Liverpool. Detailed planning went into the campaign, with a specially designed syllabus of sermons, the use of confraternities, Benediction services on the Cathedral site and acts of consecration to the Sacred Heart.[41] It is not clear how much of this ambitious programme took place; some at least of the lectures were delivered and the Catenians organised a conference on 'Christ in Business and Professional Life' in the Adelphi Hotel in August, while Dr Orchard spoke on 'Christ in the State' in September in the Picton Hall – the sessions were intended for the general public. By late 1943, however, the war was turning in the Allies' favour and the wider religious fervour of the earlier years was already waning. It would have needed a more charismatic figure than Cardinal Griffin at Westminster, and a Church more involved in national issues outside its own concerns, for the Church to give a significant lead in the work of re-constructing society from 1944 onwards.

DIOCESAN AFFAIRS AND ADMINISTRATION

Archbishop Downey had inherited a sound archdiocesan administration and needed to make only minor adjustments to it. In January 1930 he had moved out of 5 Belvidere Road, overlooking Princes Park, which had been the archbishops' residence from 1920, when Archbishop Whiteside had had to move out of St Edward's College in Everton when it passed to the Irish Christian Brothers. He moved to a secluded mansion in Woolton. The Belvidere Road house continued as the curial offices, with the Archbishop present every week on Tuesday, Thursday and Friday from 11am to 1pm. The Vicar General was in attendance every morning from 11am to 1pm. Later, when the curial offices moved to the newly acquired Cathedral Buildings in Brownlow Hill, the Belvidere Road house became a boys' grammar school run by the Vincentians.

Given his own scholarly interests and his time as lecturer at Upholland, it is not surprising to find Downey concerned about the level of his clergy's learning. He was worried about the neglect by priests of post-ordination study. In an early ad clerum of November 1928 he commented on the poor performance of some of them in the recent junior clergy examinations held at Upholland – five failed altogether and were given only temporary faculties until Lent, when they were to be re-examined. The notice ended with the warning that in future a serious view would be taken of such failure.[42] Three years later he issued a statement about the *Clergy Review,* which he had been foremost in founding and of which he was chairman of the editorial board, and which was not receiving the support from priests that he believed it deserved. It would be a great pity, he went on, if it were to fail through lack of interest among priests in their professional studies. Linked to these concerns was one about the non-attendance of some of the clergy at the Deanery Conferences. He reminded priests that absentees were required to send written answers to the questions that had been set and laid down that those who failed to do so would forfeit their right to any holiday entitlement, while those who offended a second time would be liable to be re-examined at the time of the junior clergy annual examinations.[43] There were no future references to these matters in his correspondence with the clergy so it is safe to conclude that his warnings were effective.

In the two synods held during his episcopate (in 1935 and 1945) Downey praised the clergy for their 'fine example of priestliness' and the way they had 'worthily upheld the great traditions of the diocese'. There was nothing new in his general advice to them: to strive for internal perfection through daily meditation, regular prayer and weekly confession. Externally, their vocation called for regularity of habit, reverence of demeanour, edification of life, devotion to duty, abounding charity and a willingness to 'spend and be spent for the salvation of souls'. One pastoral practice he stressed more than any other, that of visiting the people – 'the visiting priest makes the Mass-going people'; the synodal regulations decreed that it would be gravely sinful if priests with the care of souls seriously neglected this obligation. On liturgical matters he insisted that every parish should have a sung Mass every Sunday and that choirs and people should be taught plainsong – he had already taken steps to form a Liverpool Archdiocesan Plain Chant Choir, under Fr M.D. Willson OSB, with evening classes for lay men and women. Before each synod the Archbishop asked for suggestions from the clergy for new legislation, or for amending the old, but was adamant that any views they expressed were purely consultative since he alone as Bishop had legislative power. In 1945

Crowning our Lady's statue, St Joseph's, Wigan, as part of May Devotions.

he thought there was no need for any new legislation, anyway, and hoped the synod could be finished in a single day, instead of the three it had needed in 1935.[44]

Popular devotions and parish life carried on in an unchanging, and apparently unchangeable, way – attending weekly Mass and receiving the sacraments regularly, with confraternities and pious societies for the more committed. There were two confraternities in particular that Archbishop Downey thought were of great value and which he decreed should be established in every parish within a year of the 1935 synod. The first of these was the Blessed Sacrament Confraternity, the second the Confraternity of Christian Doctrine. He believed that both had a special appeal to priests and people and so provided a 'means of attaining to that all-embracing unity of prayer and action so ardently desired by the Holy Father'. He explained that the aim of the Confraternity of Christian Doctrine was threefold: to teach the children in the schools, to instruct 'growing youth that they may ever seek after a deeper knowledge of the doctrine of Christ', and lastly to teach adult men and women so that they could study the truths taught by Our Lord and draw from them comfort and strength. While the fact that he recognised the need for systematic adult instruction was welcome, the means to achieve it on a long-term basis were inadequate, with no training for the new catechists – the load fell again on the faithful parochial teachers; in each parish they should be the nucleus of this apostolate, he concluded, with confraternity members giving voluntary catechetical instruction and financial help. The later development of the Catholic Action College (see next chapter) would

help to fill the gap. By 1940 forty-four parishes across the archdiocese had branches of the Christian Doctrine Confraternity; this had slipped to thirty-eight by 1948.[45]

Lay people benefited from the development of another apostolate, that of the Retreat Movement. This had its origins back in the very early days of the diocese but flowered in the 1920s and 1930s, particularly with the provision of residential retreats – for boys and girls leaving elementary school, and groups such as the Catholic Evidence Guild, the Catholic Social Guild and the Catholic Ramblers. Parish groups of men attended week-end retreats with the Jesuits at Loyola Hall, while women and girls were catered for at the Cenacle Convent. There were a large number of one-day retreats as well, as the Jesuits in particular tried to make available to as many lay Catholics as possible what to some extent had been a spiritual luxury. In 1937 the Archbishop reported that about 5,000 individuals had made retreats at various centres across the archdiocese.[46]

Easier travel made it possible to develop another popular activity – going on pilgrimage. The first all-Lancashire pilgrimage to Lourdes took place in 1923 – the originator seems to have been Fr J.I. McKinley, first parish priest of St Malachy's, Liverpool. In announcing the pilgrimage the following year, Archbishop Keating made clear that its purpose was not to see miracles but to demonstrate enthusiastic devotion towards the Immaculate Mother of God. Those who stayed at home could become Associate Pilgrims and should enclose their intentions in a sealed envelope for one of the actual pilgrims to deposit at the Shrine. They should pray daily for the success of the pilgrimage, saying at least a daily decade of the rosary and preferably attending daily Mass and Communion, lighting a candle at Our Lady's altar and making a small offering for pilgrimage expenses.[47]

Two cures were reported during the 1923 pilgrimage. A Miss Scandrett had her full hearing restored, while Jack Traynor was fully restored after arriving in Lourdes as a serious stretcher case. Badly wounded in the head and chest during the World War and partially paralysed, he also suffered from epilepsy; his condition was so bad that he had been advised by his doctor not to travel. He left Lourdes amid scenes of great popular fervour and had to be escorted by police at Lime Street Station in Liverpool, so great were the welcoming crowds. He returned to Lourdes every year as a brancardier and ran a coal and haulage business in Liverpool; despite this, the Ministry of Pensions insisted on paying his disability pension until he died in 1943. His story was written up locally and in national publications although he himself seems to have avoided publicity as much as possible.[48] By 1927 an archdiocesan Lourdes Pilgrimage Association existed, which aimed at the personal sanctification of its members, helping the sick on pilgrimages, and raising funds to help needy sick people to go on pilgrimage.[49] The annual pilgrimage to Lourdes soon became the most important arch diocesan pilgrimage – the Archbishop led over 1,300 pilgrims there in 1939 – and parish groups also went, led by their own priests. Downey was planning to lead the 1953 pilgrimage despite his own ill-health.

Downey made a great deal of Catholic outdoor rallies and demonstrations. In 1929 he had addressed about 400,000 people in Thingwall Park, to celebrate the centenary of Catholic Emancipation. On the occasion of the canonisation of St John Fisher and St Thomas More in 1935 he called for a great 'manifestation of faith' – a 'demonstration' and not just a procession. Considerable planning went into it, with Catholics marching from St George's Hall by different routes to the cathedral site, with police involvement, marshals from each parish and special medals struck for the occasion. In September 1936 there was a great 'Demonstration of Loyalty to Christ the King' intended as a response to the 'increasing activities of the now wide-spread anti-God movement', a re-affirmation of the 'Christian principles for which we stand'.[50] These were not demonstrations against specific injustices or to try to influence imminent legislation, but a straightforward show of Catholic confidence and strength with a markedly triumphalist air about them. Whatever the immediate reasons behind them, they boosted morale and perhaps persuaded some of those who joined in, but whose attendance at church was somewhat hit and miss, that they could still regard themselves as 'good' Catholics.

One can only imagine what he would have made of a modern home-grown saint from the archdiocese – and for a time this seemed more than just a possibility. He gave wholehearted support to the cause of Teresa Higginson (1844-1905) and his backing and considerable clerical support locally led to her cause being introduced at Rome. In December 1933 Downey announced

that the new postulator supported 'the reasonableness of our expectation of its successful outcome: that God may grant this happy event should be the earnest prayer of priests and people'.[51] In the end, however, the cause failed to progress, mainly because of the unorthodox devotion to the Sacred Head that Higginson and some of her clerical supporters had pushed so energetically. Downey was taken aback by the speed of this decision, made, he believed, before the mass of evidence could have been examined, but he officially dropped the cause (See Note, page 270, below).

His ad clerum letters deal with the ordinary business of the archdiocese and, during the war years, with some extraordinary business as well. Like all the bishops, he was much concerned with the large number of children evacuated from Liverpool, some of them to Wales, where Catholic facilities were scarce, others to Chester and Sandbach – a particular worry was a proper provision of Catholic schooling for them, although the children themselves had no worries at all at being able to attend school half-days only as they shared facilities with the locals.[52] He seconded seven priests to work outside the archdiocese to care for them. There was extensive damage to churches and presbyteries as a result of the blitz – Holy Cross, St Mary's, Highfield Street, and St Alexander's, Bootle, were completely destroyed – and three priests were killed: Fr W.G. Kavanagh and Fr W. Keefe at St Anthony's, and Fr H.P. Newson at St Nicholas'; another, Fr Gerard Barry, died in action as an army chaplain and several were unable to do parish work because of injuries sustained in the blitz. The eucharistic fast was eased for those up all night because of the bombing and evening services were changed to the afternoon or cancelled altogether. But, on the whole and apart from the very worst of the

*Archbishop Downey's
funeral procession moves
up Brownlow Hill.*

attacks between September 1940 and May 1941, things returned to war-time normality fairly soon. Fr D'Andria, OSB, of St Peter's, Seel Street, reported in May 1941 that it seemed as though the parish had ceased to exist, such was the damage the whole area had suffered, yet on St Patrick's night, 1942, he held a 'most successful little social' for 150 parishioners.[53]

After the war the Archbishop's Pastoral Letters took on a decidedly gloomy tone. The optimistic reconstruction of society dreamt of and prayed for during the war did not materialise and, instead, Catholics were living in a society that was Godless and evil:

> *In truth the world is sick of a sore disease, it may be even unto death; and there seems to be no physician with the knowledge and skill requisite to heal it. There is weakness to be strengthened and lassitude to be overcome. There are cancerous growths evident, to be ruthlessly cut away ... There is madness, mania, phobia, delusional obsessions to be cured and sanity to be recovered.*

He believed that materialism was triumphant and that they were witnessing 'the apotheosis of the revolt against morality', while the social, economic and political confusion were the 'natural, logical and inevitable' result of the Protestant Reformation. Communism and the worship of the state were the principal ills, underlining the fact that the Church and the World were essentially antagonistic. Listeners to these jeremiads were saved from despair, for the only hope for the world lay in the Catholic Church:

> *... it is our opportunity ... We have a divine message for humanity, a message of faith, hope and charity; of joy, happiness and concord in this world that has shown itself patient of so much pain, misery and strife ... We must needs come to the aid of the world in which we live by every means in our power, parochial, municipal, national and international.*[54]

Phrases in these pastorals such as 'the apotheosis of the revolt against morality' highlight a rather curious feature in almost all of them: the language is very abstract and rather high-flown, with few practical examples to illustrate his points, and this despite his years of experience with the Catholic Missionary Society and his undoubted skill as a communicator on the radio or when talking off the cuff. It is almost as though he was writing with an eye more on possible publication of his pastorals than on their being read in church to a congregation who could not be expected to be much moved by being told that 'in liturgical services we re-live Christ's incarnate sojourn in a sense that is quite unique', or that Cardinal Manning had opposed someone because he was 'a Semi-Arian of notoriously heterodox views'.[55]

It must have been of some consolation to the Archbishop that Catholic expansion had continued on most fronts during his episcopate. The following statistics are taken from the archdiocesan *Directories* and are based on the very detailed returns sent in by parish priests each year. (The dates given are the dates of publication of the *Directories* but the statistics are those collected in the previous year; in the case of the numbers of Infant Baptisms and Converts, the statistics are those for two years previously.)

	1930	1935	1940	1945	1950	1955
Secular clergy	316	400	446	488	519	500
Regular clergy	142	155	175	180	191	170
Convents	65	71	82	82	84	85
Parish churches	141	160	167	175	176	186
Public chapels	20	20	21	20	18	14
Est. Cath. pop.	373,885	393,737	402,500	405,000	423,292	437,700
Infant baptisms	11,293	11,434	11,175	10,526	11,722	11,144
Converts	1,322	1,194	1,168	812	1,234	1,485

While the number of parishes had increased by 32% between 1930 and 1955, the number of Secular clergy had risen by 58%. By 1947, indeed, the archdiocese had a surplus of priests and was in a position to lend newly ordained ones to other dioceses. The surplus was composed of Irish priests, ordained in Ireland for the archdiocese – the number of Irish priests had risen significantly during the Downey years.

The figures show that infant baptisms, after an immediate post-war boom, fell back to below peak levels of the 1930s despite a rise in the general Catholic population of over 17% – were Catholic families already beginning to have fewer children as they moved out to the suburbs? There is some evidence that from the 1930s Catholic families began to follow the national trend towards smaller families and that 'natural family planning' methods were becoming better known by the 1950s, but it is impossible to know how far these trends represented what was happening in particular areas of the country.[56] Downey was worried that the true Catholic teaching on the subject of contraception might be obscured by loose talk about the 'Safe Period'; what very limited evidence there is seems to show that Irish Catholic wives, at least, held out against the general move to using contraception and family planning in the 1940s and 1950s.[57]

In his Lent Pastoral of 1946 quoted from above, Downey spoke of the duty of all Catholics to take the Gospel to the society in which they lived; this could only be fulfilled by prayer, proper organisation and study – the essentials of the Catholic Action movement that he had launched in the archdiocese and to which we must now turn.

NOTE:

The Cause of Teresa Higginson:

Rome's language in 1938 had not been decisive enough to make every devotee give up hope and the 1950s saw renewed boosts of activity. All the subsequent Archbishops had to deal with correspondence about the cause, including letters from several English-speaking countries abroad. Archbishop Heenan thought the cause might possibly be re-introduced some time but felt there were far more important issues to worry about in the meantime. As late as 1991 Archbishop Worlock noted that he received 'a steady run of letters about Teresa Higginson', even though he had written in 1975 that there seemed to be no possibility whatsoever of the cause being re-introduced. When St Alexander's church Bootle was demolished in the same year Teresa's supporters pressed for a memorial cross to be erected on the site; Worlock felt that the Salesians (who had been running the church) might want to keep it in mind if they were 'going to keep the devotees sweet'! Leaflets and prayers are still being produced with the *imprimaturs* from the 1920s and 1930s, and in 2001 one devotee wrote directly to the Pope to ask for the cause to be re-instated; the reply was that the first step would have to come from the English bishops as a body. The desire for a 'popular' modern English saint still has some life in it.

Notes

1 Archbishop Downey, *Pulpit and Platform Addresses* (1933), pp.93-107.

2 *The Tablet*, 28.2.1931.

3 The Most Rev. Richard Downey, *Some Errors of H.G. Wells* (new ed. 1933), p.59.

4 G.D. Smith (ed.), *The Teaching of the Catholic Church*, 2 vols, (1948); vol. 1, 'The Blessed Trinity', pp.111-42; 'Divine Providence', pp.214-47.

5 *The Universe*, 4.1.1935; *The Evening Standard*, 22.3.1935; *The Daily Express, The Manchester Evening News*, 15.4.1935.

6 Moloney, *Westminster*, p.18.

7 AAL Downey, S1 II, B/63, Hinsley to Downey 25.3.1935.

8 *The Lancashire Daily Post, The Daily Herald*, 25.2.1935.

9 *The Liverpool Daily Post*, 20.10.1928.

10 *The Times*, 3.12.1930.

11 AAL Press & Publicity, S2 I: Press Cuttings: there are cuttings from more than 50 different newspapers on the quarrel.

12 AAL Downey, S1 IV D/5 for detailed statistics.

13 *The Times*, 16.7.1932.

14 *Ibid.*, 17.6.1953 (obituary).

15 *The Catholic Times*, 26.11.1926.

16 Waller, p.326; *The Times*, 3,4.12.1930; 2.3.1931; *The Tablet*, 19.9.1931.

17 AAL Downey, S1 IV E: Rules and Prohibitions in Inter-Faith Relationships, 1930-53, E/10.

18 *Ibid.*, E/11, 3.9.1942.

19 *Ibid.*, E/19-25, Nov. 1945 – March 1951.

20 Waller, pp.323-4, 499; J.Davies, 'Catholic Representatives', pp.367-8.

21 J.Davies, 'Catholic Representatives', pp.376-9 and 'Conservative and Catholic: John Shute and the Liverpool Exchange By-Election, 1933', *NWCH*, XXX (2003), pp.95-109.

22 John Davies, 'A Blunt, Unsophisticated Working-Man: J.T. (Joe) Tinker, MP, and the 1944 Education Act' *NWCH*, XXI (1994), pp.27-35.

23 Waller, p.326.

24 AAL Downey, S2 I C/3, Downey to T. Lescher 19.10.1937.

25 AAL Downey, S1 III, A/3, Ad clerums 1940-53; Oct. 1951.

26 AAL Press Cuttings, *The Tribune, The Spectator, The News Chronicle, The C of E Newspaper and the Record*, all of 30.11.1951.

27 Sam Davies, 'Class, Religion and Gender: Liverpool Labour Party and Women, 1918-1939' in Belchem (ed.), *Popular Politics*, pp.217-46, at pp.217-8.

28 Waller, p.341.

29 *Ibid.*, pp.330-1.

30 John Stevenson, *British Society 1914-45* (1984), pp.270-1; J.K. Walton, *Lancashire, A Social History, 1558-1939* (1987), pp.325-54.

31 C.G. Pooley and S. Irish, 'Housing and Health in Liverpool, 1870-1940', *THSLC* vol.143 (1994), pp.193-219; M. McKenna, 'The suburbanisation of the working-class population of Liverpool between the wars', *Social History*, vol.16, no.2 (May 1991).

32 *Directory* 2003, pp.122-3.

33 *The Universe*, 12.3.1943.

34 Aspden, p.265-6.

35 Patrick Smith (ed. & trans), *The Bishop of Münster and the Nazis: The Documents in the Case* (1942), p.vii.

36 *The Universe*, 30.4.1943.

37 Aspden, p.214.

38 AAW Gr. 2/139b : Archbishop of Liverpool 1944-63: Chief Rabbi Brodie to Griffin, 17.6.1953.

39 *The Times*, 19.4.1943.

40 AAL *Liverpolitana*, Pastoral letter, 9.5.1943.

41 AAL Downey, S1 III, A/3: 'Christ in Society' programme of events.

42 *Ibid.*, A/1: Ad clerums 1928-30, Nov. 1928.

43 *Ibid.*, Nov. 1931.

44 AAL *Synods*, 22nd and 23rd Synod, 1935 and 1945; on visiting, 1935 Decrees, no.56; on Plain Chant, *The Catholic Times* 5.1.1934, 'Music in Liverpool'.

45 AAL *Synods*, 22nd Synod 1935, p.35. *Directory*, 1941, 1949.

46 Peter Doyle, 'Charles Plater SJ and the Origins of the Catholic Social Guild', *RH*, vol. 21, no.3 (May 1993), pp.401-17, esp. pp.410-3; AAL Downey, S1 III, A/2, Ad clerums 1931-9, Aug. 1937.

47 Anon., *The Liverpool Archdiocese and Lourdes: The Story of the 1st and 2nd Pilgrimages to Lourdes 1923 and 1924* (?1924), pp.18-20 for Keating's letter of 27.6.1924. The book is based on articles in *The Catholic Times* by M. O'Mahony.

48 Dom Francis Izard OSB, *The Meaning of Lourdes* (1938), pp.71-7; Ruth Cranston, *The Mystery of Lourdes* (1956), pp.119-124; Traynor's own account is in AAL Murphy Collection A/N: U/AV/LA/002, S1 A: Lourdes.

49 Details in Murphy Collection (see note 48).

50 AAL Downey S1 III, A/2 Ad Clerum 1931-9, June 1935 and September 1936.

51 *Ibid.*, Jan. 1934. See John Davies, 'Traditional Religion, Popular Piety, or Base Superstition? The Cause for the Beatification of Teresa Higginson', *RH*, vol. 24, no.1 (May 1998), pp.123-44. *The Catholic Times* ran a series of articles, starting in April 1927.

52 J. Davies, 'Evacuation during World War Two: the Response of the Catholic Church' *NWCH*, XXV (1998), pp.38-61. AAL Downey S1 III, A/3 Ad Clerum 1940-53, July and Aug. 1941, Oct. 1941.

53 J. Davies, 'Coping with the Blitz: St Peter's, Seel Street, Liverpool' *NWCH* XXIII (1996), pp.29-39; B. Plumb, 'A Liverpool Priest's Journal of the Blitz' *NWCH* IX (1982, pp.18-24; J. Davies (ed.), *Coping with the Blitz: Letters of L.J. D'Andria, OSB, 1940-41* (2000).

54 AAL *Liverpolitana*, Lent 1946; see also Lent 1947; Advent 1948.

55 *Ibid*; on Manning, Lent 1951.

56 Michael P. Hornsby-Smith (ed.), *Catholics in England 1950-2000: Historical and Sociological Perspectives* (1999), esp. pp.69-71.

57 S. Lambert, *Irish Women in Lancashire 1922-1960: Their Story* (2001), pp.79-82; AAL Downey S1 II, B, Downey, to Griffin, 1.11.1948.

CHAPTER 14 FROM CATHOLIC ACTION TO THE LAY APOSTOLATE: SEEKING A ROLE FOR THE FAITHFUL

'The Age of the Laity' had been the title proposed confidently for the twentieth century by Bishop Casartelli of Salford and a number of movements that started with his blessing seemed to point away from the highly clericalised nineteenth century: the Catholic Federation, the Catholic Social Guild and the Catholic Women's League. These movements involved a recognition of the need for both spiritual and secular preparation of the laity if they were to take on a more positive role in the Church. The Catholic Social Guild, for example, launched its study groups to provide the hard social and political knowledge that would enable its members to move beyond the generalised principles of *Rerum Novarum*, while the Jesuit-led Retreats Movement aimed at the formation of spiritual elites in each parish – as Fr Plater had put it, only working people could genuinely influence other working people, not the clergy.[1] These welcome first steps raised the issue of the relationship between lay initiatives and the bishops and clergy, and questions about the control and authenticity of any lay voice that developed were to continue for many years.

NATIONAL INITIATIVES

Pope Pius XI (1922 – 1939) became known as 'the Pope of Catholic Action', so great was his enthusiasm for the movement. He stressed its value in fighting the various evils of the day, especially communism, and the 1930s became the decade of Catholic Action as a result. He was wary of Catholic groups that had any political involvement and his ideal of Catholic Action was that of lay co-operation with the 'Apostolic Hierarchy'.[2] It became a catch-all phrase, difficult to define and pin down, though almost everyone agreed that concerted action by Catholics, as Catholics, in the interest of the Church was to be encouraged. The English and Welsh bishops at their Low Week meeting in 1933 declared themselves in favour of taking steps to support Catholic Action throughout their dioceses and talked enthusiastically of setting up a National Council for Catholic Action.[3] Archbishop Downey responded wholeheartedly (he may, indeed, have been the prime mover at the bishops' discussions) and devoted his Advent Pastoral to the topic. He defined Catholic Action as 'the co-operation of the Catholic laity of all classes and of both sexes under the authoritative guidance of the bishops, in the social activities of the Church'. The movement should not, he argued, be seen as radically new, but rather as a timely adaptation of teaching methods to modern society where, owing to the rise and triumph of democracy, political and social power was no longer vested in one dominant class, but rested very largely in the hands of the 'masses'.[4]

Downey was determined to lay down some ground rules from the start. The many movements that made up Catholic Action, he claimed, shared a unity because the bishops, appointed by the Holy Spirit, controlled them. He recognised the need for formation and allayed any fears that existing Catholic societies might have about losing their identity: the aim was rather to make them more efficient through co-operation and getting rid of wasteful overlap, and to secure the best possible results through centralised control. He believed he had already taken a step in this direction by uniting all the sodalities of the Children of Mary into a single Archdiocesan Federation which had already given abundant evidence of the 'value of the unified activities of this excellent society' – excellent in its own way, but hardly likely to rock any parochial boats.

Other bishops took some practical initiatives. The Cardiff Board of Catholic Action attracted over 12,000 members and launched a 'Clean Films' campaign, threatening to organise a boycott of cinemas that persisted in showing immoral films. The campaign caught on in other parts of the country and *The Catholic Times* helped to launch a nationwide petition and protest to keep it going; Archbishop Downey indicated that he hoped to start a similar movement throughout his archdiocese. Meanwhile the Bradford Catholic Action Board, supported by branches of the SVP and the St Joan's Social and Political Alliance, organised a protest to the Ministry of Health over the decision to extend the range of birth control advice available in public clinics.[5] It is clear that such initiatives aimed at organising Catholic opinion in support of traditional Catholic values and not at anything radically new.

The overall message of a joint pastoral in 1934 could be summarised as 'Carry on as before, but more effectively'. The letter, drafted by Downey, gave an 'authentic definition' of Catholic Action along the lines laid down by the Pope and stressed its pacific, non-political nature (a 'fundamental law' of the movement): its essentially spiritual role was to sanctify members of Catholic societies. This inward sanctification, however, should result in external vigorous and persistent activity to further God's kingdom on earth.[6] Not surprisingly, the letter stressed the complete dependence of Catholic Action on the bishops and the proposed National Board of Catholic Action was to comprise all the bishops – but no lay people. Among the issues that the Board would deal with were the press and radio; Catholic schools; Catholic morality (to be defended against the new paganism); Catholic representation on public bodies, and evangelisation. If only the many Catholic societies could be linked in 'corporate unity', the bishops argued, then they would provide a 'powerful organization for moulding public opinion and for asserting and defending our Catholic rights'.

At the 1935 Low Week meeting Downey recommended to his colleagues the Italian model of Catholic Action, a summary of which he provided for their consideration.[7] Accordingly, they issued another pastoral letter on the subject the following year, with an interesting new title, *The Apostolate of the Laity,* and published as a CTS pamphlet. Its approach was altogether different from its predecessor's: the opening sentence stated unambiguously that social injustice, the long-term scourge of Europe, had brought Christian civilization 'in this generation well-nigh to the verge of destruction'. This was followed by a resumé of the great social encyclicals, outlining the evils of the money markets and the exploitation of the workers. While English Catholics, of course, were not responsible for this evil system, the letter suggested that perhaps they might have done more to change it. The danger now lay in the rise of atheistic Communism, in itself another evil system between which and Catholicism there could be no compromise. The only way to combat organized Communism was to organize an Apostolate of the Laity, built on the spiritual renewal and education of 'lay apostles'. Three steps should be followed: the setting up of the Christian Doctrine Confraternity in every parish the establishment of the National Board of Catholic Action (the bishops), with a National Committee of lay people under it, and the mobilisation of the Catholic press to counteract the poison of all immoral literature, including that of Communism.[8]

Little happened on the national front. In September 1937 Cardinal Hinsley (Archbishop of Westminster since 1935), apologised to the bishops for having delayed so long over establishing the promised national scheme. His own enthusiasm for the new movement had been clear from the day of his installation in Westminster, when he had put forward the slogan, 'Catholic Action at home and Missionary Action abroad'. Now, however, he admitted to finding the complex issue completely overwhelming. He offered to hand over the task to any of the bishops who felt qualified and had the time to devote to it.[9] He went on to outline a scheme of national co-ordinating committees to meet twice a year – there would be a Faith Committee, a League of Catholic Youth Committee, an Industrial Relations Committee, a Women's Committee for Moral or Social Work and for the care of girls in Domestic Service, all coming under a National Board of Apostolate. He planned for councils at parish, diocesan and national level, with a special secretariat and financial organisation. Above all, however, Hinsley insisted that all those who participated in Catholic Action must be members of the Confraternity of Christian Doctrine and of the Guild of the Blessed Sacrament, to underline the essentially spiritual nature of Catholic Action and to ensure the overall direction of the movement by parish priests, the spiritual directors of the Confraternity and the Guild. It was a highly bureaucratic scheme, unlikely to appeal either to those already involved in Catholic societies or to the uncommitted.

CATHOLIC ACTION IN THE ARCHDIOCESE

Not surprisingly, there were no takers among the bishops to accept Hinsley's offer and Downey pressed on with developing his own ambitious scheme for Liverpool. He had already established a Liverpool Archdiocesan Board for Catholic Action in 1936, comprising Sir John Reynolds (President; chairman of the Executive Committee of the Liverpool Council of Social Service), Mgr Thomas Adamson (ecclesiastical assistant), and Messrs T. Lescher (vice-president), Charles Doyle (the builder of the Cathedral, treasurer) and Mr Taylor (secretary). The Board's task was 'to promote Catholic Action throughout the archdiocese by every means that shall have the approval of the Archbishop'. Its patroness was Our Lady Immaculate and its motto *Adveniat Regnum Tuum Per Regnum Mariae* ('Thy Kingdom Come through the Reign of Mary').[10] In June 1937 they published *Catholic Action. A Simple Explanation,* a sort of beginners' guide rather than a workshop manual. It defined Catholic Action as the participation of the laity, in a specially organised and directed manner, in the work of the Church: 'the official organization of the Catholic laity to enable them to take their part and assist the clergy in the work of the Church'. In this context, the work of the Church was threefold: the preservation of the faith of Catholics and the reclaiming of the lapsed; the spread of knowledge of the Faith to non-Catholics, and the solution of the 'Social Problem'.[11] This, clearly, was going beyond the traditional involvement in practical charity: there was a role for the laity in reclaiming the lapsed and in spreading the Faith to non-Catholics (as the Catholic Evidence Guild had already started to do).

Yet in some ways it was a disappointing document. It stated, for instance, that Catholic Action was necessary because it had become impossible for the clergy to deal single-handedly with the widespread indifference to religion, and it was becoming more and more difficult for priests to have access to the non-religious – a difficulty increased in many countries, the document claimed, by a shortage of clergy. From this it would seem that the laity had no specifically lay apostolate but were to help out 'Father' when he had too much to do. There were some references to the obligation on Catholics to promote the general welfare of society. Catholic Action, the Board continued, should be a lay organisation directed by lay folk, 'but co-ordinated with and subordinate to the parish priests, bishops and the Pope'.

Some of the ensuing confusion arose from the attempt to include every existing form of lay Catholic activity under the new umbrella of Catholic Action and at the same time to ensure a centralised clerical control for the movement.[12] For example, under the third arm of the movement, Catholic Social Economic Action, were grouped societies and organisations that worked for the solution of the 'Social Problem' and included groups as diverse as the SVP and the Catenians. Since Downey himself said of the latter society that it did not matter if its members did nothing more than cultivate the 'great social virtue' of meeting together as members of the universal Church, and that he admired Catenians because they were chiefly concerned 'with themselves',[13] diversity was clearly winning out over coherence. The number and variety of associations and societies at work in the archdiocese provided something appetising for even the most pernickety lay palate, even if the task of imposing a central control over it all appeared impossible.

Each parish was to have its committee or council, under a lay president, with inter-parochial councils, composed of lay people and a single priest. Downey felt confident enough to hold a Diocesan Catholic Action Congress in December 1937, bringing together in separate groups over a number of days the members of parish and deanery councils, the clergy, and the ecclesiastical assistants of the parish and deanery councils. Both Cardinal Hinsley and the Archbishop of Birmingham attended the event. It also included separate 'demonstrations' (that favoured Liverpool Catholic word) of men, women and children in St George's Hall. The Archbishop spoke afterwards of the 'splendid co-operation' of priests and people and of the interest and enthusiasm that the Congress had aroused. He was also pleased with the letter he received from the Cardinal Secretary of State in the Vatican, praising what he had already done to encourage Catholic Action and underlining the importance of national co-operation 'in this grave hour of the world's history', when the whole social fabric was being 'assailed by those poisonous ideologies which are helped on by all the forces opposed to Almighty God'. Catholic Action, the letter added, would exercise a 'most precious and healing influence on the body politic' and become a powerful help towards peace and the well-being of the nation.[14]

In a second letter of August 1938 the papal Secretary of State justified Catholic Action in defensive, rather negative, terms: it would be a powerful agency for the defence of the Christian people against every form of modern paganism, and especially against the 'greatest menace of all, which is communism'. This fear of Communism was one of Downey's principal political motivations. In a pastoral letter on the subject in 1932 he had attacked the exaltation of the state at the expense of the individual and thought that the modern world was drifting dangerously into accepting the idea of the totalitarian state. But his main focus of attack, of course, was Communism's atheism and its opposition to Christianity. He urged the world's leaders to take action against Soviet Russia and to close their ports against the Soviet commercial fleet.[15] He set up a special body, the Liverpool Archdiocesan Pro-Deo Commission, to overcome communist influence among working-class Catholics and to counter what he called the anti-God campaigns of the day. The Commission was largely a lay body though Mgr

Adamson was its chairman. In November 1936 it launched a series of leaflets (usually 4 pages in length), *The Evils of Communism and the Church's Alternative*, the first of them entitled *Communism and the Church*. It also published a poster attacking the Left Book Club because it was 'inspired and utilised by the Communist Party'.[16] The Commission developed a distribution system whereby the leaflets were dispatched to local centres for parish priests to collect, and then parish societies such as the CYMS and the Knights of St Columba distributed them to both Catholic and non-Catholic homes, to factories and offices, and at rallies. A quarter of a million copies of the first one were prepared for the archdiocese. New leaflets came out regularly, but some parishes failed to collect their copies and the Archbishop had to urge his clergy to support the venture: 'the growing menace of Communism makes us anxious that full advantage shall be taken of these leaflets in every parish'.[17]

While the Commission attacked every form of communism, its main focus became Republican Spain. *The Truth about Spain* was one of its most successful leaflets, and there was also one entitled *Spain's Red Government*. When parish lectures were organised, the topic again was Spain and an effort was made to train a special team of local speakers on this topic. The priest chosen to do this, Fr James Ellison, a young priest at St Matthew's, Liverpool, decided that he was not skilled or knowledgeable enough, which was fortunate, for he was not only rabidly anti-communist but strongly anti-semitic and pro-fascist.[18] Members of the Commission were soon reporting that it was proving difficult to organise parochial lectures. Other leaflets were *Family Rights, Save the Family, Peace and War* and *Save England First* – 40,000 copies of this last one were distributed in a few months and a second printing of 22,000 ordered. National figures were approached to write leaflets or give the lectures – Christopher Hollis was to write on 'Communism, Fascism and Democracy' but could not do it in four pages. Douglas Jerrold lectured in Liverpool in February 1938; other names suggested were Arnold Lunn and Count de la Bedoyère – mostly strongly pro-Franco. A group of priests was set up to look into the possibility of establishing cells of working men in the parishes to take on the distribution of the leaflets and work with the League of Christian Workers to deal with the threat from communists. Fr Horan of St James', Bootle, already had an Anti-Communist Vigilance Committee. Eventually, he and two priests from St Joseph's, Fr Montgomery and Fr Pownall, set up cells composed mainly of members of the League in a number of inner-city parishes.[19] These campaigns and activities did not, of course, stop Catholics becoming Communists and, in some cases, taking the lead locally in the party and then going off to fight for the republican cause in Spain. Frank Deegan, a lapsed Catholic, brings out very plainly in his autobiography the appeal of Communism to a small but active number of Catholic workers, caught up in the depression of the 1930s and impatient with promises of future happiness, whether from church leaders or politicians.[20]

The Archbishop also recommended the League of Our Lady Immaculate, a league of prayer that he launched to combat Communism; within a few months over 50,000 copies of the leaflet about the League had been requested and soon it had spread beyond the archdiocese. Within eighteen months it had a membership of 200,000 worldwide and the leaflet had been translated into several languages.[21] The Catholic Action Board suggested a campaign against Communism – 'probably at present the most important side of our work' – and suggested that the inter-parochial councils were to report on the extent of Communism in their districts. There was some confusion about the role of the Pro-Deo Commission vis-à-vis the Catholic Action Board, but in the end the Commission stayed separate though under the auspices of the Board. After eighteen months the Board reported that well over one million anti-communist leaflets had been distributed by various methods, and 25,000 copies sold of an abridged version of the pope's letter on Atheistic Communism.[22]

Other campaigns launched by the Board included the 'Sanctification of the Home' and the 'Sanctification of Sunday'. The first of these is interesting in showing how high a place personal and family sanctification enjoyed in the minds of the Board members. A Sunday in June 1938 was to be set aside for a public Act of Reparation for the sins against Christian Marriage and to ask for God's help in sanctifying family life through a greater appreciation of the Sacrament of Matrimony. The Board also suggested that the term 'monthly Communion' be dropped as it implied that that level of frequency was satisfactory. The campaign also aimed at persuading more families to consecrate themselves to the Sacred Heart, to have the ceremony at home and to display a picture of the Sacred Heart in a prominent place. Finally, the campaign was devoted to trying to ensure that a Nuptial Mass became a normal part of every Catholic wedding; its absence in a mixed marriage would, it was argued, be a rebuke and the prospect of being disgraced publicly in this way would be enough to deter the young from becoming too friendly with non-Catholics.[23] Just occasionally there is an air of pious unreality about the Board's discussions and plans. But apparently attendances at Mass and Benediction increased during the Sunday campaign, which had some of the characteristics of a religious revival, and the numbers applying for places on spiritual retreats also went up.

On the practical front, an interesting initiative involved seventy girls from all parts of the country and Ireland attending a week's training course in Catholic Action at Mount Pleasant in Liverpool, while almost a hundred attended a similar week-end course. This led to the setting up of a Young Christian Workers for working girls and Young Christian Students for those at school or college. In addition, the Board launched a Press Campaign which took as its slogan 'a Catholic paper in every household'. It wanted to increase membership of the Catholic Truth Society and to set up a CTS box in every parish. Homes were to be canvassed to obtain regular subscriptions rather than one-off sales. The campaign led to the distribution of 200,000 leaflets urging support of the Catholic papers, with marked increases in their circulation as a result and the setting up of a permanent Press Secretariat under the Board's direction – *The Catholic Times* claimed an increase of 60%.[24]

After eighteen months of encouragement and directives Downey could take some satisfaction from the fact that Deanery Catholic Action Councils existed in Chorley, Wigan, Warrington, Bootle and at least two Liverpool deaneries (St Joseph's and St Edward's). A surprising 130 Parish Councils had been established, but it was proving difficult to establish them in rural parishes. Moreover, action was not restricted to spiritual campaigns: the Deanery Councils had set up Enquiry Bureaux to help people deal with the issues of unemployment benefit, insurance and rent (the Liverpool bureau took legal action in eighty-eight cases on behalf of clients), while Fr Stan Roberts, SJ, of St Francis Xavier's, Liverpool, showed what could be done at parish level. He had approached all the parish priests and other clergy of the deanery and had organized parish bureaux to help those in need by advice and practical help. He had, for example, arranged free courses in shorthand and typing for girls who wanted office work. He was to be responsible for keeping the Deanery Council in existence during the war years – the only council to keep going without interruption since its formation, a period of fourteen years, during which it had dealt with such practical matters as compensation for the victims of street accidents, rent arrears, housing, and hire purchase schemes.[25]

Here was an example of that practical help that many priests had been good at organizing, either directly themselves or through agencies such as the SVP, and it seems that some saw the new Catholic Action as a distraction or at best an unnecessary bureaucratic addition; a few seemed to have adopted an 'emperor's new clothes' attitude to it. Early in 1937 Canon Bennett reported from his deanery the view that a priest with extensive experience of parish work in a number of towns should be co-opted to the Board, presumably to add a touch of realism to its activities. In addition, in his view the setting up of Deanery Councils should be deferred until Parish Councils had functioned for some time, in order to avoid setting up machinery whose usefulness was untried. A little later another priest wrote to complain that the various forms of Catholic Activity *(sic)* proposed by the Board had been put into operation by most parish priests for years; why interfere now?[26] In this context, when the Board's priest-consultors met in 1939 they raised a number of points that indicate a certain dissatisfaction with the way the Board had been operating. There had been, they believed, too many initiatives launched too quickly and too many directives from the Board to the clergy; it should be left to parish priests to pursue campaigns in the way they thought best suited to local conditions. The report of this meeting seems to have discouraged the Board; it noted that many of the parish councils were not working properly, and Board members asked whether it would be preferable to work through existing parish societies, and even whether the present organisation of Catholic Action should be scrapped in favour of some (unspecified) alternative.[27] Clearly there was still considerable confusion about the nature of Catholic Action.

Some people believed strongly that its main purpose should be to tackle existing social problems and the Wigan Deanery Council complained in July 1939 that the Board seemed to be doing nothing in this all-important area. The secretary of the Board replied that it was fully aware of the importance of this issue and had been waiting for a report on social conditions from the CSG. The Wigan Council did not see the need for any such report as the social problems were all too evident and it was already heavily involved in trying to deal with them.[28] It had set up a House of Hospitality in Darlington Street East, based on the New York House of Hospitality, and much of its work was clearly influenced by the radical approach of the charismatic American, Dorothy Day. The driving force was R.P. (Bob) Walsh, editor of the *Catholic Worker,* member of the Lancashire County Council and leading light of the Catholic Social Guild; after Vatican II he became secretary of the Bishops' Social Welfare Commission. He was secretary of the House's Committee, with Fr Thomas Greenhous, parish priest of Sacred Heart, as chairman and Fr Gerard Rimmer, of St Joseph's, as treasurer. *The First Annual Report* said that the project was inspired by the Sermon on the Mount: 'Give to him who asketh of thee, and from him that would borrow turn not away'. The staff of the House were there to 'serve those in need, to serve them in every possible way, and to regard nothing as being too good for them'. The *Report* also made the point that the hardest part of the work was to combat the rampant spirit of materialism. They tried to 'shock the rich into realising their brotherhood with the poor' and the essential Christian duty of helping the poor out of their surplus, while also trying to alter in a little way 'the impersonalism and ruthless efficiency' of State organisations by the personal care and love of Christianity. In a final appeal they stated:

> *Our only rules are: To love all who come in, be they deserving poor or not, and to endeavour never to say 'no'. With your material help we can live up to the second; with your prayers we have some chance of living up to the first.*[29]

Their approach was extremely practical and, unusually for Catholic activists at the time, based on an economic and social assessment of the area's needs. They pointed out that of the 20,000 families in Wigan, 7,000 had at least one member unemployed. A large proportion of the people worked in the cotton industry, notorious for its low wages, so that a large number of the employed were no better off than the unemployed. They referred to the 'insidious' effects on morale of continual or repeated unemployment and admitted that their greatest failure lay in not being able to deal with this major issue. They had to find a way to give the unemployed 'the fullness of human dignity': without that spiritual help, the giving of material help would achieve very little.

To meet the most obvious material needs, in the first year they had provided 1,260 meals and food parcels, 500 nights' shelter, either in the House itself or paid for elsewhere, and 6,000 articles of clothing. They had dealt with queries about rent and unemployment assistance (the commonest queries), invalid chairs, books for the sick, beds and bedding, railway fares, money for rent and rates, prayer books, and children's shoes. They had also given advice on matrimonial disputes, on safeguarding children's faith and on many other issues. They believed they had achieved a victory over the Communists who elsewhere were leading the national opposition to the poor quality of housing and high rents. The House had negotiated rent reductions and given tenants advice on the threatened rent strike in nearby Ince. A small number of mothers had been given a holiday away from Wigan while a holiday camp-cum-summer school was planned for the men (unfortunately the war intervened). Finally, they had put on educational courses, run a pamphlet and information stall in Wigan market on Saturdays and opened a library. They published a series of pamphlets called *Social Surveys of Wigan*. One of these, on the Public Assistance Committee (the PAC), by Bob Walsh, was so successful in getting higher benefits for the poor that the PAC took legal advice on how to ban it and sue its author – it was reckoned to have gained an extra £150 a week for claimants! It was also pirated by the local Communist Party which re-issued it with the Catholic parts left out.[30]

Clearly, Catholic Action in Wigan was alive to local problems and well ahead of other Councils in this regard, with an understanding of Catholic Action that went beyond the official definition. One suspects the work would have been done even if the archdiocesan Board had not existed. It was also clear that successful Catholic Action was totally dependent on small groups of very committed lay people and the active support of the clergy; the danger was that when those individuals moved on or 'burned out' what they had set up would fade away. And, of course, the coming of war in 1939 changed the socio-economic situation, creating full employment and reducing the need for that particular type of practical aid.

Another initiative linked to the high unemployment of the early 1930s was the Catholic Land Association. Many people at the time favoured a 'back to the land' movement, seeing in it a solution to the problems of unemployment and urban poverty, not just in economic terms but also as a means of restoring a worker's dignity. Archbishop Downey concluded one of his speeches on the subject with a touch of rural romanticism: 'Far better than huge barrack-like tenements would be the sight of a pleasant landscape, dotted with homesteads, real houses on country lanes'. Superficial similarities with the Distributism of Belloc, Chesterton, Gill and McNabb, gave the movement some philosophical respectability and perhaps was part of its appeal to Downey; he was also impressed by what he saw of Mussolini's land schemes on a visit to Italy. When *The Times* reported one of his speeches in 1932 (in which he had referred to the 'smokescreen expedient' of the allotments scheme), the Archbishop was invited to become a joint president of the national Land Settlement and Training Association and in that capacity chaired a Conference in Manchester.[31]

The Liverpool Catholic Land Association was founded in 1933, initially to provide training for those moving to the land for the first time. A year later it took over Prior's Wood Farm, Parbold, near Wigan, and appointed Dom Gregory Buisseret, OSB, as its warden – he resigned from his post as parish priest of St Benedict's, Hindley, to take on the job. He was a forceful, no-nonsense, rather awkward character and became the driving-force of the project. On Sunday, 12 May 1935, over twelve hundred people from around the archdiocese attended the solemn opening and blessing of the farm by Downey. In his speech the Archbishop claimed that with proper cultivation of the land the country could support a population of 70 million, going on ingenuously to say that there was no unemployment problem 'amongst our forefathers who had access to the land'. Other solutions to the crisis were, he argued, at best partial, and that of birth control 'utterly unsound'. England was never likely again to be the workshop of the world; what was wanted was a sane balance between town and country, between agriculture and industry. Again, his speech got national coverage in the press.[32]

The Association later took over the Salford movement and re-named itself The North of England Catholic Land Association Ltd., with Downey as president and Bishop Henshaw of Salford, Bishop Dobson (auxiliary in Liverpool), the Duke of Norfolk and Sir John Shute MP, as vice-presidents. From the start, however, Dom Gregory struggled to raise enough money and find suitable candidates for training, though at one stage the farm was able to send a wagonload of produce to a Liverpool market twice a week. There was confusion over whether the aim should be to settle the trained men on individual small-holdings or whether the original farm should become a settlement itself for twenty or so families. A few did find employment on local farms, then the emphasis changed to taking in boys aged fourteen to eighteen for training – they came from anywhere in the north of England. With the war there came refugees and evacuees and in 1940 Dom Gregory was re-called to Belmont Abbey to run the farm there – Fr Hugh Gildea took his place in Parbold. Later that year Dean Campion of Wigan wrote to the Archbishop to express his unease about the farm, although he had nothing against Fr Gildea personally: it was, he said, very difficult to find out what was going on, the laity were giving the scheme only desultory support while the clergy would have nothing to do with it. He advised against lending it any more money and complained in a later letter that local people were unhappy because few of the boys went to church.[33]

There were no more trainees after 1943 and the farm was sold, though the Association kept going as a charity until as late as 1969. As with other schemes up and down the country, the initial hope of being any sort of solution to the severe urban unemployment of the 1930s was unrealistic and owed more to Merry England medievalism than to any practical analysis of social ills. Downey enthusiastically invested time and money in the scheme, perhaps hoping that it would help to answer those critics of Catholic Action who claimed that nothing was being done about practical issues, but he refused to encourage Dom Gregory's post-war plan to re-launch it.

THE CATHOLIC ACTION COLLEGE

Meanwhile, work was going ahead on a scheme to train the 'lay apostles' who would be the leaders of the movement. Adult Catholic education had always been the very poor relative of Catholic educational policy; indeed, for most of the diocese's history it had not even had the lowly status of maiden aunt, that shadowy and neglected member of the Victorian and Edwardian family. The Catholic Social Guild was providing instruction in the Church's social teaching for a few, and the recently formed Catholic Evidence Guild was providing a training in apologetics for even fewer, but the mass of Catholics had to get by with what they had learned at school and heard in short weekly instructions from the pulpit. The Retreat Movement was having some success but was not being followed up in parishes in any systematic way.

This was the context for the establishment of the ambitious Liverpool Catholic Action College, aimed at providing the necessary intellectual training for those who responded to the call for 'crusaders in the cause of Catholic Action in all its phases'. The word 'crusaders' is interesting here, as is Downey's deliberate changing of 'leaders' of Catholic Action to 'Apostles' of Catholic Action. He announced the idea of the College in March 1938, summarising its purpose as follows: it would offer

> to many young men and women opportunities and facilities for the study
> of the most fundamental things of life which otherwise would not have
> come their way, (and) the means of attaining a commission in the army of
> Christ the King as it takes the field in the instructional campaign which
> is so vital a part of Catholic Action.[34]

A team of well-qualified staff, including two lecturers from the University of Liverpool, members of the Secular and Regular clergy and well-qualified lay men and women were responsible for delivering a comprehensive prospectus: twenty courses of twenty-four evening sessions each over two terms, covering Christian Doctrine and Apologetics, Social Studies and Social Ethics, Church History, Liturgy, Church Music, Church Latin, Economics, Public Administration, The New Paganism, Missiology and Public Speaking. All the courses were to take place in the Catholic Action Offices in the Cathedral Buildings, Brownlow Hill, Liverpool. Local affiliated centres were promised for the 'outlying districts' in the future, along with week-end, day and summer schools, and correspondence courses (for which Downey claimed to have had enquiries already from as far away as India).

The optimism of the planners is evident from the note that classes would be limited normally to forty members, and the optimism seemed justified when over 600 students registered in the first year, starting in September 1938.[35]

By any measure this was a tremendous response and must indicate substantial support for the scheme at parish level. Then came the outbreak of war, and numbers dropped to eighty on a greatly reduced programme. Eventually the nightly bombing raids that began in September 1940 forced the College to cancel its courses altogether. Yet with remarkable persistence the administrators planned a special summer session for May 1941, with a grand re-opening by the Archbishop and a full 'wartime programme' of courses.[36] Unfortunately, the worst of the blitz came in that month, when the city suffered terribly; given the generally shattered state of the city and the evacuation of people from the worst affected areas it would have been remarkable if any of the courses had even started. A course on Apologetics did run from January 1943, although with only between six and ten students. After a major re-opening in September of that year, the chief organiser, Fr Geary, complained constantly of his difficulty in getting qualified lecturers (he had no money to pay them fees) and recruiting people to serve on the College's Council. By the beginning of 1945 he was arguing to the Board that centralised classes would no longer attract any students – what was needed were study circles in the parishes.[37] It is difficult to know what led him to be so sure of this while war-time conditions still prevailed, or how he thought parish-based classes could run without a large pool of trained lay-people. After considerable discussion in 1947 and 1948 about re-opening the College, a very much reduced series of evening classes for the laity began in October 1949, with no mention of the College as such – the ambitious and far-sighted pre-war scheme was being dropped. By October 1951 the response had become so poor that the few students interested in the courses were asked to attend the Catholic Evidence Guild preparatory sessions, and the College was no more.[38] What had met with so much enthusiasm just before the war faded away very soon after it – had Catholics changed so much? Perhaps Fr Geary had read the signs of the times better than others, or perhaps there was an element of self-fulfilling prophecy in the College's demise – there was no campaign to re-launch it and little or nothing was said to the people to encourage them; the Archbishop seems to have lost interest. Nothing was done about setting up parish-based study groups.

CATHOLIC ACTION POST-WAR

The Board had kept what it could of its other activities going during the war and with the coming of peace it picked up more or less where it had left off in 1939. It was still looking for a clear role for itself, still worried about its relationship with existing societies and the role of individual parishes and the clergy. There was talk of a need to re-organise the original scheme and of the necessity to have a number of sub-committees – a Press Sub-committee, a Film Sub-committee, and a Panel of Censors. The Board recommended the setting up of parish bureaux along the lines of St Francis Xavier's and St Clare's (Mgr Adamson's parish). There were suggestions for Advisory Panels of Catholic Doctors and Solicitors and for public meetings to mark Catholic occasions such as the Feast of Christ the King and the declaration of the dogma of the Assumption. And there was talk of the need to establish an outlook which could be termed 'The Catholic Action Mind', which could be achieved by providing local training courses for the laity.[39]

In this context it is interesting that a sub-committee report about this time pointed to what seemed to be a serious weakness in the original scheme. There was, it claimed, a problem with Catholic Action groups in the outlying deaneries. There was little liaison between them and the Board and they felt isolated, even excluded from what was being organised in the city – the age-old problem of Liverpool v. the Rest. Yet the clergy as a whole were not apathetic. When a new plan for organizing the movement was launched in 1951, nine of the eleven deaneries responded positively to the idea of Deanery Councils (Wigan and Warrington were the ones not replying), and suggested priests who would act as Spiritual Directors, a name later changed to Ecclesiastical Assistants because the priests appointed would be involved in 'temporal' as well as spiritual work. The essential point of the re-organization was a move to de-centralise by giving more say to these Deanery (or, where appropriate, Borough) Councils, and the need to train competent lay people to direct local action. Dean Cartmell of Chorley reported he already had a Men's Association that was doing good work; he would bring in the women and use the combined forces as the basis of a Chorley Borough Council for Catholic Action. Dean Francis reported that the Southport Deanery already had a fully functioning Council. From these plans and discussions one gets a feeling that the Board had to some extent lost touch – as one experienced priest put it, there was a lot of Catholic Action going on in various parts of the archdiocese of which the Board knew nothing at all.[40]

As part of this re-launch the Board held a conference in December 1951 to clarify its ideas on Catholic Action and the Lay Apostolate in the light of recent papal statements to a lay congress held in Rome. In addition to the new Ecclesiastical Assistants about 120 lay representatives from a whole range of lay societies across the archdiocese attended. What they heard from Fr Denis McDonnell, a member of the Board, was much more than a re-launch: he defined the Lay Apostolate in terms of the laity's membership of the Mystical Body and their share in the priesthood of Christ through their baptism and confirmation. The Lay Apostolate was not a question of lending a hand to the Church as though they were somehow outside it: 'the laity collectively are the Church', knit together in a 'visible, indissoluble, organic unity'. This richer view of the Lay Apostolate meant that there should be less stress on official Catholic Action: lay people carried out their apostolate in their everyday lives, and perhaps also as members of societies doing specific apostolic work or even through organised Catholic Action. Fr McDonnell concluded by saying that existing societies must be aware of their apostolic role and their leaders had the duty to revitalise them along these lines.[41]

A similar conference took place in Wigan a year later. This time Mgr Adamson led the discussion with a speech that seemed to mark a step backward into the 1930s and indicated that the Board had still not made up its mind on some key theoretical issues. He put much more stress on the collaboration that was necessary between the Lay Apostolate and the hierarchy than Fr McDonnell had done – indeed, his speech can only have been planned as an indirect criticism of McDonnell's ideas. Since the laity's apostolate was a share in that of the hierarchy, Adamson argued, it had to be subject to them and to their delegates, the parish clergy; the 'single, directive force' giving the apostolate its impulse were the bishops. Existing organisations, he went on, were the key means of achieving the aims of the apostolate, provided they remembered that their purpose was 'to help the clergy to save souls'. The present-day great need for the Lay Apostolate arose, he argued, because there was a shortage of priests and, in any case, modern industrial society often made it impossible for the priest to contact the people.[42]

The Board at times was unsure how far it could rely on the laity. At its meeting of December 1950 it agreed on the need for a priest to be appointed full-time to the Board's Social Service Bureau in Truman Street in central Liverpool and to become a member of the Board. It claimed that essential work was being delayed because there was no priest in regular attendance at the office with authority to give the 'right answer'. The priest appointed would have to be experienced in Catholic Action and be able to act as liaison officer between the various sections and activities of Catholic Action – but it had to be a priest. On the other hand, by 1951 the Board had been re-organised and considerably enlarged with greater lay representation. Under the chairmanship of Charles Doyle it now comprised four ecclesiastical assistants and lay representatives of the UCM, the CEG, the Teachers' Association, the Knights of St Columba, Catholic Social Work, the University Catholic Society, and the CYMS, along with a Trade Union leader, a headmaster and a prominent city councillor, and two 'non-active' lay members.[43]

What were the main concerns of this enlarged and predominantly lay Board? It tried to keep alive interest in the three wings of the original scheme. In 1950, for example, it spent a considerable amount of time discussing how to arrange meetings on 'Mary's part in the Apostolate of Catholic Action' to mark the 1950 definition of the Assumption. The Board sent letters to all the archdiocesan societies and organisations announcing two talks on the theme, one for women and one for men (both to be given in Liverpool), as well as plans for processions in honour of Our Lady, Queen of Apostles. But the Board also showed special interest in the Young Christian Workers and praised in particular its courses on training for marriage, though there was some worry about 'how far' lectures should go. A new concern was trade unionism: what could be done to ensure that Catholic members of the unions became involved in the movement and exercised their due influence? This was partly a reflection of the Board's worry about communist infiltration, but it also linked to a general desire that lay people should take Christ into the workplace as part of their proper apostolate. There was some debate about whether the Board should support positively the Association of Catholic Trade Unionists (ACTU) or whether the CYMS could do the work better as it already had an established parish network. Again, some members of the Board were worried by the fact that branches of ACTU were operating without advice (i.e. clerical advice) and that a priest should be appointed 'to assist in its control'.[44]

The years up to 1960 were the heyday of societies such as the Legion of Mary and the Catholic Evidence Guild, and the Board minutes show an appreciation of what they were doing by way of spiritual formation and instruction. Any involvement in the relief of poverty tended to be left in the trusty but traditionalist hands of the SVP. There seems to have been no repeat of the pre-war Wigan initiatives; of course, society's needs were changing and there was now the Welfare State as a catch-all safety net (the holes in it became clear only gradually).

One very practical scheme that did flourish in these years was that organised by the Apostleship of the Sea. The work had started in Glasgow in 1922 and was taken up in Liverpool in the 1930s. It aimed to provide for the spiritual and social needs of seamen who were cut off for long periods from their families and home communities. Its first Club, known as Atlantic House, opened in Strand Road; after the war it moved to Hardman Street and eventually could provide residential accommodation for almost a hundred men. Its Guild of Hostesses and Men's Guild provided a welcoming atmosphere, with the former providing partners at weekly dances. In the late 1960s a second hostel, Stella Maris, was opened in Bootle and the Apostleship took over Gateacre Grange Nursing Home as a home for retired seamen. In the grand scheme of Catholic Action it featured as an agent of 'Catholic Preservation', to safeguard the Faith of Catholics and reclaim lapsed Catholics. It was always popular among Liverpool Catholics and its appeals for money were well received in a city that was well aware of the various dangers that faced 'those in peril on the sea'.[45]

While from some points of view Liverpool Catholicism of the 1950s was a carbon copy of that of the 1920s, there were important developments that were beginning to bring about fundamental changes. Some of the former tight parish communities had been broken up by post-war re-housing schemes. Many more Catholics were experiencing secondary and university education, often away from their parish base. Conor Ward, in his survey of a Liverpool parish in the 1950s, commented on the low level of take-up of parish activities and the problem of building inter-parish ones, partly because of unchanging clerical attitudes and a narrow parochialism.[46] Yet it was becoming clear that inter-parish co-operation was the only way ahead in some areas, and none more so than in that of adult Christian education – a pre-requisite if the laity were to be properly formed for the broader work of the Lay Apsotolate and Catholic Action.

287

Under Downey's successor, Archbishop Godfrey (1953-1956), the Board appeared to be taken up more and more with that perennial and apparently insuperable problem, the leakage of young Catholics from regular religious practice. The Board discussed at great length what could be done and in the end set up a Youth Secretariat. It also discussed setting up a Liverpool Catholic Film Unit; some parishes were experimenting with film shows but the general experience was that attendances dropped off quite rapidly after promising starts. The Board was more successful in organising day conferences on the Lay Apostolate, to be held regularly around the archdiocese. These drew good attendances of between fifty and eighty people. They were fairly basic in their approach, trying to get across the fundamental idea of the lay apostolate and dealing with youth issues, and how to co-ordinate various parish groups. This last point was a major concern for the Board itself in these years – could it direct the work of parochial and diocesan organisations, or did it have only a co-ordinating role? If the latter, how was it to achieve the co-ordination?[47]

To be still discussing this after twenty years pointed to a lack of clarity in the original scheme; it came down to the basic question of its authority, and in the end the Board decided that it had very little, despite its official status, and that it had no right to interfere in what others were doing. When Archbishop Heenan succeeded in 1956 he decided that the Board had had its day and suggested that it should be replaced by a Council of Catholic Action, with an ad hoc representation of every active organisation and the clergy. How such a Council could operate any more effectively than the Board was not clear. The Board met for the last time in February 1958, when it fell to Mgr Adamson, its principal ecclesiastical assistant since 1936, to review the successes and failures of the past twenty years – unfortunately, no account of his summary seems to exist. Catholic Action was then 'handed over' to Fr J.G. Waring in March and continued in existence for another year or so.[48]

That Catholic Action was a 'good thing' had to some extent just been taken for granted and little enough had been achieved that would not have happened anyway. It would be unfair, however, to lay much blame for this on the members of the Board. The failure to get things moving on an archdiocesan scale must, in the end, be laid at the door of the Archbishop and the clergy: he failed to translate his initial enthusiasm and grand, over-arching scheme into a clear-cut working programme for the parishes, and the clergy in too many cases failed to accept the challenge of change – if the traditional parish structures were not broken, they argued, why try to mend them? Above all, organised Catholic Action had failed to convince the clergy (and most of the laity, for that matter) that there could be (still less should be) an authentic lay voice independent of their own. When this did develop in the 1960s, with the publication, for example of *Slant,* it was far too radical and discomforting for the majority of English Catholics. It is ironic that the one lay voice that had developed in an organised way over these years had been that of the Catholic Teachers' Federation: ironic because as a body Catholic teachers had given the most invaluable and loyal support to implementing the hierarchy's plans for Catholic education; the bishops as a whole did not know how to handle it when it spoke its mind and put forward views contrary to those of their lordships. Loyal obedience was still the cardinal virtue expected of the laity.

Notes

1 Doyle, 'Charles Plater', pp.403, 411.

2 Pius XI, *Ubi arcano*, 23 Dec. 1922.

3 AAW Acta of Bishops' Meetings, Low Week 1933.

4 *The Tablet*, 1612.1933, pp.812-4.

5 *The Catholic Times*, 27 April and 27 July, 1934.

6 'Joint Pastoral Letter ... on Catholic Action', 1934.

7 Copy in AAL Downey, S1 VI: Diocesan Social Action, A./8.

8 The Hierarchy of England and Wales, *The Apostolate of the Laity* (1936).

9 AAW Hi 2/23, Catholic Action 1935-40, 18.9.1937.

10 AAL Downey, S1 VI A/12, Draft of Constitution of Liverpool Board of C.A.

11 *Ibid.*, A/7, *Catholic Action: A Simple Explanation* (1937).

12 *Ibid.*, A/12.

13 Peter Lane, *The Catenian Association 1908-1983* (1982), p.50.

14 AAL Downey S1 VI B/4-7, various addresses to the Congress and *Report on the Catholic Action Congress* (1938); also, Cardinal Secretary of State (Pacelli), Letter on Catholic Action on the Occasion ... Archdiocesan Congress of Catholic Action, Dec. 1937.

15 *The Tablet*, 10.12.1932.

16 AAL Downey, S1 II, A/2 Ad clerum 1930-9, poster attached to ad clerum of 24.9.1937,

17 *Ibid.*, ad clerum, Nov. 1936, Jan. 1937.

18 Aspden, pp.212-3.

19 AAL Downey, S2 II B/44-6: Minutes of Special Pro-Deo meetings, Feb.-May 1938.

20 Frank Deegan, *There's No Other Way: The Autobiography of Frank Deegan* (1980).

21 AAL Downey, S1 II, A/2, ad clerum 9.12.1936; S1 VI A/23, 'Eighteen Months of Catholic Action in the Arch. of Liverpool', 1938, p.5.

22 *Ibid.*, p.4.

23 *Ibid.* Also printed leaflet, 'Campaign for the Sanctification of the Home', May 1938.

24 AAL 'Eighteen Months', pp.3, 6.

25 *Ibid.*, pp.1, 4; AAL Downey, S1 VI B: Board Minutes, Jan. 1951, tribute to Fr Roberts, recently deceased.

26 AAL Downey, S1 VI A: Board Minutes, March and June 1937.

27 *Ibid.*, July 1939.

28 AAL Downey S1 XI A/56: 'Wigan House of Hospitality': 9 mainly undated items.

29 *Ibid.*, First Annual Report.

30 *Ibid.*, Newsletter July 1938.

31 J. Davies, 'The Liverpool Catholic Land Association' *NWCH*, XIX (1992), pp.21-46. AAL Downey, S1 XI A/35-38. *The Times*, Dec. 1932.

32 *The Daily Express, The Liverpool Daily Post, The Evening Chronicle, The Yorkshire Post* 13.5.1935; *The Universe* 17.5.1935.

33 AAL Downey, S1 XI A/37, Letters from Campion to Downey, May 1940.

34 AAL Downey, S1 VIII C/1, Downey's Address at launch, and draft, 13.3.1938

35 *Ibid.*, C/2, The Catholic Action College of Liverpool, June 1938; C/6, 'Aims and Objectives'; C/17, *Catholic Action in War-Time* (1941), p.6.

36 *Ibid.*, C/8, Special Summer Session: War-Time Programme, 1941.

37 AAL Downey, S1 VI A: Board Minutes 1938-49: reports of Fr Geary, Jan.-Oct. 1943, Jan. 1945; S1 VIII C/10, Minutes of the Committee ... to re-open College (1947-9); B/86 and 88, On Re-establishment of College, 1948-49.

38 AAL Downey, S1 VI A: Board Minutes, Sept.-Oct. 1951.

39 *Ibid.*, Board Minutes 1950-53, Jan.-Sept. 1950.

40 *Ibid.*, June 1950; the priest was Canon Campbell of St John's, Wigan.

41 *Ibid,* S1 VIII, 'Report on Catholic Action Conference', Liverpool Dec. 1951.

42 *Ibid,* 'The Lay Apostolate' Conference, Wigan Dec. 1952.

43 AAL Downey S1 VI A: Board Minutes, Dec. 1950; Feb. 1951.

44 *Ibid.*

45 B. Boardman, *Directory 1972*, pp.40-44.

46 Conor Ward, *Priests and People* (1961), pp.85-90.

47 AAL Godfrey Collection S1 I B/1: C.A. Board Minute Book.

48 *Ibid.*, meeting 7.12.1957; final meeting 28.2.1958; last entry 9.6.1959.

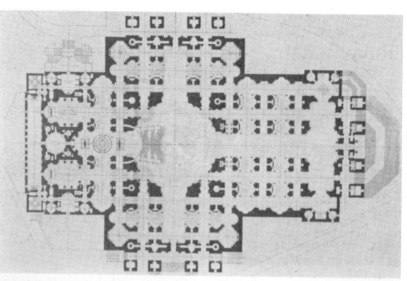
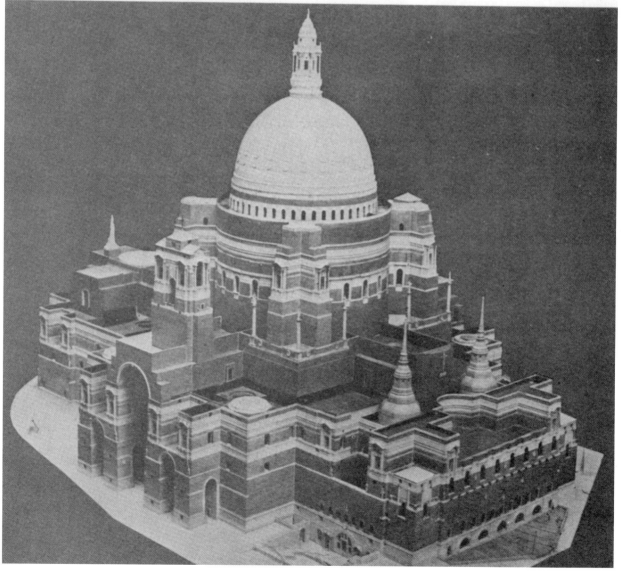

CHAPTER 15 'LET US RISE UP AND BUILD': FROM PUGIN TO GIBBERD

A SLOW START

Sometime in 1853 Bishop Brown had decided it was time to begin the work of providing his new diocese with a worthy cathedral. He had then left it to his energetic new coadjutor, Bishop Goss, to approach the architect Edward Welby Pugin, son of the famous Augustus Welby Pugin who had done so much to foster the Gothic Revival among English Catholics. There was ample room for a large building in the grounds of St Edward's College, Everton, the highest point in the north end of the town, and so this became the chosen site – as Burke put it, a cathedral of fine proportions built there would have been the dominating feature of the city, visible from every point of the estuary and the Wirral peninsula. Pugin drew up plans for a large Gothic building, dominated by a huge central spire, to be dedicated to St Edward. Building began without delay on what was to be its Lady Chapel and at the end of 1856 Bishop Goss opened it as the church of Our Lady Immaculate; until the building of the rest of the cathedral it was to serve as the church for the local Catholic community.[1]

Nothing further was done to advance Bishop Brown's project. The church of St Nicholas remained in use as the pro-cathedral in the centre of Liverpool and the church of Our Lady Immaculate in Everton continued to serve as a local church for over a hundred years (it was finally abandoned in the 1980s because it was structurally unsafe). It was not until after the first World War that the idea of building a cathedral surfaced again in a serious way; by then, even if anyone had still been thinking of completing Pugin's building, the site was no longer available (the Christian Brothers were running their school there) and most people believed that a more central position would be preferable anyway. Archbishop Keating (appointed to Liverpool in 1921) almost immediately faced the question of providing a suitable memorial to his very popular predecessor, Archbishop Whiteside. After consulting the clergy up and down the archdiocese he decided on a cathedral, dedicated to the Good Shepherd, one of Whiteside's favourite devotions.

At a public meeting in January 1922 he set up an executive committee under the chairmanship of Alderman Austin Harford, with two other laymen, Colonel Shute and Sir Alexander Maguire as treasurers, to raise funds and see the project through to completion. In addition to its officers the committee comprised a lay and a clerical representative from each deanery in the archdiocese – presumably the unusually heavy lay presence was the result of needing to raise funds, while deanery representation was

Opposite: *Sir Edwin Lutyens, the ground plan of his great design and the model exhibited at the Royal Academy in 1934.*

The original Pugin Lady Chapel at St Edward's. The students in cassocks were studying philosophy there before going to a senior seminary.

meant to ensure that interest in the project would not be restricted to Liverpool and its immediate neighbourhood. The Archbishop pledged himself to the cause: 'I shall devote the rest of my days, every ounce of my strength and every penny I save to the cause', he told those gathered for the first of what were to become annual Cathedral Demonstrations – though he was also to spend considerable energy and money on the extension of the seminary at Upholland.[2]

His pastoral letter for Good Shepherd Sunday 1922 put the case for a cathedral in the city in terms that were to become almost a mantra over the next twenty years. He argued that the liturgy could not be performed properly without a cathedral and that every year, while bishops of 'even small and impoverished dioceses' or vicars apostolic on the missions could perform the liturgy properly, he could not. Such an incongruous situation was highlighted, he went on, when his suffragan bishops and other distinguished guests visited the city:

> Our friends are shocked and puzzled at this glaring gap in our religious machinery, and the sight of the huge, enthusiastic crowds, thousands upon thousands strong, who brave all weathers and block the streets for hours during ... some ecclesiastical service from which they are necessarily excluded ... only augments the mystery why Liverpool alone, of all the notable Sees in the world, is so meanly provided.

Nor was it a case only of lacking a stage for the dignified display of pontifical functions: Catholics in Liverpool would never have more than a transient influence on the life of the city, he argued, because their efforts lacked the 'momentum' that only direction from a 'recognised centre' could impart.[3]

Finally, Keating mentioned money: building a cathedral, he insisted, was not the time for 'petty economy'. The 'magnitude of the undertaking' must determine the cost, and not vice versa. After all, he continued, the main purpose of such a building was the daily celebration of the Divine Liturgy in its fulness; it would be the centre for all the spiritual activities of 'the Diocese and the Province'. It must, therefore, be large enough to accommodate thousands and be 'crowned with beauty' fitting the house of God. He continued,

> It must woo the soul … by the sweetness of its chants, the regal ceremonial of its functions, the rich vesture of its ministers, the artistic value of all its appurtenances, and the thousand and one precious details which denote the Sanctuary of the Most High, the pride of God's people, and the nesting-place (sic) of the devout soul.[4]

Quite what Keating was imagining in referring to the Provincial role of the proposed building is not clear; certainly there was to be considerable opposition from certain parts of the Province when his successor tried to turn this grandiose notion into the basis of an appeal for money. No wonder Keating was extremely annoyed when half of his archdiocese was hived off in 1925 to form the new diocese of Lancaster: he had argued in vain to the authorities in Rome that the division was inopportune because the whole archdiocese was already committed to the cathedral project and the extension of the seminary, and that its continued support would be required to bring both projects to completion (see Chapter 11).

The Cathedral Demonstrations held each year in St George's Hall were so successful in raising funds that Bishop Dobson (the new chairman of the executive committee) was optimistic enough to announce in 1926 that the foundation stone would be laid in 1929, the centenary year of Catholic Emancipation, and not in 1933 as he had at first suggested. The project must have been popular with priests and people: by the time of Keating's death in February, 1928, £119,777 had been collected or pledged for the Cathedral Building Fund, and in 1927 a campaigning group called 'The Cathedral Crusaders' had undertaken to launch a special 'Cathedral Drive' in every parish.[5]

Deciding on a suitable site was not easy. The archdiocese had acquired land near the pro-cathedral, and one possibility would have been to demolish St Nicholas's church and build the cathedral there. Archbishop Keating, however, believed that the site was not commanding enough and set his mind instead on acquiring the nine-acre site of the former Liverpool Workhouse, at the top of Brownlow Hill and owned by the West Derby Board of Poor Law Guardians. He began private negotiations to buy the site, but found there were other interested parties – the University, directly opposite the Workhouse, and the City Council itself, which saw the site as ideal for building tenements on. He died before anything could be settled. His successor, Archbishop Richard Downey, was consecrated on 21 September 1928 and visited the proposed site the very next day. It was there, he revealed later:

> that my vision came to me; I saw in a moment … a wonderful, powerful, building situated on the highest point of this great city, tall and stately, dominating the march of commerce, the river, and smiling across the sea.[6]

It was to be two years before he could acquire the site, however, as its proposed sale to the Catholic authorities raised once again the strong anti-Catholic feeling that was never far below the surface of Liverpool's local politics.

The City Council, who would become owners of the site when responsibility for the administration of the Poor Law passed from the Guardians, decided it did not want it for house building, and suggested that it be sold for a price fixed by the Ministry of Health. They approved a price of at least £100,000 and Downey, after an independent valuation, offered £90,000 – £100,000. The Guardians, still technically the owners, held out for £125,000 although Downey's offer was the only one that approached the Ministry's price. A public auction failed to come up with anything near the reserve price and so Downey renewed his original offer; this was again refused by the Guardians by one vote, apparently on sectarian grounds, and in March 1930 the site and its buildings passed to the City Council. Its Finance Committee recommended that the Archbishop's offer be accepted and when this was debated by the full Council it was agreed by eighty-eight votes to twenty-seven. The opposition was led by the virulently anti-Catholic Rev. Harry Longbottom, leader of the Protestant Party, who said that he would prefer the site to be used for a 'poison germ factory' rather than a Catholic cathedral.[7] In August an estimated quarter of a million people attended a rally in Thingwall Park to give thanks for the acquisition of the site. Downey quipped that while he had only acquired the site 'by a short nose' that was better than 'being beaten by a long bottom!'[8]

Downey now had his vision, an outstanding site on which to realise it, and was soon to have an equally outstanding architect to share his vision, enthusiasm and ambition. Sir Edwin Lutyens, O.M., P.R.A., was the most eminent English architect of the time, responsible for the magnificently imperial viceroy's palace in India and the breath-taking Arch of the Missing in the great war memorial at Thiepval in France. It may well have been these huge public buildings, in his adapted Classical style, that made him an attractive possibility to Archbishop Downey: the latter had decided against anything even remotely Gothic, partly perhaps because he did not want to seem to be in competition with the neo-Gothic Anglican Cathedral being built only half a mile away from his chosen site, but more likely, it seems, because he saw his great cathedral being topped by a massive classical dome, modelled on that of St Peter's in Rome. He and Lutyens met for the first time at dinner in the Garrick Club in London, where the Archbishop spoke of his intention to build a cathedral in Liverpool. 'What fun for you!', was the architect's reply, and the two then discussed 'Cathedrals generally'.[9] Downey was certain that Lutyens was the only possible architect: a little later he invited him to Liverpool and they toured the proposed site together. In July 1929 he wrote with the formal offer of the commission, apparently without having seen anything on paper by way of a suggested design and without any mention of probable costs. In accepting, Lutyens wrote that the letter had given him 'the moment of my life', while the responsibility of the project filled him with 'a deep reverence' – he would need all the Archbishop's help to justify the confidence being placed in him. He ended the letter with a typical Lutyens quip (a biographer has spoken of the 'jokescreen' that the architect usually erected to hide his deeper thoughts): the Ordnance Map of Liverpool showed that the new site was thirty feet higher than that of the Anglican one – 'which is good!'[10]

Lutyens believed that one of the reasons Downey had chosen him was that he was an Anglican, while the architect of the new Anglican Cathedral was a Catholic. He was a deeply spiritual if somewhat unorthodox person; he spoke lovingly of the religious influence on him of his Irish-Catholic mother, and seems to have had for many years a 'dream of designing a great building of which the one dominant purpose was the praise of God' – presumably this was what he had meant by the commission being 'the moment' of his life.[11] Certainly the cathedral project never became for him just another commission, no matter how important: he shared his patron's vision and believed they were engaged in a holy undertaking; they went to Rome together to obtain the Pope's approval of the plans – Pius XI described the future cathedral as a bulwark against Bolshevism and suggested it should be dedicated to Christ the King. Lutyens was also alive to the symbolism of transforming the workhouse, the scene of so much suffering: he wrote to Downey:

> from the chaos of poverty and sickness rises the fane of Christ the King ...
> from out the carcase of misery and despondency comes forth love and
> mercy, and this is your cathedral church upon a workhouse site.

In a later comment that illustrates something of Lutyens' ideas on the purpose of a cathedral, he said that he wanted the narthex or space immediately inside the great west arch to be always open, day and night, 'without let or hindrance, and kept warm – a spiritual sanctuary for those cold and destitute'.[12] A little of this vision was partially realised when, many years later, part of the site was used for a time as an underground night shelter for the homeless.

Lutyens was able to release provisional plans and sketches in 1930. These were modified over the course of a year and after many conferences with Downey, a final, massive, model (magnificent in its own right) was exhibited at the Royal Academy in 1934.[13] The style of the building may best be described as a rather severe 'contemporary classic', to be executed in grey granite and browny-pink brick. It has been said that stylistically the design of the interior is in Lutyens' own version of classicism, 'sometimes rather idiosyncratic, always visually arresting'. Lutyens himself frequently compared it with St Peter's, Rome, and St Paul's, London, and coined the rather apt term '(W)renaissance' to cover what he was trying to achieve.[14] Like his two exemplars, the cathedral was to be dominated by a single great dome, 510 feet in height to the top of its cross compared with St Peter's 450 feet and St Paul's 366 feet, with an internal diameter of 168 feet, compared with St Peter's 137 and St Paul's 112. The building was to be slightly shorter overall than its

Roman counterpart, 680 feet compared with 715, but longer than St Paul's which was 510. In width, including the transepts, St Peter's would again be slightly greater (450 feet against Lutyens' 400), but St Paul's, at 250 feet, considerably narrower. One statistic that was intended to overawe visitors to the model when it was on site was that the nearby Victoria Tower of Liverpool University, itself quite a considerable landmark, would fit comfortably under the cathedral's main entrance arch. In one sense these statistics have little significance, but in another they are highly significant: while Lutyens declared it would not be fitting for any church to try to rival St Peter's, what he and Downey were trying to achieve for Liverpool was for the city to have the most impressive cathedral in Christendom.[15]

From the technical point of view Lutyens succeeded where both Michelangelo and Wren had partially failed, in overcoming the problems of attaching a huge circular dome to a square base – what has been called 'Lutyens' greatest tour-de-force in the planning of the Cathedral'.[16] Without going into the technical details, it may be said that the result would have been both structurally stable (unlike St Paul's) and aesthetically successful internally (unlike St Peter's). Whether it would have been as successful liturgically is open to doubt: while the internal space would have been immense, many in the congregation would have had their view of the altar at least partially blocked by the many columns. The post-war Scott modification of the plans, to provide a more affordable alternative (see below) would have given more people a clear view of the sanctuary.

REACTIONS

Not everyone shared the Archbishop's enthusiasm and even some of those who had been enthusiastic about the scheme to build a cathedral as a memorial to Archbishop Whiteside took fright when they saw Lutyens' plans. Apart from any other consideration, the years immediately after 1930 were years of severe economic depression and the thought of having to raise so much money from what was still a relatively poor constituency was at the very least daunting. In an article entitled 'Let us Rise up and Build' Downey dismissed as Philistines all those who queried either the need for a cathedral at all or the need to build one on the scale proposed by Lutyens. He believed that the doubters did not understand either the purpose of a cathedral or the spirit that had driven the builders of great cathedrals in the past. A cathedral, he wrote, should be a 'vast spacious place where the Bishop can address his multitudinous spiritual subjects ... (and) the place where God taught through the mouth of the Bishop'. He went on to explain that in the ages of faith a cathedral was built 'so that on occasion the whole far-flung diocese should draw nigh and listen to the authoritative words of Christ speaking in the person of the Bishop'. And these thoughts, he continued, were very relevant to the present situation: the new cathedral was not intended just for the archdiocese of Liverpool, but for the whole of the Northern Province: for the dioceses of Hexham and Newcastle, Lancaster, Leeds, Middlesbrough, and Salford. Even just in the archdiocese, however, he believed that the numbers of the faithful wishing to attend on great occasions were far too many for the pro-cathedral: 'we need a cathedral, we need it urgently, and it must be a vast one'.

To those who questioned the scale of the plans Downey put forward a number of arguments: since the sixteenth century English Catholics had always built too small, whether it was cathedrals, schools, colleges or convents – no sooner were buildings completed than they proved too small for the rapidly growing Catholic population. Moreover, a great cathedral would put the port of Liverpool on the 'ecclesiastical map' as the equal of Rheims or Cologne and enable 'men of all nations' to unite in common worship; it would lift the city to a 'higher plane than that of nationalism in religion'. With regard to the estimated cost of three million pounds, what was that, he asked, in comparison with a single bridge across Sydney Harbour (seven million), a modern battleship (eight million) or an ocean liner (at least six million) – and how long would the last two be in service? Love and sacrifice, still to be found among God's poor even in a materialist age, would overcome any financial difficulties. A cathedral would indeed be a counterblast to the machine of materialism that was 'crushing all spirituality out of men's souls' and, apart from its obvious religious role, it would be:

> a supreme expression of artistic genius, a challenge to the mediocrity of the age, a cultural standard of comparison, a masterpiece to uplift the minds and hearts of those who look upon even its exterior beauty.[17]

This was the Archbishop at his most oratorical. In one form or another these arguments and sentiments were to feature in his spoken and written appeals until the second World War eventually put a stop to building. How far he carried people with him in those years is not easy to assess: money kept coming in, and by 1932 over £216,000 had been raised in total, with the annual income averaging between £20,000 and £25,000. The site had cost £100,000 and Lutyens' fees were high – he asked for £62,500 for getting out the initial detailed plans, with a larger-scale plan of the first section of the work to be undertaken and working drawings for the building that would be covered by the first million pounds of expenditure, without finishings or furnishings. These fees were to be paid in various ways: £15,000 in transferred loan stock, an annual fee of £4,000 for ten years, an insurance on the architect's life of £10,000, and a payment of £2,500 when the first contract was signed.[18]

Despite Downey's claim that a cathedral would not be just for Liverpool, he soon found out that other dioceses regarded it as entirely his own responsibility when it came to paying for it. The Archbishop of Cardiff forbade all fund-raising for the cathedral in his diocese, while the Bishop of Salford was furious that collecting was taking place in his and insisted that the guilty fund-raiser be sacked. The Archbishop of Birmingham wrote sarcastically of 'the new wonder of the world' and of the efforts to raise money at a time when financial crisis threatened the country – he would, however, allow a film about the cathedral to be shown, but without any word of support from himself. The Bishop of Hexham and Newcastle reported that there was likely to be opposition from his clergy to the showing of the film, but he would not forbid it.[19]

A host of fund-raising initiatives were launched. The 'Golden Book', in which all those who subscribed £1 had their names inscribed and Masses said for their intentions, was the most successful and by the mid-1950s had raised over £195,000. There were appeals for specific chapels, especially those dedicated to Our Lady and St Paul of the Cross, and various groups accepted responsibility of raising the necessary funds – the priests of the archdiocese, the Federation of the Children of Mary, and the school children were some of those involved in this way. John McCormack, the famous Irish tenor, agreed to make a record to be sold in aid of the Cathedral – Elgar declined to write special music for it, but the poet Alfred Noyes wrote the words. There were home-collecting boxes in the shape of the Cathedral, a film and even cathedral tea and cigarettes! Huge annual rallies on the site and conducted tours for parish groups helped to keep the project alive in people's minds. In an interesting note written after the war, Mgr Tom Turner (appointed as Organiser and Supervisor in 1935) reported that once advertising outside the archdiocese started in 1936, the idea spread gradually throughout the country and Ireland, 'and even abroad to a limited extent', and so 'the "burden" has been shifted from the diocese', with the greater part of the funds raised coming from outside the archdiocese.[20] Downey was determined not to borrow to finance the project, and as the building costs rose above initial estimates, the Executive Committee fixed a spending limit of £2,000 a month. They were appalled when, in 1936, the builder spent over £9,500 just on buying granite from Ireland.[21]

Lutyens remained enthusiastically and wholeheartedly caught up in the undertaking. He wanted a say on every aspect and expected, for example, to be given a veto on 'unsuitable' gifts – the bane of cathedral administrators down the years – such as a statue of St Michael and even a valuable necklace given by Pius XI to adorn the statue of Our Lady, Star of the Sea. Mgr Turner, on behalf of the Executive Committee, told Lutyens, rather tartly, that the Archbishop alone would decide on the suitability of gifts and added that he felt the architect was being rather touchy about these matters – his contract contained nothing about furnishings or fittings. Lutyens complained in turn of Turner's 'narrow-mindedness' and lack of taste, and told him that modern Catholic needlework was 'terrible' – the cathedral needed a first-class needlework instructress: 'The works that are now done (by nuns) and on show in Catholic churches are mere monuments of bad taste and craftsmanship, and bring the Church into world-wide disrepute'. When Turner suggested the use of quartzite, Lutyens responded that it was too vulgar – indeed, he added in a scribbled note, it gave him a feeling of nausea.[22]

Presumably Turner had heard of some of Lutyens' more outlandish flights of fancy – the suggestion, for example, that there should be trumpeters inside the dome during Mass to play fanfares at the consecration, and that a hidden lift be installed near the sanctuary to allow coffins to be lowered to the crypt. Turner was to become synonymous with cathedral fund-raising, reporting regularly in the *Cathedral Record* and devoting his energies just as wholeheartedly as Lutyens to the project, keeping it alive during and after the war – as late as 1953 he wrote to the architect's biographer that he saw no reason to change the original plans:

> *To change or attempt to modify the plans would be to lose one of the greatest artistic creations of all time and, as you so truly say, it would be a 'terrible blow to art in this country' and an incalculable loss of 'Catholic prestige'.*[23]

He may have been, in Lutyens' eyes, unimaginative and lacking in artistic sensibility, but he was no philistine and his cautious and even penny-pinching approach was more in touch with the realities of the situation and more likely to win over the increasing numbers who began to wonder if their Archbishop's initial promise of a 'Cathedral in our time' could ever be more than a fantasy.

BUILDING

Work had begun in January 1931 on clearing the workhouse site. This was after a major difference between the Archbishop and his architect over who should do the work: Lutyens wanted to employ his favourite London firm, and at first Downey agreed. There was then a local outcry, the details of which are not clear but which centred around the provision of work for Liverpool's unemployed, and Downey backtracked, at the risk of a legal battle with the Londoners. It was all settled more or less amicably, with profuse apologies from the Archbishop. He then chose a local builder, Charles J. Doyle, a self-made successful Irish immigrant who had moved to Liverpool as a lad of seventeen to work in the building trade. At no stage was the work put out to tender and there seems to have been little or nothing in the way of initial estimates, except a vague figure of three million as a grand total.[24] Some of the old buildings were left in place – the former nurses' quarters fronting Brownlow Hill became the Cathedral offices and later the Curial Offices, housing the main archdiocesan administrative offices (and not demolished until 2003). The basement of the former Anglican chapel to the Workhouse became a chapel-of-ease to the pro-cathedral and served as the parish church of the local Catholics until the completion of the crypt chapels after the war.

The foundation stone was laid on Whit Monday 1933, when Mass was said for the first time at the temporary altar designed by Lutyens and housed under a massive canopy over the site where the future high altar of the cathedral was to stand. It was a grand occasion, attended by Cardinal MacRory of Ireland as papal legate (in place of the ill Cardinal Bourne), most

Archbishop Downey and Sir John Shute, MP, inspect the building works (The stone-mason in the trilby facing the Archbishop is the author's father).

of the English hierarchy and local civic dignitaries. The celebrations spread beyond the site: as *The Tablet* noted, 'entire thoroughfares had put themselves in festive garb' and streets and courts were hung with mottoes in true Liverpool fashion – 'God bless our Pope', 'Long Live Archbishop Downey', 'God Bless our new Cathedral of Christ the King' (but not 'God Bless the Sacred Heart', as appeared on another occasion). The same writer commented on the number of flags in evidence as part of these decorations, and that the majority of them were Union Jacks and not the Irish tricolour; the Union flag also decorated the shields that lined the approach to the site. The Archbishop must have felt well on the way to justifying his promise to the Catholics of the archdiocese in his 'The Cathedral in Our Time' speech made a few weeks after his consecration in 1928: 'you will with your own eyes see the walls of this new Cathedral rise above its foundations'.[25]

The euphoria did not last. By the following year the Archbishop was writing to Lutyens to complain that the work was not going well; nothing had been done since the laying of the foundation stone and people were beginning to complain – he feared that the psychological effect could be disastrous. He also wrote that the Executive Committee had agreed that work should begin on the east section of the Lady Chapel, the sanctuary and the Chapter house. This would have the advantage, he wrote, of committing posterity to Lutyens' design – a sign, no doubt, that some people were beginning to question its feasibility. In 1936 he complained in an *ad clerum* that 55 parishes had not contributed to the general building fund over the last twelve months; his feeling was that in some instances interest in the

cathedral scheme had been allowed to diminish.[26] By October of the following year, however, he was able to say Mass in the shell of the crypt, and work continued steadily if unspectacularly until 1941, when the Ministry of Works announced that the building should stop because it needed to transfer the skilled builders to urgent war work. Luytens was extremely concerned about the removal of the stone-masons and was able to persuade the Ministry to leave seven of the forty-one on site so that the partially completed walls of the crypt would not suffer. The Cathedral Committee agreed to pay the architect an annual retainer of £2,000 while building was suspended (and £10,000 to his heirs if he died during that time!), but he died on New Year's Day, 1944.[27]

Building restrictions remained in force for some years after 1945. Discussion about appointing a successor to Lutyens continued during that year and Adrian Gilbert Scott, the brother of the architect of the still unfinished Anglican Cathedral, emerged as the favourite candidate. Funds had continued to come in at an average of nearly £30,000 a year – between 1937 and 1953 a total of almost half a million pounds had been collected, a sign that enthusiasm for the cathedral had not waned, either inside or outside the archdiocese; by the early 1950s almost £40,000 a year was coming in, about two-thirds of it from the archdiocese (including about £450 a year from the sale of used milk-bottle tops – a typical Turner initiative). Most of this money had been given in the expectation that the original design would be completed; as late as 1953 Turner could write, 'We have superb plans, we have a vast body of goodwill, we can afford to have a little faith and trust to the future'.[28]

Despite this optimism, it was clear to most people that the future of the
original plans was highly uncertain – Scott estimated that it would take
£27,000,000 to complete them – and it was left to Archbishop Godfrey,
appointed in 1953, to take the decisive step to abandon Downey's dream. He
commissioned Scott to produce a new design that would keep the dome but
reduce the overall size of the whole, incorporate the original crypt, and be
ready for use, even if not completed, in ten years – and the cost was to be
kept below £4,000,000. Turner called it a 'wise decision' that would at last
provide the 'long-awaited cathedral;[29] Scott believed that at the current rate
of contributions it would take about 60 years to complete the project; this
could only be reduced by increasing the amounts collected. The Archbishop
was not keen on another major appeal, but believed that it was a pressing
need for the populous archdiocese, which had taken such a noteworthy part
in the Catholic life of the country, to have 'a house of God wherein Catholic
liturgical life should find a setting worthy of its beauty'. The Chapter agreed
that priests should seek ways of doubling and even trebling the amounts
given by the people; perhaps societies and confraternities could take on the
responsibility for particular fund-raising events. The burden, concluded
Godfrey realistically, must be borne by the archdiocese and not by outsiders,
'not even by the rest of the Northern Province'.[30]

Scott produced a report that was quite critical of the original plans: he
reckoned that Lutyens had allowed for only 2,500 worshippers to have a
clear view of the high altar, and even a proportion of these would hardly be
able to see what the celebrant and other ministers were doing, owing to the
great height of the sanctuary above the nave floor. Moreover, no provision

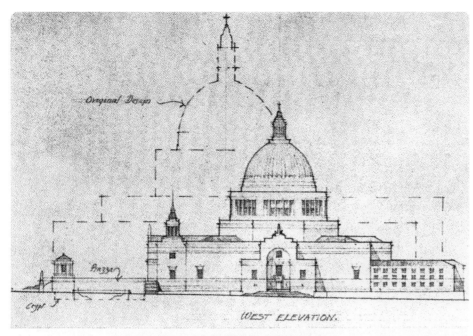

West Elevation

had been made for diocesan offices or accommodation for the residential canons who would be singing the daily office (this was the first mention of such provision). He suggested completing and roofing in the crypt, leaving a large piazza on top that would accommodate 19,000 people for open air rallies and services; a new cathedral could then be built somewhere on the remainder of the site. His eventual design had the main entrance facing Brownlow Hill; its dome was to be the same diameter as before, but only 320 feet high as against the Lutyens' 472 – just a few feet higher than the tower on the nearby Anglican Cathedral. Inside, the high altar would be under the dome and so in a central position, able to be seen by about 5,000 seated worshippers who would radiate from it in a series of nave-like spaces – an unusual 'Christo-centric' approach which allowed 'our Eucharistic Lord to come down into our midst (while) we His children are all around Him'.[31]

It was an imaginative and modern approach to the problem of having very large congregations all within easy distance of the high altar, and the piazza idea would have satisfied Liverpool Catholics' traditional need for a space for demonstrations. But from the outside the immediate impression of the plan was that it was a cut-down look-alike of the Lutyens' scheme, and as soon as it became generally known that Scott had been commissioned to 'reduce' or 'modify' Lutyens' design the architectural community were vociferous in its criticism, using such words as 'pastiche' and 'caricature'. Scott's reduced design was ready for inspection by the end of 1954 : there was general approval of the style ('Contemporary Classic'), and English and some overseas bishops declared themselves in favour – some added renewed criticisms of Lutyens' plans and some sent donations to the new fund. But the professionals were not convinced and Godfrey was involved in a lengthy correspondence on the topic throughout 1955. He and Scott had also to defend themselves against the national Fine Arts Commission, which eventually half-apologised for using the word 'caricature'.[32]

Meanwhile, no progress was being made, although work had begun on completing the original crypt. Scott wrote in November 1955 to say that he thought the project should be moved on, despite the criticisms of his designs. The Executive Committee told him that the completion of at least one chapel in the crypt must be his priority and he drew up a programme to achieve this, but a year later they were still having to push him.[33] When Archbishop Heenan succeeded Archbishop Godfrey in May 1957 he approached the whole issue of the cathedral from his usual ' no nonsense' practical point of view. After a meeting with Scott he wrote to the architect to tell him bluntly that he was not satisfied with the lack of progress on the project. They had already paid him £6,000, he went on, and yet nothing had been done on the main building, so he issued a strongly worded instruction that the architect was not to proceed with the drawings. By November 1957 it was agreed that the Scott cathedral would not be built but that the architect would carry on with the work to complete the Lutyens crypt. When the archbishop announced his intention to hold a competition for a new design and to 'go modern', Scott wrote to say he felt the decision was a wise one but hoped the new plans would not be too contemporary and 'factory-like'.[34] The Archbishop was clear what he wanted from the competitors:

> One day, and I have in mind a day of our own time, there will be a Metropolitan Cathedral on the piazza above the crypt or near the site at present occupied by the open-air altar. There is no question of not building a cathedral. The question is whether to plan a vast edifice or a cathedral to accommodate twelve or fifteen hundred people.

He spoke of the sacred trust arising from the money so far collected: the alternatives were a building that would cost millions and not be completed until the twenty-first century, or a 'small but noble cathedral church' which will cost less than £1,000,000 and be ready some time during the next decade. It was clear, he went on, that if 'we are to build quickly and economically we must begin anew'.[35]

A FRESH VISION

To call Archbishop Heenan a dreamer would normally be about as appropriate as calling Archbishop Godfrey a radical, but on this occasion he allowed himself to dream and shared his visions with his priests and people. He saw the cathedral as a centre of Catholic culture. The 'great Cathedral hall' that was soon to be completed as part of the crypt buildings would be used for music, lectures and meetings, and become a 'vital source of spiritual and intellectual power' for the city and the county. But, he went on, to achieve this there had to be Catholic men and women, both priests and laity, who would use the cathedral buildings in the spirit of apostles. There must be adult education for the growing number of Catholics who had a genuine interest in 'theology, social studies, music and Christian art', with a house they could use to meet each other and foster the work of their apostolate. This house would have another function, too: it would welcome strangers from abroad, who usually left England with an unbalanced picture, having seen London and Oxford but not the Catholic North. There would also be a convent of Religious dedicated to the service of the cathedral and its cultural life – among their many activities would be the fostering of vocations and the care of a Catholic Enquiry Centre and Library. He ended with a promise:

> But we must not sleep and dream. Within the next few months our dreams will be changed into plans … (then) I shall publish something more useful and satisfying than the story of my dreams.

The crypt was opened on 26 October 1958, the Feast of Christ the King, when Archbishop Heenan sang Pontifical High Mass. Fifteen hundred people, representatives of all the parishes in the Archdiocese, attended the ceremony, some of them watching it on screens in the side chapels. During the week of celebrations that followed about 20,000 people visited the crypt or attended Masses there. There were separate receptions for civic dignitaries, attended by the Lord Mayor, Lady Mayoress and a hundred members of the city council, and for the staff of the nearby university.[36]

What these people found was a large rectangular crypt, almost the same size in area as Westminster Cathedral and divided up by huge brick buttresses into a number of smaller areas and chapels. The overwhelming impression was of great brick vaults with granite bases and pillars. Because about half of its height was above ground it did not have the dark and gloomy character usually associated with crypts, though The Tablet's reporter was perhaps exaggerating in describing it as bright and spacious with the vaults soaring up 'with airy lightness'. Lutyens had intended that the interior brick surfaces should be plastered over, but they were left bare and, like the great brick spaces of Westminster Cathedral, they have to the modern eye their own sombre beauty. The other striking features were the massive, stark granite altars, with a minimum of decoration. Off the long processional corridor (then being used as the pontifical chapel) and cut into the rock was the chapel for the tombs of Liverpool archbishops – at present it houses the remains of Thomas Whiteside (1894-1921), Richard Downey (1928 – 1953), and George Andrew Beck (1964 – 1976). This tomb room or Relics Chapel was closed by a rolling door cut from a single piece of marble weighing six tons. Parallel to the processional corridor was what Lutyens had planned as the lower sacristy, but which had been turned into the Cathedral Hall, able to seat about 400 people. The whole crypt had a rock-like stability and a quality that provided a sense of solidity and everlastingness not found in the modern buildings of the time. A modern architectural historian has written that there is enough in the crypt to make visitors 'feel cheated that there is not more of this great building to explore'.[37] Perhaps those who still had romantic attachments to Lutyens' cathedral saw the opening of such a striking building as a vindication, if not a realisation, of their dreams. For Archbishop Heenan a feeling of relief mingled with the obvious feelings of joy: a year before he had promised that the people would soon see something 'really worth while' as a reward for their generosity and sacrifices. Now he felt justified in saying that they would be astonished when they saw the beauty of the new chapel.[38]

It was, however, still only a crypt (though Pevsner's rare cry of admiration, 'But what a crypt!' is fully justified). In 1959 Heenan launched the competition to find an architect who would design a wholly new cathedral and 299 entries came in from all over the world. Sir Basil Spence (architect of the new Coventry Cathedral) and David Stokes (a Catholic architect who had designed a number of church buildings and furnishings in the home counties) were the assessors, and the Archbishop was able to announce the winner in August 1960 – (Sir) Frederick Gibberd. Heenan was almost ecstatic:

> When the people of the North see this great Cathedral rising they will all
> – non-Catholic as well as Catholic – share our pride. I wish I could find
> words to describe the beauty of the new Cathedral.

He went on to say that over three thousand people would be able to kneel around the altar, all with a clear view and none of them more than seventy feet away from the altar rails: 'never before has it been possible to create an intimate atmosphere in so vast a church – this is one of the triumphs of our architect'. The professionals were also full of praise for the striking new design, but the general Catholic body remained to be convinced, referring to it as 'The Mersey Funnel' and one or two other even less favourable epithets.[39]

Building began in October 1962 and progressed steadily, despite fears about escalating costs and a fright when it was found that Gibberd's initial specifications included breaking into the crypt with one of the concrete supports – the problem was solved by reducing the diameter of the building, which also reduced the costs. Pevsner argues that Gibberd's 'stroke of genius' was in finishing off the crypt with a large platform for open-air services and putting his new building on the southern part of the site that was 'unimpeded by Lutyens'. It would seem that Scott had got there before him. There is no doubt, however, that Gibberd achieved something that was both striking and straightforward: striking in its overall effect when seen from a distance, especially as it dominated a city noted for its neo-classical and neo-gothic public buildings, and straightforward, given the availability of modern building techniques – two great ring beams support the main roof and the tower, and are themselves held up by huge sloping concrete ribs, with the spaces in between providing a ring of side chapels, porches and baptistery.[40] Just as Lutyens' and Scott's designs were dominated by a huge dome, the new cathedral was dominated by a large central tower, a 'unique frame for a masterpiece in stained glass'[41] designed as an abstract conception of the Trinity by John Piper and executed by Patrick Reyntiens – truly the crowning glory of the building.

The high altar, a block of white marble, is the natural focal point inside the building. It is directly below the tower and this central position allows the congregation to form almost a complete circle around it (one section is reserved for the choir and organ console), in line with the liturgical thinking of the time, but also creating difficulties in placing the president's and archbishop's seats and having some of the congregation seeing mainly the celebrant's back. The low candle holders and the narrow-stemmed cross were designed by Robert Gooden, while the unusual bronze figure of the crucified Christ was by Elizabeth Frink; together these altar furnishings 'represent all that is best in the diversity and tension of modern design, linked to an appropriate simplicity in the architecture'. The ambo or lectern is an adaptation of the traditional eagle design: two sea-eagles, sculpted in silvered bronze by the local artist Sean Rice, and symbolic of Liverpool's maritime importance, form the main part of the bookrest.[42] Apart from the multi-coloured light from the tower there is little to distract the worshipper's eye: when the building was opened for the first time, many were put off by the bare concrete surfaces and the rather cold blue light from the glass that framed the chapels and other perimeter spaces, but the single-minded focus on the altar is admirable.

From one point of view the side chapels became redundant liturgically with the demise of 'private' low Masses, and were always going to be a challenge to decorate and furnish individually without interfering with the simplicity of the whole. Three of the spaces had obvious functions – the Blessed Sacrament Chapel, the Lady Chapel, and the baptistry, the only ones that Gibberd himself designed. Two large triangular windows in a predominantly blue and gold design give the Blessed Sacrament Chapel 'an explosive but not violent' light, according to the artist Ceri Richards, who also designed the modern-style baldachino, reredos and tabernacle doors.[43] The abstract reredos was criticised at the time, but Gibberd was convinced that it was 'very original' and in time would come to be regarded as a great work of art. The tabernacle doors are very attractive and there is a unity within the chapel, though some think that it sits a little uneasily in the building as a whole. To the left of the altar is a figure of Christ sculpted in bronze by the Liverpool artist, Arthur Dooley. In the Lady Chapel is a large and very fine statue of Mary with Jesus as a young boy, cast in ceramic by Robert Brumby; it is both dignified and symbolic, with the arms of the boy stretched out to embrace but also out to prefigure the position on the cross, while Mary offers him to us all. The chapel is quietly lit by tall windows, designed by Margaret Traherne to throw a rosy light. Another of the perimeter spaces is given over to the baptistry, a circular space entered through bronze doors designed by David Atkins that were the gift of the City of Liverpool. The font, designed by Gibberd, is made of the same white marble as the high altar and is covered by a silver cover; the marble floor was designed by David Atkins.[44] Some have found the high, empty space uninteresting, others have liked its feeling of simplicity; it is certainly unusual for Catholic churches and chapels, so often victims of over-decoration and saintly clutter, to be criticised for being plain.

All the perimeter spaces now have a use and have been successfully integrated, offering places for meditation and devotion and a visual variety, with some striking works of art. Much has been done in the thirty-five years since the opening, to enhance the interior and reduce the impact of the bare (and some said, boring) interior concrete. Hangings of various kinds have been the main decorative feature, most of them designed by Sister Anthony Wilson, SND, and crafted in the Cathedral Art Workshop. Overall, as one would hope with any building designed for the worship of God, the interior is at its best when full with a congregation of worshippers (it seats 2,300 people), when it provides a deep sense of involvement and encourages concentration on what is liturgically important, and this despite drawbacks such as the difficulty of seeing the sanctuary clearly from beyond the first few rows – Gibberd had wanted a 'dished' floor but this was expensive and would have made the congregation into 'spectators' – and imperfect acoustics.[45]

THE OPENING AND AFTER

Cardinal Heenan, now Archbishop of Westminster, presided at the opening of the cathedral as Papal Legate in May 1967. The Duke of Norfolk represented the Queen and the Prime Minister, Harold Wilson, was also present (he was MP for the Huyton constituency of the city), along with the Irish Taosaich, Mr Lynch, Mr Edward Heath, and the Cardinals of Utrecht, Malines and Armagh. It was, of course, a magnificent occasion, planned in detail for a long time beforehand – though not all the plans came to fruition: Archbishop Beck had approached Benjamin Britten for a new Mass for the occasion, but in vain. *The Times* devoted over two and a half complimentary pages to the event, with a front page picture and articles on the building and the archdiocese. In his sermon the Cardinal referred to those who had criticised the whole idea of building a cathedral at that particular time:

> *there is nothing shameful in completing this cathedral when the thoughts of men of good will are with the world's hungry millions ... The opening of this cathedral is in no sense triumphalist. It is a humble act of thanksgiving to God and to the Catholics of past generations. In this cathedral men will be inspired to serve the poor and feed the hungry. There is want in the world, but that is no reason why all spiritual and cultural life should cease to exist.*

Moreover, he continued, there had never been a 'right' time to build cathedrals – they had always been the expression of the faith and love of the faithful, and the present building was no exception:

Sir Frederick Gibberd with his design for the cathedral.

This glory of glass and the crown of Christ the King above us will be paid for by humble people rejoicing that by God's grace they have some share in this superb tribute to our Lord.[46]

The national press had taken an interest in the project from early in 1967, with headlines such as 'Britain's most exciting new building for 25 years'; 'A Cathedral rises like the Phoenix'; 'An upturned cathode ray tube', and 'Magnificent new landmark of the Space Age'. *The Methodist Recorder* commented on 'Liverpool, the City of Two Crowns (and the) New Era of united Christian Concern'.[47]

The builders left the site in June, and later in the year the Cathedral Building Committee was disbanded and replaced by the Cathedral Maintenance Committee: Liverpool had its Catholic Cathedral. It had cost in the region of £2.5 million, but the architect argued that this large overshoot of the original £1 million specification was not his responsibility since it included the costs of the site, work on the crypt, the organ, the furnishings and works of art and the glass (though that was, surely, structural).[48] The cathedral has not become the throbbing spiritual-cum-cultural heart of the archdiocese dreamed of by Archbishop Heenan, though it does provide an exciting venue for a variety of occasions, spiritual and cultural. Despite Downey's and Heenan's stress that it was the Metropolitan Cathedral for the Northern Province, it has not developed a Provincial role, but then it is not clear what such a role could ever have been. Archbishop Worlock was a much more committed supporter of the Cathedral than his predecessor, Archbishop Beck, had ever been, but soon found that not everyone shared his enthusiasm. Some of the clergy found it 'unwelcoming and introverted' and objected to the 'tax' on their parishes to pay for it.[49] It is probably true that it is still developing its diocesan role. Memorable occasions have included the Hillsborough Tragedy Requiem Mass, the services for the National Pastoral Council in 1980 and the Pope's visit in 1982. The Queen visited the Cathedral in 1977, and in that same year the first of the 'Two Cathedrals' services' was inaugurated. A sympathetic though by no means uncritical art historian has concluded that the Cathedral is now in its own right associated with major civic and national occasions, and is in every sense 'a pilgrimage church, hallowed by the joys and sorrows of Liverpool'.[50]

Its essence, however, has to be regular liturgical worship, and in the English cathedral tradition that has to include music. For English Catholics, however, most of that tradition had become centred on the larger monastic houses and seminaries, with Westminster Cathedral the only serious rival to Anglican cathedrals, with a choir school and the provision of regular liturgical music. Despite the outstanding musical tradition created by Mgr Joseph Turner at Upholland, little had filtered through to parish level. Music had, of course, featured among the cultural items that Archbishop Heenan had seen in his vision for the cathedral, but no detailed plans existed for its liturgical provision. In 1960 the Diocesan Director of Music, Canon Edward Murphy of St Mary's, Woolton, had formed a voluntary choir of men's voices to sing in the crypt. Later that year Archbishop Heenan appointed Christopher Symons as the first Master of Music and sixteen boys were recruited for the choir, with Anthony Blackburne as the first Head Chorister. The boys and the men formed the first Cathedral Choir properly speaking. To begin with they sang only High Mass, then they added Friday Compline and later Sunday Vespers to their regular commitments. A little later they added a new and experimental Evening Service, a combination of Vespers and Compline similar to Anglican Evensong (though not intentionally based on it).[51] Under Terence Duffy, Organist 1963-93, and Philip Duffy, Master of Music 1966-96, the musical life of the cathedral flourished. From 1972 the choir toured abroad regularly; in 1979 it made its first commercial recording. Cathedral services have been broadcast frequently on radio and TV, and the choir and music of the cathedral have built up a national and international reputation.

If the diocese wanted a proper choir school that would be good enough to persuade parents to send their sons there, it had to find suitable accommodation and provide a high standard of teaching. At first, in September 1960, the former Jesuit preparatory school, The Gables, was bought, with Fr Wilfrid Malone as headmaster and Fr Vincent Malone (no relation) on the staff. In 1961 the Brothers of Christian Instruction (the de la Mennais Brothers) took over the school and ran it until 1973 as St Joseph's Preparatory and Cathedral Choir School. For a time the Brothers hoped to develop it into an independent boys grammar school, and it became Woolton College in 1967, taking boys aged 11-16. By 1971 it had 107 boys on roll but doubts soon arose about its future, because of the lack of a sixth form, a failure to recruit up to target and the need to appoint more lay teachers on higher salaries. The Brothers decided the grammar school had to close from July 1973, with the choir and preparatory school closing a year later. There followed an anxious period of uncertainty, during which it was not clear that the choir school could, or in the minds of some, should, continue – it was a difficult time for choir schools nationally, witness the traumas of the much longer established Westminster Cathedral school about the same time. Eventually, in 1974, the choir school was incorporated into the large existing schools, St Edward's College and Junior School in Sandfield Park, where it has remained ever since.

The liturgical changes of the post-Vatican II period created challenges for all cathedral choirs. There were demands for a much greater use of English and for much more participation by the congregation; could the choral tradition adapt to these changes without losing its essence and excellence? Archbishop Worlock took a keen interest in these questions: he saw the cathedral as the centre of worship in the diocese and a model for others 'seeking to raise the quality of liturgy in the parishes'. He did not want the congregational singing to be restricted to the singing of hymns and hoped the people could be taught the Ordinary of the Mass in English, thus setting an example for use in parishes.[52] A major difficulty here that soon became apparent was that the cathedral did not have 'a congregation' in the sense of a stable group of regular attenders: it varied from occasion to occasion, even from Sunday to Sunday.

To help develop the non-liturgical cultural side of the Cathedral, a Metropolitan Cathedral Concerts Society was founded in 1968. Its aims were ambitious: to make a valuable contribution to the musical life of Merseyside by promoting concerts and recitals of a nature that are not normally available in the area, and to attract people to the Cathedral by presenting concerts of religious music.[53] Eventually one of the crypt chapels was adapted to become a concert room, and a mixed-voice Cantata Choir and a Cathedral Orchestra were established. The crypt also houses the Archdiocesan Archives and the Cathedral's Art Workshop. The latter started in 1981 and has provided vestments, hangings and banners. Among its major outside commissions have been hangings for St Peter's, Rome (for the canonisation of the British Martyrs in 1987), the Birmingham Arena (for the Millennium Mass) and Gloucester Cathedral.[54]

From the start the experimental building techniques used in the cathedral's construction caused problems. The dignity of liturgical celebrations was spoiled by intrusive rainwater as flat roofs leaked (of course), aluminium panels split (because no allowance had been made for thermal movement) and the magnificent glass separated from its frame as sunlight affected the fixing resin. There were other serious problems, and in

The Cathedral viewed from Hope Street, with its magnificent new approach.

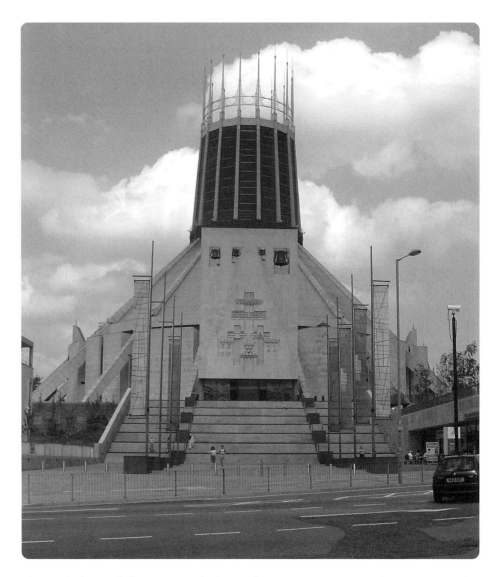

the end the archdiocese sued the architect, engineers and contractors for negligence; after five years of litigation the case was settled out of court in 1987 – the archdiocese received a substantial payment, though much less than it had claimed. This and a 'Cathedral Roof Fund' provided a total of £3 million, but it was soon clear that piecemeal repairs would not be practicable or sensible and a full restoration programme was launched, with considerable help from English Heritage. The restoration work was completed by the late summer of 2003. Also finished that autumn (with the help of European Funding) was new work to provide a grand flight of steps leading up to the main entrance, as originally planned by Gibberd, along with landscaped gardens and a Visitor Centre.[55] It was exactly 150 years since Bishop Brown had launched the original idea of a cathedral for his new diocese and the moment was suitably celebrated with a Solemn High Mass and Service of Dedication on the Feast of Christ the King.

Notes

1 Burke, p.129.

2 Swarbrick, 'Cathedral', p.873.

3 AAL *Liverpolitana*, pastoral letter Good Shepherd Sunday 1922.

4 *Ibid.*

5 Swarbrick, 'Cathedral', pp.873-4.

6 *Ibid.*, p.875.

7 Waller, p.324; AAL Cathedral Archive, S2 : The Lutyens Cathedral, I: 1929-53, A: Lutyens' Appointment and Purchase of Site. See A/12,13,22,26, May-Aug. 1930.

8 *Liverpool Daily Post*, 1.9.1930.

9 Christopher Hussey, *The Life of Sir Edwin Lutyens* (1950), pp.527-43. See also A.S.G. Butler, *The Architecture of Sir Edwin Lutyens*, 3 vols. (1950), vol.3; Arts Council of Gt Britain, *Lutyens* (1981).

10 AAL Cathedral, S2 I A/1, Lutyens to Downey, 9.7.1929.

11 Hussey, *Life*, pp.528, 543.

12 AAL Cathedral, S2 I B: Design and Build; B/4, Lutyens to Downey 18.2.1930. Visit to Rome, May 1932.

13 *Ibid.*, B/8, Lutyens to Adamson 6.9.1930; B/9, Lutyens to Downey 23.9.1930; Hussey, *Life*, p.535; currently being restored, National Museum & Galleries, Merseyside.

14 John Nelson Tarn, 'Liverpool's Two Cathedrals', D. Wood (ed.), *The Church and the Arts; SCH* 28 (1992), pp.537-69, at p.557; Abp. Heenan, *A Crown of Thorns: An Autobiography 1951-1963* (1974), p.282.

15 N. Pevsner, *The Buildings of England: Lancashire, I The Industrial and Commercial South* (1969), pp.191-3; Lutyens to *Country Life* LXXI, May 1932, p.553; Hussey, Life, p.531.

16 Hussey, Life, p.533.

17 Archbishop Downey (ed.), *Re-Building the Church in England* (1933), pp.1-9, 'Let us Rise up and Build'; among other contributors were Belloc, Chesterton, Bede Camm OSB.

18 AAL Cathedral, S2 I A/2, Insurance Co. to Downey, 24.9.1930; A/3, Lutyens to Downey 17.12.1931; Swarbrick, 'Cathedral', p.877.

19 AAL Cathedral, S2 V: General Papers and Correspondence, A/43,59,82,83, various bishops to Downey Mar.-Dec. 1931.

20 *Ibid.*, A/9,30, various publicity ideas; S2 VI:Expenditure, C/15, Mgr T.Turner 'Ways and Means', c.1952.

21 AAL Cathedral, S2 II, The Lutyens Cathedral II, A: Design and Build; A/41 Downey to Shute, 23.9.1936.

22 *Ibid.*, A/73,74,75,111, Lutyens to various, June 1937-Sept. 1938.

23 *Ibid.*, S2 VII A16 Butler to Turner 17.12.1953; Turner's reply 18.12.1953. Lutyens on fanfares, etc., S2 I B/9 to Downey 23.9.1930.

24 *Ibid.*, S2 I B/12,ff: Sept. 1930-Sept. 1931; on Doyle, *The Catholic Who's Who* (1938).

25 *The Tablet*, 10.6.1933, pp.731-4.

26 AAL Cathedral, S2 II A/2, 4: Downey to Lutyens 10 and 22 Feb.1934; AAL Downey, S1 III, A/2: Ad clerum 1931-39: Sept. 1936.

27 *Ibid.*, S2 II A/133 (bundle), Ministry of Works and Lutyens, 1 Jan. – 22 April 1941; 143, Lutyens to Ministry 2.7.1941; 151, Lutyens to Downey 16/17.3.1942; 153, on Lutyens' heirs 15.4.1942; 167, Emily Lutyens to Committee 22.1.1944.

28 *Ibid.*, A/168 (bundle), on appointment of Scott 5.1. – 19.7. 1945; AAL *Liverpolitana*, pastoral letter Oct. 1947; Turner to Butler, note 23 above.

29 Mgr T. Turner, 'Cathedral Jottings' *C.R.* April 1955, pp.83-9, for changes, costs and plans.

30 AAL Cathedral, S2 VII: Lutyens Crypt and Scott Reduction, 1953-62: A/23, Scott's proposed design, 14 – 31.12.1954; A/28, Godfrey's Pastoral Feb. 1955. Godfrey Collection, S1 I A/48, ad clerum 2.7.1955; A/53-7, Chapter discussions.

31 *Ibid.*, A/20, Scott's Report on Lutyens' plans, 13.9.1954; Turner,'Cathedral Jottings' p.84.

32 *Ibid.*, A/167-9; 185 (favourable responses); 184, 188-201 – over 100 items on the controversy, including press cuttings and letters, Feb.1955-Jan.1957.

33 *Ibid.*, A/83, Scott to Godfrey, 29.11.1955; 90, 92, 101, Committee to Scott and replies, May – Nov. 1956.

34 *Ibid.*, A/115, Heenan to Scott 16.9.1957; 118, items on end of Scott's design, 21.10 – 7.11.1957; 154, Scott to Heenan 19.1.1959.

35 Archbishop Heenan, 'The Archbishop's Dreams', in Mgr C. Taylor (ed.), *Souvenir of Solemn Opening of the Metropolitan Cathedral Crypt Liverpool* (nd).

36 *Ibid.*

37 *The Tablet,* 25.10.1958; Tarn, p.557; Pevsner, pp.192-3.

38 AAL *Lady Chapel Appeal,* 7.9.1958.

39 AAL Cathedral, S2 VIII: The Architectural Competition 1959-60; S2 IX: Gibberd Cathedral, A/1, 67, praise of design, Sept. 1961. See also S2 XX A/9 (bundle): Professional views about the cathedral; Heenan, *Crown of Thorns,* ch. 20.

40 Pevsner, pp.193-7; Tarn, pp.557-60.

41 *The Metropolitan Cathedral of Christ the King Liverpool: The History of Liverpool's Catholic Cathedral* (nd), p.20; beautifully illustrated, a guidebook as well as a history.

42 *Ibid.*, pp.22-3; Tarn, p.566.

43 Letter from Richards to Mr Walker, 5.4.1968; copy kindly supplied by Mgr P. Cookson.

44 *The Metropolitan Cathedral*, pp.31-3,38; Tarn, p.562; Pevsner, p.196; AAL Cathedral, S2 X A/136 Gibberd to Beck, 9.5.1967.

45 AAL Cathedral, S2 X A/141, 144, Beck to Gibberd and replies re floor, 12-13.7.1967; Mgr P. Cookson, *We Give Thee Thanks* (Nov. 2003) p.5.

46 *The Times,* 15.5.1967; *The Tablet,* 20.5.1967, p.569.

47 AAL Press Cuttings File, Feb.-June 1967.

48 Cookson, p.3.

49 AAL Beck Collection, Minutes of Meeting at Cathedral, Sept. 1976, p.8; letter from Mr Terry Duffy to Abp. Worlock, 20.4.1976.

50 Tarn, p.566.

51 AAL Heenan Collection, S1 II, A: pastoral letter 30.10.1960.

52 AAL Beck Collection, Abp Worlock to Terry Duffy, 25.4.1976.

53 *Ibid.*, 'Liverpool Metropolitan Cathedral Concert Society', 1968.

54 Cookson, pp.19-20.

55 *Ibid.*, pp.13-8.

CHAPTER 16 TRADITION AND TRANSITION: THE POST-WAR YEARS

Those Catholics who joined in the celebrations in 1950 to mark the centenary of the Restoration of the Hierarchy had every reason to feel proud of their Church. For the past thirty years it had experienced a steady growth, whereas the other major denominations in England and Wales had been through a period of decline. It had also spread beyond its traditional areas of strength to create strong footholds in the south and in the new towns.[1] In general terms the rest of English society accepted its presence with greater toleration than before, although for most people Catholicism was still a strange world set apart – and Catholics themselves were happy to be different. Converts were joining the Church in large numbers every year, adding to the confidence that Catholic leaders felt in their position, and Catholic lay people were active as never before in the Catholic Evidence Guild, the Catholic Social Guild, the Legion of Mary and the Young Christian Workers – all designed in their own ways to take the Catholic message out to others and to strengthen the spiritual life of their members. In the archdiocese, twenty-two new parishes were founded in the 1950s, with a further twenty-nine in the following decade – the most prolific decades in the diocese's history. It was a time when it seemed to be 'all coming together' for English Catholicism; it has even been said that it was a good time to be an English Catholic Bishop.[2]

The society in which this post-war confident English Catholicism lived, and which it was hoping to convert, was changing so rapidly and presenting so many different challenges that one may ask how justified the confidence was. Among the more obvious changes was, first of all, a greater social mobility with a growing Catholic middle-class. The old working-class communities were breaking up and the new 'towns' like Kirkby, Speke and Huyton failed to recreate the old community spirit, though some of the old Catholic loyalties remained. Secondly, the welfare state was here to stay and was welcomed in practice by the great majority of lay Catholics as freeing them from poverty, fear and disease. Some of the bishops feared the damage it might do to the rather abstract Catholic ideal of the family, and had concerns about the state taking over functions traditionally carried out by the Church, especially through its Religious Orders. But there was no going back.

A third area of change was education. Under the 1944 Education Act grammar and secondary modern schools were replacing former all-age parochial schools, from which only a small number had gone on to grammar schools and still fewer to tertiary education. A growing number of Catholics were going to university – at least 5,000 were graduating each year by 1960, with another 4,000 or so qualifying from teacher training colleges. Finally, no summary of social change in these years would be complete without mentioning the beginnings of a more even distribution of goods and increasing materialism; these were the years of Macmillan's 'You've never had it so good'. Bishop Beck's statement in 1950 that there were good reasons for believing that the drift to materialism was at an end was proving to be wildly optimistic.[3]

Would the Catholic Church in England and Wales, and more specifically in the North West, be able to cope with these changes – more importantly, would it embrace them and go forward with its people to sanctify this new society, or would it remain suspicious of it? Some of the difficulties in adapting to the changes sprang from a common Catholic mind-set prevalent at the time, a mind-set based on a solid belief in the certainty of the Catholic position. There were, indeed, some Catholic writers who were beginning to realise how the changed society might impact on the traditional Church structures and attitudes. Joan Brothers of the University of Liverpool did a survey of the attitudes and beliefs of those young Liverpool Catholics who were attending Catholic grammar schools as opposed to parish schools.[4] As we have seen, the parish school had played a major and positive role in parish life, helping to define the loyalties of parishioners, being something to be proud of and playing an important part in both the sacramental and social life of the parish – not for nothing had bishops continued to urge priests to build a school before they built a church. Clearly, the increasing number of Catholic children attending non-parochial schools could undermine that traditional role; might it not also change the relationship of the children to their parish and its priests? This was not just a question of geography: after all, grammar schools, and still more the tertiary education they increasingly led on to, aimed to develop more explicitly in their pupils ideals of leadership and independence of thought.

This was what Joan Brothers set out to examine, asking such questions as whether young Catholics who had attended grammar school regarded their home parish as part of a cultural way of living from which their education and social status had removed them, and whether the parish clergy remained their 'moral mentors'. Two of her findings stand out:

1 The old devotion and loyalty to the parochial settings have come to have little meaning to most of these young people.
2 The findings of this research reveal the inability of the parochial structure, as it is currently understood by clergy and people in Liverpool, to absorb the impact of new attitudes and ideas.[5]

In a letter to teachers soon after he moved to Liverpool, Archbishop Heenan recognised that things were changing and acknowledged that a drawback of the new inter-parochial secondary schools was a lack of contact between priest and children and their 'isolation' from parish life. As a partial remedy he wanted to experiment with appointing a chaplain to each secondary school, a local priest who would spend some hours in the school each week, giving instruction; the result should benefit not just religious instruction but 'the whole spiritual and moral tone of the school'. It might even be possible, he thought, to have the children divided into their parish groups for one period a week, to allow their home clergy to speak to them and so 'keep alive their interest in the life of the parish'.[6] This was an honest if unrealistic attempt to cope with the changes – unrealistic, because it ignored other factors that were also working against the old parochial solidarities.

As a second local example, we may take Fr Conor Ward, with his slightly earlier study of a Liverpool parish writing of the 1950s he pointed out the strengths and weaknesses of the traditional parish structure: it was ideal for priests getting to know their people, for creating a strong sense of loyalty, for weekly collections and regular home visiting by the clergy. But when it came to providing the more specialised services required by a changing situation (e.g. out of school RE for those at non-Catholic schools; adult Christian education), it appeared to be a somewhat restricted unit and the intense loyalty and rivalries created by the system made co-operation difficult if not impossible. As he put it, the structure had arisen in the different situation that was Catholic Liverpool at the end of the nineteenth century and it had not as yet adapted itself sufficiently to the new conditions and to a changed situation in the mid-twentieth century.[7]

He also commented on the relationship between priests and people. The personal relationship that existed between the priests of the parish and the parishioners, he argued, was the most important single factor in the social structure of the parish – and this depended mainly on the regular house visits by the priests. One might ask, what would replace this if either the number of clergy declined and the parish could not be covered, or when social mores made such visits increasingly difficult? Finally, Ward made a strong case for social investigation of the kind he had undertaken: if adaptation were to take place without a thorough examination of the needs of the new situation, it would be little more than ad hoc tinkering: 'A religious institution ... ought not, and in practice cannot, be isolated from the development of the social system'.[8]

Both writers were raising important questions at the start of a period of obvious change, which if considered seriously might have helped prepare priests and people for that change. Instead, the bishops seemed to regard sociologists (even good Catholic ones) as a threat to the status-quo and not as a window on life 'through which we ought to look if we are really eager for the spread of Christ's kingdom'.[9] Might it not have been useful, perhaps, if both Brothers and Ward had formed the basis for discussion at clerical conferences, for example? But it seems that the clerical authorities were certain that the traditional parish structures were the best way of organising the Church in any locality, and there was no room for discussion, least of all with lay people. As Brothers concluded, it remained to be seen how the Church would deal with the changes, but:

> *might not a preliminary step in adapting to the changing social situation*
> *be the better understanding of the behaviour and ways of thinking of*
> *those living in it, and in particular of their needs and potentialities …*[10]

There were other critics who questioned whether the efforts of organisations such as the CEG were as effective as their energy deserved because the catechetics they used were fundamentally out of date. Mgr Ronald Knox complained in 1956 that 'our Catholic apologetic, nearly all of it, strikes the modern reader as inhuman', and criticised 'the pettifogging appeal to isolated Scriptural phrases, torn from their context'; it was, he felt, 'essentially unreal'.[11] This foreshadowed Cardinal Suenens' (admittedly one of the most aware leaders in the Church) warning in 1962 of the danger of the Church not even sharing a common language with the secularised society it was trying to save. It was essential, he argued, for Church agencies to be willing to change radically to meet these challenges – 'the committed Christian must belong to two worlds, that of God and that of mankind, and can only be the mediator between the two by being loyal to both at the same time'.

Suenens also warned of the danger of taking for granted that the good times would necessarily continue or even get better. Whether the Church liked to admit it or not, he argued:

> *We no longer live in an age when daily lives were solidly framed in*
> *tradition, and institutions were there to safeguard values that were never*
> *called in question. On all sides tradition is foundering and conformism*
> *falling into ruins …*[12]

It is interesting that he mentioned the decline in conformism. One result of the certainty that marked the mindset of Church authorities was that obedience was seen as a principal virtue, to be inculcated at all times. In this context, the handbook of the excellent and popular Legion of Mary could say, 'The Legion expects from its children everywhere that spirit of *heroic and sweet docility* to proper authority of every sort'; elsewhere it spoke of the '*virtue of docility* to ecclesiastical authority'.[13] And that authority expected to be obeyed even in matters that might have been thought outside its remit: Archbishop Godfrey in 1958 forbade the Catholic Nuclear Disarmament Group to discuss the issue of war and peace.[14]

Cardinal Suenens had been talking of the situation of nuns in a changing world. One change that was affecting them was a decline in vocations, already happening although the convents were full. To take just one example of a Congregation active in Liverpool: the Religious of the Sacred Heart of Mary (RSHM) ran a large grammar school (Seafield) in the north end of the city and also taught in a number of parochial schools. Each of the three preceding decades had seen an average of 144 postulants (only 23 from Lancashire, however, in the three decades against a massive 395 from Ireland), but 1950-59 produced only 79, while in 1960-69 the number dropped to 19.[15] Clearly, the decline in vocations started in a serious way before the Second Vatican Council even met and would make a continuation of their traditional input to Catholic schooling very difficult.

It would be quite wrong to suggest that all those in authority in the Church refused to change and maintained a blind optimism that all was well. Apart from anything else, they were well aware that losses through leakage were far greater than gains through conversions. There were, too, important changes taking place in the Church's thinking in key areas. Two papal encyclicals of the 1940s were slowly revolutionising the approach to the Catholic study of Scripture and to liturgical practice and theory – *Divino Afflante Spiritu* (1943) and *Mediator Dei* (1947). Students at Upholland were fortunate to have two lecturers in Scripture who were in touch with the latest Biblical scholarship – Fr Alec Jones (1906-70) and Fr Tom Worden (1920-73). The latter edited *Scripture,* a scholarly journal that carried articles by leading Continental scholars, while Alec Jones was responsible for editing and launching the translation of the *Jerusalem Bible,* again based on up-to-date interpretations and freed from the necessity of regarding the Vulgate as the inspired text. At last there was some relief from the dead hand of anti-Modernism that had stifled genuine enquiry for so long, especially in the seminaries under rectors like Mgr Dean of Upholland.

~

The 1950s and early 1960s saw three archbishops in Liverpool of quite different stamp, but in their own ways equally certain about the traditional Catholic position. The first was Archbishop Downey, whose last years were marked by frequent illnesses, though he was still able to carry out ordinations, confirmations and the laying of foundation stones. He died in Gateacre Grange nursing home on 16th June 1953. Though he was no longer the national figure he had been, his death was covered in all the national papers with extensive photographs of the funeral procession and the thousands lining the route. The papers also published the details of his will: he had left £55,996 (duty £19,658). This was a sum certainly inexplicable, if not scandalous, to ordinary Catholics, even though he left £10,000 to the cathedral, £5,000 to each of two sisters and various sums to his housekeeper and former servants, a number of hospitals and his doctors. The panegyric was preached by Bishop Flynn of Lancaster, a life-long friend and colleague, who described the former archbishop as 'a bright meteor flashing through the sky of twentieth-century Catholicism'. He was buried in the special tomb room in the crypt of his beloved cathedral.[16]

He was succeeded by William Godfrey, who later moved to become Archbishop of Westminster in 1956. William Godfrey was a native of Liverpool, having been born in Kirkdale in 1889. After ordination in Rome in 1916, he had served as curate at St Michael's, West Derby, until 1918 when he joined the teaching staff at Ushaw, where he stayed until 1930. Then he became rector of the Venerable English College, Rome, until 1938 where, as Plumb says 'the serenity of outlook and resolute will never to be perplexed, which remained with him all his life, shone brilliantly'. He became the first Apostolic Delegate in London, and titular archbishop of Cius, in 1938, dealing with the British government during the difficult years of the war.[17] Then in November 1953 he was appointed to Liverpool.

He was to be there for only three years before moving to Westminster (appointed December 1956, enthroned February 1957), but he undertook a complete Visitation of the archdiocese and opened a number of new parishes, as well as being heavily involved with the cathedral (see Chapter 15). A speech he gave to the students at Ushaw in 1960 reveals some of his inner character:

> We must ask Our Lord to give us a spirit such as that of the English Martyrs, and a love of the priesthood, so that we may rise in the morning, go through our daily life, do our duty, say our prayers, try to be humble, patient, gentle and kind, and to give a good example to all around us.[18]

It was a far from ignoble ideal to put before aspiring priests, but it indicated a mind unwilling and probably unable to see that the times were changing and that the Church would inevitably be affected by the changes. His pastoral letters show his own deep faith and devotion to Our Lady, his high regard for the priestly office, his awareness of evil and a straightforward distrust and suspicion of the world. Sundays were to be kept holy, television was a threat, and Roman directives on all matters were to be followed rigidly.

He held a diocesan synod in 1955. There was no new legislation and little indication of any change of approach. He stressed the need for proper financial care – accounts were to be kept properly; the purchase of parish cars was to be referred to the Bishop, Mass offerings should not be allowed to accumulate. He urged the importance of parish visiting by priests, of having a children's service on Sunday afternoon 'even if only a handful come' – a difficult part of pastoral life, he admitted, but an essential one if children were to be kept in touch. Priests should always maintain due priestly reserve when dealing with lay people and with regard to recreation; it was unlawful to discard clerical dress during holidays, and the law forbidding priests to attend theatres was intended to 'lift the priest of God above the ordinary pursuits and pleasures of the world'.[19]

In one area he did make minor changes. Archbishop Downey had continued the strict line on mixed marriages, with Whiteside's unbending Instruction on the evils of mixed marriages read out each year, with only a few minor alterations in its language. It did not prevent mixed marriages, which averaged out at just over a thousand a year for the years 1943 – 53, and comprised anything from a a quarter to a third of all marriages involving Catholics in any one year. Perhaps surprisingly, given his generally cautious approach to change and rigidity over the Church's laws, in 1954 Archbishop Godfrey ordered the omission of the sentence in the Instruction that claimed

William Godfrey, fourth Archbishop of Liverpool 1953-1956, later Cardinal Archbishop of Westminister, 1957-1963.

that Catholics should have 'an abhorrence' *(sic)* of mixed marriages, and elsewhere inserted the word 'deplores' instead of 'detests' to describe the attitude of the Church to them.[20]

There were some priests, however, including the Vicar General, Mgr Alban Atkins, who were totally opposed to the annual reading of the Instruction in any form. It served no useful purpose, he argued; its language was too harsh, and damaging to children who had to listen to their parents' marriages being denigrated; it did not prevent mixed marriages – its condemnations were too generalised and its yearly repetition meant people did not take any notice of it. What was needed, he concluded, was positive instruction and proper preaching about the sacramental dignity and sacred character of marriage and the importance of choosing the right partner, not negative repetitions of the 'stark realism' of the Church's laws. He believed that the Instruction probably had no meaning at all for young Catholics until they faced the prospect of going to the priest about their particular marriage. In the case of weak Catholics, he argued, a refusal to grant a dispensation 'practically excommunicates them – and so little is gained'. Priests often found, he continued, that the prospect of marriage to a non-Catholic brought erring sheep to the door of the presbytery. Sympathy and understanding could bring them back if they were treated handsomely, though firmly; the granting of a dispensation provided the opportunity for some instruction and a return to the sacraments; it also would allow the priest later entrance to the home.

Clerical attitudes were clearly divided. According to the Vicar General, in a rather damning indictment, those parish priests who supposedly held out against all mixed marriages were those who did least about them beyond being 'unpleasant and uncooperative'. They were happy to leave other priests to deal with their people's emotional problems. A change of parish priest in a parish, or the arrival of a 'bright energetic curate', soon brought to light the excessive number of irregular marriages and a host of disgruntled people and a number of lost converts. On the other hand, he argued that those who appeared to favour mixed marriages were those who took a proper and industrious attitude to all marriages, 'who facilitate and enhance the occasion by cheerful and intelligent co-operation', who dealt conscientiously with prenuptial enquiry forms and instruction and, in general, 'displayed a priestly zeal'. In addition, they worked hard to make converts in mixed marriage cases, or used their skill and sympathy to wean the Catholic party away from the proposed union; if this failed, they tried everything to avoid it being a disastrous marriage. They promoted the ideal of a Christian home, broke down ignorance and prejudice among non-Catholics – it was 'all hard practical work'. If Atkins' portraits of the two kinds of priests are even half true, it would seem that clerical attitudes to the practical issues surrounding mixed marriages had changed little since Bishop Goss's day.

Most of this had little effect on Archbishop Godfrey. A completely revised Instruction in 1955 began with a typically cautious statement: there was safety in thinking with the Church on this question, and error and danger in departing in any way from its teaching – 'the Church is obliged to teach and we are obliged to listen with due humility'.[21] The message was as uncompromising as before, but the language was free of the derogatory words traditionally used. The Church's concern was not just with the faith of any children of a mixed marriage: the new home began with essential differences between husband and wife: 'there is a wound in the very heart of the family and it would require exceptional virtue … to escape its baneful effects'. In contrast with this was the beauty of a Catholic marriage, celebrated with a nuptial Mass in which the bride and bridegroom 'while offering themselves one to the other in true love', unite that offering with that of Our Lord to the Father. The Archbishop concluded by praying that young Catholics would understand this and that there would be an increased proportion of Catholic marriages as a result.

With regard to the more general relations of Catholics with other Christians, both Downey and Godfrey followed an equally rigid line, proving to be completely unbending on the matter and refusing all requests for permission for Catholic mayors or councillors to attend official civic services, on the grounds that scandal would ensue. Their principle was that nothing should be done by Catholics that might suggest they recognised the status of non-Catholic clergymen as genuine ministers of religion. It was the same principle that lay behind the refusal to allow Catholics to take any part in weddings in non-Catholic churches, as bridesmaids, for example. In exceptional circumstances Archbishop Godfrey was prepared to allow bridesmaids to attend, but only if they were not the official witnesses to the wedding.[22]

Local bishops, in fact, were left no opportunity to be flexible in these and related matters, even if they had wanted to be: a decree from the Holy Office in 1949 laid down an extremely rigorist approach that Catholics were to follow. The Holy Office was concerned at the unofficial ecumenical movements that had arisen during the war in a number of European countries and wished to re-establish traditional practice; it was also worried by the launch of the World Council of Churches in 1948. The decree opened with the clearest of statements: 'The Catholic Church takes no part in ecumenical conferences or meetings' and ended by supporting steps towards the re-union of all Christians in so far as that meant other Christians becoming Catholics.

In an ad clerum of May 1950, Downey explained the implications of this decree for his clergy and people as laid down by the English and Welsh bishops. Catholics were bound to view sympathetically the widely held desire 'of so many of our countrymen' for unity in religion, and they must support it with their prayers. But the main work in bringing back other Christians to the one fold of the true Church of Christ belonged to the bishops and so:

1. Meetings for discussion of religious problems should only be initiated by the local Bishop or with his written permission.
2. The subject matter to be discussed at such meetings must be approved by the Bishop in advance.
3. Any publication on these matters, including letters to the press, whether by lay people or priests (Secular or Religious), had to be submitted in advance to the Bishop for censorship.

In addition, no priest or lay person should attend meetings convened by non-Catholics to discuss religious matters, even if held privately, without the express permission of the Bishop. Finally, Downey reminded the clergy, in words borrowed from the original decree, that the best way of bringing people into the unity of the Church was 'the faith of Catholics associated with good moral conduct and an edifying life'.[23]

The decree fitted in well with Downey's life-long attitude to Christian re-union. Many years before this, in 1922, while still with the Catholic Missionary Society, he had addressed the Anglican Society of St Thomas of Canterbury on the question. His talk set out clearly the fundamentalist Roman Catholic view that reunion could only mean other Christians joining Rome, the always-undivided Church – there was no such concept in Catholic theology as 'the Church divided'. He attacked two current approaches to reunion, one which said, 'You give up some of your beliefs and I'll give up some of mine', and the other which said, 'Doctrine does not really matter, what is important is how we feel and act'. He recommended taking St Thomas Aquinas as the starting point in any discussions on the topic, because he provided a pre-Reformation synthesis of Christian belief based on a safe method of combining the use of reason and revelation. The lecture illustrated Downey's skill but also his apparent inability to pass up an opportunity to score points, in what must have seemed to his listeners a somewhat insulting manner. In this case he told his audience that 'principles of disruption and aspirations for unity' had gone hand-in-hand in England since the Reformation, because, to quote Belloc, the English people had lost the 'tradition of clear thinking at the Reformation'.[24]

Godfrey acknowledged that the rigid Catholic approach to attendance at civic services and the like might be misunderstood, but Catholics could not take part in non-Catholic worship as to do so might be interpreted as sharing the Protestant conception of a plurality of Christian Churches. The following year he consulted the Northern Bishops on these questions and reported that he found them altogether united and unwilling to budge at all because of a fear of religious indifferentism. He later made a suggestion that Catholic mayors and councillors might like to send a Protestant deputy to such services. When James Rimmer of Formby asked Godfrey for permission to attend a civic religious function as a Councillor and a JP, Godfrey laid out the Catholic principles behind his refusal:

1. Catholic mayors and Councillors should not accept invitations to attend civic services in non-Catholic churches.
2. Non-Catholic Mayors etc. should not be invited to Catholic services. We should welcome them if they ask to come but 'we ought not to embarrass them by sending an invitation.
3. With regard to weddings and funerals, Catholics in public life could attend 'provided they took no part in the service … it is understood that they are there simply as friends, and not to worship.

When asked whether a Catholic could join the Royal and Ancient Order of Buffaloes, he decided against it because their 'Hymn to the Spirit of Truth', and the fact that they had their own form of funeral service, meant there was a danger of religious indifference.[25]

John Carmel Heenan, fifth Archbishop of Liverpool 1957-1963; later Cardinal Archbishop of Westminister, 1963-1975.

Archbishop Heenan succeeded Godfrey in 1956. He announced to his rather unbelieving clergy that in general he wanted to imitate the 'calm and prudent zeal' of his predecessor – an altogether different reputation had preceded him from his previous diocese, Leeds, exemplified in a story told in his presence at a reception shortly after his arrival. According to this, when he had visited the pope the meeting had lasted an inordinately long time; the pope had eventually emerged in tears to say, 'He's moved me to Avignon!' Only the new Archbishop was not amused.[26]

In ecumenical matters, he was cautious to begin with and still afraid of 'scandal'. In 1961, for example, he corresponded with Cardinal Willebrands (of the Secretariat for Christian Unity) about the advisability of attending the coming enthronement of the Archbishop of Canterbury (Ramsey) – Willebrands had assured him that there would be an invitation from Lambeth Palace for Heenan and/or Godfrey to attend if such an invitation were likely to be accepted. After serious thought, Heenan replied that the time was not yet ripe, without risking 'very great scandal' (italics crossed out in the original). He argued that the faithful were still puzzled by the changed relations between Catholics and Protestants and it would be some time before any joint religious action could take place without fear of misunderstanding. He would, however, be willing to attend any social or civic function in Ramsey's honour. Later in the same year, when the new Coventry Cathedral was being opened, he wrote to the Anglican Bishop of Coventry to say, as tactfully as possible, that he thought it would be a mistake for any English Catholic clergy to attend, even though a number of German Catholic Bishops might be doing so – 'if Catholic clergy were to attend the service in the Cathedral the cause of Christian Unity would be hindered rather than helped ...' He offered to write to the German bishops to explain the English situation.[27]

In 1962 he wrote to his clergy to explain his thoughts about re-union; he believed that charity required them to be honest with other Christians:

> the only way to Christian unity is for our beloved but separated brethren to renounce the errors of the Reformation and to return to the fold of Peter. We need not put it so boldly as this but it is mischievous to suggest that there is any possible compromise in this matter.[28]

It was a key part of Heenan's thinking that a bishop could be, indeed should be, as pastorally pragmatic as circumstances demanded, but this was wholly divorced from any questioning of the doctrinal teaching of the Church or the value of its traditional structures.

THE BOMB AND OTHER CONCERNS

Meanwhile, a key national debate in the 1950s and 1960s concerned the morality of nuclear warfare and the role of the nuclear deterrent in maintaining peace. Archbishop Godfrey wrote to Cardinal Griffin about this in 1955. He was nervous about the bishops speaking out individually on the issues lest they failed to give a unanimous message and so gave 'a handle to pacifist propaganda'. With regard to the hydrogen bomb, he felt there was nothing they could usefully add to the Pope's messages on the subject in 1954 and until the bishops met and agreed a statement the best they could do would be to refer people to what the Pope had said. He had translated the Pope's speech for publication by the CTS.[29]

Archbishop Heenan was approached on a number of occasions for a definitive statement on behalf of those who wanted nuclear weapons and the idea of using them as a deterrent condemned as anti-Christian. He took a cautious line, in one case replying to a Quaker correspondent that the bomb did not alter the basic Christian approach to the killing of non-combatants in war. He quoted the American bombing of Japanese cities before Hiroshima, when one raid alone had killed something like 85,000 people; there was no difference between this and using the hydrogen bomb. It was, in any case, a world issue and he thought that the forthcoming Council in Rome might well deal with it (he was writing in 1959). To another correspondent he quoted the British bombing of Germany and thought men of good will should be working for general disarmament and not concentrating just on the nuclear issue; he was not at all sure that unilateral disarmament by the West would be followed by the East – more likely it would be followed by armed attack.[30]

Heenan's wrote his longest letter on the subject to Fr Anthony Kenny, a Liverpool priest who had asked for permission to accept an invitation to speak to the Crosby branch of CND. The Archbishop was worried that whatever Kenny might say would be taken as the official teaching of the Church on the subject because non-Catholics did not believe that Catholics could have differing views on moral matters. He again raised the hope that the Council would discuss the matter (it was now December 1962) and he confided to Kenny that he had raised the issue very briefly in a speech on the opening day of the Council; he would do all in his power to ensure that it did not disperse before considering the whole question. He thought the issues involved were more complex than the proponents of both sides seemed to assume. He personally thought that it was quite moral to keep the weapons as a deterrent without telling the enemy that you would never use them. Kenny was a convinced unilateralist, a point of view he put forward when commenting on Pope John's encyclical *Pacem in Terris* the following year, to balance the opposite interpretation put forward by Norman St John Stevas; both were writing for the *Catholic Pictorial.* When some of the other bishops objected to Kenny's article, Heenan stopped him writing on such matters in the *Pictorial,* though not in papers like *The Tablet,* whose readers, Heenan said, were well able to take care of themselves. What he feared was that the *Pic's* readers would be confused and take Kenny's view as official teaching – though Kenny was quite aware of the different approaches needed for different readers. What is clear is that Heenan had a very low opinion of the ability of these 'simple' Catholics to understand anything but 'the simplest statements' as they were largely 'uneducated' and only 'semi-literate'. While generally very understanding towards Kenny and his views, he did object when Kenny asked in his article whether Catholic workers at Cammell Lairds in Birkenhead should accept work on a Polaris submarine. The Archbishop was genuinely unsure about the whole question; as he wrote to Kenny, 'It is because I am in doubt that I have made no statement'.[31]

Mention has just been made of the *Catholic Pictorial.* Archbishop Heenan announced the launch of this new diocesan newspaper in October 1961, with the first issue due out in January 1962. It was to replace the monthly *Cathedral Record,* the official organ of the archdiocese for thirty years. While sales would benefit the Cathedral Building fund by as much as £2,000 a year if Catholics supported the new paper, its main aim was to provide information about what was happening across the archdiocese and entertainment for Catholic families. Heenan added, perhaps rather optimistically, that it would also inform non-Catholics of Catholic activities and spread the Catholic viewpoints on local and national issues. The editors were Mgr Cyril Taylor and Mr Norman Cresswell, managing director of the *Birmingham Catholic Pictorial Ltd,* supported by a 'competent staff' (all

Catholics and nearly all Lancastrians, the first issue boasted). Heenan asked the clergy to give their full support to the venture – apart from financial gain it could, he believed, 'powerfully serve the apostolate'.[32] The paper itself claimed to be 'an ACTION paper', not interested in 'flimsy criticism or subtle digs', but in 'CREATIVE ACTION', without explaining what that would involve.[33]

From the start it was professionally produced, lively and easy to read, with regular articles on topical issues and spiritual reflection. Not everyone was pleased with the new paper – to some it was a dumbing down, a cheapening of the image of the Church, and was quickly nick-named 'Carmel's Comic'. It could not have been more different from the rather frumpy *Cathedral Record.* But it was successful, sold well and, to some extent, united the archdiocese in a way that other means could not. The 1960s were the beginning of the modern mass media age and provided means of communication that Heenan was keen to exploit for pastoral advantage; others, perhaps, shied away from the popularisation that this entailed. In this context, a letter that Heenan wrote to Cardinal Godfrey is interesting: he was due to talk on television on a Sunday evening and asked for Godfrey's prayers because it was *'very (sic)* tricky to last out eirenically for 25 minutes without sounding either a moron or a heretic'.[34]

In the field of education, one of Heenan's concerns was that the 80% of Catholic children who attended secondary modern schools should not be labelled failures. Avoiding this, he believed, called for special qualities in the teachers: they needed to be imaginative, well-qualified and enthusiastic, gaining additional qualifications through extra-mural university courses, evening institutes and external degrees. He quoted the example of a secondary modern he had visited recently where substantial numbers stayed on after the age of fifteen, and half of those who did so went on to university or training college: the school was not pretending to be a grammar school but was catering for the needs and abilities of all its children. He claimed that he was not being starry eyed about the future of secondary moderns, nor did he think that the whole archdiocese could have schools of this type within a few years, but 'keen and well-qualified teachers rather than stream-lined buildings' were the secret of educational success.[35]

On Visitations he made sure that he spent time in the schools and spoke to the teachers. He met them as a body for the first time in the Cathedral Hall in 1962, but the occasion turned into something of a farce when the police ordered the removal of illegally parked cars and threatened summonses (Heenan promised that the archdiocese would pay all the fines). He had to end his talk prematurely but not before he had upset some of his audience with his criticisms – his usually sure touch seems to have deserted him: some teachers, he claimed, did not keep up their studies and read too little, others used corporal punishment too freely. Immediately after the aborted meeting he wrote to head teachers to say that he had only been criticising a minority of teachers and had felt free to talk to them quite frankly as a father within the family. If he had been able to finish his talk he would have made his gratitude and admiration for the 'self-sacrifice of the vast majority' clear. Even this letter, however, contained what some saw as a not-too-veiled criticism when he suggested that Catholic teachers would benefit from spending 'a week or two' in non-Catholic schools where the staff came from different training colleges and could offer fresh perspectives.[36] It was an ill-timed (and impractical) comment, especially as he was heavily involved at the time in the launch of a new Catholic Training College, Christ's College, in Liverpool.

A year later he wrote to all the teachers again and expressed his regret that some had taken his remarks amiss – he had only been trying to help. He had decided that large meetings were a mistake and in future would meet them in small groups that would allow discussion and prevent misunderstandings. Yet again, however, he struck an odd note by suggesting that young Catholic teachers in their first year or so in a school could be put off and demoralised by the attitudes of critical and cynical older members of staff. Instead, the staff should give young teachers 'a smiling welcome and do nothing to disillusion them'; they must be careful what they said in the presence of new teachers 'who are little more than children'.[37] He also apologised that the press had taken parts of an article he had written in the *Catholic Teachers' Journal* out of context and made it appear that he was criticising their approach to teaching as a vocation. This was reminiscent of his 'attack' on nurses for wanting more pay – they must always remember, he had urged, that nursing was a vocation and not subject to the same criteria as other professions when it came to pay. This had made national headlines *(The Daily Mail's* take on it was 'He said High Pay could be Degrading to Nurses') and he had had to 'explain' his meaning, which he did by claiming that he had only wanted to give prominence to their justified plea for fair treatment and that the nurses had been delighted and grateful for his intervention.[38]

THE STATE OF THE ARCHDIOCESE

These were years of tremendous growth, across the archdiocese, but at a cost. By late 1959 the archdiocese was in serious financial difficulty; the building projects currently in hand or about to start had drained it of ready cash. What Archbishop Heenan suggested as a partial remedy was for parish priests to place all their spare cash with the archdiocese so that it could be used to make loans to the parishes involved in building projects. He did not want to abandon building programmes and, indeed, financial embarrassment was a healthy sign of growth, but the financial stability of the diocese was the concern of all the clergy. A few years later he could report that £1.75 million was on loan to parishes, almost all of it money that belonged to other parishes. At the same time he announced that he had negotiated two loans of a quarter of a million pounds each with local banks to pay for the cathedral, and would soon have to borrow even more.[39] This

was the first warning of serious troubles ahead – the archdiocese became increasingly burdened with debts as it borrowed from banks, breweries and the Department of Education, and many parishes found most of their energies going into fund-raising to meet heavy interest payments. They were the years of that unique institution, the Catholic Club, with its dependence on loans from local breweries for its existence and its beer and bingo culture.

It was clear that if the traditional policy of providing a Catholic school place for every Catholic child was to continue, then more expansion and building would be required. The statistics tell a story of increasing demand over a period of thirty years that was likely to continue:[40]

Numbers of Catholic infant baptisms:

1934	11,519
1944	10,895
1950	12,277
1956	14,500
1959	14,409
1961	15,858
1964	16,288

Growth in total child population on roll in Catholic schools:

1936	58,796
1944	82,289
1950	82,607
1959	100,429
1967	119,696 (boys 60,858; girls 58,200)

And spending on education was not restricted to the schools. An area that the archdiocese had been deficient in was teacher training for men, with no provision once the out-dated pupil teacher scheme had ceased in the 1920s. The Ministry of Education approved Liverpool in 1960 as the site of a new Catholic training college that was to be co-educational – one of five new training colleges planned by the hierarchy. When it opened in September 1964 under Fr Louis Hanlon of the Salford diocese, it was jointly owned by the Ursuline nuns and the Catholic Education Council and had places for 600 students. A government grant covered 75% of the costs (excluding the chapel and convent), and the remainder was divided between the English dioceses. Additional money went to setting up a new chaplaincy building for the university.[41]

Then, just as the archdiocese had more or less come to terms with the provision of new grammar and secondary modern schools, it had to face the introduction of comprehensives. Archbishop Beck wrote to all the teachers in January 1965 on the topic and claimed that Catholics could have no objection in principle to comprehensive schooling, but adapting the existing system of secondary modern and grammar schools would be difficult. He argued that Catholics would need to make their own arrangements, which might differ from those of Local Authorities, but could not afford to bear the costs of going fully comprehensive, having already incurred such debts on establishing its secondary school system. Finally, any new system would have to take into account and respect the position of the Catholic direct-grant grammar schools – as Beck warned, all this would take time; he might have added, 'and the wisdom of a Solomon'.[42]

Meanwhile, some things did not change. Liverpool Catholics could still put on a good show when they felt it appropriate and continued to give 'Lime Street accolades' to their archbishops. Archbishop Godfrey enjoyed one as a send off when he left in 1957, as did Archbishop Heenan when he arrived. Heenan wrote to thank the clergy for encouraging their people to attend: 'These events strengthen the Faith and self-respect of the Catholic community', a rather old-fashioned sentiment, perhaps. Six years later 10,000 waved him off just as enthusiastically. Archbishop Beck arrived by car, but arrangements had still been made for people to line the last part of the route and attend the ensuing rally at the cathedral site.[43] Twenty years later Archbishop Worlock met with a similar reception: a large crowd 'of waving, smiling and hymn-singing people' welcomed him – singing, in fact, 'Faith of our Fathers';[44] was this in memory of Lancashire's martyrs, or a warning of what lay in store for him in his new diocese as it and its people faced much more radical and painful change?

Notes

1 Hastings, *English Christianity,* pp.473-8.

2 Sheridan Gilley, 'The Years of Equipoise, 1892-1943', *Flaminian Gate,* pp.21-61.

3 George Andrew Beck, 'To-day and To-morrow', in Beck, pp.585-614, at p.610.

4 Joan Brothers, *Church and School* (1964).

5 *Ibid.,* pp.10, 159.

6 AAL Heenan Collection, S1 III, A: Miscellany 1957-64: Letter to Teachers 2.10.1958.

7 Ward, Conor K., *Priests and People* (1961), p.117.

8 *Ibid.,* p.127.

9 Fr John Coyne, *C.R.* 1961, p.72, reviewing Ward.

10 Brothers, p.173.

11 Michael Hodgetts, 'The Iron Form: Catholics and Philosophy between the Councils', *Flaminian Gate,* pp.84-107, at p.100.

12 Susan O'Brien, 'Religious Life for Women', p.129.

13 *The Official Handbook of the Legion of Mary* (new ed. 1953), pp.98,193 (italics added).

14 Bernard Sharratt, 'English Roman Catholicism in the 1960s', in G. Sweeney (ed.), *Bishops and Writers* (1977) pp.127-58, at pp.146-7.

15 Figures from RSHM Archive.

16 Plumb, *Arundel; The Daily Telegraph,* 17.6.1953; *The Liverpool Daily Post,* 17, 24.6.1953; *The Irish Press,* 22.6.1953; *The Daily Mail,* 22.6.1953. Details of will in *The Times, The Daily Mail* and other papers, 25.9.1953; *The Universe,* 2.10.1953.

17 Plumb, *Arundel;* Moloney, *Westminster,* pp.90-102.

18 Quoted in Plumb, *Arundel.*

19 AAL *Synods,* 1955.

20 AAL Godfrey, S1 I A/100 for papers, extracts and statistics; Godfrey's initial change in Ad clerum, March 1954; VG to Abp, Feb., Sept., Nov., 1954.

21 *Ibid.,* 'Instruction on Mixed Marriages for use in the Archdiocese of Liverpool, 1955'.

22 AAL Godfrey, S1 I A/74-99.

23 AAL Downey, S1 III, A/3, Ad clerum 1940-53, 1.5.1950.

24 Published in his *Critical and Constructive Essays* (1934), pp.220-39.

25 AAL Godfrey, S1 I A/76 (Rimmer), 79 (Northern Bps), 83 (Buffaloes).

26 AAL Heenan, S1 III, A: 1957-64, ad clerum May 1957; personal reminiscence of author.

27 AAW, Cardinal Heenan, Liverpool Files: Heenan to Willebrands 2.3.1961; Go 2/139b, 1960-63: Heenan to Bp of Coventry, 31.5.1961.

28 AAL Beck, S2 XIV, Diocesan Matters, A/1.

29 AAL Godfrey, S2 II A/9: 1954-55 (ten items); AAW Gr. 2/139b, Godfrey to Griffin, 4.3.1955 and 7.5.1954.

30 AAL Heenan, S1 III, A: Miscellany 1957-64: Heenan to Harvey, 21.9.1959; Heenan to Heaton, 24.9.1959.

31 *Ibid.,* Kenny to Heenan and replies, 20-27.12.1962; Anthony Kenny, *A Path from Rome, An Autobiography* (1986), pp.169-90.

32 AAL Heenan, S1 III, A: 1957-64: ad clerum Oct. 1961.

33 AAL *Catholic Pictorial* files, first issue 7.1.1962.

34 AAW Go 2/139b, Heenan to Godfrey, 2.12.1960.

35 AAL Heenan, S1 III, A: 1957-64: Letter to Teachers, 2.10.1958.

36 *Ibid.,* Heenan to headteachers, 1962.

37 *Ibid.,* Letter to teachers, May 1963.

38 The Archbishop of Liverpool, 'Point of View', *Catholic Teachers' Journal* May-June 1963, pp.8-9; subsequent correspondence ran through to October. On the nurses, see his *Crown of Thorns,* pp.333-5; *The Daily Mail* 10.4.1962.

39 AAL Heenan, S1 I A: ad clerum, 30.11.1959, and March 1962.

40 *Directories.*

41 AAL Heenan, S1 IV Documents A: Miscellany, Christ's College.

42 AAL Beck, S2 XIV, Diocesan Matters, A: Ad clerums & Notices: June 1965.

43 *Ibid.,* March 1964; AAL Heenan, S1 I A: ad clerum 7.8.1957; *The Cathedral Record,* March, Aug. 1957, covers both Godfrey and Heenan; *Crown of Thorns,* pp.397-9.

44 John Furnival and Ann Knowles, *Archbishop Derek Worlock. His Personal Journey* (1998), p.170.

CHAPTER 17 THE LITURGY – RENEWAL AND REVOLUTION

To suggest to English Catholics in 1950 that they might go to Mass in the afternoon or evening would have been as strange as suggesting that they might eat meat on Fridays without feeling guilty, and yet the 1950s saw the beginning of changes that were to have an even more profound effect on their devotional life. The introduction of evening Masses and the general reduction in the Eucharistic fast to three hours made it easier to get to Mass but, paradoxically, did not lead to a corresponding rise in the number of Holy Communions. Wherever priests introduced weekday afternoon and evening Masses attendances were up compared with morning Masses, in some parishes by a factor of three or four. Some priests were disappointed that the response had not been better, but numbers were still greater than at their poorly attended morning Masses. It was encouraging that priests in some of the larger parishes reported that three-quarters of those now regularly at evening Mass on weekdays did not previously go to daily Mass. Sunday evening Masses in most cases led to a considerable increase in attendances, including young mothers, and children from lax homes who would never have got up for morning Masses; in some more rural areas, where there was no public transport on Sunday mornings, evening Masses were of obvious benefit. All this was positive, but priests across the board reported that the numbers receiving Communion at these Masses, with the exception of those on Saturday evenings, were 'most disappointing' and the three-hour fast was blamed for this. Yet the overall number of Communions throughout the archdiocese in 1959 was two million higher than in 1957 – it was unclear whether this indicated an increase in the number of communicants or, perhaps more likely, that people who had already been regular communicants were now able to receive even more frequently because they could get to Mass more often.[1]

Archbishop Heenan, enthroned as Archbishop of Liverpool in July 1957, was pastorally aware and progressive, but was also marked by that particular brand of confidence produced in many Catholic leaders of the day by an unshakeable and absolute belief in the certainty of the Church's doctrinal positions. Faced by the introduction of change in the 1950s and 1960s he reacted with sensitivity and a willingness to experiment, but seemed genuinely unable to grasp that some of the changes made no sense without a re-formulation of the doctrines underpinning them. When change led to conflict between conservatives and progressives, Heenan looked for practical solutions to tide things over until calm returned. The progressives

332

annoyed him with their constant probing of everything authority had to say, while conservatives annoyed him by refusing to accept what seemed to him to be perfectly sensible pastoral reforms imposed by that same authority.

In an attempt to increase the number of frequent communicants he launched a campaign to encourage membership of the traditional Knights and Handmaids of the Blessed Sacrament associations, whose members pledged themselves to receive Communion at least once a week. A number of plenary indulgences were attached to active membership, including one for receiving Communion on first Fridays and first Saturdays and for making 'Communions of Reparation'. He wrote to teachers to get them to encourage children to join and wear the distinctive badge, but he was at pains to stress that the movement should be as equally attractive to families and adults. The Jesuit Director of the movement nationwide had promised that Jesuits priests would happily visit churches and schools to introduce the idea of the movement – though the whole idea, Heenan believed, was so simple that it did not need special preachers; the crusade would bring great spiritual benefits to the archdiocese. In writing to the teachers he acknowledged that not everyone liked wearing badges, but children generally did, and he hoped that 'the comradeship' coming from the outward sign of membership might be of considerable help to children from homes where the religious practice was weak.[2]

The Archbishop was still worried at the end of the year that new frequent communicants were not coming forward in any substantial numbers – he reported in December 1960 that the fervent had taken advantage of the extra availability of Mass to increase the number of times they received Communion, but that on the whole there had been 'a startling decline' in the frequency of Communion. He claimed that many of those who had received once a week at Sunday morning Mass were not willing to observe the three-hour fast on a Sunday afternoon now that they had switched to evening Mass – he had to admit that it was extremely difficult for the average family to abandon the usual meal at teatime on Sundays. He asked for a detailed report from parish priests on the times of evening Sunday Mass and the numbers who went to Communion at it – they must, he concluded, consider means of bringing more to the altar rails, and in that context he hoped they were still preaching the Knights and Handmaids crusade.[3]

A year later there was a different emphasis altogether in his letters. It was as though the novelty had worn off and he was becoming rather suspicious about evening Masses – they could be 'an invitation to sloth' and priests should resist the tendency to replace morning Masses with more evening ones.[4] All that seemed to be happening, he wrote, was a shift of numbers from the morning to the evening, with no overall increase in the numbers attending and a decrease in frequent Communions – which, he pointed out, was not the original intention of the Holy See when it made the new rules. He advised priests that where several evening Masses had been introduced, their number should be cut and the people reminded that evening Mass was a 'privilege' – though he did not explain why they should regard it as such or why they should not make use of the flexibility that the new rules permitted.

Apart from the effect on the numbers receiving Communion, the growth of evening Masses also affected the traditional Sunday evening services and priests worried about the decline in the numbers attending Benediction – numbers were dwindling in every parish. It was difficult to know what to do: in some churches Benediction was put on immediately after the evening Mass, but priests felt it was unsatisfactory if people stayed on unwillingly after Mass, and disedifying if people left the church while the priest was preparing for Benediction. For his part, the Archbishop was convinced that priests should do all they could to keep the 'valuable tradition' of Benediction alive; he foresaw a generation growing up that knew no devotions outside obligatory Mass, but, he continued:

> *we cannot turn back the clock. The lure of television regrettably does not seem to be a passing fad. It is doubtful if we shall ever regain the great congregations for Sunday Devotions which were such a feature of parochial life before the war.*

He believed that this was not entirely due to the introduction of evening Masses, as the numbers attending Sunday evening devotions across the country as a whole had been in decline for some years. One solution that might bring better results, he believed, was to have Benediction immediately before the evening Mass, starting a quarter of an hour before the advertised Mass time – many were willing to come that bit earlier, and if they turned up only for the Mass they had no need to feel embarrassed. He did not comment that such an arrangement must have seemed odd to anyone with even the slightest liturgical sensitivity – it was a case of having Benediction just for the sake of having it. Even odder was his suggestion that Communion could be given out after afternoon Benediction, and then the people could go home for their tea and come back for Mass in the evening – without, of course, receiving Communion at that Mass.[5]

Heenan did suggest it would be better to have the Devotions and Benediction at a different time altogether, perhaps with the Perpetual Novena service as an additional draw, with the occasional special preacher thrown in. He concluded by saying how sad it would be if Catholics were to become strangers to the traditional service, but the fact was that some young Catholics had almost no experience of Bendiction. And so he instructed the clergy to arrange Benediction after school on one day each week and all children were to learn the prayer for the conversion of England. Of course there was a danger, he admitted, of associating religion too closely with school, but Benediction would have no attraction to future generations unless children had become familiar with it at school.[6]

In his ad clerums and exhortations on these matters there is an air of desperately wanting to keep traditional devotional practices going at all costs. He made no appeal to the changes in liturgical thinking that were behind the renewal of the liturgy and no attempt to develop new devotional practices in line with them. These changes were hardly new – they can conveniently be thought of as starting with the encyclical *Mediator Dei* of 1947 – and by 1960 it was quite common to read in popular theological works and journals explanations of the Mass as a communal meal, for example, and of Communion as being an integral part of it. It is perhaps worth noting here that one of the points made in *Mediator Dei,* and repeated in the important Instruction on the Liturgy of 1958, was that whenever possible, the faithful should receive hosts consecrated at the Mass they were attending and not those reserved from previous celebrations. This was repeated in the main conciliar document on the liturgy, issued in 1963, but it was not implemented at public Masses and so the theological reasoning behind it was not explained. With his usual sharp pastoral insight, Heenan had seen that the new regulations were causing changes in people's devotional lives, but, also as usual, he did not link the changes with any need to change his, or his clergy's (still less the people's), theological thinking.[7]

Part of the reason for later unease among many people at the introduction of liturgical changes was the lack of preparation and proper instruction about the theological reasons behind the changes – it seemed at times to be change for change's sake. Heenan's approach to Benediction exemplifies this: he wanted it to continue because it had become a worthwhile tradition in the archdiocese and it would be 'sad' if it were lost. Undoubtedly the service had played an important part in the lives of the more devout of the people, and its ability to create a sense of reverence and mystery should not be underestimated. Not that large numbers had ever attended the Sunday evening services, except, perhaps, on special occasions, but they had been a distinctive feature of every parish's spiritual life. If it were disappearing as a regular service in many parishes was this because of a deeper appreciation of the Eucharistic sacrifice as a community meal, or had the change been brought about by changes in the social and leisure life of English Catholics? To many of the faithful it must have seemed to be because it could not be fitted in at a convenient time; it gradually lost its importance, became an occasional event, mysterious in an altogether different sense, and left a gap in people's devotional lives that was not immediately filled.

The most important and more radical changes in the liturgy came about under Archbishop Beck, appointed to Liverpool in January 1964. He implemented the changes in a cautious but fully committed manner, sensitive to the worries of people and priests that so much of what they had valued for so long was apparently being destroyed in the name of modernisation. He did everything possible to encourage his priests to develop a proper theological understanding of the liturgical renewal and to explain it to the people. He wrote his first letter on the subject to the clergy in May and outlined some of the implications of Pope Paul VI's *motu proprio Sacram Liturgiam* (On the Sacred Liturgy) of the previous January. One of

these was that there had to be a homily at all Masses on Sundays and Holy Days. He made no comment on the fact that this meant the end of the syllabus of Sunday Instructions that, however imperfectly, had worked through the main points of doctrine and morality on a regular basis. There was no suggestion that this would be replaced by any other form of adult Christian instruction, though no doubt the people should have gained a better knowledge of the Scriptures if the homilies did their job. The Archbishop stressed that only the bishops could authorise other liturgical changes and added, 'We worship God more by obedience to the rubrics than by introducing unauthorized changes in the liturgy, no matter how much these may seem desirable in themselves'.[8] His own strict adherence to Roman directives is clear from a later notice to the clergy in which he explained that women or girls were now allowed to read the lessons at Mass in communities of Sisters or in girls' schools 'where a competent male reader' was not available, on condition that the female read from outside the sanctuary.[9]

He planned talks and discussions in Wigan and Liverpool for the clergy to examine the Vatican Council's Constitution on the Sacred Liturgy. This, he hoped, would help them work out practical ways in which the people could be encouraged to appreciate the significance and value of the changes, and so take a more active part in what he called 'the renewed liturgy'. Later in the year he issued a set of sermon notes to be used for this purpose on eight Sundays before the beginning of Advent. His understanding of the care with which changes had to be made is clear from two minor statements: when the people were asked to say 'Amen' to the priest's 'Corpus Christi' at Communion, he said that if the people found this 'strange' then the priest could add the 'Amen' himself. Secondly, when he gave permission in November 1964 for the *Pater Noster* at Mass to be said in English, he asked the clergy 'to guide our people with sympathy and gentleness towards a more active participation' in the liturgy (Shortly afterwards the English bishops decided as a body to keep it in Latin).[10]

At the same time he was as disturbed as his predecessor had been at the apparent drop in communicants throughout the archdiocese, despite the greater availability of Mass. He thought that the figures for Easter confessions and for Mass attendance during Lent were low, given the large Catholic population, and it was particularly worrying that there had been a decrease on the figures for the previous year. He noted that the total number of Communions had fallen by about 830,000 in two years, though he was somewhat consoled by the slight increase in those attending Sunday Benediction. Overall, he believed that the figures called for prayerful attention from the clergy and inevitably raised questions about the effectiveness of 'our pastoral work'.[11]

The first major changes in the form of the Mass came into force in Advent 1964 with the omission of the prayers at the foot of the altar at the beginning of Mass and of the Last Gospel and the Leonine Prayers at the end. Other parts, traditionally said secretly by the priest, were to be said aloud. A limited use of English became compulsory in all Low Masses on Sundays and Holy Days. In his Advent Pastoral Letter the Archbishop asked those who found these changes unwelcome to accept them 'in a spirit of loyalty to the Church and her authority' and hoped that they would not find them 'too startling', since they were, in fact, quite restricted and should help people to listen to God's word more easily and take a more active and conscious part in the prayers of the Mass. He explained the reasons for the changes in terms of the priesthood of all the faithful through baptism, the need for people to be more aware through prayer and action of their share in Christ's sacrificial offering and the desirability of people receiving Communion whenever they assisted at Mass.[12]

What people experienced in practice when they went to church in these years was sometimes less than the ideal. When Fr Brian Newns addressed the Pastoral Council in 1972 he referred to the liturgy as being for the participants 'the joyous experience of the saving Christ'. Delegates, however, questioned how often this was the real experience of those attending Mass in parish churches, where, perhaps, changes had been half-heartedly introduced, or there had been insufficient explanation and no sensitivity to the feelings of the people. This had led too often to a general opposition to the changes – what was lacking too frequently, the delegates claimed, was genuine enthusiasm on the part of both priests and people. Some also pointed out that the homily too often bore no relationship to the lives of the people and that only if the priest continued to visit his parishioners could he know their needs – a reference to another traditional practice in the archdiocese that social changes were making more difficult to continue.[13] Archbishop Heenan had, indeed, picked up on this point ten years earlier, giving it as his impression that in some parishes there was no visiting except in connection with the outdoor collection. He had described proper pastoral visiting as 'dull and laborious' but the best test he knew of priestly zeal – priests simply had to go on visiting, especially in the homes where they were least welcome.[14]

Some speakers at the Pastoral Council meeting linked the whole discussion of the liturgy to the basic issue of adult education: a 'questioning laity' would not be satisfied with a 'quick-fix' explanation but needed to mature in their faith and understanding of the liturgy. Perhaps there was some recognition in this last statement that the under-evangelisation of the adult Catholic population for generations was having its effects: had devout, unquestioning practice been accepted as the principal norm for too long?

As things turned out, the service of Benediction had roots too deeply embedded in popular devotion to wither away altogether. Attendances in the 1960s (admittedly during Lent) rose slightly and stood at about 5% of the Catholic population. The Archdiocesan Liturgical Commission issued guidelines on 'Devotion to the Blessed Sacrament', with special reference to Benediction and the Forty Hours' Exposition. It laid down two key linked principles: prayer before the Blessed Sacrament must be more than the traditional wish to 'keep Jesus company as He remains in the tabernacle'; rather, such prayer outside Mass should be related to people's union with Christ inside Mass, a union brought about especially through the reception of Communion. Only in this way, the guidelines stressed, could the traditional services of Benediction and Forty Hours' Exposition be given a deeper meaning. A re-vamped service might include suitable novena prayers, readings from Scripture, and a homily; it had to include a period of silent prayer, and should take place at least monthly, but must not be immediately after Mass just in order to give a blessing with the Blessed Sacrament. Finally, priests were encouraged to experiment, perhaps quarterly, with different forms of a more solemn Eucharistic Service. Quarant'Ore, re-named the Solemn Annual Exposition, would continue as before.[15]

The Liturgical Commission developed a range of initiatives to introduce priests and people to the new liturgy. There were regular bulletins about the new rites and model services to suit the different seasons of the liturgical year – Lenten Penance Services, Passiontide Services, etc. There were also practical guidelines on the Sign of Peace, Communion under both kinds and new Rosary services. The Commission ran basic training sessions, for example a Readers' Afternoon, and published lists of books that would be useful as introductions to the changes. Clerical conferences moved away from the traditional obsession with rubrical exactitude and discussed instead how best to explain the new liturgy to the people, how to get them involved actively and how best to disseminate 'best practice'.[16] Regular articles in the

*The new church of
St Ambrose, Speke,
designed by Weightman
& Bullen (1959-61).*

Catholic Pictorial explained the changes in straightforward language and tried to calm the fears of those who thought everything was up for grabs and that old certainties were being replaced by the shifting sands of subjectivity.

There were further major changes in 1970, with the whole Mass in English and the priest facing the people. The re-ordering of churches again meant an immediate loss of what many Catholics had come to love as essential points of focus in 'their' church, especially saints and shrines, marble altars with sets of fine altar rails, and even the tabernacle, to be replaced too often in the first instance by the utilitarian and the temporary, apparently at the whim of the individual priest. Critics of the new seemed to forget too easily that a good deal of what went in the re-ordering had itself been nondescript or even 'tacky', with the Mass sometimes hurried and almost inaudible. The advantages of the new rites were soon accepted by most Catholics as outweighing the sense of dislocation – new roles for the laity as readers and Eucharistic ministers, a greater sense of involvement and a language that all could understand. A major change was the much greater involvement of parents and other adults in preparation for the Sacraments, opening up a new field of the apostolate. For some, too much of the mystery of the Mass had been lost and the opportunities for private prayer diminished – perhaps the slow flowering of unofficial prayer and bible-study groups, usually lay led, has been a necessary and worthwhile counter-development, along with officially recognised groups like Cursillo, Focolare, the Charles De Foucauld lay fraternity and Soulcare Meditation. These new devotions have taken time to grow organically and gradually, just as pre-Vatican II devotional life had itself developed and had not sprung ready-made from the establishment of the diocese in 1850.

The introduction of lay Eucharistic Ministers came in May 1973, as the Archbishop announced rather cautiously in line with the Roman directives: it was essential not to give the impression that the new arrangements were for the convenience of priests – he stressed especially the duty of priests to continue to take Communion to the sick. So, permission to act as lay ministers would be limited to Seminarians and Religious, and it must be applied for as a privilege when a priest or deacon was not available. Proper preparation of these Minsters was, of course, essential; once trained, they would be commissioned solemnly in the cathedral. A note at the end of the Archbishop's letter seemed aimed at those who wanted to push further ahead with change on the basis of what was happening elsewhere: pastoral practices abroad and in missionary lands were not necessarily the best for this country, he warned, adding 'no doubt experience will show what the next step should be'.[17]

One surprising change that has taken place since the 1970s has been a marked decline in the popularity of Sunday evening Mass across the archdiocese. Welcomed on all sides when they were introduced, they are now, apparently, a 'minority interest'. In 1984 almost 100% of parishes had an evening Mass; by 1992 the figure had dropped to 68%, and at the time of writing the figure is only 30%. How far the decrease relates to an overall drop in the number of those attending Mass is unclear. This latter drop has been startling. In the mid-1960s Sunday Mass attendance stood at around the 255,000 mark for the archdiocese as a whole; by the early 1980s the figure was down to about 170,000, by the 1990s to under 130,000 and by 2000 it was below 95,000. It has been claimed that these figures and other similar statistics are proof that 'Catholic Lancashire is withering away'.[18] Those seeking a cause for this drop in attendance at Sunday Mass (traditionally the criterion for deciding whether someone was a 'good Catholic' or not) have variously blamed movements in population away from Merseyside, the secularisation of English society into which Catholics have been more and more integrated, the destruction of old certainties brought about by the Second Vatican Council, the failure of the Church to deal adequately with the issue of birth control, and, of course, the liturgical changes outlined in this chapter.

It would appear to be as over-simplistic to attribute the decline in Mass attendance to the liturgical revolution as to attribute the even greater decline (numerically speaking) in vocations to the Religious life to nuns changing their dress. Yet there was food for thought in the very strong impression that Archbishop Worlock received on coming to Liverpool as a complete stranger:

the intense loyalty of Northern Catholics seemed to him to be directed primarily to externals – 'our' parish, 'our' priest, 'our' archbishop, even 'our' social club – with no certainty that this was backed up by any genuine religious understanding. Many of these traditional Catholics, he believed, were more likely to be upset by the closure of a presbytery than by theological or liturgical changes, and if they were moved to new housing estates or new towns where the externals were different then their traditional loyalty could soon disappear.[19]

He had in mind places likes Kirkby, just outside Liverpool. Very large numbers of inner-city Catholics had been re-located there, so that the Catholic population amounted to more than 45% of the total. Seven new Catholic churches and primary schools were built between 1952 and 1965, along with two purpose-built comprehensives. This led to the parishes being burdened with very large debts and to the development of 'Catholic clubland' to raise money. A detailed survey in the late 1960s showed that 5,782 attended Mass on the day the census was taken – approximately 23%, of whom approximately 55% were under the age of twenty (altogether it was a young population, with nearly 60% under the age of twenty-five in 1971). 12% of adult Catholic men in the district attended, and 25% of adult Catholic women; there was little difference in the attendance rates for junior and senior school children. Yet an experienced priest added that there was still among the people a real desire to see the priest: people wanted a priest who would visit them and listen to them even if they did not go to Mass. It might be true, as he claimed, that the new liturgy offered a 'vast field' for experiment and instruction, but it seemed that the people had other priorities.[20]

Notes

[1] AAL Heenan Collection, S1 I A: Miscellany 1957-64: various ad clerum letters and notices on parish experiments and returns about impact of the changes.

[2] Ibid., ad clerum 1.10.1960.

[3] Ibid., ad clerum Dec. 1960.

[4] Ibid., ' A personal letter to my Priests', Dec. 1961.

[5] Ibid., pp.8-10.

[6] Ibid., p.9.

[7] W.M. Abbott, SJ, (ed.), The Documents of Vatican II (1966), p.156; C.Davis, Liturgy and Doctrine (1960), pp.75-7; J.D. Crichton, The Church's Worship.

[8] AAL Beck S2 XIV A: Ad clerums and Notices: May 1964; All Saints, 1964; Advent, 1964.

[9] Ibid., 2.12.1967.

[10] Ibid., June and Nov. 1964.

[11] Ibid., Sept. 1964.

[12] Ibid., Advent 1964.

[13] AAL Beck, S2 XVI Diocesan Matters, A: Archdiocesan Pastoral Council, Meeting of 4/5 Nov. 1972, p.8.

[14] Note 4 above.

[15] AAL Beck, S2 XIV A: 'Statement and Directives on Devotion to the Blessed Sacrament … Approval of the Archbishop', Jan. 1968.

[16] Ibid., Clergy Conferences, 1966-7.

[17] Ibid., ad clerum 24.5.1973.

[18] Hilton, Catholic Lancashire, p.129; statistics from Directories; The Catholic Pictorial, 10.8.1983, highlighted the drift away from Sunday evening Masses.

[19] David Sheppard and Derek Worlock, Better Together: Christian Partnership in a Hurt City (1988), p.57.

[20] AAL Beck, S2 XVI Diocesan Matters, A: Council of Clergy, Meeting Nov. 1972, p.3.

CHAPTER 18 NEW IDEAS ON PRIESTLY FORMATION AND THE CLOSURE OF UPHOLLAND

Discussions were taking place about the future of the English seminaries as early as 1960, with particular reference to two issues: how to plan for the increase in vocations required to serve the expanding Catholic population, and how far the traditional model of priestly training was still appropriate. An official report on Ushaw by the Northern Bishops stressed that extra accommodation would be needed in a matter of months rather than years. Moreover, any building programme should be planned on the supposition that students would not be required to remain in the same place 'from boyhood until ordination'. With regard to the spiritual side of the training provided, the report admitted that the traditional system allowed a student to go through his course with little or no personal contact with any of the staff and that this lack of individual spiritual direction had to be remedied. On the academic side, the tutorial system should be extended, with a series of essays and practical exercises to ensure that the students learned how to put across in an articulate way what they had been studying.[1] What effect did these ideas have on priestly training in the archdiocese?

ST JOSEPH'S COLLEGE, UPHOLLAND

The staff at Upholland (where Mgr Sidney Breen had replaced Mgr Joseph Turner as rector in 1958) were divided on the issue of keeping juniors and seniors together for the whole of their course, most believing that a break would be desirable. They also believed that too many students could get through the system because there was 'nothing against them'; some thought that life in the modern seminary had become too easy and that rules such as that of silence should be strictly enforced. Again, as at Ushaw, the need to change teaching methods in the Senior Seminary was a concern. In his report on an official visit by Bishop Beck of Salford and himself, Archbishop Heenan concluded that the visit had been both 'consoling and vastly encouraging'. It is a little odd, however, that Upholland does not receive even a mention in his account of his years in Liverpool.[2]

The early 1960s saw a large increase in the number of boys entering the Junior Seminary – for the first time there was a two-form entry. A new wing was added to the old O'Byrne buildings to increase teaching space (funded by the sale of some of O'Byrne's treasures) and under the headship of Fr Tom

Cheetham the curriculum was modernised and expanded; a full inspection in 1965 by H.M. Inspectors reported that the standards of teaching and achievement were at least equal to the best grammar schools.[3] Changes in the regime also allowed the boys home more often and encouraged open Parents' Days.

By the mid-1960s the programme of studies in the Senior Seminary had changed much more radically, from the traditional Continental approach of a total lecture and note-taking system, in which it was possible to study for six years without having to write a single essay, to a more tutorial-based system, with fewer lectures, weekly essay writing and individual tuition. The changes, introduced under the leadership of Fr Tom Worden as Prefect of Studies, reflected a changing attitude to what the student had to learn – from a set body of truths and rules that would equip him with all he needed for his priestly ministry, to an examination and reflection on God's revelation in the light of current concerns and with the help of secular as well as religious experiences. That the student might be expected to use the modern novel as a starting point for his reflection and study said it all. The new method was designed to apply the principle that the student was the person mainly responsible for acquiring an adequate knowledge of the subject taught. The most obvious change, however, was the introduction of regular Pastoral Work, with one day each week devoted to it. Final year students, the deacons, worked for the day in the parishes where they ministered on Sundays, while the fifth year students taught religion in schools; the other years did parish or hospital visiting, or worked with the elderly or in Special Schools. The aim was to give all the students the opportunity to fulfill their Christian duties to their neighbour, to relate their studies to the problems of Christian living and to gain experience of priestly pastoral work.[4]

Other changes would have had an even more radical impact if they had been implemented. Senior Seminary education and priestly training in England had long been intellectually isolated from the rest of English higher education. To many that isolation had seemed advantageous, a guarantee of orthodoxy, even. By the 1960s, however, opinions were changing. The hierarchy set up a committee to look into the 'Relations between Seminaries and British Universities'. Fr Worden was one of its members and was determined to end the traditional isolation so that students could both benefit from and contribute to the universities. Unfortunately, the intellectual isolation had led to a desire for geographical isolation when the seminaries had been established, and Upholland was badly placed when it came to establishing links with universities: the University of Liverpool was the closest, but its statutes forbade it to have a theology or religious studies faculty. Lancaster was developing a name for its Religious Studies courses, while Manchester had a well-respected Theology Faculty, but neither was within daily commuting distance. Both Lancaster and Manchester had the added disadvantage of being in other dioceses, an important factor if change meant financial investment.[5]

Early in 1967 Fr Worden wrote to Professor Ninian Smart, soon to take up his post as Head of Religious Studies at Lancaster, and to Canon Preston, of the University of Manchester, to express his anxiety about the continued intellectual isolation of the English seminaries. He received a strikingly positive response from both, with Smart saying that he had often regretted the lack of links, and Preston visiting Upholland soon afterwards and meeting staff and students there. Worden then wrote to Archbishop Beck to say that students who came to study at the age of eighteen did not want to give up their chance of studying for a degree, to which the Archbishop replied that he understood the problem but could not see any general way out of it. Eventually, several months later, the Archbishop agreed to have the matter discussed by the College Governors; Worden produced a paper on the advisability of Upholland becoming a 'recognised college' of Manchester University. The Governors reacted cautiously (but not negatively), particularly when they realised that some sort of house of studies in Manchester would be necessary.[6]

One imaginative proposal for solving the residence requirement in Manchester involved the planned re-development of Hartley Victoria College, the Methodist Training College that was already a recognised college of the university. Its authorities were planning to rebuild and hoped to be joined by two Anglican colleges; the site was large enough for Catholic extensions to be added, in so far as separate facilities would be required – other facilities would be shared, thus reducing the cost. It would have been a genuine ecumenical solution. There was obviously a reluctance on the part of some of the Catholics involved in the negotiations to 'lose' their students for two or three years – as was pointed out, training for the priesthood involved far more than academic training. On the other hand, if seminary students only attended for lectures and missed out on the social and communal life of university students, could they be said to be having a university experience?[7]

In the end the Archbishop decided in March 1968, after meeting with Canon Preston and a second time with representatives of the Faculty of Theology, that while it might be desirable for a few students to take the Certificate in Biblical Knowledge and the Certificate in Theology (involving attendance for an hour or so a week at the University for a year), any affiliation of the College to the University would be out of the question, at least in the immediate future. The overwhelming reasons seemed to be the linked geographical/financial problems, but it is not clear how far these were genuine and how far they were welcomed by some as an excuse. As a member of staff put it in a comment to the Archbishop, if the links were genuinely believed to be desirable, then a positive approach to overcoming the practical problems was possible; if the links were only half-heartedly or tokenly believed in, the practical problems would become a major inhibiting factor.[8]

The issue did not go away and in 1971 the Archbishop set up a committee to consider the professional preparation and training of priests and to make recommendations. The Committee was composed of Canon G. Walsh, as chairman, Fr Kevin Nichols of Christ's College, Fr Vincent Malone, chaplain to Liverpool University, and three members of the senior staff of Upholland, Fr William Dalton, Fr John Gaine and Fr Worden. They trod a sometimes difficult line between what was theoretically ideal and was what likely to be practicable in the given circumstances and concluded that senior aspirants to the priesthood in the archdiocese should spend:

1. a preliminary year of orientation in Liverpool;
2. the next three years in Manchester attending university courses in theology, with additional teaching from the priests in their own college;
3. a final two years, devoted principally to pastoral training, at Upholland College; here they would be in contact with the Pastoral Institute, which would be concerned with in-service training.

Other aspects of the report included an acknowledgement of the importance of the proper assessment of candidates, using modern insights from social and psychological disciplines, the importance of seeking to encourage vocations among older candidates, the expectations that an increasingly better-educated laity had of the clergy, and, perhaps most significantly, the need for a radical revision in, and much more individual approach to, proper spiritual formation.[9]

The Archdiocesan Council of Clergy discussed the report (generally referred to as the 'Red Book') a few months later. Some traditionalists (led by Canon Frank Ripley, high priest of the certainties of a by-gone age) questioned the whole basis of the report, suggesting that it ran counter to several points in the Vatican II document on priestly formation, that it was only concerned with an élite among the clergy, that universities were themselves in turmoil, and that the aim should be to produce priests modelled on the Curé d'Ars – 'our aim is to produce saints'. How could two or three years of a university-based course be fitted into the traditional training model of six years, or, to put it differently, how could a third or a half of the traditional training be lost without sacrificing essentials? Others, however, supported the report and spoke of the need to look to the future, of the value of university education, of the valuable service that Catholics could make to the universities – Mgr Breen praised the Committee for taking the long term view and for being concerned with ideas rather than buildings. After a long and very open discussion, the Council voted overwhelmingly (by 47 votes to 4) to recommend the report in substance to the Archbishop and urgently requested him to take steps to implement it, 'bearing in mind the observations expressed in this assembly'.[10]

By this time the context had altered substantially. It had become clear by the mid-1960s that earlier optimism regarding vocations had been misplaced. Archbishop Beck used his Lenten Pastoral in 1965 to outline what he saw as a future shortage of priests: between 1935 and 1949, there had been 221 ordinations for the archdiocese; but between 1950 and 1964 – in many ways a golden period for English Catholicism – there had been only 131. On the basis of these figures, he estimated a shortage in fifteen years' time of 160 priests. There was also a deficit of £11,000 in the Ecclesiastical Education Fund: the education of the archdiocese's students cost £60,000 a year; the annual collection in 1965 brought in £30,000, while in 1964 it had been £35,000; there was a small increase in 1967, when the figure rose to £32,300. A few years later, in his letter of Lent 1969, he pointed out that there were 526 Secular priests in the archdiocese, of whom 30 were retired or too ill for work, 7 were chaplains to the Forces, 19 were working outside the archdiocese in England or on the missions. The past two years had seen 16 ordinations, but 22 priests had died or retired and priests were needed for 7 new parishes. Moreover, there were only 72 students for the archdiocese in various senior seminaries who, realistically, would provide fewer than 12 ordinations per year for the next six years. The Archbishop concluded that it could no longer be taken for granted that there would be enough priests to meet all the spiritual needs of the people. Later in the same year he provided a breakdown of the clergy by number of years ordained: 211 had been ordained for 30 or more years, 174 for 15-29 years, and only 135 for 1-15 years.[11]

The Northern Bishops now had to face up to the problem that was the exact reverse of that posed less than ten years before: what could they do with the excess seminary accommodation at their disposal? They made it clear that they supported the retention of both Ushaw and Upholland as Senior Seminaries for the North of England, but wanted only a single, amalgamated, Junior Seminary, located at Upholland. This opened in September 1972, with 160 students, half of whom were for the archdiocese; numbers were expected to rise to 200 the following year, not counting the first two years which had to be located at Underley (formerly the Lancaster Junior Seminary) because of a lack of accommodation at Upholland.[12]

This, then, was the changed context of the discussions between staff at Upholland and the University of Manchester. When it was suggested later that year (1972) that some of the Bishops' Working Party should have an informal meeting with members of the Theology Faculty at Manchester, the bishops replied that great caution would be required in arranging such a meeting. While not closing the door completely on the question, the Northern Bishops made it clear that they had no intention of establishing another seminary/university link in the foreseeable future, and that it would be imprudent therefore to raise false hopes about the issue. That was January 1973. Were they unsure about how the Ushaw/Durham link was developing, or, more likely, did they already have doubts that Upholland was going to survive as a Senior Seminary? A letter from the Northern Bishops' Conference in May 1973 (incidentally the month that Fr Worden died) suggested that they were having a change of heart and going back on their decision of the previous year: it was now possible that the two Senior Seminaries might have to be merged at Ushaw and the new Junior Seminary closed.[13]

This was the rather confused background to another discussion by the Council of Clergy. Some felt that the days of junior seminaries were over anyway, a feeling that was supported by statistics about the 'success rate' of Upholland in recent years: in 1972, three students were ordained who had been through the system, out of a starting cohort of 42; in 1973 four were ordained out of an original 48; in 1974 none would be ordained out of an original 33. But the retention of the Senior Seminary at Upholland was the main issue, and eventually the Council voted to urge the bishops to retain it (the voting reflected the confusion with 29 in favour, 2 against and no fewer than 21 abstentions).[14]

The Northern Bishops and the Bishop of Shrewsbury discussed the future of priestly training in the Northern Province again in June 1973 at Headingley. This time they put forward a three-fold proposal: the Senior Seminary at Upholland should close and merge with that at Ushaw; a combined northern Junior Seminary should be located at Upholland, and a 'theological presence' should be established in the North-West as a priority to replace the loss of Upholland as a Senior Seminary. Archbishop Beck (and the Upholland staff and Liverpool clergy) objected strongly to these proposals, but at a meeting at Ushaw in July the Archbishop gave in, having decided that it would be better not to allow a public show of disagreement among the bishops, a sort of cabinet responsibility that had not always been evident. When he reported this to the staff at Upholland, however, there was an uproar and he immediately rang the bishops who were still at Ushaw and retracted his agreement! The uproar moved from Upholland to their Lordships across the Pennines who put their case to the Sacred Congregation for Catholic Education (the Roman body responsible for priestly training) in October that year. The Archbishop sent his detailed case in December.[15]

The Congregation decided in favour of all the proposals, arguing in a letter of January 1974 that amalgamation would be more successful if properly planned rather than coming about de facto as a result of falling numbers or other difficulties, especially as there were strong economic and financial pressures to amalgamate. They added that Upholland would remain as a centre for 'theological and pastoral post-ordination training and for the continuing ordination of priests'; moreover, the enlarged Junior Seminary would mean that a 'locus' for priestly training would not be completely lost to the North-West. Finally, the Congregation agreed with the Archbishop's point that any such moves were up to the diocesan bishop, and not a conference of bishops, to decide. The Archbishop, however, must consider the wider view that refusing to change might damage overall priestly training and even bring 'long range disadvantages' to Liverpool itself; the Congregation called for a spirit of sacrifice from the archdiocese.

Neither the Archbishop nor the Governors of Upholland were impressed by the arguments used by the Congregation in its letter. Indeed, they argued in return that the Congregation had made a number of false assumptions and had got a number of key facts wrong. First of all, numbers in the Senior Seminary at Upholland were as high as they had been for the previous twenty years – 75 in all, including about a dozen 'day students' from the Don Orione Fathers and the Sacred Heart Fathers who had both opened houses nearby so that their students could attend. Secondly, it was not clear either that the 'theological presence' promised by the Northern Bishops should be at Upholland or that, if it were, that the necessary changes could be made 'almost immediately' – indeed, the presence of a much enlarged Junior Seminary would militate against the use of Upholland for that purpose. Thirdly, the expensive and most uneconomic part of Upholland was the Junior Seminary and here the Archbishop quoted some frightening statistics: of 139 junior students who had entered between 1958 and 1961, only eight were ordained priests in 1971-74, at a cost of £23,000 each for the junior part of their course. On the other hand, in the four years 1965-68, 42 students had entered the Senior Seminary, of whom 11 had been ordained at a cost of just under £4,000 each. Furthermore, Upholland was cheaper to run than Ushaw and so from the economic point of view it would make sense either to amalgamate at Upholland or at least to continue to run both colleges. Then, with regard to an amalgamated Junior Seminary, the Archbishop pointed out that numbers were already declining and more and more people, including most of the priests teaching in them, were having serious doubts about their role. Finally, the Congregation's appeal to 'take the wider view' and consider the matter *coram Domino* (i.e. as a question of conscience and not in a partisan spirit) drew the response that the Governors believed that any closure might well have serious consequences on the recruitment of students for the priesthood in the most populous diocese in England and Wales.[16]

In February 1974 Archbishop Beck went to Rome with his Chancellor, Mgr George Mooney, to put his case in person. They made little impression on the Congregation, although in a letter of April its secretary stressed that the decision whether to close Upholland or not was entirely the Archbishop's and the Congregation had no intention of putting any pressure on him – its letter had no juridical status. While standing by its original decision, the Congregation urged the other bishops to consider Beck's proposal that any decision be postponed for some time.[17] The Northern Bishops discussed the question again in April 1974 at the Low Week meeting and upheld their previous decision. In the end, the Archbishop accepted this for the sake of peace, and issued an ad clerum and press release in May: this accepted the 'preference' of the Holy See for the Headingley agreement. Ushaw would be the only Senior Seminary in the North of England, and, 'as desired by the Holy See', Upholland would remain as a Theological Institute that all the northern dioceses and Shrewsbury would support. Additionally, an amalgamated Junior Seminary would be located at Upholland. All this would be put into effect as soon as possible.[18]

The Archbishop remained convinced, *coram Domino,* of the strength of his case for the retention of a Senior Seminary at Upholland. Tactically he thought he could delay any final implementation by insisting that the 'Roman Solution' was a package that had to be implemented in toto – the failure of any one part would mean he was not bound to implement the rest. In particular, he pointed out to the other bishops that a Theological Institute at Upholland would call for a considerable financial and staffing commitment on all their parts and could not be achieved quickly. Furthermore, he would have to consult his priests and the laity about any changes since Upholland was, and would remain, a major asset of the archdiocese. Finally he repeated his argument that attitudes to junior seminaries were becoming increasingly hostile to their continuation, a view now common among vocation directors. He asked the bishops take the prudent step of consulting those of their priests who would staff the new amalgamated Junior Seminary. There was no delay, however: a working party to decide on the details of the joint seminaries began to meet straight away, to plan for an amalgamation in September 1975.[19]

The last senior students left Upholland in the summer of 1975, just less than a century after it had taken in its first ones under Bishop O'Reilly in 1883 and less than fifty years after the completion of the massive extension of its buildings begun in the 1920s. The closure caused considerable bitterness, coming as it did when new ideas on the training of priests had been carefully thought through and accepted by most of the clergy: a sense of excitement turned into a sense of loss which was not eased by the nebulous idea of a Theological Institute, something that many suspected had been thought up in haste; certainly the commitment of some of the Northern Bishops to it did not last very long, as we will see.

The Senior Seminary at Upholland had contributed substantially but rarely overwhelmingly to the number of priests ordained for the archdiocese over the years – between 1940 and 1976 this amounted to 195 out of 357 (54.6%), with the highest proportion being in the decade 1960 – 1969 when the percentage rose to 64%.[20] The subsequent drastic decline in vocations to the priesthood would have made it impracticable to keep both Upholland and Ushaw going as senior seminaries for the north of England, but that was not known at the time of the closure The Archbishop was to be proved right in thinking that a Theological Institute and an enlarged Junior Seminary – two bodies with completely different aims and ethos – would sit uneasily side by side in the same buildings, no matter how large these might be. He was also right to question the Congregation's view that the transition from Senior Seminary to Theological Institute could be achieved easily and speedily. Moreover, those of his advisors who shared his belief that the days of junior seminaries were fast approaching their twilight were soon proved to have been much more in touch with 1970s realities than the other Northern Bishops and the Sacred Congregation.

The total number of Church students in the Junior Seminary in September 1975 was 197, but by 1979 it had fallen to 122, with only twelve boys (including lay students) entering the first form from the seven dioceses. The bishops refused to give the headmaster a guarantee of their long-term support. By 1986, the number of Church students had fallen to 54 out of a total of 82, and the curriculum was becoming non-viable. The Northern Bishops took the decision not to prolong the agony beyond July 1987 – Upholland was to become a hostel for the few boys who still came forward as candidates for the priesthood and they would receive their education at local Catholic schools; in December 1987 there were six 'hostelers' in residence, along with Fr Christopher Cunningham as their Director. So, in about twenty-five years Archbishop Heenan's optimistic extensions of the Junior Seminary to cope with a large increase in entrants had turned into something that a reasonably large house could have accommodated. The last boys left Upholland altogether in 1992 (the last of them to be ordained, Mark Madden, became a priest in 1996).[21]

THE UPHOLLAND NORTHERN INSTITUTE

The idea that Upholland might become a centre for in-service training for the clergy tuned in nicely with a growing realisation among many priests that they needed much more than formula-driven deanery conferences if they were to be effective pastors in modern society and not mere dispensers of the sacraments. Vatican II had made much of what they had learned in the seminary obsolete; revolutionary liturgical change could be disturbing as well as liberating for celebrant and congregation, and there was the promise (or threat) of a new Code of Canon Law. No wonder the National Conference of Priests, meeting in Liverpool in 1971, had recognized an urgent need for the organisation of post-ordination training on a serious and regular basis for all pastoral clergy. In a separate report they urged that there was as much need for the careful planning of in-service training as of seminary courses themselves. All this was in line with the Sacred Congregation of the Clergy's letter of 1968 that had insisted that on-going formation was a professional duty of priests and that a corresponding duty lay on bishops to encourage their clergy by, among other means, providing opportunities for regular sabbatical leave. In 1972 a working-party report to the Archbishop of Liverpool on Priestly Formation envisaged the setting-up of a pastoral institute and commented that if the final training of seminarians could be linked with the in-service training of the clergy and the further education of both religious and laity, then there would be advantages for all those involved. Finally, in this sketch of the background to the decisions affecting the future of Upholland, it may be mentioned that in 1973 priests of the Lancaster and Leeds dioceses had launched a number of residential courses dealing with theological renewal, one of which won national acclaim with an enthusiastic report in the *Tablet*.[22]

Post-Vatican II talk of theological renewal, of course, implied casting a net beyond priests and religious. Effective adult Christian education had always come a very poor second to school-age provision in England and Wales, and even the good work of Liverpool's ground-breaking Catholic Action and Lay Apostolate schemes had not broken that mould sufficiently.

There was now an opportunity to see the theological renewal of priests and religious, and the apostolic formation of lay-people, as part of a single operation: to energise the whole People of God in his service and worship. The National Conference of Priests had asked for a clear set of priorities, at the top of which they saw the task of forming lay apostles to promote the growth of the genuine Christian community. According to many commentators at the time, there was a crying need in the Church for mature, adult Christians, and a new theological institute could hope to make some contribution towards meeting that need.

A working-party under the Archbishop's chairmanship sought advice on the establishment of a theological foundation of some sort at Upholland. The most thoughtful Position Paper was presented by Fr Kevin Kelly. It was wide-ranging, dealing with the types of course that might be provided, the possible uses of the accommodation, the wisdom or otherwise of appointing an overall rector to head up both the Junior Seminary and the Theological Institute, as it was tentatively called at that stage, and the role of the Institute in the other northern dioceses. The fundamental part of the paper, however, did not lie in the suggestions for dealing with these practical issues, but in the approach to theology that it laid out. The purpose of Christian theology, Kelly stated, was to deepen our understanding of 'God's self-revelation in His Son, Jesus Christ, so that we may "know Him more clearly, love Him more dearly and follow Him more nearly"': theology should not be regarded as the select hobby of professional theologians, but 'a vital activity' of the whole People of God. The key purpose of the Institute, therefore, should be to assist priests, religious and lay-people to reflect as mature Christians on their Faith, and on their understanding of their lives and of the world in which they lived in the light of that Faith. The aim of the Institute could not be to teach theology to non-theologians or to up-date for priests the theology they had learned in the seminary, because essentially:

> theology is the Christian community reflecting on its encounter with
> the Risen Lord in the living world … (and) coming to recognise its
> Lord more clearly and achieving a better understanding of the life and
> demands of the Kingdom in our sophisticated, technological age.

A proper appreciation of the role of theology would assist those who rejected the Church as irrelevant, those who withdrew into their shells to seek security in the 'comforting externals of a cultic Church', and those who put up the barriers and engaged in open war against the modern world.[23] This was, truly, an ennobling vision, quite different from what most people, including, no doubt, the Northern Bishops, had in mind when they spoke about in-service training for the clergy or adult education for the laity.

At a meeting in March 1975 the Northern Bishops agreed to spend £43,000 on necessary changes and improvements to the buildings at Upholland, the costs to be shared between the northern dioceses and Shrewsbury. Fr Kelly was appointed as Director for an initial period of two years, with four other priests appointed immediately, along with a Religious

Sister, and with four other named priests as possible appointments. The name of the new foundation was to be the Upholland Northern Institute. The bishops also agreed that each diocese should appoint a pastoral director to liaise with the Institute. Perhaps less positively, there was some discussion by the bishops of a rather spirit-destroying suggestion that these directors should meet to discuss the 'degree of compulsion' to be exerted on their clergy to attend. Finally, it was established that one governing body (comprising the bishops of the Northern Province and Shrewsbury) should control and oversee the work of the three institutions – Ushaw, Upholland Junior Seminary and the Upholland Northern Institute – albeit with separate committees for each institution. This reflected the reality that between them the bishops owned and financed the three institutions, but as the Governors would also be responsible for key policy decisions, it might have been expected that their body would have had a wider membership.[24]

The Upholland Northern Institute came into formal existence in January 1976, welcomed especially by those working in the field of Adult Christian Education. In his first report six months later the Director spoke of the danger that the team might become a 'wandering band of one-night lecturers', achieving very little genuine apostolic formation among their audiences. But they had made a good start, offering a very varied range of courses, some residential, some 'on the road', some long and some lasting only a day. The initial highlight had been a residential in-service training course for the hierarchy, attended by 27 bishops and the secretary of the Bishops' Conference. Looking to the future the Director hoped to establish formal links with the Faculty of Theology at the University of Manchester and with the department of Religious Studies at the University of Lancaster, as well as with the various departments of extra-mural studies, Adult Education Colleges and the WEA.[25]

Over the first three years residential bookings rose from nineteen to eighty, with about 40% of these being for UNI's own courses. Increasingly, outside bodies began to use the facilities – the Bishops' Conference, Marriage Encounter, the Catholic Men's Society, the Middlesbrough Liturgical Commission among others – along with various non-Catholic religious and secular groups. Clearly, in a conference-conscious age Upholland was becoming relatively popular as a venue, although it suffered from the small amount of residential accommodation of a good standard that it could offer. These developments helped the financial position, but they were not part of UNI's core business, and here there were some worrying statistics. In the four years 1976 – 1979 an average of 211 secular priests attended in-service courses at Upholland each year; in 1980 this figure dropped to 184, rising again to 246 in 1981 – all in all, about 12% of the secular priests available. The staff of UNI also ran two diocesan-based courses in 1981, one in Salford that attracted 32 priests and one in Shrewsbury that attracted 10. In that year, fewer than 5% of the clergy of three dioceses, Salford, Middlesbrough, and Leeds, attended courses at Upholland.[26]

Why was UNI not attracting more clergy to its courses? This was the main question addressed by a review committee set up in 1979 by the Northern Bishops and Shrewsbury and which reported in 1982 (the *Hazlewood Report).* The review members suggested four answers: first, a natural reluctance on the part of priests to undertake in-service training, coupled with the practical difficulties of leaving their parishes. Second, they suggested that, despite the relaxed and welcoming atmosphere created by the UNI team, Upholland still carried the associations of a seminary regime (Kevin Kelly had never been happy with the juxtaposition of the Institute and the Junior Seminary and had even explored using other venues). Third, 'what was said by speakers (giving the courses) occasionally caused surprise to some people'; others felt the approach was too academic instead of being pastoral and spiritual, while some felt that the speakers sometimes resorted to 'shock tactics' in order to stimulate the audience. Finally, the reviewers believed that criticisms of UNI, which affected clerical willingness to attend, were 'frequently ill-informed or based on hearsay'. They then added a section that shows that the avant-garde nature of some of the teaching was clearly a major concern. They defended the freedom of theologians to 'penetrate further into the mysteries of the faith and to communicate them to the enlightenment of the People of God', but stressed that theologians must also be 'resolute defenders of orthodoxy' and their theology 'must be for the Church and in the Church'. There was then a long quotation from Pope John Paul II (from his *Catechesi tradendae),* dealing with the duties of theologians and catechists not to put forward as certainties what were only theories or matters of debate among experts; they had to be guided by the 'light of the Magisterium' and avoid troubling the minds of children and young people with 'outlandish theories, useless questions and unproductive discussions'.[27] That this final sentence was put into the section of the report about the presentation of theology to the clergy was, to put it politely, bizarre.

The reviewers had started their report with a more fundamental point: the all-important concept of a 'theological presence' had never been clearly defined, though it had informed the whole debate on seminary re-organisation. Moreover, they claimed that the relationship between the two basic components of UNI, clerical in-service education and adult Christian education for lay people, had been 'subject to different interpretations'.[28] With hindsight it can be seen that it was a pity that the issue of setting up a Theological Institute to serve the whole of the north of England was connected with the closure of the Upholland Senior Seminary. It was too easy to see the Institute as essentially a way of 'keeping Upholland going' under a different guise, or as a handy way of finding a use for the extensive and expensive buildings, or even as a sop to Archbishop Beck who had been so obviously opposed to closing the Senior Seminary in the first place.

The report then went on to deal with the other aspect of UNI's work, Adult Christian Education (ACE), and declared quite baldly that if UNI had confined its activities to in-service training for priests it would have been a failure. Experience had taught the team, however, that the most successful courses were those run jointly for 'priests-with-their-people': the lay people were encouraged by the participation of their own priests, while the latter did not feel themselves separated from the lay leaders 'or threatened by their advancing knowledge'. Moreover, this coming together provided an impetus to more specialised priests' courses arising from the needs of their people, and therefore more 'natural' than simple revision or up-dating of the priests' seminary-originated theology. The reviewers again resorted to the Pope's Apostolic Exhortation: this had arrived 'providentially' to show the type of institution UNI should become: its main work should be to meet the need throughout the Church to train lay catechists 'in the broadest sense of the term', for the catechesis of adults was 'the principal form' of catechesis; the Pope went on to add that such work was a suitable area for diocesan, inter-diocesan, or even national, co-operation.[29]

Fr Vincent Nichols had become Director of the Institute in January 1981 in succession to Fr Kelly. He reported that the staff remained 'happy and purposeful, aiming to deepen faith and to train local leaders in order that the basic aim of a Church in partnership might be better realised'. The main task, he went on, was the development of Adult Christian Education in the north of England, and for this there needed to be strong active links with ACE teams working in the various dioceses. The major work would be preparing, supporting and training lay leaders in partnership with the clergy.[30] It is interesting that his report made no mention of the original idea of a Theological Institute or of proper post-ordination training for the clergy, although the Institute's programme continued to put on long courses for priests and shorter courses aimed specifically at their needs.

A later report (*The Nelson Report,* 1985) painted a much bleaker picture. It included a damning financial analysis, not in terms of the overall costs but concerning the absence of proper budgeting, the lack of financial responsibility in the accepted business sense and of financial guidelines, and the practice of offering open-ended subsidies to meet estimated deficits. Furthermore, the report commented adversely on the lack of clarity about the relationship of the Institute to Upholland College (the Junior Seminary was still in existence at this stage) and particularly to its administrative processes, and on failing morale among the staff, who seemed unsure of their identity as the Theological Institute had gradually become the Provincial Centre for Adult Christian Education. At the same time it appeared to be losing the leading national position it had had for a few years in ACE itself.[31]

No doubt in answer to these criticisms, when the Director (now Fr Joseph Smith of Leeds diocese) reported to the Governors in December 1985 he was upbeat about the increased numbers attending all the courses, but stressed the need for more residential staff. The staff were even more optimistic in a document they produced a month later. They regarded the Institute as a Provincial responsibility and felt that it had delivered a 'remarkable service' to the northern dioceses in the previous ten years, gaining in the process a national and international reputation for its ACE work. Indeed, they saw its future in national terms and suggested that it should become the 'Upholland National Institute for Adult Christian Education'. This would call for further financial commitment from the bishops to realise their vision and the golden opportunity for the Church it presented.[32]

This was wishful thinking taken to extremes. Bishop Moberley of Hallam made it very clear a few weeks later that he, for one, believed that the closing of the Junior Seminary meant that the agreement to support a theological presence in the North West had been 'unwrapped' and was no longer binding. The practice of deficit funding was unacceptable to him and he had every intention of setting up his own pastoral centre that would be much more attractive to his priests and people. Finally, he believed that the idea of Upholland going national was a non-starter as others had stolen a march on them. When all the Northern Bishops met in March they raised similar concerns, but agreed to continue to support the Institute under a new, unspecified, contract.[33]

The tone of Fr Smith's report in June 1986 was altogether different from that of six months before. He described as 'distressing' the statistics of how many priests and lay people had attended courses in the previous six months: two dioceses, Hallam and Shrewsbury, had not been represented on any of the courses while the other six dioceses had provided only eleven priests between them for the long course.[34] In 1987 the long course for priests had to be cancelled through a lack of applicants and the UNI team was down to four people – Fr Smith (due to end his term of office the following summer), Fr O'Hanlon from Nottingham, a lay person (Miss Magee) and Sister Bernadette O'Malley FCJ. The governors agreed that urgent steps should be taken to define the role of the Northern Institute in the light of 'the present and future needs of the province' – a working party was set up to do this. The Institute was still running successful courses in Lay Ministry – one of them as far away as Newcastle – and for the formation of Religious. Mgr John Butchard, newly appointed overall Director of Upholland, reported that income had risen through use of the facilities of St Joseph's Conference Centre (set up in 1986) by other, often secular, groups.[35]

UNI effectively came to an end in 1988 when Fr Smith retired as its Director and was not replaced. Day and evening courses continued (e.g. for Eucharistic Ministers and other forms of Pastoral Formation), but it ceased to have any resident lecturing staff. Then in November 1988 Archbishop Worlock announced that plans had been made for a complete redevelopment of the whole site, with housing, leisure facilities and a modern conference centre. The scheme would, he claimed, take the College 'into the 21st century and beyond' and make it a 'Christian centre second to none in the country' – it was 'theologically right, ethically correct, environmentally and architecturally excellent and financially feasible'. Mgr Butchard was commissioned to close down the College altogether, issuing redundancy notices, cancelling conference bookings, emptying the estate houses, and so on. Work had already been done to win over the West Lancashire District Council, but when the detailed plans were published its promised support disappeared overnight. Eighteen months of stress and frustration later, Mgr John Devine was appointed Director in the summer of 1990, with a brief to start things up again and bring in revenue as the redevelopment seemed permanently blocked. He succeeded in getting a number of bodies to set up permanent offices there – CAFOD, the Associated Church Clubs, the Archdiocesan Youth Office and the Diocesan Commercial Services. A small number of priests lived there in retirement.[36]

The College was used for annual clergy retreats and in 1996 it became the centre for the Archdiocesan Archives with a full-time archivist. The United Reform Church ran residential training courses for its ordinands, while bodies such as the Lancashire Chamber Orchestra and the University of Central Lancashire also used the residential facilities. Some parish groups had 'away days' there and both the Council of Clergy and the Pastoral Council used it for their meetings, as did the SVP, Serra, the Catenians and the Justice and Peace Commission, the North West Catholic History Society and the Historic Churches Committee.[37] Despite all the activity, no substantial long-term use could be found for the buildings, and proper development of them as a conference centre would have necessitated a very costly up-grading of the accommodation and extensive repairs. Development of part of the grounds for housing might have brought in the huge amounts of money required for such modernisation, and several plans were drawn up, but such development was blocked by continuing Local Authority opposition to any large scale building on what was a 'green belt' area on the edge of the new town of Skelmersdale. Archbishop Kelly took the decision to close the buildings altogether in November 1999, having agreed a sale to a developer who took on the search for planning permission as part of his business risk. The benefits of sale were not to accrue to the archdiocese until such planning permission was obtained. And so Upholland College closed – a sad end to many dreams.

Notes

1 AAL St Joseph's Seminary Collection, S5 VIII: Priestly Formation, D/1 Abp Heenan to Mgr Breen, Nov. 1960; contains recommendations on Ushaw and Upholland.

2 Heenan, *Crown of Thorns*.

3 F. Callon, 'A History of the College Grounds', Pts I, II, III, *Upholland Magazine,* 1965, pp.11-5; 1966, pp.18-35; 1968, pp.4-15; AAL Beck, S1 XIV A: Council of Clergy: Fr Cheetham's Report, 20.9.1969.

4 *Ibid.,* Fr Worden's Report, 20.9.1969

5 AAL St Joseph's, S5 VIII D: University Links and Professional Training; D/2, Worden on the isolation, 15.1.1967; D/11 Worden to Governors, 24.9.1967.

6 *Ibid.,* D/12, 16, 18, 20, Dec. 1967-March 1968.

7 *Ibid.,* D/16, 26.1.1968.

8 *Ibid.,* D/19, K. Kelly to Beck, 15.3.1968.

9 *Ibid.,* 'Priestly Formation, A Report to the Archbishop of Liverpool', (1972).

10 AAL Beck, S.1 XIV A: Meeting June 1972, pp.12-6.

11 *Ibid.,* S2 XIV A: Ad clerums and Notices: Lent Pastorals 1967-9.

12 *Ibid.,* 1971 wallet, ad clerum 24.3.1971; Northern Bps' Report, April 1972.

13 *Ibid.,* S1 XIV A: Meeting 6.6.1973, Headingley Statement and summaries.

14 *Ibid.*

15 AAL Upholland Northern Institute (UNI) Collection, S1 I A/1-25: Establishment.

16 AAL UNI, S1 I A/2 'Some notes on the Letter' and Governors' Comments, 17.1.1974.

17 *Ibid.,* A/4, Sacred Congregation to Beck, 2.4.1974.

18 AAL St Joseph's, S5 IX E/1, 2 Ad clerum and press release, 13 & 15 May 1974; E/3, Upholland Students to Northern Bishops, 30.5.1974.

19 AAL UNI, S1 I A/5, Dalton to Beck, 7.5.1974; St Joseph's, S5 IX E/4, Agenda for Joint Staff Meeting, 4.6.1974.

20 *Directories; The Upholland Magazine* gave detailed ordination figures each year.

21 AAL St Joseph's, S5 IX E; UNI, S1 I A and S1 IV A, cover the closure. I am very grateful for correspondence and conversations on the material in this chapter with Dr K. Kelly, Mgr John Butchard and Mgr George Mooney.

22 Kevin T. Kelly, 'A New Venture in the North: Upholland Northern Institute', *Clergy Review,* vol. LX, no.10 (Oct.1975), pp.623-43; AAL UNI, S1 I E/17, 'The Hazlewood Report', (1982), p.32.

23 AAL UNI, S1 I A/7: 'The Upholland Theological Institute', 9.10.1974.

24 *Ibid.,* A/10: 'Meeting of the Northern Bishops and Shrewsbury', 12-13.3.1975.

25 *Ibid.,* A/40: Report on Jan.-June 1976.

26 *Ibid.,* A/26-63: Director's reports, 1976-81.

27 *Ibid.,* S1 I E/17, 'The Hazlewood Report' (1982), esp. pp.35-6.

28 *Ibid.,* p.32.

29 *Ibid.,* pp.36-7.

30 *Ibid.,* E/16-25, Directors' Reports to Governors, Nov. 1981.

31 *Ibid.,* E/29, 'The Nelson Report', May 1985.

32 *Ibid.,* E/25, Director to Governors, 4.12.1985; S8 IV A/6: 'Reflections on the Future of Upholland: The Perspective of the UNI Team', 14.1.1986.

33 AAL UNI, S8 IV A/8: Moberley to Worlock, 17.2.1986; A/11: Minutes of Hazlewood Meeting, 5.3.1986.

34 AAL UNI, S1 I E/30, Director to Governors, 10.6.1986.

35 *Ibid.,* E/33, Butchard to Governors, Dec. 1987; E/27, Minutes of Governors, 10.12.1987.

36 Correspondence with Mgr Butchard Nov. 2003, in author's possession. The re-development plans, announced in Nov. 1988, are covered in *The Catholic Pictorial,* Nov. 1988.

37 AAL UNI, Buildings and Maintenance, S1 IV A: Closure and Future Use, A/1-26.

CHAPTER 19 CATHOLICS AND THEIR NEIGHBOURS

S creaming women and children attacked the Archbishop, some wielding brooms, some throwing stones and tomatoes at him and his car. The large Catholic crowd began to sing 'Faith of our Fathers' (with more venom than religious fervour, according to the Archbishop's own account) and the Protestants feared an invasion of 'their' streets. This was in Robsart Street, in St Anthony's parish, not in the 1930s but in March 1958 – Archbishop Heenan had been visiting a house-bound Catholic parishioner. In the end tempers were fairly easily quieted and the Archbishop played down the event as much as he could, but the incident shows some of the difficulties inherent in the pursuit of Christian unity at ground level.[1] The extent to which that pursuit had been successful may perhaps be illustrated by the fact that at Christmas 2003 the Catholics and the Anglicans of Hough Green, Widnes, most of whom had been re-located from inner-city Liverpool, celebrated a shared Eucharist in their shared parish church.[2]

THE GROWTH OF ECUMENISM

There had been little attempt at serious ecumenical action among English Catholics until the setting up of the Secretariat for Christian Unity in Rome prior to the Second Vatican Council, and no demand for it, either, at parish level, although some complained about restrictions that did not allow them to take part in non-Catholic weddings and funerals or attend civic services. Even Archbishop Heenan continued the fundamental attitude of his predecessors, although he wanted more friendly relations with other Christians and allowed the saying of the 'Our Father' and 'Apostles' Creed' in common. He became a member of the Vatican Secretariat and set up its English office, or ecumenical headquarters as he called it, in Liverpool (because Cardinal Godfrey was not keen to have it in Westminster), so that Christians of all denominations would have, in his words, 'a place to go' and there would be a Catholic body to give guidance to priests and people.[3]

After attending the first session of the Second Vatican Council he showed some movement from his previous position: the fortress still stood intact, but perhaps its battlements looked a little less forbidding. He pointed out to the clergy that Pope John XXIII had Church Unity very much at heart when he called the Council, wishing it to be both pastoral and ecumenical (although he later described the Pope's approach to ecumenism as 'rudimentary' and old fashioned).[4] Therefore, he went on, the English Bishops while in Rome had decided that the coming Octave of Prayer for Christian Unity in 1963 should be celebrated with more emphasis, with special Masses and sermons. He suggested that those preaching during the week should make it clear that Christian Unity entailed the return of the Separated Brethren to the Mother Church – Catholic doctrine could never be changed to suit non-Catholics, but better ways of talking about and explaining it could be found. Scholastic terminology should be avoided and efforts made to show that Catholic doctrine 'stripped of the extravagance often used by Catholic writers' did not differ from the beliefs of the early Church. On practical issues, he was against visits by non-Catholic groups to Mass during the Octave, though courtesy would make it difficult to refuse them if they insisted on coming. It was unfortunate, but such visits could give non-Catholics the idea that all Christian services had the same value, and, of course, Catholics could not return the visit – there was a world of difference, he argued, between praying in common and encouraging joint religious services.

The Archbishop went on to say that Unity in the sense of a return of Protestants to the Church was most unlikely for some generations to come. It was essential, therefore, to persuade would-be converts not to put off becoming Catholics. The times were more opportune than ever for people, freed of religious prejudice, to examine seriously the claims of the Catholic Church, and any priests who did not have prospective converts under instruction should examine their consciences. When priests spoke of Christian Unity, he concluded, they should always do so 'with compassion', letting the people see that their zeal for souls was genuine, while always being 'firm but very gentle' on the point that a a return to the Catholic Church could be the only form of true unity.

There is an interesting section in Clifford Longley's account of Mgr (later Archbishop) Derek Worlock at the Second Vatican Council.[5] According to this, Bishop Beck (at the time Bishop of Salford) wanted to speak at the Council to criticise the ecumenical movement because of the adverse effect it was having on individual conversions to Catholicism. Archbishop Heenan (by then at Westminster) heard of this through Worlock, who described what Beck had intended to say as the 'most die-hard and ultra-conservative stuff', and so the Archbishop persuaded Beck not to give the speech. When Heenan himself spoke on the subject at the Council shortly afterwards he claimed to be speaking for all the English hierarchy who, he said, were prepared to do anything, short of denying the faith, 'to obtain the unity of Christians'.[6] It is quite clear that the hierarchy were anything but united themselves and Beck's blocked speech would not have been expressing just his own views. Worlock himself had already gone through a conversion experience as a result of attending the Council and working with Heenan (he had earlier shared Cardinal Godfrey's conservative views); Bishop Beck took somewhat longer to make that journey.

Little changed in practice until late 1964, after the promulgation of the Council's decree on Ecumenism. This left it up to national hierarchies to determine the extent and methods of common prayer between Catholics and other Christians, while making it clear that it would be a false ecumenism to act as though all Christians were already united in faith and so could join in joint worship. The English and Welsh bishops issued a statement that altered practice radically and overthrew a number of long-established prohibitions.[7] In future, they said, elected representatives and public officials might attend services in non-Catholic churches as part of their civic duties. Moreover, all Catholics were allowed, out of friendship or courtesy, to attend non-Catholic weddings and funerals, and could even be bridesmaids or best men at weddings between non-Catholics. As friendship between Christians grew, the bishops expected that some Catholics would be invited to attend services such as the induction of a new clergyman; those invitations could be accepted. On the issue of attendance at Remembrance Day services at war memorials (as we have seen, a very sensitive issue that had given considerable offence to non-Catholics in the past), there was now nothing to stop Catholics attending; priests might even plan combined services with other ministers. The Week of Prayer for Christian Unity had, according to the bishops, been observed 'with growing enthusiasm in recent years'; in future, as well as services in each church, there should be an evening set aside for a meeting in some suitable hall of all the Christians in an area for joint prayer, talks from different ministers, Scripture readings and hymns. Priests or lay people who were invited to speak in non-Catholic churches still needed episcopal permission and their addresses must not constitute a formal part of a service.

The bishops ended by hoping that clergy and laity would wholeheartedly follow the lead given by the Council. There could be no sharing by Catholics in non-Catholic Eucharistic services nor could a Catholic take any official part in a non-Catholic service. The norms they had laid down would, they believed, avoid any danger of indifferentism and ensure that 'true ecumenism' would not be jeopardised by 'injudicious action which could easily give a wrong impression on both sides'. After this statement, read out in all the churches of the archdiocese in December 1964, relations between Catholics and other Christians had to change, despite the fears of those who believed that the martyr-fed heritage of Catholic Lancashire was in danger of being thrown away – and the equally strong fears of evangelical Protestants that they would be expected to regard Catholics as their 'brothers and sisters in Christ'.

Archbishop Beck (at Liverpool since January 1964) was quite clear how the Decree of the Vatican Council should affect the whole of Catholic thinking and not just occasional practice. He wrote in a pastoral letter that, although Christ had founded only one Church, his followers were divided into hundreds of separate groups, in clear contradiction to his will. This was, he was sure, *a scandal to the world, and a dishonour to all who bear the Christian name. It is a serious obstacle to the fulfilment of Christ's command that the Gospel should be preached to every creature.*[8]

It was the first time that people had heard the call to unity in such plain terms and realised that it involved more than being kind to other Christians, who, in the Archbishop's words, also loved and worshipped God and acknowledged 'Jesus Christ as Lord and Saviour'. He picked out Anglicans for special mention – their love of the Scriptures, their noble forms of worship, their prayers and hymns full of Catholic truth and their works of practical charity often put Catholics to shame – and quoted Pope John XXIII's declaration that they would 'never cease to be our brothers until they cease to say "Our Father"'.

What could be done to translate these ideas into practice and so create and foster an ecumenical outlook, especially at parish level, throughout the archdiocese – and how far could one go? The Archbishop had already set up an Ecumenical Commission to encourage closer contacts between Catholics and other Christians, to plan joint meetings of theologians and to help priests meet other ministers in their area. Parish sodalities of men and women should, he believed, meet similar groups from other churches in the neighbourhood, and there should be common action to help the sick and deprived and to improve society. On suitable occasions, Christians should pray together, though the full sharing in Eucharistic services was not allowed since the Eucharist was the sign of unity already achieved. Above all, the work for unity depended on a renewal of the individual's inner life. Obviously, the Archbishop added, Catholics must never sacrifice their beliefs, but they might well have to abandon their old prejudices.[9]

Here were all the essentials of the call to unity that was to echo and re-echo over the next thirty years. It was only to be expected that some priests answered the call with greater enthusiasm than others and that some of their people, fully committed to their faith in many ways, failed to make their own the conviction of popes and archbishops that division was a scandal and a sin. Perhaps what was remarkable was how much progress was made in overcoming this understandable conservatism, under the general guidance of the Commission. There were meetings of deanery representatives, united services of prayer, the setting up of local Councils of Churches, regular 'fraternals' between clergy of different denominations, joint schemes for house visiting, joint study of the social problems facing the new towns and even ecumenical hot pot suppers. Fr James Geary (forty years ordained) reported from Southport that they were finding ecumenism 'a most rich and rewarding experience … manifestly the work of the Holy Spirit', while Abbot Byrne, OSB, from Leyland thought that ecumenism was still a 'young and tender plant' but was already showing 'fair promise of future fruitfulness'.[10]

Church leaders of every persuasion recognised that their committed followers were a minority in English society and that there was an urgent need to find some way to evangelise both the un-churched and those who were nominal Christians; would a united approach be effective? Late in 1969 the Archdiocesan Council of Clergy discussed the possibility of joining in an ecumenical 'Mission to the North', an idea that had come from a meeting of Christian leaders and formed the essence of the 'Bishopthorpe Statement'. The Northern Catholic Bishops had reacted cautiously to this, the Liverpool Pastoral Council (composed of lay people and priests) rather more enthusiastically. Archbishop Beck was undecided about the proposal and so were most of his clergy, though as much because of doubts about the value of general missions to the uncommitted as because of its ecumenical nature. There was a danger, some felt, of ecumenical window-dressing, especially if tried and genuine ecumenical structures did not exist in a locality – how could they try to convert the uncommitted if they themselves did not speak with one voice? As one speaker put it, until there was a clearer idea of how 'all may be one', personal and local initiatives, accompanied by much study and prayer, were more likely to be fruitful.[11] Behind the discussion lay some questions that no one at that stage could answer: what did 'unity' mean in terms of doctrinal agreement and how far did it demand unified structures?

What was taking place ecumenically across the archdiocese showed that it was at least as well advanced in its practice as any other Catholic diocese in the country. Without wanting to read too much into a resumé of a report, it is interesting that in 1970 the Maghull deanery felt it had nothing exciting to report, just the usual 'run of the mill' ecumenical gatherings – were united services, fraternals, joint Good Friday walks of witness and a shared week-day Mass already in danger of becoming humdrum or at least routine?[12]

The Commission, however, was soon voicing concern about its own effectiveness: it was an old problem in a different dress – members felt their activities and interests were too connected with Merseyside, with the rest of the archdiocese in danger of neglect. This was especially so as its original plan to have a priest in each deanery responsible for ecumenical matters had not worked out. It now wanted an ecumenical committee in each deanery, with at least six members (to include lay people); this would be able to organise and react to local events more immediately than the central Commission, which was itself to be re-constituted with a membership made up of representatives from the deanery committees. The new arrangement should invigorate ecumenical work throughout the archdiocese – once again, local initiatives were seen to be the effective way forward, rather than grand central designs. One of the first tasks of the new deanery bodies was to see how they and their non-Catholic counterparts could agree on the message to be presented in the proposed 'Call to the North' (the new name for the Bishopthorpe initiative), to be launched in 1973.[13]

No one should have been surprised that it was taking time to get the structures for fruitful co-operation right and especially to inaugurate serious theological discussion at local levels. Where this did take place it was usually based on a discussion of a set book of the Bible – safe ground on the whole, avoiding the complex issues inherent in discussions of papal authority or the authenticity of non-Catholic orders. It was much easier, and for most Catholics probably more satisfying, to talk about and undertake joint social work of the 'Good Neighbour' type. A comprehensive report in March 1972 praised what had been achieved by a range of initiatives and the good will of most priests, but believed that the general picture across the archdiocese was far from satisfactory. There were still some deaneries where the fences were as high and as thick as in pre-Council days, and others where the fences were crossed, unwillingly, now and again for an ecumenical service, usually on the initiative of the local non-Catholics.[14]

It is tempting in retrospect to divide 1970s Catholics into three groups with regard to ecumenism. There were those (perhaps more numerous than was admitted) who wanted no part in ecumenical dialogue about re-union with non-Catholics (though they were quite prepared to be polite to them and even to buy their Christmas raffle-tickets), because it would mean throwing out too much of traditional Catholic belief and practice and was already leading to a decline in conversions. For these Catholics Archbishop Heenan had had the right idea: the only true unity would come when 'our separated brethren re-joined their Roman Mother'. Then there were those who were all in favour of ecumenical initiatives (the ecumaniacs, as they were called), attended joint services and waited impatiently for the day when they could share Communion together – or did not wait, but went ahead, seeing the refusal to share the Lord's Supper as only a continuation of the scandal of division; after all, all baptised people were already one in Christ, were they not?

There was a third group, perhaps the majority and including committed Catholics, who could not see what all the fuss was about and who fairly soon became tired of going to joint services that were planned on a lowest-common-denominator basis. If ecumenism was the work of the Spirit, as popes and bishops stressed it was, then re-union would come about in God's own good time. In the meanwhile, no progress would be made, humanly speaking, until 'They' sorted out a few real problems, such as, would non-Catholics ever accept the pope, and would the pope ever accept birth-control?

Most commentators agreed that by the mid-1970s or so the ecumenical movement at ground level was losing its earlier dynamism. Three reports in a Commission Newsletter of 1973 illustrate this in minor ways. The main service in Unity Week had taken place in the Anglican Cathedral and had been only moderately attended, with a congregation of 'perhaps 500'. Secondly, one of the deanery reports (St Thomas', Waterloo) was 'not at all happy, even rather pessimistic', with the main problem being a lack of leadership and initiative. Thirdly, and perhaps most tellingly, the report from St Joseph's (Liverpool) deanery, which comprised seven inner-city Catholic churches, said that good ecumenical work was being done at St Mary's, Highfield Street, but that a huge gap remained between the middle-class congregation that attended, usually from outside the area entirely, and the 'nominally 100% R.C. local population'.[15]

Commentators were also agreed that the 1960s and 1970s had witnessed a welcome decline in sectarian bitterness and hostility in Liverpool – and the size of the small demonstration by Ian Paisley and about 150 die-hard Protestants at the time of the papal visit in 1982 only underlined the changed relations. What commentators could not agree on was the cause of this development: it is not easy to know how far the reduction in sectarianism was due to greater understanding and tolerance of other people's religious standpoints, or to a growing indifference to all religion, even nominal religious adherence. One suspects that the latter played the more important role, along with shifting housing patterns that had broken up the former close-knit neighbourhood, almost tribal, communities. There was also the economic crisis of the 1970s, with heavy unemployment and social deprivation across the region, that led to the alienation evident at the time of the Toxteth riots in 1981: it united against authority those who in previous years might have relied on sectarian loyalties to bolster their sense of identity.

In most areas of English Catholic life, and especially in the more traditional heartlands of the industrial towns and cities, the influence of the priest was still key, despite any greater importance that was being given to the laity. It would be very unusual to find parishioners who were enthusiastic about elements of Catholic life if there were no corresponding enthusiastic priests involved. On the issue of ecumenism, only one attempt seems to have been made to measure the attitudes of the priests in the archdiocese and this was in a carefully constructed survey carried out in 1972-3. The survey was based on the detailed replies of nearly 200 priests, 52% of whom were parish priests and 63% of whom had been ordained more than twenty years. The priests generally declared themselves to be in favour of the ecumenical movement (but to a lesser degree than non-Catholic clergymen surveyed elsewhere), and even, to a surprisingly large extent (about 75%), to favour organic union with Churches that were similar in their theology and churchmanship. When it came to explaining what 'organic union' might mean in practice, however, most thought of it as consisting of absorption of other traditions into the Catholic Church or the formation of some sort of loose federation.[16]

While the priests surveyed supported joint meetings, discussions, and sharing in social projects and jointly organised services, a small majority were against shared churches and shared missionary work, and a small majority in favour of preaching in non-Catholic churches. A very small number (1.6%) admitted to having celebrated the Eucharist in another denomination's church, while a rather larger number (10.8%) had received Communion during a joint service in a non-Catholic church. One gets the impression overall from the survey of a certain amount of enthusiasm for 'run of the mill' ecumenical attitudes and practices, but an understandable reluctance to go any further until authority sorted out some very contentious issues. It is interesting in this context that a few years later a speaker at the Council of Clergy felt that parish ecumenical groups would work 'if they were backed by the priests' – lay people were depressed by the little support they received.[17]

364

This was more or less the ecumenical situation in the archdiocese when Derek Worlock moved from being Bishop of Portsmouth to become Archbishop of Liverpool in March 1976. His commitment to the cause of Church Unity was total, usually symbolised by his relationship with David Sheppard, the Anglican Bishop of Liverpool. It was much wider and deeper than that and was never intended by either of them to be just a duet – a point made obvious when from 1986 the partnership included Dr John Newton, the Methodist District Chairman and Moderator of the Free Churches, to form 'The Liverpool Three'. Other Free Church leaders were heavily involved in the search for Christian Unity, especially Norwyn Denny and John Williamson. Nor was Archbishop Worlock the initiator of this special relationship – he himself paid tribute to the quiet laying of foundations that had gone on between Archbishop Beck and Stuart Blanch, the former Anglican Bishop, as well as with Bishop Sheppard.[18]

Archbishop Worlock's striving for a genuine ecumenism cannot be separated from his striving for a genuine social justice. During his first press conference he said that he wished to close the gap between religion and life:

> to make our Faith a living reality that can be a sign of hope to people in rather troubled times; and at the same time to secure justice and human dignity in the ordinary affairs of life.[19]

He believed passionately that church leaders should be able to speak with one voice, or individually on behalf of the others, on the social problems or tragic events of the moment, and should respond as a united group when consulted by government or other bodies. It might seem, indeed, that at times he was more interested in this external face of ecumenism than in furthering it theologically or spiritually. He certainly believed that an ecumenism that was not 'at the service of the people' was worth very little, and would do nothing to attract people to adopt it as their own Christian outlook. At the same time he strove to put in place structures and institutions that would allow the deeper theological issues to be explored, and not just at a local level. He was one of the leading forces behind the creation of the new Council of Churches for Britain and Ireland, to replace the former British Council of Churches.[20]

In May 1982 Pope John Paul II visited Liverpool as part of his pastoral visit to England, Wales and Scotland. He took part in a service in the Anglican Cathedral on 30 May, accompanied by Cardinal Hume and Archbishop Worlock, and this was followed by Mass in the Catholic Cathedral. In his address before Mass the Pope dealt with the issue of Christian Unity, which he claimed was a vital concern for everyone. As Christians worked for reconciliation throughout the world, they felt the need more urgently than ever before to be reconciled among themselves:

> For the sin of disunity among Christians which has been with us for centuries, weighs heavily upon the Church. The seriousness of this sin was clearly shown at the Second Vatican Council, which stated: 'Without doubt, this discord openly contradicts the will of Christ ...' Restoration of unity ... is one of the main concerns of the Church in the last part of the 20th century ... No one can claim exemption from this responsibility.[21]

Archbishop Worlock took up the theme in his welcome to the Pope: referring to the Pope's historic journey along Hope Street between the two Cathedrals, he prayed that it would light a torch for reconciliation. The need for reconciliation at the local level, and the continuance of intransigent hostility, had been clear during the Unity Octave earlier that year: Mgr (later Bishop) Vincent Malone had been shouted down by a small group of the Orange Order in the Anglican Cathedral while preaching on that very topic, and Bishop John Rawsthorne had suffered the same fate when he had dared to preach in St George's, Everton, at the same time. To show that the ultra-Protestants were nothing if not consistent in their opposition, it should be added that they also shouted down Archbishop Runcie of Canterbury in March when he tried to preach at St Nicholas' Anglican parish church, apparently for being pro-papal and, they claimed, pro-IRA.[22]

There were a number of practical initiatives. The setting up of the Liverpool Institute of Higher Education (now Hope University College) was important for more than symbolic reasons. What happened was that the two Catholic colleges, Christ's and Notre Dame, amalgamated on the site of the former, which was next door to the site of St Katherine's, the Anglican college. Negotiations had already begun under Archbishop Beck to see if a merger or some sort of federation between the Catholic and the Anglican colleges would be feasible – partly on ecumenical grounds but also, it must be admitted, to stave off possible closure of one or more of the colleges under the government's programme of reducing the number of teacher-training places across the country. Lengthy negotiations led in the end to the formation of the Liverpool Institute of Higher Education, in which the amalgamated colleges would each keep their own character and so provide an example of ecumenical training in a Christian institute for would-be teachers.[23] The ecumenical character features clearly in the current prospectus.

Other initiatives included the LIMEC project – the Liverpool Industrial Mission Ecumenical Council – built on the long experience of the Anglican Liverpool Industrial Mission, the Catholic Young Christian Worker movement and Free Church lay people and ministers. There were Youth Pilgrimages to Taizé, Lindisfarne and Iona, each made up of ecumenical groups of people aged eighteen to twenty-five and led by a 'mixed' team of Church leaders. And then there were the shared churches.

The Directory of Liverpool Archdiocese for 1984 contained a short article, 'Shared Church in Hough Green'. It is worth quoting the opening statement:

> *The first church in the north built to be shared by Anglicans and Roman Catholics was opened … on Tuesday 22 March 1983. The church … is dedicated to St Basil and All saints and is used by the Anglican and Catholic communities of Hough Green.*

The Pope had blessed the foundation stone in May 1982, and the laying of the foundation stone ceremony had included the act of faith used by the Pope and Archbishop Runcie in Canterbury Cathedral. The buildings included the common church, with separate presbytery and vicarage. In a sense the building of a common church had been a natural development. The site had been bought by the archdiocese as far back as 1968, when the area was developed as a new estate for 15,000 people. The archdiocese had opened a school and a parish centre the following year and a presbytery in 1970. On the Anglican side, a mission was founded in Hough Green in 1981. A series of public meetings and other consultations took place when it was suggested that a common church be built; the voting at the public meetings was unanimously for a shared building, while of 432 written replies received only 32 were against the project. Some of the respondents said that they wanted something different for their children from the sectarian divisions of their own childhoods.

The management of the shared facilities is controlled by the Shared Church Agreement established by Act of Parliament of 1969 (The Sharing of Church Buildings Act). Archbishop Worlock stressed at the opening that it was a joint venture and a brave one, symbolised by the font of the new church that was an amalgam of the fonts previously used by the Anglicans and the Catholics. Moreover, he continued, it was a permanent arrangement, and not just a convenient alliance, involving a single group of Christians 'reconciled and joined in a common commitment to the Lord of their baptism'. The church has a single tabernacle, divided internally into separate Anglican and Catholic sections – an honest sign to some of the official lack of agreement on the Eucharist, but a disappointment to others that they could not share that 'Lord of their baptism' in Communion. There is another shared church in Warrington New Town, jointly owned by Catholics and Anglicans, and one in Liverpool.[24] In all three examples the support of local congregations on both sides has been a key element in the successful setting up of the joint ventures, for forced ecumenism is no ecumenism.

These and other initiatives bore fruit eventually in a joint agreement between Church leaders on Merseyside. On Pentecost Sunday 1985 six of them, including Archbishop Worlock, signed a Covenant of Unity or 'Call to Partnership' in the Anglican Cathedral. A good example of a local covenant occurred in Kirkby when in 1992 a Methodist, three Anglican and seven Catholic churches signed one. This was, perhaps, especially meaningful and even poignant because so many of the forebears of the Kirkby people had been riven by sectarian hatred; one of the things that had brought them together now, they said, was common action to 'repel attacks on the dignity and helplessness of our people' (see pages 384-5 below).

There were some, however, among the Catholic clergy who thought that the Archbishop spent too much time on these initiatives and neglected dealing with the day-to-day problems of priests throughout the archdiocese, as they coped with falling numbers and in some cases a loss of self-identity. Old certainties and practices were disappearing and with them the tasks that had at least provided a daily structure, such as visiting the sick and taking Communion to the house-bound – now handed over to the laity – or spending long hours in the confessional, now no longer necessary. One priest commented recently that he was expected to be more and more a manager of other people, which was not what he was trained or ordained for. Other criticisms centred on the time and energy spent on the problems of inner-city Liverpool and even of South America through LAMP (see below page 381).[25] Some felt that others saw more of their leader than the clergy and people in the archdiocese did; one is reminded of the spoof headline during World War II, when Churchill was under criticism for being abroad too often: 'Prime Minister Spotted in London!'

MIXED MARRIAGES

It is necessary to go back a few years to catch up with what was happening in this key area of the relationship between Catholics and their non-Catholic neighbours. As we have seen, successive archbishops had adopted a very strict line against them to discourage Catholics from entering such unions, but this had failed in many cases, and the regulations were as likely to alienate as to convert – although there had always been a stream of 'marriage converts'.

In 1958 Archbishop Heenan issued an ad clerum that dealt with both wholly Catholic and mixed marriages. He argued that the best way to discourage the latter was to perform Catholic marriages with every possible solemnity, especially that of a nuptial Mass – priests must try to establish everywhere the tradition of nuptial Masses 'which happily already exists in a small number of parishes', a telling admission of failure, surely, on the part of the clergy. He had already given permission for afternoon nuptial Masses and these had proved popular. To create a public opinion in favour of nuptial Masses priests should preach occasionally on their beauty, and should announce the times of their celebration and encourage parishioners to attend them. He referred to the time when he had been a parish priest and his practice of sometimes having the last, usually sung, Mass on Sunday as a nuptial Mass; this practice, he claimed, had been extremely successful and had made more young couples want one for their own wedding.[26]

Moving on to mixed marriages, he first declared that if possible he would refuse all requests for dispensations for such marriages. As the Church allowed them under certain conditions, however, he could not adopt that line. As a result, what concerned him most was the way mixed marriages were celebrated once a dispensation had been obtained. The couple and their families often felt slighted at the lack of decent celebration, the absence of organ music and flowers, and the use of 'a small altar obscurely sited'. Such things could become a lasting source of contention after the wedding, with the Catholic party becoming bitter and the non-Catholic hostile and disinclined to keep the promises; even good Catholics could feel resentful about it all. He had, he went on, listened to some priests whose opinions he valued and knew that they would deplore any relaxation of the regulations, but his conscience forced him to change them: in future, mixed marriages should take place before the high altar, though without lighted candles, and the organ could play before and after the service; the regulations of the previous diocesan synod were revoked. He had consulted the Chapter and had prayed over the issue for six months and, despite the obvious risks, was now certain that the changes would be for 'the greater good of souls' – his only motive in making them. He ordered the clergy, however, to read out the warning against mixed marriages every month.

It would be difficult to find a more sensitive, pastorally-aware statement on a difficult issue than this letter from Heenan. He went against the advice of some, or even most, of his senior clergy and against a diocesan tradition that dated back at least to Archbishop Whiteside, one of the great heroes of Liverpool Catholicism. Heenan was to urge a similar relaxation in 1964 during the Vatican Council, making the point that:

> if the Church grants a dispensation she should do graciously, magnanimously and in an open-handed way. The wedding should be both beautiful and happy ...[27]

It was a good example of true leadership and illustrates again his pastoral pragmatism.

Attitudes to mixed marriages were changing rapidly anyway with the growth of ecumenical insights. Archbishop Beck issued some guidelines (agreed by all the bishops) to help implement an Instruction on Mixed Marriages issued by the Sacred Congregation for the Doctrine of the Faith in March 1966. There were still promises to be made regarding the Catholic's religious practice and the bringing up of the children – usually in writing by both partners, but if necessary an oral promise by the non-Catholic would suffice. A bishop could permit mixed marriages to be celebrated with all the ceremonies, including a nuptial Mass and blessing. The ceremony, however, was not to be conducted jointly by priest and non-Catholic minister, although the latter could 'say a few words of congratulation and encouragement' and could offer prayers with the congregation after the ceremony. Finally, the penalty of excommunication formerly incurred by Catholics who attempted to marry before a non-Catholic minister was abolished, and, moreover, the abolition was retrospective.[28]

So far, so good. But the more theologians and Church leaders stressed the importance of baptism as bringing about a fundamental Christian unity (it was 'the sacramental bond of unity', according to the *Roman Ecumenical Directory* of 1967), and pointed to the acceptance of 'one Lord and Saviour, Jesus Christ' as a sign of that unity, the more difficult it became to continue with any remnant of traditional Catholic attitudes and to treat committed non-Catholic partners as second-class Christians. Might not mixed marriages between committed Christians, one of whom was a Catholic, be more fruitfully regarded as experiments in Christian unity calling for the involvement of both parties' ministers in their pastoral care before and after the wedding? The Ecumenical Commission's 1970 *Spring Newsletter* touched on these points: its report on a national Catholic conference on ecumenism included a resolution urgently requesting the bishops to initiate discussions with other Christian leaders. The conference delegates felt that this would be a proof of Catholic sincerity in dealing with practising non-Catholic Christians for whom the present Catholic regulations were a troublesome burden. They asked the bishops to consider in particular whether such marriages might be celebrated in non-Catholic churches, as well as the question of the religious education of the children of such marriages. The delegates considered that the pastoral care of mixed marriages should be shared between the priest and the minister of the non-Catholic party.[29]

By 1974, mixed marriages were allowed to take place in non-Catholic churches. Indeed, a number of priests felt that some fresh guidance from the Archbishop on the whole subject of mixed marriages would be very welcome, as they were becoming very common in a large number of parishes and it was so easy to obtain a dispensation that there was a danger of making a mockery of the impediment.[30] The new Code of Canon Law, promulgated in 1983 and described by the Pope as the final document of the Second Vatican Council, not surprisingly dealt with mixed marriages in a much more sympathetic way than its 1917 predecessor. Only the Catholic party has to make a promise to do all in his or her power to have the children baptised and brought up in the Catholic Church, and the wedding may be celebrated in due style and, with the bishop's permission, in the church of the non-Catholic party. In 1974 a special training course for clergy, 'The Pastoral Care of Mixed Marriages', was put on by a team of three – a Catholic priest (Fr Peter Ryan), an Anglican vicar and marriage counsellor, and a psychologist from the University of Liverpool. Mixed marriages may still cause pastoral problems, but as one commentator has put it, if approached properly they can be a unique sign of the unity that is Christ's desire for his Church.[31] From another perspective, the end of the strict attitude to mixed marriages brought with it a further weakening of the traditional Catholic identity created for so long by separateness from others.

~

As we have seen, a constant warning by those who opposed any rush into ecumenical activity was that it would result in a decline in individual conversions to the Church. The following statistics would seem to support their point of view:

	1960	1965	1970	1975	1980	1985	1990	1995	2000
Converts	1,563	1,308	695	419	369	371	226	252	207

It is, of course, impossible to determine why unknown people do not take a particular action, but in trying to find reasons for this remarkable decline over the last forty years one would need to take into account such factors as the drop in mixed-marriage conversions (formerly a high percentage of all conversions), the general falling off in religious practice and the unwillingness of many in a post-modern society to make long-term commitments of any sort. An interesting case study here would be the Catholic Evidence Guild, active in the archdiocese since 1920 with its work of explaining the Catholic religion to the uncommitted and the hostile. Its open-air sessions at Liverpool's Pier Head ended in 1983 because of a lack of members, and a strong recruitment drive in 1986 failed to attract a single recruit; the group held its last meeting in 1991.[32] Did this decline come about because of uncertainty about the truths of the Faith, a lack of commitment, changed ecumenical relations or the growing indifference of society to religious issues? In all this we have fields of psychology and sociology that a simple historian should not enter alone.

Notes

1 *The Daily Mail*, 4.3.1958; Heenan, *Crown of Thorns*, pp.235-8.

2 Service card, St Basil and All Saints Church, Widnes, Christmas 2003, in author's possession.

3 Heenan, *Crown of Thorns*, pp.314-5.

4 AAL Heenan, S1 III, A: Miscellany 1957-64, ad clerum 18.12.1962; *Crown of Thorns*, pp.322-3.

5 Clifford Longley, *The Worlock Archive* (2000), pp.160-3.

6 *Ibid.*, p.163.

7 AAL Beck, S2 XIV A: Ad clerums and Notices: Hierarchy Statement 6.12.1964.

8 *Ibid.*, Pastoral letter, Jan. 1968.

9 *Ibid.*

10 *Ibid.*, 'Bulletin of the Archdiocesan Ecumenical Commission', No.1, Summer 1969.

11 *Ibid.*, S2 XVI A: Council of Clergy, 3 Dec.1969.

12 *Ibid.*, S2 XIV A: 'Bulletin of the Arch. Ecumenical Commission', Spring 1970.

13 *Ibid.*, ad clerum, 8.11.1971.

14 *Ibid.*, Fr E.K. Taylor, 'Ecumenism in Practice' 11.3.1972.

15 *Ibid.*, 'Bulletin of the Arch. Ecumenical Commission', Feb. 1973.

16 *Ibid.*, C.R. Hinings, S. Ranson, A. Bryman, 'Priests and the Church: Liverpool Catholic Priests, A Preliminary Report', Nov. 1973, for Archbishop Beck.

17 AAL Beck, S2 XVI A: Council of Clergy Nov. 1976.

18 Sheppard and Worlock, *Better Together*, p.83-113, at p.83.

19 Furnival and Knowles, *Worlock*, p.169.

20 *Ibid.*, pp.184-5; Longley, *Worlock Archive*, p.307.

21 *The Pope in Britain: Collected Homilies and Speeches* (1982), p.20.

22 *The Catholic Pictorial,* Jan., March 1982.

23 Furnival and Knowles, *Worlock*, pp.212-4

24 Sheppard and Worlock, *Better Together*, pp.97-8.

25 Furnival and Knowles, *Worlock*, pp.215-6.

26 AAL Heenan, S1 III, A: ad clerum, Jan. 1958; *Crown of Thorns*, pp.229-35.

27 *Crown of Thorns*, p.234-5.

28 AAL Beck, S2 XIV A: ad clerum 12.5.1966.

29 *Ibid.*, 'Ecumenical Commission Newsletter', Spring 1970.

30 *Ibid.*, S2 XVI A: Council of Clergy, Propositions for meeting Nov.1974.

31 *Ibid.*, S2 XV A: April 1974; J. McAreavey, *The Canon Law of Marriage and the Family* (1997), p.164.

32 Conversation with Mr John White, CEG Secretary, Feb. 2004; the Guild still features in the *Directory*.

CHAPTER 20 A POST-CONCILIAR CHURCH?

What sort of diocese, parish and everyday Catholic would come about if the decrees of Vatican II were implemented? What changes in traditional structures and practices would be necessary to accommodate and support these new entities? Some changes appeared to be relatively easy to achieve because externals could be altered fairly quickly – the liturgy is probably the most obvious example, or relations between Catholics and other Christians. But changing the externals did not of itself bring any inner changes of mind or any positive understanding of what lay behind the changes. New ideas such as collaborative ministry and the co-responsibility it required could not be tacked-on to traditional Catholicism – they demanded radical changes in outlook and structures if the hundred years of largely passive service since the 1850s were to bear different fruit.

What was required was a translation into local practice of the Conciliar decrees, through sensitive adult Christian education and in-service training for the clergy. Just as it had taken centuries for the Council of Trent to be implemented everywhere and for its influence to filter into outlook and practice to bring about a truly Tridentine Church, perhaps Vatican II would only be implemented gradually and even then not as a uniform package. This chapter examines some of the attempts in the archdiocese to alter traditional structures and introduce some of the Council's new thinking – against a background of crises in manpower and finance and a post-modern society denying the importance or even the desirability of long-term commitment and a questioning of authority of every kind.

The Council's decree on the Apostolate of the Laity (1965) had answered some of the questions raised during the previous attempts to set up a structure for Catholic Action in the archdiocese (see chapter 14). According to the Council, lay people had their own 'proper and indispensable' role in the mission of the Church, a role that derived from their Christian baptism. Through that baptism lay people shared in the priestly, prophetic, and royal office of Christ; this in turn imposed an obligation to live out the Gospel in their own lives and to do all in their power to spread that Gospel to others. Personal holiness and proper formation were necessary for lay people devoted to this apostolate. The decree recommended the traditional works of charity but also included a strong statement that the lay apostle must work to remove the causes of the suffering and problems that made that charity necessary. At the same time, the decree seemed unsure of the relationship of lay people with the bishops and clergy – leaning, in Clifford Longley's judgement, towards a rather 'clericalised laity'.[1]

Mgr Derek Worlock, at that time secretary at Westminster, was one of the group that had prepared the documents for discussion at the Council. He was friendly with Pat Keegan of the YCW who had the distinction of being the first English lay person to address the Council: he spoke of the need for 'close collaboration' between the clergy and the laity – 'family dialogue' was how he described it.[2] The model he recommended was strongly influenced by YCW practice, based on its 'see, judge, act' approach. The more detailed working out of these ideas during the preparatory Commissions at the Council was a turning point in Worlock's own thinking about the laity, and indeed in his whole theology of the Church.[3] He was later to become president of the Bishops' Laity Commission, and a member of the Vatican's Council for the Laity.

THE ARCHDIOCESAN PASTORAL COUNCIL

The first steps towards changing structures in the archdiocese were taken in the late 1960s. The Archdiocesan Pastoral Council, consisting of lay people, priests and religious, met in 1968: it was a consultative body with permanent Working Groups on Social Justice and Political Action, Community Development (with particular reference to new towns and housing areas), Communications, Education, and Family and Social Welfare. More important than the individual discussions and reports, although many of these were directly to the point and marked by fresh thinking, were some general issues raised right from the beginning – how to ensure 'authentic' representation on the Pastoral Council, and, above all else, how to develop communications within the archdiocese. Delegates soon realised that the Council could only work if there existed a network of Deanery or, preferably, Area, Councils and Parochial Councils. Time and again this issue was raised, but it was always left up to the clergy whether to have a parochial council in their parish or not. In practice, they were always the exception and not the rule – by 1973, they existed in only twenty-six parishes across the archdiocese. In this context it is worth quoting from a report of the Social Justice and Political Action Group as early as 1968:

> … for anything worthwhile at ground level, the enthusiastic encouragement of the Clergy, the willingness to put real responsibility and decision making in the hands of the laity, and the willingness and ability of the laity to accept these responsibilities, are all necessary and they cannot at present be assumed to exist in many cases.

Without some such structures to enable communication and genuine consultation 'upwards and downwards' across the archdiocese, there remained only the Archbishop's pastoral letters and the *Catholic Pictorial*.[4]

Archbishop Derek Worlock, seventh Archbishop of Liverpool (1976-1996).

So, it came down to the attitudes of the clergy. An independent report into those attitudes in 1973 enquired about the role of the laity as a possible area for reform. Nearly half (48.9%) of the 200 priests surveyed (just over half of whom were parish priests) felt that such a reform was 'most important', and an additional 41.1% thought it was 'quite important' – only the reform of priestly training received a higher rating of 'most' or 'quite' important. Over 40% thought that the laity should be present in all structures to ensure their direct participation in all decision-making, while over 85% favoured the introduction of a Christian stewardship scheme. Nothing appears to have been done directly to implement the report.[5]

Three years later, as part of an exercise to re-structure the archdiocese so that both priests and people might share in the mission of the Church, Archbishop Worlock told his priests that a proper role for the laity was not something the clergy allowed the people or was necessary because of a shortage of priests:

> It is something which is the right and duty of all our people by virtue of their baptism and confirmation. There is really no aspect of the Church's mission which we do not share, even though we have different roles and the prime sphere of the layman's apostolate is the secular surroundings in which he spends the greater part of his life.

He proposed that each priest should choose twelve lay people from his parish and begin discussing with them the task of the Church in their parish. The group were not necessarily to form a parish council (though the Archbishop clearly hoped they would) but a group of 'disciples or companions' with whom the priest would eventually begin to share responsibility. The Archbishop hoped, rather tentatively, that there would be some practical significance in his 'twelve apostles' scheme and that priests would be able to say to their people, 'We are the Church. In all the changes about us, let us together show the face of Christ to the world'.[6] It was as though the archdiocese were starting from scratch to release its lay potential.

Then there was 'Liverpool 1980', the nearest the English and Welsh bishops have ever come to calling a national lay synod – 79% of the 2,115 who attended the four days of discussion and prayer in Liverpool were lay people (200 of them from the archdiocese). Preparation for it was as thorough as possible and national consultation was meant to involve every parish in the country through a series of discussion documents and questionnaires. Reading through the responses now one gets a clear impression of the heartfelt seriousness of the vast majority of the respondents, even of those who had particular bees buzzing in their lay bonnets. The logistical exercise of organising the event was huge and involved hundreds of Liverpool Catholic families and their local parishes. As an event it was an outstanding success, and its discussions pointed up the insights, the frustrations and the hopes of the laity.[7]

Delegates were very critical of the general failure to implement and even to understand the imperatives of the decrees of Vatican II. When dealing with the major causes of lay apathy, they identified the failure of the clergy to ask enough of the laity, with the latter, by and large, being happy not to be asked! Too many priests, they felt, were dragging their feet over parish consultation and there had been too great a stress on the laity's taking on 'churchy things' – being lay readers and Eucharistic ministers, for example. Their main apostolate should be in the world where they lived and worked, with their essential formation springing from their Eucharistic life in the parish. Delegates stressed that the clergy at all levels had an obligation to listen to lay people and to trust their 'distinctive insights and experience ... (of) the many social and moral issues which form so central a part of our apostolic programme'. Finally, they felt a lack of formation for their role, and that this was a major deficiency; they called for a permanent and structured provision, available in every parish and deanery. Again they admitted their own past apathy in making use of what had been provided.

The bishops' response to the Congress, *The Easter People*, was almost entirely Archbishop Worlock's work, with help from Fr J. Mahoney, SJ, the well-respected theologian, Pat Jones, a young lay woman and later Assistant General Secretary to the Bishops' Conference, and Mgr G. Leonard of Shrewsbury Diocese. In many ways it was a very good document, but it did not pick up specifically on the points about the laity and their apostolate. The Archbishop's biographer pointed out its main weakness: neither the Congress resolutions nor the bishops' response had any binding force in parishes, and any success they might have relied on the 'understanding and acceptance ... of the local parish communities and the priests'.[8] The Congress showed what could be done when the Church in England and Wales got together as one body; unfortunately, so far it has not done so again and both *Liverpool 1980* and *The Easter People* remained reports, not programmes.

As elsewhere throughout the Church, the archdiocese witnessed the growth of new (or re-constituted) lay movements and secular institutes. These reflected the charisms of particular founders and the spirit of Vatican II, with their members living the Gospel in the ordinary circumstances of their lives – and in some cases sealing their dedication with religious vows – for example, Christian Life Communities, the Cursillo Movement, Caritas Christi, the Servants of Mary and St Philip Benizi Group (both linked to the Servite Order), the Focolare Movement (with a men's and a women's house), Consecrated Widows and Widowers, and The Grail.[9]

The Pontifical Council for the Laity, the new Code of Canon Law, and the Roman Synod of the Laity in 1989, helped to define the place of these movements in the Church. Pope John Paul II has spoken of an 'age of ecclesial maturity' that calls for a fuller integration of the laity into the structures of the Church and sees the new movements as the instruments for this: they are 'providential expressions of the new springtime brought forth by the Spirit with the Second Vatican Council'. It is too early to assess their impact throughout the archdiocese and there are still unresolved issues about their relationship to the parish and the role of the clergy in their organisation. In many parishes there are also new interests, and groups to serve them – Justice and Peace and Third World groups seek to meet the concerns of the age, while Prayer and Bible Study groups run by lay people, often without clerical input, meet some of their personal spiritual needs as the new apostles. Parish Councils have been slower to develop and there are few signs of lay people being integrated into the structures of the Church at a local level (the only level that matters to most of them), or of having a distinctive voice of their own, although they have become a significant presence on archdiocesan commissions and other bodies.

THE ARCHDIOCESAN COUNCIL OF CLERGY

The Archdiocesan Council of Clergy first met in November 1966. It consisted of a number of ex officio members (the auxiliary bishops, vicar general, two members of the Upholland staff, etc.), all the deans and two priests elected by each deanery (one under fifteen years ordained, one over) – 86 priests in all; every priest in the archdiocese received the agenda and minutes of each meeting. Propositions for discussion came from deanery conferences or individual priests and could be grouped roughly under five headings: i. Priestly life and ministry; ii. Liturgy; iii. Ecumenism; iv. Administration (parochial, diocesan, and financial); v. Education (including in-service training for priests and general catechetics). General issues that underlay many of the specific discussions included collegiality, at all levels, and the functions and relationships of the Clergy and Pastoral Councils and the Chapter. As with the Pastoral Council, there was a constant question of communication – up, down and sideways.[10]

Openness in discussions developed quickly and everything was allowed (shades of Worthy in the 1850s!): plans for new forms of ministry and parochial organisation, restructuring of the archdiocese, the appointment of clergy and voting for future bishops, the new liturgy, seminary re-organisation, the Church's mission to the uncommitted, and *Humanae Vitae* – all were covered in greater or lesser detail. Archbishop Beck accepted any resolutions passed by what he called a morally unanimous vote and implemented them as far as he thought possible – he wrote to the clergy after the sessions to announce what he intended to do.[11] On some issues, no matter how dear to clerical hearts, he could only promise sensitivity in handling them. The question of clerical appointments and tenure came up on a number of occasions – the large number of priests in the archdiocese had meant that many had celebrated their silver jubilees as curates, and clerical wits had suggested that Samuel Beckett had got the initial idea for 'Waiting for Godot' from talking to Liverpool curates waiting to become PPs! The Archbishop claimed that 'A greater sense of co-responsibility for the well-being of the archdiocese as a whole' had become perceptible among the Clergy since the setting up of the Council.[12] Two of the topics discussed deserve some detail here.

The papal encyclical *Humanae Vitae* came out in the Summer of 1968. Archbishop Beck gave an interview to a reporter from the *Catholic Herald* and appeared on '24 Hours' on television. His approach won praise and his replies to the large number of letters from priests and lay people around the country were full of concern and marked by gentleness and understanding. He agreed in private letters to priests that the argument of the encyclical was 'flawed' and that the mind of the Church was still evolving on the question. Some priests and lay people in the archdiocese welcomed the Pope's upholding of traditional teaching, others thanked the Archbishop for his helpful approach and were grateful that they lived in a 'fortunate diocese' – only a few priests seem to have offered to resign because they disagreed with the encyclical, and these he recommended to stay and be patient. He advised his clergy in general not to make severe judgements about their people and there should be no denunciations from the pulpit or in private – the full rigour of the law must not be invoked on those who were learning 'slowly and with difficulty' not only how to keep it but even that it ought to be kept. Divided opinions were obvious at the Council of Clergy and various more general points were brought out – one was that the idea of authority was changing and would take time to evolve; another concerned the inadequacy of the traditional Catholic theology on sex and marriage. Beck thanked the clergy for the sense of responsibility and the spirit of charity that had enabled such a frank discussion – pastoral responses would, he acknowledged, remain very difficult, but he warned them not to be 'tragic about the situation'.[13] His sensitive leadership meant that public clerical crises were avoided.

How to re-organise the archdiocese was a recurring topic of discussion from the late 1960s on – not changing the boundaries (although this was raised, with the suggestion of a new diocese for Central Lancashire to include the area around Chorley, where priests and people felt remote from Liverpool), but trying to enhance the importance of localities and communities which meant more to people than deaneries or even, some argued, than parishes. The discussions take us back to Cardinal Bourne and his belief that smaller dioceses would improve active evangelisation (see Chapter 5). One possibility put forward now was to appoint a series of auxiliary bishops with territorial responsibility and to be known as Pastoral Bishops; another was to appoint Episcopal Vicars (non-bishops) who would hold office for a limited period and could be either territorial or 'job specific', and therefore allow greater flexibility – it was a time of rapid change that called for experiment rather than firm new structures. Those who favoured Pastoral Bishops (and that included the official working group) argued that they would not be regarded just as another type of administrator – glorified deans or substitute vicar generals; the stress in their title would be on 'pastoral', and they would have greater status and therefore authority. This met with the counter-argument that the days of status were limited and it was now performance that counted, and, anyway,

Rome was most unlikely to agree to a multiplicity of bishops in a diocese. (It is interesting that questions about the function of auxiliary bishops went right back to the 1850s.) A series of articles in the *Catholic Pictorial* in 1975 attempted to test lay opinion on the issue through painting a picture of what it would mean to have Area Bishops – a Bishop of Kirkby, a Bishop of Wigan, and so on. News of the working group's model for six Pastoral Bishops was picked up and highly praised under the heading, 'Liverpool Leads the Way' in *Herder Correspondence*, which described the suggested model as one to be followed by other dioceses in the future.[14] All these discussions were overtaken by the resignation of Archbishop Beck through ill-health and the appointment of Archbishop Worlock in February 1976.

By then neither Episcopal Vicars nor Pastoral Bishops had been established; there were two auxiliary bishops, Bishop Augustine Harris (appointed 1966) and Bishop Joseph Gray (appointed 1969). From the start the new Archbishop clearly favoured Episcopal Vicars over Pastoral Bishops. His grand Pastoral Plan launched in September 1976 proposed a structure of Archbishop, two Auxiliaries, one Vicar General (these four being the core of a Council of Administration), and five Episcopal Vicars – for Education, Finance and Development, Pastoral Affairs, Missionary Activity, and the Religious. The plan also stressed the importance of the Dean as leader of the Church in his locality, with responsibility for the welfare of the clergy and charged with promoting collaboration between priests, Religious and lay people in the Church's apostolate – the deanery could be an effective unit at the heart of pastoral strategy, where the work of the local church could be co-ordinated and given effect.[15]

The clergy discussed the plan and gave it general support, although some jibbed at the size of the task facing some of the Episcopal Vicars, especially whoever would be responsible for Education. There was considerable discussion about 'super-deans' – did people not still relate to parishes? But most acknowledged a need for area-wide planning by people on the ground and not outsiders, and while the rigidity of structures could be an obstacle, there was a need for structures if consultation between parishes was to be more than ad hoc. The Vicariates that emerged initially were Finance and Development; Schools and Colleges; Christian Formation; Sick and Retired Clergy; Missionary Activity, and Religious (with an Epsicopal Vicar chosen from the Religious). Three of these Vicariates comprised a number of Committees or Departments and there were also a number of Archdiocesan Commissions – for Schools; Justice and Peace; Ecumenism, and Liturgy.[16] These and other discussions led eventually to the setting up of a Pastoral Institute and the Archdiocesan Council for Evangelisation.

While the above discussions and arrangements were essentially inward looking, mention should be made here of an initiative that arose from the archdiocese's commitment to the Church overseas. By 1977 four of the Secular clergy were working in South America (Fr Vincent Hughes had been there for over ten years) and one in Africa, and in 1979 LAMP was established – the Liverpool Archdiocesan Missionary Project – after the Archbishop had visited South America. This aimed at having six archdiocesan priests working in Peru and Ecuador at any one time, under the aegis of the American Society of St James the Apostle. An annual collection supported the work – in 1981 this raised over £48,000, and the money went to help build chapels, provide transport and in aid to the poor.[17] The laity were also extremely active in missionary work overseas and in 1982 there were 102 men and women engaged in the work – the archdiocese could claim to top the 'diocesan league' in this respect.[18] One local lay initiative that became a national movement was 'Survive – International Mobile Medical Aid' (now 'Survive-Miva'). It started when Sean O'Leary and Margaret Price visited Ethiopia to look into setting up a hospice, but found that a mobile clinic and operating theatre would be of much greater benefit; back in Liverpool they began collecting and by the mid-1970s were supplying specialist vehicles and medical staff to Africa. The movement later expanded to include the provision of vehicles for general pastoral use throughout the developing world.[19]

A FINANCIAL CRISIS

As early as 1959 the clergy had been warned that the archdiocese was facing mounting financial difficulties; by the late 1960s this had become a crisis. While there were 110 parishes without debts, there were others that faced twenty to thirty years of debt repayment – the 109 parishes in debt had repaid over £450,000 in 1966, with the ten most heavily in debt repaying a huge £166,000. Additionally, the cathedral debt involved a repayment of £150,000 a year. An assessment scheme on all parishes was planned to raise an annual £321,000, from which new and poor parishes could draw on £150,000, with £10,000 going to the national fund for Catholic Teacher Training Colleges and £11,000 to meet the deficit on the archdiocesan Priests' Training Fund. An increasing use of covenanted-giving would increase the archdiocese's annual income substantially.[20] The scheme was largely successful – the cathedral repayment of interest and capital was reduced to just over £100,000 – until the massive inflation and price rises of the early 1970s made a nonsense of everyone's calculations.

Parishioners did increase their offertory giving to compensate, but by nothing like enough to make up for the rise in costs: a rise of 26.5% in cash terms between 1969 and 1975 could not match a rise in the retail price index of 94.35% (and in wages/salaries of 120.3%); in real value, therefore, the offertory collections had dropped to approximately 65% of their 1970 value. If the money brought in from covenant schemes were added to cash collections, then there was a 41% rise compared with 1970, but in real terms this was still only 73% of the 1970 income. Over the same period attendances at Sunday Masses remained almost exactly the same.[21] In 1971 Archbishop Beck had appealed for more money in a pastoral letter, pointing out that in twenty years no fewer than 47 new churches and 137 new schools had been built – the biggest Catholic school-building programme in the country. A report to the Council of Clergy three years later highlighted one of the problems: in Kirkby, the two new schools built as comprehensives had cost half-a-million pounds in interest payments on a capital debt of a quarter-of-a-million pounds – money originally borrowed at 5.25% interest was being repaid now at 14% – and so it was essential that future building would have to be done without outside borrowing; DES loans, in particular, were becoming cripplingly expensive at around 17% over twenty-five years.[22] And all this when the prospect of school-reorganisation to allow for a general change to comprehensives had to be faced – when many of the existing secondary schools had not yet been paid for. Fortunately, the government contribution to the capital costs of building voluntary aided schools had risen steadily, to 75% in 1959, 80% in 1967, and 85% in 1975, so future building could be undertaken without the heavy borrowing of the past.

What could go wrong with the best of intentions may be illustrated by the example of Netherley, a suburb of Liverpool designated in the 1960s to grow to a total population of about 20,000. A parish was founded in 1967, dedicated to St Cyril of Jerusalem. The first building was a parish club, opened in February that year with a loan of £24,000 from a brewery (at 3% interest). The first Mass was said, for a congregation of sixteen people, in Advent, and a mixed infants and junior school followed two years later – built for 560 children, this time with a loan of £25,000 (at 8% interest) from the Department of Education; by now there were over a 1,000 Catholics in the area. A church and presbytery were finally built in the early 1970s. By the early 1980s the Catholic population had risen to 1,500, but the planned expansion of the area did not take place – in 1981 the population was only 12,500 and a fifth of the dwellings were empty, because people refused to move into the high rise 'terraces in the sky' (they were later demolished) and the City Council decided to concentrate on regeneration of the older areas; by 2001 the total population was down to 8,000. By the early 1990s the school had closed and by 1997 there were only 400 Catholics living there.[23] The parish was eventually 'clustered' with Our Lady's, Gateacre, which had been founded in 1949. The debts, incurred at a time of optimistic expansion, remained a burden on a small congregation.

The clergy in general supported the efforts to share the burdens more equitably between parishes, though some felt that any centralisation might destroy the parish as the basis for people's giving and so be counter-productive. Surveys seemed to show that many parishioners thought the archdiocese could not be short of money as there were so many collections and so much building going on. Such financial 'ignorance' was hardly surprising – for well over a hundred years the clergy had elevated Bishop

Goss's distrust of the laity in financial matters into a principle of natural law. What an increasing number of priests objected to was the reliance on social clubs and bingo, with loans from breweries (a few priests even stated openly that they wished the same efforts would go into other pastoral concerns as went into money-raising). It is interesting that when Archbishop Worlock arrived in 1976 one of the first things he commented on was this reliance – he said he found it hard to accept that up to a third of archdiocesan income came from that source. They could not just be abolished, however, as they were tied into existing loans and financial arrangements; what he urged was that they should never be open in competition to liturgical services and he recommended closing them altogether on Christmas Eve, and during the Easter Vigil – they must never clash with the spiritual interests of a parish and ways should be found of relieving priests of the management burden of running them.[24]

It remains to be seen what effects on the financial situation the massive decline in regular Mass attendances, the closure of parishes and sale of church sites, and the sale of Upholland, will have. Diocesan debt could be taken as a sign of life and growth, perhaps, but it could also become a burden that required too much energy to be diverted from pastoral concerns.

CATHOLICS AND THE WIDER SOCIETY

English Catholics had never been completely isolated from the society in which they lived, and lay people had been involved in its concerns through work-place and ordinary social involvement, trade unions and politics. For their leaders there had always been something of a tension between wanting Catholics to integrate more fully into English society, and their pride when they gained positions of preferment, and wanting them to keep apart from its evils. 'Building communities' in this context meant building up parishes so that people kept the Faith; a range of parish societies, spiritual and secular, provided alternatives to the outside world. If the new lay apostolate and post-conciliar more positive attitudes to 'the world', meant anything, however, 'building communities' now implied that Catholics should play their part in building the local secular community into something that would provide and support human dignity, empowering local people to have some input into, and some control over, processes that affected their lives. The aim was not to dominate or control these communities but to make a proper Christian input into them as fellow concerned citizens, with this involvement being essential to building the kingdom of God.

As mines, mills and docks closed or contracted, and companies 'downsized' to cope with inflation and rising energy prices, both old and new towns suffered. The economic and social evils of unemployment became major obstacles to building God's kingdom in south west

Lancashire. The welfare state could help but it could not provide respect, confidence or human dignity to the unemployed, and the Church had to be 'caught up' in the urgency of this situation, never allowing the unacceptable to become accepted through drifting.[25] Many lay Catholics and some of the clergy had already taken up the challenge, or were about to do so; they became involved in forming new communities, no longer parish-based or even Christian in some cases, but each with something to teach about living out the Gospel message in a new society. Just two examples will be examined in a little detail here, Eldon Street and Kirkby.

Preparations to build a second Mersey road tunnel in 1968 involved the demolition of housing, neighbourhood shops and two churches in the north end of Liverpool (the churches were St Brigid's and All Souls'). Some residents were re-housed in the Eldon Street area as a result. When a second phase of re-housing was proposed in 1978, these people faced another move, this time out of the area altogether to out-of-town housing estates and new towns. They did not want to leave and formed themselves into 'The Eldonians' as a community group. In 1980 another blow came when the Tate and Lyle factory closed with the loss of 1,700 jobs – it had been the main provider of non-dock work in the area for as long as people could remember. As the people began to develop their own housing policy, aimed at redeveloping the area, they clashed with the City Council, dominated since 1983 by the Militant Tendency. Both Derek Worlock and David Sheppard became involved controversially in a public row with the Council in 1985 after they had written to *The Times* to condemn what they claimed was the confrontation deliberately provoked by the Militant leadership, and its refusal to support housing co-operatives and other voluntary groups.[26]

The people eventually won their case on appeal (at which Church leaders supported them) and in 1986 there were great celebrations in Our Lady's, Eldon Street, to mark the final approval of their scheme and their obtaining financial backing. The first people moved into the Eldonian Village two years later and by 1995 almost 300 houses had been built, with a residential care home, a sports hall, day nursery, a village hall and the Eldonian Development Trust to encourage inward investment. These successes were a tribute to the leadership, skills and initiative of local people planning from the inside and collaborating with official and voluntary organisations. Although by no means a utopia, Christian or secular, – there were still higher than national rates of unemployment, problems of drug abuse and youth disaffection – their slogan, 'We do it better together', had proved to be much more than an empty token.[27]

The problems in Kirkby had different origins. By 1971 it had a population of almost 60,000, about half of whom, as we have seen, were at least nominally Catholic. At the best of times the provision of social and leisure amenities had lagged far behind the provision of houses. Then the local economy began to collapse in the 1970s as factories closed and unemployment rose above 50%; the people had not had time to form communities in the traditional Eldonian sense but were brought together by a sense of injustice and, in particular, by a sense of powerlessness to do anything about their situation. Radical action was encouraged by Fr J Collins, the local dean – so that, at least, the Church was 'there' where people were suffering. His involvement pointed up the importance of local leadership, this time at deanery level, to win clerical support and action in areas traditionally avoided as 'too political'. He was responsible for a Flat Dwellers Association to work for justice and a power base from which to negotiate with the police and local politicians. He also helped to start a Workers' Co-operative (it failed after three years) and a still flourishing Credit Union, and co-founded an Unemployment Centre that led demonstrations and picket lines, and a major advice centre for the whole town. All this was done with the support of other priests and in collaboration with politicians of different hues and lay people – a truly collaborative ministry. As a particular case, when the Birds Eye factory closed in 1989 with the loss of 1,000 jobs he organised a day of fasting and prayer outside the factory during the negotiations between unions and employers; this got TV coverage and, perhaps partly as a result, the company gave a grant of £1m for community facilities and retraining. There was a strong ecumenical side to this involvement as Catholics were joined by Anglicans and Methodists: what have been described as the 'politicised' and 'pious' wings of religion worked together to provide a voice and active support to the under-privileged.[28]

These examples of 'building communities' (and even of 'collaborative ministry') in strongly Catholic areas were not in themselves Catholic, but they raised the question of how local churches should react to such processes; could they learn anything about how to collaborate with people who were no longer their loyal members and what kinds of ministry would best serve these areas? *The Pastoral Plan* of 1974 picked out seven areas as requiring special ministries – the Isle of Man, Skelmersdale, Kirkby, Warrington and Padgate, and three sectors in the city of Liverpool. If nothing else, this acknowledged that different areas called for different approaches rather than the traditional 'one size fits all' centralised model, although there was no guarantee that the new pastoral approaches would be radically diverse. The Isle of Man was an obvious natural community and could be regarded as a pastoral unit under its dean. Skelmersdale – a new town of about 43,000 people, of whom approximately 25% were Catholics – was not a natural community in that sense, but might be seen as a pastoral unit calling for a collaborative ministry. The clergy there had already decided that some form of team ministry, comprising priests and Sisters, would be the most suitable and after 1976 they established seven 'Eucharistic communities' that fitted the physical make-up of the town; three of these communities had parish churches and four had 'Mass centres' in schools. A united Pastoral Council and agreed Mission Statement acknowledged the need for the Church in Skelmersdale to be a Gospel-based community fully involved in creating a whole-town community. The town experienced serious social problems linked to high unemployment (in the 1980s this rose to over 30%, with male unemployment over 40%). One of the priests in the original team, Fr Michael McKenna, had started a youth employment scheme called 'Tomorrow's People Today' (or TPT), run by local lay people and still operating over twenty years later; it became a model for such schemes elsewhere.[29]

Keeping such ministries going depended among other things on having sufficient priests. At the time of writing the town has four churches (a new one was built in 1993), served by two priests and two sets of religious Sisters (Ursulines, and Sisters of the Holy Family, Bordeaux); the idea of the seven smaller Eucharistic communities seems to have been given up. Other 'natural communities', such as Chorley and Southport, were not given 'special ministry' status, which seemed to depend on initiatives from groups of clergy as much as on any pastoral insights or central planning.

~

Meanwhile, the archdiocese was involved in its own 'downsizing'. The heavily Catholic wards in Liverpool – Central, Everton, Melrose, Sandhills and Vauxhall – lost 48% of their total population between 1961 and 1971 because of population movements.[30] These losses led to declining parish numbers and, given a general decline in attendances and a shortage of clergy, to a number of parish closures. Not surprisingly, the heaviest loss has been in the Liverpool docklands and inner-city areas – as we have seen, two churches were closed to make way for the new Mersey Tunnel – St Brigid's (1967), and All Souls' (1968). Other closures have been St Nicholas (the former Pro-Cathedral, 1972), St Augustine's (1976), St Peter's (1978), St Alban's (1991), St Alexander's, Bootle (1991), St Gerard's (1996), St Mary's, Highfield St (2000), St Alphonsus' (2001), Holy Cross (2001), St Joseph's (2001), St Malachy's (2001), St Mary of the Angels' (The Friary – the Franciscans moved out in 1981 and the Jesuits ran the parish until its closure in 2001), St Philip Neri's (2001 – now the University Church and Chaplaincy), and St Cuthbert's (2002). Two post-war churches have also closed – St Finbar's and St Brendan's (both opened only in 1960 and closed in 2002). Outside Liverpool, three have closed: St Anselm's, Chorley (opened in 1953, closed 1992), St Patrick's, Widnes (1888, closed 1997) and Sacred Heart, Pulrose, IOM (1939, closed 2001). At the time of writing, a number of parishes have been 'clustered' (they have no resident priest but the church remains open for regular services): 38 out of a total of 222.

The decline in the number of clergy working in the archdiocese over a twenty year period is shown in the following table:

	1983	1993	2003
Secular clergy			
active in archdiocese	328	284	187
active elsewhere	22	20	18
retired	55	58	67
Regular clergy, including those retired	155	?	103
Permanent deacons	25	61	97

The decline may be explained by a substantial falling-off in the number of ordinations and by the number of priests who left the ministry. Religious Orders have continued to play an essential role in staffing parishes – the Benedictines still run eight parishes, and the Jesuits, Franciscans, Redemptorists, Passionists and Oblates of Mary Immaculate, one each. Other Orders/Congregations have taken on parishes: the Augustinians, the Divine Word Missionaries, the Mill Hill Missionaries, the Missionaries of the Sacred Heart, the Sacred Heart Fathers, the Salesians, the Vincentians, and the Priests of the Sacred Heart, Betharram.

The large increase in the number of Permanent Deacons is striking – as a comparison, Westminster Archdiocese had only four in 2000. The development came from a particular post-Conciliar initiative of Archbishop Worlock and led to the first ordinations in 1979. Since then, while there has not been a deliberate recruitment campaign, clergy have been encouraged to be on the look-out for vocations to the permanent diaconate, as they would be for any other religious vocations. A three-year training programme, which includes study for the Catholic Certificate in Religious Studies alongside teachers, precedes ordination. Normally the deacons are appointed to their home parishes but some are also involved in special ministries and a small number sit on archdiocesan bodies.[31]

The decline in parish populations had an inevitable effect on that constant of Catholic effort, the provision of schools. We have seen how the policy of providing a place for every Catholic child was largely achieved by the 1960s and how the demand for justice for the Catholic position had proved to be a uniting call over several generations. Additional re-organisation became necessary as the national educational system became comprehensive, but here there were several complicating factors affecting any such re-organisation in the archdiocese. There was the question whether schools should be single sex or mixed – support for single sex schools remained strong in some areas. There was also the existence of direct grant grammar schools, usually run and owned by Religious Congregations (St Edward's College went Independent for a time, and St Mary's College, Crosby, altogether), and the use of secondary modern buildings on different sites to form new comprehensives – the archdiocese could not afford even to think about building wholly new comprehensive schools. In addition, there were a large number of different Education Authorities across the archdiocese with their own schemes for re-organisation – this could affect decisions about Sixth Form Colleges, for example. Lastly, but by no means the least important, there was concern about the effects on a local community of closing a school, often particularly important in a deprived area with few other facilities. The re-organisation was originally to take place in September 1981, but was postponed for a year to allow further consultation and did not take place until 1983, by which time some of the secondary schools were down to intakes of only a dozen pupils or so.[32]

The following table shows the result of the immense task carried out by the Archdiocesan Schools Commission with as much consultation as was practicable, but inevitably not without creating bitterness and, in some cases, disillusion among parents and teachers:[33]

	1982		1984		1992	
	schools	pupils	schools	pupils	schools	pupils
Voluntary aided						
Primary	235	57,040	232	52,063	213	49,069
Secondary Modern	30	8,783	–	–	–	–
Bilateral	1	899	–	–	–	–
Comprehensive	42	35,012	55	48,199	44	34,158
Grammar	7	4,707	–	–	–	–
Sixth Form College	1	682	1	697	2	1,575
Direct Grant						
Grammar	3	1,674	–	–	–	–
Independent	7	2,233	7	2,126	5	1,825

~

It is very much a case of unfinished business with regard to the implementation of the second Vatican Council across the archdiocese, as it is throughout the Catholic world, but in other ways a complete transformation of the Catholic community has taken place, willingly or unwillingly. Clerical authority has been under severe scrutiny since the publication of *Humanae Vitae* and the general social acceptance of a subjective approach to morality; perhaps it was always so to a greater extent than the clergy liked to admit and the difference is that those who question it now on serious matters still regard themselves as good Catholics. There has been a growing laicisation, most obviously in education, but there is still far to go if the laity are to be integrated into key church structures and collaborative ministry (the use of the talents of all for the good of all) is to be the norm. Bishop Goss in the mid-nineteenth century lamented the demise of traditional Catholic devotions and values, and many, priests and lay people, might echo his laments today. But he also accepted that times were changing and Catholics had to change with them. The tension between the traditional and the modern is as evident in the Catholicism of south-west Lancashire as it is anywhere else; will clergy and people ensure that it is fruitful, for the good of the wider communities of which they should now be an integral part?

Notes

[1] Abbott, *Documents of Vatican II*, pp.489-520; Longley, *Worlock Archive*, pp.179-80.

[2] Furnival and Knowles, *Worlock*, p.119.

[3] Longley, *Worlock Archive*, pp.183-7.

[4] AAL Beck Collection, S2 XVI A: The Pastoral Council: meeting of Oct. 1968; on parish councils, S2 XV A: Catholic Information Office, 27.6.1973.

[5] See above, p.352 for the Report.

[6] AAL Beck Collection (*sic*), S2 XV A: 1976 Folder: Archbishop Worlock, 'Pastoral Plan for the Archdiocese of Liverpool', 1976, p.15.

[7] *Liverpool 1980* (1981); Furnival and Knowles, *Worlock*, pp.207-10; Longley, *Worlock Archive*, pp.284-7; *The Easter People* (1981).

[8] Furnival and Knowles, *Worlock*, p.209.

[9] *Directories*.

[10] AAL Beck, S2 XVI, Bishop and Clergy, A: The Council of Clergy.

[11] For example, AAL Beck, S2 XIV A: 'Decisions and Suggestions of the Council of Clergy', Oct. 1967.

[12] AAL Beck, S2 XVI A: Beck to Sacred Congregation for the Clergy, 31.3.1969.

[13] AAL Beck, S2 XIV A: Pastoral letter, 11.8.1968; ad clerum, 15.8.1958; Folder of correspondence; *The Catholic Herald*, 23.8.1968; Council of Clergy, 20-21.11.1968.

[14] AAL Beck, S2 XIV A: Council of Clergy, 30.4.1969, pp.1-3.

[15] See note 6; also, 'The Way Ahead', Address of Abp Worlock to the Clergy, 30.3.1976.

[16] AAL Beck, S2 XIV A: Council of Clergy, 9-10.11.1976, pp.1-5.

[17] AAL Pastoral letter, Nov. 1981; *The Catholic Pictorial*, series of articles by Worlock on his South American visit, May-June 1983.

[18] AAL *Newsletter*, Oct. 1982.

[19] Information kindly supplied by Survive-Miva Office, Liverpool, March 2004.

[20] AAL Beck, S2 XIV A, and S2 XV A: e.g. Pastoral letter 31.3.1964; ad clerum letters, 5.5.1968; 10.10.1968; 23.1.1969; 20.10.1969; Council of Clergy, June 1972.

[21] AAL Beck, S2 XV A: 1976 Folder: Report on Offertory Income 1969-75

[22] *Ibid.*, S2 XIV A: Council of Clergy, 9.5.1974.

[23] I am grateful to Michael Chitty, formerly of Merseyside County Council's Planning Dept., for information on Netherley; see also AAL *Newsletter* 1969, and *Directories*.

[24] 'The Way Ahead', p.7 (note 15 above).

[25] AAL Beck, S2 XIV A: Pastoral letter, Nov. 1971, 'The Kingdom of Christ'.

[26] *The Times*, 1.10.1985; *The Catholic Pictorial*, 6.10.1985.

[27] Kevin T. Kelly, *From a Parish Base* (1999), pp.36-56; Frank Boyce, 'Catholicism in Liverpool's Docklands 1950s-1990s', in Hornsby-Smith, *Catholics in England*, pp.46-66; Sheppard and Worlock, *Better Together*, pp.195-212.

[28] Boyce, 'Docklands', pp.46-9; *The Tablet*, 24/31.5.2003 – correspondence; I am grateful to Fr Collins for sending me extra information, letter 16.1.2004.

[29] Kelly, *From a Parish Base*, pp.56-65, 217 (Fr Kelly was dean of Skelmersdale 1980-85); Sheppard and Worlock, *Better Together*, pp153-4.

[30] Boyce, 'Docklands', p.49; *Directories* for closures and statistics; information on clustered parishes kindly supplied by Chancellor's office, Aug. 2003.

[31] Information kindly supplied by Mgr Austin Hunt, Director for the Permanent Diaconate.

[32] *The Catholic Pictorial*, 8.12.1974 and 14.7.1983; AAL Beck S2 XV A: Pastoral letter 27.7.1975; Final Report of Working Party, June 1977.

[33] *Directories*.

APPENDIX

Biographical details of Bishops and Archbishops of Liverpool[1]

BROWN, George Hilary: born at Clifton, in the Fylde, 13 January 1786, he studied at Crook Hall and Ushaw and was ordained 13 June 1810. He lectured in theology at Ushaw for ten years, becoming vice-rector. He was then appointed rector of St Peter's, Lancaster. Ordained titular Bishop of Bugia (later changed to Tioa) and Vicar Apostolic of the new Lancashire District in 1840, he was appointed first Bishop of the new Diocese of Liverpool on 29 September 1850; he was a poor administrator but did much to enable the young diocese to expand. He died 25 January 1856 and was buried at St Oswald's, Old Swan, Liverpool.

Residences: Bishop Eton; Sandfield Park.

GOSS, Alexander: born in Ormskirk 5 July 1814, he studied at Ushaw and the English College, Rome, where he was ordained 4 July 1841. He served for a short time on the mission, probably at Ss Peter and Paul's, Mawdesley, before becoming vice-president of St Edward's College in October 1842. He was appointed co-adjutor to Bishop Brown in June 1853 and consecrated Bishop of Gerra in that September. He succeeded as Bishop of Liverpool 25 January 1856 and became an outspoken defender of his own and his people's rights, a rigorist in interpreting the law, and a successful missionary Bishop. After some years of ill-health he died suddenly 3 October 1872 and was buried in Ford Cemetery.

Residence: The Gatehouse, St Edward's College, Everton.

O'REILLY, Bernard: born 10 January 1824 in Ballybeg, Co. Meath, Ireland; his mother Mary was a member of the Blundell family of Ince Blundell – thus he combined in himself the Irish and old recusant traditions that shaped Lancashire Catholicism. He studied at St Finian's, Navan, and Ushaw and was ordained 9 May 1847. He served as curate at St Patrick's, Liverpool, and parish priest of St Vincent's, Liverpool. He was appointed Bishop of Liverpool in succession to Bishop Goss and was consecrated 19 March 1873. A quiet, somewhat shy manner (he spoke with a stammer) and a ready smile were deceptive if taken as a lack of determination to have things just as he wanted them. He died 9 April 1894 and was buried at Upholland College, which he had founded.

Residence: He lived for a short time in Rodney Street and/or Catharine Street, in central Liverpool, but moved to St Edward's College, Everton, for reasons of economy.

WHITESIDE, Thomas: born 17 April 1857 in Lancaster, he was educated at St Edward's, Liverpool, Ushaw and the English College, Rome, where he was ordained 30 May 1885. He taught for nine years at Upholland, where he became vice-rector (1887) and rector (1893); he was then appointed fourth Bishop of Liverpool and was consecrated 15 August 1894. He was very strict and even severe in manner, minutely conscientious and seemingly unable to delegate any duties to others; he fought hard for Catholic schools and other causes and became surprisingly popular. When the diocese was made an archdiocese in 1911 he became its first archbishop, with metropolitan jurisdiction over the new Northern Province. He died suddenly 28 January 1921 and was buried in Ford Cemetery; in 1936 his remains were moved to the crypt of the cathedral which had been planned as his memorial.

Residence: St Edward's College, Everton; moved to 5 Belvidere Road, Princes Park, Liverpool, in 1919.

KEATING, Frederick William: born 13 June 1859 in Birmingham. He studied at Sedgley Park School, Douai (France) and St Bernard's Seminary, Olton, and was ordained 20 October 1882. After some years of teaching, in 1888 he became parish priest of St Mary's, Wednesbury, and later administrator of St Chad's Cathedral in Birmingham. In 1908 he became fourth Bishop of Northampton and developed a national reputation on Catholic social teaching. He was appointed to succeed Archbishop Whiteside in 1921. He oversaw the division of the archdiocese and the extension of Upholland, and launched a major cathedral appeal. He died unexpectedly 7 February 1928 and was buried at Upholland.

Residence: 5 Belvidere Road, Princes Park.

DOWNEY, Richard: he was born in Kilkenny, Ireland, in May 1881; his parents moved to Everton, Liverpool, while he was still young and he was educated at St Edward's and Upholland. He was ordained 25 May 1907 and then studied in Rome. He was with the Catholic Missionary Society from 1911 to 1926 when he joined the staff at Upholland, where he became vice-rector before his appointment as archbishop of Liverpool in 1928. He was a national figure and the favourite internal candidate for Westminster in 1935, but Archbishop Hinsley was appointed instead. He was very overweight and suffered from ill-health for several years, though he remained active; he died 16 June 1953 and was buried in the crypt of his grandiose cathedral.

Residence: Belvidere Road, Princes Park; Archbishop's House, Church Road, Woolton, Liverpool.

GODFREY, William: born in Kirkdale, Liverpool, 25 September 1889, he studied at Ushaw and the English College, Rome; ordained 28 October 1916. Curate at St Michael's, West Derby, then lectured in Philosophy and Dogmatic Theology at Ushaw until 1930 when he became rector of the English College, Rome. On 21 December 1938 he was ordained titular archbishop of Cius, having been appointed Apostolic Delegate in London in November; took up his post in February 1939. On 14 November 1953 he was appointed archbishop of Liverpool. Three years later he was appointed archbishop of Westminster and was enthroned on 11 February 1957. He became a Cardinal in November 1958. He died 22 January 1963 and was buried in Westminster Cathedral.

Residence: Archbishop's House, Church Road, Woolton.

HEENAN, John Carmel: born Ilford, Essex, 26 January 1905. After studying at Ushaw and the English College, Rome, he was ordained 6 July 1930. He served as curate in Barking and then as parish priest in Manor Park until he became superior of the Catholic Missionary Society. He was appointed Bishop of Leeds in March 1951 and translated to Liverpool 2 May 1957 where he was enthroned 16 July. An able controversialist and national figure, he was translated to Westminster 2 September 1963 and created Cardinal 22 February 1965. He died 7 November 1975 and was buried in Westminster Cathedral.

Residence: Archbishop's House, Church Road, Woolton.

BECK, George Andrew: born in Streatham, London, 28 May 1904, he joined the Assumptionists and studied in Louvain. He was ordained 24 July 1927. He became co-adjutor of Brentwood 21 September 1948, as Bishop of Tigra; succeeded as Bishop 23 January 1951. He was translated to Salford, November 1955, and to Liverpool 29 January 1964. He was the hierarchy's spokesman and chief negotiator on Catholic education. He suffered from ill-health for much of his time in Liverpool, but initiated the implementation of the decrees of Vatican II. He retired to Upholland 11 February 1976; he died 13 September 1978 and was buried in the crypt of the cathedral.

Residence: Church Road, Woolton; in 1972 moved to 87 Green Lane, Mossley Hill.

WORLOCK, Derek: Born in London 4 February 1920, he studied at St Edmund's, Ware, and Allen Hall, and was ordained 3 June 1944. He became secretary to Cardinal Griffin that same year, and then to Cardinals Godfrey and Heenan until 1964. He served as parish priest for a short time in Stepney before becoming Bishop of Portsmouth in December 1965. From there he was translated to Liverpool 7 February 1976 and installed 19 March 1976. A prominent national figure, he was awarded honorary degrees from a number of universities, received the freedom of the city of Liverpool and was created a Companion of Honour, January 1996. He died 8 February 1996 and was buried in St Joseph's Chapel in the cathedral.

Residence: Green Lane, Mossley Hill.

KELLY, Patrick Altham : born in Morecambe, Lancashire, 23 November 1938. He was ordained 18 February 1962 and appointed Bishop of Salford in April 1984. He was translated to Liverpool 21 May 1996 and installed 3 July 1996.

Residence: Lowood, Carnatic Road, Liverpool 18.

AUXILIARY BISHOPS

GOSS, ALEXANDER: born Ormskirk 1814; titular Bishop of Gerra and co-adjutor, 1853-56; then Bishop of Liverpool.

DOBSON, ROBERT: born New Orleans, USA, 1867; grew up in the Fylde. Ordained 1891; titular Bishop of Cynopolis and auxiliary 1922-42.

HALSALL, JOSEPH: born Ainsdale, Lancs., 1902; ordained 1930; titular Bishop of Zabi and auxiliary 1945-58.

HARRIS, AUGUSTINE: born Liverpool 1917; ordained 1942; titular Bishop of Socia and auxiliary1966-78; Bishop of Middlesbrough to 1992; retired.

GRAY, JOSEPH: born Cavan, Ireland, 1919; ordained1943; titular Bishop of Mercia and auxiliary 1969-80; then Bishop of Shrewsbury.

O'CONNOR, KEVIN: born Liverpool 1929; ordained 1954; titular Bishop of Glastonia and auxiliary 1979-93.

HITCHEN, ANTHONY: born Chorley, Lancs., 1930; ordained 1955; titular Bishop of Othona and auxiliary 1979-88.

RAWSTHORNE, JOHN: born Crosby, Liverpool, 1936; ordained 1962; titular Bishop of Rotdon and auxiliary 1981-97; then Bishop of Hallam.

MALONE, VINCENT: born Liverpool 1931; ordained 1955; titular Bishop of Abora and auxiliary 1989.

WILLIAMS, THOMAS: born Liverpool, 1948; ordained 1972; titular Bishop of Mageo and auxiliary 2003.

~

The Rt Rev René Boisguerin, Bishop of Sui-Fu, Vietnam, lived in exile in Liverpool and carried out some of the duties of an auxiliary in the 1960s and 1970s.

1 Plumb, Arundel to Zabi, is the most comprehensive source. See also Beck, pp.187-222, and for the early bishops, W. Maziere Brady, *The Epsicopal Succession in England, Scotland and Ireland*, 3 vols. (1876; repr. 1971); details of Archbishop Worlock from *Directory 1997*, pp.140-1; for later bishops, *Directories*.

BIBLIOGRAPHY

Abbott, W.M., SJ, (ed.), *The Documents of Vatican II* (1966).

Altholz, J., *The Liberal Catholic Movement in England* (1962).

Anon., 'The End of an Epoch', *Upholland Magazine* (1943), pp.87-97.

Anon., *St Vincent De Paul's, Liverpool* (1952).

Anon., *The Liverpool Archdiocese and Lourdes: The Story of the 1st and 2nd Pilgrimages to Lourdes 1923 and 1924* (nd; ?1924).

Archdiocesan Board of Catholic Action, *The Catholic Action College of Liverpool* (June 1938), and *Catholic Action in War-Time* (1941).

Arts Council of Gt Britain, *Lutyens* (1981).

Aspden, Kester, *Fortress Church: The English Roman Catholic Bishops and Politics 1903-63* (2002).

Aspinwall, B., 'Catholic Teachers for Scotland: the Liverpool Connection', *The Innes Review* XLV no.1 (Spring 1994), pp.47-70.

Austin, Alfred, *The Autobiography of Alfred Austin Poet Laureate, 1835-1910* (1911).

Battersby, W.J., 'Educational Work of the Religious Orders of Women: 1850-1950', in Beck, pp.337-64.

Beales, A.C.F., 'The Struggle for the Schools', in Beck pp.365-409.

Beck, Rt Rev George Andrew, AA. (ed.), *The English Catholics 1850-1950. Essays to commemorate the centenary of the restoration of the Hierarchy of England and Wales* (1950).

.. 'To-day and To-morrow', in Beck, pp.585-614.

Belchem, J., 'Class, Creed and Country: the Irish Middle Class in Victorian Liverpool', in R. Swift and S. Gilley (eds.), *The Irish in Victorian Britain: the Local Dimension* (1999), pp.190-211.

.. 'Liverpool in 1848: Image, Identity and Issues', *THSLC,* vol. 147 (1998), pp.1-26.

.. *Merseypride. Essays in Liverpool Exceptionalism* (2000).

.. (ed.), *Popular Politics, Riot and Labour. Essays in Liverpool History 1790-1940* (1992).

Bellenger, Dominic Aidan, *The French Exiled Clergy in the British Isles after 1789* (1986).

Bennett, Canon J., 'The Catholic Emigration Association', in *CR,* vol. XX (1950).

.. 'The Story of Father Berry's Homes', *CR,* XXI (1951).

.. *Father Nugent of Liverpool* (1949).

Bennett, E.K., *Archbishop Whiteside* (CTS 1926).

Blundell, Dom F.O., OSB, *Old Catholic Lancashire,* 3 vols. (1925-1941).

Bohstedt, John, 'More than One Working Class: Protestant-Catholic Riots in Edwardian Liverpool', in Belchem (ed.), *Popular Politics,* pp.173-216.

Bossy, John, *The English Catholic Community 1570-1850* (1975).

Boyce, Frank, 'Catholicism in Liverpool's Docklands 1950s-1990s', in Hornsby-Smith, *Catholics in England,* pp.46-66.

Brady, L.W., *T.P. O'Connor and the Liverpool Irish* (1983).

Bridge, J., *The Lowe House Story 1743-1993* (1993).

Brothers, Joan, *Church and School* (1964).

Burscough, Margaret, *The History of Lark Hill, Preston, 1797-1989* (1989).

Butler, A.S.G., *The Architecture of Sir Edwin Lutyens,* 3 vols. (1950).

Butler, C., *The Life and Times of Bishop Ullathorne,* 2 vols. (1926).

Callon, F., 'A History of the College Grounds', Pts I, II, III, *Upholland Magazine,* 1965, pp.11-5; 1966, pp.18-35; 1968, pp.4-15.

Carus, J., *History of St Lewis' Church, Croft* (1977).

Champ, Judith, 'Bishop Milner, Holywell, and the Cure Tradition', *SCH,* vol. 19, pp.153-164,

Connolly, G.P., 'The Transubstantiation of Myth', *JEH,* vol. 35 (1984).

Cookson, Peter, *We Give Thee Thanks* (2003).

Coyne, John, *Cathedral Record* 1961, p.72, reviewing Ward.

Cranston, Ruth, *The Mystery of Lourdes* (1956).

Crichton, J.D., *The Church's Worship.*

Cwiekowski, F.J., *The English Bishops and the First Vatican Council* (1971).

Davies, J. (ed.), *Coping with the Blitz: Letters of L.J.D'Andria, OSB, 1940-41* (2000).

.. 'A Blunt, Unsophisticated Working-Man: J.T. (Joe) Tinker, MP, and the 1944 Education Act', *NWCH,* XXI (1994), pp.27-35.

.. 'British Catholics and the South African War. 1899-1900', in Hilton, *Turning the Last Century,* pp.47-65.

.. 'Catholic Representatives in Parliament: the North West of England 1918-1945', *RH,* vol. 26, no.2 (Oct. 2002), pp.359-83.

.. 'Conservative and Catholic: John Shute and the Liverpool Exchange By-Election, 1933', *NWCH,* XXX (2003), pp.95-109.

.. 'Evacuation during World War Two: the Response of the Catholic Church', *NWCH,* XXV (1998), pp.38-61.

.. 'Father James Nugent, Prison Chaplain', *NWCH*, XXII (1995).

.. 'Palliative and Expedients: The 1944 Education Act: Archbishop Downey and the Catholic Response', *NWCH*, XX (1993), pp.47-70.

.. 'Parish Charity: The Work of the SVP, St Mary's, Highfield St, Liverpool, 1867-8', *NWCH*, XVII (1990), pp.37-46

.. 'Rome on the Rates: Archbishop Richard Downey and the Catholic Schools Question, 1929-39', *NWCH*, XVIII (1991), pp.16-32.

.. 'The Liverpool Catholic Land Association', *NWCH*, XIX (1992), pp.21-46.

.. 'Traditional Religion, Popular Piety, or Base Superstition? The Cause for the Beatification of Teresa Higginson', *RH*, vol. 24, no.1 (May 1998), pp.123-44.

.. (ed.), *Thomas Anselm Burge: St Austin's Log 1899-1929* (1999).

Davies, Sam, 'A Stormy Political Career: P.J. Kelly and Irish Nationalist and Labour Politics in Liverpool, 1891-1936', *THSLC*, 148 (1999), pp.147-89.

.. 'Class, Religion and Gender: Liverpool Labour Party and Women, 1918-1939' in Belchem (ed.), *Popular Politics*, pp.217-46.

Davis, C., *Liturgy and Doctrine* (1960).

Davitt, Thomas, CM, 'St Vincent's, Gateacre, Liverpool', in *'Colloque', Journal of the Irish Province of the Congregation of the Mission*, no.22, (Autumn 1990), pp.273-95.

Deegan, Frank, *There's No Other Way: The Autobiography of Frank Deegan* (1980).

Denvir, J., *The Life Story of an Old Rebel* (1910; republ. 1972).

Dominic Savio, (Hamer) Sr., CP, 'Some Passionist Parish Missions in the Victorian North West', *NWCH*, XXII (1995), pp.9-14.

Downey, Abp Richard, *Some Errors of H.G. Wells* (new ed. 1933).

.. *Critical and Constructive Essays* (1934).

.. (ed.), *Re-Building the Church in England* (1933).

.. *Pulpit and Platform Addresses* (1933).

Doyle, P., 'A Link Between Priests and People: The *Parishioner* Magazine', *NWCH*, XXIX (2002), pp.101-8.

.. '"A Tangled Skein of Confusion": The Administration of George Hilary Brown, Bishop of Liverpool 1850-1856', *RH*, vol.25, no.2 (Oct. 2000), pp.294-303.

.. 'Bishop Goss and the Gentry: the Control of Private Chapels', *NWCH*, XII (1985), pp.6-13.

.. 'Bishop O'Reilly and the Franciscans', *NWCH*, XXVII (2000), pp.45-54.

.. 'Charles Plater SJ and the Origins of the Catholic Social Guild', *RH*, vol. 21, no.3 (May 1993), pp.401-17.

.. 'Episcopal Authority and Clerical Democracy: Diocesan Synods in Liverpool in the 1850s', *RH*, vol. 23 (May 1997), pp.418-33.

.. 'Lancashire Benedictines: The Restoration of the Hierarchy', *EBC History Symposium* 1983, pp.4-21.

.. 'Missed Opportunities: Clerical Conferences in the Nineteenth Century', *Downside Review (*Oct. 1982), pp.263-73.

.. 'The Education and Training of Roman Catholic Priests in Nineteenth-Century England', *JEH*, vol. 35, no. 2 (April 1984), pp.208-19.

.. 'Bishop Goss of Liverpool (1856-1872) and the Importance of Being English', in *SCH*, vol.18 (1982), pp.433-447.

.. 'Jesuit Reactions to the Restoration of the Hierarchy: the Diocese of Liverpool,1850-1880', *RH* vol. 26, 1 (May 2002), pp.210-28.

Doyle, Peter & McLoughlin, Leslie, *The Edwardian Story* : *The History of St Edward's College, Liverpool* (2003).

Dudley, Sr Margaret Mary, SND, *Treasured Memories of St Joseph's 1845-2001* (2001).

Dye, Ryan, 'The Irish Flood: Famine, Philanthropy, and the Emergence of Duelling Catholic Identities, 1845-1865', *THSLC*, vol. 150 (2001), pp.97-120.

Edwards, Francis, SJ, *The Jesuits in England:From 1580 to the Present Day* (1985).

Fielding, S., *Class and Ethnicity: Irish Catholics in England, 1880-1939* (1993).

Foster, Harry, *New Birkdale: The Growth of a Lancashire Seaside Suburb* (1995).

Furnival, John, and Knowles, Ann, *Archbishop Derek Worlock. His Personal Journey* (1998).

Garvin, J., 'James O'Byrne', *Upholland Magazine* (Jan. 1934), pp.3-5.

Giblin, J.F., 'The Gerard Family of Bryn and Ince and the Parish of SS Oswald and Edmund', *NWCH*, XVII (1990), pp.1-17.

.. 'The Molyneux Family and the Missions at Scholes Hall and Our Lady's Portico', *NWCH*, XXI (1994), pp.1-13.

.. 'The Orrell Family and the Mission of St Mary's, Blackbrook, in Parr, St Helens', *NWCH*, VII (1980), pp.6-19.

Gillespie, William, *The Christian Brothers in England 1825-1880* (1975).

Gilley, Sheridan, 'The Years of Equipoise, 1892-1943' in *Flaminian Gate,* pp.21-61.

Goddard, Gillian, 'St John's, Lathom: The Sociology of a Parish as Viewed Through Fr Eager's Log Book 1880-1918', *NWCH,* XXIX (2002), pp.90-1.

   .. *St John the Evangelist Catholic Church, Burscough, A Celebration of the Tercentenary … of the Burscough Hall Mission 1700-2000* (2000).

Gooch, Leo (ed.), *The Revival of English Catholicism: The Banister-Rutter Correspondence 1777-1807* (1995).

Goss, Bp Alexander, *A Sacred History, comprising the leading facts of the Old and New Testament* (1856).

   .. *Abbott's Journal 1689-91*, and *The Trials at Manchester 1694* (1864).

   .. *Chronica Regum Manniae et Insularum … (*1874).

Guide to the Catholic Church Services and Quarant'Ore in Liverpool for 1861 (1861).

Hamer, Edna, *Elizabeth Prout 1820-1864. A Religious Life for Industrial England* (1994).

Hanley, L., 'John Sadler: An Eighteenth-Century Liverpool Catholic', *NWCH,* VIII (1981), pp.16-24.

Hastings, Adrian, *A History of English Christianity 1920-1985* (1986).

Heenan, Abp J.C., 'Point of View', *Catholic Teachers' Journal* May-June 1963, pp.8-9.

   .. *A Crown of Thorns: An Autobiography 1951-1963* (1974).

Heery, Pat, *The History of St Francis Xavier's College, Liverpool, 1842-2001* (2002).

Heimann, Mary, *Catholic Devotion in Victorian England* (1995).

Hewlett, M.J., *Our Lady of Mount Carmel, Centenary of the Opening* (1978).

Hierarchy of England and Wales, *The Apostolate of the Laity* (1936).

Hierarchy of England and Wales, *The Easter People* (1981).

Hilton, J.A., *Catholic Lancashire* (1994).

   .. (ed.), *Turning the Last Century: Essays on English Catholicism c1900* (2003).

   .. (ed.), *Catholic Englishmen. Essays presented to the Rt. Rev. Brian Charles Foley* (1984).

   .. *St Joseph's Wrightington. A History* (1994).

   .. 'A Catholic Congregation in the Age of Revolution: St Benedict's, Hindley', *NWCH,* XVII (1990), pp.20-28.

   .. 'Catholic Congregationalism in Fleetwood, 1841-42', *NWCH,* XXVI (1999), pp.62-9.

   .. 'Lingard's Hornby', in Hilton, *Catholic Englishmen,* pp.37-44.

   .. 'The Case of Wigan: Catholic Congregationalism in the Age of Revolution', *NWCH,* X (1983), pp.1-7.

Hindle, Alban, *A Centenary History of the Catholic College, Preston* (1971).

Hodgetts, Michael, 'The Iron Form: Catholics and Philosophy between the Councils', *Flaminian Gate,* pp.84-107.

Holmes, J. Derek, *More Roman than Rome* (1978).

Holt, G., SJ, 'Croxteth-Gillmoss: The Development of a Mission', *NWCH,* XXII (1995), pp.1-8.

Holt, T.G., SJ, 'Joseph Dunn of Preston from his Correspondence', Hilton, *Catholic Englishmen,* pp.29-36.

Hornsby-Smith, M.P., (ed.), *Catholics in England 1950-2000: Historical and Sociological Perspectives* (1999).

Hughes, Philip, 'The English Catholics in 1850' in Beck, pp.71-2.

Hussey, C., *The Life of Sir Edwin Lutyens* (1950).

Izard, Dom Francis, OSB, *The Meaning of Lourdes* (1938).

John-Paul II, Pope, *The Pope in Britain: Collected Homilies and Speeches* (1982).

Kearns, G., Laxton, P. and Campbell, J., 'Duncan and the Cholera Test: public health in nineteenth-century Liverpool', *THSLC,* vol. 143 (1994), pp.87-115.

Kelly, Kevin T., 'A New Venture in the North: Upholland Northern Institute', *Cl.R* vol. LX, no.10 (Oct.1975), pp.623-43.

   .. *From a Parish Base* (1999).

Kenny, A., *A Path from Rome, An Autobiography* (1986).

Kollar, R., OSB, 'The Reluctant Prior: Bishop Wulfstan Pearson of Lancaster', *RH,* vol. 20, no.3 (1991), pp.403-13.

Ladyewell, Past and Present (nd, but c. 2000).

Lambert, S., *Irish Women in Lancashire 1922-1960: Their Story (*2001*).*

Lane, P., *The Catenian Association 1908-1983* (1982).

Leetham, C., *Luigi Gentili, a sower for the second spring* (1965).

Legion of Mary Official Handbook (new ed. 1953).

Longley, Clifford, *The Worlock Archive* (2000).

Lowe, W.J., *The Irish in Mid-Victorian Lancashire* (1989).

Machin, G.I.T., *The Catholic Question in English Politics,1820-1830* (1964).

MacRaild, D.M., *Culture, Conflict and Migration; The Irish in Victorian Cumbria* (1998).

Maher, M., 'Holywell in 1894', *The Month* (1895), p.154.

Mallin, D., 'Rome on the Rates in Wigan: the Founding of the Sacred Heart School,1904-6', *NWCH,* V (1978), pp.34-41.

Manning, H.E., *The Good Soldier's Death* (1872).

Marsden, W.E., 'Social environment, school attendance and achievement in a Merseyside town 1870-1900', in P. McCann (ed.) *Popular education and socialization in the 19th century* (1977), pp.194-230.

McAreavey, J., *The Canon Law of Marriage and the Family* (1997).

McCarren, Mary Campion, FCJ, Trotman, Frances & Piggin, Marion, *With Devotedness and Love - 150 Years of service to Catholic Education* (1994).

McClelland, V.A., 'The making of Young Imperialists; Rev. Thomas Seddon, Lord Archibald Douglas and the Resettling of British Catholic Orphans in Canada', *RH,* 19, no.4 (Oct. 1989), pp.509-29.

McClelland, V.A., and Hodgetts, M. (eds.), *From Without the Flaminian Gate. 150 Years of Roman Catholicism in England and Wales 1850-2000 (*1999).

McEntee, G.P., *The Social Catholic Movement in Great Britain* (1927).

McGrath, T.G., 'The Tridentine Evolution of Modern Irish Catholicism, 1563-1962', *RH*, vol. 20, no.4 (Oct. 1991) pp.512-23.

McKenna, M., 'The suburbanisation of the working-class population of Liverpool between the wars', *Social History,* vol.16, no.2 (May 1991).

Metropolitan Cathedral of Christ the King Liverpool: The History of Liverpool's Catholic Cathedral (nd).

Milburn, D., *A History of Ushaw College* (1964).

Miller, A., *Poverty Deserved? Relieving the Poor in Victorian Liverpool* (1988).

Moloney, Thomas, *Westminster, Whitehall and the Vatican: The Role of Cardinal Hinsley 1935-43* (1985).

Morgan, N., *Deadly Dwellings: Housing and Health in a Lancashire Cotton Town: Preston from 1840-1914* (1993).

National Pastoral Congress, *Liverpool 1980* (1981).

Neal, Frank, *Black '47: Britain and the Famine Irish* (1998).

    ..   *Sectarian Violence. The Liverpool Experience 1819-1914* (1988).

O'Brien, Susan, 'French Nuns in Nineteenth Century England', *Past and Present,* 154 (Feb. 1997), pp.142-64.

    ..   'Religious Life for Women', in *Flaminian Gate* (1999), pp.108-41.

O'Day, A. (ed.), *A Survey of the Irish in England* (1872, repr. 1990).

O'Mara, P., *The Autobiography of a Liverpool Irish Slummy*

(1934, republ. 1967).

Panikkar, M., 'A Catholic Scarlet Pimpernel and the Dames of Ghent: the Benedictine Convent in Preston 1795-1811', *NWCH,* XXIX (2002), pp.50-60.

Parkinson, Anne C., *A History of Catholicism in the Furness Peninsula, 1127-1997* (1998).

Peters, M., Plumb, B., et al., *St Charles Borromeo Parish Centenary 1892-1992* (1992).

Pevsner, N., *The Buildings of England: Lancashire, I The Industrial and Commercial South* (1969).

Phillips, P., 'St Joseph's College, Upholland. A Brief History', *Ushaw Magazine* (1983), pp.3-17.

Plumb, B., *Arundel to Zabi. A Biographical Dictionary of the Catholic Bishops of England and Wales (Deceased) 1623-1987* (1987).

    ..   *Found Worthy. A Biographical Dictionary of the Secular Clergy of the Archdiocese of Liverpool (Deceased) since 1850* (1986).

    ..   'A Liverpool Priest's Journal of the Blitz', *NWCH,* IX (1982), pp.18-24.

    ..   'Hymnbooks Revisited', *NWCH,* XXVII (2000), pp.68-91.

    ..   'The Founding Fathers of Lancaster Diocese' in Hilton (ed.), *Catholic Englishmen*, pp.53-8.

    ..   *Our Glorious Chapter, The Story of St Mary's, Warrington* (1977).

    ..   *St Mary's, Little Crosby. A History* (1997).

Pooley, C.G. and Irish, S., 'Housing and Health in Liverpool, 1870-1940', *THSLC* vol.143 (1994), pp.193-219.

Pooley, C.G., 'Segregation or integration? The residential experience of the Irish in mid-Victorian Britain', in Swift and Gilley, *Irish in Britain*, pp.60-83.

Pope, D.J., 'The Liverpool Catholic and Maritime Business Community', *NWCH,* XXX (2003), pp.28-56.

Questions Addressed to the Clergy … at the Visitation of 1855, (Liverpool 1855).

Quinn, Dermot, *Patronage and Piety. The Politics of Roman Catholicism, 1850-1900* (1993).

Report on the Catholic Action Congress (1938).

Ripley, F.J., *The Diary of a Small Town Priest* (1979).

    ..   *Another Diary of a Small Town Priest* (1987).

Rockett, J., *Held in Trust: Catholic Parishes in England and Wales 1900-1950* (2001).

Rowlands, Marie B. (ed.), *Catholics of Parish and Town 1558-1778* (1999).

Ryan, N., SJ, *St Francis Xavier's Church Centenary, 1848-1948* (1948).

Savage, M., *The Dynamics of Working-Class Politics. The Labour Movement in Preston 1880-1940* (1987).

Scarisbrick, J.J., *Selly Park and Beyond* (1997).

Schiefen, R., *Nicholas Wiseman and the Transformation of English Catholicism* (1984).

Sexton, James, *Sir James Sexton, Agitator* (1936).

Sharp, John, *Reapers of the Harvest: The Redemptorists in Great Britain and Ireland 1843-98* (1989).

Sharples, Joseph, *Liverpool (Pevsner Architectural Guides)* (2004).

Sharratt, B., 'English Roman Catholicism in the 1960s', in G. Sweeney (ed.), *Bishops and Writers* (1977), pp.127-58.

Sheppard, David, and Worlock, Derek, *Better Together: Christian Partnership in a Hurt City* (1988).

Singleton, F.J., *Mowbreck Hall and the Willows* (1983).

Smith, G.D. (ed.), *The Teaching of the Catholic Church*, 2 vols, (1948).

Smith, Tom, 'Preston Catholics Before Emancipation', *NWCH*, XXVI (1999), pp.33-61.

.. 'Turning the Century: Catholics Decadent and Prestonian', in Hilton, *Turning the Last Century*, pp.10-26.

Snape, M., 'British Catholicism and the British Army in the First World War', *RH*, vol.26, no.2 (Oct. 2002).

Stevenson, John, *British Society 1914-45* (1984).

Swarbrick, J., *Marriage, A Sermon Preached at St Augustine's by the Rev. James Swarbrick … 1858* (1858).

Sweeney, Garrett, *St Edmund's House, Cambridge, the First Eighty Years* (1980).

Sweeney, M.V., 'Mixed Marriages: Some Statistics of the Eighteenth Century', *Cl.R*, XXIV (Sept. 1944), pp.402-6.

Swift, R. and Gilley, S. (eds.), *The Irish in Britain* (1989).

Swift, R. and Gilley, S. (eds.), *The Irish in the Victorian City* (1985).

Tarn, J.N., 'Liverpool's Two Cathedrals', D. Wood (ed.), *The Church and the Arts; SCH* 28 (1992), pp.537-69.

Taylor, Mgr C. (ed.), *Souvenir of Solemn Opening of the Metropolitan Cathedral Crypt Liverpool* (nd).

Thurston, H., 'Holywell in Recent Years', *The Month*, vol. 128 (1916), pp.38-51;

Toole, Janet, *The Parish is a Beehive* (2002).

Trappes-Lomax, J., *The Letters of Dr John Lingard to Mrs Thomas Lomax (1835-51)*, C.R.S. vol.77 (2000).

Turner, J.F., 'St Edward's', *Upholland Magazine* (1943), pp.71-86.

Virgoe, J., 'Thomas Fleetwood and the Draining of Martin Mere', *THSLC*, vol. 152 (2004), pp.27-49.

Waller, P.J., *Democracy and Sectarianism: a Political and Social History of Liverpool 1868-1939* (1981).

Walsh, Michael J., 'Ecumenism in War-time Britain', *Heythrop Journal* XXII, no. 3 & 4 (July & Oct. 1982).

.. *A Dictionary of Devotions* (1993).

Walton, J.K., *Lancashire, A Social History, 1558-1939* (1987).

Ward, B., *The Dawn of the Catholic Revival in England, 1781-1803*, 3 vols. (1909).

Ward, B., *The Sequel to Catholic Emancipation 1830-1850*, 2 vols. (1915), pp.205-22.

Ward, Conor K., *Priests and People* (1961).

Warren, Leo, *Through Twenty Preston Guilds. The Catholic Congregation of St Wilfrid's, Preston* (1993).

Whitehead, M., 'Briefly and in Confidence: Private Views of HMI on English Catholic Elementary Schools, 1875', *RH* vol. 20, no. 4 (Oct. 1991), pp.554-62.

.. 'The English Jesuits and Episcopal Authority: The Liverpool Test Case, 1840-1843', *RH*, vol.18 (Oct. 1986), pp.197-219.

.. 'The Gillows and their work in Georgian Lancaster', in J.A. Hilton (ed.), *Catholic Englishmen* (1984), pp.21-27.

.. 'A View from the Bridge: The Catholic School', in *Flaminian Gate*, pp.217-44.

Worrall, Jennifer, SND, *Jubilee: Sisters of N.D. de Namur celebrate 150 years in Britain* (1995).

Unpublished Theses

Feehan, L., 'Charitable Effort, Statutory Authorities and the Poor in Liverpool, c.1850-1914', PhD thesis, University of Liverpool (1987).

Lynch. P., 'Southport and the Catholic Church in the 19th Century', MA thesis, Liverpool Hope University College (2002).

Whittle, M., 'Philanthropy in Preston: The Changing Face of Charity in a Nineteenth Century Provincial Town', PhD thesis, University of Lancaster (1990).

INDEX

403